Sunk Costs and Market Structure

Sunk Costs and Market Structure

Price Competition, Advertising, and
the Evolution of Concentration

John Sutton

The MIT Press
Cambridge, Massachusetts
London, England

Second Printing, 1992
© 1991 Massachusetts Institute of Technology

This book was set in Baskerville by Asco Trade Typesetting Ltd., Hong Kong and printed and bound in the United States of America.

Library of Congress Cataloging-in-Publication Data

Sutton, John, 1948–
    Sunk costs and market structure: price competition, advertising,
    and the evolution of concentration / John Sutton.
        p.   cm.
    Includes bibliographical references and index.
    ISBN 0-262-19305-1
    1. Industrial organization (Economic theory) 2. Game theory.
3. Advertising—Costs—Mathematical models. 4. Costs, Industrial—
Mathematical models. I. Title.
HD2326.S88   1991
338.6—dc20   90-22722
                                                            CIP

To my parents

There are such things as historical and theoretical temperaments. That is to say, there are types of mind that take delight in all the colors of historical processes.... There are other types that prefer a neat theorem to everything else. We have use for both. But they are not made to appreciate one another.

Joseph Schumpeter,
History of Economic Analysis

Contents

Part V Summing Up 305

Acknowledgments

In preparing this book, I have accumulated many debts. My first is to my longtime collaborator Avner Shaked. This book represents an attempt to further develop, and implement empirically, a theoretical approach that we set out in a series of papers published between 1982 and 1987.

My second debt is to my research assistants Yukiko Abe, Dan Aronoff, Magda Bianco, Cara Funk, and Yves Mertens, who assisted me in assembling and processing information on various groups of markets and in organizing a lengthy program of company interviews; and to Alan Shcr and Mike Sadler, who helped me in the later stages of the work.

My thanks are also due to the several specialists on particular industries, or groups of industries, who assisted me generously in the course of my research. I would like in particular to record my gratitude to Hartmut Berg, Umberto Bertele, Elizabetta Bianchi, Patrizio Bianchi, Tim Cooke, Bruce Marion, Jürgen Müller, Luca Pellegrini, M. J. L. Rastoin, Joachim Schwalbach, David Stout, Christian Von Weizsäcker, and Bernard Yon.

In certain cases, I benefited enormously from earlier studies of particular industries. I would especially like to acknowledge my debt to the major study of the U.S. food processing industries by John Connor, Richard Rogers, Bruce Marion, and Willard Mueller; to Alfred Eichner's classic study of the U.S. sugar industry; to Carolyn Fost's valuable thesis on the U.S. salt industry; and to the several FTC and MMC reports cited throughout the text.

I was extremely fortunate to enjoy the invaluable assistance of a small number of leading market research organizations, without which this study would not have been possible. They are: Euromonitor (London), Agra-Alimentation (Paris), Databank (Milan), MEAL (London), Nielsen Werbeforschung (Hamburg), and AGB Italia (Milan).

A preliminary draft of the book was inflicted upon colleagues and students in the Economics of Industry Group at LSE, on my graduate class of 1989–90, and on several friendly critics. I benefited greatly from the criticisms and suggestions of Dan Aronoff, Stephen Berry, Richard Caves, Vittoria Cherasi, Stephen Davies, Marie-Thérèse Flaherty, Katrien Kesteloot, Paul Klemperer, Bruce Lyons, Kjerstigro Lindquist, James MacDonald, Massimo Motta, Willard Mueller, Georg Noldeke, Ariel Pakes, Louis Phlips, Robert Porter, Margaret Slade, Paul Stoneman, and Mike Whinston. The final version was read by John Black and Sang-Seung Yu, for whose suggestions I am most grateful. The econometric analysis of chapter 5 benefited greatly from the advice and assistance of Richard Smith, Mark Schankerman, Hugh Wills, and Tore Ellingsen.

The research was made possible by grants from STICERD at LSE and the Leverhulme Foundation. I am very grateful to both organizations for their support. The many drafts of the manuscript were typed by Enid Gowing, Sue Kirkbride, and Ann Clarke, for whose patience I am more than grateful.

I owe the various quotes at the opening of parts II–V to Stephen Jay Gould, *An Urchin in the Storm*, Norton, 1987 (II, IV), and *Ever Since Darwin*, Burnet Books/André Deutsch, 1978 (V); and to Richard Dawkins, *The Selfish Gene*, Oxford University Press, 1978 (III).

I would like to acknowledge a particular debt to the very many individuals and organizations who gave so willingly of their time and expertise in allowing me to assemble the basic information on the various markets. With the exception of a number who preferred to remain anonymous, their names are listed in the references section. Last, but by no means least, is my debt to my wife Jean for her sound advice and untiring support throughout the entire project.

Foreword

The literature on industrial organization has undergone a radical change over the past decade. This change has involved the reformulation of many traditional arguments within the subject in terms of (explicitly game-theoretic) oligopoly models. In developing this program, researchers have rediscovered an old difficulty. There are usually many ways of designing a game-theoretic model, which appear equally reasonable a priori. Moreover, within any particular model there are often many outcomes that can be supported as equilibria. This richness in modeling has made it much easier to provide a theoretical rationale for a wide range of observed phenomena: from predatory pricing to vertical restraints, our tool kit has been greatly enriched. The sting in the tail, however, lies in the old taunt, "With oligopoly, anything can happen." In explaining everything, have we explained nothing? What do the theories exclude?

Put more constructively, if the results of game-theoretic analyses depend delicately on a range of factors that are impossible to identify or proxy empirically, then how can we implement and test such theories? The currently popular response is to focus on some particular industry for which we can tailor-make a specific oligopoly model. By relying on arguments specific to this industry, it may be possible to restrict the class of admissible specifications quite tightly a priori and so generate a range of testable predictions. This approach has proved to be quite fruitful over the past few years, and has provided the beginnings of a response to the above line of criticism. At the same time, an increasingly skeptical attitude has been evident as to the usefulness of the kind of cross-industry studies that formed the staple of the traditional literature.

In this book I attempt to develop a different, though complementary, approach to these issues. I draw out, within a general theoretical framework, some fairly robust results that hold across a broad range of model specifications. These properties do not depend delicately on such nonmeasurable features of the model as might be expected to vary substantially from one industry to another. They can therefore provide a framework within which we can analyze a relatively broad class of industries and provide a new foundation for the kind of cross-industry comparisons of structure that became popular in the earlier literature, following Bain's pioneering work. Thereafter, by exploring the experience of each industry, or group of industries, in some detail, it is possible to explore various special cases arising within this general theoretical framework.

One of the most striking features of the industrial organization field generally is the cleavage between the traditional empirical literature on the one hand and the recent game-theoretic literature, with its associated single industry empirical studies, on the other. This book constitutes a first step toward building some bridges between certain recent theoretical advances and one major part of the traditional agenda of the subject.

I
The Framework

I have argued that inter-industry research in industrial organization should generally be viewed as a search for empirical regularities.... And I have attempted to show that research in this tradition has indeed uncovered many stable, robust, empirical regularities.

Richard Schmalensee (1989)

1

An Introductory Overview

1.1 A Statistical Regularity

Many authors have observed that the ranking of industries by concentration level tends to be closely similar from one country to another: an industry that is dominated by a handful of firms in one country is likely to be dominated by a handful of firms elsewhere too.[1] This "statistical regularity" has occasioned a wide range of response in the literature. The large majority of studies argue in favor of the existence of such a regularity and interpret it as a reflection of the fact that the pattern of technology and tastes that characterize a given market may be expected to be similar across different countries. For this reason, the industry's equilibrium structure may in turn be similar from one country to another. While some authors have regarded this similarity of structure as rather trivial and of little interest, many, if not most, authors have seen it as providing considerable encouragement for the view that the underlying pattern of technology

1. The issue was raised by Bain (1966). An ambitious early study by Pryor (1972) covered twelve countries. That study suffered from one serious limitation, however, insofar as it used official statistics on concentration ratios that involved different levels of aggregation for certain industry groups, in different countries. Phlips (1971) avoided this problem by taking advantage of the newly available statistics for EEC countries, which were based on a common set of industry definitions. A similar approach was followed by George and Ward (1975). More recently, Connor et al. (1985) have carried out comparisons for industries within the food and drink sector over OECD countries. All these authors conclude that a high degree of correlation exists, whether comparisons are made on a pairwise basis (regressing U.K. concentration levels on U.S. levels, etc.) or otherwise. Many studies indicate an unusually wide disparity of experience between the United Kingdom and the United States; the relatively poor correlation obtaining in this case was emphasized by the early study of Shepherd (1961).

and tastes strongly constrains equilibrium structure (Scherer 1980, Caves 1989, Connor et al 1985).

Closely related to this empirical regularity is an important strand in the traditional literature on industrial structure, which aims to explain differences in concentration across industries by reference to a small number of candidate explanatory variables that are taken to reflect basic industry characteristics. Typically, the degree of scale economies, the intensity of advertising, and the level of R&D expenditure have been regarded as key variables. This study attempts to develop a new approach to this issue.

Most of the existing empirical work on cross-sectional differences in structure is based on an appeal to the structure/conduct/performance paradigm of Bain (1956). Within that paradigm, it is supposed that a one-way chain of causation runs from *structure* (the level of concentration) to *conduct* (the degree of collusion), and from conduct to *performance* (profitability). Structure, in this setting, is explained by the presence of certain barriers to entry, whose height can be measured by the degree of scale economies in the industry and by observed levels of advertising and R&D outlays relative to industry sales. This approach has for example motivated various empirical studies that seek to explain structure by regressing observed concentration levels on measures of scale economies, advertising intensity, R&D intensity, and so on (see chapter 5).

Bain's pioneering studies laid the foundations for a generation of subsequent work. His approach, however, has been subjected to considerable criticism both by empirical researchers during the 1960s and 1970s and by contributors to the game-theoretic literature of the past decade. The approach taken in this study, like many contributions to the recent game-theoretic literature, differs sharply from that of the Bain paradigm. The key theoretical differences between the two approaches are set out in section 1.4.

This volume also differs from much of the earlier literature in terms of its empirical focus. Here the starting point of the analysis lies in an alleged tendency for a given industry to be less concentrated, in those countries in which the size of the market (as measured by the total volume of sales) is larger. This negative relationship between market size and concentration has been noted by several authors (Phlips 1971, George and Ward 1975, Schmalensee 1989), but it has not received much attention in the past. After all, it seems a "natural" result and one that can be immediately explained by reference to traditional ideas. Put loosely, we might expect that given any particular configuration of barriers to entry, an expansion in the size of the market will raise the profitability of incumbents and so induce more potential entrants to surmount that barrier, thus leading to a fall in concentration.

This relationship between market size and market structure stands at the center of my analysis, which is developed in three steps. The first step lies in describing a new theoretical rationale for the appearance of a negative relationship between market size and concentration, which is quite different to that embodied in the post-Bain literature. The second step involves the central claim of the present study. It says that this size-structure relationship, which has traditionally been seen as holding across industries generally, is in fact only valid for a certain group of industries. Most important, it is not valid for those industries in which advertising and R&D outlays play a significant role. In this latter context, it is argued that the negative relationship between market size and concentration levels breaks down for reasons that are quite fundamental.

The third step in the argument lies in developing some implications. Once the mechanisms leading both to the appearance of this negative relationship and to its breakdown in advertising and R&D intensive industries is understood, we are led to a new way of organizing many long-standing ideas regarding the determinants of cross-industry differences in structure. Those few empirical relationships that have emerged consistently in earlier empirical work now emerge as corollaries of certain relationships implied by the present theory. At the same time, we are led to a series of new approaches to a wide range of phenomena, noted in earlier empirical work, and to some new insights regarding a number of long-standing controversies.

But why should the relationship between market size and market structure merit such attention in the first place? The reason for this lies in the fact that the present characterization of the size-structure relationship represents one of the relatively few robust theoretical results to have emerged from the recent game-theoretic literature. To see the point of this remark, it is necessary to digress a little.

1.2 Game-Theoretic Models

Within the recent game-theoretic literature, numerous authors have sought to examine the long-run issues surrounding the determination of industrial structure (see Dasgupta and Stiglitz 1980, Shaked and

Sutton 1982, and Vickers 1986). One feature basic to this game-theoretic literature, however, is that the results of such analyses tend to depend delicately on the precise form of the underlying game.

Game-theoretic oligopoly models employ various simple building blocks that carry key distinctions of empirical interest. For example, we may capture the notion of the toughness of price competition by distinguishing a "Bertrand" formulation, a "Cournot" formulation, or a "joint profit maximization" formulation. Again, we may capture the presence or absence of some strategic asymmetry in the firms' relations to each other by contrasting a sequential moves formulation with a simultaneous moves formulation.

But these distinctions can often be mapped into empirical categories only in a rather loose and informal way. We may be willing to accept some particular formulation as a reasonable representation for some specific market, at least in the sense of a "prior" or null hypothesis. But if we aim to investigate statistical regularities that are presumed to hold across a range of different industries, between which the toughness of price competition or the degree of strategic asymmetry may vary, it may be extremely problematic to identify any measurable market characteristic that can act as an adequate proxy in capturing such distinctions.

Many researchers have come to feel that a natural response to such difficulties is to focus analysis on some specific market, or some set of virtually identical markets, so that we can tailor-make the oligopoly model to fit that specific context. The "ultra-micro" work to which we are led along this route is now one of the most lively areas of empirical research in industrial economics.[2]

These observations have led to a growing skepticism about the value of searching for statistical regularities that hold across a broad run of different industries. After all, if current theory indicates that most results are delicately dependent upon certain factors that are liable to vary widely across different industries and we cannot measure or proxy these in any satisfactory way, then the basis of running cross-industry regressions might appear to be somewhat dubious.

A central thesis of the present study is that this currently popular view is unduly pessimistic. Moreover, a too-rigid adherence to such

---

2. For a selection of such studies, see the *Journal of Industrial Economics* symposium of June 1987. Influential contributions include Hendricks and Porter (1988) on the auctioning of offshore oil leases, Slade (1987) on gasoline price wars, and Bresnahan and Reiss (1990) on the relationship between the size of towns and the number of retail outlets.

a view runs the risk of abandoning a central part of the traditional agenda of the subject, which concerns the investigation of regularities of behavior that hold across the general run of industries.

The point of departure lies in the observation that a fundamental trade-off exists between the degree of precision of predictions that obtain across a class of models and the breadth of applications of that class. Tight predictions may demand quite stringent a priori restrictions on the model(s); but it may nonetheless be possible to find some (necessarily weak) predictions that are robust in the sense that they hold across a wide class of models—and so lend themselves to implementation across a correspondingly broad set of different industries.

The approach taken in what follows, then, is to begin by looking to such robust predictions as will hold across a wide class of reasonable models, and to use these predictions as a basis for cross-industry regressions. What kind of results can be obtained at this level of generality? It turns out that certain robust results can be obtained that relate to the specification of a *lower bound* to the equilibrium level of concentration as a function of the size of the market. The properties of such bounds are studied in detail, and their role is examined empirically by reference to cross-country comparisons of industry structure. A number of ancillary results are also obtained at this general level, which again can be investigated by reference to cross-country comparisons.

In parallel with the development of this general framework, various special cases within the theory are investigated, and these may be used as a vehicle both for tracing the evolution of particular industries and for generating a richer menu of testable predictions appropriate to a correspondingly narrower domain. The next three sections are devoted to providing a chapter-by-chapter summary of the study as a whole.

1.3 An Outline of the Theory

The theory developed below derives from the recent vertical product differentiation literature. The starting point of this analysis, as developed by Shaked and Sutton (1982, 1987) and elaborated in Sutton 1989a, lies in the observation that advertising and R & D can both be thought of as sunk costs incurred with a view to enhancing consumers' willingness-to-pay for the firm's product (s). Focusing attention on this relationship makes possible a simple unified treatment of these two contributory factors. Now R & D and advertising outlays are choice variables to the firms, and so their levels must be determined endogenously as part of the specification of industry equilibrium. The role of scale economies, on the other hand, can be introduced by treating the acquisition of a single plant of minimum efficient scale as involving an element of sunk cost that must be incurred by all entrants, and whose level is determined exogenously by the nature of the underlying technology.

The central focus of the present theory lies in unraveling the way in which these *exogenous* and *endogenous* elements of sunk cost interact with each other in determining the equilibrium pattern of industrial structure. This theoretical framework is set out in detail in chapters 2 and 3. In what follows, a brief description of the main features of the theory is presented, as a prelude to summarizing the contents of later chapters.

Exogenous Sunk Costs (i)

The way in which the central notion of *sunk costs* is captured in the present study is by modeling industry equilibrium in terms of a two-stage game. At stage 1 of the game firms incur fixed outlays, which are associated with acquiring a single plant of minimum efficient scale (setup costs), and developing and establishing a product line (possibly incurring advertising and R & D outlays). These fixed outlays incurred at stage 1 of the game are treated as sunk costs in analyzing price competition at the second stage of the game. In the latter stage of the game, all firms are assumed to operate at the same constant level of marginal cost.

Consider first the case in which the only sunk costs involved are the exogenously given setup costs. Within this case it is useful to distinguish two subcases. The first subcase is that in which the various firms produce a homogeneous product. In this setting, as the size of the market (measured by the population of consumers) increases, the equilibrium number of firms entering the market increases, and so concentration declines indefinitely. To see this, note that entry occurs up to the point at which the (stage 2) profits of the last entrant cover the sunk cost incurred on entry at stage 1. But, for any given level of concentration in the industry, any increase in the size of the market will tend to raise these profits and so induce further entry. Thus concentration declines indefinitely as market size increases (except under very special circumstances; see chapter 2).

This case, then, corresponds to some familiar limit theorems of the standard theoretical literature; and it offers one way of characterizing the traditional idea that scale economies become unimportant as a constraint on equilibrium structure in large economies. What may be less obvious is the way in which this process is affected by the nature of price competition at stage 2 of the game. When analyzing stage 2, concentration is taken as fixed—being inherited as a result of decisions made at stage 1, which are now irreversible (i.e., they embody sunk costs). Now this means that we can properly build into our analysis of this stage of the game (i.e., the stage 2 subgame) the traditional Bain hypothesis on conduct: that prices (and so unit margins) decline as concentration falls. Within the present theory, this notion is embodied in the form of a *function* linking concentration to prices or unit margins. This *function* will be affected by such features of the market as the physical nature of the product (homogeneous versus differentiated products) and the climate of competition policy (a strict or acquiescent approach to price coordination by firms). In what follows, references to the "toughness of price competition" in a market will always refer to this *function*—and *not* to the level of prices or unit margins observed at equilibrium. (In other words, differences in the toughness of price competition across two different markets relate to the way in which margins *would* differ between those markets were concentration held at the same arbitrary level in both.)

It is shown in chapter 2 that according as price competition is tougher in this sense, the equilibrium level of concentration will be correspondingly *higher*. The intuition underlying this result is simply that the anticipation of a tougher competitive regime makes entry less attractive, thus raising equilibrium concentration levels. One of the main attractions of the two-stage game formulation is that it allows a neat unraveling of this latter effect from the traditional Bain effects (higher concentration implies higher margins, and higher profitability). To sum up: where sunk costs are exogenous, and where firms offer a homogeneous product, the equilibrium level of concentration declines with the ratio of market size to setup cost and rises with the toughness of price competition.

Exogenous Sunk Costs (ii)

The next subcase to be considered is that in which firms offer products that are differentiated, but in which sunk costs are still exogenously determined. This case has been widely explored in the horizontal product differentiation literature; the archetypal example arises in simple locational models of the Hotelling kind (a brief description of these standard models is provided in chapter 2). In these models, consumers are spread over some geographic region, and they incur (psychic or transport) costs in purchasing from distant suppliers. Each firm may establish any number of plants, incurring a given setup cost per plant. Consumers thereafter make their purchases from the lowest-cost supplier, where the cost to the consumer consists of the price paid to the firm plus a transport cost that increases with his distance from the supplier.

In models of this kind, multiple equilibria are endemic. In general, for any given market size, we may find fragmented equilibria, in which a large number of firms each sell at one location, and concentrated equilibria, in which a small number of firms each sell at many locations. In chapter 2 the factors underlying the appearance of these two types of equilibria are set out; these factors are likely to vary widely from one industry to another. Thus, if we are interested in finding properties robust enough to be of interest in cross-industry studies, we cannot constrain possible equilibrium configurations here, beyond saying that the bound corresponding to the most fragmented configuration (single-product firms) forms a *lower bound* to equilibrium concentration. This bound declines with market size in the manner of the schedule described above for the homogeneous product case.

The case, then, is that in which the present theory *least* constrains the data; and so this set of industries provides the first of several illustrations of the inherent limitations of this theory, insofar as robust predictions appropriate to a broad cross-section of industries are involved. It is perhaps worth remarking, therefore, that even in this case the theory *does* in fact yield some quite sharp predictions. But these predictions depend in all cases upon market features that are likely to vary widely from one industry to another and that are difficult to measure or proxy in many instances. (Shaked and Sutton 1990).

Bringing together these remarks on the two subcases, then, a central conclusion for the *exogenous sunk cost* regime may be phrased as follows: an increase in the size of the market relative to setup costs may lead to the appearance of indefinitely low levels of concentration in these industries. It is precisely this property that breaks down once we turn to the next case.

Endogenous Sunk Costs

We now turn to the case of *endogenous sunk costs*. These cost components may be of various kinds; the two most obvious examples, though not the only ones, are advertising and R & D outlays (see chapter 14). Suppose that, by incurring greater advertising (or R & D) outlays at stage 1 of the game, a firm can enhance the demand for its product at stage 2 (i.e., for any prices set by other firms, the demand schedule of the firm in question shifts outward). Then it is fairly obvious that the game played at stage 1 might involve a competitive escalation of outlays by firms and so lead to higher sunk costs being incurred at equilibrium. It is also fairly obvious that the larger the size of the market—and so the profits achievable at stage 2—the greater might be the sunk costs thereby incurred at equilibrium.

What is not obvious is that this is not merely a *possible* outcome; rather, on examining a range of different oligopoly models, an unusually robust result arises in this case, which runs contrary to that found in the exogenous sunk cost case. This result says that under very general conditions a lower bound exists to the equilibrium level of concentration in the industry, no matter how large the market becomes.

The level of this lower bound depends on the degree of demand responsiveness faced by an individual firm to increases in its fixed (advertising or R & D) outlays at stage 1 of the game. The higher the degree of responsiveness, the higher will be the lower bound to equilibrium concentration levels in the industry.

The central assumption of this study, then, is that across a certain range of industries, advertising works; loosely stated, it is postulated that the degree of responsiveness of demand to advertising outlays for any one of a number of competing firms always exceeds some minimal level. An exact statement of this assumption must be deferred to chapter 3.

Under these circumstances, increases in market size cannot lead to a fragmented market structure as the size of the market increases. Rather, a competitive escalation in outlays at stage 1 of the game raises the equilibrium level of sunk costs incurred by incumbent firms in step with increases in the size of the market—thus offsetting the tendency toward fragmentation.

The importance of this simple but basic result lies in the fact that it holds over an extremely wide class of oligopoly models. For example, the result holds independently of whether each firm offers a single product or a range of products. It holds independently of the form price competition takes at stage 2 of the game (Bertrand, Cournot, etc.). Furthermore, it is not affected by altering the sequence of moves in the entry stage of the game (simultaneous entry, sequential entry, etc.). The degree of robustness of this result to changes in model specification makes it a suitable candidate for investigation in a cross-industry setting.

The above comments on the *exogenous* sunk costs case imply that, if we confine attention to some set of industries in which advertising and R & D outlays are insignificant and examine how concentration varies with the size of the market across different countries, then we should expect the lower bound to observed concentration levels to fall as the size of the market rises relative to the setup costs incurred in entering the industry. The central prediction of the theory is that this relationship should break down among advertising-intensive industries. The precise way in which the relationship fails, and the testable implications of this result, are developed in chapter 3.

Further themes explored in chapter 3 include the question of how exogenous sunk costs *interact* with endogenous sunk costs in determining industrial structure. Attention is also directed toward various special cases arising within this general theoretical framework. The most important of these special cases relates to the role played by "first-mover advantages" in determining equilibrium structure and to the factors leading to the evolution of dual structure—in which a small number of leading firms spending heavily on advertising and enjoying large market shares coexists with a possibly large fringe of nonadvertisers who sell on price.

1.4   Econometric Tests

The theoretical framework developed in chapters 2 and 3, then, leads to a basic prediction about the way in which the market size/market structure relationship will vary between industries in which sunk costs are exogenously given and those in which endogenous sunk costs such as advertising or R & D play a significant role. This book is concerned with exploring this and other predictions of the theory within the context of a group of advertising-intensive industries.[3] In chapter 4, the rationale underlying the selection of this group of industries is set out in some detail. Broadly, the aim was to find a group of cognate industries in which R & D played an insignificant role and in which levels of advertising intensity were high on average, but varied widely across different industries within the group. Based on these criteria, the food and drink sector provided an obvious choice. This sector, which comprises about one-eighth of all manufacturing industry in the countries studied, has both the highest level of advertising intensity among all two-digit SIC groups and is among the lowest of all such groups in terms of R&D intensity.[4] This study is based on the experience of twenty narrowly defined food and drink industries across six countries (France, Germany, Italy, Japan, the United Kingdom, and the United States). These industries divide into two groups. In the first group, advertising outlays are extremely low in almost all cases; and these industries provide a benchmark case corresponding to the exogenous sunk cost case of the theory. In the other group of industries, the levels of advertising intensity are moderate to high; and the evolution of this group is examined by reference to the endogenous sunk cost case.

In chapter 5, a cross-sectional econometric analysis of observed concentration levels is presented, the results of which are consistent with the theory. These results, moreover, are *not* consistent with the

---

3. There are good reasons to divide the task of implementing the theory in this way, in spite of its emphasis on the similarities of the advertising and R & D cases. In the case of advertising-intensive industries, a great deal can be learned from cross-country comparisons of structure, since the sunk costs incurred by a firm in advertising its product in one country do not carry over to other countries. (Its brand image must be established anew in each country.) This is not so for R & D outlays, and most R & D-intensive industries are best treated as unified global markets. It is also worth remarking at this point that even at the theoretical level, the case of R & D is somewhat more complex than that of advertising, and an adequate treatment of the R & D case requires some extensions of the theoretical framework developed here (see chapter 14).

4. In the United States, for example, the food and drink sector accounted for 12% of the total value of production in manufacturing in 1980 (Connor et al. 1985). The level of private R&D expenditure as a proportion of sales was equal lowest with textiles and apparel, at 0.4% in 1975 (Scherer 1980, p. 410). The level of advertising expenditure relative to sales far outruns that of any other sector. Food and tobacco advertising accounted for 32% of advertising of all manufactured products in the United States in 1979, but for only 12% of all sales of manufactures (Connor et al. 1985, p. 80).

alternative view, that observed advertising levels can be regarded as exogenously given, that is, determined by product characteristics and other factors, independent of market size.

A second important theme developed in chapter 5 is that those few statistical regularities that have emerged more or less consistently in the earlier literature in this area can be shown to follow as a *consequence* of the basic regularity identified here. Thus the present theory, as well as generating new findings, appears successfully to provide an explanation consistent with these well-known empirical relationships.

Cross-industry regression results always invite alternative interpretations, however, and in the following industry studies an attempt is made to probe the validity of the interpretation offered here by investigating whether the pattern of evolution of structure in these two industry groups exhibits those different qualitative features implied by the theory.

1.5 Industry Studies

The core of this book consists of a matrix of industry studies, which has been compiled using a combination of published market research reports and a lengthy program of meetings with senior marketing executives in the industries concerned. An attempt was made, whenever possible, to provide accounts of the industry that were complete relative to the theory. One aim of this exercise is to provide the appropriate background information to readers who may wish to explore alternative explanations for the statistical regularities of chapter 5.

By building up a detailed profile of each industry, it was possible to go much further in probing the validity of the theory than would have been possible solely on the basis of a cross-sectional econometric analysis. Apart from directly testing the implications of the theory, moreover, these industry studies make possible a number of ancillary exercises. The presentation of these studies has, for expositional reasons, been arranged around a number of major themes.

(a)   Testing the Theory I: Two Mechanisms

The central idea of the theory lies in the claim that two qualitatively different mechanisms operate to prevent certain fragmented configu-

rations from persisting over time—the claim is that such configurations are not (Nash) equilibria, that is, they will be broken because,
in such a configuration, it will always be optimal for one firm to
deviate in a way that destroys that configuration.

(i) With the exogenous sunk costs model, a too fragmented configuration will break down because it is impossible to maintain price-
cost margins sufficient to generate a normal rate of return on the setup
costs incurred in establishing plants; and while this is perfectly possible in the *short run*, it is not consistent with a *long-run* equilibrium
situation in which obsolete plants need to be replaced periodically.
Attempts by firms to coordinate prices to a degree sufficient to recover
these outlays will fail unless a level of concentration is achieved that
exceeds the lower bound consistent with equilibrium (see chapter 2
for details).

(ii) Within advertising-intensive industries, a second mechanism operates to exclude the persistence of certain fragmented configurations.
In this setting, as has already been noted, the mechanism involves a
competitive escalation of advertising outlays in the initially fragmented industry.

The first theme explored in the industry studies lies in examining
whether the histories of these two groups of industries provide any
evidence for the alleged operation of these two distinct mechanisms.
Although these mechanisms recur throughout many of the chapters
that follow, the contrast between them is best illustrated by reference
to chapters 6 and 8.

Chapter 6 is devoted to the application of the exogenous sunk cost
model to a study of the salt and sugar industries. These two industries
are characterized by a high degree of product homogeneity and a
fairly high level of setup cost relative to market size. The theory
predicts that, in this setting, a process of free competition will lead to
a highly concentrated structure. The experience of the salt industry
offers a striking example of this mechanism. In the case of U.S.
and British industries, whose history is relatively well documented,
the market was initially quite fragmented. Both industries were characterized by strong price cutting, especially in periods of declining
demand and repeated attempts to bring about price coordination
among the many firms ended in failure. In each case, poor profitability led to a mixture of exit and of merger and acquisition activity, and it was this process which in turn led to a consolidated industry

structure within which unit margins were stabilized and profitability recovered. Current concentration levels in these industries greatly exceed those levels that have been considered "warranted" by previous observers (the traditional notion of warranted concentration levels is discussed in the next section).

The central novelty of the present theory in this context is that the equilibrium level of concentration is argued to depend inter alia on the toughness of price competition in the market. The theory predicts that if institutional factors cause price competition to become less tough (in the sense that higher unit margins can be sustained at any *given* level of concentration), then the *equilibrium* level of concentration will be correspondingly lower. The obvious way to probe the validity of this argument is to look to cases in which institutional factors impinge to a varying degree on the free play of competition in different markets. Except where state monopolies exist, the salt industry has in most cases operated with minimal intervention by the authorities. Policy measures in the industry have for the most part been "pro-competitive," in that they have involved no more than occasional attempts to limit or prohibit price fixing. But the sugar industry, in contrast, usually enjoys the support of a strong agricultural lobby, and the authorities' approach to price determination in the industry has varied widely, both across countries and over time. In some cases, the authorities have favored unfettered competition; in others they have effectively determined industry margins, with a view to either stabilizing or rationalizing industry structure. In others, policy has varied sharply in different periods.

In contrast to the salt industry, which is highly concentrated everywhere, the sugar industry shows a wide divergence of structure across countries. In chapter 6, it is argued that these differences in structure can be traced directly to the differences in policy regime in a manner consistent with the theory.

The cases of salt and sugar, then, illustrate the way in which the toughness of price competition impinges on the determination of structure in those industries where setup costs are high in relation to market size. The evolution of concentration in these two industries stands in sharp contrast to the pattern observed in advertising-intensive industries.

Chapter 8, a pivotal chapter, begins the exploration of advertising intensive industries by examining the evolution of structure in the frozen food market. This case is of special interest, as this is one of the rare examples of an advertising-intensive industry within the food and drink sector whose origin is both recent and sharply defined. The industry's beginnings can be traced to the development of certain freezing processes in the 1930s, and the early history of the industry, especially in the United Stated and the United Kingdom, is well documented.

The themes explored in chapter 8 provide a clear illustration of the mechanism postulated in the present theory as applying to industries that exhibit endogenous sunk costs. The setup costs incurred in entering the frozen food industry are quite low; and the market includes both a retail segment (within which advertising is quite effective) and nonretail segments in which buyers choose suppliers almost wholly on the basis of relative price. Under such circumstances, the theory predicts that increases in market size may lead to an indefinite expansion in the total number of firms, but that the (advertising-sensitive) retail sector will remain concentrated, while advertising outlays by leading sellers in the retail sector expand in step with the size of the market. (The theoretical basis for the evolution of this dual structure is described in chapter 3.) A competitive escalation of advertising outlays will necessarily lead to a situation in which only a small number of firms survive and dominate the retail segment of the market.

This process is well illustrated by the history of the frozen food industries of the United States and the United Kingdom. In each case, it is possible to pinpoint the exact phase at which firms became partitioned into two discrete groups: a high-advertising group selling primarily to the retail sector, and a nonadvertising group selling solely to the nonretail sector. Indeed, it is possible to trace the way in which firms situated between these two groups faced declining profitability until this split was achieved.

While the frozen food industries provide an unusually clear-cut illustration of this process, the same process can be seen to operate in a wide number of instances explored in later chapters. In many of these cases, however, the appearance of the high advertising group can be traced to the turn of the century, and documentation of the structure of the industries at that time is often sparse. Moreover, the partitioning of firms into two groups appears to have taken place in a more gradual and less dramatic fashion than in the case of the frozen food industry. This may in part reflect the lesser scale and effectiveness of advertising prior to the advent of television. These qualifications apart, however, the same process appears to have operated across a wide range of those advertising-intensive industries that are explored in later chapters.

(b) Testing the Theory II: Comparative Static Predictions

A central issue concerns how the exogenous and endogenous elements of sunk costs *interact*. How does a higher level of setup costs affect equilibrium advertising outlays and equilibrium structure, other things being equal? Since other things are rarely equal, examining this question empirically poses considerable difficulties. As far as theoretical predictions are concerned, chapter 2 shows that a rise in setup cost will lead to a more concentrated equilibrium structure; this modest result, however, is the only robust comparative static result within the endogenous sunk cost model. In respect of advertising, a rise in setup costs from an initially very low level will at first imply a rise in the advertising-sales ratio. As setup costs continue to rise, however, the advertising-sales ratio may continue to rise, or it may fall. The outcome will depend delicately on the details of the model— and most importantly on the extent to which increases in total *industry* advertising affect total *industry* sales. This feature of the market will differ sharply across different industries, so that no robust result is available.

Investigating such comparative static properties is made difficult, in general, by the presence of a multitude of industry-specific characteristics whose effect may be extremely hard to quantify. The analysis of chapter 12 takes advantage of the fact that two pairs of industries within the present sample offer an unusually helpful context in which to examine this issue, for in each case the two industries in question have setup costs that differ by a very large factor, while the other economic characteristics of the industry are closely similar. The production of instant coffee involves setup costs very much greater than those incurred by the typical producer of ground (or roast and ground) coffee. Within the confectionery industry, the setup costs incurred by producers of mass-market chocolate confectionery items exceeds by an order of magnitude the costs incurred by the typical producer of sugar confectionery. In each of these cases, we find that the industry with the higher setup costs is more highly concentrated. Furthermore, differences in setup costs vary across different market segments; and a detailed analysis of how concentration differences mirror these differences in the pattern of market segmentation offers further support to this interpretation. Finally, it is shown that, within the confectionery sector, the high-setup cost (chocolate confectionery) industry displays a systematically higher advertising-sales ratio. This is not true within the coffee industry, however: here the advertising-sales ratio in the instant coffee market may be higher or lower than the ratio obtaining in the ground coffee market. While considerable caution is needed in interpreting these differences in experience, they appear in part to reflect the extent to which *total* advertising outlays for instant coffee are likely to expand total instant coffee sales (at the expense of total sales of ground coffee)—as the present theory implies.

(c)   Special Cases: First-Mover Advantages

One important role played by the industry studies that follow lies in allowing an exploration of various special cases arising within the general theoretical framework. One such special case arises in respect of "first-mover advantages": to what extent do strategic asymmetries between early entrants to an industry and firms that enter later impinge on the equilibrium pattern of structure? Here, the results of a game-theoretic analysis suggest that the outcome depends delicately on the details of the model; and so in this context the focus is *not* on testing theory, but is merely exploratory. The aim is to examine on the basis of industry histories how such influences may play a part in accounting for the often wide divergence of structure in the same industry from one country to another.

It is often extremely difficult in practice, however, to decide whether or not a particular firm enjoys this kind of strong strategic asymmetry relative to its rivals. But there are some instances in which the historical and institutional background point to a sharp asymmetry between firms, of a kind that can reasonably be represented by a simple sequential entry model. Chapter 9 examines three industries in which a very clear-cut first-mover advantage was present and traces the apparent consequences of this strategic asymmetry for the evolution of structure.

In the prepared soups industry the contrast between the United Kingdom and the United States is of particular interest, as the same two firms dominate each of these markets. Their roles in the two markets are precisely reversed, however, with the U.S. market leader Campbell filling the same role in the United Kingdom market as does the U.K. market leader Heinz in the U.S. market. This similarity of roles extends to such areas as the two firms' pricing policy, their decisions as to whether to supply retailers' own-label products, and so on; and these differences can be traced to the fact that each country's current market leader enjoyed a first-mover advantage over its rival in that country. In this case, the structure of the industry is closely similar in both countries, and only the roles of the leading players differ.

A second example illustrates how the presence or absence of first-mover advantages may exert an apparently profound effect on the overall structure of the industry. In the margarine market, Unilever enjoyed a strong first-mover advantage in the various European markets, where it still enjoys a leadership position. In the U.S. market, however, a strong agricultural lobby effectively stifled the development of the margarine market until the 1950s, by which time a number of major U.S. food producers had developed a position in the industry. Thus, no one firm had a first-mover advantage on the eve of the rapid takeoff in margarine sales, which coincided with the growth of television as the dominant advertising channel during the 1950s. The outcome was a less concentrated overall structure, in which Unilever competes on a more or less equal basis with two major indigenous food producers (Kraft and Procter & Gamble).

A third example of a first-mover advantage arises in the soft drink market. The Coca-Cola Company and Pepsico enjoy rough parity in the U.S. market, and the escalating competition between the two has played a central role in shaping the evolution of the U.S. industry. In Europe, however, a sharp asymmetry exists between the two, which can be traced to a series of events that took place during the Second World War. In return for its commitment to "put a Coke in the hand of every U.S. serviceman" for 10 cents, the Coca-Cola Company was made exempt from wartime sugar rationing, and the resulting ubiquity of Coca-Cola set the stage for the continuing dominance of Coca-Cola over Pepsi throughout postwar Europe. It is argued in chapter 9 that this asymmetry may be one of the contributory factors underlying the wide divergence in structure in this industry in the United States and Europe.

(d)   The Limitations of the Theory

Another theme that runs through the industry studies relates to the limitations of the theory—indeed, one of the main virtues of constructing such a matrix of industry studies is that it provides an unusually detailed feel for both the strengths and the limitations of the theory. The limitations are of two kinds:

1. The theory predicts only a *lower bound* to equilibrium concentration levels. The lower this minimal equilibrium level, the less the theory constrains the data.

This implies an inherent limitation in the theory, the importance of which varies across different groups of industry. This issue is explored in chapters 7 and 8.

2. The usefulness of this theory rests on the assumption that the advertising response function depends only on certain (unspecified) product characteristics, which may be assumed similar across countries, and on *observable* institutional factors, which may differ across countries.

While this assumption appears, on the basis of the evidence, to be broadly reasonable, occasional instances arise in which idiosyncratic factors peculiar to certain firms or markets profoundly influence the extent to which advertising "works." A good illustration of this kind of effect, which highlights a potentially serious limitation to the value of theories of this kind, is provided by the experience of the mineral water market. Perrier's success in the French market, and its competitors' reaction to that success, transformed the structure of the industry within a few years. In no other country has Perrier, or any other company, achieved a similar success. Indeed, in the three main European markets (France, Germany, Italy), apparently closely similar market conditions coexist with levels of concentration that diverge very widely from one country to another (chapter 11).

(e)   Controversial Cases

The final theme explored in the industry studies relates to the reexamination of some cases that have received heavy emphasis in the recent literature in terms of the present theoretical framework.

One of the most crucial U.S. antitrust cases in recent years was that brought by the Federal Trade Commission (FTC) against the Kellogg Company and its main rivals in the ready-to-eat (RTE) breakfast cereals industry. The case was interpreted in some quarters as constituting a test for a new departure in antitrust practice—a departure in favor of government intervention in markets on the basis of an examination of structural features (concentration) per se, independent of any observed anticompetitive practices. Under these circumstances, it is not surprising that the case attracted an unusual degree of interest among industrial economists, and the causes of concentration in the industry became a much debated issue. The most popular theory to emerge was that proposed by Schmalensee (1978), who proposed that Kellogg's dominant position could be traced to a process of monopolization by product proliferation. By taking advantage of its status as a first-mover, Kellogg could allegedly fill all available product niches, leaving little scope for rivals to enter.

How does this view fit in with the present theory? In chapter 10, it is shown that the strategy of product proliferation can be seen as a special case of the general framework developed here; but placing it within this setting introduces as a additional and primary mechanism the same competitive escalation of advertising outlays that appears across the general run of advertising-intensive industries. It is argued that this difference in interpretation has possible implications for the effects of the type of remedy proposed by the FTC.

The evolution of concentration in the beer industry is the subject of the last of the industry studies presented in part II. Few industries have been more intensively studied; and particular attention has been focused on the U.S. industry, in which a steady rise in concentration over the past generation has led to a situation in which the emergence of a triopoly was becoming evident by the late 1980s.

The causes of this massive and sustained rise in concentration have been variously explained. Two lines of argument stand out in the economics literature. One emphasizes changes in brewing and bottling technology, which have led to a substantial rise in the minimum efficient scale of operation (m.e.s). Another view emphasizes the role of escalating advertising outlays by the major brewers and the consequent pressure on small and medium-sized firms. Some authors take an eclectic view, arguing that both of these factors have contributed to the changes in industry structure.

The central theme of chapter 13 is that within the context of the present theory, these two contributory factors, while both relevant, are not independent. Rather, they both play a part within the same unified mechanism that underlies the evolution of all of the advertising-intensive industries studied here. Under this interpretation, the exogenous changes in technology that have raised the minimum efficient scale—and so the level of setup costs—have thereby stimulated and fueled the concomitant increases in advertising outlays, thereby accentuating what would otherwise have been a comparatively modest trend toward higher levels of concentration.

A central implication of this analysis relates to the likely effect of recent changes in technology, which appear to favor the relative efficiency of smaller breweries. It is argued in chapter 13 that such a reversal of earlier trends toward higher m.e.s. levels will *not* tend to lead to a dilution in industry concentration.

1.6 The Bain Paradigm Revisited

It may be of interest to readers familiar with the earlier literature to see how the ideas set out above relate to the Bain paradigm. Two points of difference are obvious. The first point relates to difficulties arising with the chain of causation story. As noted earlier, the Bain paradigm posits a one-way chain of causation running from structure to conduct to performance. The determination of structure, in this setting, is explained by reference to various barriers to entry, whose nature is taken to be exogenously given. It is not only within the recent game-theoretic literature that one finds the adequacy of such a story challenged: various early empirical studies drew attention to the need to consider a possible reverse link from conduct or performance to structure; but this was often presented as an econometric issue, in the sense that it might be dealt with by writing down a simultaneous equations system linking structure, conduct, and performance. This line of response did not prove very fruitful, however (see Schmalensee 1989 for a review). Within the present framework, the problem is tackled by looking rather to a reformulation of the basic theoretical model. The key contribution of the two-stage game formulation is that it offers a neat way of unraveling the two-way link between structure and conduct.

The second point of difference with the Bain paradigm lies in its treatment of observed advertising levels as a barrier to entry, whose level might be appealed to in explaining industry structure . This view of advertising as a barrier to entry was taken to its logical conclusion in a series of studies that regressed observed levels of (or changes in) concentration on a series of explanatory variables, including the level of scale economies, the level of advertising intensity, and so on. (See chapter 5 for a comparison of the results of such studies to this study.)

Within the present approach, observed advertising levels are endogenously determined. This difference is of fundamental importance, and it raises some serious questions about the way in which the barriers to entry concept is commonly used. The role of this concept in the post-Bain literature lay in providing a rationale for why apparently high profits could be consistent with an absence of entry. If the height of such a barrier is endogenously determined, however, then considerable care is needed in formulating explanations of why observed concentration levels are high, or why high measured profit levels do not seem to stimulate new entry in certain industries.

Beyond these two rather obvious differences, however, there are a number of further ways in which the present approach departs from the traditional literature. One such feature relates to the relationship between product differentiation and advertising. In the traditional literature, these were often closely identified; advertising intensity was in fact widely used as a proxy for the degree of product differentiation. Such an approach is highly dubious on purely empirical grounds: many industrial sectors (such as engineering) involve both a high degree of product differentiation and minimal advertising. Within this study, a sharp analytical distinction exists between the effects of product differentiation per se and the effects of advertising outlays. In making this distinction, the concepts of horizontal and vertical product differentiation outlined above turn out to be extremely useful (section 3.5).

There is one final difference between the present approach and the earlier empirical literature that deserves a relatively full remark. This relates to the way in which a lower bound to industry structure was introduced by some contributors to the traditional literature, in the guise of a warranted level of concentration . The idea ran as follows: Consider an industry in which advertising and R&D play no role, so that a firm's costs may be identified with the (fixed and variable) costs of production alone.

Imagine that each firm operates subject to an average cost schedule that declines up to some critical level of output (the minimum efficient scale (m.e.s.) of operation) and is flat after that point. Any firm operating at a level of output below this point will suffer a competitive disadvantage, and at equilibrium the industry will be populated by a number of firms operating at a level of output at or above the m.e.s. Thus a lower bound to industry concentration exists, corresponding to a configuration in which the industry consists of a number of firms operating at a level of output *equal to* the m.e.s. level. The associated level of concentration is referred to as the warranted level of concentration throughout much of the empirical literature of the 1960s and 1970s (see Anderson et al. 1975).

It was noted by many observers, however, that actual concentration levels seem to lie far above the levels warranted on the basis of such arguments (see Scherer 1980, and for a specific example, Anderson et al. 1975), whether the m.e.s. level used in calculating such bounds came from estimates of median plant size, or from independent engineering studies (see chapter 4).

How does this relate to the present approach? A strict formulation of the preceding argument depends necessarily on the assumption that the average cost schedule becomes perfectly flat once the m.e.s. level of output is exceeded. In applying the idea empirically, however, it was (and remains) customary to adopt an arbitrary definition of m.e.s. as corresponding to the level beyond which further increases in output would lead to a reduction in average cost of no more than 10%. Engineering studies would otherwise often imply an implausibly high value for m.e.s., and one that might lie far above those generated by the other popular measure of m.e.s., viz., the size of the median plant operating in the industry. It was in terms of these definitions that the warranted levels of concentration were seen to be very low compared to actual levels. While this procedure may lead to plausible answers, it actually hides the central analytical issue behind an empirical guess, for it rests upon a judgment as to the size of cost disadvantage a firm may suffer without being driven from the market.

But such questions obviously depend on the intensity of price competition in the market, and this will depend in turn not only on product characteristics (the degree of product differentiation) and on the state of competition policy, etc., but also on the degree of concentration in the industry. But if this is so, it would appear that there is no escaping an explicit analysis of the kind undertaken in chapter 2.

Within the present approach, it is assumed that the firm's average cost (including the contribution of sunk outlays incurred in setting up production) are declining, so that the m.e.s. level—on a strict definition—is infinite. On the other hand, the toughness of price competition is considered explicitly, and the equilibrium level of concentration is ground out by the interplay between setup costs, market size, and the toughness of price competition.[5]

5. Thus, the warranted degree of concentration does not figure in the present scheme. The use of m.e.s. levels, as estimated from either engineering studies or median plant size, enters only insofar as it is assumed that differences in the cost of establishing a single m.e.s. plant, as defined along traditional lines, may provide a very rough proxy for differences in the level of setup cost across different industries (see chapter 4).

2

The Analytical Framework I: Exogenous Sunk Costs

2.1 Introduction

This chapter and the next are both concerned with the formulation of hypotheses. Since the underlying aim is to examine cross-industry regularities, the primary focus in setting out the theory lies in developing hypotheses appropriate to a pooled sample of different industries. As noted earlier, the class of models on which the analysis rests admits of a wide range of detailed specifications, and many results of these models depend delicately on such details. The central thesis is that only those results that do *not* depend on such details but hold good across the entire class of models considered will be of interest in looking at cross-industry relationships.

Hypothesis formulation is, of its nature, judgmental. The central judgment made in what follows relates to the choice of the class of models over which the results should hold. It will be argued, in fact, that it is appropriate to work in terms of a very broad class, and this argument reflects the judgment that no tighter restrictions could reasonably be justified for the entire run of industries to be considered here. Given the breadth of this class of models, it is unsurprising that the resulting regularities are very limited.

In special circumstances, however, there is a second kind of regularity that is of some interest. These circumstances arise when comparisons are made between the same industry across different countries, or between two closely cognate industries (which differ, say, in respect of one attribute, such as setup cost). In these circumstances, though it would not be possible to identify any specific model as the best representation, it might nonetheless be reasonable to suppose that the *same* specific model is appropriate to the industry, or pair of industries. This implies that comparative static results that hold across the entire class of models defined below are of potential interest. A secondary aim of this chapter and the next lies in drawing out results of this latter kind.

This chapter looks at the case of exogenous sunk costs, and the next chapter is concerned with endogenous sunk costs. Each chapter begins with a specific example, which is used to illustrate some basic ideas. We then go on to ask whether any of the properties illustrated in the example hold across an appropriately broad range of model specifications. It is at this point that we discuss and define the class of models over which we wish the results to be robust. Within the exogenous sunk costs case, two subcases arise. The next section deals with the homogeneous good subcase. The following section is concerned with the situation in which products are differentiated.

2.2 The Role of Setup Costs

In this section we consider the determination of structure in a homogeneous goods industry in which all firms offer an identical product. We identify the setup cost incurred by firms on entering such an industry with the cost of acquiring a single plant of minimum efficient scale, net of any resale value. (This identification is, at best, a somewhat crude approximation.)

Since this irrecoverable element of fixed cost incurred on entering the industry constitutes a sunk cost, its level plays no role in determining the firm's day-to-day pricing policy. This idea is neatly captured using the simple device of a two-stage game . We represent the firm's decision as taking place in two stages: at the first stage, each of a number of potential entrants decides whether or not to enter. Then, at the second stage, those firms that have entered set their respective prices.

This two-stage game device also serves to capture in a relatively simple manner the traditional distinction between long-run and short-run decisions. Those variables labeled long run are chosen at the first stage and are treated as fixed parameters when analyzing equilibrium in the short run, as depicted in the second stage of the game (figure 2.1).

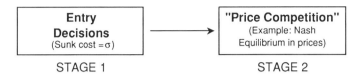

STAGE 1   STAGE 2

Figure 2.1
The two-stage game.

This way of representing the setup costs associated with entry has an immediate implication that is of interest in what follows: prices set at the second stage of the game depend on the setup costs only *indirectly*, that is, only by way of their influence on the entry decisions of firms in the first stage . It follows that mistakes involving excessive entry to the industry may lead to losses, as prices set in the second stage may not suffice to cover the setup costs incurred in entering the industry.

The entry decisions of firms in this kind of model will depend on the *interplay* between the level of setup cost incurred at stage 1 and the intensity of price competition that firms face at stage 2. The greater the degree of price competition at stage 2, the lower the post-entry profits and the fewer the number of firms choosing to enter. Thus equilibrium structure reflects a tension between the level of setup costs that must be recovered to justify entry ex-post, and the intensity of price competition following entry: more entrants mean lower prices, but the lower the prices (for any given number of entrants), the less attractive will entry be.

Three Examples

The results of this analysis hinge on the form of price competition that is assumed to hold in the second stage of the game. To fix ideas, we begin by looking at the three examples most widely used in the literature: Cournot competition (Nash equilibrium in quantities), Bertrand competition (Nash equilibrium in prices), and joint profit maximization. Although none of these cases should be thought of as an adequate depiction of price competition under oligopoly, taken together they nonetheless provide a useful point of reference. (We assume throughout that the firm pays a sunk cost $\sigma > 0$ on entering the industry and thereafter produces at constant marginal cost $c > 0$.)

The Cournot Case

We begin by looking at the Cournot case, which has been the most popular point of departure in the theoretical literature. Here each firm produces the profit-maximizing quantity of output, taking its rivals' quantities as given (i.e., we seek a Nash equilibrium in quantities). Market price is then determined as a function of these output levels, by reference to a given industry demand schedule.[1]

It will be clear that the qualitative features of all three examples hold good for any downward-sloping demand schedule. For expositional reasons, however, we shall illustrate these features by reference to one particular demand schedule. (This schedule has been chosen with a view to keeping the algebra as simple as possible throughout the various extensions of the example presented in later sections.) We take, then, the case of the isoelastic demand schedule

$$X = S/p,$$

where p denotes market price and X is the quantity sold; S represents total expenditure, which in this setting is independent of price and which measures the size of the market. Since the above demand schedule has the property that (for positive marginal cost) the monopoly price goes to infinity, we further assume that sales become zero above some cutoff price p_0; hence p_0 becomes the monopoly price.[2]

Suppose then, that N firms enter the market at stage 1. To find the Cournot equilibrium, note that firm i's profit in stage 2 is given by

$$p_i(\Sigma x_j) x_i - c x_i.$$

---

1. Although this procedure might seem hard to motivate in a realistic manner, Kreps and Scheinkman (1983) develop a rationale for the Cournot story, as follows. Imagine a two-stage game in which firms choose a capacity level in stage one. Let stage 2 competition be characterized as a Nash equilibrium in prices, that is, each firm sets the profit-maximizing price, taking his rivals' prices as given (so that, given capacity constraints, we have a Bertrand-Edgeworth game at stage 2). Kreps and Scheinkman show that the (perfect) equilibrium of this two-stage game (between two firms) corresponds to the solution of the elementary Cournot duopoly model. (This result rests on certain special assumptions on the rationing of output when prices are such that demand exceeds supply.)
2. This schedule may be derived from the linear utility function $U(x, y) = x + y$, where y denotes consumption of an outside good (Hicksian composite commodity) whose price is fixed at p_0. The market demand schedule depends, then, only on the sum of consumers' incomes, which we denote S.

Differentiating this expression with respect to x_i yields the first-order conditions that specify firm i's optimal reply x_i to its rivals' strategies $(x_1, \ldots, x_{i-1}, x_{i+1}, \ldots x_n)$. Setting $x_i = x$ for all i yields the (symmetric) Cournot equilibrium, at which price equals

$$p = c\left\{1 + \frac{1}{N-1}\right\},$$

unless this expression exceeds p_0, in which case $p = p_0$.

In the former case, equilibrium output per firm becomes

$$x = \frac{S}{c} \cdot \frac{N-1}{N^2},$$

and the equilibrium level of profit earned at stage 2 is

$$\Pi = (p - c)x = S/N^2.$$

In the latter case $(p = p_0)$ we have $\Pi = (p_0 - c)x(p_0)$, the monopoly profit level.

Now consider the firms' entry decisions at stage 1. Given the entry decisions of its rivals, firm i incurs a sunk cost σ on entering the market and so earns net profit $S/(k + 1)^2 - \sigma$, where k denotes the number of its rivals who choose to enter. Entry is profitable if this expression is positive, and so it follows that the number of firms entering at equilibrium is given by (the integer part of)

$$N^* = \sqrt{\frac{S}{\sigma}}$$

as obtained by simply setting $\Pi = \sigma$. (A formal statement of the foregoing procedure is given in footnote 3).

Within this model, then, we obtain an equilibrium outcome in which the number of entrants to the market increases steadily as the level of setup cost falls from the level of monopoly profits, at which we have one entrant, to zero, where the number of entrants becomes

---

3. The procedure adopted above may be specified more formally as follows: A firm's *strategy* in this game takes one of two forms: *either* "don't enter," or "enter, and set output at stage 2 as a function of the number of firms that have entered at stage 1." The firm's *payoff* is either zero (if it chooses not to enter), or else it equals the profit earned at stage 2 less the sunk cost incurred at stage 1 (which we denote as σ, and which we assume to be strictly positive). Equilibrium is specified as a subgame-perfect equilibrium of the two-stage game. In what follows, we shall confine our attention to equilibria that involve the use of a pure strategy at the entry stage (see footnote 4).

arbitrarily large. This result constitutes the most elementary form of limit theorem, according to which an increase in the size of the market relative to the level of setup costs leads to a more fragmented structure.

The Bertrand Case

The Cournot model can be contrasted with the results of a Bertrand formulation, which runs as follows. We describe competition in stage 2 of the game by a Nash equilibrium in prices (Bertrand equilibrium), that is, each firm chooses its price to maximize profits, taking as given the prices chosen by its rivals.

From the standard Bertrand undercutting argument, it follows that if two or more firms enter, then price equals marginal cost in the second stage, so that profits are zero—and each firm makes a net loss of σ at equilibrium.[4] If, on the other hand, only one firm enters, it sets a monopoly price and enjoys monopoly profits at stage 2. We assume that the market is viable, in the sense that the setup cost does not exceed the level of monopoly profits. Turning to the entry stage, then, it is clear that firm i's optimal reply to its rivals' decisions is to enter if and only if no rival enters. We have, therefore, the following result: *For any $\sigma > 0$, exactly one firm enters and sets the monopoly price.*[5]

---

4. Formally, we define the strategies in a manner analogous to the Cournot case. The firm's payoff is defined in terms of the stage-2 profit function, as before. Let m denote the number of firms setting the equal lowest price, $\underline{p}$. Then firm i's profit in stage two equals $(p_i - c)x(p_i)/m$ if $p_i = \underline{p}$, and zero otherwise.

Suppose two or more firms enter. Then, at equilibrium, at least two firms must be setting an equal lowest price $\underline{p} = c$; and all firms with $p > \underline{p}$ will have zero sales. For otherwise at least one firm is not using an optimal reply to its rivals' prices. To see this, note that if $\underline{p} < c$, the lowest-price firm(s) can raise profit (to zero) by setting $\underline{p} = c$; if $\underline{p} > c$, then any (equal) highest-price firm can raise its profits by slightly undercutting $\underline{p}$; while if only one firm is setting $\underline{p} = c$, then that firm can raise its profits by increasing its price.

Hence, if two or more firms enter, each entrant makes zero profit in stage 2.

5. As noted earlier, we confine attention to equilibria involving pure strategies at the entry stage; there is also a symmetric mixed-strategy equilibrium in which each firm enters with the same (positive) probability. The pure-strategy equilibria are asymmetric and so come in mirror-image sets, that is, there is nothing within the model that determines *which* firm enters. This feature arises in a wide range of game-theoretic models in industrial economics and sometimes causes comment. The theory can tell us something about equilibrium outcomes, but cannot distinguish which player follows which strategy. Attempts to select any one equilibrium (the symmetric mixed-strategy equilibrium, say) must rest on arguments that are less than compelling. This issue is discussed again, from a practical standpoint, in chapter 8.

The Monopoly Case

Our third example relates to a situation in which firms maximize joint profits in the second stage of the game . This outcome may be supported as a noncooperative (Nash) equilibrium if we modify the present setup by replacing the one-shot representation of stage 2 by an infinite-horizon dynamic game in which firms set prices, and receive payoffs, over successive periods.[6]

In this setup, joint profits remain invariant to the number of entrants; denoting monopoly profit by Π_0, the equilibrium number of entrants is now given by (the integer part of) Π_0/σ.

The results of our three examples are illustrated in figure 2.2. These examples illustrate the simple property noted earlier: given any market size, as we make price competition tougher (moving from joint profit maximization to Cournot, to Bertrand), equilibrium structure becomes more concentrated.[7]

As noted in chapter 1, the phrase "toughness of price competition" is used in a very special sense. It does *not* relate to the size of observed price-cost margins; rather, it relates to the *function* linking concentration levels to equilibrium price (the function $p(\mathcal{N})$). This function summarizes the properties of stage 2 of the underlying game: in other words, it describes what happens to prices, *given* any historically determined level of concentration $(1/\mathcal{N})$. As such, the function simply summarizes the link that Bain emphasized between (the histori-

---

6. The details are as follows: let the constituent game played in each period be the Bertrand game, as specified above. A *strategy* for firm i in the repeated game is a function that maps the prices set by all players in periods $1, \ldots \tau - 1$ into a price $p_{i,\tau}$ for firm i in period τ. Firm i's payoff is the discounted sum of its profits in each period, $\Sigma \delta^\tau \Pi_\tau$, where Π_τ is computed as specified earlier.

The following (trigger) strategies support the cooperative outcome as a noncooperative (Nash) equilibrium in the repeated game: firm i sets the monopoly price p_0 in all periods, if and only if no price set in any earlier period is less than p_0; otherwise firm i sets price equal to marginal cost.

(This example constitutes an elementary folk theorem; for a full discussion of such results, see Friedman 1986).

7. This idea was familiar to many contributors to the traditional literature (see, for example, George and Ward 1975, pp. 15–16), and it featured in some early thinking on policy regarding restrictive practices in the United Kingdom. In the recent literature, its representation in terms of multistage games has been noted by several authors. Compare Shaked and Sutton 1982 and Bonanno 1985; see also Vickers 1986. The above presentation follows that of my 1987 Einaudi lecture, published as Sutton 1989a. An analogous presentation is found in Dasgupta and Stiglitz 1988.

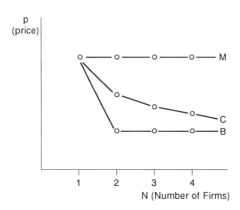

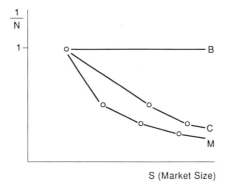

Figure 2.2
Equilibrium price as a function of the number of entrants, N, and equilibrium
concentration $(1/N)$ as a function of market size, for three simple examples
(B = Bertrand, C = Cournot, M = joint profit maximization).

cally given) level of concentration and the (short-run equilibrium) price.[8]

The main virtue of the two-stage game formulation is that it permits a neat unraveling of this short-run nexus, summarized by the function $p(\mathcal{N})$, and the long-run link between this factor and the determination of equilibrium concentration levels (via the entry decision of firms). Interpreting the toughness of price competition in this sense, then, our analysis implies a fundamental trade-off between tough price competition and equilibrium concentration levels.

This trade-off is a basic feature of two-stage models. For any symmetric model, we can summarize the stage 2 subgame in terms of some (nonincreasing) function $p(\mathcal{N})$ linking the number of firms in the market to the equilibrium price. If any two models can be ranked in the sense that these $p(\mathcal{N})$ schedules are nonintersecting, so that one regime is characterized by tougher price competition, then for a given market size equilibrium structure will be more concentrated under this regime (in the sense that $\mathcal{N}$ will be smaller). The property that will be of central interest is illustrated in figure 2.2: it relates market size to equilibrium structure (as measured by $1/\mathcal{N}$). For a wide class of homogeneous goods models, including the Cournot and joint profit maximization models, the industry converges to a fragmented structure $(1/\mathcal{N} \to 0)$ as S/σ becomes large. For the Bertrand model, this property fails. The Bertrand model can be seen as a limiting case, in which the fact that entry would cause a very sharp fall in price suffices to deter entry and maintain a monopoly outcome.

---

8. This may suggest a question to the reader: why not specify the basic features of the model that determine $p(\mathcal{N})$ and work directly in terms of these? Why use this *function* as a primitive of the analysis? It is true that this procedure is both unfamiliar and perhaps puzzling. Yet it is natural in the present setup, given the objectives of the study. For one central lesson of the recent game-theoretic literature is that models of *dynamic* price competition involve acute difficulties of the kind alluded to in chapter 1. The results are delicately dependent on many unobservable features of the model, and within any particular model specification, multiple equilibria are common (the Bertrand, Cournot, and joint profit maximization examples considered above are only three of a very wide class of models).

Under these circumstances, the only way to proceed to characterize robust results appears to be to work directly in terms of $p(\mathcal{N})$ and to take advantage of the fact that even though it is not possible to measure or proxy the full set of determinants of $p(\mathcal{N})$, it may nonetheless be possible to identify certain exogenous influences that shift $p(\mathcal{N})$ in a known direction—thus making possible empirical tests of the theory (see chapter 6).

It is of interest, therefore, to consider the behavior of these models when the schedule $p(\mathcal{N})$ is close to, but does not coincide with, the Bertrand limit. Let us assume that $p(\mathcal{N})$ is nonincreasing[9] and that $p(\mathcal{N}) > c$ for all $\mathcal{N}$. As long as this is so, equilibrium concentration, as measured by $(1/\mathcal{N})$, will fall monotonically as market size S increases,[10] relative to setup cost σ. This property is of central interest in what follows. At the Bertrand pole, this property fails (figure 2.2).[11] On the other hand, for any nonincreasing function satisfying $p(\mathcal{N}) > c$ for all $\mathcal{N}$, however close to the Bertrand case, convergence occurs—though the rate at which concentration falls as S/σ increases may be arbitrarily slow. Within the class of homogeneous goods models set out above, the minimal assumption that $p(\mathcal{N}) > c$ for all $\mathcal{N}$ suffices to ensure that increases in market size relative to setup cost lead to an arbitrarily fragmented structure.

Finally, it is worth remarking on one other property of these models that is robust enough to be of some general interest. As market size increases by replication of the population of consumers, unit margins fall in general (except in the limiting case of joint profit maximization). It follows that increases in economy size are accompanied by

---

9. While it might seem almost compelling to assume that the equilibrium price level is nonincreasing in the number of firms, some theoretical examples have been presented in the literature in which entry actually raises prices. Such examples, however, either rest on extremely contrived assumptions regarding the nature of demand (tastes), or else they pertain to situations characterized by rather special informational asymmetries that are unlikely to hold in the usual run of product markets. The interested reader is referred to Sutton 1989b for details; in the class of models to be considered here, such cases are excluded.

10. Increases in market size are understood here in the sense of a replication of the population of consumers. This, together with our assumption of constant marginal cost, implies that equilibrium prices are *independent* of market size (the first-order conditions defining the optimal reply of each firm are independent of S). Hence $p(\mathcal{N})$ can be defined independent of S.

11. The Bertrand limit case has some further interesting properties. First, it has the feature that for *any* $\sigma > 0$, however small, the outcome is monopoly. If $\sigma = 0$, however, a continuum of equilibria exist, including equilibria in which two or more firms enter, and the (minimum) market price is $p = c$. This polar case, in which we combine "no sunk cost" with Bertrand competition, corresponds to the notion of a "contestable market," as introduced by Baumol, Panzar, and Willig (1982). It is of interest to note that this result is a "knife-edge" result, which requires that sunk cost be *exactly* zero. Any sunk cost, however small, implies a switch to a *monopoly* outcome. It is at this point that the present study parts company with the "contestability" approach. In what follows, we shall always assume that entry involves *some* sunk cost, however small.

a less-than-proportionate increase in the number of firms and an increase in the level of output per firm (a higher output level being required to permit recovery of the sunk cost σ at equilibrium, in the presence of tighter unit margins). This property will be relevant to our observations in chapter 5, in respect of those (few) statistical regularities that have been reported with some consistency in the earlier literature.

2.3   The (Horizontal) Product Differentiation Subcase

Up to this point, it has been assumed that rival firms produce a homogeneous product subject to an exogenously given level of sunk cost. Very few products are strictly homogeneous in nature, however. Even among commodity products like salt or sugar, the existence of transport costs is sufficient to introduce some degree of product differentiation among sellers located in different places. Even if transport costs are unimportant, there may still be small differences in the physical characteristics of rival sellers' offerings, or in the allied services offered by different sellers, that make them different in the eyes of consumers. Such differences may exist even though the sunk costs incurred by all sellers are equal and exogenously given, and so the treatment of the exogenous sunk cost model needs to be extended to encompass this feature.

This kind of product differentiation is usually modeled in the literature in terms of the standard models of horizontal product differentiation. (Readers unfamiliar with the standard literature on this topic may consult pp. 38–39 for a summary.) Equilibria in models of horizontal product differentiation have been explored to some degree in the recent literature, some notable contributions being Schmalensee 1978, Lane 1980, and Bonanno 1987. A full discussion of their properties lies outside our present scope; the interested reader is referred to Shaked and Sutton 1990 for a characterization of equilibria. Here only a brief summary of those features relevant to the present analysis is attempted.

Within models of this kind, if each firm is confined to producing a single product, a limit theorem holds regarding the relationship between concentration and market size which is directly analogous to that developed above for the homogeneous goods case (for details,

Horizontal Product Differentiation

Any model of competition among differentiated products consists of two elements. The first element is a set of potential products, together with a specification of the (fixed and variable) costs associated with the production of any particular variety or set of varieties. The second element is a set of consumers, each of whom is described by an income level and a utility function defined over the appropriate domain of products.

A general model of this kind would be quite complex to analyze, and so the literature has tended to focus on some special cases, which have interesting empirical counterparts. By far the most widely studied case is one in which some set of alternative varieties are possible, each of which involves the same (fixed and variable) cost[12] and in which consumers differ in respect of their ranking of alternative varieties. Models of this kind are known as horizontal product differentiation models.

The simplest example is the elementary location model in which both products and consumers are distributed over some space (a line, say); each consumer prefers, ceteris paribus, the product located closest to him along the line. The first model of this kind was introduced by Hotelling in 1929. In Hotelling-type models, consumers are taken to be distributed along some line (figure 2.3). Suppose to begin with that each firm offers a single product, whose specification is represented by a point on the line. This construction can be interpreted in two ways, literally or figuratively. In the former case, the line is taken to represent some geographic space,[13] and each consumer is assumed to buy (a single unit) from the lowest-cost firm, where the cost of acquiring a unit equals the price plus a transport cost given by the distance from the consumer to the firm multiplied by a given unit transport cost, $t > 0$. In the alternative (figurative) interpretation, the line is taken to represent some abstract space of product characteristic, and a consumer's location represents his most preferred attribute. A consumer buys (one unit) from the firm that yields him maximum utility, where his utility function takes the form $U(p, d) = U^* - p - t \cdot d$ where U^* is a constant, d is his distance from the firm, and t now measures the intensity of his preferences. Under either interpretation, firms' market shares are determined by the intersection

12. A widely studied extension of these models involves the introduction of economies of scope that may arise when a firm produces several varieties (Panzar and Willig 1981).

13. Hotelling invited his readers to imagine consumers and firms as being located along a transcontinental railroad; in today's more modest terminology, the line is usually called "Hotelling's beach" and the firms are labeled "ice-cream sellers."

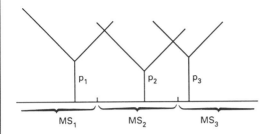

Figure 2.3
The determination of market shares in Hotelling's model. The price and market
share of firm i are denoted p_i and MS_i respectively.

points of "Hotelling's umbrellas" as shown in figure 2.3. The Hotelling
model is by no means the only popular model of horizontal product
differentiation. A very different example is that of Dixit and Stiglitz
(1977). In this model, no explicit representation of the product space
is offered. Instead, each product is simply assumed to be different; all
consumers are assumed to have identical tastes, and each consumer
purchases a mixture of all goods on offer—the relative quantity of
good i purchased varying inversely with the price of good i, given any
prices for the other goods.

The properties of such a model depend inter alia on the form of the
consumers' utility function. While the Dixit-Stiglitz model rests on a
CES function, another well-known model is obtained by using a
quadratic utility function, which ensures that the demand schedule
for each good is linear (this is the linear demand schedule model
popularized by Shubik and Levitan (1980) and others).

What all of these models of horizontal product differentiation have
in common is that

• all products are produced subject to the same exogenously given
level of sunk cost and the same level of marginal cost;

• for any vector of distinct products on offer, if all prices are equal (to
marginal cost, say), then *all* products enjoy a strictly positive market
share.

These are clearly rather special properties. The latter property
turns out to be extremely important in generating the result that
increases in market size can induce a fragmented market structure. It
is this that may fail to hold once we move to the vertical product
differentiation case (see pp. 70–71).

see Shaked and Sutton 1987). As market size increases, industry structure becomes fragmented.[14]

Once firms are permitted to produce more than one product, however, *multiple equilibria are endemic* within models of this kind. Depending on the nature of demand (and cost) conditions, the models may permit—for a given level of setup cost and market size—both fragmented equilibria, in which a large number of firms each offer one product, and concentrated equilibria, in which a small number of firms each offer several products.

It may be helpful to illustrate this point by reference to one very simple situation, which is of particular relevance to later chapters. This case arises when a number of distinct varieties may be produced that are quite independent on the demand side (i.e., they are neither substitutes nor complements). If a setup cost of σ must be paid to produce any such variety (i.e., there are no economies or diseconomies of scope), then the market breaks down into a number of independent submarkets or segments. A firm's strategy now decomposes into a separate strategy for each segment. Given a large number of potential entrants, this model will have a range of equilibria. At one extreme, the firms entering each submarket are different, leading to a fragmented structure; at the other extreme, the same group of firms enters all segments, leading to a more concentrated structure. In this special polar case, there is one equilibrium at which each firm produces only one product, and this single-product firm configuration is associated with the most fragmented equilibrium of the model. There are various other equilibria in which each firm occupies several niches, leading to a more concentrated structure.

The situation in general is more complex. While a full treatment lies outside the scope of the present discussion, the basic intuition underlying the appearance of fragmented or concentrated equilibria may be described as follows. The range of equilibria reflects three features of the model:

(i) Demand-side characteristics. The role of demand-side characteristics in determining equilibrium outcomes in horizontal product differentiation models is set out in Shaked and Sutton 1990. Here we confine ourselves to a brief outline of results. The demand side of any model of this kind can be characterized in terms of two effects. The *market expansion effect* measures the extent to which the addition

---

14. Technically, the maximal market share goes to zero as market size increases.

of new products expands total industry sales, prices being fixed (at the monopoly level, say). On the other hand, the *competition effect* measures the extent to which, the list of available products being fixed, prices are lower when each of these products is owned by a different firm, as opposed to the situation where all products are owned by a monopolist. The intuition underlying the appearance of different equilibria may now be stated. A stronger competition effect favors the appearance of concentrated outcomes, and the reason for this is directly analogous to the idea set out in section 2.2: tougher competition in the post-entry stage of the game makes the entry of rival producers less attractive. The role of the expansion effect is best seen by considering the incentives that encourage a monopolist to add to his product range: returns to the monopolist accrue from sales to new consumers who hitherto purchased none of his offerings. The returns to an entrant additionally comprise sales captured from the incumbent's existing products. Hence a stronger expansion effect favors the appearance of more concentrated equilibria, and vice versa.

(ii) Cost-side characteristics. Insofar as certain elements of sunk costs can be shared between several product lines (economies of scope), concentrated equilibria are favored.

(iii) Strategic asymmetry. If some firms enjoy a strategic advantage (usually modeled in terms of a first mover advantage, by assuming sequential as opposed to simultaneous entry) then concentrated outcomes are favored. The first-mover may preempt the market by offering a range of products sufficiently broad to forestall further entry. This tactic, known as monopolization by product proliferation, was first described by Schmalensee (1978) and is discussed at length in chapter 8.

It will be clear from the foregoing remarks that once products are (horizontally) differentiated and firms produce multiple products, equilibrium outcomes will be delicately dependent on the exact structure of the model specified. Progress in developing and testing empirical predictions for models of this kind must largely depend on confining attention to certain specific markets in which the detailed characteristics influencing equilibrium outcomes can be pinned down empirically.

But if attention is to be confined to those robust results that are independent of such details of the model, the only statement that can

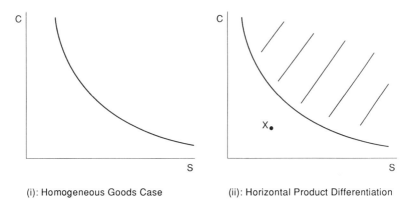

(i): Homogeneous Goods Case   (ii): Horizontal Product Differentiation

Figure 2.4
The market size—market structure relationship for the exogenous sunk cost model.
The configuration X can not be supported as an equilibrium (see text, section 2.4).

be made runs as follows: First, insofar as products are differentiated
horizontally, the implied relaxation of price competition causes the
concentration–size schedule to shift downward and to the left. Second, the appearance of multiple equilibria implies that this schedule
now specifies only a *lower bound* to equilibrium concentration at any
market size (figure 2.4). It is the latter interpretation (of a negatively
sloping *lower bound* to equilibrium concentration levels) that will
provide the basis for the empirical studies of chapter 4.

2.4   Empirical Implications

What, then, are the testable predictions of the model? The first, which
will be taken up in looking at cross-industry regressions in chapter 5,
is summarized in figure 2.4. Over a cross section of industries for
which sunk costs are exogenously fixed, it is predicted that the lower
bound to observed concentration levels should converge to zero as
market size increases. The form of this schedule implies that the
theory places only a weak constraint on the data when the S/σ ratio
is high; to the right of the figure, almost any level of concentration is
consistent with equilibrium. Where S/σ is low, however, the theory
constrains the data. A point such as X in figure 2.4 (ii) cannot be an
equilibrium. Moreover, the theory tells us something about the reason for this: in a configuration such as X, firms are failing to recover

their sunk costs. In the short run, attempts may be made to achieve normal returns on existing capacity by means of price coordination; but such attempts will founder because of price cutting by deviants (this is the story implicit in the *definition* of the toughness of price competition schedule set out in section 2.2, which was used to derive the lower bound of figure 2.4). The only route to raising margins and thus allowing a recovery of sunk costs must lie in a change of structure, and this may happen in two ways. Either consolidation of ownership—whether by means of acquisition or merger—may bring about a rise in margins; or else in the longer run the failure to recover sunk costs will lead to an unwillingness to renew plant as it becomes obsolete, so that concentration rises as exit occurs. Either of these changes may be interpreted in terms of a movement along the $p(N)$ schedule of figure 2.2.

The second prediction of the theory in this context relates to the determinants of the lower bound itself, whose height has been shown to depend inter alia on the toughness of price competition in the market (in the sense of the *function* mapping concentration level to market price). Insofar as institutional or other factors cause the toughness of price competition to weaken, the model predicts that equilibrium concentration levels may be lower. This prediction is taken up in chapter 6.

This, then, completes the treatment of the exogenous sunk cost model. The next chapter develops the complementary analysis for the case of endogenous sunk costs. There, the focus lies in showing how the convergence property developed for the exogenous sunk cost model fails to hold good once advertising outlays by firms are effective in raising consumers' willingness-to-pay for their respective offerings.

What this chapter has done, then, is to set out a new rationale for an old empirical relationship: the negative correlation between market size and concentration levels for the same industry across different countries. The rationale for this relationship rests crucially on the notion that the level of sunk costs is exogenously fixed. The task of the next chapter is to show how, once endogenous sunk costs are present, the mechanism explored in this chapter will be overriden by a new and quite different mechanism, which will cause this convergence property to fail.

3

The Analytical Framework II: Endogenous Sunk Costs

3.1 Introduction

This chapter develops the central analytical argument, extending the analysis of the preceding chapter to the case in which endogenous sunk costs are incurred with a view to enhancing consumers' willingness-to-pay for a specific firm's product(s). In analyzing this issue, the simplest way forward is to describe each firm's product in terms of a single attribute, labeled u, which may be thought of as the perceived quality of the product. In discussing advertising-intensive industries, we will interpret u as the advertising-based brand image enjoyed by the product. In terms of the literature on the economics of advertising, the function linking the endogenous element of sunk cost to u, labeled $A(u)$, may be seen as playing a role analogous to that of the advertising response function.[1]

In other contexts the variable u could be thought of as a measure of desirable physical characteristics achieved through enhanced R & D outlays. Even more generally, it can encompass any feature of the good or of associated services that raises consumers' willingness-to-pay for this product as opposed to rival products. All that matters to the analysis is that this enhancement of consumers' willingness-to-pay involves an increase in fixed outlays by firms—possibly accompanied by a *limited* increase in unit variable costs.

---

1. An alternative way of interpreting the vertical attribute u is to think of it simply as a shift parameter in the consumer's demand function, such that an increase in u leads to an unambiguous outward shift in the demand schedule. Some readers may prefer this formulation to one in which u enters the consumer's utility function directly.

In what follows, classical advertising outlays (i.e., television, radio, and press) will be interpreted as a fixed cost incurred prior to the final stage of the game (and so as a sunk cost). On the other hand, promotional outlays (associated with coupons, special terms to retailers, etc.) involve an outlay roughly proportionate to current sales volume, and these will be interpreted as an element of variable cost incurred in the final price (or quantity) competition stage of the game. In practice, both of these cost elements are incurred as a flow of expenditure over time, and the use of the multistage game formulation is intended not as a literal representation but merely as a way of capturing the fact that classical advertising outlays represent an investment in the product's image, the value of which depreciates only gradually over time.

It will be assumed, then, that the fixed cost that must be incurred in the preliminary stage (s) of the game is described by an increasing function of u. In defining consumer tastes over this attribute, we suppose that the willingness-to-pay of *all* consumers is nondecreasing in u (i.e., in the language of the product differentiation literature, u is a "vertical" attribute).

The cost $A(u)$ is both *fixed*, in the sense that it is independent of the volume of output produced and sold by the firm, and it is *sunk*, in the sense that it is incurred in some earlier stage of the game and is irrecoverable once the final stage is reached. As to the determinants of the function $A(u)$, we bypass the question of *why* consumers respond to advertising (an issue that lies midway between economics and psychology) and rely instead on the well-established empirical observation that advertising is indeed effective in stimulating demand for an individual firm, at least, over a wide range of goods and services (Lambin 1976, Broadbent 1981. On persuasion versus information, see section 14.3). This leaves open the question of whether it raises total *industry* sales. The answer to this latter question will clearly vary from one market to another. Here we are concerned solely with the issue of analyzing the implications of the observation that increases in an individual firm's advertising outlays are effective in stimulating demand for *that firm's* offerings.

Extending the analysis of the preceding chapter to this new domain raises a number of issues regarding the robustness of the results obtained below in the face of reasonable changes in model specification. In the case of homogeneous products, this issue was relatively simple. The only factor of interest that was difficult to indentify or proxy empirically was the degree of toughness of price competition, and it was possible to find a limit theorem result that held across almost all possible specifications (i.e., for all nonincreasing functions $p(\mathcal{N})$ satisfying $p(\mathcal{N}) > c$ for all $\mathcal{N}$).

But once we turn to the analysis of differentiated products, the range of model specifications that seem reasonable a priori and differ only in respect of aspects that are difficult to identify or proxy empirically is very much wider. A major focus of this chapter lies in specifying a wide range of admissible model specifications over which certain key results should be robust. The range of admissible model specifications is discussed in section 3.5. Briefly, this range encompasses

(i) Product differentiation and multiproduct firms: the results should hold good for a context in which each firm may offer a range of products and in which differences between alternative products may be modeled in various ways;

(ii) Toughness of price competition: the results should be robust with respect to alternative forms of price competition, as in the preceding chapter;

(iii) Strategic symmetry/asymmetry: the results should hold across alternative model specifications incorporating different degrees of strategic asymmetry between firms (symmetric entry models, sequential entry models incorporating first-mover advantages, and so on).

As these remarks imply, any usefully robust results must be framed within a very broad class of models.

But while most results in the area of product differentiation depend in a more or less delicate way on the precise specification of the model used, there is one argument that turns out to be extremely robust. Stated loosely, it runs as follows:

If it is possible to enhance consumers' willingness-to-pay for a given product to some minimal degree by way of a proportionate increase in *fixed* cost (with either no increase or only a small increase in unit variable costs), then the industry will not converge to a fragmented structure, however large the market becomes.

Now the degree to which willingness-to-pay can be enhanced in return for an increase in fixed outlays depends inter alia on the shape of the advertising response function. What the above result implies is that if we can place a bound on the elasticity of the function that links firms' fixed outlays to consumers' willingness-to-pay, then we can deduce a corresponding lower bound to the degree of concentration in the industry.

This very vague statement can be made precise only by specifying some suitable class of models within which the result can be developed; and an obvious trade-off exists between the sharpness of the associated proposition and the breadth of the class of models over which it holds good. The interested reader may find alternative formulations in Shaked and Sutton 1983 and 1987; and an overview of these results is given in Sutton 1986. In section 3.4, a very general formulation is set out, which corresponds to a negation of the idea captured in the limit theorem of chapter 2; in other words, we merely ensure that it is impossible to converge to a fragmented structure, as the market becomes large.

This result rests on an appeal to a very simple mechanism, which seems to be fundamental to this broad class of models. Suppose that the structure of the market is fragmented. Then, as each firm's market share is relatively smaller, the proportionate gain in market share that it can achieve by undertaking a given proportionate increase in its fixed outlays is correspondingly greater. This leads to a tendency for any fragmented outcome to be broken, as some firms jump to successively higher levels of fixed outlays. The outcome of this process is that increases in market size are associated, not with a more fragmented pattern of market shares, but rather with escalating levels of fixed outlays by a limited number of firms. In what follows, these ideas are first illustrated using a simple example, which builds on the Cournot case reviewed in the preceding chapter. This example is then extended in various ways to illustrate a series of ideas that arise in the industry studies. Readers who prefer to skim briefly over the next section will find a self-contained discussion of the main results in section 3.3.)

3.2 A Specific Example

The Cournot Model with "Perceived Quality"

To keep matters simple, suppose all consumers have the same utility function of the form

$$U = (ux)^{\delta} z^{1-\delta}$$

defined over two goods, the good that is the focus of analysis, and some other "outside" good. (The latter can in fact be thought of as a Hicksian "composite commodity" consisting of a bundle of goods all of whose prices are fixed.) The quantities of these two goods are denoted x and z respectively. Increases in u, the index of perceived quality, enhance the marginal utility derived from the former good. We will, henceforward, refer to this first good x as the "quality" good, in order to distinguish it from the "outside" good.

Rival firms are assumed to offer various quality goods; let u_i and p_i denote the index of perceived quality and the price of firm i's offering. Then, the consumer's decision problem can be represented as follows: for any $\{u_i\}$, $\{p_i\}$, the consumer chooses a product that maximizes the quality-price ratio u_i/p_i; and the consumer spends fraction δ of his income on this chosen quality good, and fraction $(1 - \delta)$ of his income on the composite good.[2] Total expenditure on the quality goods is therefore independent of the levels of prices and perceived qualities and equals a fraction δ of total consumer income. Denote this level of total expenditure on all quality goods by S.

The first step in the analysis involves looking at the final stage of the game. Here the perceived qualities $\{u_i\}$ are taken as given (having been chosen by firms at the preceding stage). Equilibrium in the final stage of the game is characterized as a Nash equilibrium in quantities (Cournot equilibrium). This equilibrium can be calculated as follows: since each consumer chooses the good that maximizes u_i/p_i, the equilibrium prices of all those firms enjoying positive sales at equilibrium must be proportionate to their perceived qualities, that is, $u_i/p_i = u_j/p_j$, all i, j.

If all firms offered the same perceived quality level $\bar{u}$, then the equilibrium price level would be obtained by equating sales revenue to consumer expenditure, whence $p = S/Q$, where Q denotes the total volume of output. Now suppose all firms but one offer the same level of perceived quality $\bar{u}$, while one "deviant" firm offers some level u. At equilibrium, $p = (u/\bar{u})\bar{p}$, whence, equating sales revenue to consumer expenditure, it follows that

---

2. This elementary property of the Cobb-Douglas utility function follows immediately from the first order conditions for the problem:

$$\max_{\{x_i\}, z} (u_i x_i)^\delta z^{1-\delta}$$

subject to $p_i x_i + p_z z \leqslant M$.

$$\bar{p} = \frac{S}{Q + (u/\bar{u})q},$$

where $\bar{Q}$ denotes the combined output of all nondeviant firms, while q represents the output of the deviant firm.

Let each firm have a unit variable cost (marginal cost) equal to c, independent of its perceived quality level. (It is at this point that we introduce a key assumption, that the burden of quality improvement falls primarily on fixed cost. The present example involves the simplest case, in which u depend *solely* on fixed cost; this strong restriction is relaxed in the general formulation (section 3.5).)

Using the above expression for $\bar{p}$, the profit functions of the deviant firm and of the remaining firms may be written down. By writing down these profit functions and differentiating with respect to output to find the first-order conditions for an optimum, the Nash equilibrium in quantities for the final-stage subgame can be calculated. It is easily shown that this equilibrium corresponds to a common output level for the $N - 1$ nondeviant firms equal to

$$\bar{q} = \frac{S}{c} \cdot \frac{(u/\bar{u})(N-1)}{[(u/\bar{u})(N-1)+1]^2}$$

and a corresponding price

$$\bar{p} = c\left\{1 + \frac{1}{(u/\bar{u})(N-1)}\right\}.$$

The price of the deviant firm at equilibrium equals

$$p(u|\bar{u}) = c\left\{\frac{u}{\bar{u}} + \frac{1}{N-1}\right\},$$

and its output level is given by

$$q(u|\bar{u}) = [(N-1) - (\bar{u}/u)(N-2)]\bar{q}.$$

From the above expressions for equilibrium price and quantity, it follows that the net profit earned by the deviant in the final-stage subgame equals

$$\Pi(u|\bar{u}) = S\left\{1 - \frac{1}{\frac{1}{N-1} + \frac{u}{\bar{u}}}\right\}^2$$

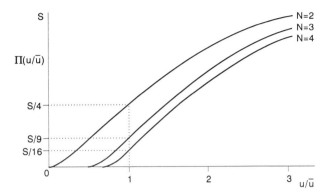

Figure 3.1
The profit function for the final-stage subgame.

The function $\Pi(u|\bar{u})$ is S-shaped, as illustrated in figure 3.1 . Note that u and $\bar{u}$ enter the function only through the ratio $(u/\bar{u})$; in particular, in a symmetric configuration where all firms set $u = \bar{u}$, then $\Pi = S/N^2$ independent of $\bar{u}$. As can be immediately checked by differentiating, this symmetric solution corresponds to a point on $\Pi(u|\bar{u})$ where the curve is concave or convex, according as $N \lesseqgtr 3$.

The Determination of Sunk Costs

Armed with the above expression for profits, it is now possible to look at the game as a whole and to discuss the firm's choice of u. There are several ways of doing this. We defer a discussion of the various alternatives until the next section. In what follows, we proceed by simply taking the basic two-stage game analyzed in the preceding chapter and inserting a new intermediate stage, at which each of the N firms that entered in the first stage, at cost σ, choose a value of u at some additional cost $A(u)$ at the second stage. Finally, there is a third stage, at which firms compete à la Cournot, taking the $\{u_i\}$ as fixed, as described in the preceding section.

At this point, we need to specify the function that links perceived product quality u with the firms advertising outlays, $A(u)$. Two empirical features regarding advertising response functions are well established: first, threshold effects may exist (in the sense that advertising below a certain threshold level has little impact). Second, apart from the possible existence of such thresholds, the effectiveness of advertising outlays is subject to diminishing returns. (See, for example, Lambin 1976.) Here it is simply assumed that increases in fixed outlays raise consumers' willingness-to-pay according to a smooth convex schedule $A(u)$, defined on the domain $u \geqslant 1$, and with $A(1) = 0$ (no threshold effects).

Two properties of the schedule $A(u)$ play a central role in influencing the relationship between market size and market structure. The first property relates to the extent to which returns to marginal increases in outlays diminish as these outlays increase. This is measured by the convexity of $A(u)$. The second property relates to the returns the firm achieves from a small initial outlay, measured by the slope of $A(u)$ at $u = 1$. The latter quantity depends both on the unit cost of sending advertising messages and on the initial impact of these messages on consumers' willingness-to-pay. In choosing a suitable family of functions $A(u)$ for the purpose of this example, we will "normalize" by setting the initial impact per message at unity and introduce the cost per message, denoted a, as a parameter of the model. A suitable functional form is

$$A(u) = \frac{a}{\gamma}(u^{\gamma} - 1), \qquad \gamma > 1.$$

Note that $A(1) = 0$, and $A'(1) = a$, independent of γ. Higher values of γ correspond to more rapidly diminishing returns to increases in outlays.

In what follows, it will be useful to combine the setup cost σ incurred at stage 1 with the advertising outlay $A(u)$ incurred at stage 2 in a single function labeled $F(u)$, such that

$$F(u) = \sigma + A(u) = \sigma + \frac{a}{\gamma}(u^{\gamma} - 1).$$

Thus $F(u)$ represents the firm's total fixed outlays.

There is one feature of the special functional form chosen here that is worth noting at this point. The elasticity of the function $F(u)$ can be written

$$\frac{u}{F}\frac{dF}{du} = \gamma\left\{1 - \frac{\sigma - a/\gamma}{F}\right\}.$$

Now as $u \to \infty$, $F(u) \to \infty$, so this elasticity tends to γ, independent of σ and a. On the other hand, for any finite u (and so $F(u)$), the elasticity lies above or below γ according as $\sigma < a/\gamma$ or $\sigma > a/\gamma$. When

$\sigma = a/\gamma$, the elasticity is constant for all u. This property should be borne in mind in interpreting the results that follow. It turns out that the nature of the relationship between market size and market structure depends on the ratio of σ to a/γ, and the special case $\sigma = a/\gamma$ is an interesting benchmark.

Equilibrium Advertising Levels

We are now in a position to analyze the second stage of the game. Here the number of firms $\mathcal{N}$ is taken as a parameter, representing the outcome of choices made at stage 1. All entrants have, at this point, incurred a sunk cost σ in entering the industry. Now each decides what level of advertising outlay to incur.

Remembering the shape of $\Pi(u|\bar{u})$, illustrated in figure 3.1, it will be clear that certain assumptions regarding the convexity of $F(u)$ may be required to obtain "well-behaved" solutions in the advertising game. Appendix 3.1 shows that so long as the advertising response function is sufficiently convex, the solutions to the game take a very simple form. Specifically, for any range of possible values of setup cost, $[\underline{\sigma}, \bar{\sigma}]$ with $\underline{\sigma} > 0$, and advertising cost a, there exists some finite $\gamma > 0$ such that the advertising choice game has a symmetric solution in pure strategies. In what follows, we confine ourselves to this simple case. We assume[3]

$$\gamma > \underline{\gamma} = \max\left\{1, \frac{2}{3}\frac{a}{\sigma}\right\}$$

A characterization of these solutions is quite straightforward. We aim to characterize a symmetric Nash equilibrium in advertising levels. Consider a firm whose rivals set a common value of perceived quality $\bar{u}$. The firm's payoff if it sets a level u then equals

$$\Pi(u|\bar{u}) - F(u).$$

The equilibrium outcome takes one of two forms, according as

---

3. If $\gamma < \underline{\gamma} = \max\{1, \frac{2}{3}a/\sigma\}$, then for certain values of σ, it may be the case that the only solution to the advertising game involves mixed strategies. A characterization of these strategies is relatively difficult. For $\gamma = 1$, additional (asymmetric) pure-strategy equilibria appear. Such asymmetric solutions, when they appear, correspond to a higher level of concentration than do the symmetric solutions that characterize the lower bound.

$$\left. \frac{d\Pi}{du} \right|_{u=\bar{u}=1} \leqslant \left. \frac{dF}{du} \right|_{u=1}$$

or otherwise.

The interpretation of this condition is as follows. Consider a no-advertising configuration. The marginal gain in final-stage profit π for a deviant firm that sets u slightly above $\bar{u}$ outweighs the marginal cost if and only if the above condition fails. If the above condition holds, equilibrium corresponds exactly to that of the elementary Cournot model described in chapter 2. In other words, all firms incur setup costs σ on entering, incur no advertising outlays, and offer a common level of perceived quality $\bar{u} = 1$ at equilibrium.

On the other hand, if the above condition fails, then at equilibrium all firms offer a common level of perceived quality $\bar{u} > 1$, where $\bar{u}$ is determined by the condition

$$\left. \frac{d\Pi}{du} \right|_{u=\bar{u}} = \left. \frac{dF}{du} \right|_{u=\bar{u}}.$$

Using the expressions for $\Pi(u|\bar{u})$ and $F(u)$ to write this condition in explicit form, and multiplying across by $\bar{u}$, we obtain

$$2S\frac{(\mathcal{N}-1)^2}{\mathcal{N}^3} = \gamma[F - (\sigma - a/\gamma)]. \tag{1}$$

This equation defines the level of fixed outlays incurred by firms at equilibrium as a function of the number of firms that entered at stage 1. We denote the value of F implicitly defined by equation (1) as $F^*(\mathcal{N}; S)$ in what follows.

The fact that the first-order condition (1) does indeed define a global maximum of $\Pi(u|\bar{u}) - F(u)$ is guaranteed by the restriction $\gamma > \underline{\gamma}$ (see appendix 3.1).

Equilibrium Structure

We may now consider the entry decisions of firms in the first stage of the game and so determine the equilibrium structure of the industry. Notice first that all those firms that enter at stage 1 will, at equilibrium, set the same level of u at stage 1 and will therefore all incur the same level of fixed outlays $F^*(\mathcal{N}; S) \geqslant \sigma$. At stage 1 of the game, firms will enter up to the point at which $\mathcal{N}$ is the (largest integer) value satisfying

$$\frac{S}{N^2} \geq F^*(N; S).$$ (2)

To simplify the exposition, write N as a continuous variable for the moment, and replace the above inequality by an equality. We may then combine equations (1) and (2) to solve for the equilibrium values of N and $F^*(N; S)$ as functions of σ, S, γ, and a.

Before describing how to solve (1) and (2) for N and F^*, we first introduce some notation. Our focus of interest lies in describing the relationship between market size S and the equilibrium number of firms. Within the advertising regime, this relationship is specified by the equation

$$N + \frac{1}{N} - 2 = \frac{\gamma}{2}\left[1 - \frac{\sigma - a/\gamma}{S}N^2\right],$$ (3)

obtained using (2) in equality form to substitute for F in (1). The limiting behavior of this relationship as $S \to \infty$ will be of central interest. For any given value of N, the right-hand side of equation (3) takes the value $\gamma/2$ as $S \to \infty$, independently of σ and a. It will be convenient to denote the (unique) value of N that solves

$$N + \frac{1}{N} - 2 = x \qquad x \geq 0,$$

on the domain $N \geq 1$ as $\tilde{N}(x)$ in what follows. In this notation, the solution to equation (3) in the limit $S \to \infty$ is denoted $\tilde{N}(\gamma/2)$, and we label this N_∞ in the figures that follow.

We are now in a position to describe the solution to the model. For expositional reasons, it is convenient to proceed in a slightly round-about fashion, as follows. Using (2) in equality form to substitute for S in equation (1), we obtain

$$N + \frac{1}{N} - 2 = \frac{\gamma}{2}\left[1 - \frac{\sigma - a/\gamma}{F}\right].$$ (4)

This equation describes a locus in (N, F) space; and equilibrium in the advertising zone is described by the intersection of this locus with the zero profit relation

$$F = S/N^2,$$ (2')

which describes a downward-sloping family of curves in (N, F) space, parameterized by S (figure 3.2). The locus described by equation (4) is upward sloping, vertical, or downward sloping according as σ is greater than, equal to, or less than a/γ. The form of the size-structure relationship is different in each of these cases.

Consider first the case $\sigma = a/\gamma$, illustrated in panel (i) of figure 3.2. Here, the locus described by (4) is vertical.

For S sufficiently small, the equilibrium involves zero advertising and the market size/market structure relationship is as for the elementary Cournot model described in chapter 2, that is, equilibrium is given by

$$\Pi = \frac{S}{N^2} = F = \sigma.$$

(This corresponds to the values S_1, N_1 in Figure 3.2 (i).)

As S increases, however, we eventually reach a value of N at which advertising begins. This value is determined by the condition

$$\frac{d\Pi}{du}\bigg|_{u=\bar{u}=1} = \frac{dF}{du}\bigg|_{u=1}.$$

Using (1), and noting that $F(1) = \sigma = a/\gamma$, this becomes

$$2S\frac{(N-1)^2}{N^3} = a,$$

or, setting $S/N^2 = \sigma$,

$$N + \frac{1}{N} - 2 = \frac{1}{2}\frac{a}{\sigma}.$$

The critical value of N implicitly defined by this equation is labeled $\tilde{N}(\frac{1}{2}a/\sigma)$. In the present case, that is, where $\sigma = a/\gamma$, this coincides with $N_\infty = \tilde{N}(\gamma/2)$, and once market size reaches the level that supports this number of firms in the no-advertising regime, further increases in market size involve only increasing levels of advertising, with no further change in market structure.[4] The size/structure combination for this case is illustrated in figure 3.3 (i).

---

4. Notice that the expression $N + (1/N) - 2$ increases monotonically with N on the domain $N \geq 1$. For S greater than the critical value specified above, the intersection of the zero profit locus $F - S/N^2$ with the horizontal schedule $F = \sigma$ in figure 3.2 does not correspond to an equilibrium configuration.

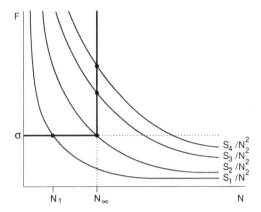

Case (i): $\sigma = a/\gamma$, Here $\tilde{N}\left(\frac{1}{2}\frac{a}{\sigma}\right) = \tilde{N}\left(\frac{\gamma}{2}\right) = \tilde{N}_{\infty}$

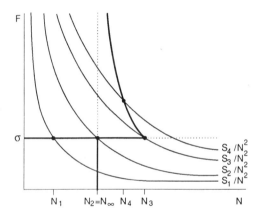

Case (ii): $\sigma < a/\gamma$, $\tilde{N}\left(\frac{1}{2}\frac{a}{\sigma}\right) = N_3 > N\left(\frac{\gamma}{2}\right) = N_{\infty}$

Figure 3.2
The equilibrium configuration as a function of market size S, for the case $\sigma = a/\gamma$ (panel (i)) and $\sigma < a/\gamma$ (panel (ii)). This figure illustrates equations (2) and (4) of the text. Four values of S are shown, with $S_1 < S_2 < S_3 < S_4$. The "switch" value at which we move from the nonadvertising to the advertising zone is S_2 in case (i) and S_3 in case (ii). In both cases, $\mathcal{N}$ converges asymptotically to $\mathcal{N}_{\infty} = \tilde{\mathcal{N}}(\gamma/2)$ as $S \to \infty$. In panel (ii), the relationship between S and $\mathcal{N}$ is nonmonotonic. As S increases, we pass through the value $\mathcal{N}_2$ when $S = S_2$; further increases in S raise $\mathcal{N}$ until $\mathcal{N} = \mathcal{N}_3$, but beyond this level, $\mathcal{N}$ falls as S increases and as $S \to \infty$, $\mathcal{N}$ converges asymptotically to the value $\mathcal{N}_{\infty}$ (which has been drawn to coincide with $\mathcal{N}_2$ in the figure).

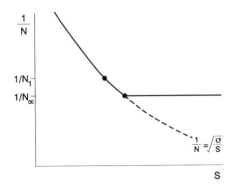

Case (i): $\sigma = a/\gamma$

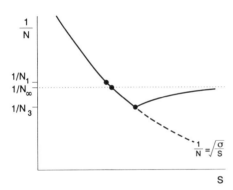

Case (ii): $\sigma < a/\gamma$

Figure 3.3
Concentration and market size, for alternative values of σ.

We now turn to the second case, in which $\sigma < a/\gamma$, as illustrated in panels (ii) of figures 3.2 and 3.3. In this case, the schedule described by equation (4) is downward sloping and intersects the horizontal line $F = \sigma$ at the value $\tilde{N}(\frac{1}{2}a/\sigma)$, which is greater than the (asymptotic) value $\tilde{N}(\gamma/2)$. It is shown in appendix 3.1 that the restrictions placed on σ, a, and γ above (footnote 3) imply that the zero profit schedule $F = S/N^2$ cuts this downward-sloping schedule from below at the "switch" value $\tilde{N}(\frac{1}{2}a/\sigma)$. As S increases, N first increases until the switch value $\tilde{N}(\frac{1}{2}a/\sigma)$ is reached, but after that point further increases in S cause a *decrease* in N throughout the advertising zone. As $S \to \infty$, N converges asymptotically to $\tilde{N}(\gamma/2)$, labeled N_∞ in figure 3.2(ii). In this latter case, then, the relationship between market size and concentration is nonmonotonic. This case is of central importance in the analysis that follows. The reason underlying the appearance of a nonmonotonic relationship is discussed in the next section.

The third and final case is that in which $\sigma > a/\gamma$ (not illustrated in figures 3.2 and 3.3). Here a similar diagrammatic analysis indicates that the level of concentration $1/N$ falls monotonically through both nonadvertising and advertising regimes. These three cases are combined in figure 3.4, which shows how the market size/market structure relationship varies with the parameter σ.

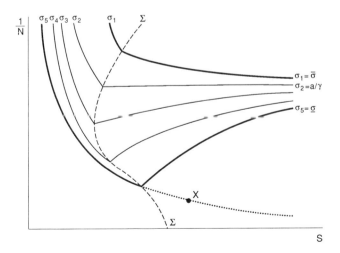

Figure 3.4
Concentration and market size, for various values of σ, where $\bar{\sigma} = \sigma_1 > \sigma_2 = a/\gamma > \sigma_3 > \sigma_4 > \sigma_5 = \underline{\sigma}$.

The switch point at which we move from one regime to the other traces out a locus in $(1/N, S)$ space, labeled $\Sigma\Sigma$ in figure 3.4. This locus is described in the appendix. It is defined by the condition that if N firms set a zero advertising level, that is, $F(\bar{u}) = \sigma$, then it will be *just* profitable for a single firm to deviate. Given the restrictions on γ and σ introduced above, this collapses to the first-order condition (for local deviations)

$$\left.\frac{d\Pi}{du}\right|_{u=\bar{u}=1} = \left.\frac{dF}{du}\right|_{u=1} \qquad \text{or} \qquad 2S\frac{(N-1)^2}{N^3} = a,$$

and this latter equation traces out a nonmonotonic locus in (N, S) space as illustrated in figure 3.4. The lowest value of S is attained when $N = 3$, as is easily checked by differentiation. Below the curve labeled $\underline{\sigma}$ in the figure, however, the locus must be defined by reference to the (global) condition that no (finite) increase in u can raise profits. As shown in appendix 3.1, this condition leads to a specification of the critical locus as illustrated in figure 3.4. The property of the locus that will be relevant in what follows is that it cuts the horizontal axis at some finite value of S.

The effect of increasing the unit cost of advertising, a, on the market size/market structure relationship is easily seen from figure 3.4. Such an increase shifts the locus $\Sigma\Sigma$ to the right. This implies that the equilibrium level of concentration $(1/N)$ will be lower for some intermediate range of market sizes (at which we revert from an advertising to a nonadvertising regime), but that the asymptotic value of concentration (which depends on γ alone and is independent of a and σ) remains unchanged.

3.3 Discussion

The relationship between market size and market structure, as depicted in figure 3.4, illustrates two features of general interest, which play a central role in all that follows. The first is the failure of the convergence property: increases in market size do not lead to an indefinite fall in the level of concentration. The second feature relates to the fact that the market size/market structure relationship is not even necessarily monotonic.

In the figure, low values of setup cost are associated with a concentration-size relationship that is initially falling, and thereafter rising.

Why does this happen? The answer comes in two steps. Firstly, there is the fact that advertising becomes profitable only when a certain minimal market size is attained: this size, which itself varies with the level of concentration, is specified by the hatched curve $\Sigma\Sigma$ in figure 3.4. A lower value of σ implies that the level of concentration may decline to a correspondingly lower value before this switch point between the two regimes is reached.

The second step in the explanation is that, within the advertising regime, increases in market size are accompanied by an indefinite increase in advertising outlays. This implies that, in the limit as market size becomes indefinitely large, equilibrium concentration becomes *independent* of setup cost, for the latter element of cost becomes small as a fraction of total fixed outlays. So a low value of setup cost permits a low value of concentration to emerge only over some intermediate range of market size, and this leads to the appearance of a nonmonotonic schedule.

The preceding argument makes it clear that the failure of the monotonicity property is not just special to the present example; in fact, over the broad class of models discussed in section 3.4, there is no reason to assume that the concentration-size relationship will either rise or fall within the advertising regime. This feature of the theory sharply distinguishes the present approach from the traditional view of advertising as an exogenous barrier to entry, in terms of which the cost of advertising simply added a fixed increment to setup cost and so merely shifted the conventional negative relationship between concentration and market size.

One final remark is in order regarding the market size-market structure relationship. This relates to the way in which configurations lying below the present schedule break down. Consider a concentration-market size combination corresponding to the point marked X in figure 3.4. At this point, it will be optimal for some firm to break the configuration by raising its level of advertising. An interesting feature of the present example relates to the *size* of deviation that is profitable for such a firm. Will a *marginal* increase in advertising lead to an increase in profitability? Routine calculations indicate that the answer is yes only if the point X is sufficiently close to the

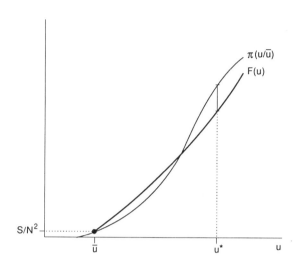

Figure 3.5
The profitability of a global deviation in a nonequilibrium configuration, which is very fragmented. The optimal reply to $\bar{u}$ is u^*.

equilibrium schedule. For any values of the underlying parameters, it can be shown that if the level of concentration is sufficiently low, a local deviation to some low level of advertising will *not* be profitable, but a discrete jump to some high level *will* be profitable (figure 3.5). This feature of the example is of interest in the context of many of the industry studies reported in chapters 8 to 15.

While the above features of the example turn out on further examination to be extremely robust to changes in model specification, this example also incorporates a number of features that are quite special. It has been assumed, for example, that all consumers have the same utility function, and that this function has a special form. One immediate consequence of this choice is as follows: if the perceived quality level u offered by every firm is increased by the same proportionate amount, then the vector of equilibrium prices remains unchanged. A second special feature of the example relates to the form of $F(u)$: the form chosen has the property that the elasticity of response of perceived quality to changes in fixed outlays converges asymptotically to a constant value γ as u increases. It is the combination of this property and the special form of the utility function chosen that leads to a special feature of the model shown in figure 3.4: as S increases, equilibrium concentration converges asymptotically to a *constant* value. (In the more general setting explored in section 3.5, all that can be said about this asymptotic relationship is that it is bounded away from zero.)

Within the example, a special case arises when the setup cost σ equals γ/a: here concentration remains constant as market size increases throughout the advertising regime. This simply reflects the fact that, for this particular value of σ, the elasticity of $F(u)$ takes a constant value for all u.

That equilibrium is *symmetric* in the example follows from a combination of three assumptions: consumers are identical, $F(u)$ is continuous (no threshold effects), and competition is Cournot (contrast Shaked and Sutton 1982). Symmetry combined with the fact that the number of firms is treated as a continuous variable underlies the last special feature of note: that firms have zero profits at equilibrium.

In this regard, it is important to remark on the fact that N was treated as a continuous variable above and that this led to a replacement of the non-negative profit constraint by a zero-profit condition. Treating N as an integer modifies the above results as follows: the equilibrium number of firms equals the integer part $[N]$ of the solution value calculated above; while the equilibrium level of advertising outlays is now $F^*([N])$. Firms now earn positive profits at equilibrium, for almost all parameter values—though an additional entrant would earn zero or negative profits. This obvious point carries a rather important implication in the present context: because N does *not* go to infinity with S in the present model, the usual disclaimer about such profits merely reflecting integer effects has little force. Profits as a fraction of sales revenue do *not* approach zero as market size increases.

One last special feature of the example deserves comment. This relates to the use of a three-stage game in which firms choose first whether to enter the industry and then—given the number of firms that have entered—choose their respective levels of u at the second stage. An obvious alternative to this is to use a two-stage structure in which firms choose at stage 1 both whether to enter and, if so, what level of u to set.

There is in fact an interesting difference between the three-stage and two-stage formulations. In using the three-stage setup, it is assumed that were some additional firm to enter the industry, the N

incumbent firms would react to this entry by altering their levels of u (in stage 2). The use of a two-stage game embodies the alternative assumption that such an entrant may take as given the levels of u chosen by the N incumbents. Clearly, the reasonableness of either assumption will depend on the context. The general results developed in section 3.5 encompass both possibilities.[5]

3.4 Extending the Example: Sources of Asymmetry

Before proceeding to general results, it will be worth pausing briefly to look at two extensions of the example set out above, which will be helpful in discussing the industry studies presented in later chapters. Both these extensions correspond to relaxations of certain restrictive assumptions used in the example, and both lead to the appearance of asymmetric solutions in which advertising levels differ across firms. The assumptions we relax here relate to (i) differences in consumer tastes, and (ii) sequential entry.

Differences in Tastes

The assumption that all consumers have identical tastes is clearly restrictive. If consumers differ in their tastes, then at equilibrium different firms will offer different levels of perceived quality, u. In many of the industries studied, a clear dichotomy exists on the demand side between retail markets, where buyers are more or less sensitive to advertising outlays, and nonretail markets, where it is widely assumed that buyers choose their suppliers largely on the basis of price (and the physical characteristics of the good) alone and are relatively insensitive to the advertising-based brand image. If, in the above example, it is assumed that some fraction θ of consumers have the utility function cited earlier, while the remaining group simply choose the lowest-priced product, then a dual structure emerges. Above some critical value of S, it can be shown that the market splits into two groups of firms. The first group sells in the retail segment, and

---

5. Within the present example, the results are changed by the use of a two-stage formulation as follows: for all S corresponding to integer values of N in the above solution, the equilibrium is as before. There exist, however, certain subintervals of S immediately below the values corresponding to integer solutions for which the only equilibrium in the first stage of the two-stage game may involve the use of mixed strategies.

the evolution of firm numbers and quality in that segment is described by the equations of the basic example cited above (where the S appearing in these equations is replaced by θS, the total expenditure in the retail segment). The nonretail segment of the market evolves as described by the equations of the exogenous sunk cost model (with S replaced by $(1 - \theta)S$, the total expenditure in the nonretail segment). Once S is sufficiently large, all consumers in the retail segment *strictly* prefer the products of the advertised group, and vice versa, so that the two segments behave independently.

For values of S intermediate between the switch point at which advertising begins and the point at which the two submarkets become independent, we obtain solutions in which the price of advertised products is constrained by that of the low-price offerings of the competitive fringe, in that purchasers of advertised products are *indifferent* between these products and the low-price nonadvertised products, at equilibrium. As in the preceding case, it may happen that over some intermediate range of market size the only equilibria involve the use of mixed strategies; and the explicit computation of these strategies is difficult.

An Illustration of Dual Structure

The analysis of the present example becomes much more complex once discrete consumer groups are introduced; a full characterization lies outside the scope of this chapter. A specific numerical example is illustrated in figure 3.6, and this will serve to introduce some possible configurations that will be of interest in what follows.

The relationship between market size and market structure in the example is as follows. Once some critical value S_1 is reached, some firm begins to advertise (in contrast to the basic example, this firm makes a discrete jump to some level $u > 1$ at market size S_1).

In this regime, the equilibrium prices of the advertised and non-advertised goods are such that retail customers are *indifferent* between the two offerings (i.e., $p = u\bar{p}$).

As S increases further, however, we reach a second critical value S_2 beyond which the (p, u) combination offered by the advertising firm (s) is *strictly preferred* by retail customers (i.e., $p < u\bar{p}$). Beyond this point, the two submarkets are essentially independent. The size-structure relationship in the retail sector is identical to that described by the basic example of section 3.2. The size-structure relationship

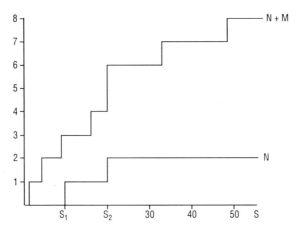

Figure 3.6
The evolution of dual structure: an example. The example corresponds to a choice of
parameter values $a = 1$, $\theta = 1/4$, $\gamma \gtrsim 1$, $\sigma = 1$. The diagram shows how the numbers of
firms selling in the retail sector (N) and in the nonretail sector (M) respectively vary
with market size. Note that for all values of S beyond some critical value, N takes the
constant value 2. Over this domain the retail sector behaves exactly as in the simple
example illustrated in figure 3.4 for the corresponding case ($\sigma = a/\gamma$). Regime shifts
occur at $S_1 = 10$ and $S_2 = 64/3$ (see text).

in the nonretail sector is as specified by the exogenous sunk cost model
of chapter 2. In other words, increases in market size are consistent
with an indefinite degree of fragmentation of the nonretail sector, but
the retail sector remains concentrated however large the market
becomes. The (n-firm) concentration ratio for the market as a whole
is bounded away from zero.

Sequential Entry

A final direction in which the above example may be modified is by
allowing one or more firms to enjoy a first-mover advantage vis-à-vis
rivals. This kind of strategic asymmetry can be captured by using a
sequential entry formulation. In this setting, we allow some (large
but finite) number of firms to make their entry and product choice decisions in some predetermined sequence, that is, the first stage of the
game is replaced by a sequence of n stages, and at stage i, firm i decides
either not to enter or to enter a product of perceived quality u_i.

Under these circumstances, the first mover can monopolize the
market by setting a value of u so high that no later firm will find it

profitable to enter at any u. Whether or not it does so depends on the parameter values γ, a, σ, and S. It is easy to show that for γ sufficiently close to 1, such preemption occurs, but that for larger values of γ, this may not occur. In the latter case, asymmetric equilibria can arise in which further firms enter, but with lower advertising outlays and lower equilibrium market shares. A full analytical characterization of this case lies outside the scope of this chapter; an illustrative example is shown in figure 3.7.

The example shown corresponds to a simple extension of the basic example developed above (all consumers are identical and have tastes described by the same advertising-sensitive utility function). The parameters in this example satisfy $a = \sigma = 1$, and $\gamma = 2$, so that in the corresponding simultaneous entry model the market size/market structure relationship is extremely simple: advertising begins at a market size $S = 4$, at which point two firms enter the market, and further increases in S have no effect on structure.[6]

Under sequential entry, the outcome depends on the value of γ, as noted above. Figure 3.7 illustrates two cases, $\gamma \gtrsim 1$ and $\gamma = 2.2$. In the former case, the first entrant completely preempts. In the latter case, a critical market size is reached beyond which a second firm enters. The entry of the second firm is associated with a fall in advertising outlays, and in profitability, for the leader. Further increases in S lead to growth in both firms' advertising levels—but the size disparity between the two remains.

The difference between the two cases can be related to the level of equilibrium profits earned in the simultaneous entry case. Where γ is close to 1, duopoly profits are approximately zero; equilibrium advertising outlays exhaust the profits earned in the final stage. It follows that the first mover, by only slightly increasing its outlays above those undertaken in a symmetric equilibrium, can successfully preempt. In the latter case, duopoly profits in the symmetric situation are positive and increase with S. In this case, preemption proves impossible at large values of S, though it is still possible for the leader to maintain a substantial gap vis-à-vis his rival.

These illustrations complete the discussion of the present example. The next section is devoted to an exploration of the robustness of the

---

6. To see this, refer to equation (3) of section 3.4 and note that the integer part of $\tilde{N}(\gamma/2) = \tilde{N}(\frac{1}{2}a/\sigma)$ equals 2; and that in the no-advertising regime where $S/N^2 = \sigma$, the value $N = 2$ is reached at $S = 4$.

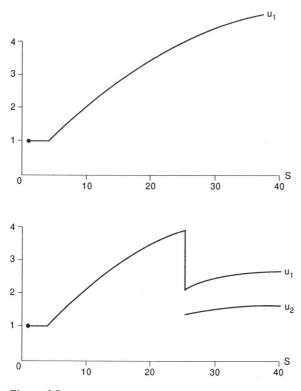

Figure 3.7
Sequential entry equilibrium in the basic example. The top panel shows the
relationship between market size and the choice of u, for the case $a = \sigma = 1, \gamma = 2$.
Here, the first firm preempts by setting a quality level u_1. The bottom panel shows the
case $a = \sigma = 1, \gamma = 2.2$. Here, u_1 and u_2 denote the quality levels of firms 1 and 2
respectively.

basic nonconvergence property that it illustrates. (It is possible to skip forward at this point, without loss of continuity, to the final section of the chapter, which sets out the empirical implications that form the basis for the remainder of the study.)

3.5   A General Treatment

This section focuses on the central result developed above—the nonconvergence property—which holds good across a very wide range of models. To avoid a sharp discontinuity in exposition at this point, it will be convenient to begin by developing the main argument within the three-stage game framework of the above example. This argument will then be shown to extend to a very broad class of models.

The starting point of the argument lies in the following observation: what matters for the nonconvergence result is the relationship between consumers' willingness-to-pay as indexed by u and the firm's costs. The latter comprises two parts: the fixed cost component $F(u)$ and the variable cost component. The latter component was taken as a constant, labeled c, in the example. In general, increases in u will affect both cost components, and we label these $F(u)$ and $c(u)$ accordingly. It is worth emphasizing that $c(u)$ represents the firm's marginal cost level, and we maintain the assumption that marginal cost is constant over all levels of output, hence $c(u)$ is the firm's unit variable cost. (Recall that $F(u)$ may be identified as classical advertising outlays, while $c(u)$ will include many promotional outlays such as discounts to retailers, coupons, packaging, inserts, etc.)

Raising u involves a mixture of both variable and fixed outlays, and various mixes might in principle be employed to achieve the same net impact on demand. The central argument may be stated briefly, if rather vaguely, as follows: Suppose, first, that (one possible way of) raising consumers' willingness-to-pay involves the use of more *fixed* outlays than are incurred by rivals, and that this involves no increase, or only a limited increase, in unit variable costs relative to that of rivals. Second, suppose that however high the *absolute* level of outlays incurred by rival firms, it is still possible to achieve some limited impact on demand by outspending rivals in this way; then the nonconvergence result follows. This idea lies at the center of the vertical product differentiation literature (see pp. 70–71).

Vertical Product Differentiation

The vertical product differentiation literature is concerned with the study of situations in which firms' offerings differ in terms of some attribute u in respect of which all consumers share the same ranking, that is, if two distinct products with qualities $u > v$ are offered at the same price, then all consumers choose the (higher-quality) product u. Consumers differ in their willingness-to-pay for a given quality increment, however, so that at equilibrium we may have prices $p_u > p_v$ such that each product commands a positive market share.

Now the obvious question that arises in this setting is: why should these models work any differently from the classical horizontal product differentiation models? An intuitive answer may be given by reference to figure 3.8, which illustrates the relationship $c(u)$ between the firm's unit variable cost of production c (i.e., its marginal cost) and the level of perceived quality u.

Imagine that all possible products (u-values) on some interval $(\underline{u}, \overline{u})$ are offered to consumers, and the price of each product is constrained to be equal to the level of unit variable cost $c(u)$. Two situations can arise: it may be that different consumers prefer different products, as in panel (i) of figure 3.8. In the case shown in this panel, a one-to-one mapping exists between some interval of consumer incomes and an interval of most-preferred products. In this

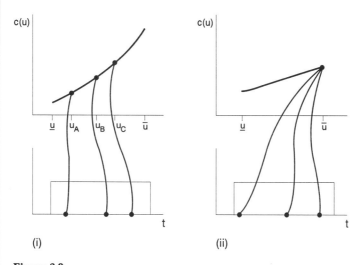

(i)   (ii)

Figure 3.8
The mapping from consumer types t into preferred product specifications u in the setting where price is constrained to be equal to unit variable cost $c(u)$. (i) the Chamberlinian case, (ii) the oligopoly case.

case the model has a structure *identical* to the classic Hotelling model. The reason for this is as follows: no matter what vector of products are offered, it is always possible to insert a new product between two adjacent products, which will capture a positive market share consisting of consumers who hitherto chose one or other of the two neighboring products. In the figure, u_B may be entered between u_A and u_C, and at equilibrium it will certainly enjoy a positive market share: since by setting price sufficiently close to marginal cost $c(u_B)$ it can achieve positive sales *even* if its rivals A and C set prices at the lowest possible level $(p_A = c(u_A), p_B = c(u_B))$.

Now the above construction breaks down if $c(u)$ is sufficiently flat. Here, the situation is as shown in panel (ii): if each possible product is offered at a price equal to marginal cost, then *all* consumers rank the products in the same way, that is, all prefer the highest quality on offer.

In the Hotelling model, market shares could always be made arbitrarily small by means of a successive entry of new products between preexisting products. This is no longer true in case (ii). Here, the entry of new products and the consequent reduction in product prices may simply drive some preexisting products (of lower quality) out of the market. Certainly, there is no reason to suppose that such a process of entry can lead to a fragmented structure.

Various theorems exist that categorize the properties of pure vertical product differentiation models of this type. The most widely used formulation is that developed by Gabszewicz and Thisse (1980) and Shaked and Sutton (1982). The latter paper develops the description of the relationship between the nature of technology and tastes (as captured by the $c(u)$ function in figure 3.9) and the emergence of fragmented or concentrated equilibria.

Matters become more complex once *both* vertical and horizontal attributes are present. The question now arises: why could we not have a fragmented equilibrium in which all products shared the *same* vertical attribute and differed only in their horizontal attributes? The answer to this question turns on the form of the fixed cost schedule $F(u)$: and the discussion in the main text is aimed at specifying conditions under which such configurations are not consistent with an optimal choice of product specification by firms.

The argument is developed by writing down two conditions that are sufficient to imply nonconvergence . These conditions are stated in general terms, independent of the details of any particular model of product differentiation. The first condition carries the idea that increases in u involve only a limited increase in $c(u)$: so long as this is true, it will be possible for the deviant firm to find a u sufficiently high to allow it to capture some given fraction of consumers, while maintaining a price that exceeds its unit variable cost by some—possibly very small—margin. In other words, if it raises $F(u)$ sufficiently high, relative to its rivals, it can guarantee some minimal level of profit Π in the final stage of the game, and this minimal level of profit will increase in step with the size of the market. To state this condition formally, a little notation is required.

Let $\mathbf{N}$ denote the number of consumers in the market. Consumers differ in their incomes and in their tastes, and these incomes and tastes are distributed according to some given functions, to be specified later. An increase in the size of the economy is understood to mean an increase in $\mathbf{N}$, the distribution of incomes and tastes remaining unchanged. The mean income of consumers is denoted y, and so total consumer income equals $y\mathbf{N}$.

CONDITION 1:   There exists a pair (α, k), $\alpha > 0$, $k > 1$, such that by offering a product with vertical attribute $k\overline{u}$, where $\overline{u}$ denotes the maximum level offered by any of its rivals, a firm may ensure an equilibrium payoff $\Pi \geqslant \alpha y \mathbf{N}$ in the final-stage subgame.

Condition 1 ensures that a sufficiently high value of u will imply a certain minimal level of profit in the lower stage of the game. This leaves open the question of whether that level of profit will suffice to allow a recovery of the sunk costs $F(u)$ incurred in raising u; this latter consideration turns upon the nature of $F(u)$:

CONDITION 2:   The function $F(u)$ is continuous and increasing on $u \geqslant 1$; and its elasticity is bounded above, viz., for some β,

$$\frac{u}{F}\frac{dF}{du} < \beta, \qquad \text{for all } u \geqslant 1.$$

The parameter β specified in condition 2 will be linked directly to the lower bound to the concentration-market size relationship. (In the context of the example of section 3.4, notice that for small values of σ, the elasticity of the schedule $F(u)$ takes its maximum value at

$F = \sigma$, and this corresponds to the minimum level of concentration, which is attained at the "kink" in the market size-market structure schedule.)

It is slightly unnatural to frame these conditions in terms of the (arbitrarily chosen) labeling of perceived quality levels embodied in the index u. All that matters, in what follows, turns only on the derived mapping from the firm's costs F, c into consumers' willingness-to-pay, and so into the profit function for the final-stage subgame. The above pair of conditions can be restated independently of u, as follows:

There exists a pair (α, K), $\alpha > 0$, $K > 1$, such that by incurring K times more fixed costs than any of its rivals, a firm may ensure an equilibrium payoff $\Pi \geqslant \alpha y \mathbf{N}$ in the final-stage subgame.

(Simply write the elasticity in condition 2 in log form and integrate. The constant K equals k^β.)

We now show that conditions 1 and 2 suffice to imply the non-convergence property.

PROPOSITION: Under conditions 1 and 2, there exists some $B > 0$ such that some firm must enjoy at least a fraction B of total industry sales at any (subgame perfect) equilibrium, independent of the size of the market $\mathbf{N}$.

Proof: We show, in fact, that $B = \alpha/(1 + k^\beta)$.

Consider an equilibrium, and denote by $\bar{u}$ the highest value of u offered by any firm, and by ε the highest share of industry sales enjoyed by any firm.

The sales revenue of each firm at equilibrium is less than or equal to $\varepsilon y \mathbf{N}$; hence the profit of each firm in the final stage of the game cannot exceed this value. Moreover, the fixed cost incurred by every firm is at most $\varepsilon y \mathbf{N}$; whence $F(\bar{u}) \leqslant \varepsilon y \mathbf{N}$. Now suppose any firm deviates in its choice of u, by setting $u = k\bar{u}$, the values chosen by its rivals being taken as given. Then it follows from conditions 1 and 2 that the firm's net profit is at least

$$\alpha y \mathbf{N} - F(k\bar{u}) \geqslant \alpha y \mathbf{N} - k^\beta F(\bar{u})$$

$$\geqslant \alpha y \mathbf{N} - k^\beta \varepsilon y \mathbf{N}$$

$$= (\alpha - k^\beta \varepsilon) y \mathbf{N}.$$

But since the firm's profit level in the supposed equilibrium cannot exceed $\varepsilon y \mathbf{N}$, it follows that this deviation would be profitable if

$$\alpha - k^\beta \varepsilon > \varepsilon,$$

i.e., $\varepsilon < \dfrac{\alpha}{1 + k^\beta}.$

Hence the maximal market share must exceed $\alpha/(1 + k^\beta)$ at equilibrium. This completes the proof.

We now turn to a discussion of the role of condition 1. This condition has been stated in a quite general form, and the next task lies in showing how it can be restated in concrete terms by reference to the primitives of some specific model of product differentiation. In terms of the example developed in section 3.3, for instance, it is easy to see that condition 1 holds. For, take the profit function $\Pi(u|\bar{u})$ as specified above (p. 50) and set $k = 2$, $y\mathbf{N} = S$, and an immediate calculation shows that condition 1 is satisfied with $\alpha = 1/4$.

Rather than multiply examples of how this condition can be made specific within various models of product differentiation, we here confine ourselves to illustrating this point for one type of model, viz., one in which products are differentiated according to two attributes, one of which is vertical (u), and the other of which is a horizontal attribute (h) of the locational or Hotelling kind.

Within this model, each consumer is assumed to buy either one unit of one of these goods, or none. The consumer's utility function takes the form $U(u, d, m)$, where u denotes the vertical attribute of the chosen product; $d = |h - \tilde{h}|$ denotes the absolute distance between the horizontal attribute of that product and the most preferred value of that attribute, labeled $\tilde{h}$; and $m = Y - p$ denotes the money remaining from the consumer's income Y after purchasing the product at price p. A consumer consuming none of the goods on offer achieves utility $U(u_0, 0, Y)$ where u_0 is a given constant and Y denotes income as before. Consumers differ in income Y and in their tastes over the horizontal attribute, that is, in $\tilde{h}$. (A trivial extension allows them also to differ in respect of the intensity of their preferences over the vertical attribute.) The distribution of income and tastes is described by some function $f(Y, h)$ defined on a rectangle $\underline{Y} \leqslant Y \leqslant \bar{Y}$, $0 \leqslant h \leqslant 1$.

It is well known that models of this kind exhibit various problems in respect of existence of pure strategy equilibria. Here no attempt is made to impose restrictions sufficient to ensure existence; rather, we keep the class of models as broad as possible and seek only to *character-ize* equilibria, whenever they exist. Existence problems may arise both within the second stage of the game and for the game as a whole. For example, in the case of pure horizontal differentiation, a (pure strategy) price equilibrium may fail to exist at the second stage (D'Aspremont, Gabszewicz, and Thisse 1979). To ensure existence, suitable convexity assumptions need to be imposed on consumer preferences (Neven 1985). The case of pure vertical differentiation is relatively well behaved in this respect (Gabszewicz, Shaked, Sutton, and Thisse (1981)). Assuming that a price equilibrium exists for any set of products, existence problems may still arise at the first (product choice) stage, if firms choose their products simultaneously. If, on the other hand, (a finite number of) firms choose products sequentially, existence of a pure strategy equilibrium (in quality choices) is assured (Börgers 1987, Harris 1985).

As regards *characterization* of equilibria, however, matters are straightforward. The following assumption is easily shown to imply condition 1 above:

ASSUMPTION 1:

(i) There is some bound $\bar{c}$ such that $c(u) < \bar{c}$ for all $u \geqslant 1$.

(ii) The utility function $U(u, d, m)$ satisfies $U_u > 0$, $U_m > 0$ and $U_d < 0$. Moreover, there exist bounds b_1, b_2, b_3 and some $\underline{m} \geqslant 0$ such that for all $u \geqslant 1$, $m \geqslant \underline{m}$ and $d \in [0, 1]$,

$uU_u > b_1;$

$U_m < b_2;$

$U_d < b_3.$

(iii) $\bar{Y} > \underline{m} + c.$

(iv) For some $\underline{f} > 0$, $f(Y, h) \geqslant \underline{f}$ for all $Y \in [\underline{Y}, \bar{Y}]$, $h \in [0, 1]$.

Part (i) requires that unit variable costs remain bounded as u increases. Part (ii), apart from placing some mild regularity conditions on $U(.)$, also requires that the marginal utility of outside goods (or money) should remain bounded, at least once some threshold level of income $\underline{m}$ is surpassed. In combination with (iii) and (iv), this ensures that at least some fraction of consumers will be willing to pay a price in excess of unit variable cost for a product of sufficiently high u.

Assumption 1 is a statement about consumer preferences; condition 1, on the other hand, relates to the level of profits and so depends inter alia on the equilibrium concept used in modeling competition in the final-stage subgame. Under Bertrand or Cournot competition, the proof that assumption 1 implies condition 1 is routine and will be found in Appendix 3.1.

Discussion

How robust are the results set out above? The four relevant aspects in respect of which we might require that results be robust were noted earlier:

(i) *Representations of product differentiation.*
For any of the standard models of product differentiation, a reformulation of assumption 1 in terms analogous to those employed in the horizontal and vertical case is routine.

(ii) *Strategic asymmetries.*
The above proof applies to models involving either two-stage or three-stage games in which firms make simultaneous choices of u. It can also be applied immediately to sequential entry models: all that is required is that the firm chosen as the deviant in the proof should come last in the sequence—so that it can take its rivals' choices of u as given.

(iii) *Multiproduct firms.*
The above proof uses the notion that a firm choosing a single product of quality u incurs fixed cost $F(u)$. It extends immediately to the case in which firms are also free to choose more than one product. In this latter setting, various cost functions may seem reasonable. For example, a firm might be required to spend an exogenously given setup cost *per product*, followed by an advertising outlay $A(u)$, which determines the perceived quality level u of *all* its products (complete spillover). It might, on the other hand, be assumed that an amount $A(u)$ must be incurred on *each* product (no spillover). The above argument extends immediately to both these cases.

(iv) *Equilibrium concept.*
Assumption (i) is a statement about consumer preferences. What it ensures is that there exists some fraction of the **N** consumers, say μ, who will strictly prefer the deviant's product at some price $p^* > c(u)$ *whatever* the prices of its rivals' products.

As was noted above, condition (i) is a statement about the firm's equilibrium profits, and it rests on both assumption (i) and on the form of competition that takes place in the final-stage subgame.

Under Bertrand or Cournot competition, it is clear that the deviant firm's profit must be at least $\mu(p^* - c(u))\mathbf{N}$; for the firm can guarantee this level of profit by setting its price equal to p^* (in the Bertrand case) or by setting its quantity equal to $\mu\mathbf{N}$ (in the Cournot case).[7]

What must be excluded here is the case of joint profit maximization by firms. Under this assumption, there may be no incentive to raise u as market size expands. This point is readily illustrated by reference to the example of section 3.5, in which the optimal level of advertising under monopoly is zero (in the notation of that section, $F^*(1; S) = \sigma$.

3.6 Empirical Predictions

General Results

The preceding analysis leads to a number of empirical predictions that are sufficiently robust to provide a basis for looking at cross-industry regressions. The first prediction relates to the nature of the lower bound to the concentration-market size relationship. In the preceding chapter, an appeal to the horizontal product differentiation concept was used to argue that insofar as the presence of physical differences between rival firms' offerings reduces the intensity of price competition, this lower bound is shifted downward and to the left. In this chapter, it is argued that the presence of advertising competition introduces an additional and tighter lower bound to concentration for larger values of market size. Two features of this new bound are of interest:

(i) It is *not* necessarily decreasing (or even monotonic).

(ii) It does *not* converge to zero as market size increases. In fact,

---

7. Notice, incidentally, that in the Cournot case an expansion in the firm's output, taking its rivals' equilibrium output levels as given, may cause rivals' prices to fall below unit variable cost. It is for this reason that assumption 1 is designed to ensure that these μN consumers will choose the deviant's product, even if its rivals' prices fall below marginal cost. In the Bertrand case this does not arise, and a weaker version of assumption 1 is sufficient to ensure condition 1. (This point was not made clear in Shaked and Sutton 1987.)

independent of the detailed structure of the model there exists a minimal level of concentration that can never be surpassed no matter how large the market becomes.

These properties are illustrated in figure 3.9. The figure shows how the lower bound to equilibrium concentration is shifted in two ways once we move from a set of homogeneous goods to differentiated products for which advertising is effective in raising willingness-to-pay. In the traditional literature, the distinction between the effects of product differentiation per se and the effects of advertising has often been confused. Since advertising-intensive industries typically involve more highly differentiated products, it is tempting to identify these two concepts: indeed it is common practice in empirical work to use the level of advertising intensity as a proxy for the degree of product differentiation. It is not true, however, that all those industries with negligibly small advertising-sales ratios sell nondifferentiated products. The archetypal counterexample arises in the engineering industry, where many highly differentiated products are sold primarily to industrial buyers and for which advertising levels are usually extremely low.

One of the advantages of the present framework is that it allows a neat analytical separation between two familiar ideas that are often juxtaposed in discussing product differentiation as a barrier to entry, following Bain 1959:

1. The higher degree of product differentiation *per se* will facilitate entry insofar as it provides new niches for potential entrants. This is captured by the leftward shift of the lower bound for small values of market size in figure 3.9.

2. Insofar as product differentiation renders advertising more effective, this will tend to raise concentration levels. This is captured by the upward shift in the lower bound at high values of S in figure 3.9.

Advertising as an Exogenous Barrier to Entry

The general results just cited all turn on one key property, which relates to the effectiveness of fixed (advertising) outlays in stimulating consumers' willingness-to-pay. It is time to focus attention on the precise role played by this property. It may be helpful to begin with a clarification: It is *not* assumed that consumers' willingness-to-pay can be increased indefinitely by means of increases in fixed (advertis-

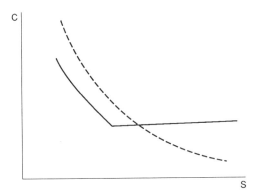

Figure 3.9
The lower bound to concentration in advertising-intensive industries. The hatched line shows the equivalent bound for homogeneous goods industries.

ing) outlays. Such an assumption would be quite implausible. What *is* assumed is that such outlays can induce *some* fixed fraction of consumers to choose some particular firm's offerings at a price level that exceeds that firm's unit variable cost. What matters to the present results is that this statement should continue to hold good, even if the advertising levels of all firms become very high. It is assumed that, even though absolute outlays become high, a given proportionate increase in outlays vis-à-vis rival firms will still be effective in drawing away that given fraction of consumers.

A failure of this property, then, would arise in a situation where there is some *absolute* level of advertising outlays beyond which further increases become ineffective. What matters in practice is whether such a saturation level is achieved across the empirically relevant range of parameter values. What happens if such a saturation level exists? In terms of the theory, we might model this by letting the $A(u)$ schedule become vertical beyond some point (u_∞, A_∞). If this case holds, then that increases in market size may lead to an indefinite fragmentation of the market, as an indefinitely large number of entrants each undertake an advertising level A_∞. (The details of this construction can be found in Shaked and Sutton 1987.) This variant of the present theory captures the view of advertising as an exogenous barrier to entry; equilibrium behavior is similar to that of the exogenous sunk cost model of chapter 2, with σ replaced by $\sigma + A_\infty$. This provides a counterhypothesis against which the theory may be tested, as well as a useful point of reference in examining the differences between the present approach and other approaches to the analysis of particular industries (see especially chapter 10).

Beyond the few general results set out above, is anything else sufficiently robust to be of potential interest in looking at cross-industry regularities? The obvious candidates to consider here relate to comparative static results linking setup costs, advertising, and concentration. The link between setup costs and concentration can be seen from figure 3.4: increases in setup cost imply an increase in equilibrium concentration $(1/N)$ within the example. This result follows directly from equilibrium condition (2); restated in general terms, and written as an equality, this is

$$\Pi(N) = F^*(N; S) = \sigma + A^*(N). \tag{2'}$$

The function $\Pi(N)$ is strictly decreasing. Moreover, at equilibrium it must be the case that $\Pi_N - A_N < 0$ (since otherwise, further entry would be profitable). Differentiation of $(2')$ and an appeal to this stability condition implies that

$$\frac{dN}{d\sigma} = \frac{1}{\Pi_N - A_N} < 0 \text{ as required.}$$

The general form of this argument suggests that it might be extended to a fairly wide class of models. This is indeed the case;[8] though it is *not* as robust a result as the nonconvergence properties just summarized, it does appear to be of potential interest in looking at cross-industry relationships.

The same is not true, however, for the relationship between setup costs and advertising levels (or measures of advertising intensity). A

---

8. A full treatment of this result lies outside our scope. Here, we confine ourselves to a few remarks as to how the result may be extended. The argument, as stated above, covers all models having symmetric equilibria, irrespective of the shape of the function $A^*(N)$. One special feature of the example of section 3.2 was that the final stage profit is a function of N alone, independent of any common level of advertising undertaken by firms at the preceding stage. More generally, it might be assumed that equilibrium profits also depend on the level of advertising undertaken, viz., the final-stage profit function might be written as $\Pi(N, A^*(N))$. In this setting, the comparative static results continue to hold, so long as the total derivative $d\Pi/dN$ remains negative, that is, entry may affect advertising and so partially, but not wholly, offset the tendency for profits to decline. The result can also be extended to cases in which multiple equilibria are present, by framing it in terms of the minimal level of concentration supportable as an equilibrium. Finally, it can be extended to cases in which equilibria are nonsymmetric if both final-stage equilibrium profit and equilibrium advertising outlays can be expressed in terms of some scalar index of concentration.

case has sometimes been made in the literature for some form of systematic relationship between concentration and advertising levels; in particular, it has been claimed by Kaldor (1950) and Greer (1973) that advertising should first rise, and then fall, as concentration rises.

This type of relationship can certainly be supported as a *possibility* within the present theory.[9] Such a result depends delicately, however, on the form of the mapping from advertising outlays to consumers' willingness-to-pay. In particular, it turns on the question of how an increase in advertising affects *total* industry sales—a consideration that in turn determines a monopolist's incentive to advertise. Insofar as increases in advertising stimulate total *industry* sales, the tendency for increases in setup costs to lead eventually to a fall in equilibrium advertising levels may be reversed.

---

9. The example of section 3.4 provides an illustration of this: in figure 3.4, imagine a vertical line that cuts the $\Sigma\Sigma$ locus at two points. An upward movement along this line brings us from a region of low concentration and zero advertising, through a region of medium concentration and positive advertising, and finally to a region of high concentration and zero advertising.

4

From Theory to Measurement

4.1 Introduction and Summary

This chapter is primarily concerned with developing some relations
between the theoretical categories introduced in the preceding chapters and their empirical counterparts. The first part of the chapter
deals with some preliminary issues regarding industry definitions. A
number of criteria are introduced, and all industries within the food
and drink sector that meet these criteria are included in the study.
The primary criterion is simply that it should be possible to arrive at
an industry definition that can be applied in a consistent way across
each country, so that cross-country comparisons are likely to be both
valid and informative. The criteria determining the set of countries
to be studied here are also discussed briefly, and some mention is
made of a number of country-specific factors whose influence is noted
occasionally in later chapters.

The central part of the chapter is concerned with finding empirical
counterparts to the concepts of setup cost, market size, and market
structure, and with classifying industries into two groups: those in
which advertising plays a negligible role, so that the exogenous sunk
cost model of chapter 2 may reasonably be applied, and those in
which advertising outlays appear to play a potentially important
role.

Problems of measurement, then, take up much of the discussion,
and a wide range of empirical problems arise in relation to the
measurement of each of the variables. The econometric tests set out
in the next chapter have been designed with these difficulties in mind;
in particular, it is argued below that an important distinction arises
between two sets of measurement issues.

• The key predictions of the model are about the relationship between market size and market structure (concentration), and the way in which this varies between two groups of industries. It is very important, therefore, to obtain reliable measures of market size and industry concentration, suitably defined, and to arrive at a classification scheme that is well motivated a priori.

• On the other hand, quite severe problems of measurement arise in estimating the levels of sunk costs incurred in any particular industry. These problems relate both to (exogenous) setup costs and to (endogenous) advertising outlays. Fortunately, the more important test of the model employed in the next chapter is *independent* of any measures of setup cost. Moreover, all procedures used in the next chapter rely on measures of advertising intensity only as a classificatory variable in dividing the industries into two groups. Because the divide between the two groups is rather sharp, this classification scheme would not be affected by moderate errors in measuring advertising outlays in particular industries.

The final section turns to problems of data collection and related issues. The raw data take the form of a matrix of industry profiles, which were built up using a combination of published market research reports and official industry studies. The information thus collected was augmented and cross-checked by over 100 interviews with senior marketing executives in various companies. Further checks were made possible by the generous assistance of leading market research companies in several countries.

4.2 The Industries

It was noted in chapter 1 that the set of industries studied here has been drawn from the food and drink sector. As explained earlier, the reason for choosing this sector is that among all broadly defined industry groups (two-digit SIC level), the food and drink group has one of the lowest levels of R & D intensity, together with the highest level of advertising intensity. For this reason, it offers an opportunity to study the effects of advertising in isolation from the similar (but more complex) mechanisms associated with the role of R & D outlays as an endogenous sunk cost. Moreover, the intensity of advertising in the food and drink sector is not only high on average but varies extremely widely from one product market to another, thus providing an unusually good context in which to examine its effects.

Before turning to the question of defining individual industries within this sector, it may be helpful to remark on two familiar issues that arise in respect of industry definitions. First, an industry may be defined either by reference to market criteria (i.e., in terms of substitutability of products in consumption) or by reference to similarities in production techniques. Typically, official statistics tend to be influenced by the latter criterion: for example, the U.S. four-digit SIC classification distinguishes the beet sugar industry from the cane sugar industry on this basis, though from a marketing point of view both products are perfect substitutes. Given the aims of this study, it is appropriate to work in terms of industry definitions that are chosen primarily by reference to market criteria; but it is useful, nonetheless, to maintain a rough concordance between the list of industries used and the four-digit SIC industries described in (U.S. and other) official statistics. The reason for maintaining this concordance is to facilitate the estimation of setup costs by industry.

In seeking a suitable market-based definition, a second difficulty arises: if we define an industry broadly enough to include all close substitutes for its core products, then it is likely that the industry thus defined will in fact be segmented into a number of product areas, in the sense that many, or most, firms will confine their activities to one or more market segments and will effectively compete only with the set of firms operating within that segment. (In Caves's terminology, these sets of firms are dubbed "strategic groups.")

If we try, on the other hand, to narrow our definition so as to confine our attention to one such specific market segment, we may miss the fact that many of the industry's major firms operate across many, or all, segments, and that a firm's activities in one segment may influence its success in another. This can happen not only because some firm may enjoy a cost advantage (economies of scope, in the sense of Panzar and Willig 1981), but—more pertinently to the present analysis—that its image advertising for one product line may enhance the demand for its entire product range (indeed, such a firm may devote a substantial fraction of its advertising budget to range advertising, that is, advertising its product line as a whole, across all market segments).

Under these circumstances, it seems appropriate to adopt a compromise solution: define markets fairly broadly to begin with, and then look at the pattern of segmentation within each market, on a case-by-case basis.

Bearing these observations in mind, the aim was to identify as large and comprehensive a set of markets as possible, subject to a number of criteria designed to ensure that like is being compared to like in carrying out cross-country comparisons. A preliminary examination of the market research literature on the food processing industries suggested a set of market definitions that recurs, with few exceptions or modifications, across all of the countries studied here. The level of aggregation involved in these studies is not dissimilar to that of the standard four-digit SIC industry, and a rough concordance between the definitions is possible (table 4.2).

One potential shortcoming of this approach, however, is that it runs the danger of undercoverage in respect of commodity-type industries, in which advertising expenditure is virtually nil—and in which there is relatively little interest by the market research community. For this reason, the set of products examined here has been broadened to include a number of commodity-type products—salt, sugar, flour, and bread—for which market research reports are rarely available and for which information must be sought through other channels (including, in particular, company interviews). In the case of salt, only a modest fraction of output enters the food industry; the bulk of output is used in other areas (de-icing roads, the chemical industry, etc.). Nonetheless, the industry provides a valuable point of comparison with other industries.

In this way, a preliminary list of industries was compiled and a rough concordance with four-digit SIC definitions established. Four criteria were employed in excluding certain industries from this preliminary list or in modifying industry definitions to avoid problems of comparability.

1. The product mix within the industry should not vary so widely across countries as to render comparisons overly problematic or meaningless.

On the basis of this criterion, wine, spirits, and pasta products were excluded entirely. In less extreme cases, the use of a narrower industry definition than that customarily used permitted a reasonable degree of comparability across countries. Thus, the meat processing industry is here defined narrowly to encompass processed pork products only. The canning industries are represented here by canned vegetables. The SIC category "canned specialties" includes part of the prepared soups industry, as well as the baby food industry, both of which are treated as separate industries here. The canned vegetables industry is defined to exclude canned tomatoes, which constitutes a very large category in Italy but is relatively unimportant elsewhere. In the oils and fats sector, it was decided to use the narrowly defined margarine market as a representative of the group.

Finally, in a few instances, the market in a single country was anomalous, and this market alone was excluded (canned vegetables in Japan (see chapter 7), prepared soups in Italy (see chapter 9), and mineral water in the United States (see chapter 11)).

2. Some industries include one or more segments that differ widely in respect of the level of setup cost incurred by entrants. It is necessary to formulate industry definitions in a way that respects these differences.

Here, two approaches were used. In some cases, it was possible to split the industry into two broad subindustries and to consider each of them independently (sugar and chocolate confectionery, instant and roast and ground coffee). In other cases, a subindustry with setup costs widely different from the rest of the industry was simply excluded from the industry definition. The production of chewing gum involves extremely high setup costs, but this activity is normally classified as part of the sugar confectionery, where setup costs are generally extremely low. For this reason, in defining the sugar confectionery industry, the market for chewing gum was excluded.

3. Some food and drink markets lie midway between the industrial and agricultural sectors, and the institutional arrangements in the latter sector may vary widely, and in a complex manner, across countries.

Because of the difficulty of making satisfactory comparisons in this context, the dairy products sector as a whole was excluded from the study.

4. The markets should be independent.

This analysis assumes that each market is supplied by producers who each incur a minimal setup cost in entering the market. In a few of the industries considered here this condition is violated, either because the market is very small and is largely supplied by imports from abroad, or because a group of adjacent countries have a highly integrated market. For example, in the ready-to-eat (RTE) breakfast

Table 4.1
The twenty industries (the number in parentheses indicates the chapter in which the industry is discussed)

Salt	(6)	RTE cereals	(10)
Sugar	(6)	Mineral water	(11)
Flour	(7)	Sugar confectionery	(12)
Bread	(7)	Chocolate confectionery	(12)
Processed meat	(7)	Roast and ground coffee	(12)
Canned vegetables	(7)	Instant coffee	(12)
Frozen food	(8)	Biscuits	(12)
Soup	(9)	Pet foods	(12)
Margarine	(9)	Baby foods	(12)
Soft drinks	(9)	Beer	(13)

cereals industry, the leading seller (Kellogg) supplies all continental European markets from a single plant located in Germany, and it would be inappropriate to treat these three markets as independent; all three are omitted from the data set used in chapter 5. Furthermore, several markets in which the import penetration ratio exceeds 20% are excluded (see below).

These criteria led to the list of twenty industries shown in table 4.1. Readers who wish to see how the above exclusion criteria were applied, in terms of the standard list of four-digit SIC industries within the food and drink sector, may consult table 4.5. Finally, certain of these industries are omitted from the data set employed in the next chapter on the basis of criterion 4 (independence of supply). These are

France:	RTE cereals
Germany (F.R.):	RTE cereals, canned vegetables
Italy:	RTE cereals, pet foods
Japan:	salt, RTE cereals, baby foods
United Kingdom:	processed meat.

Some brief comment on each of these cases will be found in the relevant appendix.

The Countries

This study is confined to the six largest Western economies: the United States, Japan, Germany (Federal Republic), France, the

United Kingdom, and Italy. The primary reason for not extending the sample further relates to the problems posed by the fact that import penetration ratios are much larger in the case of small economies, so that structure is heavily influenced by the role of imported (leading) brands. As has just been noted, this would violate the maintained assumption that each seller incurs the same setup cost in commencing production, in each market in which it operates. A secondary reason for not extending the study to more countries lies in the lack of adequate coverage of many of these industries in the market research literature.

In comparing industrial structure across these six countries, it is of interest to ask whether any country-specific factors exist that might operate across the general run of the industries studied. It has sometimes been observed in cross-country comparisons of structure that concentration levels tend to be higher in the United States and United Kingdom than in France, Germany, and Italy (see, for example, George and Ward 1975). The reasons for this are not generally agreed, and while the present data set supports the existence of such a difference, the theory set out here does not offer an explanation.

Within the present framework, systematic cross-country differences would arise if institutional factors specific to some country or countries affected either the toughness of price competition in the market or the degree of effectiveness of advertising outlays. Differences of this kind do indeed operate in specific industries, and their influence will be traced (see especially chapters 6 and 13). As to the existence of other cross-country differences that might impinge in a systematic way on structure, two are worth noting:

• The much greater geographical extent of the U.S. market might make it easier to achieve a relaxation in the toughness of price competition by means of geographical market segmentation. This is indeed evident in several of the industries (see, for example, chapter 6).

• Another respect in which the six countries differ relates to the degree of success achieved by retailers in developing their own brands ("private label" products) in competition with the manufacturers of leading branded products. This appears to vary in line with the degree of concentration in the retail sector. The retail sector is relatively concentrated in the United Kingdom, France, and Germany, but is relatively fragmented in the United States, Japan, and Italy.[1]

The degree of success of retailers' own brands has been greatest in the United Kingdom, where they accounted for 28% of total retail sales in 1985. The degree of penetration by category varies widely, being greatest when brands are least strong (canned vegetables and frozen food) and weakest where brands are strongest (pet foods and RTE cereals). Some leading retailers in the United Kingdom, notably Sainsbury's and Tesco, now advertise their own brands quite heavily. In the United States, on the other hand, the impact of retailers' own brands has been extremely weak. The relevance of this difference between countries will be seen in several of the industry studies. In the United Kingdom, for example, the strength of retailers' own brands appears to have grown to the point when it may be more costly for manufacturers to achieve a given market share by dint of advertising support for a new brand.

4.3   Measurement Issues I: Market Size and Concentration

This section deals with the measurement of the two key variables on which the central econometric tests of the present model will rest: market structure, or concentration, and market size.

The Reference Year

Basic research for study was carried out over the period 1987–88, and the figures for market size and market shares were established for the reference year 1986, or, if that figure was unavailable, for a date as close as possible to 1986. In the large majority of markets studied here, year-to-year fluctuations in sales and market shares are not very

---

1. In the United Kingdom, ten leading retailers were estimated to hold about 42% of retail sales of food in 1986. The four largest chains were Tesco, J. Sainsbury, Dee (inc. Fine Fare) and the Co-op. In France, the major supermarket chains cooperate as buying groups, thereby enjoying considerable bargaining power vis-à-vis food-processing firms. The three largest buying groups, A.R.C.I., Contact, and Di Fra, together accounted for 28% of retail sales of food in 1984. In Germany, thirteen leading retail groups accounted for 53.2% of retail sales of food in 1986, the largest being Aldi, RGG Leibbrand, Co-op AG Frankfurt, and Tengelman Gruppe. At the other extreme, the largest food retailer in the United States (Safeway) accounts for only 2% of total sales. In Italy, only 12% of total retail sales of food occurs through supermarkets (or hypermarkets). See the report *Own Brands*, published by Keynote (U.K.), 1986.

great, and figures reported for 1985 or 1987 differ little from those reported for 1986. Where occasional exceptions arise, due either to an unusually volatile share pattern or to the occurrence of mergers or acquisitions during the mid-1980s, attention is drawn to this in the relevant chapter.

Relative Market Size

The problem of measuring market size and its relation to setup cost can be divided into two steps. Assuming that the setup cost incurred in entering the market in any industry is the same across all countries, it suffices to estimate setup cost relative to market size for a single reference country (the United States) and to estimate as a separate exercise the relative size of each market relative to the U.S. market. The former step is quite problematic and is deferred to the next section. The latter step, of estimating relative size, is dealt with here.

The procedure applied is to estimate relative market size on the basis of total output volumes, wherever this is appropriate. In fact, this turns out to be feasible for ten of the twenty industries. In the remaining cases, relative market size is computed by reference to measures of the value of total sales (retail and nonretail) in the various markets, converted to U.S. dollars at the average rate of exchange prevailing over the reference year chosen.

Measuring Concentration

Two questions arise in regard to the appropriate measure of concentration. The first relates to the choice of index; some summary measure is needed which will distinguish concentrated from fragmented patterns of market share. An a priori defense of a particular measure may be developed if one is willing to presuppose some specific (oligopoly) model underlying the observed share pattern.[2] Since the aim here is to avoid imposing any precisely specified oligopoly model on the data, it would clearly be inappropriate to seek some "ideal" measure. The most important of the results presented in chapters 2 and 3 were framed in terms of the maximal market share, this is, the share enjoyed by the single largest firm. In most of

---

2. The standard example relates to the imposition of the standard Cournot model as a basis for employing the Herfindahl index. For a particularly helpful approach to the choice of index, based on certain intuitively appealing criteria, see Hannah and Kay 1977.

what follows, we adopt the conventional course of using a more or less arbitrary summary measure; specifically, we use the most popular measure, the four-firm concentration ratio (the sum of the shares of the top four firms). The results obtained, however, are checked against various alternative measures. To allow readers to examine their preferred choice of measure, the data presented in the industry appendices include individual market shares for the four largest firms. Furthermore, since we focus some attention on the "tail" of small firms active in the industry, an estimate of the total number of firms active in the industry is also provided, wherever a reliable estimate is available.

The second question that arises in regard to a measure of concentration relates to the choice between a sales concentration ratio as defined, for example, by the sum of the market shares of the four largest firms; or a production concentration ratio, defined as the sum of their shares of industry production. It has already been noted that the former measure is more appropriate in the present context, and this is adhered to in almost all industries. A few exceptions arise, in which it is not possible to ascertain firms' shares in total sales, and, in these cases, shares in total production, or in industry capacity, have been used an an approximation.

It may be worth noting the reasons for the often very large discrepancies between the sales concentration ratios reported here and the official estimates for the corresponding four-digit SIC industries in official statistics. A minor problem arises insofar as some domestically produced output is exported, while part of domestic sales consists of imports, thus leading to a difference between sales- and production-based measures. A much more important problem relates to the fact that the procedures used in official census estimates rely on the convention that each plant (establishment) is allocated to a particular industry, as defined by an SIC code. All sales revenue deriving from the plant is then attributed to this industry. The census must, of its nature, aim to be comprehensive; every plant must be allocated to some industry. This means, however, that the range of products falling within a particular SIC definition may encompass not only a central core of products that are more or less close substitutes in consumption, but may also include ancillary products that share a common production technology with the core products but that are not substitutes in consumption with these products.

A final problem that arises in using production-based concentration measures relates to products that can be produced using different technologies. For example, beet and cane sugar, as noted earlier, are classified in different four-digit SICs in the United States. Official estimates of concentration ratios relate, therefore, to two separate "industries." Some sugar producers operate only in one of these, while others operate in both. Unless the firms in question can be identified, the concentration ratios for these two industries do not suffice to determine the concentration ratio for the combined sugar market.

But while these considerations underline the value of working with sales concentration ratios computed directly from the market research literature and related sources, it should be emphasized that this approach has a number of shortcomings too. The most obvious of these relates to the accuracy of available market share statistics. In the food and drink industry, the fact that well-established procedures for monitoring retail sales have been developed over the past two decades by leading agencies means that quite accurate and reliable measures are often available. On the other hand, quite serious limitations arise whenever the nonretail market is relatively important—for even among the leading companies themselves, considerable uncertainty often surrounds the market share pattern in the nonretail segment.

In the market share tables shown in appendix 1 a range of values, rather than a single figure, is indicated in many instances. In a few cases, shares are reported for both the retail market and (with less accuracy) the total market. In all but two of the industries it has been possible to obtain reasonably satisfactory share estimates for the total market (i.e., retail and nonretail), or else the nonretail segment is so small that the sales concentration ratio for the retail sector provides a reasonable approximation to that of the market as a whole. There are, however, two industries in which neither of these circumstances holds (margarine and frozen food). The econometric estimates in chapter 5 are presented with these two industries excluded. Their inclusion (using the best measures available) does not materially affect the results.

4.4 Measurement Issues II: Setup Cost

The difficulties that arise in estimating the level of setup cost by industry are of a different order than those encountered in the preceding section. In what follows, a simple proxy measure of the *relative* level of setup costs across different industries is proposed. A number of criticisms of this measure are then listed. It is argued, in light of these criticisms, that it is desirable to proceed as far as possible in the subsequent analysis without employing these estimates of setup cost.

Defining a Proxy for Setup Cost

In chapters 2 and 3, the setup cost σ was defined as the minimal level of sunk cost that must be incurred by each entrant to the industry prior to commencing production. In the present section, it is argued that these sunk costs might reasonably be assumed to vary across industries in proportion to the cost of constructing a single plant of minimum efficient scale (m.e.s.).

This assertion raises two kinds of difficulty:

(i) It assumes that the proportion of initial outlays that might be recovered on exiting the industry is constant across industries. A less strict requirement, which would suffice in the present context, is that the proportion of such costs which are recoverable should not vary in a systematic way with the size of the market or the structure of the industry. Even this latter condition, however, might be challenged. No systematic body of data is available that throws light on the way in which such recovery rates vary across the present set of industries.

(ii) If some minimum efficient scale of operation could be identified, and if all new entrants necessarily operated at or above that level, then the present procedure would be justified, subject only to (i). A less strict requirement, which is still sufficient for our purposes, is that the ratio between the minimal outlay that must be incurred by a new entrant and the cost of establishing a single m.e.s. plant does not vary in a systematic way with the size of the market or the structure of the industry. No data on the outlays incurred by new entrants exist that allow this assertion to be directly tested.[3]

The two preceding assumptions, though not directly testable, appear at least to be plausible. A more serious difficulty arises when we turn

---

3. Moreover, even if such data were available, it will be clear that new entrants will often confine themselves to some single segment (niche) of the market, and setup costs may vary across different segments. As noted, the principles of industry delimitation used here are aimed at avoiding the most serious instances of such heterogeneity—but, even using the present set of definitions, this issue remains serious.

to the measurement of minimum efficient scale.[4] The most natural measure of m.e.s., in the present context, is that provided by engineering estimates based on studies that aim to identify the level of average cost achievable using alternative technologies and plant sizes. The m.e.s. level is defined as corresponding to the smallest level of output at which, using any available technology or plant size, a firm can attain a level of average cost within a given percentage (usually 10%) of the lowest achievable level (see section 1.6).

Such an estimate falls short of providing information on the *degree* to which firms operating below this level will be penalized. In some studies, supplementary estimates give the percentage increase in average cost suffered by a firm operating at some specified fraction of the m.e.s. level. Estimates of this kind would be extremely useful,

---

4. Within the theory, what meaning can be attached to the notion of minimum efficient scale? This concept is normally defined in the empirical literature as the scale of operation at which average cost can be brought to, or within some specified percentage distance of, the lowest level achievable. The interpretation of this idea varies according as different assumptions are made about the nature of the underlying technology. It has been assumed here that only one technology is available, and that this requires a sunk outlay of σ, whereupon output may then be produced at constant marginal cost c. More generally, it might be assumed that a range of possible technologies were available, and that increases in σ were associated with decreases in c. Two cases now arise. In the first case, the effectiveness of increasing σ eventually diminishes as c reaches some point beyond which further efficiency improvements become arbitrarily costly. In the second case, the elasticity of c with respect to σ is bounded above; a proportionate increase in σ always achieves a certain minimal proportionate reduction in c.

In other words, it is possible to embed the choice of technology (σ) within the richer framework of the endogenous sunk cost model. This means that the maintained assumption of the theory, that σ is exogenously fixed, is replaced by the weaker assumption, corresponding to the first case identified above, that is, that increases in σ eventually become ineffective in reducing c. This is precisely analogous to the discussion of advertising as an endogenous sunk cost in section 3.5. There, it was noted that if a ceiling to the effectiveness of advertising was reached at some point, increases in market size would eventually lead to a structure in which an arbitrarily large number of firms all operated arbitarily close to that ceiling—and the model collapsed in the limit to the exogenous sunk cost model. (The complementary case, in which increases in σ continue indefinitely to exert an effect on c, is of independent interest. It offers a model appropriate to industries characterized by constant process innovation. The properties of this case were developed by Dasgupta and Stiglitz 1980.)

This, then, is a route along which a concept analogous to the traditional m.e.s. notion may be incorporated into the present framework. On this reading, different firms may choose to incur different outlays at equilibrium in setting up plant, but there is a minimal outlay below which firms will suffer a serious cost disadvantage in stage two of the game—and, at equilibrium, all firms will incur at least some minimal outlay on plant and equipment.

because they might in principle help to identify more precisely the minimal outlay needed for viability. Unfortunately, estimates of this kind are available for relatively few industries, and it is customary in the industrial organization literature to represent m.e.s. instead by a more easily available measure: the size of the industry's median plant.

The rationale underlying this proxy is less than compelling, but it can be claimed that—at least within the food and drink sector— median plant size correlates quite well with engineering estimates of m.e.s. For a set of thirteen four-digit SIC industries in the U.S. food and drink sector, Connor et al. (1985), using the results reported by Culbertson and Morrison (1983), report a correlation coefficient of 0.83 between median plant estimates based on the 1972 census of manufactures and engineering estimates published over the period 1970–80. In Figure 4.1, scatter diagrams of these estimates are shown, both for the 1970–80 period and for the period 1950–63 (as compared with 1958 Census data). While the overall correlation is good, one clear outlier occurs. The engineering estimate for the canned vegetables industry lies far above m.e.s. estimates for the latter period, though not for the earlier period. This may reflect the fact that demand in the canned vegetables industry has been stagnant or declining since the 1950s, and new plant construction embodying best-practice technology may have been slowed as a consequence (see appendix 7.4).

This exception apart, the correlation is quite good for both periods and, on the basis of this observation, it may not seem unreasonable to employ m.e.s. estimates. Median plant size estimates, unlike engineering estimates, are available for all four-digit SIC industries in the case of the United States (but not in the case of the other countries studied here); and, as noted, a rough concordance can be established with the present set of industries. The measure of m.e.s. used here, then, is the ratio between the output level of the industry's median plant, relative to industry output. The estimates used are those of Culbertson and Morrison (1983) for 1972, as reported by Connor et al. (1985, pp. 154–156).

In two of the industries studied here, coffee and confectionery, the industry subdivides into two subindustries that differ greatly in respect of their m.e.s. ratio. In the case of confectionery, the median plant estimate can be identified with the m.e.s. appropriate to sugar confectionery: for the large majority of firms in the industry specialize

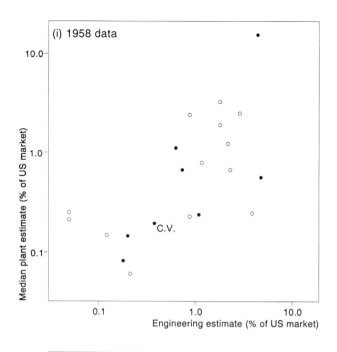

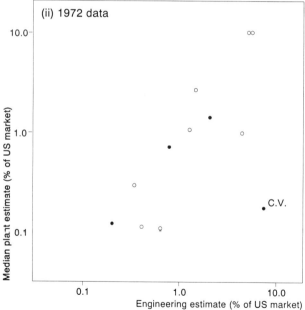

Key: Industries shown as ● are among those included in the present study

C.V. denotes canned vegetables (see text)

Figure 4.1

Engineering estimates of m.e.s. versus median plant size estimates for a set of four-digit SIC industries in the food and drink sector (double log scale). The estimates are those reported by Connor et al. (1985), following Culbertson and Morrison (1983).

in only one segment, and the number of firms producing mainstream chocolate confectionery products, which involve relative high setup costs, is extremely small (<100) as compared with the number producing sugar confectionery (about 1,000). In the case of the coffee industry, however, the estimates for the combined U.S. industry are less easily identified with either subindustry (see chapter 12). In the table of estimated setup costs presented later in this chapter, the chocolate confectionery industry and both parts of the coffee industry have been omitted. A detailed discussion of these industries can be found in chapter 12.

Given some measure of m.e.s., we may proceed to estimate the level of setup cost relative to the size of the market as follows: Let μ denote the measure of m.e.s., that is, the output of the median plant relative to industry output. Assume (rather heroically) that the capital-output ratio of the median firm stands in the same proportion to the capital-output ratio of the industry as a whole, across all of the industries studied here. Let K/S denote the capital-output ratio of the industry as a whole, that is, the total value of plant and equipment[5] in the industry divided by the value of annual industry sales.

Under the above assumptions, the value of plant and equipment owned by the median firm is porportionate to μK, and an index of setup cost relative to market size is given by

$$\frac{\sigma}{S} = \frac{\mu K}{S}.$$

Estimates of this measure for the United States in 1976 are presented in table 4.2 for each of the relevant four-digit SIC industries. (This procedure is similar to that of Kessides 1988.)

The measure of capital stock used in deriving these estimates is the book value of plant and equipment, divided by annual industry sales. The book value of assets, valued at historic prices, seriously underestimates the current replacement cost of plant and equipment; this further reinforces the point that little weight should be attached to the absolute value of the index σ/S thus computed. Assuming that the age structure of plant and equipment does not vary greatly across the set of industries, however, this index still provides a (fairly crude) indicator of the *relative* level of σ/S across these industries.

---

5. The industries' capital stock will also include land; but this part of the firm's capital stock is likely to be more readily recoverable on exit and is here assumed not to constitute a sunk cost.

To compute the σ/S values for the remaining five countries, we estimate the ratio of the value of sales for the U.S. industry to the value of sales for the industry of the country in question. This ratio is labeled ρ_{ij} in what follows, where i is an industry index and j a country index. (In computing ρ_{ij}, the value of sales used for both countries is that of the industry as defined in the present study, and *not* that of the corresponding four-digit SIC industry.) Thus, if S_i/σ_i denotes the ratio of market size to setup cost for the U.S. industry, the corresponding ratio for country j is simply $\rho_{ij} \cdot (S_i/\sigma_i)$. The results of these computations are set out in table 4.3.

Criticisms

It will be clear at this point that the estimation of setup costs by industry poses serious difficulties. In addition to those problems raised above, a further objection may be added, which has some force: as Davies (1980) has noted, the use of median plant estimates in explaining differences in structure across industries may involve a potentially serious bias; put crudely, concentrated industries have large firms, and large firms tend to operate large plants. Thus even if the average cost schedule were flat above some minimal level of operation, median plant estimates would tend to be higher where concentration was higher.

This objection has considerable force where differences in m.e.s. are used to explain differences in structure *across industries* within a single country; and it is therefore worth emphasizing at this point that the primary focus of this study is to look at a *within-industry* relationship between market size and concentration by examining the same industry across several countries. In principle, the exercise could be carried out industry by industry, avoiding all interindustry comparisons, thus obviating the need for an estimate of σ. In practice, the paucity of data points means that some pooling of information from different industries is inevitable—but the key test in chapter 5 is independent of the σ_i/S_i measures and rests only on the relative market size estimates, ρ_{ij}.

4.5 Measurement Issues III: Advertising

The most serious measurement problems relate to advertising outlays; and, as with m.e.s. estimates, the design of the econometric analysis is designed to rely as little as possible on problematic measures in this area. In this section, the difficulties involved are set out at some length in order to motivate the route chosen in what follows. This involves the use of measures of advertising intensity only as a simple classificatory variable.

The Issues

The study aims to analyze the role played by advertising outlays in influencing the development of structure; and this is carried out by treating advertising as an endogenous sunk cost. It is doubtless true that many other elements of sunk cost in these industries are also endogenous; several elements of sunk cost may indeed be *complementary* to advertising outlays. Such elements include not only product development costs (which have been argued to be relatively low in the food and drink sector) but also ancillary elements of sunk cost incurred in such activities as building up a sales network. The presence of such ancillary sunk costs will not vitiate the validity of the model, but it would lead to a serious problem of measurement if an attempt was made to estimate the total sunk costs incurred in these industries.

If attention is confined to the role of advertising alone, then matters might appear more straightforward. In modeling advertising as an endogenous sunk cost, what we would like to measure, ideally, is an *exogenous* advertising response *function* analogous to the $F(u)$ of chapter 3. In practice, advertising response functions are extremely difficult to measure, both because (i) they will vary to a greater or lesser degree over time and across product lines, within any industry, and (ii) the response to any stream of advertising depends not only on the level of outlay but on other factors (the quality or effectiveness of a particular campaign), so that any function mapping outlays into response for a particular industry, or group of firms, must be treated as being stochastic in nature. (For a discussion of some aspects of this problem from an economist's standpoint, see Lambin 1976; for some attempts at estimation within particular advertising campaigns, see Broadbent 1981.)

In the present study, we eschew all attempts to estimate an equivalent of the function $F(u)$, and confine ourselves to looking at the level of (endogenously determined) advertising outlays. This clearly adds to the (already serious) limitations that arise in trying to formulate precise tests of the hypotheses. But even in estimating the level of advertising outlays actually incurred by firms in a particular industry, some serious difficulties arise. The simple multistage structure of the games presented in chapter 3 embodies an analytically useful distinction between sunk costs incurred in product development over the long run and current costs incurred in the short run, over which it was assumed that the main focus of competition was on price. In practice, advertising outlays are incurred in a more or less continuous stream, both with a view to enhancing the product's image and in attempting to influence month-to-month fluctuations in share. In the latter context, price changes, promotional outlays (price support to retailers, etc.) involving variable costs, and advertising outlays that may properly be identified as a fixed cost are all involved.

In trying to suggest some suitable mapping from theoretical to empirical categories, it would in principle be appropriate to estimate the net present value of outlays incurred by firms over the history of the industry in supporting brands and products currently on offer. Even this modest task, however, lies outside the scope of the study. As was noted above, this book merely attempts a single broad-brush distinction between those industries that can be identified with the exogenous sunk cost model of chapter 2 and those in which endogenous advertising outlays play a substantial role. This is done by reference to a simple comparison of the range of current advertising-sales ratios observed for the industry across the six countries studied.

Even in regard to the relatively straightforward matter of estimating advertising-sales ratios, however, a number of routine difficulties arise that deserve mention. The advertising-sales ratio, which constitutes the most commonly used measure of advertising intensity, is defined as the ratio of total current advertising expenditure to industry sales. The level of advertising expenditure can be measured in two ways:

(i) by measuring the volume of advertising (seconds of TV time, numbers of magazine pages, and so on), and converting this to a value figure by using standard unit costs. This method tends to overstate total expenditure, insofar as (some) firms obtain rates more favorable than the list price of the advertising in question (the card rate). The values thus estimated may be compared either with total industry sales, or with the value of *retail sales* in the industry.

(ii) by computing the total expenditure on advertising reported by firms in their census returns. This figure, based on SIC definitions, can then be compared with the *value of production* in the industry in question.

We follow the first route. The values of A/S reported below are based on the ratio of measured advertising expenditure either to the total value of industry sales or to the value of retail sales. The reason for choosing a measured advertising value is that such advertising measures for most countries are based on market (industry) definitions close or identical to those employed here in computing the market share statistics. The reason for the use of a measure based on retail sales is that the impact of advertising falls primarily on the retail sector. As noted in chapter 3, it is widely argued that the industrial and catering buyers who constitute the nonretail sector tend to be less concerned about brand image, and their purchases appear to be more heavily influenced by reference to a comparison of price and intrinsic product characteristics.

The ratio of advertising outlays to retail sales for the six countries in 1986 are shown in table 4.4. The median reported values for six of the industries lies below 1%, and the remaining fourteen industries have values lying above this level. The six industries with levels below 1% are salt, sugar, bread, flour, canned vegetables, and processed meat. All of these are widely regarded as commodity products, and their identification as a low-advertising group appears reasonable a priori.

This split between the two groups is fairly sharp. Out of thirty values for the commodity group, only three lie above 1%. Of the seventy-one values for the advertising-intensive group, only two lie below 1%. A ranking of the twenty industries in terms of the advertising to *total* sales ratio for the United States, as shown in the first column of table 4.4, indicates that these six commodity products are again the six lowest ranked products. The split between the two groups of industries, then, appears to be a fairly sharp, and even fairly substantial measurement errors in advertising outlays would be unlikely to affect this classification. It seems reasonable, on the whole, to hypothesize that the structure of the first group of industries might be adequately described by the simple exogenous sunk cost model of chapter 2, whereas advertising outlays may play a potentially important role as an endogenous sunk cost in influencing the evolution of structure in the latter group.

A final remark is in order, regarding the fact that the A/S values shown in table 4.5 (whose magnitude corresponds to the values cited in the relevant market research literature), are substantially higher than certain values reported in the industrial economics literature (compare, for example, these values with those reported in Connor et al. 1985). There are three sources of discrepancy, which reflect the considerations noted above:

(i) The estimates usually cited in the industrial economics literature employ a sales value equal to the total sales revenue of the appropriate (four-digit) SIC industry.

This may lead to a *downward* bias in these figures, whenever (a) a nonretail segment is present, (b) the (four-digit) SIC industry encompasses activities peripheral to the narrower definition of the core market implicit in the definition used in the marketing literature.

(ii) Our values are biased *upward* by our failure to allow for the (often very substantial) discounts over card rates enjoyed by some firms.

(iii) Estimates based on official statistics will differ from those used here, due to the valuation of sales at producer rather than consumer prices.

One common reason for using SIC-based measures, in preference to the kind of estimates used here, is to take advantage of the large body of available data—notably in respect of concentration ratios. Once a decision is made to employ sales concentration ratios based on market research studies, rather than the official production-based figures, this consideration becomes less weighty.

In spite of these biases noted above, the A/S values reported here probably serve as a fairly reliable guide to the *relative* levels of advertising intensity across different industries. As to the absolute size of these values, it is worth noting that—qualifications regarding possible biases notwithstanding—the values reported in table 4.5 are very high in comparison with manufacturers' profit margins in the food and drink industries. The median value of the ratio of measured advertising outlays to total industry sales for the United States, over 11 advertising-intensive industries, is 3% (table 4.5). This figure can be compared with the ratio of net after-tax income to total industry sales, which stood at 4.2% in 1986.[6]

---

6. See the *Quarterly Financial Report for Manufacturing, Mining, and Trade Corporations*, First Quarter 1987, U.S. Dept. of Commerce, Bureau of the Census, p. 6. In comparing these figures, it should be borne in mind that these advertising-sales ratios may be biased upward (see section 4.5).

Table 4.2
Setup Costs for Equivalent Four-Digit SIC Industries (United States)

Industry	Nearest four-digit SIC (U.S.)		m.e.s.[a] (% of output)	Gross book value (plant and equipment) ($ millions, 1976)	Value of shipments ($ millions, 1976)	Estimated σ/S (%)[b] (based on m.e.s. of 0.8)
Salt	1476	Rock salt	0.8–3.52	103.2	159.8	0.52
	2899	Chemicals and chemical preps, n.e.c.	0.43			
Sugar[c]	2063	Beet sugar	1.87	622.1	1,483.2	0.78
	2062	Cane sugar refining	12.01	409.8	2,596.0	1.90
Flour	2041	Flour and other grain mill products	0.68	379.0	4,095.9	0.063
Bread	2051	Bread, cake, and related products	0.12	1,809.3	9,511.5	0.023
Processed meat	2013	Sausages and other prepared meats	0.26	533.8	7,098.7	0.020
Canned vegetables	2033	Canned fruit and vegetables	0.17	1,145.3	6,217.5	0.031
Frozen food[d]	{2037 2038	Frozen fruit and vegetables Frozen specialties	0.92	559.7	2,830.4	0.18
Soup[j]	2034	Dehydrated fruit and vegetables, soup	2.26	216.9	1,048.8	0.47
	2032	Canned specialties	2.59	439.7	2,863.5	0.40
Margarine	2079	Shortening and cooking oils	1.75	417.7	3,325.8	0.22
Soft drinks[h]	2086	Bottled and canned soft drinks	0.08	211.3	2,421.2	0.006
	2087	Flavoring extracts, syrups, etc.	1.23	211.3	2,421.2	0.11
RTE cereal	2043	Cereal breakfast foods	9.47	416.7	2,158.2	1.83
Mineral water	2086	Bottled and canned soft drinks[i]	0.08	1,810.7	8,780.1	0.016

Sugar confectionery / Chocolate confectionery	2065	Confectionery products[e]	0.64	619.1	3,804.1	0.10
R & G coffee / Instant coffee	2095	Roasted coffee[f]	5.82	442.7	4,623.6	0.56
Biscuits	2052	Cookies and crackers	2.04	459.8	2,718.2	0.35
Pet foods	2047	Dog, cat, and other pet food	3.02	475.9	2,675.6	0.54
Baby foods	2032	Canned specialties[g]	2.59	439.7	2,863.5	0.40
Beer	2082	Malt beverages	1.37	2,432.6	6024.5	0.55

a. The m.e.s. figure represents the ratio between the output of the median plant expressed as a percentage of industry shipments for the United States in 1977. All figures except that for salt are those estimated by Culbertson and Morrison (1983), as reported in Connor et al. 1985. The figures for salt are computed as described in appendix 5.1.

b. σ/S is estimated as m.e.s. $\times$ (gross book value of plant and equipment) $\div$ (value of shipments). See text.

c. Sugar refining encompasses two four-digit SIC codes, 2062 (cane sugar refining) and 2063 (beet sugar refining). To estimate the *minimal* setup cost required to enter the industry, the value used is that for beet sugar refining, where scale economies and so estimated setup costs are both lower.

d. Frozen food encompasses two four-digit SIC industries, 2037 (frozen fruit and vegetables) and 2038 (frozen specialties). No m.e.s. estimates are available for the latter industry.

e. The number of sugar confectionery plants is very much greater than the number of chocolate confectionery plants in the United States, and the m.e.s. figure for SIC 2065 provides a good approximation to the value for sugar confectionery plants. This is used in what follows in estimating S/σ for sugar confectionery.

f. The estimate for SIC 2095 is no. taken in the present study as providing a suitable measure for *either* R & G or instant coffee; see text, and chapter 12.

g. SIC 2032 (canned specialties) includes inter alia the five-digit industries 20321 (canned baby foods) and 20322 (canned soups).

h. The relationship between industries 2086 and 2087 is discussed in chapter 9. On the issue of combining the two industries, see Connor et al. 1985, p. 146. Here we take the higher setup cost associated with syrup manufacture as the appropriate figure; it can be argued that the lower value derived from 2086 is appropriate as a measure of the *minimal* outlay involved in entering the industry, as syrup is bought in by small drink firms. Under the latter interpretation, the arguments developed in this chapter and in chapter 9 are further strengthened.

i. The use of SIC 2086 as a point of reference in estimating setup costs in producing mineral water is somewhat arbitrary, but it appears to be the best available proxy.

j. Canned soup is included in SIC 2032 (see footnote g); dehydrated soup is SIC 2034. The associated values of σ are fairly close; the value 0.47 is used below.

Table 4.3
Market size to setup cost ratios, and four-firm sales concentration by country

Industry	France		Germany		Italy		Japan		United Kindgom		United States	
	S/σ	C_4 (%)	S/σ	C_4 (%)	S/σ	C_4 (%)	S/σ	C_4 (%)	S/σ	C_4 (%)	S/σ	C_4 (%)
Salt	39	~98	62	~93	24	~80	(*)	(*)	39	~99.5	194	82
Sugar	46	81	40	~60	31	72	49	41.5	41	94	128	46
Flour	392	29	580	38	652	6.7	392	67	346	78	1,590	55
Bread	2,845	4.5	3,824	7	3,015	~4	1,144	~48	2,114	~58	4,350	~25
Processed meat	745	~23	1,465	~22	1,245	~11	1,340	51	(*)	(*)	5,000	19
Canned vegetables	1,569	40	(*)	(*)	93	80	(*)	(*)	480	81	3,230	~50
Frozen food	(≠)	(≠)	(≠)	(≠)	(≠)	(≠)	(≠)	(≠)	(≠)	(≠)	(≠)	(≠)
Soup	14	91	25	84	(*)	(*)	18	71	36	75	556	75
Margarine	79	(≠)	181	(≠)	34	(≠)	87	(≠)	154	(≠)	213	(≠)
Soft drinks	16	~70	89	57	20	84	53	88	47	~48	455	~89
RTE cereal	(*)	(*)	(*)	(*)	(*)	(*)	(*)	(*)	7.4	79	910	86
Mineral water	400	77	350	27	337	~55	9.8	62	9.4	73	55	(*)
Sugar confectionery	143	51	353	39	116	29	142	48	279	38	1,000	~27
Biscuits	88	62	43	49	69	46	57	49	130	62	286	68
Pet foods	30	86	16	93	(*)	(*)	9.3	39	33	83	185	64
Baby foods	50	88	40	83	41	88	(*)	(*)	27	80	250	90
Beer	18	82	68	~25	9.8	55	35	99.85	46	59	181	81

(*) Omitted from data set, see text. (≠) Figures relate to retail only, and the nonretail sector is large. See tables M7, M9 (appendix 1).

Table 4.4
Advertising to retail sales ratios for six countries, and advertising to total sales ratios for the United States. Figures are for 1986 except where indicated.

Product	Advertising/ total sales (%) United States	Advertising/retail sales (%)					
		France	Germany	Italy	Japan	United Kingdom	United States
Salt	0.26	—	—	—	(×)	0.45	1.3
Sugar	0.10	—	—	—	—	0.06	0.24
Flour	0.54	0.55	N.A.	N.A.	—	0.96	0.17
Bread	0.02*	0.12	0.40	0.04	1.14	0.29	0.42
Processed meat	0.32	0.70	0.30	0.40	3.2	(×)	0.54
Canned vegetables	0.71*	0.55	(×)	0.50	(×)	0.58	0.29
Frozen food	1.35	N.A.	1.2	7.1	2.5	2.6	2.0
Soup	N.A.	5.7	5.6	(×)	2.7	6.0	3.3
Margarine	3.04*	N.A.	2.6	N.A.	9.5	10.2	2.3
Soft drinks	2.80†*	2.2	3.8	5.4	4.4	1.2	3.2
RTE cereals	8.34	(×)	(×)	(×)	(×)	12.9	10.8
Mineral water	( )†	5.0	1.5	4.1	3.0	2.7	(×)
Sugar confectionery	2–3	~1.4	4.2	6.0	3.8	2.1	2–3
Chocolate confectionery	3–4	2.9	5.9	6.5	6.0	3.5	3–4
R&G coffee ⎱ Instant coffee ⎰	2.19	14.0 11.1	2.9 3.5	~3 N.A.	16.7 9.6	1.9 6.4	~1 2.2
Biscuits	1.87	2.9	5.1	8.0	3.0	1.9	2.5
Pet foods	4.35	4.2	8.4	(×)	8.0	4.3	4.0
Baby foods	~0.9	1.3	1.2	4.2	(×)	2.2	0.9
Beer	5.43	~5	1.0	N.A.	2.7	1.0	3.6

Source: Author's estimates based on Leading National Advertisers (U.S.), MEAL (U.K.), Schmidt and Pohlman (Germany), Secodip (France), AGB Italia, and Fuji Keizai (Japan).
(−) Value very low and omitted from published statistics.
N.A. Not available.
(×) Market omitted from study.
† Soft drinks, including mineral water.
* 1905 figure.

Table 4.5
Relationship between four-digit SIC industries in the U.S. food and drink sector and the present set of industries. The criteria referred to in the table are those set out in section 4.2.

Four-digit SIC industries	Scope of industry group	Comment
2011–2017	Meat packing, processing	Represented by processed pork products
2021–2026	Dairy products	Excluded (criterion 3)
2032–3, 2091	Canning	Represented by canned vegetables, baby food, prepared soups
2034	Dehydrated fruits, vegetables, soups	Represented by prepared soups
2035	Pickles	Excluded (criterion 1)
2037–8	Frozen foods	Included
2941, 5	Flour	Included
2043	RTE cereals	Included
2044, 6	Rice milling, wet corn milling	Excluded (criterion 1)
2047	Pet foods	Included
2051	Bread, etc.	Included
2952	Cookies and crackers	Included
2061–3	Sugar	Included
2065–7	Confectionery	Represented as sugar confectionery and chocolate confectionery (criterion 2)
2074–9	Oils and fats	Represented by margarine
2082, 3	Malt, malt beverages	Represented by beer
2084, 5	Wines, spirits, liquors	Excluded (criterion 1)
2986	Soft drinks	Included
2092	Fish	Excluded (criterion 1)
2095	Coffee	Represented as R & G coffee and instant coffee (criterion 2)
2097	Manufactured ice	Excluded (criterion 1)
2098	Pasta products	Excluded (criterion 1)

The "miscellaneous" groups 2048, 2087, and 2099 were excluded under criterion 1. In addition to the above, a number of specific industries were excluded, as follows:
Criterion 1: Canned vegetables in Japan; prepared soups in Italy; mineral water in the United States.
Criterion 4: Salt in Japan; processed meat in the United Kingdom; canned vegetables in Germany; RTE cereals in France, Germany, Italy, Japan; baby foods in Japan; pet foods in Italy.

4.6 Statistical Tables

Table 4.2 illustrates the concordance between the present set of industries and the equivalent four-digit SIC industries, together with the estimated σ/S values for the United States.

Table 4.3 shows the corresponding S/σ values for each country, the four-firm sales concentration ratio, as computed by multiplying the reciprocal of the σ/S value for the U.S. industry shown in table 4.2 by the ratio of industry sales in the country in question to the sales of the corresponding U.S. industry. Further statistical details on each industry are presented in the relevant industry studies presented in chapters 6–13.

5

Econometric Evidence

5.1 Introduction

This chapter presents some econometric evidence regarding the predictions of the theory, as summarized in the concluding sections of chapters 2 and 3.[1] Before turning to that evidence, it is of interest to first look at the way in which concentration ratios for each of the industries differ across the several countries. As noted in chapter 1, various earlier studies have found that the pattern of concentration levels across different industries is broadly similar from one country to another.

This relationship is illustrated in figure 5.1. The median value of the four-firm sales concentration ratio for each industry is plotted on the horizontal axis, and the actual values for each of the six countries on the vertical axis. Thus, each vertical bar in the figure indicates the range of concentration levels found for a particular industry.

It is clear that a substantial degree of correlation is present. This can be confirmed by regressing C_4 for the pooled sample on a set of industry and country dummies; the resulting R^2 equals 0.57 (a regression on industry dummies only yields an R^2 of 0.55). It is also clear from the figure that, in a small number of industries, the range of concentration levels is unusually high, and this in some instances reflects the presence of some obvious anomalies. Particularly noteworthy are the cases of beer (where Japan and Germany are outliers at the top and bottom of the range respectively) and flour (where

1. I would like to thank Richard Smith for his advice and help on the estimation of lower bounds, and Mark Schankerman and Hugh Wills, who suggested the proof set out in the annex.

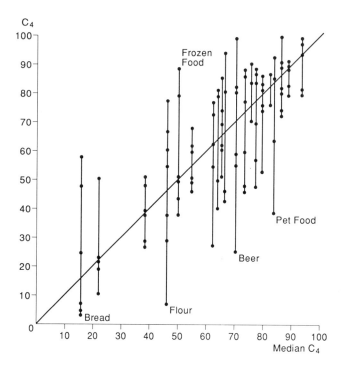

Figure 5.1
The range of four-firm sales concentration ratios across countries, for each product. For each industry, the horizontal axis shows the median value, while individual values are shown on the vertical axis. The height of the vertical bar indicates the range of values for the industry.

the United Kingdom has the highest level of concentration). Other outliers include the German and Italian frozen food industries, which are both highly concentrated. These and other cases will be discussed in later chapters. Some, but not all, of the variation observed in figure 5.1 can be attributed to differences in market size across different countries; this issue forms the subject of the next section.

5.2 Testing the Theory

The central implication of the theory is that, where the level of sunk costs is exogenously fixed, the minimal level of concentration decreases to zero as market size increases; but within advertising-intensive industries where sunk costs are endogenous this relationship breaks down.

Specifically, there are two predictions that are of interest:

(a) Within advertising-intensive industries, the minimal level of concentration is bounded away from zero independent of the size of the market.

(b) The most distinctive proposition to emerge from the model is that, within advertising-intensive industries, the function describing the lower bound to concentration as a function of market size need not be monotonic. (See figure 3.4 and the accompanying discussion of the determinants of this function.)

The second prediction, despite its negative character, turns out to be very helpful in distinguishing this theory from the alternative view, that advertising may be treated as an exogenous barrier to entry. Under the latter view, the level of the barrier might of course vary from one industry to another, and it might also depend on certain country-specific factors. What is important is that its level is independent of the size of the market per se, as measured here by the value of total sales. Under this exogenous sunk cost view, the relationship between concentration and market size in advertising-intensive industries should be identical to that in homogeneous goods industries, except insofar as the setup cost σ is augmented by some unknown constant, representing the height of the advertising barrier. This prediction is tested in what follows.

5.3   The Evidence

The relationship between the four-firm concentration ratio, C_4, and the ratio of market size to setup cost, S/σ, is shown in figure 5.2. For the homogeneous goods group, shown in part (i) of the figure, a strong negative correlation is evident, and the minimal levels of concentration attained at large values of S/σ are quite small (less than 5%).

Among the advertising-intensive group, however, the lowest observed level of C_4 is 25%; several industries, all with relatively high values of S/σ, have values in the 25%–30% range.

The analysis that follows is developed in two steps. We take as our null hypothesis the traditional view under which advertising outlays constitute a barrier to entry whose size is exogenously fixed. Under

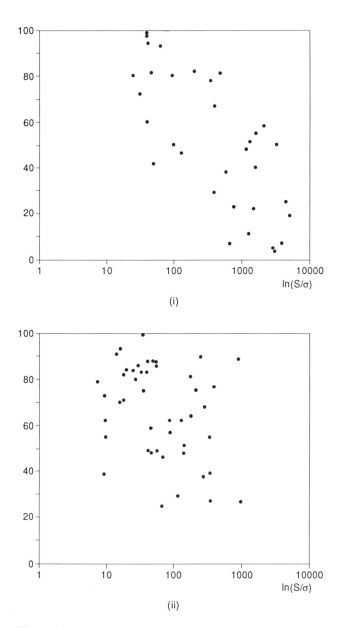

Figure 5.2
Scatter diagrams of the four-firm concentration ratio C_4 versus the market size to setup cost ratio S/σ (log scale) for (i) homogeneous goods industries and (ii) advertising-intensive industries.

the hypothesis, the presence of advertising outlays will shift the schedule that describes the lower bound to concentration as a function of market size, but this schedule will still approach zero as market size increases, just as it does in the homogeneous goods case.

The first part of this section is devoted to a preliminary exercise in which we estimate lower bounds to the scatters of points shown in figure 5.2, and we argue that the results do not support the null hypothesis; rather, the results are consistent with prediction (a). The schedule for the pooled sample of all advertising-intensive industries appears to tend to a different (higher) limiting value as market size increases.

Under our null hypothesis, the schedule describing the lower bound to concentration tends to the same limit (i.e., zero) for *all* industries as market size increases, and so estimating this schedule for the pooled sample of all advertising-intensive industries is reasonable. But under the present theory, this schedule will tend to a different limit in different industries. The paucity of observations in the sample makes it infeasible to estimate a separate schedule for each industry. We can, however, make further progress by turning to prediction (b), which forms the main topic of this section.

Estimating Lower Bounds

A lower bound to the scatters of observations shown in figure 5.2 can be estimated using standard techniques if we regard the chosen measure of concentration in each industry as generated by some underlying distribution function. A natural choice of distribution function is the Weibull distribution, for two separate reasons. First, the Weibull is a highly flexible functional form that has been widely and successfully used in fitting bounds to various empirical distributions. Second, some special features of the present data set make the Weibull form particularly attractive. This argument runs as follows: Suppose we regard a concentration ratio C_n as the sum of the n largest values in a sample (of firms' market shares) drawn from some distribution whose form is unspecified. Thus, C_1 can be treated as an extreme value of this unknown distribution. The limiting distributions of extreme values were first studied by Fisher and Tippett (1928). The classic reference to the use of such methods is Gumbel 1958. The central result is that the distribution of extreme values converges asymptotically to a distribution that takes one of three forms; only one of these three forms (the Weibull distribution) corresponds to the case in which the extreme values are bounded below. Thus, on this statistical model, a scatter of values of C_1 would be expected to converge asymptotically to a Weibull distribution. The case of C_n, $n > 1$, is more complicated, but the limiting form of distribution is closely similar to the Weibull distribution, and it would be difficult to distinguish the two in small samples.

Methods for estimating lower bounds using the Weibull distribution are well established. These methods can be extended to deal with the case where the lower bound b is a function of some independent variable z (see Smith 1989 for a recent review of the literature). These methods involve modeling the distribution of residuals between the observed values $y_i(z_i)$ and the bound $b(z_j)$, as a Weibull distribution, that is, $x_i = y_i - b$ should be distributed according to

$$F(x) = 1 - \exp\left[-\left(\frac{x - \mu}{s}\right)^\alpha \right] \qquad \alpha > 0, s > 0$$

on the domain $x \geq \mu$. The case $\mu = 0$ corresponds to the two parameter Weibull distribution. Nonzero values of μ correspond to a horizontal shift in the distribution illustrated in figure 5.3. The shape of the distribution varies with parameter α, a lower value of α corresponding to a heavier degree of clustering of observations at the lower

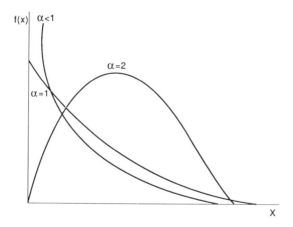

Figure 5.3
The form of the Weibull distribution.

bound, while the parameter s measures the dispersion (scale) of the distribution.

The obvious way to proceed here would be to fit a lower bound to the data using maximum likelihood methods. For $\alpha > 2$, the usual asymptotic results for maximum likelihood methods hold; they are consistent, asymptotically efficient, and asymptotically normally distributed. For $\alpha < 2$, however, these results break down, and an alternative approach is called for. For $1 < \alpha \leqslant 2$, a local maximum of the likelihood function exists, but it does not have the usual asymptotic properties; for $0 \leqslant \alpha \leqslant 1$, no local maximum of the likelihood function exists. (See Smith 1985, 1989 for details.) Low values of α correspond to the case in which observations are heavily clustered on the lower bound, and a visual examination of figure 5.2 suggests that it would be unwise to exclude this case a priori (an impression confirmed by the estimates presented below).

A method of fitting lower bounds that avoids these problems and is both computationally tractable and reasonably efficient[2] over the entire range of α has been suggested by Smith (1985, 1990).

It involves the use of a two-step procedure. As with any parametric method, some a priori decision must be made as to the form of the schedule $b(z)$ that describes the lower bound. Given some (one or many) parameter family of candidate schedules, a consistent estimator of the actual schedule may be obtained by choosing parameters to minimize the sum of the residuals $y_i - b(z_i)$ subject to the constraint that all residuals shall be non-negative. (Thus, a k-parameter bound will pass though k of the data points.) The second step in the procedure is to check that the pattern of residuals thus estimated (the k zero observations being deleted) fits the Weibull distribution and that the hypothesis $\mu = 0$ cannot be rejected.

The procedure rests on the assumption that the distribution of residuals is identical at all values of the independent variable (here S/σ). This would clearly be unreasonable if applied directly to the scatters shown in figure 5.2, given the presence of an upper limit of $C_4 = 1$; and so we first take a logit transformation of C_4, viz.,

$$\tilde{C}_4 = \ln \frac{C_4}{1 - C_4}.$$

---

2. Its rate of convergence is $n^{-1/\alpha}$, which is the optimal rate. More efficient (Pitman) estimators involve much more complex computations.

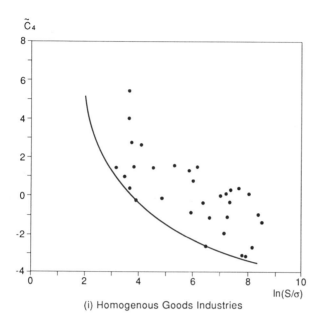

(i) Homogenous Goods Industries

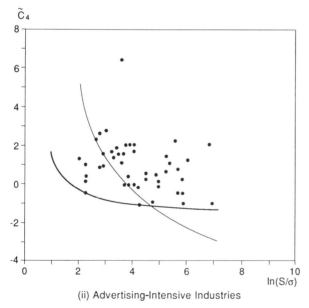

(ii) Advertising-Intensive Industries

Figure 5.4
Scatter diagrams of the logit transformation of C_4 against $\ln S/\sigma$ for (i) homogeneous
goods industries and (ii) advertising-intensive industries. The fitted bounds are
(i) $\tilde{C}_4 = -6.08 + 22.3/(\ln S/\sigma)$; (ii) $\tilde{C}_4 = -1.83 + 3.08/(\ln S/\sigma)$. The estimated bound
(i) is shown also for comparison in panel (ii). The outlier in panel (ii) is the Japanese
beer industry (see chapter 13).

Table 5.1
Estimation of lower bounds (standard errors in parentheses). The values of μ correspond to the three-parameter Weibull distribution, ΔNLLH indicates the difference in the negative log likelihood between the three-parameter Weibull and the two-parameter Weibull ($\mu = 0$). The two-parameter Weibull cannot be rejected (see text); the shape of parameter α reported in the table is that corresponding to the fitted two-parameter Weibull.

		$\tilde{C}_\infty$	μ	ΔNLLH	α
$\tilde{C}_4$	H	-6.08	-0.70	0.4	2.00
			(1.51)		
	A	-1.83	-0.03	0.0	2.90
			(0.51)		
$\tilde{C}_1$	H	-7.23	-0.54	0.5	1.66
			(1.01)		
	A	-3.71	-0.21	0.8	1.75
			(0.10)		

The scatters of $\tilde{C}_4$ are shown in figure 5.4. An examination of these scatters suggested that a reasonable family of candidate schedules would be

$$\tilde{C}_n = a + \frac{b}{ln\,(S/\sigma)}.$$

The fitted schedules are illustrated in figure 5.4. The associated set of residuals fits the Weibull distribution well in both cases, and the hypothesis $\mu = 0$ cannot be rejected.[3] Finally, the estimated values of α are below 2, in some cases, so that a maximum likelihood approach would not be appropriate (table 5.1). The lower panel of figure 5.4 shows the estimated schedule for the homogeneous goods group overlaid on that estimated for the advertising-intensive group. The relationship between the two schedules is *not* suggestive of a horizontal shift, as would be implied by the hypothesis that advertising was an exogenously determined element of sunk cost. On the

---

3. Checking that $\mu = 0$ amounts to testing the two-parameter Weibull against the three-parameter Weibull; this can be tested using a likelihood ratio test. Twice the difference of the fitted negative log likelihood (NLLH) has an approximate chi-square distribution with one degree of freedom. The 5% rejection point of this distribution is 3.84, corresponding to a difference of NLLH of 1.92. The NLLH values reported in table 5.1 are all far below this level; so that the two-parameter Weibull ($\mu = 0$) cannot be rejected. This conclusion is further supported by comparing the estimated values of μ in table 5.1 with their standard error.

other hand, the relationship between the two schedules does appear
to conform nicely to that predicted on the basis of the present theory:
this can be seen by comparing panel (ii) of figure 5.4 with figure 3.9.
The limiting value of the estimated bound for the advertising group,
as $S/\sigma \to \infty$, corresponds to a value of $C_4 = 19\%$. The corresponding
limit of C_4 for the homogeneous goods group is 0.06%. These procedures were also applied to the scatter of maximal market shares, that
is, to $\tilde{C}_1$, with closely similar results (table 5.1). To test the null
hypothesis that the estimated schedules for both industry groups
converge to the same value as $S \to \infty$, we can compare the difference
in the estimated asymptotic values (shown as $\tilde{C}_\infty$ in table 5.1) with
the standard errors on μ. It is clear that the difference in the means
is very large compared to these standard errors in all cases, so that
the hypothesis can be rejected.[4]

The procedure just described involves a pooling of observations for
all advertising-intensive industries. As noted, this is satisfactory under
the null hypothesis, but is not appropriate in the context of the
present theory. To proceed further, we need to adopt a different
approach.

The Second Prediction

A useful line of attack in discriminating between the present theory
and the view of advertising as an exogenous barrier to entry lies in
examining the second prediction set out above. Suppose that the level
of sunk costs is exogenously fixed. Then, we predict that the expected
level of concentration is negatively related to the ratio of market size
to setup cost. An obvious specification for this relationship would be

$$C_{ij} = a_i + b_j + c\, ln\left(\frac{S}{\sigma}\right)_{ij}$$

$$= a_i + b_j + c\, ln\left[\left(\frac{S}{\sigma}\right)_i \rho_{ij}\right], \tag{1}$$

where C denotes the (n-firm) concentration ratio, and where industries are indexed by i and countries by j. As explained in chapter

---

4. In the case of the estimates for C_1, caution is needed in interpreting these standard
errors, as the estimated α lies below 2, implying that the distribution of μ is not asymptotically normal.

4, the ratio of market size to setup cost for industry i in country j is computed by estimating S/σ for industry i in the U.S. market and multiplying by the ratio ρ_{ij} of the size of market i in country j to the size of the corresponding market in the United States. Hence it is the latter form of equation (1) that is estimated below.

One possible objection to specification (1) is that values of C_{ij} must lie between 0 and 1, so that this linear specification in inappropriate. This objection can be met by taking a logit transformation of C_{ij}, that is, by estimating

$$ln \frac{C_{ij}}{1 - C_{ij}} = \tilde{C}_{ij} = a_i + b_j + c\, ln\left[\left(\frac{S}{\sigma}\right)_i \rho_{ij}\right]. \tag{2}$$

Now equation (2) can be written in the alternative form

$$\tilde{C}_{ij} = a_i + b_j + c\, ln\left(\frac{S}{\sigma}\right)_i + c\, ln\,\rho_{ij}$$

$$= a_i' + b_j + c\, ln\,\rho_{ij}. \tag{2'}$$

As equation (2′) indicates, errors in the estimated values of σ will affect equation (2) only via the industry dummy and will *not* affect the slope parameter c. In view of the difficulties surrounding the measurement of σ noted in chapter 4, this point deserves emphasis.

If advertising outlays can be treated as an (industry-specific) exogenous sunk cost, which merely augments the level of setup cost σ, then the coefficient c estimated in equation (2), (2′) should take the same negative value for both the homogeneous goods group and the advertising-intensive group. On the other hand, the theory predicts a negative relationship between ρ_{ij} and C_{ij} for the homogeneous goods group, but it implies that there is no reason to expect any systematic (negative or positive) relationship between ρ_{ij} and C_{ij} for the advertising-intensive group.

Estimates for specifications (1) and (2) for both groups of industries are shown in table 5.2. (A full set of industry and country dummies are included in all cases.) In the homogeneous goods group, the coefficient b is negative and statistically significant (at the 5% level) in both cases[5]; for the advertising-intensive group, the coefficient is

---

5. The estimates of the slope parameter for the first equation reported in table 5.2 imply that a doubling in S/σ implies a fall of 13 percentage points in C_4; the corresponding equation for the logit formulation indicates that a doubling of S/σ implies a fall of 19 percentage points in C_4.

Table 5.2
Regressions of concentration ratios on market size to setup cost ratios. A full set of industry and country dummies are included in all specifications; the table lists those that are significant at the 5% level. The estimated equations correspond to equations (1)–(2) in the text. $\tilde{C}_4$ denotes the logit transformation of C_4.

Dependent variable	Industry group	$\ln(S/\sigma)$	No. of obs.	R^2	Significant dummies
C_4	H	-0.187	32	0.86	Sugar $(-)$;
		$(t = 3.2)$			U.K. $(+)$, U.S. $(+)$
	A	-0.02	58	0.49	Sugar con. $(-)$
		$(t = 0.63)$			
$\tilde{C}_4$	H	-1.12	32	0.89	Sugar $(-)$;
		$(t = 3.4)$			Italy $(-)$, U.K. $(+)$, U.S. $(+)$
	A	$+0.006$	58	0.35	Sugar con. $(-)$
		$(t = 0.02)$			

small, its sign is unstable, and it is not statistically significant in any specification. These equations were reestimated using various alternative measures of concentration (C_3, C_2, etc.), and the same pattern of results was confirmed.

The equations shown for the advertising-intensive group in table 5.2 relate to the subsample of industries for which satisfactory measures of σ and C were available (table 4.3). Specification (2′) can also be estimated for various extended samples of industries. These results (not shown in the table) confirm the same lack of any relationship.[6] All in all, these results offer encouraging support for the predictions of the present theory, as against the view that advertising outlays constitute a barrier to entry whose size is exogenously fixed.

It would be attractive to try to probe the predictions of the theory further along these lines. What *determines* the slope of the lower bound to the size-structure relationship, for example? As shown in

---

6. Frozen food and margarine were omitted from the reported regressions, as nonretail market shares are difficult to estimate (see chapter 4). Their inclusion, using the C_4 for retail sales only, does not materially affect the results reported above. Chocolate confectionery, instant coffee and R&G coffee were also omitted from the reported regressions because of problems in measuring σ and/or ρ. The market size/market structure relationship for these industries is illustrated in chapter 12.

chapter 2, while this depends delicately on the details of the model, two influences are clear: the lower bound to the concentration-size relationship varies with the absolute size of setup cost and the responsiveness of demand to advertising outlays. While this might lead in principle to a more powerful test of the theory, the difficulties involved in obtaining satisfactory estimates of advertising response functions make this a rather problematic route.

5.4   Some Implications

The present theory has led us to a novel econometric specification, which differs from the several specifications employed throughout the traditional literature. One desirable feature in any new approach is that it should succeed in accounting for such empirical regularities as have been well established in the earlier literature, albeit on the basis of quite different arguments. In the present context, such regularities are few. There are, however, three observations that merit attention.

(i) As noted in chapter 1, earlier cross-country studies have indicated some support for a negative relationship between market size and market structure. In reviewing the various cross-country studies of industry structure in 1975, George and Ward reported that "there is a general tendency for concentration to be inversely related to the size of the domestic market." This conclusion rested heavily on the results of Phlips's (1971) study. George and Ward's study, which, like that of Phlips, was based on the 1963 industrial inquiry in the EEC countries, indicated limited evidence of a negative association between concentration and industry size, and the authors concluded that the association, "where it does exist, is rather weak."

(ii) A second finding that emerged consistently from the literature surveyed by George and Ward, and that was replicated in their own study, was that (median) plant and firm size tended to increase with the size of the market. This finding has received further confirmation in more recent surveys (Caves 1989).

(iii) A number of authors have attempted to account for cross-industry differences in concentration within a single country by regressing some measure of concentration on (a) the degree of scale economies, as measured by m.e.s. estimates, (b) market size, (c) some measure of advertising intensity (usually the advertising-sales ratio), and (d) some measure of R & D intensity. Studies of this kind have tended to find that concentration is related positively to m.e.s. and negatively to market size (or that it is negatively related to m.e.s. expressed as a fraction of market size). (For the United Kingdom, for example, see Hart and Clark 1980.)

The results on advertising intensity, however, are mixed. Most studies that include this variable also include, among the independent variables, a measure of concentration at some earlier date. In several studies, the latter variable enters with a positive coefficient that lies between (and is significantly different from) zero and unity. The advertising intensity measure is reported as insignificant in some of these studies (see Hart and Clark 1980 for the United Kingdom and Ornstein and Lustgarten 1978 for the United States); but it is found to be significant in others (Rogers 1984, Mueller and Hamm 1974).

We now turn to the question of whether the results of the present study are consistent with observations (i)–(iii). Observation (i) is concerned with scale economies (m.e.s. levels) and market size. The estimate of setup cost used in the present study is closely related to the m.e.s. value, with the only difference caused by differences in capital-output ratios across industries. Thus, the regressions underlying observation (i) can be compared to those of the present study. On the basis of the present theory, it has been argued that it is inappropriate to pool the observations of homogeneous goods industries, and advertising-intensive industries. If such pooling is employed, however, the theory predicts that this will lead to a weaker but still negative relationship between concentration and the ratio of m.e.s. to market size. Here the present study is *consistent* with the earlier findings, while leading to a different specification and a sharper empirical result.[7]

Observation (ii) concerns the relationship between market size and the median sizes of firms and plants. Such a finding is consistent with the basic model of chapter 2: given some level of sunk cost σ, increases in market size lead to a *less than proportionate* increase in the number

7. If the data used in the study is pooled, a regression of concentration on the ratio of market size to setup cost yields a much weaker result. The estimated coefficient is less than that obtained for the homogeneous goods group alone; if industry and country dummies are included, the relationship is statistically insignificant.

of firms present, since unit margins decline with entry—and so to an increase in *output per firm*. In fact, this is a very robust prediction of this class of models, one that is of central empirical interest (for a discussion, see Sutton 1989b). The model of chapter 2 does not, however, allow for multiplant operation and so does not distinguish between firm size and plant size. For this reason, the present analysis falls short of providing a full account of the empirical relationship.

Observation (iii) relates to those results obtained by regressing concentration levels on a series of explanatory variables that include both some measure of scale economies (or setup cost) and a measure of advertising intensity. As noted above, some authors have reported both a strong negative coefficient on the scale economies variable and a weak positive coefficient on the advertising variable in regressions of this kind.

If the present theory is correct, such a regression constitutes a misspecification. It is important to note, moreover, exactly in what sense it is misspecified. As noted in chapter 1, it has long been accepted that such equations could be objected to on econometric grounds, insofar as advertising levels might not be exogenous, but might themselves be affected by concentration levels. This observation has led some researchers to treat problems of this kind as simultaneous equations problems, but the estimation of simultaneous equation systems in this area has not proved fruitful.

The theory suggests a different diagnosis. What it implies, in econometric terminology, is that the underlying problem is not a simultaneous equations problem, but rather a switch of regime problem. It asserts that the relationship linking market size to concentration is different in kind as between homogeneous goods industries and advertising-intensive industries. But can this way of looking at the problem explain why the earlier regression procedures led to the results cited above? A pleasing feature of the theory is that it leads to a resolution of this issue.

Suppose, consistent with the theory, that a negative relationship exists between concentration and market size for the homogeneous goods group, and a null relationship exists for the advertising-intensive group. Suppose, again consistent with the theory, that the mean level of concentration within the advertising-intensive group is higher than that of the homogeneous goods group. Then if concentration is regressed on the market size/setup cost ratio and the level of advertising intensity, for the pooled sample, the present theory predicts a negative coefficient on the market size/setup cost ratio and a *positive* coefficient on the advertising-intensity variable. (A full explanation of this point is set out in the annex at the end of the chapter.) Hence, the theory provides an explanation of why such traditional specifications have occasionally found a significant positive coefficient on the advertising variable, while also suggesting that such a specification is inappropriate.

Observations (i)–(iii) have focused on those results in the literature that have been corroborated to a greater or lesser degree across various independent studies. It remains to note briefly one relationship that has been adduced in the past on the basis of arguments similar to those developed here, but that has not been reproduced across a range of independent studies.

Several authors, notably Kaldor (1950) and Greer (1973), have suggested that the advertising-sales ratio should show a nonmonotonic relationship to the level of concentration. The arguments offered by these authors are not *inconsistent* with the present theory, as noted in chapter 3 (section 3.6). Although it is easy to construct particular examples within the theory that are consistent with such a relationship, it is also easy to construct examples in which it fails. Thus, this is *not* a relationship that is robust in the sense of chapter 3. By regressing the advertising-sales ratio on C_4 and C_4^2 for the sample, it is possible to test for such a relationship. The estimated equation, however, offers no support for a nonmonotonic relationship of the form proposed.

5.5 Summing Up

How much weight should be placed on the regression results reported above? The number of industries involved is small. Moreover, the size of the sample cannot easily be extended without doing violence to the criteria set out in chapter 4. We are left, however, with an encouraging result. It suggests that the data set is *consistent* with the theory. These results, moreover, appear to imply such empirical regularities as have been consistently reported in the literature. Nonetheless, the results fall short of a convincing demonstration that the explanation proposed here is indeed the right one. Any such limited set of statistical regularities, taken in isolation, might always be explained away by reference to alternative stories.

The central question, then, is whether the difference in the size-structure relationship between these two groups of industries does in fact reflect a fundamental difference in the underlying mechanism that constrains equilibrium structure, as proposed by the theory. To defend the validity of the interpretation proposed here, we must dig deeper. That is the task to which we turn in part II.

Annex

The model implies that a conventional regression of concentration on some measures of scale economies and advertising intensity will yield a (possibly very weak) positive coefficient on the latter term. Suppose the true model generating the data is as follows: there are two groups of industries, for which advertising intensity $A_i \equiv 0$ (the H-industries) and $A_i > 0$ (the A-industries) respectively; and

$$C_i = \beta_0 + \beta_1 \tilde{S}_i + \varepsilon_i \qquad \text{if } i \in H$$

$$C_i = \beta_0 + \varepsilon_i \qquad \text{if } i \in A,$$

where $\beta_0 > 0$ and $\beta_1 < 0$, $\tilde{S}$ represents some measure of the market size/setup cost ratio, and ε_i is an i.i.d. random error.

Define: $\alpha_i = 0 \qquad \text{if } i \in H$

$\qquad\qquad = 1 \qquad \text{if } i \in A.$

Then the true model is

$$C_i = \beta_0 + \beta_1 \tilde{S}_i + \beta_2 \alpha_i \cdot \tilde{S}_i + \beta_3 A_i + \varepsilon_i, \tag{1}$$

where $\beta_2 = -\beta_1 > 0$ and $\beta_3 = 0$.

Suppose we run the regression

$$C_i = \gamma_0 + \gamma_1 \tilde{S}_i + \gamma_2 A_i + \eta_i, \tag{2}$$

that is, equation (1) with the variable $\alpha_i . \tilde{S}_i$ omitted.

Define the regression of $\alpha_i . \tilde{S}_i$ on $[\mathbf{1}, \tilde{S}, A]$, yielding coefficients $\hat{\delta}$. (Here $\mathbf{1}$ denotes a vector 1's.) Then

$$E(\hat{\gamma}_1 - \beta_1) = \hat{\delta}_2 . \beta_2$$

$$E(\hat{\gamma}_2 - \beta_3) = E(\hat{\gamma}_2) - \hat{\delta}_3 . \beta_2.$$

Now $\beta_2 > 0$ and $\hat{\delta}_2 > 0$. Moreover, we expect $\hat{\delta}_3 > 0$ since both $\alpha_i.S_i$ and A_i are zero for all H-industries and positive for all A-industries. Hence the estimated coefficient γ_1 in equation (2) is biased upward (toward zero) while the estimated coefficient γ_2 is biased upward from zero.

II
Setup Costs and Structure

For God does dwell in the details, and visceral comprehension can only arise from immersion in the particulars.

Stephen Jay Gould

6
The Evolution of Homogeneous Goods Industries

6.1 Introduction and Summary

In this chapter and the next, we look at those six industries in which advertising levels are normally extremely low and whose evolution may be understood by reference to the simple exogenous sunk cost model developed in chapter 2. The exogenous sunk cost model makes two predictions that will be of central interest. The first of these runs as follows:

(i) There is a lower bound to the level of concentration that can be sustained as an equilibrium, and this lower bound decreases to zero as the size of the market (relative to the level of setup costs) increases.

This implies that the theory constrains the data more tightly when the ratio of setup cost to market size is large, and so it is natural to divide the group of industries on this basis. This chapter focuses on the salt and sugar industries, where setup costs are large relative to market size, so that the theory constrains the data tightly. The next chapter looks at the other four industries in this group, for which setup costs are moderate to low relative to market size, so that the theory is consistent with a wide range of structures.

The second prediction developed in chapter 2 relates to the relationship between industry structure and equilibrium prices (or price–cost margins). It was argued in chapter 2 that this relationship plays a fundamental role in determining equilibrium structure. The phrase "toughness of price competition" was introduced to label this functional relationship between structure and equilibrium prices (or margins). When two markets differ in respect of the toughness of price competition, what is meant is that, were structure constrained to be the same in these two markets, prices (and margins) would be lower in one (that is, it does *not* relate to *actual* or *equilibrium* margins).

The theory predicts that:

(ii) If two markets are similar in terms of size and setup costs, but the toughness of price competition is greater in one, then the lower bound to equilibrium concentration in that industry is correspondingly greater. In other words, tougher price competition leads (somewhat paradoxically) to a more concentrated equilibrium structure.

How can such a prediction be tested? At first glance, there appears to be a serious problem here: for in practice we observe just one point on the function in question, that is, one which corresponds to the actual or equilibrium level of concentration and prices (margins). It is possible, however, to make some progress by asking whether there are any identifiable exogenous influences that can safely be assumed to *shift* this functional relationship in a given direction.

There are two such influences. The first relates to *product characteristics*. Insofar as all firms offer a physically homogeneous product, it should be expected that price competition is tough, whereas if products are differentiated, price competition should be less tough. The commodity nature of these six products means that the only relevant form of product differentiation is that associated with the regional segmentation of markets. The second influence relates to the nature of *competition policy* in the industry: if firms are permitted to coordinate prices or operate a legal cartel in one industry while an active antitrust policy prohibits price fixing in another, then a second route toward testing the prediction becomes available.

The first theme of the chapter is concerned with exploring this prediction by means of a comparison of industries both across countries and over time. The second theme involves the study of industry histories as a way of probing the validity of the theory. The central idea is that two distinct mechanisms operate to place a lower bound on the range of industry structures that can be supported as equilibria. Insofar as the present group of industries are concerned, the mechanism underlying that lower bound runs as follows: for a market of any given size, if the level of concentration is less than that corresponding to the lower bound prescribed by the theory, then firms will be unable to sustain prices high enough to generate a normal rate of return on the sunk costs incurred in setting up production. It is of course possible that such a situation might be observed in the short run; the theory says that firms' long-run decisions, taken in light of their beliefs regarding the intensity of post-entry competition, will be inconsistent with the maintenance of such an industry structure.

If firms fail to achieve profits adequate to cover their sunk outlays, one possible reaction would be to attempt to coordinate prices in order to restore profitability. However, the degree to which prices can be maintained above marginal cost in short-run equilibrium is already subsumed within the theory in the form of the functional relationship linking concentration and prices (i.e., by the toughness of price competition). Implicit in our construction of the lower bound is the notion that for any level of concentration lying below that bound, no such attempt to coordinate prices can succeed in restoring profitability. According to the theory, the route toward long-run equilibrium must take the form of a switch toward a more concentrated structure. The dynamics of such a switch in structure are not specified by the theory: this might take the form of exit, by way of a failure to renew plant when it becomes obsolete, or it might take the form of a consolidation of ownership via merger and acquisition, or both. What the theory *does* specify, however, is the nature of the *deviation* that precludes a fragmented structure from being an equilibrium, as emphasized earlier (see section 2.4). The deviations in question are as follows: if concentration lies below the bound in question, then in the short run prices cannot be sustained at a level consistent with the recovery of normal profits, because at such price levels it will become worthwhile for deviant firms to undercut market prices, given the degree of fragmentation of market structure. Second, the failure to recover normal returns on sunk costs will lead to changes in structure by way of exit or consolidation of ownership.

The discussion of industry histories that follows focuses on the mechanisms underlying the high levels of concentration observed today. Many of these industries passed through an early phase in which a highly fragmented structure persisted for a short time. Did the collapse of that structure follow the route suggested by the theory? This theme is linked to that of chapter 8 (on advertising-intensive industries). In that context, the theory predicts a quite different mechanism as underlying the breakdown of a fragmented structure. By juxtaposing the histories of the advertising-intensive industries

with those explored in this chapter, it is possible to develop some feel
for the plausibility of the central thesis.

The Salt and Sugar Industries

The salt and sugar industries provide a valuable context in which
to explore the predictions set out above. Both are commodity products, whose nature is conducive to the appearance of tough price
competition. Moreover, as noted, the level of setup cost to market
size is high, so that the theory constrains the data and so has some
useful predictive content. In spite of these similarities, however, there
is one crucial difference between the two industries that makes the
comparison particularly interesting. This difference relates to the
varying stance of the authorities in respect of price competition across
these two industries.

   In the case of the salt industry, price competition has long been
allowed free play in all the countries considered here, with the competition policy authorities taking a neutral or hostile stance toward
attempts to coordinate prices. The salt industry is small in terms of
employment, and it has never had a strong lobbying base. This is in
sharp contrast to the sugar industry, which represents the outlet for
a major agricultural product and enjoys the indirect support of a
powerful agricultural lobby in many countries. The degree to which
this has affected the authorities' view of the sugar-refining industry
varies widely, and the complex reasons for the authorities' position
are often hard to unravel. Whatever the detailed reasons, however,
it is relatively easy to identify certain broad differences that have
appeared, both between countries and over time, in respect of the
authorities' stance toward price determination.

   Within the United States, sugar refiners have faced an active if
intermittent policy aimed at restricting attempts to coordinate prices
(though price-support schemes to protect the prices received by
farmers for raw sugar have been in place for decades). Within Continental Europe, on the other hand, under the EC sugar regime
refiners operate under a quota system in which price competition
between refiners is extremely muted. A particularly useful point of
comparison is afforded by the experience of the Japanese sugar
industry, whose early history divides into two clear phases. In the
pre-1914 period, the industry was characterized by a tightly operating cartel, but this cartel collapsed during the interwar years. The

evolution of structure during these two phases is of particular interest in the context of the theory.

What we find, briefly, is that the differing experiences of the various industries appear to be broadly consistent with the predictions of the model. The salt industry, as the theory implies, is highly concentrated in all countries. In the sugar industry, however, concentration levels vary widely, in a way that broadly mirrors the differences in the toughness of price competition. In the United States, the industry discovered a modus vivendi in the late 1920s, following a decade of antitrust action, in which a geographical segmentation of markets became established. Within each region, a highly concentrated structure emerged. In Europe, on the other hand, a wide range of concentration levels exists across different countries, consistent with our prediction that once price competition is weak, the lower bound to possible equilibrium concentration levels is low, and a wide range of structures is consistent with equilibrium. Finally, in Japan, the cartel phase of the pre-1914 period coincided with a relatively fragmented structure; but the collapse of the cartel in the interwar years was associated with a steady change in structure, culminating in a highly concentrated structure by the end of the period.

The second theme of the chapter relates to the history of the various industries. (It may be helpful, in reading the industry histories that follow, to bear in mind the schematic representation of the theory shown in figure 6.1.) As noted, several of these industries have passed through an early phase during which a highly fragmented structure appeared for a limited period. This early phase was in each case characterized by a relatively low ratio of setup cost to market size. In some cases, this reflected a low level of setup cost associated with an early production technique that was later superseded by other methods. In other cases, this ratio was sustained for a period by a high level of industry sales, associated with a relatively large export market. In each case, the ratio of setup cost to market size rose during some intermediate phase of the industry's history, whether by virtue of changing techniques or the dwindling of export markets. In the case of the United States, these changes were accompanied by another influence that operated in the same direction: as national transport links unified hitherto separated regional markets, the intensity of price competition faced by the typical producer increased, exerting a downward pressure on price–cost margins. Thus, in various cases the industry inherited a structure that was too fragmented

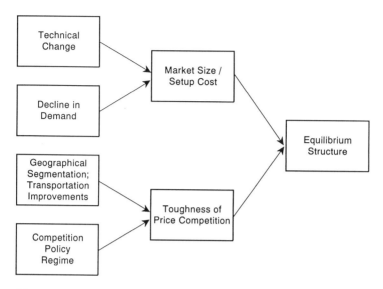

Figure 6.1
A schematic representation of the influences impinging on the evolution of structure in the salt and sugar industries.

to survive as an equilibrium under these new circumstances. What is of interest is the way this fragmented structure dissolved over time.

Good documentation of the early history of these industries is unavailable in some cases. Where good documentation exists for those industries in which price competition had free play, the development of structure appears to be closely in line with what the theory suggests—the early fragmented phase was marked by continuous failed attempts to coordinate prices—and in each case, this process culminated in a mixture of exit and consolidation, which established a highly concentrated structure.

6.2   The Salt Industry

The highly concentrated nature of the market for common salt is indicated in table 6.1. In the United States and the United Kingdom, the industry went through a transition from an initially quite fragmented structure to a highly concentrated one, the details of which are well documented. The development of structure in the French and German industries, described in appendix 6.1, is not well documented, but the available evidence suggests some broad similarities

Table 6.1
Four-firm sales concentration ratios for salt in the mid-1980s

	%
France	~98
Germany	~93
Italy	~80
United Kingdom	~99.5
United States	~82

of experience with the British and American markets. The Italian market, also described in appendix 6.1, was until recently dominated by a state monopoly. Japan has very limited domestic salt deposits and imports most of its requirements; the small Japanese industry is omitted from the study.

The Evolution of Structure: The U.S. Industry

The Competitive Phase

The history of the U.S. salt industry[1] throughout the nineteenth century was marked by a sequence of alternating phases of aggressive price competition and sporadic attempts to achieve price coordination. The successive failures of such attempts led to the consolidation of the industry, which began around the turn of the century. The first important attempt to control output and prices occurred among the producers of the Kanawha Valley in West Virginia, who in 1817 formed a cooperative association called the Kanawha Salt Company in response to a steady decline by over 90% in the price of salt from its 1897 level of 10 cents per pound to less than 1 cent. This price decline was precipitated by imports from other areas via the Great Lakes and the Mississippi River, which began to penetrate the region from 1797 onward as improvements in transportation began to unify separated regional markets. Other regional associations followed, but this and other early attempts at price coordination on a local basis ran into difficulties with competition from outside producers.

---

1. This section draws on the excellent study by Fost (1970), and for the more recent period on the various publications of the U.S. Bureau of Mines, as well as on information acquired via interviews.

The first attempt at coordination that achieved success at a supra-regional level grew out of the efforts of the Michigan Salt Association in 1876. The association had itself been formed in the wake of a failed attempt at coordination by the Michigan producers, which had ended in a phase of intense price competition, a steady fall in price, and serious financial difficulties for smaller producers. The association's president, J. E. Shaw, issued a circular to the salt manufacturers of Michigan pointing out the need for new and more effective organization:

The oldest manufacturers of the Syracuse, Kanawha and Ohio districts tell us that their experience, dating back forty years in some cases, has *always* been this: "*Organized we have prospered. Unorganized we have not.*". . . . The other salt districts of the United States are now organized, and are ready to treat with us . . . relative to fixing and maintaining prices, dividing the territory, and making other arrangements which will inure to the advantage of the trade. But we must first be organized. They cannot treat with individuals.

The upshot of Shaw's appeal was the formation of the Michigan Salt Association in 1876, the member firms of which operated a pooling arrangement. Each firm held stock in proportion to its average daily capacity. Members contracted to sell their salt through the association; but if a member sold some salt privately, the contract would not be forfeit, though the member would be required to pay the association a charge of 10 cents a barrel on that salt.

This new arrangement lasted for nine years, over which period the rate of decline of salt prices was considerably reduced, but its success was mixed. A surge in membership in 1877 boosted prices, but a number of members defected in 1880, sparking off a price war to which the association responded. Further problems followed in 1881, when the Michigan association withdrew from its pooling agreement with New York producers. Finally, in 1885, the Michigan producers' pooling arrangement broke down, leading to a phase of stronger competition in the industry, particularly in the New York area, where the effects of fierce competition among local firms were compounded by the ready supply of imported salt arriving in New York as ships' ballast.

Toward Consolidation

Although the passage of the Sherman Act in 1890 rendered price coordination illegal, the salt industry's previous experience indicated that such coordination was in any case extremely difficult to achieve. In light of repeated failures in supporting prices, the National Salt Company of New Jersey was formed in 1899, with a view to acquiring salt firms outright, beginning with twelve New York producers. Acquisitions in Michigan, Kansas, and Texas gave it nominal control of several major salt fields by the turn of the century and, through a series of agreements with the Michigan producers and others, it was marketing two-thirds of the nation's evaporated salt by that stage. Its effect on prices was sharp: in New York, for example, prices rose from $2.50 per coarse ton in 1897 to $4.00 in 1899, over the two years during which the new organization was taking shape. The ambitious venture was, however, relatively short lived. By 1901, it had overextended itself financially in its acquisitions and was placed in receivership.[2]

The National Salt Company set a model for the next major attempt to unite the industry, which came with the formation of the Salt Producers' Association in 1914. From that date onward, the industry shifted to a regime in which tight coordination was achieved. The association's eighteen members sold almost 90% of the salt produced by the country's thirty-five salt firms. Firms operated within assigned natural market areas, and prices were uniform in each area of the country for comparable grades of salt for about twenty years following the association's formation. For evaporated salt, the Morton Salt Company acted as price leader, and several firms simply issued Morton's price list with their own company name printed on top.

The Federal Trade Commission investigated the salt industry in 1922 and threw considerable light on the association's methods of operation. The FTC's judgment, however, was limited to a cease and desist order requiring that the association abandon its practice of restricting offers of discounts to an approved set of wholesalers.

An Era of Stability

The newfound stability within the industry lasted until the early 1930s; and from 1933 onward, the National Recovery Administra-

---

2. It is believed that the failure of the authorities to take action against the company under the Sherman Act of 1890 simply reflects the short span of the company's activities.

tion's Code of Fair Competition for the industry effectively enforced a regime of stable prices.[3,4] But while the cooperative arrangements established under the NRA were subsequently declared unconstitutional, the industry continued to operate under this regime through the period 1935–1940. The Federal Trade Commission, following an investigation of various price-fixing practices, issued a cease and desist order. Ensuring compliance with the order proved problematic, however, and throughout the 1940s the industry was repeatedly fined (relatively modest amounts) for failure to supply information on its activities. Throughout the postwar years, the FTC continued to intervene in the industry. Cases involving price fixing arose in 1956 (against the Morton Salt Company and others[5]) and in 1965 (against four companies, including three of the four largest sellers, Morton, International, and Diamond[6]).

The period from 1914 to the 1950s, then, was one of comparative stability for the industry, whose pattern of operation had been established by the formation of the Salt Producers' Association in 1914. Over this period, a gradual consolidation of ownership occurred. During the 1920s, a number of firms were acquired and their plants closed. Entry to the industry virtually ceased from the mid-1920s onward. Meanwhile, a series of mergers and acquisitions established and strengthened the three firms that came to dominate the industry by mid-century. The Leslie Salt Company grew over time via a sequence of mergers, which eventually evoked a challenge from the

---

3. Price rebates and secret price cuts were explicitly prohibited. Prices were to be listed openly and adhered to. No outside firm was permitted to undercut, in any field, the lowest of the prices offered by those firms producing salt within that field.

4. Over the lengthy period of relatively stable prices from 1914 onward, a modest fall in the number of operating plants occurred (from 102 in 1912 to a low of 74 in 1935). Fost (1970) identifies five cases in which a firm was acquired and its plants shut down during the period 1925–1930, but no such instances after 1930. Between 1925 and 1952, no new firm entered the industry (apart from a number of established chemical companies, and one water authority producing salt for its own needs).

5. *Morton Salt Co., Royal Crystal Salt Co., Deseret Live Stock Co., and Deseret Salt Co. -v- U.S. 235F (2d.) 573 (1956).* The companies were convicted and fined amounts between $3,000 and $5,000 each.

6. All of whom were acquitted by a federal jury; but in a related civil suit, Carey and International filed consent decrees, while the other two defendants—Morton and Carey Salt Company—were found guilty of conspiring to fix the price of rock salt in the Upper Midwest from 1956–1960 (Fost 1970, p. 72).

Federal Trade Commission.[7] The Diamond Salt Company also met with a demand by the FTC for divestment when its acquisition in 1958 of the Jefferson Island Salt Company boosted the market share of the top three dry salt producers in a nine-state area from 86.9% to 90.1%.

By the 1950s, the market was not only concentrated on a regional basis, but was dominated at the national level by three major producers. While market share figures for the industry are not published,[8] Fost (1970) cites estimates by Watt (1962) for 1957: by that date, only three large companies produced salt as major product for sale. These were International Salt Company, Leslie Salt Company and Morton Salt Comapny. A fourth supplier of salt for sale was the Diamond Crystal Company, a chemical firm producing both rock and evaporated salt.[9]

Recent Developments

Salt is nowadays produced widely across the United States; in 1985, fourteen states produced salt but seven of these accounted for 93% of output. Transportation costs in the industry are high. Fost (1970) reports that, "in 1956, shipping one ton of rock salt 250 miles would almost have doubled its value at the mine." The market, therefore, is heavily regionalized.

---

7. A second challenge involved one of the Big Four, the Leslie Salt Company, in respect of its acquisition of the Deseret Salt Company in 1958. The Leslie Salt Company had grown over time through a sequence of mergers. In 1924, through a series of mergers and consolidations with Continental Salt Company, California Salt Company, and Leslie Salt Refining Company, it had come to dominate salt production in the San Francisco Bay area. Subsequent absorptions of Turk Island Salt Company in 1927, Oliver Salt Company in 1931, and Arden Salt Company in 1936 left it as the sole producer in that area. The FTC's objection to its acquisition of Deseret in 1958 was based on the fact that Deseret competed with Leslie in two states (Washington and Oregon) in which Leslie already had very high market shares (90.7% and 83.5% respectively), and Leslie was ordered to divest itself of the assets acquired.

8. Official statistics reveal that the number of firms *producing* salt showed only a slow decline over time (62 in 1931, 57 in 1967, 39 in 1985), and concentration *in production* remains moderate. In 1985, nine firms accounted for 80% of total production. Official statistics relate, however, to *all* salt production, including the large fraction of salt produced by chemical firms for their own internal use (salt in brine accounted for 46% of all salt produced in 1985). The concentration of sales in the industry is much higher.

9. As to the nonmarketed salt in brine, six companies produced 95% of this in 1957—leading to the overall conclusion as to concentration in *production* that ten companies supplied 88% of total domestic output in that year.

Apart from some changes in ownership, the structure of the industry has changed little over the past generation. In 1986, the three leading producers were the Morton Salt Company, the International Salt Company (owned by AKZO), and Cargill (the grain conglomerate—see chapter 7). Apart from these three firms, only four other producers marketed salt: the Diamond Crystal Company, Carey (owned by Processed Minerals Inc.), Great Salt Lake Minerals and Chemicals (GSL), and American Salt. Further changes in ownership structure occurred during the latter half of the 1980s, when DOMTAR emerged as a new group incorporating GSL, Cargill, and American. By 1989, the four-firm sales concentration ratio for marketed salt was close to 100%.

The Evolution of Structure: The U.K. Industry

By the mid-nineteenth century, Britain's salt producers, operating from the rich Cheshire salt beds, came to dominate the world salt markets.[10] A small firm could, at that time, set up production facilities with a very small capital outlay by simply drilling down to the salt bed, pumping up brine, and evaporating it in open pans. In the last decades of the century, however, the industry entered a long phase associated first with declining demand and later with changes in technology, which together induced a shift toward a more concentrated structure. The events surrounding that shift in structure have much in common with the U.S. experience.

The Changing Environment

Transport costs operate heavily against the export of salt, and by the 1880s the gradual expansion of salt production in other countries led to a decline in demand for British salt; a decline exacerbated by changing techniques in the chemical industry, which began to use more brine directly, as opposed to salt. The decline in demand from 1875 onward precipitated a period of intense price competition

---

10. This account draws on Calvert 1913a, b and, for the recent period, on the report of the Monopolies Commission (1986). Calvert was a leading critic of the Salt Union, and his account is not that of a detached observer. He had the unusual virtue, however, of publishing his primary sources together with his own account (Calvert 1913a).

among the many small producers then operating and led to a wave of bankruptcies.

Attempts to stabilize the situation began in 1882, when a pooling arrangement was established . A new and higher price was fixed and, to support it, any member operating more than half his pans paid a fixed amount per pan into the pool, the receipts then being paid to those firms operating less than half their pans, in proportion to the number of pans unused. The pool effectively collapsed within a year, as a result of the entry of a substantial new producer located outside the Cheshire region. By 1888, prices reached an all-time low, as the industry failed to find any way of managing its now enormously excessive capacity.

This crisis precipitated an attempt at consolidating ownership in the industry. In 1888, a firm of London solicitors, backed by financial institutions, took the initiative in bringing together sixty-four salt firms that together accounted for over 90% of total capacity. A new publicly quoted company, the Salt Union, was formed, which then bought out the assets of the constituent firms. Over the following decade, however, the Salt Union ran into continuing difficulties; declining demand led to a situation in which the fringe of competing producers could supply a substantially greater part of total sales (one half by 1897, according to one contemporary account). In 1898, the several producers in the Middlesbrough area (including the Salt Union, whose main interests lay in Cheshire) formed the North Eastern Salt Company Ltd., but attempts to form similar associations that would bring in producers outside the Cheshire and Middlesbrough areas failed. These fringe firms did agree, however, to an arrangement to maintain higher prices, and in the following year a new combination emerged in the form of the British Salt Association. The new venture survived for six years; but in 1905, the Salt Union discovered that its partners were in fact not only exceeding their quotas, but were in some cases installing additional capacity—and the agreement collapsed.

A new venture immediately emerged. The North-Western Salt Company, set up in 1906 under the joint ownership of the Salt Union and the United Alkali Company, devised a scheme to regulate prices and output that attracted the support of virtually all salt makers. The new scheme foundered in 1911, largely due to competition from the growing chemical concern of Chance Hunt, which had established substantial production capacity (10,000 to 25,000 tons/annum) and which stood outside the new group. Following the demise of this arrangement, a short-lived attempt to reestablish the British Salt Association collapsed within a year, as ten important producers refused to join, and prices remained low. The threat from the growing chemical industry was to play an important part in the years that followed. A key step in the consolidation of the industry emanated from the growing importance of the leading chemical firm of Brunner Mond, which had developed a strong presence in the Cheshire area. In the early years of the century, Brunner Mond and the Salt Union controlled most of the salt lands of Cheshire. Brunner Mond held a small stake in the Salt Union, and both companies had agreed to discourage further entry into the region.[11] In 1926, Imperial Chemical Industries (ICI) was formed by the amalgamation of Brunner Mond & Co. Ltd. with three other chemical concerns, and in 1937, ICI acquired the Salt Union.

Throughout the postwar period, a further series of consolidations occurred, culminating in the current duopoly structure in which ICI and British Salt dominate the market. The first phase of that process arose during the 1950s and 1960s, when a series of mergers and acquisitions, followed by plant closures, left only five substantial producers: ICI, Staveley Industries, BP Chemicals, Cerebos Foods, and the New Cheshire Salt Works. Staveley Industries, by origin an engineering firm, entered the salt industry in 1919. It came to prominence in 1967 when it formed British Salt as a joint venture with Rank Hovis McDougall Ltd., the leading flour company, whose acquisitions via its Cerebos subsidiary during the 1950s had made it the leading producer of domestic salt. The pooling of the Cerebos and Staveley interests led the way to a program of replacement of older plant by a single larger modern plant. Staveley subsequently bought out RHM's interest in British Salt, though it retains the packing plant and markets domestic salt supplied from the British Salt works next door to its own plant under the Cerebos and Saxa brands.

Apart from British Salt and ICI, the other firm now producing salt by the vacuum process is the New Cheshire Salt Works Ltd., which produces salt for industrial, domestic, and pharmaceutical use and

---

11. In 1905, the Salt Union introduced the modern vacuum technique of salt production from the United States, and the economies achievable using the new technique encouraged the opening of new plants, by the Salt Union and other companies. By 1945, there were twenty-seven plants in operation, nine of which employed the vacuum process, and these nine accounted for over half of total output.

accounts for around 3% of industry capacity. Two other firms produce small quantities of salt using an open-pan method: Ingram
Thompson & Co. Ltd. (rock salt) and Maldon Crystal Salt Ltd. (sea
salt).[12]

To sum up, then, the U.K. market is in effect a duopoly, in which
ICI and British Salt enjoy a combined market share of about 95%.[13]
Of the two firms, British Salt is the low-cost producer, as noted by
the Monopolies Commission during its investigation of price behavior
in 1986. The commission found that British Salt typically followed
ICI in its pricing and commented that British Salt believed that if
they "sought to undercut ICI this would have provoked a damaging
retaliation" (MC 1986, p. 86). The commission concluded, "We do
not accept that these reasons demonstrate the existence of a competi-
titive market. If anything they merely serve to show the lack of
effective competition by a company well placed to offer it." The
commission recommended that prices be controlled through the use
of an index based on the costs of the low-cost producer, British Salt.

Summing Up

The two industry histories just summarized have a number of features
in common:

• In each case, the highly homogeneous nature of the product appears to have made firms particularly vulnerable to price cutting by
rivals, a process in which less efficient (often smaller) producers may
be particularly vulnerable.

• Attempts to achieve some kind of price coordination within a
fragmented industry met with repeated failures.

---

12. Less than 10% of salt production in the United Kingdom is sold through the retail
trade for household use. In this segment of the market, there are two long-established
brands, Cerebos and Saxa, both now owned by Ranks-Hovis McDougal (see chapter 7),
which operates a packing plant next door to British Salt's production plant, from which
they obtain their salt supplies.

13. The capital employed in salt production by the two U.K. majors, in their respective
plants, provides some feel for the order of magnitude of capital outlays involved in the
industry. ICI's main (Weston Point) plant had fixed assets valued at £25.4 million in
1984, while British Salt (whose activities are confined to salt production) had assets valued
at £27.1 million in the same year (Monopolies Commission 1986). These figures can be
compared with the two companies' sales revenue in the same year (£17.8 million and
£23.5 million respectively).

• A concentrated structure emerged as a result of exit and consolidation, and this concentrated structure in turn permitted an avoidance of future price wars.

It is interesting to compare this pattern of events with the corresponding evolution of the sugar industry.

6.3   The Sugar Industry

Sugar, like salt, combines a high degree of product homogeneity with a level of setup cost that is moderately high relative to the size of the markets considered here. However, the level of concentration varies widely across countries, as indicated in table 6.2. Further details on the current structure of the market by country, with tables of leading firms and their market shares, are provided in appendix 1 and appendix 6.2.

In interpreting the concentration levels for national markets reported in table 6.2, it is important to bear in mind the highly regionalized nature of the U.S. market. Much of the difference in experience in these markets can be traced to differences in the degree of price competition. In the case of the United States, the industry developed a highly concentrated structure during an early period of free price competition, and today the industry remains highly concentrated within each marketing region.

We begin by looking at the history of the U.S. industry and then contrast this with the experiences of France, Germany, and Italy,

Table 6.2
Four-firm concentration ratios for the sugar industry, by country, for 1985/6. In some cases, these figures have been estimated from reported capacity levels, as opposed to sales. (See appendix 6.2 and the market share table in that appendix for details.)

	%
France	81
Germany	~60
Italy	72
Japan	41.5
United Kingdom	94
United States	46

which operate within the EC's sugar regime. Finally, we look at the several phases of development through which the Japanese industry has passed. The U.K. market, which developed under rather unusual institutional conditions, is described in appendix 6.2.

The Development of the U.S. Sugar Industry

The evolution of concentration in the U.S. industry can be traced to the period 1870–1920, after which its structure remained more or less stable for half a century. Prior to 1870, the industry evolved under conditions of unfettered competition to a quite concentrated structure, in a manner remarkably similar to that of the salt industry. This phase was followed by a period during which the industry became a tight oligopoly, a pattern that had emerged by the turn of the century. These developments have been documented in detail in the classic study by Eichner (1969), on which the following account draws.

Competition and Instability

Prior to 1830, the production of sugar was a notoriously complex business. The European industry was relatively well established, and the production process was overseen by highly skilled sugarmasters. One of the main problems facing potential entrants to the U.S. market lay in the need to bring a skilled sugarmaster from Europe to supervise the refining process. By mid-century, however, the use of improved filtering agents to whiten sugar, together with the new vacuum-pan technique for boiling, had made the production of high-grade sugar a fairly routine industrial process. These technical developments eased the entry of new firms into the industry, at the same time making refined sugar a more standardized commodity product; this change in itself was conducive to an increase in the intensity of price competition among refiners.

But just as these technical developments were easing entry into the industry, parallel developments in transportation were in progress, which further exacerbated the degree of price competition faced by refiners. The development of the railroads brought East Coast refiners into competition with their Louisiana counterparts in the growing markets of the Midwest. The twin influences of production standardization and the unification of localized markets set the stage for the first major developments in the structure of the industry.

The period up to 1870 was marked by a substantial flow of entry as well as exit. The main Eastern seaboard markets of New York, Philadelphia, and Boston supported thirty-eight independent refiners in 1878. In each year from 1869 to 1875, three or four new firms entered the market in New York alone. Price competition was severe, and refiners' margins were declining more or less steadily, in spite of market growth. Efficiency levels, and unit margins, varied widely. Refining margins varied across firms from around 5/8 of a cent to 2 cents at mid-century; by 1870 average margins stood at 3.47 cents, and by 1877 this figure had fallen sharply to 1.62 cents.[14] But this era of unfettered competition in an initially fragmented industry led to the increasing dominance of a handful of major concerns. The more intense the price competition, the greater the disparity in market shares generated by small efficiency differences,[15] and in this era of intensifying price competition a small group of relatively efficient refiners came to dominate the market.

The highest levels of efficiency were attained by some half-dozen large refiners based at major ports. By setting up an integrated operation, loading sugar directly from ships to warehouses, firms such as Havemeyer and Elder (New York) achieved substantial economies. Combining this with the use of the most recent technology available, these few firms produced 75% of U.S. output by 1877. Alongside these firms, a very substantial range of small inland refiners offered more or less effective competition. As Eichner (1969) remarks, pricing behavior in this first era of the industry's history appeared to be consistent with a competitive story, in the sense that prices and margins fluctuated positively with demand, a fringe of smaller firms brought refineries in and out of operation as demand fluctuated, and, when margins rose, new entry to the industry followed.

---

14. Wells, D., *The Sugar Industry and the Tariff*, quoted by Eichner (1969), and Anderson et al. 1975. The figures cited are measured as the difference between the price of Muscovado raw sugar and standard 'A' refined.

15. See chapter 2. The most elementary illustration of this point is provided by a comparison of the basic Bertrand and Cournot models for the case in which one firm enjoys a slightly lower level of marginal cost than its rivals.

This first era in the industry's history was marked by a strong upward trend in total demand. From the 1870s, however, this picture changed, and stagnating demand was accompanied by a varying degree of excess capacity over the next decade. The events of that decade, as Eichner (1969) notes, "suggest that a competitive industry was inherently unstable."

Toward Consolidation

In terms of the theory, the configuration of the industry in the late 1870s can be seen as corresponding to a regime of tough price competition, where small efficiency differences were magnified into large differences in market share. In such a configuration, it is the least efficient firms that face the greatest threat of ruin from small changes in market conditions, and they are likely to perceive the greatest advantage from consolidation. Thus, it is not surprising that the smaller refiners, with their typically lower efficiency levels, first proposed some form of price coordination for the industry as it entered a phase of stagnating demand from the 1870s onward.

The large refiners initially refused to cooperate. In 1880, however —by which time the refining margin had fallen to 1.4 cents per pound—both groups of firms entered a pooling arrangement. This arrangement held for only one year, but it represents the starting point of the next phase of the industry's history. This phase was marked by the emergence of the Sugar Trust, which encompassed all but one of the important East Coast refineries and came to dominate the sugar industry in the East. As refinery margins rose in the East, the trust turned to the West Coast, where only two important refiners operated. The larger of the two, the California Sugar Refinery Company, owned by Claus Spreckels (dubbed the "Hawaiian Sugar King"), imported raw sugar from Hawaii to refineries in the United States. Spreckels initially refused to join the trust, which responded by acquiring his West Coast rival, the American Sugar Company, and a price war ensued. Spreckels carried the price war back to the East Coast, building a refinery in Philadelphia in 1890. A subsequent agreement between Spreckels and the trust brought the price war to an end, giving Spreckels control of the West Coast market in return for which the trust acquired a 45% stake in Spreckels's Philadelphia refinery. The trust, reorganized as the American Sugar

Refining Company, went on to acquire two small Philadelphia-based firms. This acquisition, which left only one independent active (the Revere refinery, with a 2% market share), gave the company a near monopoly position.[16]

Problems and Developments

Serious problems soon arose as the rise in margins achieved by these developments attracted a steady stream of new entrants to the industry. Refining margins, which had fallen to 0.72 cents per pound during the price war of 1890, recovered to 1 cent per pound in 1892–1893. Three new refineries entered the industry in 1892; the three later merged to form the National Sugar Refineries Company, which remains one of the major firms in the industry. The new entrants agreed to follow the price set by American. All companies were to quote the same price, under a basing point system that has persisted in the industry to the present day.

To discourage further entry, following this episode, American decided to lower its target for refining margins with a view to limiting entry. In spite of this, two important new entrants appeared over the next few years. A further threat to American's position was posed by the strategy of *threatened* entry, a technique developed by Adolph Segal. The so-called Segal strategy involved constructing a new plant with a view toward being bought out by the market leader. In 1895, Segal built a new refinery. Shortly after its completion, he was approached by American with an offer to buy the plant, which, after some delay, he sold at a profit estimated at between $50,000 and $100,000. (Segal then proceeded to use the same strategy with some success in steel, shipbuilding, and asphalt; and he even returned for a second, unsuccessful attempt in sugar in 1901.)

Until the turn of the century, sugar production in the United States was based almost entirely on cane. A further potential threat to American's position arose from a decision by Congress in 1898 to impose a duty on imported raw sugar, which stimulated the development of a domestic beet sugar industry. As the new industry developed, American acquired a controlling interest in many of the

16. It also provoked the first suit against the company under the recently passed Sherman Act. The case, however, was dismissed on the grounds that the matter lay outside federal jurisdiction.

emerging companies; by 1907, the Havermeyer family and/or American owned 69% of total sugar beet slicing capacity.

The major legal battle faced by the trust began with a case brought by the authorities in 1911 and ended with a consent decree in 1922. Justice Department officials claimed that "competitive conditions have been entirely restored" (Eichner 1969, p. 329). At the time the suit was commenced, American and its allied interests controlled about 75% of the U.S. refined sugar industry. By 1922, it was pointed out, the control of American had decreased to the point where it controlled only about 24% of the industry.

This claim notwithstanding, Eichner (1969) concludes that the consent decree, far from reestablishing competition, in fact acquiesced in the maintenance of an oligopoly, for American was not required to divest itself of any of its plants or subsidiaries.

It was allowed to retain its holdings in other companies, and though these were considerably less extensive than had been the case in 1911, they were nonetheless substantial: 25% of the stock in the National Sugar Refining Company, 31% of the stock in the Great Western Sugar Company, and 34% of the stock in the Michigan Sugar Company. As Eichner (1969, p. 369) remarks,

Approximately three times the size of its largest competitor, it remained the undisputed price leader. And when it thought that other firms were secretly shading the price, it did not hesitate to match them, concession for concession, until it was convinced that its own announced price list was once again being adhered to.... The one time competitive character of the sugar refining industry had not been restored; the government had merely acquiesced to the continued existence of oligopoly.

The decree thus left the structure of the sugar refining industry essentially as it was. Moreover, that structure remained largely unchanged in the half century that followed. American had a 31.5% share in 1918 and (as "Amstar") a 27% share in 1972. The leading firms in the industry in the 1970s included several that were controlled by American in the first decade of the century (Great Western, Amalgamated). American's main rival at the time of the consent decree, National, had fallen to fifth place in the industry by 1972. The second-ranking firm was Californian and Hawaiian, which had been founded in 1906 by a group of Hawaiian planters who were dissatisfied with the prices paid for cane by Claus Spreckels.

Table 6.3
Federal Trade Commission estimates of four- and eight-firm concentration ratios for refined sugar in the United States by market region, 1972 (%)

Marketing region	C_4	C_8
Northwest	80.0	96.0
Southeast	85.8	97.4
Gulf	79.7	97.5
Southwest	80.0	91.9
Lower Pacific	95.3	100.0
Intermountain Northwest	93.5	100.0
Chicago-West	52.7	79.0

Source: Anderson et al. 1975.

The structure of the industry during most of this century has been marked by a modus vivendi between a small number of major producers, most of whom operate on a regional basis. Weiss (1972) notes that 90% of sugar produced in the United States is sold within 921 miles of the plant at which it is refined. Seven major regions are recognized in the setting and reporting of wholesale sugar prices. The four- and eight-firm concentration ratios for each of these regions were estimated by the Federal Trade Commission's Bureau of Economics for the year 1972 (table 6.3).

Four firms had a share of 80% or more in all but one of these regions. The pattern of industry leadership varied substantially from one region to another, leading to an overall concentration level for the national market that was very much lower. Amstar, with a 25% share nationally, was the only producer that ranked among the top four producers in each of the seven marketing areas. It was ranked first in two areas (the Northeast, where it had a 50% share, and the Gulf area, where it accounted for about one-third of sales). The regional concentration ratios may be compared with the shares of the national market accounted for by each firm in the same year (table 6.4). Until the 1970s, the structure of the industry had changed little for half a century. Since then, the main threat to the industry has come from the growing importance of high fructose corn syrup (HFCS) as a sugar substitute within the food industry. This has led to the growth of serious competitors to Amstar, and it represents a form of competition from which the protected European industry has been largely immune.

Table 6.4
U.S. market shares in refined sugar, 1972

Company	1972 market share (%)
Amstar	27.1
California and Hawaiian	9.4
Great Western United	7.0
Savannah Foods and Industries	5.2
National Sugar Co.	4.8
Amalgamated Sugar Co.	4.9
American Crystal Sugar	4.4
Barden, Inc.	4.0

France, Germany, and Italy

Whereas the U.S. industry evolved to a highly concentrated structure in an early period of unfettered competition, its European counterpart was from its early days more highly regulated—a pattern that persists in the form of the European Community's sugar regime, under which a system of producer quotas effectively blunts price competition between refiners. This has meant that the structure of each of these industries has to a considerable extent reflected deliberate policy choices by the authorities.

All three industries currently operate under the regime, which allocates production quotas to each country and guarantees a minimum intervention price for sugar produced within the quota (i.e, the so-called A and B quotas—see appendix 6.2). In practice, each country partitions its country quotas among domestic refiners, roughly in proportion to their production in the years immediately preceding the introduction of the scheme in 1968. This has the effect of freezing the structure of the sugar refining industry at its 1968 configuration.

Germany's industry had already assumed a relatively concentrated structure by that date. France, on the other hand, had retained a rather fragmented structure; but on the eve of the scheme's operation, the French authorities undertook a major scheme of rationalization, leading to a relatively concentrated structure that still persists. Italy is the community's high-cost producer, largely for climatic reasons. The domestic industry had long enjoyed a system of intervention and subsidies, and until fairly recently this had allowed a relatively fragmented structure to persist. In 1984, however, a major rationalization program was initiated, which has led to a consolidated structure.

Japan's Sugar Industry

As noted earlier, Japan's sugar-refining industry has passed through a number of distinct phases, marked by major changes in the strength of price competition in the market.

The Early Period

From the turn of the century up to the 1920s, the Japanese industry enjoyed steady or growing demand and a relatively stable cartel arrangement. The period was marked by substantial entry and increasing fragmentation in the industry. By the turn of the century, world sugar prices had for long been affected by the continued entry of new producer countries, and this had spurred attempts at achieving international coordination on sugar supply. In 1902, a key agreement was reached in Brussels that ended the dumping of sugar on European markets and so led to a period of relatively stable world prices. Japan, as a nonsignatory to the Brussels agreement, benefited doubly from the new regime, in that it enjoyed the new stability in world prices while being free to continue subsidizing its domestic producers. Two distinct groups of producers were active on the Japanese market during this period, one based in Japan and the other in Taiwan. The activities of the Taiwanese companies, which supplied raw sugar to the Japanese refiners, were overseen by the Taiwanese authorities, who encouraged the industry with subsidies, and—until 1915—regulated producers' capacity. In 1910, the Taiwanese producers formed a cartel (under the auspices of their trade association, the Taiwan-Togyo-Rengokai); this was extended to encompass the Japanese producers and renamed the Togyo-Rengokai shortly afterward. This cartel arrangement established a regime of stable prices that lasted until 1914.

This regime of stable prices encouraged a process of entry into the industry in the early years of the century; a steady stream of new companies was established, both in Taiwan and within Japan, in the period before 1925. At the same time, several of the emergent companies grew by acquisition; between 1907 and 1919, six major Taiwanese companies acquired a total of twenty-four producers. The same tendency operated to a lesser degree within Japan: Dainihon Seito, itself a product of a 1906 merger of Nippon Seiseito and Nippon Seito, acquired two Japanese producers in 1907–1908. These acquisitions notwithstanding, the relative stability of prices and the industry's prosperity—especially from 1915 onward, as sugar exports began to expand sharply—allowed a relatively fragmented structure to persist for a lengthy period. Sugar firms grew rapidly by diversification, turning to railroads, shipping, confectionery, and alcoholic drinks in their search for new areas of expansion.

The Cartel Collapses

The cartel arrangement, which had protected producers throughout the prewar years, had always been threatened to some degree by rivalry between Taiwanese and Japanese refiners. In 1914, the two groups failed to reach an agreement, but the immediate consequences were masked by the huge surge in export demand that followed the outbreak of war in Europe. It was not until the slump in demand that accompanied the postwar recession of the 1920s that problems began to emerge. Throughout the late 1920s, financial difficulties among refiners began to induce consolidations. A number of majors grew, in part by acquiring assets of firms in financial difficulties. The continuing difficulties of smaller refiners led to the increasing dominance of these few firms; but forming a successful cartel among them proved difficult in the presence of substantial excess capacity. The rivalry between the top two producers, Meiji Seito and Dainihon Seito, was seen as a major bar to progress; throughout the 1920s, the two repeatedly failed to strike a workable agreement. But as prices fell to a new low toward the end of the decade, the majors agreed to set up a new cartel (the Satokyokyu Kumiai), which encompassed Meiji Seito, Danihon Seito, and Shinko Seito (which it managed), as well as Taiwan Seito (with its Ensuiko subsidiary), Hokkaido Seito, and Chuou Seito. Even then, a relatively small refiner, Tokyo-Seito, remained outside the new arrangement; it imported its raw sugar directly from Java and conducted its affairs independently of the cartel, for which it remained a serious problem until demand recovered as the Japanese economy revived in 1932.

Over the course of the interwar years, then, continuing difficulties in coordinating prices went hand in hand with an increasing degree of consolidation among refiners. The increasingly concentrated structure that emerged throughout this period persisted up to the end of the Second World War; only six independent producers survived by that date.

The Postwar Years

In the early postwar years, a new regime was devised under which the sugar industry operated for almost two decades (1945–1963). From 1945 to 1963, sugar refiners were subject to a rationing of foreign currency with which to buy their raw sugar needs. The quota of foreign currency made available to each producer depended on that producer's level of capacity. The resulting restriction on supply meant that sugar prices on the domestic market were rising, and profits grew. Meanwhile, the link between foreign currency allocations and firms' capacities stimulated both entry into the industry and capacity expansion by existing refiners.

In 1963, foreign currency rationing was abolished, and the price of sugar on the Japanese market fell rapidly. The government reacted with the Sugar Price Stabilization Act of 1965 . This new act aimed to protect producers against excessive fluctuations in sugar prices: sugar producers would receive subsidies when the world price of raw sugar went above a given price band and pay taxes when the price fell below the band. As it happened, the world price of raw sugar declined over the years that followed; but, the new system notwithstanding, Japan's refiners raised their production levels to a point where the price of refined sugar on the Japanese market declined, several small refiners experienced losses, and a number of acquisitions of such refiners by the majors ensued.

In 1977, the government decided to introduce more direct controls. The industry's profitability was restored by imposing a production quota on each refiner based on its total sales in that year, and these quotas have remained in force. These arrangements permit the sales of an individual firm to fluctuate from one year to the next, with consequent fluctuations in inventories. (Mitsui, for example, has a quota of 12.85%, as compared with its 1981 market share of 14%; see the market share table in appendix 1.)

The new regime has not entirely frozen the industry's structure; total demand has been falling in volume terms, and with fixed percentage quotas, this has led to some difficulties for certain of the smaller refiners. The Kobe Sugar Company went bankrupt, for instance, in the early 1980s; following such an exit, quotas are re-allocated to surviving firms in proportion to their 1977 shares. The government has, moreover, pursued a policy of rationalization under the Industrial Structure Improvement Act of 1982. The number of factories operated by various companies has been reduced and their production concentrated in their remaining plants (Mitsui, for instance, closed one of three plants under this scheme).

The Japanese industry, then, experienced a phase of consolidation in the era of tough price competition during the interwar years, following a process akin to that experienced at an earlier date in the U.S. industry. Before that period, however, a more relaxed price competition regime had led to entry and increasing fragmentation. During the postwar period, a series of government policies has moved the industry back toward a less concentrated and a more or less stable structure.

6.4 Summing Up

The aim of this chapter has been to probe the explanation offered in chapter 5 for the observed negative relationship between concentration in homogeneous goods industries and the ratio of market size to setup costs. The explanation proposed in chapter 2 posits that the (minimal equilibrium) level of concentration depends positively on the ratio of setup cost to market size and positively on the toughness of price competition. To probe that explanation further, this chapter has been devoted to examining the salt and sugar industries, both of which exhibit a ratio of setup cost to market size that is relatively high in all of the countries studied here, and for which the degree of product homogeneity is extreme.

It has been argued, first, that certain broad differences in experience across these markets can be traced to differences in the intensity of price competition. Second, it has been argued that the difficulty of maintaining adequate price-cost margins in a fragmented industry appears to lie at the root of the historical tendency for these industries to move to a highly consolidated structure. It was argued that these industries are well represented by one polar case of the simple model set out in chapter 2, viz., that in which any departure from a high level of concentration leads to a sharp fall in unit margins, so that the only equilibrium configuration for the industry is a highly concentrated one (an extreme illustration of this is provided by the Bertrand case of chapter 2).

An important feature of the explanation proposed here is that the level of concentration resulting from the present mechanism is liable to far exceed any level that might have been considered warranted by the estimated m.e.s. of plants, on the basis of traditional arguments. A comparison of m.e.s. levels as reported in chapter 4, table 4.3, with the concentration levels shown in table 6.3 makes it clear that actual levels do indeed far outrun such warranted levels. (See, for example, Anderson et al. 1975 and appendix 6.2. On the concept of warranted concentration levels, see chapter 1.)

One caveat is called for, in regard to the characterization of equilibrium structure. The preceding discussion suggests that the process of consolidation in these industries can be interpreted as a response by firms to the difficulty of avoiding price wars within the fragmented industry. It might appear that this argument would imply that the final outcome will be a degree of consolidation that just suffices to maintain margins yielding a normal rate of return on the sunk costs incurred. *Such a conclusion is unwarranted.*

The reason why such an argument does not hold good is illustrated by reference to the Bertrand example of chapter 2. In fact, in that example, the equilibrium structure is a monopoly, and equilibrium profits can be made arbitrarily large by letting market size increase. This, of course, is an extreme case, but it does serve to illustrate a general point. What dissuades potential entrants from entering the industry, at equilibrium, is the level of *expected post-entry* margins. If it is assumed, as has been done throughout this chapter, that any fragmentation in structure causes a sharp fall in margins, then it follows that large *pre-entry* margins may be consistent with the absence of entry. Of course, it may still be argued that—the implausibly extreme Bertrand case apart—we are dealing with "merely an integer effect." The key point to note in this regard is that in these industries the number of significant players is typically quite small, and so the entry of one further significant player may plausibly exert a substantial impact on equilibrium prices.

Capacity Limits

One route by which unit margins might be kept high enough to recoup sunk costs, however intense is price competition, is by striking a balance between rigid capacity limits and a static level of industry demand. The experience of the industries examined above suggests— unsurprisingly—that many problems of price cutting were initiated or exacerbated by factors that led to an imbalance between total capacity and industry demand. Would it not be better to model the effect of such fluctuations explicitly? Such an extension is in principle straightforward (though it drastically complexifies the mathematics of these models; chapter 2, footnote 1), once we confine attention to the case in which demand is static.

But capacity limits are often quite flexible, while industry demand is likely to fluctuate to a greater or lesser degree over time, and firms must build capacity in an environment that is both uncertain and stochastic. The issues of interest above are precisely those that arise when some exogenous change in market conditions renders a hitherto persistent structure unstable; our focus has been on examining the mechanisms that then come into play and bring the industry back to a new equilibrium structure. These mechanisms may be adequately captured by our simple model.

Price Competition

The functional relationship between structure and price (the toughness of price competition) is simply taken as given here. This is not ideal—in principle, it would seem desirable to explain this function in terms of some more primitive concept. The game-theoretic literature on dynamic oligopoly and cartel stability indicates, however, that the determinants of this function are delicate and subtle and include many (informational and other) factors that would be extremely difficult to identify or proxy empirically. Indeed, viewed against this background, the device of simply taking this functional relationship as a primitive of the theory seems an attractive way forward. Its success, of course, depends on the extent to which it is possible to couch explanations in terms of shifts in this relationship. The shift variables proposed above relate to product characteristics (degree of homogeneity) and institutional factors (the stance of the authorities vis-à-vis competition policy). Most of the arguments developed above have been couched in terms of exogenous changes in the institutional regime. In looking at the Japanese sugar industry, however, the key shock to the system lies in the breakdown of a long-standing cartel arrangement between the Japanese and Taiwanese producers, the explanation for which lies outside the scope of the model. This disagreement had little impact, however, until the postwar collapse in demand led to a sharp fall in prices. This observation again raises the point made above regarding the role played by capacity limits. It also echoes the fact that, in spite of the emphasis in the recent game-theoretic literature on the richness and complexity of the influences affecting cartel stability, one result common to many (but not all) models is that cartel breakdown may be triggered by falls in demand—a factor heavily emphasized in the traditional literature on cartels.

Alternative Explanations?

The theory appears to be fairly successful in providing an explanation for a series of features of these industries by reference to one simple principle. Any one of these features, taken in isolation, will invite alternative explanations. One of these alternative explanations is worth noting here. This relates to the U.S. sugar industry, in which a period of consolidation occurred around the last decade of the nineteenth century. This change in structure coincided with the first great merger wave in U.S. industry. One possible explanation for the increase in mergers is that it represented a reaction to the Sherman Act of 1890: firms that previously practiced some form of price coordination rendered illegal by the act entered into mergers as a way of legally effecting the same outcome as before, in respect of prices and profits.

This explanation does not conflict with the theory—indeed, the argument proposed here is very much in the same spirit. It is interesting, in this regard, that a similar type of argument has been adduced in respect of U.K. experience in the 1950s, when the banning of resale price maintenance agreements led to a regime of more intense price competition and precipitated a wave of exits and consolidations. Indeed, explanations of this kind run very much along the same lines as the above discussion of the determinants of cross country differences in the structure of the sugar industry. The aim of the present approach is to seek some *general* economic mechanism, the operation of which may be admittedly influenced by country-specific institutional forces, but which will, to a greater or lesser extent, operate in all countries and periods. Within the framework of this general argument, any country-specific institutional change that affects the toughness of price competition may of course be adduced as the proximate cause of particular shifts in structure within particular industries.

7

The Limitations of the Theory I

7.1 Introduction and Summary

This chapter is short, and though its theme is negative in character, it nonetheless constitutes an essential step in the argument. Two key ideas emerged from the analysis of the exogenous sunk cost model in chapter 2. The first idea was that the size-structure relationship depends upon the toughness of price competition in the market. The second idea is that the size-structure relationship derived in that chapter constitutes only a *lower bound* to equilibrium concentration: when market size becomes large relative to setup cost, a more fragmented structure *may* be supported as an equilibrium, but we cannot exclude the appearance of other, more concentrated, equilibria.

The preceding chapter was concerned with the case in which the ratio of market size to setup cost is low; this chapter focuses on the complementary case, in which the ratio of market size to setup cost is relatively high (flour, canned vegetables, bread, processed meat). In the cases examined in the preceding chapter, the lower bound to equilibrium concentration is high, and so the theory constrains the data quite strongly. As seen in the studies of the salt and sugar industries, it is possible in this setting to trace the role played by various factors that affect the toughness of price competition and thereby impinge on this lower bound. These include both institutional differences and the presence of horizontal product differentiation in the form of plant location (geographical market segmentation).

In the cases examined in this chapter, the theoretical model is much less informative. The lower bound to concentration is lower in this setting, and so the theory places correspondingly weaker constraints on the data. This feature represents a central and intrinsic limitation of the present approach. The aim of this chapter lies *not* in testing any predictions (the model has little predictive content here), but rather in attempting to convince the reader that it would be inappropriate and unjustified to seek to improve the predictive content of the model by adding additional structure. The argument developed below is that, at the present level of cross-industry studies, no more precise model is justified. The search for more refined predictions in this area must rather be directed toward studies of particular industries, within which further structure can validly be imposed on the underlying model. To justify this stance, an attempt is made here and in the associated appendices to describe the rich variety of industry and country-specific factors that appear to have played a significant role in leading to the diversity of experience encountered in the present group of industries.

A second feature of the studies that follow deserves mention. This relates to the diminished role played by the toughness of price competition in influencing industry structure in this setting. As shown in chapter 2, the toughness of price competition affects the *lower bound* to equilibrium structure. As this lower bound falls, so that the model constrains equilibrium structure less tightly, the influence of differences in the toughness of price competition becomes less evident. By looking in detail at the influences underlying the evolution of concentration in this group of industries, we are led to conclude that the absence of any tight constraint on industry structure within the theory seems to be mirrored in the lack of any strong *systematic* pattern of influences bearing on the evolution of structure. The picture, rather, is one of widely diverging experience.

In surveying the various industries, it is natural to begin by looking at the extent to which current concentration levels are explained by the regression equations developed in chapter 5. An examination of the regression residuals indicates that in one industry, the flour industry, they are very large. This industry shows a very wide divergence of structure, which is not to any substantial degree explicable by reference to differences in market size, and so it provides a particularly useful context in which to illustrate the theme. While these remarks serve to illustrate the main focus of this chapter, the conclusions offered below must, of their nature, rest on a rather detailed examination of each industry. Readers who wish to trace the details of each of the industries will find the relevant material in appendices 7.1 to 7.4.

7.2 The Flour Industry

The French, German, and Italian flour industries are all more fragmented than would be expected in the sense that their regression residuals (section 5.3) are large and negative. A number of possible explanations are worth recording, though we are not able here to discriminate between them. First, a certain amount of caution is needed in using a measure of σ based on U.S. data, because concentration is relatively high in the United States and plant size may reflect this. However, estimates based on engineers' studies of m.e.s. are available, and these corroborate the median plant measure. This makes it somewhat implausible to attribute the negative residuals for France, Germany, and Italy to a mismeasurement of m.e.s. A second line of explanation, which falls within our model, is that price competition might be relatively muted in these markets. An examination of the three industries, however, offers only limited support for such a view. The most striking observation arises in the case of the German market. Here, a sharp difference in structure exists between the north, where milling is relatively concentrated, and the south, where it is extremely fragmented. Some industry sources attribute this observation to allegedly tougher price competition in the north German market. No evidence is available that might allow this to be tested, however, and the question remains open.

Whatever the reason for the continuing fragmentation of these three markets, they provide a striking contrast to the experience of the U.S., U.K., and Japanese industries. In these three markets, concentration is substantially higher than would be expected on the basis of the regression equations reported in chapter 5, and the origins of these higher concentration levels differ widely across these three cases. In the Japanese market, two major companies, Nisshin Seifun (Nisshin Flour Milling Co., Ltd.) and Nippon Seifun (Nippon Flour Mills Co., Ltd.), play a leading role in the industry, a position that can be traced to the industry's beginnings at the turn of the century.[1]

---

1. This account draws on the company histories of Nisshin Seifun and Nippon Seifun. (All company histories are listed separately at the end of the references section.)

Flour was, until after 1945, regarded as a Western product, and the total size of the market was very small. Large-scale production began around 1905–1910, and during that period the millers attempted to form a cartel, which quickly collapsed. The government, however, shared the view of a number of the companies involved that flour production should be rationalized, and a phase of mergers and acquisitions followed, from which Nippon Seifun and Nisshin Seifun emerged as the two major millers.

The early lead achieved by these two companies, in what was then a relatively small industry, is one they have retained ever since. Throughout the interwar period, the two companies responded to depressed flour prices by forming a price agreement and segmenting the market. In the early postwar years, the government first attempted to stimulate entry to the now rapidly growing industry, but a later reversal of policy led to the exit of many of the firms that entered at that time. Further policy changes since 1975 have tended to stabilize shares, with Nisshin Seifun and Nippon Seifun as the only first-rank producers.

This pattern of early leadership followed by long-term stability contrasts with the pattern followed in the United States, where an initially very fragmented industry moved through three discrete phases of consolidation in the 1890s, 1920s, and 1980s. The factors that sparked each of these three merger waves were very different in kind: The first wave appears to have reflected a defensive reaction by rivals to one major acquisition; the second seems to have had its origins in a response to consolidation in the downstream baking sector; and the third phase was driven by the entry into this and other sectors of the food industry of a number of expanding conglomerate concerns.

The evolution of concentration in the U.K. industry is perhaps the most striking case of all. Here the highly concentrated structure of the industry can be traced to two separate phases of consolidation.[2] The first phase was marked by a response to the appearance of serious overcapacity in the industry at the turn of the century. At that time, the attractiveness of constructing new large-scale mills in the immediate vicinity of major ports led to an expansion of new plant, with no offsetting closure of older mills. These problems were

---

2. This account draws on Hart, Utton, and Walshe 1973 and the Commission of the European Communities 1977.

exacerbated during the First World War, when transport restrictions inhibited the operation of some mills, leading to compensating entry and expansion elsewhere. By the time government control of the industry ended in 1921, a serious overcapacity problem existed. Some 90% of flour production came from some 300 of the 650 mills then operating. The overcapacity problem prompted a period of severe competition throughout the 1920s, which in turn stimulated three responses:

• the formation of an association of millers, the Millers' Mutual Association, which set production quotas and recommended selling prices;

• an industry initiative aimed at the purchase and closure of redundant mills;

• a process of acquisition by two of the larger firms, Ranks and Spillers, which resulted in these two producers, together with the Co-operative Wholesale Society, accounting by 1935 for some 39% of the output of the grain milling industry. Further acquisitions in the late 1930s left these three firms in control of two-thirds of U.K. flour production. (The initial round of acquisitions in 1928 was said by Spillers's chairman in his 1929 speech to shareholders to have been an essential preliminary to their taking a lead in promoting the industry initiative toward reorganization.)

Concentration in the industry remained moderate, however, until the early 1950s. Between 1935 and 1951, the share of total output accounted for by the four largest millers fell from 39% to 33%. The three largest millers operating in 1951 were Ranks, Spillers, and the Co-operative Wholesale Society.

This first phase of consolidation in the U.K. industry bears some similarity to the processes described in the preceding chapter. The second phase of consolidation, however, had an entirely different character. It began with an incident in 1953, the year in which wartime controls on the importation of grain were finally lifted. In that year, one of the United Kingdom's leading bread producers, Allied Bakeries Ltd., fell into dispute with Ranks and Spillers in respect of discount terms on purchases of flour. Allied reacted to the millers' refusal to grant favorable terms by turning to Canadian sources for flour supplies. Though Ranks and Spillers subsequently reached an agreement with Allied on discount terms, they set out thereafter to acquire additional bakeries in the United Kingdom to ensure a secure outlet for their flour production (Maunder 1970).

The result was an escalating process of acquisitions throughout the bread and flour industries, with all three companies—Ranks, Spillers, and Allied—competing for bakeries. As this process continued, Allied proceeded to integrate backward and meet Ranks and Spillers on their own ground, through a series of acquisitions of flour producers. Allied acquired twenty-nine mills in 1961–1962 alone, and by 1967 it operated thirty-nine flour mills and seventy-six bakeries. Ranks's merger and acquisition activity meanwhile had led to the emergence of Ranks-Hovis McDougall Ltd. (RHM) in 1962. A separate series of mergers, centered on the Co-operative Wholesale Society, led to the emergence of a new grouping, which was in turn acquired by Spillers, forming Spillers-French Holding Ltd. in 1972. By 1972, the process had run its course; by that date, the three leading firms accounted for 70–75% of flour production.

All in all, then, the widely diverging experiences of the flour industry across these countries appear traceable neither to any differences in the pattern of technology and tastes nor to any differences in institutional arrangements that might for example impinge on the toughness of price competition in the industry. Rather, these differences appear to reflect idiosyncratic factors particular to each industry's development, whose nature lies outside the scope of any theory of the present kind. This impression is reinforced on turning to the three other industries in the group.

7.3   Other Industries

Bread

We already noted that the relatively high level of concentration in the U.K. industry was the outcome of a scramble for bakery outlets among major bread and flour producers during the 1960s. In the United States, on the other hand, where the bread industry is also moderately concentrated, the evolution of structure has been little influenced by the upstream flour industry. Rather, it reflects a gradual process of expansion by one leading bread producer, Continental, whose growth in market share over different periods has been achieved by varying strategies: advertising played a central role for a limited period during the 1960s, whereas aggressive price competition was the central element in the company's strategy in the 1970s.

Meat Processing

The experience of the meat-processing industry also indicates a wide range of differing influences at work across different countries. Moderate levels of concentration exist both in the United States and Japan. In the United States, these can in part be related to the presence of a relatively concentrated upstream sector (meat packing) and in part to the (very limited) success achieved in establishing well-known brands in certain submarkets. In Japan, on the other hand, the dominance of two leading producers stems from the early days of the industry's development . In contrast to Western countries, Japan's meat-processing industry is of recent origin and did not evolve out of a traditional artisan sector. The two firms that first succeeded in overcoming technical production problems in the early postwar years established a leading position that they still retain.

Canned Vegetables

Canned vegetables represent a middle ground between the homogeneous goods industries and the advertising-intensive industries. The canning industry was one of the first to be shaped by heavy advertising outlays, and the history of the U.S. industry up to 1960 closely parallels the experience of the advertising-intensive industries studied in later chapters (especially that of the frozen food industry). Over the past generation, however, the decline of the industry—due in large part to the displacement of canned by frozen food—has been associated with a gradual decline in advertising outlays. Today canned goods are thought of as a commodity product, which sell basically on price, and the decline in advertising outlays has been so sharp as to place them within the homogeneous goods category on the basis of our criterion.

   As this process has developed, price pressures have played a more important role in determining the evolution of structure. Changes in technology have favored larger plant sizes, but the industry in many countries has suffered from excess capacity. These pressures have induced consolidation in some cases, though in a few instances a handful of firms with relatively strong brands have succeeded in maintaining a significant price differential vis-à-vis rival products.

In the United States, two such firms (both drawn from among the eight top brands of the 1960s) have succeeded in retaining a substantial market share, and these two firms were clear leaders in the U.S. industry in the mid–1980s. In contrast to this, the leading U.K. firms have failed to retain any brands that can command a significant price premium. The history of the U.K. industry in recent years has been marked by a sharp phase of consolidation—driven by strong price competition—which closely parallels the experience of the high setup cost industries examined in the preceding chapter.

7.4 Concluding Remarks

These remarks illustrate the kinds of arguments that lead to the main conclusions of the chapter, though a full defense of the stance taken here must rest on a blow-by-blow account of each industry's experience, as set out in the accompanying appendices. These conclusions can be stated succinctly:

• When market size is large relative to setup cost, a fragmented structure can emerge as an equilibrium outcome, but the theory is also consistent with the emergence of a wide range of more concentrated structures. This points to one of the central limitations of the theory. We argue, however, that this limitation is *inherent* in the approach: it would not be justifiable to add additional structure in order to sharpen predictions, for any such particularization of the basic model(s) used here could only be justified by appealing to features that are certain to vary widely across industries.

• The chapter attempts to justify this point of view by illustrating the fact that the divergence of experience encountered among these industries cannot be traced to any systematic influences operating across the entire group. Rather, a range of highly specific factors appears to have played a primary role in shaping structure.

• In particular, the influence of the toughness of price competition, which was easily identified as a primary influence in the case of the industries we examined in the preceding chapter, is overshadowed in the present set of industries by these industry-specific influences.

III
Advertising and Structure

Darwin's "survival of the fittest" is really a special case of a more general law of "survival of the stable." The universe is populated by stable things.

Richard Dawkins

8

The Evolution of Advertising-Intensive Industries

8.1 Introduction and Summary

In this chapter, and in those that follow, we turn to the structure of advertising-intensive industries. The role of advertising in shaping several of these industries can be traced to the beginnings of modern advertising at the end of the nineteenth century. In the United States, for example, today's market leaders in several of these industries had established leading brands by the turn of the century [see, for example, soft drinks (chapter 9), prepared soups (chapter 9), and biscuits (cookies and crackers; appendix 12.2)], but the details of these histories are for the most part incompletely documented. For that reason, this chapter focuses on one of the few food and drink industries to have emerged in recent times, the frozen food industry, which came into being during the interwar years and only began to develop rapidly during the late 1940s. Its development is very fully documented, and it provides a useful starting point in examining the evolution of concentration in advertising-intensive industries.

The First Theme

This chapter develops two themes: the first of these relates to the central prediction of the theory, which states that increases in market size cannot lead to the emergence of a fragmented market structure in these industries. The argument underlying this prediction posits the existence of a simple mechanism that will induce the breakdown of any fragmented configuration, and the first theme of this chapter relates to the identification of this mechanism. This chapter, then, provides a counterpoint to chapter 6, in which the corresponding mechanism characteristic of the exogenous sunk cost model was set out. As in that chapter, the underlying logic lies in an attempt to use industry histories as a way of exploring predictions based on the Nash equilibrium concept, that is, on models whose content lies in assertions that certain configurations cannot emerge, because some firm would, in such a setting, find it optimal to deviate. This chapter, then, explores these deviations.

Within advertising-intensive industries, then, what does the theory exclude? As market size increases, the theory permits an indefinite increase in the number of firms entering the industry. What it precludes, loosely stated, are configurations in which no firms advertise, or configurations in which all firms advertise a little, thus permitting a fragmented structure to emerge. The latter configuration might appear a perfectly reasonable outcome on intuitive grounds. It is possible to envisage a situation, for example, in which each firm needs to devote a fixed sum of advertising outlays in order to inform consumers of the virtues of its product. In such a setting, advertising might be treated as an exogenous sunk cost (see chapter 3), and convergence to a fragmented market structure could occur.

What the theory implies, however, is that some small set of firms must at some point emerge as high advertisers, whose combined market share exceeds some lower bound, however large the market becomes. A remaining fringe consisting of an indefinite number of firms that do little or no advertising may coexist with these market leaders at equilibrium.[1]

The viability of this large fringe of small firms will depend on a number of factors. First, it will depend on buyers' responsiveness to advertising outlays. Buyers in the nonretail sector are notoriously unresponsive to advertising outlays, and typically buy on price. The larger the size of the nonretail sector, the greater the maximal number of fringe firms. Second, the maximal number of fringe firms will be greater insofar as the level of setup costs is lower. In the frozen food industry, setup costs are extremely low, and the nonretail part of the market is significant, ranging from about one-fifth of the total sales

---

1. The split between the two groups need not necessarily be as sharp as this: if several distinct market segments exist, and if advertising spillovers between segments are weak, a firm might succeed by confining its operations to some specific market segment, say, and advertising at some level intermediate between those leading firms that sell across all segments and the fringe firms.

in the United Kingdom to over three-quarters in Japan. Thus the industry affords considerable scope for the emergence and viability of second-tier firms.

As to the predictions of the theory, however, all that is claimed is that a fragmented structure must break down, as market size increases, and that the collapse of such a fragmented structure will be driven by a competitive escalation of advertising outlays by some small number of firms. Beyond this, the theory tells us little . How will such a competitive escalation evolve? What factors will determine which firms will succeed? Will a number of firms vie for position over some period of time? Will firms avoid such a potentially costly process and achieve some kind of coordination, whereby an equilibrium outcome is achieved rapidly?

While the theory is consistent with many of these scenarios, the choice between them depends delicately on various nonobservables —notably, the firms' beliefs concerning both the eventual size of the market and the strategies of their rivals. While it will be easy to offer a plausible rationale within the context of the theory for the cross-country differences in experience documented below, it should be emphasized that there are no robust predictions to be had regarding the dynamics of this process.

In what follows, we begin by examining the U.S. and U.K. markets, in which the frozen food industry first developed. The evolution of structure in these two cases shows a quite remarkable degree of similarity. In each case, it is possible to identify a precise period at which a dual pattern emerged and hardened. During that period, escalating advertising outlays eroded the profitability of middle-ranking firms, thus making it increasingly unattractive for this group to persist with a high advertising strategy.

A strikingly different pattern emerged, however, in the German and Italian markets. These two markets developed relatively late, and in both cases the slow and costly battle for a leading niche in the market, which had marked the evolution of the industry in the United States and the United Kingdom, was avoided. Instead, a cooperative solution rapidly emerged between the two leading firms, whereby their interests were merged. This led both to an extremely high level of concentration and to a much more rapid convergence to a clear dual pattern.[2]

---

2. The Japanese and French markets have a number of special features; the French market is discussed in section 8.4, and the Japanese market in appendix 8.1.

The Second Theme

The second theme relates to those limitations of the theory discussed in the preceding chapter. The theory implies only the existence of a *lower bound* to equilibrium concentration and is consistent with a— possibly very wide—range of equilibrium outcomes. The multiplicity of outcomes emerging within the exogenous sunk costs framework, once (horizontal) product differentiation is present, was discussed in chapter 2. There it was pointed out that an extreme example of such multiplicity of equilibria arises when markets are subdivided into a number of more or less independent segments. In that setting, we may have both concentrated equilibria, in which the same set of firms operates in each segment, and other more fragmented equilibria, in which a different set of firms occupies each segment.

This same observation continues to hold good within the endogenous sunk cost model. The range of equilibrium configurations will depend delicately on the details of the model (in particular, on the extent to which advertising outlays supporting a firm's offerings in one market segment enhance the firm's brand image and so generate spillovers in respect of its offerings in other segments). A comparison between the current structure of the U.S. industry and that of the other countries studied here provides a striking illustration of this point. In the United States, a number of separate market segments can be defined, within each of which a different set of leading firms is active. Elsewhere, the same set of firms dominates all segments. This persistence of a segmented structure within the U.S. industry is one of the factors underlying the wide divergence in over-

Table 8.1
The frozen food industry by country

	Four-firm sales concentration ratio (retail only, %)	Number of firms	Relative market size (total sales)	Retail sales as a fraction of total sales
France	43	~70	~0.05	N.A.
Germany	81	~90	0.2–0.3	0.5
Italy	89	~70	0.1	0.75
Japan	46	~500	0.15	0.25
United Kingdom	37	50–100	0.2	0.76
United States	~40	1,500–1,600	1	N.A.

all concentration levels observed across the present set of countries (table 8.1).

Market Definition

Throughout, we follow the usual convention of defining the frozen food industry to include frozen fish, (prepared) meat, vegetables, and prepared meals and desserts. We exclude ice cream and frozen carcass meat.

8.2   The U.S. Frozen Food Industry

Today's most visible brand name in frozen food derives from the industry's founder, Clarence Birdseye, who formed a company in New York in 1923 to freeze fish fillets.[3] A number of other firms were already producing frozen food by that date, but Birdseye's innovation lay in realizing the advantage of freezing sufficiently rapidly to avoid damage to the cellular structure of the food. He also had the distinction of being the first to freeze food in a package designed to be sold at retail.

Birdseye's first venture ended in bankruptcy, but he went on to launch a new firm, General Seafoods Corp., with share capital of $60,000. The parent firm for Birdseye's company was known as General Foods Company. In 1929, the Postum Company, a rapidly diversifying firm, purchased Birdseye's company, paying $20 million for its patents and $2 million for its assets. The name of the company was immediately changed to General Foods Corporation. Throughout the 1930s the market grew slowly but steadily; by 1939 total industry production was still below 400 million pounds (a figure that doubled by the end of the war and increased tenfold by the mid-1950s). The main barrier to growth throughout the 1930s lay in the costs retailers faced in installing display cabinets; developed by C. V. Hill in 1929, these glass-fronted cases were extremely expensive —a small four-foot unit cost $400 during the Depression years. General Foods, trading under the Birds Eye brand name, developed a number of initiatives designed to circumvent the problem. In 1931

---

3. This account of the U.S. industry draws on the Federal Trade Commission report of 1962 and the 35th anniversary retrospective published as a supplement to the industry's leading trade paper, *Frozen Food Age* (1987).

it contracted with the Commercial Credit Company to finance retailers' purchases of display cases. In 1934 it contracted the American
Radiator Corp. to manufacture a new, low-cost unit in the form of a
closed chest. This sacrificed the display element, but the cost reduction (to $260) was substantial. It then proceeded to rent these new
"Amerad" units to retailers at the modest rate of $7.50 a month.

Hand in hand with this strategy went the use of a sales force, not
to take customer orders (these were phoned in by the retailer directly
to the company's warehouses), but rather to oversee the retailer's
sales strategy: ensuring that rented cases contained only Birds Eye
products, talking to shoppers with the aid of charts designed to
demonstrate the value offered by frozen foods, and educating the
retailer's staff on selling the company's products. General Foods's
lead was followed, over the course of the 1930s, by a number of large,
diversified food firms, including most of those that would come to
dominate the postwar industry.

General Foods specialized throughout the decade in marketing
and distribution; much of its product was "bought in" from subcontractors that operated freezing plants in agricultural areas. With
the coming of the Roosevelt administration in 1933, the company
responded to the growing antitrust climate by licensing these subcontractors (or "copackers") to use its patented freezers on a royalty
basis. More important, by the late 1930s the Birds Eye patents had
become relatively unimportant as new types of freezing systems were
developed, which involved freezing vegetables in loose form rather
than in a block.

In this environment, many firms that had produced for Birdseye
or distributed Birds Eye products were encouraged to set up independently. The first major breakaway involved two partners from
Waterman & Co., one of New York's major food wholesalers, which
had been distributing Birds Eye products to institutional buyers. In
1933 the company dropped the Birds Eye line and set up its own
company, Honor Brand Frosted Foods. At first, Honor Brand focused
its attention on the nonretail sector, but in 1937 it entered the retail
market with a strategy somewhat different to that of General Foods.
Rather than lease display cases, the company sold them outright to
retailers, who could pay by installments over two years. On the
distribution side, General Foods used two routes: it sold the majority
of its retail volume through its own regional branches, while selling
the remainder through a net of independent wholesale distributors

who were paid a percentage of sales revenue. Honor Brand, on the other hand, avoided developing its own expensive distribution network by selling its product outright to a number of exclusive wholesale distributors; many of these were dairy jobbers who already had refrigerated trucks and storage equipment. The resulting distribution net was patchy, relative to that of General Foods, but by 1939, Honor Brand's retail sales had risen to half the level of the market leader's. In the same year Stokely-Van Camp, one of the country's major canners, until then a minority shareholder, took complete ownership of Honor Brand. Stokely integrated Honor Brand into its own frozen food division in 1954.

Throughout the prewar period, however, the retail market remained very small, and it played a secondary role to the nonretail segment. The war years saw a substantial increase in total volume as the shortage of tinplate hit canners. The resurgence of the canning industry in the immediate postwar years led to a short-lived fall in frozen food sales, but then the industry entered a decade of steady growth.[4] In this decade the basic pattern of the industry took shape.

The Crucial Decades

In the late 1940s, signs were beginning to appear that the retail segment was to become a major mass market. One of the most significant trends concerned the demise of the independent distributor, who had played a pivotal role in the prewar industry. Most prewar entrants to the industry were canners, to whom frozen foods represented a minor sideline to their main business (FTC 1962, p. 57); they chose for the most part to sell their products through independent distributors. It was in the immediate postwar years that a new trend in marketing developed; the main innovator was Snow Crop, which subsequently became part of Minute Maid.

Snow Crop's founder was an ex-General Foods marketing manager, John I. Moone, who left to set up his own company in 1945. At first the company followed the established pattern in the industry of working through exclusive wholesale distributors. It relied, moreover, on outside processors for its entire supply of product, thus specializing purely in the marketing function. Snow Crop was, in effect,

---

4. Total sales volume stood at 700 million pounds in 1942, peaked at 1,486 million pounds in 1946, fell to a low of 1,132 million pounds in 1947, and thereafter grew steadily to reach 5,661 million pounds a decade later (FTC 1962).

a national marketing arm for the twenty-one contract freezing companies that supplied it, simply taking 6% of sales as its commission.

Snow Crop's key innovation lay in the central role it assigned to advertising: one-sixth of the revenue it received was devoted to an advertising fund, with an equal contribution being made to the fund by the distributors with which it worked. Snow Crop introduced TV advertising of frozen foods for the first time in 1949. The response was so strong, and the growth of the brand so rapid, that the company decided to begin producing for itself,[5] on the argument that it could earn a margin on its own product greater than the 6% commission it then earned on bought-in products. Moreover, it was felt that the company could produce at lower cost than it could buy in and so support a round of price reductions.

With growing competition for scarce display space in retail outlets, Snow Crop set out to use price cuts to raise its share of space. A second element in its attempt to cut costs, in order to underpin this strategy, was to bypass the well-established distribution route via independent wholesalers and to market directly to retail chains. It tested the new policy in 1946 with First National Stores in Boston and A & P in Chicago. The latter chain reported a tripling in sales within ninety days on price reductions of 16%–17%. The new high advertising/low price policy pursued by Snow Crop led to an extremely rapid rise in the company's market share and sparked off a wave of competitive advertising.[6] Throughout the 1950s Snow Crop emerged as General Foods's main rival, and as brand competition intensified, a new pattern began to emerge in the industry.

Looking back over the period in its 1962 report on the industry, the Federal Trade Commission distinguished three groups of firms among the 270 firms covered by its 1959 survey.

(i) Somewhat over one-third of the firms (101) were established before 1940. These were mostly canning companies that had diversified into frozen foods, and these accounted for 53.2% of total sales.

---

5. The immediate impetus for the move was provided by the decision of Vacuum Foods Corp., Snow Crop's supplier of frozen orange juice, to begin marketing under its own label and cease supplying Snow Crop. Vacuum Foods Corp. was subsequently renamed Minute Maid.

6. Minute Maid's answer was to hire Bing Crosby to sing on radio five times a week. In return he received, inter alia, an issue of shares on favourable terms, as well as an exclusive sales franchise to eight Western states, for which he put up a $50,000 stake. The singer's name became synonymous with Minute Maid for a decade.

(ii) The next major group of seventy-five firms had entered in the immediate postwar period 1945–1949, and these accounted for 31% of 1959 sales.

(iii) The sixty-seven firms that had entered the industry in 1950–1958 accounted for a mere 7.8% of industry sales. These new firms were almost all small, highly specialized concerns for which frozen food production was the main or sole activity, and which confined themselves to some small specialized market niche. As the FTC report noted, "their operations can be classified as 'fringe'. They generally produced only one or a few minor products, rather than large volume products; they generally were not diversified into related activities; they generally were limited to local markets" (FTC 1962, p. 6).

In the new climate of the 1950s, with intensifying brand competition led by Birds Eye and Snow Crop, the only recent entrants that could effectively compete across the board were a handful of major food producers that had diversified into the area during the early postwar years. Among them was Libby, McNeil & Libby, which began national distribution in 1948.[7]

By the 1950s, then, the barriers to entry that marked the early phase of development had collapsed: the FTC's 1962 report found that entry to the industry had long been easy and postwar market growth had been accompanied by a steady inflow of new firms. The new pattern of competition that had emerged in the retail market rested on marketing and advertising expenditures; entry was easy— but competing with the market leaders across the board was not.

Competition in Advertising

By 1959, the pace was being set by General Foods (Birds Eye) and Minute Maid. As the FTC report concluded, "these two firms were clearly in an advertising class of their own; they spent $9.8 million in advertising during 1959, which was 46.2 percent of the total advertising expenditure of the industry, and 6.1 percent of their combined packer label[8] sales" (FTC 1962, p. 99).

---

7. Established in the mid-nineteenth century, the company ranked as one of the country's leading canners, and its brand image was well established in both canned foods and tomato juice.

8. That is, their sales under their own (Birds Eye and Minute Maid) brands, as opposed to own-label supplies to retail chains.

This ratio of advertising to sales was characteristic only of a small group of leading firms; the FTC cited a ratio of advertising to (total) sales of 5.2% for the largest six firms, of 2.2% for the next twelve, and of 2.7% for the industry as a whole. The leading firms also accounted for most of the other promotional expenditures: the top five spent $6 million on customer promotion deals in 1959—71% of all such expenditures by the industry.

As the role of advertising changed the shape of the retail market, a clear difference in pattern vis-à-vis the nonretail segment became evident. The four-firm concentration ratio, as reported by the FTC for 1959, was 35% overall; in the retail segment it was 39%, but if own-label products are excluded, the top four brands accounted for 52% of the total. Most own-label product was supplied by small firms who supplied the larger retail chains. The nonretail segment remained more fragmented, and the smaller firms specializing in nonretail sales remained relatively profitable compared to those firms of similar size that faced severe competition from the majors in the retail segment, where profit rates were strongly and positively related to firm size.[9]

The small number of firms that competed on a more or less equal basis with the two market leaders found it increasingly difficult to do so throughout the decade (figure 8.1). The third- to fifth-largest sellers each spent over $1 million on advertising in 1959; whereas their absolute spending levels lay far below that of the two leaders, it nonetheless represented a higher advertising to sales ratio.[10] As the FTC remarked, however,

This heavier advertising burden for the third to fifth packer-label leaders apparently did not generate a sufficient total revenue to permit these firms to earn a very high rate of profit. Their before taxes profit rate of 0.6 percent was considerably lower than the before taxes ratio of 5.1 percent for the two leaders. . . .

Advertising expenditures for the two leaders . . . were only slightly higher than their before tax profits but the other three firms among the five leaders spent nine times as much on advertising as they received in profits.

9. The FTC noted: "Financial Data indicated that not only large freezers, but also those selling primarily to the non-retail market had more favorable profit ratios than those selling primarily to the retail market. The group of 58 of the latter firms, with sales less than $1 million, reported net operating losses on sales of frozen fruits and vegetables" (FTC 1962, p. 5).
10. 7.8% of their packer label sales, as opposed to 6.1% for the two leading firms.

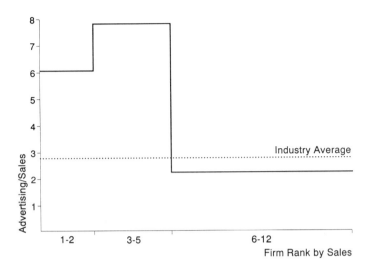

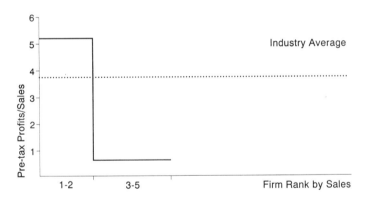

Figure 8.1

Advertising/sales ratios and profit rates by firm rank in the U.S. frozen food industry, 1959. The dotted line in each diagram shows the average value for the industry as a whole. The advertising/sales ratio relates to packer label sales only, for firms ranked 1–5, but to all sales for firms ranked 6–12. All these firms sold most of their output in the retail market. The average profit rate of firms ranked sixth to twelfth was not recorded by the FTC, but the average for the top thirteen firms in the industry was 4.2%, slightly higher than the industry average of 3.8% (FTC 1959, pp. 105, 107, 109–110).

This indicates that even relatively large firms found it difficult to make advertising-created product differentiation pay for itself. Since there was an inverse relationship between the relative burden of advertising expenditures and the size of firms, it appears that the advertising requirements alone could provide an effective barrier to new entry into the packer-label sector of the industry. (FTC 1962, p. 109).

Price Competition and Consolidation

As this new structural pattern developed throughout the 1950s, price competition intensified as leading brands sought to combine high advertising[11] and low prices in an effort to capture market share. The pace was set by PictSweet,[12] whose strategy was based on using only a small number of price classes across a wide range of product lines (most vegetables carried a retail price of 19 cents, for example). The disadvantages of such a policy, which was followed by others in the industry,[13] were seen to be outweighed by the fact that retailers were encouraged to shelve products by price band rather than by type, and so PictSweet built up increased visibility in supermarkets, which carried long continuous facings of PictSweet lines. The strategy, in combination with heavy advertising (shared between Pict Sweet and the retailers), led to an impressive growth of sales. By the late 1950s, however, others had followed to such a degree that the 19-cent pack was no longer a novelty, and this so-called group pricing strategy survives today only in a few small special categories of frozen food. A second feature of price competition in the 1950s, was a steady decrease in pack size as sellers attempted to offer lower and lower retail prices; the process went so far that vegetable packs reached sizes of 8 ounces. At this point the trend reversed in favor of the slightly larger 9–10 ounce packs, which became an industry standard.

The price competition of the 1950s represented in one way, however, an important turning point. Consumers could now buy grade-A

11. The industry history prepared by the leading trade journal *Frozen Food Age* on its 35th anniversary cites one contemporary observer as remarking, "At times it seems that they're selling advertising, rather than frozen food" (p. 62).

12. Known originally as Bozeman Canning Company, the company had become one of the top three or four fruit and vegetable processors by 1952. The company name had been changed to PictSweet in 1946.

13. The "19-cent band" was introduced by a group of food brokers, Ayres & Roberts This strategy was not supported by an exclusive dealer net, however, and when Birds Eye distributors carried it, General Foods revoked their franchises. What caused the demise of 19-cent brand, however, was the emergence of the new PictSweet strategy.

frozen vegetables at prices equal to those of leading canned brands. From this point forward, the trend was set for the long-term decline of the canning industry (see chapter 7). It was against this background of intensifying price competition and tightened margins that the frozen food industry experienced its first major wave of consolidations.

For the period 1950 to 1959, a total of sixty-two acquisitions (of which forty-four were of food-processing facilities) were recorded by thirty-one of the frozen food firms covered by the FTC report of 1962. Most of the acquired companies were small; of the fifty-seven for which asset data were available, forty had assets below $1 million. Many of the important acquisitions were undertaken by leading firms: of the forty-four food-processing facilities acquired, fourteen were acquired by the eight leading companies in the industry. The first of the big mergers occurred in 1954, when Stokely-Van Camp acquired PictSweet. By far the most important acquirer, however, was Minute Maid, whose two acquisitions accounted for 42.3% of all assets acquired.

In 1954, Minute Maid Corp., hitherto a frozen juice specialist, acquired all assets of the Snow Crop Division of Clinton Foods Inc., thus bringing the company into the mainstream frozen vegetable area and making it second only to the Birds Eye brand in the frozen food industry. Minute Maid's new venture sparked off a price war with the two leading brands in frozen vegetables, Birds Eye and Seabrook Farms. Prices to retailers were cut by up to 60 cents per dozen, and Seabrook carried the war into Minute Maid's home territory by offering its concentrated orange juice for 5 cents a can if purchased with a Seabrook vegetable. As the *Frozen Food Age* retrospective on the industry remarks, "Fundamentally, the battle was lost before it began. Minute Maid had entered the fruit and vegetable field too late. Competitive brands were too deeply dug in" (p. 70). In 1957 Minute Maid capitulated, selling the rights to its Snow Crop fruit and vegetables to Seabrook Farms. But it was Minute Maid's key market, frozen orange juice, that attracted most attention.

As the country's leading producer of frozen citrus juice concentrates, Minute Maid accounted for 20% of industry capacity and 15% of sales. Snow Crop held a further 15% of industry capacity. As a result of an FTC complaint, Minute Maid divested itself in 1960 of the frozen orange juice production facilities acquired from Clinton Foods. In the same year, Minute Maid merged with the Coca-Cola

Company, which had, shortly before, launched its Fanta orange drink (see chapter 9). This merger, the FTC noted in 1962, "eliminated as an independent firm an innovator that was willing to try new products, new processing techniques, and new packaging methods" and "brought to an end any rivalry that existed or might have developed between the Coca-Cola Co. and Minute Maid" (FTC 1962, p. 124).

Later Developments: 1960–1986

Throughout the 1950s, a small number of companies that had entered the industry in its early days retained their strong share position, building their first-mover advantage via heavy brand-promotion activity. By the end of the decade, high absolute outlays on advertising had become crucial to building a major position in the retail segment. Most new entrants aimed to enter, and confine themselves to, a particular niche of the market, and all but a few remained small.

Over the next quarter-century, the dual structure of the industry remained in place. The number of firms has increased from less than 300 in 1960 to over 1,500 today. The scale of the industry has grown enormously; retail sales alone accounted for about $14 billion in 1985. Nonetheless, a small number of highly visible, well-promoted brands dominate retail sales. The smaller producers concentrate on supplying products to the majors, selling to the nonretail sector, or selling within special retail categories at the local or regional level. However, underlying this continuity, a number of major structural changes have impinged on the pattern of industry leadership.

• As the size of the industry and the range of frozen food categories expanded, some of the firms that entered small, new segments of the market in its early days have grown with the market to become some of today's leading firms. The most notable example is C. A. Swanson & Sons, which introduced the "TV dinner" in 1953, and Stouffer Foods, which began producing frozen entrees in the same year.

• The pattern of entry set in the 1950s, whereby entrants began small and stayed small, was sometimes broken. The last entrant to rapidly establish itself as a leading seller in an established market segment— other than through an acquisition—was Pillsbury, which in 1962 introduced its Green Giant brand into the frozen vegetables area.

Following a failed attempt to enter the market some years before, the company hit upon a new approach, offering prepared frozen vegetables (i.e., the vegetables were combined with a seasoned butter sauce). The new category succeeded rapidly, at a time when branded frozen vegetables were coming under increased threat from own-label suppliers. Pillsbury responded to this challenge with a heavy, steady stream of advertising support and a continual flow of new product lines. Several leading retailers withdrew their own-label lines of frozen vegetables, and by 1970 a pattern emerged that has remained stable ever since: in regular frozen vegetables, own-label products account for over half of all sales, but their share in prepared frozen vegetables remains very low.

• Although market growth attracted a large number of major food processors into the area, few followed Pillsbury's strategy. The other majors that have entered in recent years did so by acquisition. All three leading firms in the highly concentrated prepared meals segment were acquired by food industry leaders: Campbell acquired Swanson in 1955, Nestlé acquired Stouffer in 1973, while Banquet, owned by RCA, was acquired by ConAgra in 1980. By 1985, the three majors had over 80% of sales in the segment (which accounted for annual sales of around $4 billion, as compared with $13 billion for frozen foods as a whole).

• Continuing competition between the majors accentuated the dual structure of the industry, as majors returned to increased reliance on small "coprocessors" (subcontractors) for their supply of product. General Foods has moved strongly in this direction; its current philosophy is that production should be dropped in favor of coprocessing wherever product can be bought in more cheaply than it can be produced in-house. The role of General Foods is seen as being that of contributing what is described in the trade press as the "marketing magic" associated with the Birds Eye brand.

• Some of the "Big Eight" that dominated the market in the 1950s still enjoy a major presence (Birds Eye, Minute Maid, Seabrook Farms, Simplot). Others have survived in spite of ownership changes. (Stokely-Van Camp sold its PictSweet brand to United Foods, now one of the top names in frozen vegetables. Stokely was later bought by Quaker Oats, which sold the canned vegetable business to Oconomowoc, a Wisconsin canner now known as Stokely U.S.A., which markets under the Stokely brand.) Libby exited from the market, selling its frozen food interests to Winter Garden, another of the Big Eight of the 1950s.

Current Structure

Overall, the degree of concentration in the U.S. frozen food industry as a whole appears very modest by international standards. This, however, reflects the fact that different firms dominate different segments, in striking contrast to the picture found in the other countries described below. The structure of the U.S. market is one in which high levels of concentration within various segments, combined with a differing pattern of market leadership across segments, produces an overall level of concentration that appears relatively low.

The major segments and their 1985 value shares are shown in table 8.2. In the largest segment, frozen prepared meals, the three leading firms account for about 80% of total sales (table 8.3). Even within this segment, some further specialization is evident: almost all of Campbell's sales are of complete dinners, whereas almost all of Nestlé's sales are of single-dish products. In the frozen vegetables sector, two brands dominate: Birds Eye (General Foods) and Green Giant. In

Table 8.2
Segment shares in the U.S. frozen food industry

Segment	1986 retail sales ($ billions)
Prepared meals (complete dinners)	2.8
Prepared meals (single dishes)	0.9
Other prepared foods (including pizzas)	1.4
Vegetables excluding potatoes (regular)	1.3
Vegetables excluding potatoes (prepared)	0.5
Potatoes	0.7
Meat and fish	1.0

Table 8.3
Market shares in frozen prepared meals in the United States

Firm	Share, 1987
Campbell Soup Co. (Swanson, Le Menu)	~40%
Nestle (Stouffer, Lean Cuisine, etc.)	15%–20%
ConAgra (Banquet)	15%–20%

frozen potatoes, the Heinz subsidiary Ore-Ida accounts for about half of retail sales. Ore-Ida is strong both in retail and nonretail; its two major competitors, Simplot and Lamb-Weston, concentrate almost exclusively on the nonretail sector.

The most striking feature of this pattern of segmentation in the U.S. market relates to the evident difficulty market leaders have experienced in broadening their scope across segments. Minute Maid's early difficulties in moving out of its frozen juice specialty have already been noted. General Foods experienced similar difficulties in frozen potatoes, a market long dominated by an early entrant: Ore-Ida, acquired by H. J. Heinz in 1965, still retains a 47.5% retail share in spite of the appearance of many new entrants over the years. Birds Eye finally abandoned its attempt to build up a presence in that segment in 1985.

The appearance of this segmented pattern is consistent with the theory. Whether or not it constitutes an equilibrium pattern depends inter alia on whether the advertising incurred in one segment carries over effectively in supporting a firm's brand image in another. If such advertising spillovers are very weak, each segment can be treated as an independent market. Entry to the top of any segment is unattractive at equilibrium simply because it entails heavy incremental advertising outlays.

But if such advertising spillovers are strong, then cross-entry by market leaders to new segments would become less costly, and a segmented configuration would collapse. This alternative assumption is plausible a priori, and so it is interesting to ask whether the mechanism implicit in the model tells the whole story. One recent U.S. case is of interest, in that it suggests an additional reason for the continued segmentation of the U.S. industry.

The case in question relates to the battles between Stouffer and Sara Lee in the 1970s. By the early 1970s, Stouffer was the leading "quality" producer of frozen prepared meals, while Sara Lee was the market leader in frozen baked goods. Stouffer entered the frozen baked goods segment in the early 1970s, with an advertising campaign that invited customers to "try a delicious alternative to Sara Lee." Sara Lee retaliated by launching a new twelve-item line of frozen entrees within the segment dominated by Stouffer. The competition proved too costly to maintain; within a few years, both companies withdrew their new offerings (Sara Lee in 1975, Stouffer in 1979).

8.3   Frozen Food in the United Kingdom

In this section, we turn to the very similar pattern of development followed within the U.K. industry in its early stages, and we remark on the more recent erosion of concentration in the industry as own-label products came to compete with increasing effectiveness against leading brands.

The First Phase

Although small-scale quick freezing was initiated by several U.K. companies in the 1930s, the manufacture of consumer-size packs of frozen foods for national distribution through the retail trade was pioneered by Birds Eye in the immediate postwar years.[14] Birds Eye Foods Ltd. was incorporated in 1938, with Frosted Foods Ltd. holding 35% of the shares. Frosted Foods Ltd., incorporated in the United Kingdom earlier that year, was 85% owned by Frosted Foods Inc., the U.S. subsidiary of General Foods. In 1943, Unilever became the major shareholder in Frosted Foods Ltd., and four years later it bought out the minority shareholders, and the name of the company was changed to Birds Eye (Holdings) Ltd. (This led to the unusual situation whereby the leading Birds Eye brand is owned by General Foods in the United States, but by Unilever in the United Kingdom.)

With its ownership of the Frosted Foods patent rights and strong links with Unilever subsidiaries (Macfisheries, Bachelors Peas Ltd., Poulton and Noel Ltd.) as sources of supply, Birds Eye rapidly expanded throughout the late 1940s and 1950s. As in the United States, the early development of the market was limited by the lack of retail display space and the inadequacy of distribution channels. The retail market remained very small up to 1956; over the next five years, however, it grew at a rate of 36% per annum; from then on, until the mid-1970s, growth continued at a more modest rate (around 10% per annum).

It was during the crucial period of rapid growth of the 1950s that Birds Eye achieved a strong leadership position in the industry. Its strategy focused on the building up of a strong national distribution network, with its raw materials largely supplied by other Unilever

---

14. Monopolies and Mergers Commission 1976, Commission of the European Communities 1976.

subsidiaries. Its distribution was undertaken by another Unilever subsidiary, S.P.D. Ltd., a general distribution company whose refrigerated transport division acted solely for Birds Eye. As for retailer displays, Birds Eye persuaded two suppliers, Prestcold and Frigidaire, to design and market an open-top display cabinet in 1953–1954 and thereafter sought new business only with retailers that installed such cabinets. Birds Eye did not, however, normally provide cabinets to retailers.

By the end of the 1950s, Birds Eye accounted for 80% of total sales value[15] of quick-frozen foods in the United Kingdom. By then, however, the rapid growth of the market had begun to attract a stream of new entrants.

The Second Phase

The new entrants were of two kinds. The majority were subsidiaries of major food manufacturers that aimed to carve out a small presence in some specialized niche of the frozen food business. Two of the new arrivals, however, aimed to challenge Birds Eye across the board. Their experience offers some striking parallels with that of the second tier of leading firms in the U.S. industry of the 1950s (i.e., those ranked fifth to eighth; see figure 8.1).

The first of the new challengers was the Swedish company Findus, which began operations in the United Kingdom in 1956 and was acquired by Nestlé in 1962. By 1968, Findus, which had set out to create a high-quality image to rival Birds Eye, had attained an 8% market share, but was trading at a loss. In that year it merged with Fropax Eskimo Foods Ltd., which had itself been formed by the merger of three frozen food producers. Following its rationalization of production and of the brand mix (eliminating all but the Findus brand), the company achieved an 18% market share.

The second challenger to Birds Eye was Ross Group, a long-established fish merchanting business that had entered the frozen food business in the 1940s. In 1959, Ross Group acquired Young's, a firm specializing in fresh and frozen seafood; by 1965, the two companies together accounted for about 5% of retail sales and 12% of catering pack sales. In 1969, Ross Group was acquired by Imperial Group as part of the tobacco firm's drive into the food and drink

---

15. Its volume share was probably closer to 60%.

sector—a drive that inter alia led to the acquisition of Smedley's, the canning specialist, whose frozen food business was integrated with Ross Foods, with the consequent phasing out of the Smedley brand in frozen food. The growing importance of Findus and Ross constituted the main threat to Birds Eye throughout the 1960s. The small niche entrants, though numerous, had relatively little impact, whereas the own-label market accounted for little more than 5% of sales at the end of the decade.

The asymmetry in strength between Ross and Findus, on the one hand, and Birds Eye on the other, stood in marked contrast to the stronger position enjoyed by Birds Eye's closest competitors in the United States. One result of this was that the tendency toward a competitive escalation of advertising expenditures was more muted in the United Kingdom. Birds Eye, devoting around 2% of its sales revenue to (classical) advertising, had an absolute level of expenditure so far ahead of its main rivals that Ross Foods's parent company (Imperial Group) reported to the Monopolies and Mergers Commission (MMC) that it "considered massive brand support, aimed at achieving dramatic increases in sales, to be far beyond the means of its frozen food companies, and it had never sought to answer Birds Eye's intensive advertising in kind. In 1973 Ross Foods virtually ceased advertising its retail packs since advertising was not making it more competitive in the retail trade" (p. 44). (The basic mechanism involved here—that reduced access to retail outlets reduces the incentive to escalate advertising expenditure—recurs in chapter 14 in our examination of the difference in experience between the U.S. and U.K. beer industries.)

Overall, Findus and Ross found it extremely difficult to overcome the first-mover advantage enjoyed by Birds Eye, and their growing share of the market was achieved at the cost of extremely tight margins. By the early 1970s, the pattern of price competition had settled down to one of clear price leadership by Birds Eye in the retail sector. Evidence given by the companies to the Monopolies and Mergers Commission in 1976 indicated that neither Ross nor Findus could afford to overprice Birds Eye at retail, given the strong image of Birds Eye products. Moreover, both companies were operating on such thin unit margins that it was almost invariably worthwhile for them to price up to Birds Eye's level. The outcome was that Birds Eye's price changes were closely followed by its two main rivals. Birds Eye, in an effort to maintain share, however, tried to hold price rises below the rate of increase of food prices generally. Birds Eye's return on capital employed, as estimated by the MMC, fell from 22.2% in 1967 to 15.9% in 1974 (for manufacturing industry as a whole, the rate of return over the same period rose from 12.0% to 17.4%).

If Birds Eye's profits were falling, however, its main competitors were faring worse again. The Commission summed up its comparison by remarking: "Findus and Ross Foods have consistently achieved lower returns on capital employed (on an historic cost basis) than has Birds Eye. The low profitability of Ross Foods and Findus is due, in part, to the cost advantages derived by Birds Eye from economies of scale in distribution, advertising and selling expenses" (MMC 1976, p. 60). In 1974, for example, while Birds Eye's return on capital stood at 15.9%, Findus earned 8.9% (frozen food only), while Ross Foods earned 4.3% (all operations). By the early 1970s it had become clear that the challenge to Birds Eye's position offered by Ross and Findus was a limited one. Unilever (via Birds Eye, and the very small Tempo company) retained a 60%–61% share of total sales, as against 18% for Findus and 8% for Ross.

Despite their well-developed distribution system,[16] both Ross and Findus faced considerable difficulty in obtaining display space in retail outlets. In January 1974, Ross Foods's market research data indicated that the Ross brand was represented in only 31% of grocery outlets, compared to 51% for Findus and 71% for Birds Eye.[17] The outcome of these events was that Ross began to focus, from the early 1970s onward, on the nonretail sector. A new but growing segment

---

16. Both Ross and Findus had succeeded in building up a national distribution system throughout the 1960s. By the early 1970s, Ross Foods operated primarily via its own two national distribution centers and twenty-five regional depots (though some of its sales were made via nine frozen food wholesalers by way of an exclusive franchise arrangement). Findus sold most of its output through Alpine Refrigerated Deliveries Ltd , which it owned jointly with J. Lyons & Co. Like Ross Foods, it also used franchise distribution arrangements with wholesalers to deal with areas not covered by its own system.

17. Retailers would often choose to carry only two lines—and Birds Eye was almost invariably one of the two. The introduction of a retailer's own-label would endanger the carrying of Ross or Findus, rather than Birds Eye. Partly for this reason, both companies had begun, by the early 1970s, to try to build up a significant presence in own-label sales. The difficulty involved in acquiring display space led both Ross and Findus to offer special arrangements to retailers. Ross Foods had about 8,000 refrigerated cabinets on free loan to retailers in the mid-1970s; these were lent on condition that they were used exclusively for Ross products. Findus offered free cabinets in order to gain entry to new retail outlets; it also operated a scheme with retail chains whereby it provided one cabinet free out of every eight installed, in return for a certain percentage of display space.

of the U.K. market was developing as consumers installed home freezers and purchased relatively large "home freezer" packs, usually from specialist outlets.[18] Ross's advertising, from 1974, was largely targeted toward this submarket.

The advertising expenditures of the "Big Three" during the 1970s illustrate the differences between their respective strategies: In 1974, Birds Eye's expenditure on advertising and sales promotion activities as a percentage of total sales stood at 3.6%. The equivalent figure for Ross Foods was 2.1% (almost all aimed at its new offerings for the home freezer submarket) and about 0.5% for Young's, Ross's sister company. Findus, too, decided to cut back on advertising in the early 1970s; advertising and sales promotion fell from 2.1% in 1973 to less than 1% in 1974.

Thus, the pattern of competition during the 1970s between Birds Eye, on the one hand, and Ross and Findus, on the other, closely parallels the competition between first- and second-tier producers in the U.S. market during the 1950s (figure 8.1). While small firms focused almost exclusively on the nonretail market (even Ross and Findus expanded in that area), the difference in structure between retail and nonretail segments began to harden. In 1974, Birds Eye estimated that its overall *volume* share in the U.K. market had fallen from 60% in the late 1950s to 49% in 1970 and 35% in 1974. In the retail market, however, in 1974 it still retained a volume share of 42% and a value share of over 60%. Birds Eye's value share in the catering submarket was probably less than 30% at the same period (MMC 1976, p. 19).

The Third Phase

The major trend that has shaped the market between the mid-1970s and the mid-1980s was the rise of retailers' own labels. Food retailing in the United Kingdom is highly concentrated, with a handful of major chains accounting for the larger part of food sales. The emergence and growth of these major retailing groups, led by Sainsbury's,

---

18. This growth of home freezer ownership might have been expected to stimulate the growth of freezer centers (specialist retail outlets selling larger packs). These outlets had represented, even in the mid-1970s, a relatively easy port of entry for the smaller firms. In fact, the number of freezer centers stabilized at around 1,000 in the mid-1970s, and from then on the centers found themselves under increasing competitive pressure from the major retail chains as the latter offered an ever widening range of products.

Marks and Spencer, and Tesco, has been accompanied by the increasing strength of their own-label products relative to leading brands. Own-label sales of frozen food accounted for a mere 6% of retail sales in 1972; by the mid-1980s, it accounted for 35%. By the latter period, the largest of the retailers' own brands had sales equivalent to those of leading manufacturers (Sainsbury's, with over 10% of the market, outsold both Ross and Findus).

This growth in own-label sales, above all, put pressure on the market leaders from the 1970s onward. By 1987, Birds Eye's share had fallen to just over 25% of total retail sales. It nonetheless remained strong across all segments, yielding its leading position in only one area (frozen potatoes, where international market leader McCain had a strong position). Findus suffered most heavily over the decade, slipping from second position to a clear third, while Ross maintained its 8% share. The Big Three did not yield their positions easily. Birds Eye maintained its high advertising levels in an attempt to preserve its brand image vis-à-vis increasingly prestigious own-labels, while attempting to constantly introduce new products, particularly in newer, high-value-added niches. As in the U.S. market, though to a dramatically lesser degree, the leading brands have fared better in these high-value-added areas; in frozen prepared meals, for example, Birds Eye retains a 37% share of retail sales (table 8.4).

At the other end of the product spectrum, the market leaders have fared less well. In the core product area of frozen vegetables, own-label now takes almost half of total sales, while Birds Eye's share has fallen to little over a fifth (table 8.5).

The decline in sales has left the majors in something of a dilemma regarding advertising expenditures. Given the externalities enjoyed by the major retailers, whose own-label products are highly visible

Table 8.4
Retail shares in quick frozen foods in the United Kingdom

	Market share (%)	
	1972	1987
Birds Eye	60	25
Ross	8	8
Findus	18	4
Own-label	6	35

Source: EEC 1976 and figures supplied by Unilever.

Table 8.5
Market shares by segment in quick frozen foods in the United Kingdom, 1987

	Prepared meals (%)	Frozen vegetables (%)
Birds Eye	37	21
Findus	9	1
Ross	12	9
Own-label	20	49

Source: Unilever.

to their huge clientele in the absence of any advertising support and have become increasingly well regarded vis-à-vis leading brands, what response is open to the majors in the face of declining sales? The advertising-sales ratio, which stood at around 2.5% in the late 1980s, showed no sign of falling, in spite of the weakening position of branded goods. Individual companies, however, had reacted in very different ways during the decade. Birds Eye's response was to maintain its traditionally high advertising-sales ratio. As its market share fell, its share of industry advertising also declined: in 1978, it accounted for 71% of total frozen food advertising; in 1984, its share of industry advertising fell below one half for the first time (to 42%). Findus, in contrast, responded to a very substantial decline in its market share by trying to maintain advertising levels and retain its traditionally strong image with consumers. Despite falling to third position in sales, it continued to rank as the second largest advertiser and even outran Birds Eye in certain categories during the 1980s.

The catering segment of the market, which accounts for only one-fifth or so of total frozen food sales in the United Kingdom, declined slowly in relative importance from the mid-1970s to the mid-1980s. Birds Eye's share of the catering segment remained small, while Ross still retained a major presence. Findus decided to quit the segment completely in the early 1980s.

An Interim Summary

At first glance, the U.S. and U.K. markets both appear to share a relatively low level of concentration when compared with the other markets studied here. This apparent similarity in structure, however, dissolves on closer examination. The origin of the low overall level of concentration in the United States can be traced to the fact that market leadership differs sharply across segments; concentration within segments is relatively high. In the United Kingdom, the low level of overall concentration reflects quite a different phenomenon: the steady growth of retailers' own labels has gradually eroded the position of the market leaders across the board.

Thus, the recent history of the two markets has differed rather sharply—a fact to which we return at the end of the chapter. On the other hand, the early history of these two industries shows a remarkable similarity of experience. In each case, a new and steadily growing market both attracted a wave of new entrants and stimulated a number of leading firms to escalate their advertising outlays. This process came to a head as middle-tier firms found it increasingly unprofitable to vie with the industry leaders in creating successful retail brands. The process ended, in each case, with the emergence of a relatively clear division between a group of leading brands, and the others.

8.4   Frozen Food in France, Germany, and Italy

In this section, we turn to a group of countries in which the market developed later: by this juncture, experience gleaned by leading firms in the U.S. and U.K. markets may have played a major part in influencing the rather different pattern of events. The beginning of the modern frozen food industry in much of Continental Europe can be traced to the early 1960s, when both Unilever and Nestlé (Findus) began operations in several countries. In Italy, Nestlé remained unchallenged until 1969, when Unilever entered with its Langnese-Iglo brand and mounted a vigorous advertising campaign under the slogan "Let's take frozen food seriously." Within a year, the two companies had pooled their interests in Italy and Germany by way of a joint venture, in which Unilever held a 75% stake and Nestlé a 25% share. During the 1980s, Unilever bought out Nestlé's interests. Under the terms of this agreement, Unilever retained the Findus brand name in Italy, where the brand was relatively strong, and Nestlé agreed not to sell under the Findus label for a five-year period (1986–1991) within Germany, where Unilever markets under its own Langnese-Iglo brand.

The exception to this pattern of events arose in France, where the frozen food market was relatively slow to develop. Following an unsuccessful early attempt to enter via the ice cream market, Unilever remained inactive in the market for some time, and Nestlé built up a strong leadership position that it still enjoys. Although these events preempted any escalation of advertising outlays akin to that found in the United States and the United Kingdom, they did not protect the new market leader, in either case, from later losses of market share to medium-size firms. The extent to which this occurred, however, was quite different in each country.

Italy

In Italy, the success of later entrants to the market was relatively limited. In the retail market, Unilever has followed a strategy of high, consistent advertising, which has allowed it to retain a strong position across all categories. A wide gap exists between Unilever's advertising level and that of its nearest competitors. The divergence of experience between the market leaders and the remaining firms is, as in most other countries, more evident in the high value added prepared meals sector. Unilever's share of total retail sales stood around 60% in the late 1980s; in frozen prepared meals, it stood at 75%.[19]

Unilever's main competitors include a number of early entrants that began producing in the late 1960s and early 1970s: Surgela (now owned by Italgel), Arena (now S.I.P.A. Arena), and Brena. During that period Findus still had a share exceeding 85% in an extremely small market (8,400 tons in 1965, as opposed to 320,000 tons in 1987). The strategies of these early entrants varied widely. Arena focused

---

19. At the other end of the spectrum, Unilever's position in the low-value-added frozen vegetables segment appears at first glance to be relatively strong: Unilever retains a 60%–63% share in this segment. It is helpful, however, to distinguish two subdivisions in this market, between which the pattern of competition differs greatly. The first relates to sales of the traditional small pack (carton) of frozen vegetables; this business is dominated by leading brands: Unilever, Surgela, Arena, and Brena. The second relates to sales of large (1-kilo) bags, which retail at two different price levels. Leading brands in the area (Unilever's Iglo brand and the French brand, Bonduelle) retail at prices per kilo about 20%–25% less than the traditional small pack. The less established brands of small sellers typically retail at around 40%–50% less, per kilo, than the small pack. It is in this latter (kilo bag) area of the market that Unilever faces the most serious competition, given the very large price differential that must be carried by its brand image in the segment.

Within the meat and fish submarkets, too, certain segments are extremely price competitive. In meat, for example, the hamburger segment remains broad and sensitive, and Unilever retains a strong share. The same is true in coated fish products, such as fish fingers. In basic frozen fish fillets, however, its position is relatively weak.

its attention on the frozen poultry segment, and its major strength is still in that area. Surgela, on the other hand, set out to offer a broad range of frozen foods from the outset. None of these firms, however, succeeded in establishing a position commensurate with Unilever's in the retail market. The catering market, which accounts for one quarter of total sales, is the domain of medium-to-small firms. Unilever ranks fourth in the segment, behind three medium-size companies. The own-label segment, meanwhile, remains unimportant in the Italian market. The only major retailer with a long-standing own label is Esselungha, which introduced its brand in the 1970s.[20]

Germany

Unilever's relatively strong position on the Italian market contrasts with its much weaker position vis-à-vis its main rivals in the German market. This difference is at least partly due to the greater role played in Germany by medium-size domestic producers, whose main strength lies in the catering area—but whose products are also sold at retail, where they have in some cases succeeded in establishing a strong market position. (Nonretail sales account for 47% of total sales in Germany and 32% in Italy.)

Unilever remains a clear market leader within the retail area, where its share stands at around 35%, while its three major rivals each have a share in the 10%–17% range. Its most important rival, Bofrost, is a private company whose founder began by selling farm produce, and which grew to the point where, by the mid-1980s, it operated a fleet of 1,500 refrigerated trucks in a national distribution network. Within the high value added ready meals segment, Bofrost is now the leading seller (see table 8.6).

Unilever's second rival in the retail segment is Eisman, a company owned by an agricultural cooperative, which manufactures ice cream and frozen pastries. It buys in its other frozen food lines from a number of sources, including Hansa Tiefkühlmenu. The last of the "Big Four" in retailing is the Oetker Gruppe, a widely diversified German food firm with a strong quality image. Unlike Bofrost and Eisman, it operates only on the retail market. It is the only company

---

20. Several retailers, however, launched own labels during the 1985–1987 period. Both they, and Esselungha, buy in their supplies from small producers.

Table 8.6
Market shares in frozen prepared meals in Germany (including nonretail sales)

Rank	Company	Market share (%)
1	Bofrost	26
2	Iglo (Unilever)	17–20
3	Eisman	16–17
4	Oetker	10
5	Hansa Tiefkühlmenu	8

Source: Company interviews.

besides Unilever that offers a full range of frozen food items at retail and is, in this sense, Unilever's main rival.

The catering market attracts both medium- and small-size firms; there is a small prepared meals segment, in which medium-size firms are prominent (table 8.6), but 95% of catering sales consist of basic commodity products (frozen vegetables, etc.), and here small firms play an important role. Many small firms specialize narrowly in particular lines, which they sell in the catering segment via brokers.[21] The own-label sector has, until recently, been relatively small. However, Germany's leading food retailer, Aldi, has now achieved a share of 20% for its own-label frozen food within its own outlets, and this is seen in the industry as indicating a serious potential threat to the leading brands in the long run. The most striking feature of the German market, then, is the way in which firms have built up a substantial position in the low-advertising, price-sensitive catering sector and have successfully built on this position to establish themselves as major rivals to Unilever on the retail market.[22]

---

21. Some small firms supply their product directly to leading firms: in frozen French fries, for example, where the leading international brand (McCain) has 40% of sales, its main rival Stoever sells both under its own label (Agrafrost), while also producing for Oetker, as well as for own-label sellers. The third firm in the segment, Scheekamp, produces for both Bofrost and Langnese Iglo.

22. Indeed, of Germany's six leading frozen food firms apart from Unilever, three confine themselves exclusively to the large catering sector. Gerbrüdde Bratzler, a private company, began as a caterer supplying prepared meals (to airlines, etc.) and subsequently moved into the frozen food area. Apetito, also a private company, was for a period owned by the major international catering group AEA. Hansa Tiefkühlmenu has wide interests in catering, with specialist ranges for institutional, industrial, and general food service. It also markets a range of items designed for the retail market, which it explicitly presents as a high-quality, low-cost alternative to the major brands.

France

Unilever first entered the French frozen food market by way of the closely related ice cream market, as it did in several other European countries. In the case of the French market, however, its ice cream venture proved a failure and it withdrew from the market in 1964. During the 1960s and 1970s, the French market developed slowly. The canned food industry, already in decline in many countries, remained very strong in France, and a wide variety of prepared meals became available in canned form. Many canners chose to freeze (less fresh) foods as an alternative to canning them, and the image of frozen foods suffered for a time. On the other hand, leading canners such as Bonduelle could develop well-regarded frozen food lines on the strength of a long-established brand image in canned foods.

It was only in 1970 that Unilever reentered the market, in a relatively slow and tentative manner, operating by way of its Belgian subsidiary. It was not until 1978, with its acquisition of the ice cream maker Motta, that it reestablished itself as a major presence in the market. Throughout the 1980s, its main focus was on building a successful operation in the ice cream market, and its frozen food interests played a secondary role.

Against this background, Nestlé faced much weaker competition from Unilever within frozen foods. Nestlé entered the market in the 1960s by way of the ice cream sector, purchasing the Gervais business.[23] Nestlé built up its position in the frozen food industry as the market developed slowly through the 1960s and 1970s, in competition with the leading canning companies, which remain among its main competitors today. Nestlé's main competitor in the French market is the ice cream maker Ortiz-Miko. The third-largest producer is the leading canned goods producer, Bonduelle, whose market share slightly exceeds that of Unilever.

8.5   Concluding Comments

The main aim of this chapter has been to explore the idea that a simple mechanism precludes the persistence of a fragmented structure

---

23. Which is now part of the BSN-owned Gervais-Danone, though Nestlé retains the Gervais brand for ice cream.

within advertising-intensive industries. The notion that a qualitatively distinct mechanism, involving the competitive escalation of advertising outlays, is at work in these industries represents a central theme. The evolution of concentration in the frozen food industry offers a clear illustration of this mechanism at work, and it also serves to illustrate the emergence of dual structure in industries of this kind.[24] It has been widely noted that many food and drink industries are typified by this twofold division of firms into high-advertisers and nonadvertisers. Within the theory, as noted in chapter 3, such a configuration emerges as an equilibrium outcome, once setup costs are low and some fraction of buyers have a relatively low degree of responsiveness to advertising outlays. Beyond these general features of equilibria, however, the simple static model employed in chapter 3 is relatively uninformative. As to the dynamics of industry evolution, it leaves matters open. A wide variety of dynamic stories, consistent with the model, could be formulated; their results, however, would depend delicately on the assumption made in regard to firms' beliefs about the eventual size of the market and the strategies of their rivals.

The cases examined here can be interpreted plausibly, if rather loosely and informally, as corresponding to two special polar cases. Within the United States and the United Kingdom, where the market first developed, a middle tier of firms suffered very low profits throughout a critical phase, as they vied for survival at the top end of the industry. Such actions may easily be rationalized by positing that the eventual winner will achieve long-run profits sufficient to

---

24. One feature of the frozen food industry that might seem to make it a rather special case is that the period of rapid expansion in sales in the United States and the United Kingdom coincided with a general upsurge in national television advertising. To what extent might the experience of this industry be no more than an artifact of that general movement? There are good reasons for believing that this line of argument is ultimately unconvincing. The experience of the frozen food industry mirrors the experience of a range of other industries that underwent the same pattern of development prior to the advent of television: for example, see the cases of soft drinks, biscuits (cookies and crackers), and soup. Most tellingly of all, the evolution of dual structure in the frozen food industry coincided with the decline of the canned vegetable industry. The latter, within the United States, had been one of the most heavily advertised products at the turn of the century, and the industry had evolved a clear dual structure closely analogous to that of the frozen food industry. The advent of television advertising coincided with its decline to commodity status.

The experience of the U.S. frozen food industry during the 1950s was not an accident of the "television age," but merely the most recent example of a long-existing phenomenon.

cover these losses. In other words, this intermediate phase of the industry's history has something of the character of a bidding game or a war of attrition in which firms accept short-run losses at the margin equal to the expected long-term gains to be achieved by winning.[25]

Nonetheless, such a game has a clear "prisoner's dilemma" character. If some way could be found of signaling who the eventual winners will be, losses by all parties could be avoided by moving immediately to the equilibrium configuration. It is arguable, at least, that this kind of learning is relevant to an understanding of the very different experience of the German and Italian industries. In both cases, the two established multinationals avoided an escalation of advertising outlays, while no domestic middle tier of firms emerged to challenge them at first. Indeed, insofar as domestic firms came to the fore, they did so by way of a slow accretion of reputation in the nonretail sector.

The difference in experience between the United States and the United Kingdom on the one hand and the Continental European markets on the other extends to several other industries. In each case, the product was first established in the United States and the United Kingdom, and the market developed only later in France, Germany, and Italy. In several such cases (notably pet food and RTE cereals), the prior success of the multinational brands generated a sufficiently strong signal to deter any major challenge from indigenous producers in the industry's early days. In such cases, the reputation of the multinational firm(s) may of itself be sufficient to allow it (them) to establish a leadership position without any costly escalation of advertising outlays. It is clear, at least, that first-mover advantages may play an important role in determining the dynamics of these interactions. It is to this topic that we turn in the next chapter.

---

25. Various games with this character are familiar in the recent literature. See Tirole 1989, for example.

9

How History Matters

9.1 Introduction and Summary

An idea that has attracted widespread attention in the recent industrial organization literature is that the presence of first-mover
advantages may exert an important influence on the evolution of
industry structure. The role of such strategic asymmetries within the
theory was explored in chapter 3, where it was pointed out that results
in this area are far from robust, and outcomes may depend in a
sensitive fashion on the details of the model used. For that reason,
this chapter is concerned, not with the testing of predictions, but
merely with illustrating a number of special cases arising within
the general theoretical framework.

The ideas explored here are those described in section 3.6: a first
mover may spend more on advertising than would be the case under
strategic symmetry, but may thereby succeed in relegating an equally
efficient late entrant to a weak second place. It may be unprofitable
for such a later entrant to attempt to achieve parity with the leading
firm at the top end of the market, and its advertising efforts may be
correspondingly muted. One major difficulty in investigating such
effects empirically is that it is often hard to identify the presence of
sharply defined strategic asymmetries of this kind—and it is rarer
still to find cases in which the pattern of advantage differs in a
clear-cut fashion from one country to another, thus permitting a
comparative analysis. Within the present set of industries, there are
only three cases in which these conditions are met, and these three
cases form the subject of this chapter. In the first two cases, it is argued
that the clear structural differences found across countries can indeed

be traced to the presence of first-mover advantages. In the third instance, clear structural differences also exist across countries, but here there are two possible explanations for these differences between which we cannot discriminate.

The first case is that of prepared soups. Here, the Campbell company had a clear first-mover advantage in the United States, and it has retained its leadership. Campbell's main rival, Heinz, is a weak second, and it has for long played a major role in supplying retailers' own-label products. The U.K. market is very similar to that of the United States in terms of its state of development, the composition of demand across categories (canned versus dried), and so on. But in the U.K. market, it was Heinz that entered first; when Campbell's entered the U.K. market, Heinz was already well established. The U.K. industry today is a virtual mirror image of the U.S. industry. Heinz plays the leading role, while Campbell's is a relatively weak second in the canned soups category, with strong interests in supplying retailers' own-label products. In the United States, Campbell's success is in part attributed to being the low-cost producer; in the United Kingdom, Heinz is identified as the low-cost producer whose pricing policy effectively shapes the pattern of market shares. In each case, it seems compelling to assume that these cost advantages are endogenous, with first-mover advantages as the exogenous influence driving the pattern of industry leadership. The presence of scale economies in production will merely accentuate a tendency toward concentration generated by competition in advertising outlays (see chapter 3), while leaving the market leader with an apparent cost advantage. This case appears to offer an unusually clear illustration of the way in which first-mover advantages may drive a significant wedge between two leading firms even in the absence of any important difference in their intrinsic efficiency levels.

The second industry examined here is the margarine industry. Here, a sharp contrast in respect of first-mover advantages exists between the European countries and the United States. In Europe, two of Unilever's parent companies, Van den Berghs and Jurgens, jointly established an early leadership position, and Unilever has enjoyed a clear dominant position within each of the European markets ever since. In the United States, on the other hand, a series of legal restrictions on margarine production and marketing hampered the growth of the margarine market until the 1950s, and the U.S. market remained relatively small up to that time. A number of leading food firms had each begun margarine production on a small scale by that period, however. When demand and output surged dramatically from the 1950s onward, a number of firms developed more or less in step with each other, and no single firm has achieved a dominant position.

A third case of interest arises in the soft drinks industry. In the United States, the development of the market has been driven for over a generation by a competitive escalation in advertising outlays between the Coca-Cola Company and Pepsico, which enjoy a rough parity in the dominant cola segment. In contrast to the United States, where the overall level of concentration in the soft drinks market is extremely high, the four European markets have a much lower level of concentration and (much) lower advertising-sales ratios. To some degree, this disparity may be attributable to the relatively small size of these four markets (the disparity in size between the U.S. market and the others is unusually wide in this instance). Indeed, such an interpretation is consistent with a widespread belief in the European industry that future growth in European markets will bring the industry closer to the U.S. pattern, in which a small number of heavily advertised national brands dominate the market.

A second feature that may help to explain the disparity of structure between the U.S. market and the other markets studied here relates to a (historical) first-mover advantage enjoyed by the Coca-Cola Company over its main rival Pepsico in these latter markets. This has apparently led to a much more muted approach to advertising competition, in contrast to the United States, where a competitive escalation of advertising outlays between Coca-Cola and Pepsico has fundamentally influenced the development of the market. On the basis of the evidence presented here, however, it is not possible to assess the relative influence of these two factors in determining the observed cross-country differences in the structure of the soft drinks market.

9.2 The Soup Market

The United States

Campbell began operations in 1869 in the form of a partnership established to can a wide range of food products. (The company's current name, the Campbell Soup Company, dates from 1922.) Its introduction of canned soups[1] dates back to the invention in 1897 by one of the company's chemists of a simple technique for producing condensed soups, which became the company's main product. Campbell established the market for condensed canned soup on the basis of a heavy magazine advertising campaign combined with a low-price policy and soon became the leading soup producer. It acquired its main rival, Franco-American, in 1921, and so reached a market share of over 80%. Campbell's major competitor thereafter was the Heinz company, which sought to establish its position on the basis of heavy advertising linked with promotional deals and an unusually widespread and expensive sales network. In the early years of the century, Heinz's total selling costs exceeded one-third of its sales revenue. In spite of these efforts, Heinz failed to significantly erode Campbell's share, and it subsequently switched strategy, focusing on supplying soup for retailers' own-label sales; it became the leading seller in this segment.

Given Campbell's continued dominance in the canned soup market, the main development in the U.S. industry in recent decades has concerned the (slow) growth of the dried soup segment. The leading seller in this segment is the major food conglomerate Lipton, which acquired a small Chicago-based dried soup maker, Continental, in 1940. For many years, dried soups received little advertising support, and their share in the soup market remained small. More recently, however, they have been more heavily advertised, and they now account for one-quarter of total sales. Campbell, hitherto a negligible presence in the segment, began during the mid-1980s to rival Lipton in advertising newly launched varieties of dried soups. Following an unsuccessful launch at the beginning of the decade, Campbell launched a new ("Quality") line in 1985. Campbell's (measured media) advertising expenditure on soups in 1986 was $42.4 million, and $5 million of this was spent on the Quality line of dried soups. Lipton spent $16.9 million in advertising its dried soups in the same year, of which $4.8 million was devoted to its main line of dried soups, (Cup-A-Soup). (*Advertising Age* 1987). The current rivalry between Campbell and Lipton in this still-fragmented market segment has much in common with industries such as frozen food prior to the phase in which escalating advertising outlays led to a more concentrated structure (table 9.1).

---

1. The first half of this section draws on Connor et al. 1985.

Table 9.1
Brand shares in the U.S. soup market, 1986

Canned soups (%)		Dried soups (%)	
Campbell	82	Lipton Soup	22 ⎱ 32
Progresso	3	Lipton Cup-A-Soup	10 ⎰
		Radama Pride	9
		Oodles of Noodles	7
		Top Ramen	5 ⎱ 9
		Ramen Supreme	4 ⎰
		Campbell (Quality) <	4

Source: Euromonitor.
Canned soups accounted for 75% of total sales, and dried soups for 25%. Own-label sales accounted for 10% of canned soup sales and 5% of dried soup sales.

The United Kingdom

Heinz established an initial lead in the U.K. canned soup market in the 1930s, which it has retained by means of sustained advertising outlays. Until the 1950s, its main rival was a U.K.-based firm, Crosse & Blackwell. Both Heinz and Crosse & Blackwell sold ready-to-serve canned soup, in contrast to Campbell's condensed product,[2] which had achieved popularity in the United States. In the late 1950s, Campbell entered the U.K. industry with its standard condensed soups range. The initial reaction of the industry leaders, Heinz and Crosse & Blackwell, was to counter Campbell's entry by launching their own ranges of condensed soups. As advertising outlays in support of the rival brands of condensed soups rose, the combined sales of the three firms' condensed offerings rose to a peak of 30% of all canned soup sales.

At this point in the process, Heinz realized the weakness of this strategy: by inducing consumers to switch to a condensed product, they were effectively easing Campbell's difficulty in switching U.K. consumers out of their established ready-to-serve segment. Heinz thereafter shifted strategy dramatically: in a move much admired in marketing circles, the company altered its price structure, selling its condensed offering at half the price of ready-to-serve. Apart from its obvious direct effect on Campbell's position, this move had the more

---

2. Campbell's condensed soup is prepared by adding an equal volume of water before heating; ready-to-serve soups simply require heating.

important secondary effect of undermining the image of the condensed category, making it seem an inferior product. The move effectively eroded the position of condensed soups within the U.K. market; and although they now sell at rough parity[3] with ready-to-serve soups, the condensed category has never recovered a substantial market share. Both Heinz and Crosse & Blackwell later withdrew their condensed offerings.

Thereafter, both Campbell and Crosse & Blackwell vied for market share with Heinz. The advertising-sales ratio for canned soups stood at about 3% in the early 1970s, with 90% of this advertising being undertaken by the three market leaders. Heinz, with a market share of just over 60%, accounted for just over 58% of total advertising. Campbell, with a 1973 market share of 12%, increased its advertising expenditure during the early 1970s; between 1968 and 1973 its advertising increased from £247 million to £359 million, the latter figure constituting 6% of its sales revenue in that year. Crosse & Blackwell, with a 1973 market share of 8%, began to spend less on advertising during the early 1970s; in 1973, it spent £134,000, which was just over one-third of Campbell's expenditure.[4] From that stage onward, the pattern of market shares in the canned sector remained fairly stable. By the mid-1980s, Heinz had a share of about 58%, Campbell had about 12%, and Crosse & Blackwell, 9%. Various specialist soups had much smaller shares (led by Baxter's with 3%), while own-label sales accounted for 15%.

Just as Heinz plays a leading role in supplying own-label products in the United States, Campbell plays a similar role in the United Kingdom, producing both condensed and ready-to-serve products for leading retail chains. Campbell is the single largest producer of own-label canned soups and accounts for just under half of total

3. The rough price parity that is believed in the industry to correspond to a more or less stable market share pattern is defined as follows: Heinz's standard offering is a 15-ounce can of ready-to-serve, which retailed in U.K. supermarkets in 1989 at about 31 pence. To maintain parity, Campbell pitches its standard offering, a 10-ounce can that produces 20 ounces in prepared form, at about the same price.
4. The relative degree of success achieved by Campbell and Crosse & Blackwell in vying for the number two slot in the industry turned not only on their respective advertising strategies but also on their respective product offerings. In spite of the weakness of the condensed category, Campbell nonetheless gained considerably from the fact that its offering was different from that of Heinz. Retailers could easily be persuaded to stock Campbell as the second brand on this basis, whereas Crosse & Blackwell competed for shelf space with own-label ready-to-serve products.

supply. Other suppliers of own-label products include Crosse & Blackwell and a handful of own-label specialists.

The dried soup segment of the U.K. market is also dominated by three firms. The market leader, Bachelors (now owned by Unilever), achieved a strong initial position in the segment in 1968 by introducing a dried soup with a relatively short preparation time (5 minutes as opposed to 20). In 1970, Bachelors had a 50% market share in the segment; its main rival was the U.K. subsidiary of an American company, CPC International, which marketed dried soups under the Knorr brand. Having faced severe competition from Bachelors throughout the 1960s, Knorr soups recovered during the 1970s by way of intensive advertising outlays. Over the same period, the Nestlé company, having had limited success with its Maggi brand, launched a new brand, Chef, and escalating advertising outlays between Chef and the two market leaders brought the advertising-sales ratio for dried soups to 12% by 1972.[5] These three firms have continued to dominate the segment, though Nestlé, having acquired Crosse & Blackwell, now markets its dried soups under that name.

9.3   The Margarine Market

As noted above, the development of the margarine market in Europe, where Unilever successfully built an early leadership position, differs sharply from that of the United States, where the market developed relatively late and a number of major food firms operated on a more or less equal basis before the takeoff in the industry's growth from 1950 onward. In what follows, we look at the events underlying the development of the European markets (the details for individual European markets and for the Japanese market will be found in appendix 9.2). We then turn to the evolution of the U.S. market.

The European Markets

In 1870 Holland was the leading butter exporter in the world. Most of its exports went to England, where industrialization was well

---

5. 1972 advertising outlays were £869,000, while the value of retail sales stood at £11 million.

advanced and where most of butter consumption was supplied by imports. In the early 1870s, the Dutch butter wholesaler Jurgens began to manufacture margarine, initially following a process developed by the French research chemist Mège Mouriès. The process involved the combination of two inexpensive ingredients (skimmed milk and beef tallow) and offered the possibility of producing a relatively cheap butter substitute. Within a few years, several Dutch firms were active in the new industry. Among them were the Van den Berghs company, to whose owners Jurgens had shown his initial product and who had sent representatives to Paris to study the Mouriès process. The technology developed rapidly in the early years; beef tallow was replaced with its derivative, "oleo"; and in the course of time vegetable oils came to replace these animal fats as the basic raw material. The newly developing industry suffered a severe setback in the depression years of the late 1890s. With excess capacity in the business, a wave of price cutting ensued, and many manufacturers faced financial difficulties. This was especially true in Germany, where Van den Berghs had begun manufacturing in 1888. In the wave of difficulties that ensued, Van den Berghs acquired several rival manufacturers. Nonetheless, Van den Berghs continued to produce on a smaller scale than Jurgens. But at the turn of the century, Van den Berghs achieved considerable success on the German market with a new product, Vitello, based on a patent taken out by a German chemist. The new product, manufactured at Van den Berghs's German factory, was technically superior to rival offerings, and the company supported it with substantial advertising outlays. Van den Berghs's output rose about sevenfold between the mid-1890s and 1906. Between 1904 and 1906, the company responded to sagging sales by sharply raising its advertising outlays. The German margarine manufacturers had agreed to keep in touch with each other to avoid a mutually damaging escalation of advertising outlays, but Jurgens was unwilling to bind itself to any agreement; in 1906, in an attempt to counteract Van den Berghs's success with Vitello, it raised its outlays dramatically, supporting its "Solo" brand with a wide range of promotional devices. Between 1904 and 1906, advertising outlays increased more than threefold. The favored media were wall posters, enameled plates in shops, and cards.[6] By 1906,

---

6. In Rotterdam, at the same period, special show-cases began to appear on the main street to display advertising posters.

the two companies had rough parity on the German market,[7] but profits had declined relative to their 1904 levels.

Many of the industry's difficulties in its early years could be traced to fluctuating conditions in raw material supplies, and these difficulties appear to have weighed more heavily on smaller firms. Holland, the home of the industry, had seventy factories in 1880, but following two periods of recession this number had declined to twenty-eight by 1912. From the last decade of the century onward, American meat packers had become a major source of beef fat for the industry and had entered margarine production and export in their own right. A worsening situation in respect of raw material prices in 1907, combined with low butter prices, stimulated a pooling arrangement between Van den Berghs and Jurgens in 1908, which was to operate in both the German and U.K. markets.[8] Throughout the 1920s and 1930s, continued periods of recession in the European margarine industry led to phases of price cutting. This was particularly so in the United Kingdom, where Lever Brothers had entered the industry with government support during the First World War. Prior to the war, the only sizable U.K. firm competing with Jurgens and Van den Berghs was the Maypole Dairy Company, which Jurgens acquired in 1927. In 1929, one of the largest amalgamations in European history combined Jurgens, Van den Berghs and Lever Brothers as Unilever. Since then Unilever, through its U.K. subsidiary Van den Berghs and Jurgens, has dominated the U.K. margarine business and has played a leading role in all other European countries. Currently, Unilever (via its local subsidiary) holds a retail market share of 50% in the United Kingdom, 52% in West Germany, and 40%–45% in Italy.[9]

The U.S. Market

The development of the U.S. margarine market during the first half of the century was seriously hampered by a series of legislative mea-

---

7. Van den Berghs's output stood at 720 tons per week as against Jurgens's 620 tons.

8. The initial agreement did not include any constraints on advertising outlays. In 1911, Jurgens enjoyed a rise in profits, and rather than share this with Van der Berghs, they pumped the gains into increased advertising outlays. A revised agreement in 1913 incorporated limits on advertising.

9. The Italian market developed only recently in the immediate postwar period; it was essentially developed by Unilever. Unilever also has a strong presence in Japan. The Japanese market is unusual in that the retail sector is relatively small; for details, see appendix 9.2.

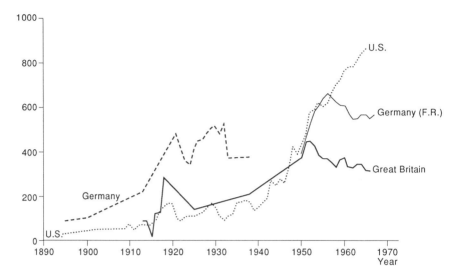

Figure 9.1
Annual margarine production in the United States and Western Europe, 1895–1965.

sures that held back its development until the 1950s. Western European production exceeded that of the United States by a factor of about five in 1938; from the 1950s onward, however, U.S. consumption rose rapidly, reaching almost half the combined production of all Western European countries by 1965 (see figure 9.1).

The limited development of the U.S. market up to the 1950s can be traced directly to a series of policy measures designed to protect the interests of the dairy industry. A detailed account of these measures is set out in van Stuyvenberg 1969, chapter 7. The process began with a federal law of 1886, which required that the product be sold only under the name "oleomargarine" and which introduced license fees on manufacturers, wholesalers, and retailers as well as a manufacturing tax of 2 cents per pound. More far-reaching measures were introduced in 1903 and 1931, with the imposition of substantial taxes on any margarine that was colored to resemble butter. These measures were rescinded by the House of Representatives in 1949 and by the Senate in 1950. The abolition of associated legislation at the state level occurred from the 1940s onward; one state (Wisconsin) retained restrictions up to 1967. The early 1950s, however, represented an effective turning point in the industry, and the coincidence of the easing of legislation with the rise of television advertising made the 1950s a key period in the industry's development.

The beginnings of the U.S. margarine industry can be traced to the 1870s, when the growth of the meat-packing industry led to the availability of vast quantities of animal fats as a raw material. Though the first meat packers to enter the business were Boston firms, the industry's center of gravity quickly shifted to Chicago, and within a few years virtually all U.S. margarine production was in the hands of five Chicago meat packers (Armour & Company, Swift, Nelson Morris & Company, Hammond and Company, and John Cudahy). By 1877, U.S. firms had begun to export margarine to Holland and later to other European countries.

By 1900, only one major producer other than the meat packers was in operation (Jelke). In the 1930s, however, two important new producers entered: Kraft and Standard Brands. Both were general food firms, and for them, as for the meat packers, margarine was a secondary product that could be distributed conveniently alongside their other offerings to the retail trade. Another early entrant to the U.S. market was Unilever's main rival in the related soap industry, Procter & Gamble. While all other U.S. manufacturers employed animal fats, Procter & Gamble had successfully launched a vegetable-based cooking fat under the brand name "Crisco." Underwritten by substantial advertising, the Crisco brand achieved considerable success, and this attracted the interest of Jurgens in the U.S. market. On the eve of the First World War, Jurgens entered into a joint venture with Spencer Kellogg, the leading linseed oil crusher in the United States, which led to the launching of yet another margarine on the U.S. market—where the new venture met with stiff competition from the fifty competing brands. At around the same time, Lever Brothers also entered the U.S. market by way of a joint venture with a Philippines-based supplier of coconut oil.

Today's three leading firms—Unilever, Kraft, and Procter & Gamble—were already active in the U.S. market in some form in its early days. At that time, though a sizable number of brands were on offer, the industry was highly concentrated. In 1935, the four leading sellers accounted for 79% of the total value of shipments. By 1947, the figure had declined to 64%. Over the crucial decade of the 1950s, two trends emerged. First, the rapid growth in the size of the market led initially to a fall in concentration: the four firm sales concentration ratio fell to 39% by 1954. Second, escalating advertising outlays by the industry's leading firms began to establish a number of strong national brands, and from 1954 onward, the four-firm sales concentration ratio began to rise steadily, reaching 50% in 1963.

What distinguished the U.S. experience from that of the main European countries, however, was the presence, on a more or less equal footing, of three major food firms, which enjoyed similar opportunities in launching and establishing new varieties and brands. In summing up the differences in U.S. and European experience, Tousley (1969) notes that the U.S. industry has outdone most European markets (the United Kingdom being an exception) in the variety of products offered and in the rapidity of introduction of new varieties. Moreover, in contrast to the European markets, where the majors typically operate in both the high-price segment and in competition with own-label products at the low-price end of the spectrum, American manufacturers have tended to abandon the low-price end of the market to own-label products. No brand in the U.S. has succeeded in achieving a share comparable to that enjoyed by Unilever in European markets. Despite subsequent entry and changes in ownership, the three main sellers in 1986 enjoyed retail shares in the range 9%–20% by the mid-1980s, while a fourth seller, Land O' Lakes, had a share of 4%.

9.4 The Soft Drinks Industry

The soft drinks industry in the United States offers one of the most clear-cut examples of the way in which a competitive escalation of advertising outlays by leading firms can mold the evolution of industry structure. Yet this process, which is so central to the development of the U.S. industry, is either highly muted or completely absent in European markets. In what follows, we first look at the evolution of structure in the U.S. industry before turning to a comparison with European experience.

Preliminary Remarks

The industry, as defined here, excludes both mineral water (see chapter 11) and pure fruit juice. Apart from a few special categories noted below, it coincides with the widely used market definition of carbonated soft drinks. The classification of market segments preferred in the industry varies across countries, but in the interest of uniformity we shall here work in terms of a rather crude division, which represents a useful lowest common denominator: colas, clear lemonade, and a residual category of fruit-based drinks. This last category includes two quite different kinds of product: the lemon-lime subsegment is the preserve of the majors, while the orange-juice subsegment includes both offerings by the majors (Coca-Cola's Fanta) and those drinks with a higher orange juice content that are more traditional in many European countries (France's Orangina is probably the most widely known example). Some countries have product categories lying outside this group (root beer in the United States, lactic drinks such as Calpis in Japan, and concentrates in the United Kingdom); these are classified separately.

The nature of the soft drinks market hinges on a dichotomy between two kinds of operation. At the risk of oversimplifying, it may be roughly described as follows. Almost all producers of carbonated soft drinks manufacture their product not from fruit or other primary inputs but from a syrup or concentrate produced by a specialist firm. Syrups or concentrates in many cases constitute a basic commodity product, and the firms purchasing such inputs produce drinks under their own brands; such firms are often small to medium-size firms operating in a local or regional market. At the other end of the spectrum stand the major multinational groups, of which the Coca-Cola Company is the archetype. Specializing in the manufacture of a soft drink concentrate, these firms typically license a net of local and regional bottlers to produce and market their range of drinks over a specified area. Here, the brand belongs to the upstream producer of the concentrate; though the advertising and marketing of the brand may be carried out jointly, control over its franchisees allows the concentrate producer to extract the rent earned on its brands.[10]

The Evolution of Structure in the United States

The origins of the U.S. industry can be traced to a bottling innovation in the mid-nineteenth century. Prior to that, carbonated drinks were

---

10. The two kinds of operation just distinguished differ substantially in respect of their setup costs. Statistics for the United States distinguish the bottling operation (SIC 2086) from syrup manufacture (SIC 2087); but in the light of the features of the U.S. industry just noted, economists have chosen in the past to identify the m.e.s. for the industry with that of syrup manufacture, SIC 2087 (see Connor et al 1985). This is the convention we have followed in chapter 4. It may, however, be argued that the lower level, associated with SIC 2086, is more appropriate in certain contexts. On either estimate, however, the setup costs in soft drinks manufacture are relatively modest.

widely sold in pharmacies (drugstores) where flavors and carbonated water were mixed on the premises for immediate consumption. With the introduction of manually operated filling and bottling machines, thousands of local bottling works began to offer carbonated soft drinks under their own brands to a local market.

The drugstore image left its mark on the industry, however. Coca-Cola was first introduced as a remedy for various ills, but soon developed into a popular drink in the drugstore trade; the name Coca-Cola was copyrighted in 1886. Pepsi Cola, invented in the 1890s by Caleb Bradham, a North Carolina pharmacist, was designed specifically as a cure for dyspepsia. Bradham applied for a trademark in 1902, the year in which he began to issue stock and market the product in earnest. He spent $1,900 on advertising in that year—an extremely large sum relative to the revenue earned on the limited sales of 8,000 gallons. The advertising campaign was extremely successful; five years later sales stood at 100,000 gallons a year, and in 1907 Pepsico hired a New York advertising agency to promote its product.

Coca-Cola, however, became even more successful than Pepsi; with its characteristic bottle and its imaginative advertising campaigns, it became the leading American soft drink in the first two decades of the century. Pepsi Cola, meanwhile, ran into serious financial difficulties following an unlucky speculation by Bradham on post-World War I sugar prices. Bankruptcy and a change of ownership followed. The company's fortunes recovered during the Depression years, however, as it took advantage of the easy availability of used twelve-ounce beer bottles to offer twice the volume of cola at the same 5 cent price that rivals charged for the standard six-ounce size. Underwritten by a large-scale advertising campaign,[11] the strategy reestablished the company's fortunes, and the dynamics of the soft drink industry from that point forward turned largely on the rivalry between the two market leaders.

Pepsi Cola took some time to live down the image of the cheap alternative to Coke in the affluent postwar years, and its position advanced only gradually. Its periodic attempts to achieve a significant improvement in its position relative to Coca-Cola have done much to shape the development of the industry over the past gen-

---

11. The campaign's centerpiece was an advertising jingle that, by 1940, outran the "Star Spangled Banner" as the most widely known tune in the United States.

eration. Every decade has seen a major initiative. In the 1960s, the company launched a highly successful advertising campaign under the "Pepsi Generation" slogan. By the mid-1970s, however, market research showed a poor level of brand awareness, but the results of "blind tasting" experiments appeared very encouraging. This prompted a new bout in what the trade press termed "the cola war" as Pepsico launched a new advertising campaign featuring blind tasting tests (the "Pepsi Challenge"). Coca-Cola responded with a series of advertisements questioning the tests' validity[12] and with substantial price cuts (most of these being followed by Pepsico). In 1985 Coca-Cola responded to what it saw as signs of an erosion of its market share by changing its formula in launching "New Coke." The new product met with a great deal of consumer resistance, and Pepsi's share advanced relative to Coke's. Coca-Cola responded by reintroducing the old formula "Coke Classic"; the net result was a substantial net gain in overall share for Coca-Cola.[13]

The shape of the industry over the postwar period has largely been determined by the rivalry between Coca-Cola and Pepsico in the large cola segment. The two companies regularly figure as numbers one and two in the league of top advertisers in the United States, and their combined share of the cola segment now exceeds three-quarters. The only other company that retains a significant presence in the cola sector is Royal Crown. Ranking fifth among the Big Six, Royal Crown Cola is the only cola maker that effectively competes with Coca-Cola and Pepsi. Royal Crown's strength in the late 1960s and early 1970s rested heavily on its position in diet cola, in which it was a leader (with a share equaling that of the diet versions of Pepsi and Coke for several years).[14]

Royal Crown's position in the market is akin to that of middle-tier producers in many other advertising-intensive industries in that its modest market share means that it can equal the absolute advertising outlays of its main rivals only by accepting an advertising-sales ratio

---

12. Consistently with the marketing adage that number one should never compare itself with number two, this had the effect of further increasing consumer awareness of Pepsi. As attitudinal research began to demonstrate this, Coca-Cola decided to drop all comparative advertising worldwide.

13. The combined sales of New Coke, Coke Classic, and Cherry Coke rose by 10% in nominal terms in 1985, as against a 5% rise for all carbonated soft drinks.

14. The combined market share of all Royal Crown's brands in the soft drinks market in the late 1960s was around one-third of Pepsico's figure, which in turn was two-thirds that of Coca-Cola (table 9.3).

Table 9.2
Market shares in the U.S. soft drinks market 1966–1975 (%)

	Market share (%)		
	1966	1972	1975
The Big Six	·		
Coke	33.4	34.7	35.3
Pepsico	20.4	19.8	21.1
Seven-Up	6.9	7.2	7.6
Dr. Pepper	2.7	3.8	5.5
Royal Crown	6.9	6.0	5.4
Canada Dry	4.2	3.6	3.4
Total Big Six	74.5	75.1	78.3
Other producers			
Small nationals and regionals	7.5	11.5	11.9
Supermarket private labels	.2	2.4	1.1
Shasta	.9	1.9	2.5
All others (small local firms)	16.9	9.1	6.2
Market size (billion cases)	2.91	3.68	4.46

Source: From C. Roland Christensen, Note on the Soft Drink Industry in the United States, Note 377–213. Boston: Harvard Business School, 1977. Used with permission.

so high as to drastically reduce profit margins. During the early 1970s, Royal Crown more than doubled its advertising expenditure from $5.3 million in 1970 to $14 million in 1975—a figure two-thirds that of Pepsico and half that of Coca-Cola. Its underlying strength in the diet segment notwithstanding, Royal Crown's slow decline in share went on throughout these years (table 9.2).

Other Big Six Producers

The remaining three producers among the Big Six are all market leaders within their respective segments. Two of the three, Seven-Up and Dr. Pepper, strengthened their position vis-à-vis the two market leaders during the 1960s and 1970s (table 9.3). Just as Coke and Pepsi first established their positions among a sea of small local companies through heavy advertising in the early years of the century, so Seven-Up emerged from among 600 companies offering lemon-lime drinks in 1937, when the brand's name was introduced (replacing the somewhat less catchy earlier name, "Bib Label Lithiated Lemon-

Table 9.3
Market segmentation in carbonated soft drinks in the United States

Segment	Fraction of market (by volume, %)	Structure
Cola	63	Dominated by Coca-Cola and Pepsico, with Royal Crown a weak third.
Lemon-lime	12	Seven-Up is the market leader, with competition from Coca-Cola's Sprite and Pepsico's Slice.
Orange	7	Coca-Cola's Fanta is the only major brand, but it commands no strong price premium over own-label.
"Pepper"-type	7	Dr. Pepper is the leading brand.
Root beer	5	Several smaller national brands are of significant size (Hires, Dad's, A & W).

Lime Soda"). In its early years the company enjoyed the advantage of a medicinal image, fostered by its characteristic green bottle. But by the mid-1960s, this was identified as a factor holding back growth, and the company's advertising shifted direction to change the product's image. In the early 1970s, defying conventional advertising wisdom ("never use negatives"), the company began advertising heavily under the slogan "7-Up, the Uncola," in a move designed not only to establish leadership in the lemon-lime sector but to build up share at the expense of the much larger cola category. The move succeeded on both counts; the lemon-lime category advanced from 12% to 13% of total sales between 1970 and 1975, while Seven-Up's share also showed a modest advance (table 9.3).

The strongest gain in sales over the 1960s and 1970s was made by Dr. Pepper, whose share more than doubled between 1966 and 1975. Throughout the early 1970s Dr. Pepper's advertising level remained fairly static, though at a high level—around one-third of Pepsico's (Dr. Pepper's market share, on the other hand, was about one-fifth of Pepsico's at the start of the decade). Dr. Pepper's advance was in large part based on a highly successful strategy of broadening its distribution system by "piggybacking" on Coca-Cola's unrivaled net of franchised bottlers. The rules under which all the majors operate their net of bottling franchises are simple: the bottler undertakes not to bottle any rival product in the same soft drink category, and in return he enjoys territorial exclusivity over a specified region. In this way, intracategory competition is eliminated.[15] The Dr. Pepper company, with a product effectively in a category of its own, succeeded in the early 1970s in inducing leading Coca-Cola franchisees to carry Dr. Pepper also—first in New York, and then on Coca-Cola's home ground in Atlanta.[16] By the end of the 1970s, the pattern in the U.S. market was one of strong segmentation, with a single clear-cut market leader in each of the main noncola segments, and this pattern persisted during the 1980s (table 9.3).

The Role of Small Firms

Intense rivalry among the Big Six was accompanied by a slow but steady rise in their aggregate share. An intermediate group of small national and regional brands showed modest growth also; this group included several root beer brands (Hires, Dad's, etc.). Small local firms showed a steady decline, however, and their combined share of the market fell to 6% by the mid-1970s.[17] The decline of the smaller independents in part reflects the fact that many lacked the minimum efficient scale required for survival in a price-competitive market. Among franchised bottlers of major brands, a steady exit of the smallest operators has occurred over the past twenty years (Katz 1978, Boston Consulting Group 1987).[18] This exit has been overseen by the majors, which in some cases have arranged a program of mergers among the smallest units. In 1986, both Coca-Cola and Pepsico made major acquisitions of bottling companies; both companies will henceforth bottle and distribute about 30% of their U.S. sales.

---

15. This arrangement evolved historically as a response by the concentrate producers to the fact that high unit transport costs for bottled drinks necessitated the use of a large net of local bottling plants. In order to sidestep the capital requirements involved in building up such a net, the concentrate producers offered local bottlers territorial exclusivity. This arrangement also makes feasible the use of local advertising campaigns financed jointly by the majors and the bottler. In return, the concentrate producer requires that the bottler carries no rival brand of soft drink falling in the same category.

16. Much to Coca-Cola's chagrin, it would seem (Christensen 1977).

17. One firm to break from the mold in the 1970s was Shasta Beverages, a division of Consolidated Foods. Shasta avoided the concentrate producer/bottler split, producing drinks for direct delivery to both food stores and catering outlets.

18. Indeed, industry observers feel that the industry has now stabilized, with almost all the remaining bottlers working at m.e.s. Returns in this part of the industry are modest, as the price of concentrate and other parameters (advertising cost share, etc.) can be set to transfer rents to the concentrate supplier.

As for the small independents, their role in the U.S. market is severely restricted by two features of the soft drinks business. The first is the tiny size of the own-label sales; this amounts to a mere 1%–2% of total soft drink sales. The second feature working against small independents is that, while a very large nonretail segment exists, this segment is one in which brand awareness is not much less important than it is at retail.[19] Market shares in the food service (catering) segment are notoriously difficult to assess, but industry observers estimate Coca-Cola's share to lie between 60% and 90%, and the company's strength in this area is one reason for the limited success of minor brand colas (an interesting parallel exists with Kellogg's in the RTE area—see chapter 10).

Recent Developments

In 1986, however, a rapid and complex series of acquisitions produced a major consolidation in the pattern of ownership in the industry. The sequence of events began with the decision by the Philip-Morris Company to divest itself of the Seven-Up Company. Pepsico proposed to purchase the company, and Coca-Cola responded with a bid to acquire Dr. Pepper. The Federal Trade Commission voted in June 1986 to oppose both acquisitions. Pepsico did, however, acquire Seven-Up's international interests, a move that will strengthen the company considerably vis-à-vis Coca-Cola outside the United States.

In May 1986, Hicks and Haas, a Dallas-based investment firm, entered the soft drinks industry by purchasing a major stake in A & W Brands Inc., a leading root beer company. Later in the year, Hicks and Haas acquired both Dr. Pepper (in a joint arrangement with other investors) and Seven-Up's domestic interests. In the same year, the U.K. group, Cadbury Schweppes, whose Schweppes brand took second place to Canada Dry in the tonics segment, purchased both Canada Dry and the orange juice specialist Sunkist from RJR Nabisco, Inc. The overall result of these moves was a consolidation of the industry leaders into five major companies, Coca-Cola, Pepsico, Hicks and Haas, Royal Crown, and Cadbury Schweppes, which to-

---

19. A fast-food-chain customer is highly unlikely to know what brand of coffee is on offer, but is more likely to know whether he is offered Coke or a generic cola. Trivial though the point might seem, it has strong implications—in that the nonretail (catering) segment is an area in which unbranded substitutes are usually relatively strong.

gether account for 93%–94% of industry sales (see the market share table M.10, appendix 1).

Soft Drinks in Europe

The soft drinks market in the four European countries studied here[20] shows a sharp divergence of structure from that of the United States. As table 9.4 indicates, these markets are much smaller than that of the United States—the difference in size being much greater than in the case of the other industries studied. The level of concentration in the European markets is also much lower, as is the advertising-sales ratio. This suggests one obvious line of explanation, within the present theory. As we saw in chapter 3, industries with low setup costs, such as the soft drinks industry, may exhibit an increasing relationship between market size and (minimal) concentration levels, simply because advertising may become worthwhile only when the market

Table 9.4
The soft drinks market

	Volume of sales 1986 (billion liters)	Relative market size	Four-firm sales concentration ratio (%)	Share of cola segment (%)	Coca-Cola's share of cola segment (%)
France	0.9	0.02	64	33	80
Germany	4.0	0.08	57	40	75
Italy	1.1	0.02	—	—	over 80
Japan	2.9	0.06	88	33	90
United Kingdom	2.6	0.05	47	35	50 (Pepsi = 17)
United States	50.0	1	89	63	(*)

*Coca-Cola and Pepsico had similar retail shares in the United States, though Coca-Cola had a much larger nonretail share.

20. The soft drinks market in Japan does not afford an enlightening point of comparison, as its structure is heavily influenced by Japan's leading brewers (appendix 9.3). In contrast to the United States, Japanese breweries are permitted to distribute soft drinks alongside beer, and Japan's beer industry is dominated by four major brewers, who account for over 99% of domestic production—a fact that itself reflects a deliberate policy decision by the Japanese authorities in the postwar years.

reaches a certain critical size (see figure 3.5). Although this might seem a plausible reason for the observed difference in structure, a more detailed examination of the structure of the market suggests that a second factor may be relevant.

Table 9.4 shows the size of the cola segment and the share of Coca-Cola within that segment. In all countries, the size of the cola segment is smaller than in the U.S. market, while the share of Coca-Cola relative to Pepsi within the segment is much higher. The asymmetry in the position of Coca-Cola relative to its main rival derives from an initiative taken by the company during the course of the Second World War. Coca-Cola, pledging to put a Coke in the hand of every American serviceman overseas, won exemption from wartime sugar rationing and a level of government support that extended to building 100 overseas bottling plants. This episode appears to have been crucial in the postwar development of the cola market outside the United States. A substantial asymmetry between Coke and Pepsi was established in Europe, which has persisted ever since.

This strong asymmetry between Pepsico and Coca-Cola, allied with the small size of the European market, greatly diminishes the incentive for Pepsico to mount an expensive advertising campaign in European markets. The spillover effect of this for other market participants is suggested by a comparison with U.S. experience. In the United States, a virtual elimination of small independent producers has occurred, as the major national brands have come to dominate the market.[21] Within Europe, on the other hand, a substantial fringe of smaller producers continues to operate.

The experience of each of the European markets is described in appendix 9.3. Many industry analysts argue that these markets are in a state of transition and that, as market size increases, the structure will come to approximate more closely the structure of the U S industry. There appears to be some evidence for such an underlying trend, particularly in the case of the French market. On the other

---

21. It is true in many of the industries studied here that one result of the process of competition between the majors is the squeezing out of middle- and bottom-tier firms (see chapter 12 on coffee, in particular). What is unusual in the soft drinks market is the manner in which this tier of small firms has been in effect absorbed as bottlers to the majors. Viewed within the context of the theory, there is an obvious logic to this outcome, one that is directly analogous to the phenomenon whereby leading producers of branded goods at times buy in their product, so that they in effect sell the brand name (see chapter 8, on frozen food).

hand, the continuing asymmetry between Pepsico and Coca-Cola may slow any such trend.

9.5   Summary and Conclusions

This chapter illustrates some effects of first-mover advantages in advertising-intensive industries. In the soup market, we have seen how a reversal of first-mover status between the United States and the United Kingdom led to the appearance of industry structures that are virtual mirror images, with the roles of the two key firms reversed. In the margarine market, we have seen how the absence of the first-mover advantage that underpinned Unilever's dominance of European markets has been associated with the evolution of a much more fragmented market structure in the United States.

Finally, we have looked at the archetypal example of competition via escalating advertising outlays—the U.S. soft drinks market. The market differs sharply in structure from its European counterparts. While the dominance of Coca-Cola in Europe has led to a highly concentrated cola segment, the advertising-sales ratio in the industry remains much lower than in the United States, and the cola segment has not expanded to take such a large share of soft drinks sales. The noncola segments of the European markets remain large, and they support a substantial fringe of small and medium firms. Two factors appear to underlie this difference: the small size of the European market and the stong strategic asymmetry between Coca-Cola and Pepsico. It does not seem possible on the basis of the evidence presented here, however, to distinguish the relative importance of these two factors.

10

Endogenous Advertising Outlays and Brand Proliferation

10.1 Introduction and Summary

This chapter continues the theme of looking at special cases that arise within the general theoretical framework developed in chapter 3. Here, we turn to the case of the ready-to-eat (RTE) breakfast cereals industry. The RTE cereals industry was the subject of one of the most famous actions brought by the U.S. Federal Trade Commission during the 1970s, in what was generally seen as a crucial test case for a new approach to antitrust proceedings by the commission (see appendix 10.2). Consequently, the market has been the subject of intensive study by industrial economists, and Schmalensee's important 1978 paper on the determinants of concentration and profitability in the industry is one of the most widely read articles in the industrial organization literature. In this chapter, the RTE cereals industry is explored as another special case arising within the theory, and this analysis of the industry is compared with that of Schmalensee (1978).

The RTE cereals industry has two special features, and these two features underlie much of the analysis that follows. First, many observers have argued that the Kellogg company, the market leader worldwide, enjoys a first-mover advantage of the kind explored in the preceding chapter. In addition to this, the industry also exhibits a second distinctive feature. Each of the main manufacturers offers a wide range of product varieties or brands. (Kellogg's leading brands include Corn Flakes, Rice Krispies, Sugar Puffs, and so on.) Even though the U.S. market is dominated by a mere six firms, brand shares remain quite fragmented in the sense that all but a handful of the many varieties on the market have extremely small market shares. The dynamics of competition in the market turn primarily on the constant flow of new offerings—most of which will have a fairly short lifetime. A high proportion of advertising expenditure is devoted to supporting new products in the first year or so following their introduction.

This chapter is largely concerned with unraveling the roles played by two mechanisms in determining the equilibrium level of concentration in this industry. The first mechanism is the one emphasized in the present theory, as illustrated in the two preceding chapters: a process of competition in endogenous advertising outlays imposes a lower bound to the equilibrium level of concentration. Within this setting, as we saw in the last chapter, a first mover can exploit his advantage by setting a high level of advertising outlays. The second mechanism is a specific one whose operation rests on the particular characteristics of the RTE market just noted: this mechanism involves the first mover exploiting his advantage by entering so wide a range of products as to fill all available niches, thus preempting entry by later arrivals. This second mechanism is consistent with the present theory and can be developed as a special case within the general framework set out in chapter 3. However, it is also consistent with its contrary view, that advertising outlays can be treated as an exogenous sunk cost. This second mechanism forms the basis of the Schmalensee model. In terms of the present theory, *both* these mechanisms operate.

Does it matter which view we accept? As we argue in the final section, the policy implications differ sharply depending on which view is taken . In particular, a form of intervention proposed by the FTC on the basis of the FTC-Schmalensee model may be largely ineffectual, if the present theory is correct. How can we discriminate between the two views? In what follows, three arguments are developed that appear to lend strong support to the view that a process of competition in endogenous advertising outlays plays a central role in the RTE cereals industry, as the present theory suggests. On this view, the brand proliferation mechanism, though it may indeed have been an important contributory element in the U.S. market over the past thirty years, seems not to be the primary influence underlying the evolution of concentration. Before setting out these arguments, however, it is necessary to look a little more fully at the two theoretical views.

10.2   Some Theoretical Ideas

The Brand Advertising Model

Up to this point, it has been tacitly assumed that we can treat the advertising outlays of any firm as benefiting that firm's entire product range, even though any individual advertisement will more often than not be focused on a single product. It is now time to question whether this is always a reasonable assumption. One view of the RTE market holds that advertising in this industry should be thought of as supporting individual products (brands); in other words, a firm's advertising outlay for one of its varieties generates no spillovers that benefit sales of other varieties. This view is based in part on the observation that most RTE cereals are eaten by children, that the main channel of advertising used (in the United States, at least) is children's television, and that market research indicates that children are only aware of the brand (product) name, and not the manufacturer's identity. (Children are also, incidentally, said to display little brand loyalty, thus making it relatively easy to draw them away to newly launched brands via heavy advertising, often focused on current television characters or on "gifts" included in boxes.)

As against this view, it can be pointed out that most RTE cereals are *purchased* by adults, who are much more aware of the Kellogg name, say. It is arguable that the degree to which Kellogg's advertising carries over to the company's general image is very substantial. But for the moment, we focus on some implications of the brand advertising interpretation. What are the implications of this notion for the theoretical framework of chapter 3?

Brand Advertising within the Theory

To see how the brand advertising view fits into the theory, it is helpful to begin by thinking in terms of the model of section 3.5, in which products differ both in a vertical and a horizontal attribute. The vertical attribute can be identified with the advertising-generated product image, whereas the horizontal attribute can be thought of as corresponding to the different physical characteristics of the different RTE cereal products.

In modeling consumer tastes over the horizontal attribute, the intensity of preferences is represented by the slope of Hotelling "umbrellas" (see in figure 2.3). Steeper umbrellas correspond to a fuller degree of segmentation of the market. A fall in price, or an increase in u, is represented by a vertical shift in the umbrella. According as the umbrellas are steeper, a given reduction in price or increase in the value of the vertical attribute (product image) is less effective in drawing away consumers from adjacent products (segments).

It is useful to distinguish two polar cases. The first corresponds to the situation in which a given level of outlays $F(u)$ suffices to establish a common level u of the vertical attribute for *all* the firm's products. The opposite pole is that of brand advertising: in this case, expenditure $F(u)$ is needed to raise the image of any one product to level u.

Now in the latter case, how is the analysis of chapter 3 affected? The answer is that the formal analysis goes through exactly as before —the only thing that changes is the *value* of the lower bound to concentration. Since this bound depends on the degree to which advertising is effective in raising market share, the diminished effectiveness of advertising in raising market share in this setting simply means the bound will now be lower. There will in general be many equilibrium configurations corresponding to various concentration levels lying above that bound. This situation arises whenever we have a horizontal attribute: there are many possible configurations including concentrated configurations in which there are only a few firms, each with many products, and fragmented configurations in which many firms operate, each offering few products. The range of such configurations that will emerge as equilibria will depend, as usual, on the details of the model. Among the factors influencing this is the presence or absence of first-mover advantages: a first-mover advantage implies a strong bias in favor of concentrated outcomes in which the first mover monopolizes the market by means of a strategy of product proliferation. It is this mechanism on which the Schmalensee model focuses, and the mechanism can operate whether advertising outlays are endogenous or exogenous.

Exogenous Advertising Outlays and Brand Proliferation

Suppose we treat advertising outlays *per product* (brand) as exogenously fixed, so that a new entrant incurs some exogenously determined setup cost, defined to incorporate these advertising outlays. We may then imagine each product as a point on the Hotelling line, as before. But if one firm has a first-mover advantage and is free to enter many products, then it may be optimal for that firm to fill up the line with an array of products—leaving the gap between adjacent products small enough to render entry by a new producer unprofitable. In fact, a moment's reflection makes it clear that this gap can still be big enough to allow the first mover to earn positive (supernormal) profits, while still deterring entry. The higher the sunk costs a new entrant must incur, the higher can the incumbent's profits be, without inducing entry. This, then, is the argument developed by Schmalensee (1978), and it offers a possible explanation both for the high concentration in the industry and for the high profitability of the market leader.[1]

So, even if the lower bound to concentration implied by the present theory is inoperative, it is still possible to explain the high concentration of the industry by appealing to the notion that Kellogg has a first-mover advantage, which it exploits, not by way of preemptive advertising outlays *per se* (as in the case examined in the preceding chapter), but rather by way of a strategy of product proliferation designed to preempt available market niches that might provide a point of entry for rivals.

One final theoretical remark is in order. We noted in chapter 3 how the exogenous sunk cost view of advertising can be derived as a limiting case of the present theory, corresponding to a situation in which the advertising response function $F(u)$ becomes vertical beyond some ceiling level $\bar{u}$. Under these circumstances, the lower bound to concentration proposed by the theory goes to zero as market size becomes large, and the constraint on equilibrium structure implied by the theory becomes inoperative. All the interest now resides in the question of *which* equilibrium will emerge—and this is the focus of the Schmalensee model.

Discriminating between the Models

How, then, can we discriminate between the two views? In what follows, we will focus on three points that illuminate this issue:

(i) Brand proliferation has been a very salient feature of the U.S.

---

1. This argument was elaborated further in the course of the case brought by the FTC. It was argued that few new RTE products achieved a market share sufficient to support a single m.c.s. plant. Several costly product launches would be needed, and so the sunk costs faced by new entrants were correspondingly high—and this in turn meant that the profits that could be earned by the first mover were very substantial (see section 10.3).

market over the past three decades. However, the high levels of concentration in this industry are observed in all countries and can be traced in all cases to the industry's early days. The range of products offered at this stage was relatively narrow: in the United Kingdom, for example, a single Kellogg product (Corn Flakes) accounted for 68% of Kellogg's total sales volume in 1955 and 57% in 1970. This suggests that the origins of concentration in the industry might be sought elsewhere.

(ii) The early history of the industry offers some striking parallels with the experience of other advertising-intensive industries. A process of escalating advertising outlays appears to have played a central role in the United States, according to Scherer (1982). In the United Kingdom, this process is very well documented and offers a striking parallel to the evolution of the frozen food industry. This suggests that the primary cause of high concentration in the RTE cereals industry lies in a mechanism common to a wide range of advertising-intensive industries, and that the special features of the RTE cereals industry modify rather than replace this basic mechanism.

(iii) The two models differ in respect of the factor that is assumed to deter entry to the industry in spite of its high profitability. The present theory suggests that entry would precipitate an escalation of advertising outlays among incumbents and that this would erode the entrants' profitability. The product proliferation model suggests that the closure of available niches is the key to entry deterrence; within this model, if some deviant enters, no change occurs in the (exogenously determined) level of advertising outlays. It is argued below that the observed response of incumbents to new entry in the RTE market offers further support for the present theory.

These four themes underlie the discussion of the industries in the next section.

10.3 The Markets by Country

The RTE cereals market consists of two segments, whose relative importance varies widely across countries. The first segment consists of mainstream products of the cornflakes kind. These are made from a range of grains (mostly corn, oats, wheat; some rice, barley, and soy flour is also used) using several production techniques (granulation, flaking, shreddmg, puffing, and extrusion). Designed to be eaten uncooked with milk added, their use gradually spread, in most Western economies, at the expense of cooked cereals (porridge, etc.). Setup costs in this part of the market are relatively high.

The second market segment consists of muesli-type products. Mueslis are a traditional European product, a simple mixture of various grains with dried fruit, etc. As their production merely involves the mixing of various standard ingredients, setup costs in this sector are minimal, and nonindustrial production is common (some 1,000 health food stores producing their own mueslis supply a substantial share of German consumption, for example).[2]

Both the size of the total market and the relative importance of the two market segments vary widely across countries. Per capita consumption of RTE cereals is relatively high in the United States and the United Kingdom (over 5,000 grams per annum), is substantially smaller in France and Germany (200 grams and 400 grams), and is extremely low in Italy and Japan (less than 50 grams). The relative importance of muesli-type cereals also varies considerably: they form a very small but steadily growing part of the market in the United States and the United Kingdom; whereas in France and Germany they constitute 40% and 50%, respectively, of total consumption by volume.

As in the case of the frozen food market, the market for mainstream RTE cereals developed relatively early in the United States and the United Kingdom. The Kellogg company, established in the United States in 1906, is the clear market leader internationally. More than 40% of the company's assets are held outside the United States, and it operates twenty-two plants in seventeen countries. By the time the market began to develop in other countries, Kellogg had become a clear market leader in both the United States and the United King-

---

2. The sharp difference in setup cost between these two market segments might appear to afford an opportunity for a pairwise comparison of structure, with a view to isolating the impact of setup cost on structure (in the manner of chapter 12). However, it is not true of the RTE cereals market that the two segments are similar on the demand side. The age profile of consumers varies sharply between the segments, with muesli-type products being aimed heavily at a health-conscious adult segment, and mainstream cereals being directed much more heavily toward children. This leads, in itself, to a sharply different approach to the channels, style, and intensity of advertising in the two segments.

dom, and it enjoyed an extremely strong position vis-à-vis any indigenous rivals in the newly developing markets. The main focus in what follows lies in a comparison of the U.S. and U.K. markets. Appendix 10.1 describes the relationship between Kellogg, its main multinational competitors, and its indigenous rivals in the four remaining markets.

The U.S. Market

RTE cereals first appeared on the scene[3] in the late nineteenth century as a health food. Henry D. Perky's "Shredded Wheat" was an early success. Heavily promoted by its 55-year-old founder at the 1894 World Food Fair as the key to his own vigorous good health, the product achieved fame at home and abroad. In 1923, Perky's Shredded Wheat Company was acquired by the National Biscuit Company (later, Nabisco), one of today's Big Six in the U.S. industry (Kellogg, General Mills, General Foods, Quaker Oats, Ralston Purina, and Nabisco). Two of today's Big Six had their origin in Dr. J. H. Kellogg's sanitarium, where he developed various prepared cereals in the 1880s and 1990s. One of Kellogg's patients, C. W. Post, began to develop and market products of his own, and—realizing that the products' potential transcended the health food category—he embarked on a national advertising campaign. Post's endeavors led to the formation of a company that later became the Post division of General Foods. It was Dr. Kellogg's brother, W. K. Kellogg, who in 1906 founded the Kellogg Company.

A fourth member of today's Big Six had its origins in the then-dominant hot cereals industry, which had become relatively concentrated as a number of companies (which previously operated an industry cartel) merged to form the American Cereal Company, later Quaker Oats. Quaker entered the RTE market in 1905, when it acquired the assets of a small RTE firm. The other two members of the Big Six are firms whose primary interests lie in other markets: Ralston Purina and General Mills.

The success of the early entrants prompted a substantial inflow of new firms; the number of RTE producers "may have come close to

---

3. The U.S. industry is unusually well documented, thanks in large part to the FTC case (appendix 10.2). An excellent overview is provided by Scherer (1982), on which this section draws.

100 during the first decade of the twentieth century. From the available qualitative evidence, it would appear that the RTE market leaders of the 1970s pulled ahead relatively early in the game through the use of aggressive advertising and marketing techniques aimed at achieving a large nationwide sales volume" (Scherer 1982). In the case of Kellogg, as Scherer notes, "a third of the company's working capital was devoted to a full page advertisement in the *Ladies Home Journal*, which offered a free season's supply of corn flakes to any woman who persuaded her grocer to stock the Kellogg's product. In its first year, the Kellogg company distributed 4 million free samples."

Unfortunately, this crucial phase in the development of the U.S. industry is not well documented. (The equivalent phase in the U.K. industry, however, is more fully documented; see below.) The industry grew steadily at the expense of hot cereals until the early 1950s, by which time RTE sales accounted for over half of the breakfast cereals market. The share of hot cereals declined rapidly thereafter, and the segment is now very small. The volume of consumption of RTE cereals per capita began to reach a plateau from the end of the 1950s onward, and since then total volume has grown more or less in line with population. By 1987, 92.4% of U.S. households purchased RTE cereals, and the median number of packages in stock in a household was four.

Advertising levels in the industry are among the highest found anywhere. The advertising-sales ratio for the industry as a whole stood at 8.34% in 1986. The ratio is currently much lower than it was during the 1960s and 1970s. Ornstein (1977) reports advertising-sales ratios for 324 narrowly defined industries for 1967; RTE cereals rank second in this list, with a ratio of 18.5% (a ratio exceeded only by perfumes and cosmetics, etc.). The pattern of market shares for 1986 is shown in the Table 10.1. Kellogg, with a share of 41%, is about twice as large as its nearest competitors, a clear leader in a market where four firms (Kellogg, General Mills, General Foods, Quaker Oats) account for 90% of industry sales. Table 10.1 also shows the share of industry advertising by each of the four leading firms. As these figures indicate, Kellogg's advertising-sales ratio is substantially lower than that of its leading rivals—a pattern that commonly emerges in advertising-intensive industries (see chapter 8, especially figure 8.1).

Table 10.1
Market shares and shares of industry advertising outlays in the American RTE cereals industry, 1986

	Market share (%)	Share of industry advertising (%)
Kellogg	42	37
General Mills	24	30
General Foods	12	16
Quaker Oats	8	8

Sources: Euromonitor, Leading National Advertisers.

Brand shares are much more fragmented than are market shares. No brand had a share exceeding 6% in 1986, and the top twenty brands had a combined share of 61% (Euromonitor 1987). The total number of brands offered by the Big Six has grown steadily over time, from 26 in 1950 to 44 in 1960, 69 in 1970, and to about 100 by the mid-1980s (FTC, *In re Kellogg et al.*). Accompanying this growth has been a series of waves of new product introductions and an ongoing process of withdrawal of small brands. In the most volatile children's category, the ten top brands have retained their status for a decade, but a long tail of smaller brands cycle over time, with a typical lifetime of one to two years. A number of factors drive the pattern of new brand introductions. New methods in production have increased the range of shapes on offer. Market research tracks changing consumer preferences, leading to sequences of highly similar offerings by several majors in new growth categories.[4]

Companies' success in maintaining or increasing their market shares appears to be loosely related to the intensity with which they keep up the flow of new introductions to offset the otherwise slow decline in the share of their portfolio of brands. Analysts associate the weaker record of General Foods and Quaker Oats in the 1980s, for example, with their relatively slow rate of new product introduction, while

---

4. Several variants of Ralston Purina's CHEX, for example, have been targeted at a health nut taste combination. Ralston, General Mills, and Kellogg all introduced almond-type products in the 1980s. In the children's market, a number of majors—notably Ralston—have bought the rights to market cereals featuring television characters to market ranges of "short-life" cereals. The children's segment is characterized as a "fun and games" segment; free gifts are normally included in packages in this category, and market researchers remark on the low brand loyalty of children, who readily switch varieties in response to new marketing angles.

Ralston Purina's retention of its market share is seen as reflecting its steady stream of new products. On the other hand, a small number of long-established brands have retained a strong position for decades: Nabisco depends heavily on its Shredded Wheat, which has enjoyed a strong boost as part of recent trend toward healthy eating.

Setup Costs, Advertising, and Brand Shares

The costs incurred by a new entrant in RTE cereals have been analysed by Scherer (1982) following Stern (1966), Headen and McKie (1966), and FTC, *In re Kellogg et al.* Various studies indicate that efficient production processes require only a modest scale of operation, and that the minimum efficient scale of plant is determined primarily by the packaging operation. Economies of scale achievable in packaging in the 1960s, for example, persisted up to a scale of 50–60 million pounds per year, or 4%–6% of industry output at that time. The lack of important economies beyond this level of operation was consistent with the fact that the two leading firms, Kellogg and General Mills, both split their production among five plants at that date, while new plants constructed in the industry had capacity in the range of 40–60 million pounds per year.

One of the central arguments developed in the FTC's case against Kellogg et al. ran as follows: because of the market features just noted, the sunk costs involved in entering this market should be computed by reference to the simultaneous launch of a number of new products, sufficient to keep a single m.e.s. plant operating near full capacity. The advertising outlay incurred by firms in establishing and maintaining a new product is substantial. Scherer's (1982) estimates indicate that during the 1960s the fixed costs incurred in advertising a new RTE cereal brand in the first year of sales were of the order of $3.2 million. Outlays in the third year averaged $1.6 million. Thus the launch costs of a single brand over the first three years were around $5 million, or around 1% of annual industry sales.

Given the level of fragmentation in brand shares noted earlier, the *typical* newly launched product cannot reasonably be expected to capture substantially more than 1% of sales—many will fail. On the other hand, only those reaching something of this order are thought of in the industry as being viable in the long run, given inter alia the ongoing advertising support needed to support the brand. On this basis, a new entrant planning to operate efficiently in production would need to plan on achieving some four or five viable brands; the fixed costs incurred in launching and establishing such an array— on the optimistic assumption that all launches succeeded—would be of the order of 4%–5% of annual industry sales. If both the launch costs of a brand and the market share achievable by any brand (and so, in particular, the number of brands on the market) are regarded as exogenously given, this type of estimate would be appropriate and would appear to explain the limited degree of entry to the market.

In contrast to the foregoing type of argument, our present argument runs in terms of the notion that the estimates of advertising costs incorporated in the above calculation should be regarded as endogenous. While their current levels may offer a proximate explanation for the observed lack of entry, the ultimate explanation for observed industry structure lies in the operation of the same basic mechanism explored in the preceding chapter and the process of advertising competition that determined the equilibrium levels of these outlays.

Attempts at Entry

The pattern of industry leadership has been more or less settled for a generation. Over the same period, the fringe of smaller producers has had only limited success in retaining a role in the own-label and nonretail sector. Where new entry has occurred during the postwar period, it has been confined to a segment of the market where these problems were minimized: natural or granola-type cereals, which became fashionable in the 1960s and 1970s. These, like muesli, are relatively simple to produce, and the problems of achieving a viable scale in production were largely avoided.

This segment of the market was quite unexploited by the majors throughout the 1960s and early 1970s, by which time a number of very small firms had already achieved a substantial success in selling these new varieties. These first entrants, however, lacked the resources needed to market and distribute the product effectively and were rapidly followed by a wave of major food companies not hitherto involved in RTE cereals (see Scherer 1982). These included Pet Inc., Pillsbury, and Colgate.

This wave of entry was followed by a rapid response by the RTE majors: in 1973 Quaker entered with its 100% Natural brand, General Mills with Nature Valley, and Kellogg with Country Morning.

All three were supported by a large-scale advertising campaign, and the new entrants' market shares dwindled rapidly; that of Pet, the most successful, reached 1.8% of total RTE sales in 1974, but fell to 0.2% within four years. Pillsbury and Colgate withdrew from the market, and Quaker—the first of the majors to enter—became the leading brand in the segment with a 1.8% share of the overall RTE market.[5] The lack of success of small and medium-size firms in this low setup cost segment is mirrored by their equally limited impact in the nonretail (catering) segment and in the supply of own-label products.

The catering segment of the RTE market is unusual, relative to that of most food products, in that Kellogg not only strongly dominates its rivals in the segment, but it has succeeded in creating some degree of brand awareness, so that the RTE catering segment is more analogous in this respect to the soft drink industry than to say, frozen food. Kellogg's name is regularly featured in company logo style on hotel and restaurant menus, which describe the product not simply as "corn flakes" but as "Kellogg's Corn Flakes."

Own-label sales account for a mere 4% of the U.S. market. Virtually all of these sales come from one company, Ralston Purina. This rather unusual outcome reflects a number of strategic decisions by the majors in the market. Kellogg and General Mills both have a firm, publicly known policy of never supplying own-label products. In 1943, when three own-label producers operated, Kellogg acquired one of the three, the Miller Cereal Company, and switched its facilities over to the production of Kellogg's branded cereals. General Foods acquired another of the three, the Jersey Cereal Company, and, having continued private label business for some time, gradually ran down its scale of operation throughout the 1960s. The third of the private label suppliers, Ralston Purina, continued to operate a private label business alongside the sale of its own brands. As the sales of its own brands declined during the 1960s, Ralston offered its corn

---

5. The history of these natural or granola-type products suggests that the fringe of small producers associated elsewhere with the muesli sector may be preempted in the United States, if and when this segment of the market (currently negligible) begins to develop. Market research suggests that Americans are, by and large, fairly resistant to standard European-type offerings in this area. Although the best-selling U.K. muesli brand, Alpen, is available in the United States, its impact on the market has been small. By the late 1980s, Kellogg had developed a muesli-type product designed for American tastes as reflected in market research studies.

flakes—judged "equal or better than Kellogg's corn flakes quality" by a General Foods Technical Research group[6]—at a wholesale price 16% below Kellogg's.[7] As Ralston's share began to grow at Kellogg's expense, Kellogg replied with improved terms to wholesalers, finally reducing its wholesale price to equal Ralston's. Ralston in turn replied with a new price cut, this time bringing its wholesale price below Kellogg's by 10%.[8] At this smaller differential, the market stabilized, leaving Ralston earning satisfactory margins as sole supplier of own-label products and operating at a price differential such that the company captures a small but valuable segment of price-sensitive consumers (including a high proportion of adults buying for their own consumption).

The U.K. Market

The U.K. market is similar to that of the United States in many respects. Unlike most of the countries studied here, the market is relatively large (per capita consumption is around 6,000 grams/year, which is about fifteen times that of Germany, the next largest market). The market developed early and was largely shaped by the arrival of the U.S. majors in the early part of the century. Ready-to-eat cereals have for long dominated hot cereals, which now account for only 6% of 1985 sales revenue in the total cereals market. Within RTE cereals, muesli is a small but growing category, accounting for about 11% of RTE sales revenue in 1985.

As in the United States, only a handful of sellers are active: the four leading firms are the privately owned British company Weetabix, with a 1985 share of 17%, and the three U.S. majors, Kellogg, Nabisco, and Quaker, with 1985 shares of 49%, 8%, and 5% respectively. In own-label sales, which account for 18% of total sales, the most important supplier is Viota, a member of the Avana group, which specializes in supplying own-label food products generally. Branded products other than those supplied by the four market leaders, on the other hand, took less than 4% of 1985 sales, and the handful of companies making up this modest total are specialists in

---

6. Cited by Scherer (1982) from evidence in *In re Kellogg et al.*

7. 6% being retained as an enhanced wholesaler margin; the price differential to the consumer was 10%.

8. As Kellogg's margins became squeezed, its advertising levels were cut back. Scherer (1982) quotes this as an illustration of the Dorfman-Steiner effect.

the small but growing health segment (muesli, etc.) of the market (Jordans, Harmony Foods, and others). This segment has also favored the own-label suppliers, as it is a weakly branded sector: prior to its development, own-label suppliers had confined themselves to basic cornflakes and "bix" (own-label versions of Weetabix's basic offering).

The U.K. market mirrors that of the United States in having gone through a phase in which escalating competition between the majors was accompanied by a gradual shrinking of the fringe of small producers. Whereas, in the U.S. case, this process involved a direct conflict between Kellogg and the leading own-label supplier, Ralston Purina, the fortunes of the fringe in the U.K. market evolved almost purely as a by-product of advertising competition among the majors themselves—a theme echoed in many of the other industries studied here (see in particular chapter 12 on coffee and chapter 13 on beer).

The Evolution of Structure in the U.K. Market

RTE imports began to appear in the United Kingdom[9] at the turn of the century, and during the interwar years the market began to develop rapidly. By 1938, consumption levels, at around 900 grams/capita, stood at more than twice the present-day level for Germany. Kellogg had opened a London office in 1924 and had embarked on an extensive campaign to promote its products; in 1938 it switched from importing to domestic production. Quaker had set up a London agency in 1899 and had begun production in 1920. The Shredded Wheat Company Ltd. of Canada, now Nabisco, was formed in 1908 to handle imports of Shredded Wheat, which remains Nabisco's leading RTE product in the United Kingdom. The leading domestic producer, Weetabix, was formed in 1932 under the name of the British and African Cereal Co. Ltd.

The process of development of market structure can be divided into two key phases: the interwar years and the 1950s and 1960s. In the interwar years, Kellogg built up a very strong position in a small but steadily growing market. As the Monopolies Commission report of 1973 remarks, "Kellogg's buildup of its sales before the War was

---

9. This section draws on the Monopolies Commission Report of 1973, and on Keynote 1983.

achieved with the help of a high rate of expenditure on advertising and promotion. The ratio of advertising to sales was 12 per cent, 11 per cent and 17 per cent for 1930, 1931, and 1932, and from 1933 the percentage spent on advertising and promotion together rose from 20 per cent to a peak of 27.7 per cent in 1935, thereafter falling gradually to 18.2 per cent in 1939. Kellogg said that between 1936 and 1940 its sales by weight of cereals increased by 78 per cent" (p. 5).

The heavy expenditures incurred from 1935 onward bit heavily into Kellogg's margins, and Kellogg's ratio of operating profit to net sales was very low in 1935, 1936, and 1937 (1%, 2%, and 4% respectively). But as advertising began to decline during the late 1950s, the company's profits recovered, and with the opening of its U.K. factory in 1938, net returns jumped to 15% in 1938, 33% in 1939, 26% in 1940, and 34% in 1941. In the years immediately following the war, Kellogg's operating profits returned to a level of 30% by 1949 (Monopolies Commission 1973). Sacrificing short-run returns with a view to building up a strong brand image, Kellogg established a position of clear market leadership in the interwar years, a position that allowed it to command a substantial net rate of return, and the company entered the crucial era of the 1950s and 1960s as an unchallenged market leader, with somewhat over one-half of the total sales by volume.

The growth of the market in the interwar years had attracted an inflow of new producers, however. Kellogg's evidence (cited in MMC 1973, p. 5) described the industry as entering a new phase from 1948–50 onward, during which "a highly competitive market situation developed and Kellogg's ... faced an intensive struggle for market share with a number of manufacturers offering a wide range of cereal products." During the early 1950s, certain wartime restrictions on advertising still remained in force, and competition focused on a range of promotional devices. With the easing of these restrictions, however, and with the arrival of commercial television in 1955, the main focus of competition switched to advertising expenditures.

Kellogg's ratio of advertising and promotion[10] to sales rose from its postwar low of 1.1% to 12.4% in 1955, and to a postwar peak of 15% in 1959. It averaged 14% between 1960 and 1965, and then fell slowly to reach 11.6% in 1971. The Monopolies Commission reported that figures obtained from Weetabix and Nabisco for 1966–1971 and from

---

10. In 1970, 80% of this total was devoted to advertising.

Quaker Oats for 1966–1970 indicated an average ratio of advertising and promotion to sales appreciably in excess of Kellogg in the case of two of these companies and an average ratio similar to that of Kellogg in the case of the third (in reporting this, the commission did not cite estimates for individual companies).

In this period of intensifying competition for shares, Kellogg made modest gains (from a 51.2% market share in 1950 to a high of 59.0% in 1961, after which its share fell back to 54% by 1976); but these gains were made at the cost of a squeeze on net margins, and Kellogg's operating profit to sales ratio began a slow decline from its 1949 high of 30% to around 25% by the end of the 1950s.[11] As Kellogg's share slowly inched ahead in the 1950s and then fell slowly back in the 1960s, only one of its three major competitors, Weetabix, gained ground. In spite of matching or exceeding Kellogg's ratio of advertising and promotion to sales, both Nabisco and Quaker saw their shares erode, albeit slowly, over the period. An important feature of the market share pattern over this period is that Kellogg's leading product, Corn Flakes, continued to account for over half the company's sales volume until the early 1970s (figure 10.1).

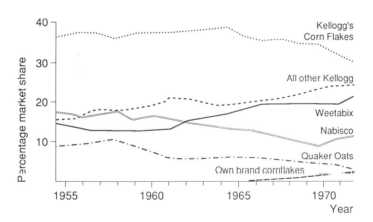

Figure 10.1
The evolution of RTE market shares in the United Kingdom, 1955–1971. Source: Monopolies and Mergers Commission 1973.

---

11. Taking the sum of profits with advertising and promotional expenditures as a percentage of sales, the Monopolies Commission found that this ratio was fairly steady from the mid-1950s to the mid-1960s (about 40% for 1956–1960 and 39% for 1961–1964); advertising and promotional expenditures rose over the period, as net profits fell. Throughout the latter half of the 1960s, however, both components declined.

The major losers in this process were the eight small producers, which together accounted for 7.2% of volume sales in 1950. By 1961, their combined share had fallen by more than half, to 3.2%. By 1970 it had fallen further to 1.9% while own-label products, which had first appeared on the market in the 1960s, took 3.1%. The future of the fringe, then, lay from the late 1960s with the own-label sector. In 1963, Viota Limited, a subsidiary of Robertson's Foods Ltd., the well-known jam producer, acquired a factory from the American General Mills, which had been supplying cornflakes to the Tesco supermarket chain. The business grew rapidly from 1968 onward, and by 1971 Viota had twenty-five customers. Selling at a price of the order of 10% below Kellogg, own-label products produced by Viota accounted for half of cornflake sales through (small) grocers in 1971, but their share in supermarkets was much lower (of the order of one-fifth or less).

By the time the own-label sector developed, however, the Big Four already accounted for about 95% of sales. Kellogg told the Commission (MMC 1973, p. 22) "that it did at one stage consider whether it should attempt to counter the threat of Viota competition to the volume of sales by reducing its prices by 5 per cent but that it rejected this on the ground that the increase of 21 per cent in volume of sales that would have been necessary to maintain profits was greater than the share of the market obtained by Viota." The own-label sector grew steadily, however; today it accounts for over 10% of sales, although continuing high levels of advertising relative to sales serve to strengthen the position of the established brands.[12]

10.4 A Summing Up

Does it Matter?

The central argument here relates to the distinction between the present endogenous advertising outlays explanation for concentration and the brand proliferation argument. But does this distinction

---

12. The Monopolies Commission concluded that Kellogg was a price leader in the U.K. market, and its recommendation was that Kellogg's profit rates should be kept under review and that the company should be required to seek government approval for any price increases.

matter? To see its relevance, it is useful to look at the type of remedy put forward by the Federal Trade Commission in the Kellogg case, which rests on the notion that the observed levels of advertising outlays may be treated as exogenous. On this basis, it was argued that it would be feasible to break up the industry leader(s) into a larger number of firms of "viable size." If we treat advertising as an exogenous sunk cost, there is a lower bound to equilibrium concentration, and this bound goes to zero as market size becomes large. Above this bound, a wide range of equilibrium structures exist, so it becomes feasible to choose one of these equilibrium structures for the industry.

But what range of choice is available? What the present theory suggests is that this range may be narrower than would seem to be the case on the basis of a calculation that takes currently observed levels of advertising as an exogenous datum. Specifically, the theory implies that as industry structure becomes more fragmented, the greater is the incentive for some firm to deviate and so spark off a competitive escalation of advertising outlays, which in turn would lead back to a more concentrated structure. If, as is argued here, the origins of concentration lie in a process of competition in endogenous advertising outlays, then freezing in a fragmented structure may not in itself be a viable option. If, for some reason, it was decided to attempt to alter the structure of the industry, then the policy instruments employed would need to be focused on the advertising mechanism itself.[13]

Distinguishing the Theories

The brand proliferation argument turns on some features special to the RTE market. Yet, as we have seen above, a comparison of the evolution of structure in the RTE industry suggests that a familiar mechanism is in operation, which is independent of these special features of the market. While documentation of the early history of the U.S. industry is sparse, it appears to have followed a path analogous to that which led to the evolution of dual structure in such other industries as frozen food, soft drinks, biscuits, and beer. Throughout

---

13. The point being made here is, of course, a point of principle; it is *not* argued that those specific (and quite limited) structural changes actually proposed by the FTC would be unstable—merely that the degree to which changes of this nature would be feasible differs crucially as between the two theories. It is also worth emphasizing that no welfare argument in favor of intervention has been offered here (see chapter 14).

the 1960s and 1970s, the advertising-sales ratio of the market leader, Kellogg, was substantially below that of its three (four) main rivals in the retail (branded) sector. This is a characteristic feature of our mechanism, and one that we note elsewhere to be a feature of the frozen food and soft drinks industries, for example. It is, moreover, a feature that is difficult to account for if we regard advertising outlays as an exogenous barrier to entry mechanism.

The better-documented early phase in the evolution of the RTE cereals industry in the United Kingdom offers a close and striking parallel with the experience of many of those advertising-intensive industries described in other chapters. The evolution of concentration in the U.K. market can be traced to a competitive escalation of advertising outlays, and during this key phase of the industry's development a single variety (Corn Flakes) accounted for two-thirds of Kellogg's sales. There seems to be no evidence of any brand proliferation activities by firms. A second type of argument that helps to distinguish this explanation from the pure brand proliferation argument relates to the behavior of incumbent firms in response to new entry. Under a brand proliferation story, the lack of new entry to the industry is attributed to the fact that new niches open up only slowly, and these are filled by incumbents as they arise. It was argued in the FTC case that a single m.e.s. plant might need four successful product launches to maintain full capacity—and it would be difficult to launch four successful new varieties at any one time. This confers an advantage on incumbents, who can release marginal capacity on existing plants to produce new products as they are introduced.

Against this argument, however, it can be pointed out that the existence of own-label and nonretail sectors permits the survival of producers, like Ralston Purina in the United States or Gram in Italy (see appendix 10.1), that already possess the production capacity required to enter the retail sector with a single product, while maintaining full capacity operation via own-label sales. The lack of new entrants to the U.S. retail sector is probably best explained along other lines.

But if advertising outlays are endogenously determined, the factor that deters entry will lie *not* in the above kind of computation of costs (based inter alia on current advertising levels), but rather in a belief concerning the post-entry response of incumbents. The experience of the markets considered in this chapter suggests that when an entrant does choose to compete in the retail sector, the likely response is one of escalating advertising outlays, leading to increased pressure on one or more of those firms vying for a position in the retail market.

• In the granola sector of the U.S. market, the problems of entry are minimal, as setup costs are extremely low. Here, the brand proliferation mechanism is consistent with a fragmented outcome. However, the growth of the granola sector in the United States has been marked by escalating advertising competition by the majors, who rapidly overtook the early entrants to this sector.

• This same process is also illustrated by the recent development of the small but growing Italian industry (see appendix 10.1). In that market, the indigenous producer, Gram, which specializes in own-label sales, has recently begun to expand its retail sales. Gram's expansion in the retail segment has required it to set an advertising-sales ratio above Kellogg's, and has led to a dwindling market share for the industry's number two producer, Chiari e Forte (Quaker).

For all of these reasons, it seems that those special features of the RTE market alluded to earlier serve only to *modify*, and not to *replace*, the basic process we have argued to be characteristic of all the advertising-intensive industries considered here. The presence of diminishing returns to advertising on any single brand may of course encourage brand proliferation. But once the equilibrium level of advertising support per brand and (possibly) the equilibrium number of brands are endogenously determined, the basic mechanism involved is a special case of that described in the model of chapter 3.

11

The Limitations of the Theory II

11.1 Introduction and Summary

This chapter, like chapter 7, focuses on the limitations of the theory. Chapter 7 looked at some *inherent* limitations of the theory. There, the focus lay in examining the consequences of the fact that many results in this area depend in a delicate way on the details of the underlying model—and if we focus attention only on robust results, we are necessarily left with a theory that places only mild constraints on the data. That problem was further exacerbated by the fact that, even within any particular model, multiple equilibria may appear that correspond to different patterns of structure so that, once again, the theory places only mild constraints on the data.

These same limitations that formed the focus of chapter 7 have reappeared in the discussion of advertising-intensive industries. In looking at the frozen food industry in chapter 8, it was noted that the theory had little to say regarding the difference in structure between the U.S. market and the other markets examined. Those differences lay in the fact that the market was highly segmented, and the overall level of concentration depended crucially on whether or not it was the same handful of leading firms that dominated each of these segments. This source of cross-country differences could be interpreted in terms of the appearance of multiple equilibria within the theory. A second limitation of this same kind arises in respect of the first-mover advantages explored in chapters 9 and 10. There, crucial differences in structure can be traced to the presence or absence of first-mover advantages by particular firms. Here again, the range of equilibrium outcomes permitted by the class of models considered here may be wide and may depend on factors other than the measurable technology and tastes variables that characterize the industry.

But all of these observations constitute limitations of the theory only in the weak sense that they reflect the limited explanatory power of a model that places only weak restrictions on the data. In this chapter, we turn to a quite different type of limitation of the theory —and one that is potentially more damaging. One of the central maintained assumptions on which the theory rests runs as follows: there are certain product characteristics that—though they may be difficult to identify, let alone measure or proxy empirically—will serve to determine the extent to which price competition is tough or weak and the degree to which advertising outlays are effective in stimulating demand for the product.

It is perfectly in order that the toughness of price competition or the advertising response function should additionally be influenced by a series of identifiable institutional factors, which may differ across countries. Indeed, throughout various chapters, we take advantage of just this kind of cross-country institutional difference to test the predictions of the model. What is *not* consistent with this maintained assumption, however, is that the advertising response function should depend crucially on various idiosyncratic features of individual firms' advertising campaigns. Of course, the effectiveness of any particular advertising campaign is notoriously difficult to predict, but this is not what is at issue here. What is at issue is whether over many such campaigns some more or less stable pattern emerges that allows us to classify the product as one in which advertising either is, or is not, generally effective in stimulating demand. Is this a reasonable assumption? A central argument of this study is that it is. In this chapter, we play devil's advocate by drawing attention to a case in which the huge divergence of experience across apparently similar markets can be traced to differences in the effectiveness of leading firms' advertising efforts.

The mineral water market offers a striking example of divergences in structure within apparently similar market environments. Here, we will be concerned with the French, German, and Italian markets, all of which are closely similar in their characteristics:

- market size varies across these three markets by less than 20%;
- the three markets are quite independent; import penetration is

extremely low (5% or less), and no multinational firms operate across different markets;

• the patterns of consumer demand, and of growth, are similar. In each case, there has been a steady trend toward the use of mineral water as table water, a trend associated with rising disposable income over the past three decades, and total sales have risen steadily over time.

Each of the remaining three markets has some quite distinctive characteristics, which make comparisons less helpful. These three markets are described in appendix 11.1.

Our main theme in what follows relates to the fact that these three apparently similar markets exhibit widely different levels of concentration. Concentration is moderately high in France, very low in Germany, and intermediate in Italy. While it could be argued that these differences are merely transitional, an examination of firms' strategies in these markets strongly suggests that the most important difference in experience relates to the different degree of effectiveness achieved by leading firms in building up their market shares by way of advertising outlays, and in the consequent reactions of their rivals to these advertising activities.

11.2   The Mineral Water Market

We begin by looking at the French market, in which a surprisingly effective advertising campaign by Perrier led to a major shift in the structure of the market. We then contrast this with the experience of the German market, which remains fragmented, in spite of a steady and substantial flow of advertising outlays by the industry's leading firm. Finally, we look at the experience of the Italian industry, in which a combination of consolidation and rising advertising outlays has been leading to rising concentration over the past few years.

We define "mineral water" quite broadly. In particular, we include the French categories "eaux minerales," a name reserved for waters having a specified mineral content, and "eaux de sources," to which no such restriction applies. Our definition includes both still and sparkling waters, the relative importance of which varies greatly by country. We exclude the category of sodas and seltzers, which can be seen as representing the bottom end of the market in the

United States; these are produced by introducing carbon dioxide, along with other additives, into water.[1]

France

The French mineral water market has its origins in the mineral springs, whose medicinal properties were greatly valued a century ago. Many of today's top brands, including Vittel, Evian, and Contrexeville, come from sources already renowned as thermal springs at the turn of the century. Patients returning from their "cure" brought some supplies of the waters with them and continued their cure at home. In so doing, they generated a modest demand for these waters, which were widely available from pharmacies throughout the country. Perrier was something of an exception. The original owner, Dr. Louis Perrier, sold the company to a member of the British Harmsworth family who envisaged building up an export trade directed toward the British aristocracy. Dr. Perrier invented the characteristic Perrier bottle, whose shape was inspired by that of the old-fashioned Indian clubs with which he exercised. The company's sales had fallen to 20 million bottles by the 1940s, when the Lever brothers began to acquire shares prior to a buyout. The two brothers currently share control of the company with the Greek Mentzelopoulos family.

Until the 1950s, the French mineral water market remained tiny, and—Perrier apart—the image of the product was a severely medical one. The volume of sales of still waters, for example, stood at a mere 80 million liters in 1955. Today, annual consumption is around 3 billion liters. A number of developments occurred during the 1960s that sparked off major changes in the nature of the market. The period was one of rapid real growth in consumer spending; a wide range of food products, from yogurt to beer, enjoyed substantial increases in sales volume over the decade. The birth of large-scale "hypermarkets" in 1964–1966 gave a boost to this trend, and it was this change that first led to the crucial switch of mineral waters from a

---

1. The issue of market definition in this area is relatively straightforward in the case of five of the countries studied, the United States being the exception. The issue is whether to use a narrow definition incorporating only those waters used as a soft drink substitute (which may or may not have some specified mineral content), or a broad definition, which also includes bottled water sold in large containers and used as a substitute for tap water. Only in the United States is the latter segment relatively large; we take up this point in appendix 11.1.

pharmacy category to a grocery category, as the newly established hypermarkets began to carry the products.

One of the most important changes in the market came in 1968 with the introduction of plastic bottles. This led to a switch from the small 90-centiliter bottle, which had been standard, to the larger 1.5-liter size familiar today. These bottles were originally suited only to the still waters, and only five years later were some of the sparkling waters (those with a relatively low carbon dioxide level, such as Badoit) packaged in plastic.[2] The availability of still waters in this new format accentuated a trend in consumption that had been running in their favor, as French consumers preferred still to sparkling waters for table use—a growing category of consumption. Still and sparkling waters were of roughly equal importance in the small market of the 1950s; by the mid-1980s, sparkling waters accounted for just one-fifth of volume sales.

Against this background, Perrier was something of an outlier: its traditional image was not a medicinal one, but rather that of a mixer, popular with the older generation of whiskey drinkers. It found no favor as a table water, and its highly carbonated nature barred any switch—whether desirable or not—to the new plastic bottles. The new strategy the company developed over the next few years was, to say the least, imaginative. No changes were made to the product or its packaging; but a substantial and sustained advertising campaign was directed toward changing the image of the product in the eyes of a younger generation of consumers. The first major slogan, "Perrier, c'est fou" (captured imperfectly in translation as "Perrier, it's crazy") was launched in commercials filled with dancing youngsters, creating an image of Perrier as "très 'in,' très 'à la mode.'" So effective was the slogan that later campaigns could be launched by distorting it: "Ferrier, c'est pou" was meaningless, but instantly recognizable.

Perrier's expensive campaign paid off, in a way much admired by others in the industry, for the company succeeded in the difficult task of changing its image to capture an entirely new clientèle without losing the old one. But for both of its target groups, Perrier's image, in contrast to that of its main rivals, was and remains one of fun as

---

2. Waters that were highly carbonated, like Perrier, could not be packaged in plastic until the relatively recent introduction of the "PET" bottles; Perrier's glass bottle had by that time become a hallmark, and it has never changed to plastic.

opposed to health. This notwithstanding, its success sparked off a reaction from Evian and Vittel, which began to advertise heavily. The image projected by each of the three market leaders was quite different. Evian, for example, had from the 1960s targeted its efforts toward sales for infants (the baby bottle segment), and much of the company's advertising emphasized this idea. But the changing pattern of consumption in the market made it inevitable that much of the efforts in the advertising campaigns of the 1970s and 1980s would be directed toward deemphasizing the traditional medical image in favor of the idea of everyday use. In competing for the middle ground, all three leaders moved to a strategy of high, steady advertising support. Currently, all three spend a roughly similar amount on advertising, and each holds a market share in the range of 20%–25%. The sustained efforts of its two main rivals allowed them to draw level with, or slightly ahead of, Perrier by the late 1980s. In 1983, Perrier's two brands, Perrier and Contrexeville, took slightly over a quarter of total sales; by 1987, they took slightly less than a quarter. By that year, BSN, which acquired Evian in 1970, had become a market leader, its Evian and Badoit brands accounting for about a quarter of total sales.

While the three majors, together with the (much smaller) Volvic, accounted for some 80%–85% of sales in the mid-1980s, the growth of the market had stimulated the opening or reopening of many springs. There are at present over 150 firms operating; less than 20 are classified as producers of eaux minerales. The rest are classified as producers of eaux de sources. All this latter group sell on price with no advertising support, at the bottom end of the price spectrum. The price spectrum in the mineral water market is a broad one: a typical eau de source retails at 1.50–2.00 French francs for the standard 1.5-liter bottle, while the prices of eaux minerales (Perrier apart[3]) are in the range 2.50–3.00 French francs.

For the more recent arrivals, however, the outlays required to compete at the high-price end of the market are now extremely high. The pattern of shares has altered little over the past decade, and the structure shows little sign of changing as the market develops.

---

3. Sparkling waters are generally priced higher, and Perrier sells for substantially more than other mineral waters. (The latter differential may in part be attributed to the fact that Perrier is still sold in glass, rather than plastic, bottles.)

Germany (F.R.)

The polarization of the French market into two distinct groups of producers stands in sharp contrast with the German experience. Germany's mineral water market is in many respects similar to that of France. Total sales have grown substantially over the past decade, as increasing concern with a healthy diet has caused consumers to switch to mineral water. Total volume consumption, at 2.8 billion liters, outran France's level for the first time in 1983. (The mix of still versus sparkling waters in the French market, on the other hand, is precisely reversed in the German case, where sparkling waters account for 72% of sales by volume.)

As in France, the industry was well established traditionally, with a large number of small local producers sited around the mineral springs of the Alps and in a number of mountainous regions (the Bayerische Wald, the Lippisches Bergland, and elsewhere). The growth of the industry in recent times has attracted new entrants: there were 159 producers in 1970, compared to around 200 in the mid–1980s.

The difference, vis-à-vis the French experience, lies in the continuingly high degree of fragmentation. Up to now, no firm has succeeded in capturing a market share exceeding 10% or so, and the leading four firms account for less than 30% of sales. Some of the leading firms in the industry are subsidiaries of major food and drink producers. Apollinaris, the market leader, is a subsidiary of Germany's leading brewing conglomerate. Deutsche Granini, a subsidiary of the Melitta-Bentz coffee group, is a major producer of fruit juice. The Nestlé group holds a majority stake in the fourth largest producer, Blaue Quellen.

The strategy of the industry's leading firm, Apollinaris, has always been based on relatively heavy advertising expenditure. Its advertising has built up a sufficiently prestigious image to allow the company to achieve a market share of about 9%, while charging a price premium of around 50% as compared with its competitors. Like Perrier, Apollinaris is sold in glass bottles only; its packaging is sophisticated and distinctive: the small print in German sets out its mineral content, while above it the company name is underwritten with an English slogan ("The Queen of Mineral Waters"). In contrast to Perrier, the vast bulk of whose sales derive from its leading Perrier brand, Apollinaris sells several other waters, each under its own label: Heppinger and Bad Neuenahrer (both in the small Heilwasser category) and Johannis Quell (a still water). The top-quality image of the Apollinaris label permits the product to sell at a high-price premium, but it has not led to the kind of volume expansion Perrier has enjoyed. Its image, moreover, is very different, in one sense, from that of Perrier. The Apollinaris company describes its product as being "the 'classic' of the mineral water market since 1852"; Perrier's image appears almost decadent compared to the austerity of Apollinaris.

If Apollinaris has failed to achieve the kind of mass-market volume gained by the French market leader, it nonetheless enjoys a very strong position vis-à-vis its domestic rivals. Arguably, its strong image has helped it to avoid being threatened by imports at the premium end of the market: total mineral water imports to Germany totaled only 5% in the mid–1980s.[4]

Italy

The Italian market is roughly similar in size to the French and German markets, with volume sales of 2.7 billion liters in 1985. The market has been little affected by imports, which constituted less than 1% of consumption in the mid–1980s. The industry has a strong historical base, with a tradition of spas and thermal springs, particularly in the north of the country (which remains the main source of supply as well as demand). As in France and Germany, the main long-term change in the sector has been the growth of demand associated with everyday use as a table water, or an alternative soft drink as opposed to a medicinal one. Growth has been strong in the recent past; consumption rose by a quarter between 1980 and 1985. The medicinal character of mineral water remains important, however. Italian waters are broadly divided into two classes, "salutistica" (health oriented) and "da tavola" (table waters). These categories describe the image under which the product is sold, rather than mineral content, etc. The former group sells at a premium, and

---

4. Another interpretation of the low degree of import penetration lies in the very strict German regulations on the mineral content and bottling of waters. Under a decree of 1934, mineral waters were required to contain a minimum level of dissolved salts and to be bottled at the source. The former restriction was abandoned in 1984 under EEC pressure. EEC regulations, however, are in themselves quite strict. A 1984 directive not only requires bottling at source, but requires that all water from the same source must be labeled identically.

represents the top end of the market, while the latter sells basically on price.

Three separate groups of firms are active in the market:

(i) The market leaders are three major groups. Each markets the waters from several separate springs, and the three together account for 54% of total sales. While Italian law requires the water from each different source to carry its own brand name, the three groups have achieved nationally recognizable brands, either by using composite brand names or by prominently displaying the group name on each label.

(ii) A number of midsize producers operate from a single source and have established a large market share in their own localities, equivalent to a share of 1%–4% of the national market (San Bernardo, Sant'Antonio, Levissima, Sant'Andrea, Recoaro, Vorola, Crodo, and others).

(iii) The large majority of the 248 companies active in the market in 1986 were small local concerns selling in their immediate vicinity in the low-price "acqua da tavola" segment.

Of the three major groups, two are long established. Sangemini, a family-controlled firm until the 1980s, when it was acquired by the French BSN group and the Italian Fiat group, sells several brands (Sangemini, Boario, Ferrarella, Fabia). Its Sangemini brand sells in the premium "salutistica" segment, while its recent advertising campaigns have been aimed at bringing Boario and Fabia into the premium segment, with a campaign associating their use with healthy outdoor activity. San Pellegrino, controlled by the Mentasti family, sells a wide range of mineral waters via its many subsidiaries. Its main brands are Panna (the leading brand for still water in the standard 1.5-liter plastic container, which alone accounts for 7% of total sales); San Pellegrino, its leading brand, which sells at the premium end of the market (with a much smaller market share of just below 2%); Pracostella; Claudia; and Sandalia.

Unlike Sangemini and San Pellegrino, which are long established, the third major group was formed quite recently. The Ciarrapico group entered the market in 1983 and have followed a strategy of building up a portfolio of brands each of which is strong in its own region. The group controls Acque e Terme di Bognanco, through which it holds seventeen brands (sources). All of these are now marketed under names reflecting group ownership; thus, for example, one of the seventeen, "Fonti di Lurisia," is now marketed as "Fonti di Lurisia Bognanco." The Ciarrapico group has also acquired several other springs; in particular, through its financial holding company Gruppo Italfin 80, it controls Nord Terme Italia and Terme di Recoaro. These are now marketed with the designation "Italfin 80" on their labels.

Advertising expenditure rose rapidly in the Italian market during the 1980s; total expenditure more than doubled in nominal terms between 1981 and 1985, by which year the advertising-sales ratio reached the 5% level. Advertising expenditure is concentrated heavily on a handful of brands. In 1985 ten brands (out of over 200) accounted for 90% of advertising expenditure. Of these ten brands, six belonged to the three main groups[5] and these accounted for just over half of total advertising. The other five main advertisers were strong regional brands, and all but one of these received a relatively low level of support.[6]

In spite of the high and rising advertising-sales ratio, the Italian market remains much less concentrated than its French counterpart. Although the level of concentration far outruns that of the German market, this largely reflects a recent consolidation of the industry achieved by way of a series of acquisitions. One possible interpretation of recent developments in the Italian market is that such consolidation forms the preliminary to building up a strong advertising-based image for a group that encompasses a sufficient total capacity (number of sources) to permit it to support a substantial share of domestic consumption .

11.3 Summing Up

As with the soft drinks industry, it can be argued that the mineral water market is in transition. This line of argument seems plausible when applied to the Italian case, but less so in regard to a comparison of French and German experience. The argument offered here is that

---

5. They were Fiuggi (Chiarrapico); Ferrarelle and Sangemini (Sangemini); San Pellegrino and Panna (San Pellegrino).

6. The exception, Levissima—which alone accounted for 30% of all mineral water advertising in 1985—was a company whose financial problems had recently led it to sell off some of its other interests in the nonalcoholic drinks sector, and which had set out to build up its (2%–3%) share of the growing mineral water market.

these cross-country differences in structure appear to reflect wide differences in the efficacy of firms' advertising efforts across countries. This market is an unusual one in this regard, and it has been chosen to illustrate this point, precisely because it seems to constitute an outlier within the sample of industries. Were such wide differences in the apparent efficacy of advertising outlays the norm rather than the exception, this would constitute a serious challenge to the usefulness of attempting the kind of categorization of industries that lies at the base of this study.

IV

How Setup Costs and Advertising Interact

The charming notion that true science can only be based on unbiased observation of nature in the raw is mythology. Creative work ... is interaction and synthesis.

Stephen Jay Gould

12

Setup Costs and Structure in Advertising-Intensive Industries

12.1 Introduction and Summary

Having examined the separate roles played by setup costs and advertising outlays in earlier chapters, it is now time to turn to the question of how these two elements interact. The analysis of this interaction provides the focus of this chapter and the next. The specific issue addressed in this chapter is as follows: within advertising-intensive industries, does any relationship hold between the level of setup cost, the level (or intensity) of advertising outlays, and the equilibrium structure of the industry? Now equilibrium structure obviously depends not only on setup costs but on a wide range of industry-specific characteristics—including in particular the degree of responsiveness of the firm's sales to advertising outlays—and many of these industry characteristics are difficult to measure or proxy empirically. How, then, can we isolate the effect of a change in setup cost from other influences?

The approach taken in this chapter is to focus attention on pairwise comparisons between industries whose economic characteristics are closely similar in most respects, but which differ dramatically in respect of the setup costs incurred by the typical entrant. The theoretical basis for this approach is set out in chapter 3. It was shown in section 3.6 that a certain comparative static property holds good *within any particular model* drawn from a very wide class of models. In comparing some pairs of closely cognate industries, we posit a priori that both can be represented by the *same* underlying model —even though we cannot, and need not, specify *which* particular model this is. On the basis of this supposition, we may then invoke the prediction developed in chapter 3, viz., an increase in setup costs implies a rise in equilibrium concentration.

This property was illustrated in chapter 3, figure 3.4, which shows the relationship between concentration and market size in the context of a specific example. One clarification is in order. The example used in chapter 3 was one in which each firm produced a single product. Once we turn to the (empirically relevant) case of multiproduct firms, however, multiple equilibria are endemic. In this setting, the above statement must be reinterpreted as an assertion concerning the *lower bound* to concentration levels.

What, then, should be expected empirically? Insofar as an industry has higher setup costs, then the scatter of points showing the concentration level and market size of that industry in different countries should be shifted upward. This is the relationship to be investigated in what follows. As to the effect of an increase in setup costs on advertising outlays, the theory suggests that no robust results are available. The effect depends crucially on various industry-specific features. For example, as noted earlier, one key factor influencing the outcome relates to the extent to which increases in advertising outlays expand total *industry* sales (as opposed to attracting sales from rivals). As setup costs and equilibrium concentration rise, the level and intensity of advertising outlays *may* eventually decrease (as posited by Greer (1973) and Kaldor (1950)), or they may not. The stronger the tendency for advertising to expand total *industry* sales, other things being equal, the weaker the tendency for advertising levels to fall as setup costs and concentration rise.

This chapter aims to investigate these relationships in the context of two pairs of cognate industries. The first part of the chapter compares the experience of the chocolate confectionery industry, in which setup costs are relatively high, with that of the sugar confectionery industry, where such costs are relatively low. This simple characterization of the two industries, however, needs considerable elaboration, for both industries are highly segmented, and the level of setup cost varies widely between segments. Nonetheless, an examination of the overall level of concentration in each industry supports the prediction that equilibrium concentration rises with setup costs. More interesting, it turns out that the *extent* of the difference in structure between the two industries is closely related to the overall size of the difference in setup costs—the latter difference being determined by the pattern of market segmentation across countries. In the United States and the United Kingdom, where the dominant sectors within the chocolate confectionery industry are those with the highest setup cost, the observed difference in concentration between the chocolate and sugar confectionery industries is relatively large. In the other four countries, the difference in setup costs between the two industries is less sharp (in the sense of a weighted average across market segments). In these countries, the differences in overall concentration between the two industries are also relatively low. (The one exception to this pattern arises in the case of France, and the reasons for this are explored at some length in what follows.)

As to the levels of advertising, a fairly uniform pattern emerges. The advertising-sales ratio in chocolate confectionery is in all cases higher than in sugar confectionery. (Again, the French experience is slightly unusual here. The level of concentration in the French sugar confectionery industry is relatively high, and levels of advertising are also relatively high.)

Finally, we consider the possibility that increases in concentration might eventually induce a *lower* advertising-sales ratio. While no reversals of this kind occur across the two confectionery industries, the recent history of the U.S. chocolate confectionery industry throws some interesting light on this idea, and we take up this point in section 12.2.

The second part of this chapter compares the experience of the instant coffee market, in which setup costs are very high, with that of the roast and ground (R & G) coffee market, where setup costs are much lower. Again the relationship between setup cost and concentration is as predicted by the theory. As to advertising intensity, however, the pattern is less clear. While advertising intensity is usually higher in the (high setup cost) instant sector, some exceptions arise and these are discussed at some length.

While the main theme of the chapter is the investigation of these comparative static propositions, a secondary theme is explored in the final section of the chapter, within the context of the U.S. R & G coffee market. This market has been characterized, for the past decade, by escalating competition between the market majors, with an associated decline of middle-ranking firms. The overall pattern of events in the market bears a close resemblance to the mechanism of escalating advertising outlays. What is novel is that this process of competition between the majors is more complex than that explored elsewhere, in that it has taken place across a clearly defined sequence of regionally separated markets. This gives the process the character of the now familiar "chain store paradox" of the theoretical literature (Selten 1978)—in fact, this market formed part of the motivation for the classic Kreps-Wilson (1982) and Milgrom-Roberts (1982) analysis of predatory pricing. (See Hilke and Nelson 1987a.) The way in which this geographical segmentation of the market affects the present analysis is taken up in the final part of the chapter.

12.2 The Confectionery Industries

The markets for chocolate and sugar confectionery appear closely similar on the demand side. They are bought by the same groups of consumers, through the same channels of distribution, with a similar unit cost of purchase and frequency of purchase, and are advertised in the same media. Both markets are almost wholly retail in nature, the nonretail sector being extremely small.[1] The assumption underlying our comparison is that these similarities on the demand side of the market imply that the advertising response function is probably not very different in these two cases. On the other hand, the setup costs that must be incurred by a new producer of mass-market chocolate confectionery typically exceed by an order of magnitude the setup costs incurred by a typical entrant to the sugar confectionery industry. Within each of the two industries, however, there are a number of well-defined market segments, and the level of setup costs varies quite substantially from one segment to another. For this reason, a short digression on the pattern of market segmentation is in order before turning to the evidence on setup costs and concentration levels.

Market Segmentation in Chocolate Confectionery

Within the chocolate confectionery industry, products are customarily divided into three basic categories, together with a number of special subcategories. The three basic categories are:

(i) *Chocolate bars* (which may or may not be filled). The typical product is a standard bar of say, Cadbury's or Hershey's.

---

1. Details of these aspects of the two markets, including statistics on the slightly different age profiles and personal attributes of consumers in the two markets, can be found in the several market research reports cited in the reference section.

(ii) *Countlines* (so called because they are normally sold in single units, that is, by "count" as are chocolate bars, but involve a mixture of chocolate with other ingredients). The quintessential countline is the Mars bar, but the category covers a broad range of items including light products such as chocolate-covered wafers of the Kit-Kat type .

(iii) *Assortments*. These consist of individual sweets normally sold by weight, in bags or boxes. The typical product here is the box of chocolates.

It is useful to distinguish two more segments. The first consists of seasonal items such as Easter eggs and other simple molded chocolate items; the nature and role of this seasonal business varies widely across countries. The second relates to "panned goods" such as sugar-coated chocolate sweets (typified by M & Ms, Skittles, or Smarties).

Our basic assumption as to the high level of setup costs in the chocolate confectionery industry is most clearly satisfied in the countline sector, which involves the use of relatively sophisticated production techniques in the preparation of mass-market items. It is satisfied to a lesser degree in the case of chocolate bars, in that substantial scale economies may be achieved in mass-production plants, but the basic production process simply involves the blending and molding of chocolate, and production on a small scale (and even at the artisan level) is feasible, albeit not efficient.

The distinction between countlines and chocolate bars extends further, for the countlines offered by rival manufacturers are heavily differentiated, while the basic chocolate bar varies little from one manufacturer to another. In fact, where the market is dominated by this category of product, the industry may take on the character of a homogeneous goods industry with substantial scale economies, in which competition revolves primarily around price and the pressure on unit margins provides the main impetus toward consolidation of the industry (similar to the cases of salt and sugar).

As regards the third basic category, that of assortments, it is appropriate to distinguish two subcategories—though the distinction is far from sharp. On the one hand, the assortments segment in some countries (notably the United Kingdom) is dominated by relatively low-price mass-market chocolates produced by some of the industry's leading firms, and, the underlying technology is akin to that of the

Table 12.1
Market segmentation in chocolate confectionery in the mid-1980s. All figures
should be regarded as approximations, as many minor differences exist between
classification schemes used in different countries

	France	Germany (F.R.)	Italy	Japan	United Kingdom	United States
Countlines and panned items	17	25	7	30	55[a]	70
Bars	47	50	32	15	15	20
Assortments/seasonals	20	}40	}59	}40	15–20	8
Other	15				10–15	2

Market share (%)

a. Including filled blocks and bars.
Sources: Author's estimates based on various sources and company interviews.

countlines segment. In other countries (notably Italy), the assortments sector is dominated by high-price quality chocolates in whose
production scale economies matter little and in which a strong artisan
fringe is active. With regard to the remaining segments, mass-market
panned goods (such as M & Ms, etc.) involve a relatively sophisticated production technology and high setup costs. Most seasonal
products (Easter eggs, etc.), on the other hand, involve a simple
molding process, and their production may involve extremely low
setup costs.

The way in which the relative importance of each segment differs
across the six countries is illustrated in table 12.1.

The dichotomy between the chocolate and sugar confectionery
sectors, in terms of their difference in setup costs experienced by a
typical producer, is sharpest in the case of the United States and
the United Kingdom. In the United States, countlines dominate
the chocolate confectionery sector, whereas the (exceptional) assortments sector is extremely small. In the United Kingdom, while
assortments play a major role, sales are almost entirely accounted for
by mass-market items. The French and German markets, on the
other hand, are dominated by the chocolate bar segment, and countlines play a minor (though rapidly growing) role. In Italy, where per
capita consumption of confectionery is very low, the market is heavily
dominated by high-price quality assortments—indeed, in Italy chocolate retains a luxury rather than mass-market image. Countlines,
on the other hand, are relatively unimportant. Thus the median

producer of chocolate confectionery in Italy incurs quite modest setup costs.

The Japanese chocolate confectionery industry is divided into two roughly commensurate parts. The first consists of panned items and bars, for which setup costs are relatively high. (Countlines, however, account for only a few percent of sales.) The other major segment consists of items lying outside our classification, the most important being chocolate-covered biscuits sold in boxes (rather than as countlines). These are included in the customary Japanese definition of chocolate confectionery, but they are closer in their production characteristics to some segments of the Western biscuit (cookies and crackers) industry and involve relatively modest setup costs. The inclusion of this group, and the relative unimportance of countlines, blurs the distinction as to setup costs in regard to the Japanese industry.

In light of these differences in the pattern of segmentation across countries, a more refined prediction may be drawn from the model. It is expected that a wide difference in concentration should be present between the chocolate and sugar confectionery industries in the United States and the United Kingdom. As to France and Germany, it is clearly necessary to draw a distinction between the relatively small countlines sector of the chocolate confectionery industry (where we expect this difference in concentration vis-à-vis the sugar confectionery industry to be present) and the dominant chocolate bar segments in which the commodity nature of the product makes our model inappropriate. As to Italy and Japan, where the differences in setup costs between the chocolate and sugar confectionery industries are less marked, the difference in concentration should be relatively small.

Market Segmentation in Sugar Confectionery

In the case of sugar confectionery, the picture is much less complex. Sugar confectionery products may be divided into three main categories: (i) sugar confectionery (boiled sweets), (ii) toffees and caramels, (iii) gums, jellies, and pastilles, as well as a number of specialist segments such as chewing gum, mints, and licorice. Setup costs are relatively modest throughout most of these areas and are minimal in the case of boiled sweets. An exception arises in the case of chewing gum, a subcategory often included in compiling sugar confectionery

statistics; this segment involves high setup costs and is largely dominated by a handful of multinationals. In this chapter, we omit this
subcategory from the sugar confectionery industry. The only other
exception of note relates to what in American terminology is called
"hard roll candy" (mints or similar sweets, packed in a tube). Here,
the *packaging* technology effectively determines the minimal level of
setup costs incurred by entrants, which are high relative to other
sugar confectionary categories.

To sum up: the broad distinction between the level of setup costs
involved in chocolate confectionery, as opposed to sugar confectionery, is somewhat blurred insofar as the hard roll candy sector and
the chocolate assortments sector constitute an intermediate "gray
area." The extent to which this matters to our comparison depends
on the relative importance of the several product categories across
the countries in question. The hard roll candy segment is fairly small
and well defined, and its presence poses few problems. The assortments segment, on the other hand, varies greatly in its importance
across countries, being negligible in the United States but dominant
in Italy. A second substantial consideration relates to the commodity
nature of the chocolate bar segment, which plays a dominant role in
the French and German markets. To these issues we now turn.

Setup Costs and Structure: The Evidence

In this section, and the next, we look at the differences in concentration and in advertising intensity across the two industries. Detailed
profiles of all these industries are provided in appendix 12.1, which
also presents a table of market share patterns, relative market size,
and import penetration. In gauging relative market size, it would in
principle seem natural to use the *value* of sales as a measure. However,
the most reliable and consistently based measures available are based
on production volume, as compiled by the International Office of
Cocoa, Chocolate, and Sugar Confectionery, and these figures are
employed throughout.[2] The four-firm concentration ratio for each
industry is shown in table 12.2, and the relationship between market
size and concentration is shown in figure 12.1 . This figure indicates
a clear upward shift in the scatter of points for chocolate confectionery

2. This procedure relies on the fact that differences in the value to weight ratio for the
products of the two industries are very small in comparison to differences in setup costs.

Table 12.2
Four-firm sales concentration ratios for sugar and chocolate confectionery,
by country

	Sugar confectionery (%)	Chocolate confectionery (%)
France	51	38
Germany (F.R.)	39	77
Italy	29	48
Japan	42	60
United Kingdom	38	80
United States	27	86

relative to sugar confectionery, as predicted. Since it is plausible that certain country-specific factors might operate across both industries, it is of some interest to look at the comparison country by country. The figures for individual countries shown in table 12.2 indicate that concentration is higher in the chocolate confectionery market for five of the six countries studied, the exception being France.[3]

Our earlier remarks on setup costs suggest that the U.S. and the U.K. markets offer a natural point of departure. Here, the pattern of market segmentation induces a sharp difference in setup costs across the two industries; as table 12.2 indicates, both countries also exhibit a wide difference in structure, the four-firm sales concentration ratio for chocolate confectionery being over twice as great as for sugar confectionery.

In the remaining countries, the disparity in setup costs is less sharp, as are the differences in concentration recorded in table 12.2. In both France and Germany, the chocolate confectionery industry is dominated by the commodity-like chocolate bar segment. In appendix 12.1, it is noted that both markets are characterized by strong price competition and relatively low unit margins, but the current structure of the two industries differs considerably. In the German case, the chocolate confectionery industry has experienced a wave of consolidations in recent years, leading to a relatively high level of concentration. These changes have involved both mergers between

---

3. A comparison of the total number of producers in each segment also conforms to the expected pattern, there being more sugar confectioners than chocolate confectioners in each country except Italy. In the Italian case, the presence of an unusually high number of chocolate confectioners can be traced to the dominant assortments sector, with its low setup costs (appendix 12.1).

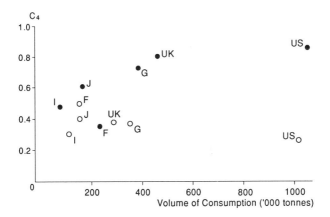

Figure 12.1
Concentration versus market size in chocolate confectionery (black circles) and sugar
confectionery (open circles) for six countries.

Table 12.3
Advertising-sales ratios for sugar and chocolate confectionery, by country, 1986

	Sugar confectionery (%)	Chocolate confectionery (%)
France	~1.5	2.9
Germany (F.R.)	4.2	5.9
Italy	6.0	6.5
Japan	3.8	6.0
United Kingdom	2.1	3.5
United States	2–3	3–4

domestic firms and an important acquisition by the multinational, Jacobs Suchard. In the French market, on the other hand, the strength of leading branded products has been eroded to an unusual degree by the growth of retailers' own-label products. The largest supplier of own-label chocolate bars, Cantalou, now accounts for more sales than any other manufacturer (24%). Meanwhile, no one of the three main branded producers (Poulain, Nestlé, Suchard) has been able to advance its share much beyond its rivals; all have segment shares of 13%–17%. Both Italy and Japan exhibit relatively low disparity in setup costs across the two industries, as noted above. As table 12.2 indicates, they also show a relatively modest disparity in structure. Chocolate confectionery, which in each case is dominated by low setup cost segments (assortments in Italy, biscuits in Japan) is much less concentrated than its U.S. and U.K. counterparts.

When we look to the pattern of concentration within segments, moreover, the same regularity is evident. This is most striking in the case of chocolate countlines, where setup costs are highest. Even in those countries where the overall level of concentration in chocolate confectionery is low, the countline segment remains highly concentrated (appendix 12.1). The overall pattern observed between these two industries conforms fairly well to our prediction, then. One clear anomaly arises, however: the French industries exhibit a reversal of the usual pattern of relative concentration levels. This reversal reflects both a low level of concentration in chocolate confectionery and an unusually high level of concentration in sugar confectionery. The latter observation must be traced to factors lying beyond the model. The evolution of the French sugar confectionery industry is described in appendix 12.1.

Setup Costs and Advertising Outlays

As noted, the theory predicts that an increase in setup costs may initially lead to an increase in the advertising-sales ratio, but whether this positive relationship continues to hold as setup costs become higher depends on the details of the model—and no general prediction is possible. The data presented in table 12.3 indicate a fairly clear empirical regularity. The advertising-sales ratio in the chocolate confectionery industry exceeds that in sugar confectionery in all cases. A closer examination of each industry reveals two interesting features, however. The first relates to the experience of the Italian and Japanese industries; the second relates to the U.S. market.

The Italian and Japanese industries, for somewhat different reasons, do not conform very well to the pattern found in the four other countries. In Japan, the boundary between the two industries is blurred, insofar as a number of leading firms operate in both segments and pursue similar advertising and marketing policies across both categories of confectionery. Thus, the relatively small difference observed in respect of advertising intensity may, at least in part, reflect this feature of the Japanese market.

The Italian market is anomalous in that the advertising-sales ratio in sugar confectionery is high relative to the values found in other countries; it is also very close to that found in the Italian chocolate confectionery industry. In appendix 12.1, the pattern of market segmentation in the Italian industry is analysed from a different angle to trace the origin of the relatively high advertising levels found in the sugar confectionery industry. It is argued that these high outlays can be linked to a recent process of escalating expenditures by a handful of firms, which have vied for a leading position in one rapidly developing segment of the sugar confectionery market.

We remark, finally, on the experience of the U.S. industry. Over the past two decades, the advertising-sales ratio for chocolate confectionery has exceeded that found in sugar confectionery. However, the earlier experience of the U.S. chocolate confectionery industry throws some interesting light on the theoretical possibility raised in chapter 3: that very high levels of concentration might be accompanied by relatively *low* advertising outlays.

Until the 1960s, the Hershey company enjoyed a comfortable leadership position in the U.S. chocolate confectionery industry and retained, up to that point, a long-standing policy of not advertising its products. This situation came to an end when Hershey's leadership was challenged by Mars, which launched a massive and well-planned advertising and promotional campaign. Mars increased its market share to just exceed Hershey's by the early 1970s. Hershey's belated response was to break with its no-advertising policy in 1969, by which time it had lost a significant share of the market. By meeting the scale of Mars's advertising spending, Hershey reestablished parity with Mars by 1980.

In its efforts to catch up, Hershey changed, in the words of industry analyst John McMillin, from "a sleepy company" to a "marketing powerhouse," turning out a steady stream of heavily innovative products (*Prepared Foods*, May 1987). Mars, on the other hand, rarely introduces new products. Between 1980 and 1986, Hershey launched nine new candy bars, and Mars launched one—the highly successful Twix bar. While Hershey has seventeen of the sixty top-selling bars in the United States, Mars has nine. Mars's strength, rather, is attributed within the industry to a combination of high efficiency on the production side and strong promotional activity. The company is known throughout the industry—both in the United States and elsewhere—for delivering excellent value, in the sense of the weight-price ratio (Messenger 1986).

Competition in the U.S. chocolate confectionery industry since the 1970s has revolved heavily around advertising expenditure. Price competition plays a very secondary role. In fact, one of the most remarkable features of the U.S. candy bar market is that prices are uniform for an extremely broad range of standard bars offered by all of the major suppliers.[4]

12.3   The Coffee Industries

The coffee market divides into two basic segments: roast and ground coffee (sometimes referred to as "regular" or ground coffee) and instant coffee (sometimes referred to as soluble coffee). (Decaffeinated coffee may be either roast and ground or instant, and it will be classified as part of one or the other of these categories in what follows.) In the roast and ground (R & G) segment, the technology is simpler, and setup costs are relatively low. The production process involves roasting the (imported) coffee beans and grinding them to a consistency suited to local preparation methods (percolation, filtering, espresso, etc.). Many firms in this sector operate with a handful of employees and a minimal capital outlay. Economies of scale in production are extremely limited. Economies of scale in packaging, on the other hand, may be substantial (see appendix 12.3). The production of instant coffee involves a high capital outlay. Its scale

---

4. Mars's standard price was 30 cents in the early 1980s, by which time Mars was recognized as the established industry price setter. But in 1983, Hershey attempted to break the pattern by raising the price of the standard Hershey bar from 30 to 35 cents. Mars responded by refusing to follow the price lead: instead it began advertising that Mars bars were "still the same price." The strategy failed; retailers across the country marked up Mars products to 35 cents, the company's advertisements notwithstanding, and a uniform industry price was reestablished.

is difficult to quantify, since it varies across producers and is related to the quality of the final product (a point to which we will return). Details of the differences in setup cost are set out in appendix 12.3. An important distinction arises between the powdered product produced using a "spray-dried" process and the increasingly familiar granules obtained using a "freeze dried" process. It is accepted within the industry that the latter process is particularly difficult to perfect and requires considerable know-how. The former process is much less demanding; both processes, however, require substantial capital outlays. Freeze-drying is now standard among the relatively small number of leading firms in the industry worldwide. On the other hand, a relatively large number of low-cost producers of spray-dried powdered coffee now operate internationally. (This has led to a growing—and unwarranted—identification of powdered coffee as low quality; in fact, it is quite feasible to make a very high quality freeze-dried coffee in powdered form, albeit at a higher cost.) From the consumer's point of view, the only differences lie in flavor and in ease of preparation. The two products are sold through the same channels of distribution, advertised in similar style in the same media, and lend themselves equally well to the creation of an effective brand image.

One problem with our comparison is that a certain degree of overlap is present in some countries between the leading firms in the R & G sector and those in the instant sector. This is most striking in the United States, where the market leaders in R & G (the larger of the two segments) are the same group of firms that dominate the instant market. It is clear that, insofar as a company's brand image in one market enhances its position in another, a major degree of interdependence between the R & G and instant markets is present in the United States. This qualification apart, the coffee market affords a valuable opportunity to look at the effects of differences in setup costs on market structure. Indeed, in one respect the coffee market offers an ideal opportunity to explore this issue, for the serious complications posed by complex patterns of market segmentation in the confectionery industry are largely absent here.

Setup Cost and Structure: The Evidence

In figure 12.2, the scatter diagram of concentration versus market size is shown for the two industries. The measurement of relative

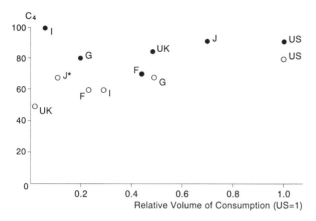

Figure 12.2
Retail market concentration versus total market size in the instant coffee market (black circles) and the R & G coffee market (open circles). (Measures of market size are notoriously problematic in these two industries, and the estimates used in this figure should be regarded as approximations only. See appendix 12.1.)

market sizes poses unusually serious difficulties. In the figure, market size is measured in terms of the volume of coffee consumed in each segment, as measured in terms of the primary input (green beans); the details of the calculations underlying these measures are set out in appendix 12.3. The scatter of points for each industry is consistent with the predictions of the theory.

An examination of the market share tables in appendix 12.3 shows that the instant market is more highly concentrated in each country. In fact, while the number of sellers of instant coffee is limited in each of these markets to no more than a handful of producers, in some cases accompanied by a few importers of a cheaper, powdered product, the "tail" of small producers operating in the R & G market is quite extensive. The number of producers of R & G coffee ranges from around 50 in Germany, for example, to some 400–500 in Japan, to around 1,000 in Italy.

The pattern of advertising intensity is illustrated in table 12.4, in which the fraction of total coffee advertising attributable to istant coffee is compared with the fraction of retail coffee sales accounted for by instant coffee. In interpreting table 12.4, it should be borne in mind that the measurement of relative advertising intensity in these two markets is complicated by the fact that a certain fraction of advertising is carried out by firms that are active in both sectors, and

Table 12.4
Advertising intensity in the coffee market

	A_I	I_r
France	.45	.37
Germany (F.R.)	.10	.115
Italy	.13	.04
Japan	.66	.78
United Kingdom	.97	.89
United States	(*)	.22

A_I: Fraction of all coffee advertising attributable to instant coffee
I_r: Fraction of retail coffee sales accounted for by instant coffee
(*): Figures for the United States are not meaningful here, as "whole line" advertising by firms active in both sectors is quite substantial (see text).

some of this advertising is not identified with specific (R & G or instant) products but supports the firm's product line as a whole. Such brand support advertising is omitted in computing the figures reported in the table.

It is clear from the table that instant coffee is more intensively advertised in most countries, but the pattern is less clear here than in the case of the confectionery industries. In two of the markets—Japan and Italy—Nestlé has a virtual monopoly on instant coffee sales. This affords an unusual opportunity to examine the idea that advertising intensity might fall as the industry becomes (very) highly concentrated. It was noted in chapter 3 that advertising intensity *may* fall at high concentration levels, depending inter alia on the degree to which advertising expands total *industry* sales.

In the Japanese market, where instant coffee dominates R & G, Nestlé maintains a low advertising to sales ratio. In Italy, on the other hand, Nestlé's share of all coffee advertising (13%) far outruns its modest 4% share of the instant coffee segment, in which it is the sole supplier. This difference in strategy may reflect a wish by Nestlé to exploit a perceived opportunity to raise the still-tiny category share of instant coffee in the Italian market. Such an interpretation is consistent with the theoretical possibility just noted.

One notable feature of table 12.4 is that advertising intensity in the two sectors is closely similar in Germany. This observation is in fact one reflection of a major realignment of the R & G coffee market in Europe during the past decade. The R & G coffee markets have been in a state of transition in most of the countries studied here since the mid–1970s. The manner in which the market has been changing is in many respects analogous to the changes noted in the frozen food market in chapter 8. One effect of this shifting pattern of structure has been an escalation of advertising outlays in R & G coffee, which occurred in several countries. In the case of the United Kingdom, for example, this led to a short-lived reversal during the late 1980s of the usual tendency for advertising intensity to be greater in the instant sector.

Competition in the R & G market has revolved no less around advertising than around aggressive price competition, underwritten by the long purse of the market majors—a development most evident in the United States and to a lesser degree in France. Entry and expansion by acquisition have also played a central role, notably in France and the United Kingdom. The evolution of structure in the French, German, U.K., and Japanese R & G markets is discussed in appendix 12.3. In what follows, we look at the experience of the U.S. market. This case is of particular interest because the expansion of the R & G majors in the United States has been viewed by some observers as an important illustration of predatory pricing. Viewed in the context of the other industries examined, however, it is probably best seen as a further illustration of the tendency for escalating competition between market majors to result in an outcome in which the main losers are middle-tier firms. In fact, the experience of this market has much in common with the development and hardening of dual structure in other cases. What distinguishes these cases from the archetypal example of the frozen food industry is the close complementarity between the use of fixed cost (advertising) and variable cost (price promotions and retailer discounts) elements as part of a composite strategy.

Coffee in the United States

The American coffee market has changed greatly over the past generation. At the start of the 1960s, three leading suppliers accounted for about half of retail sales. General Foods, with its Maxwell House brand, operated in both the instant and R & G markets and accounted for about one-third of all coffee sold. Procter and Gamble operated via its subsidiary, the Folger Coffee Company, a regional R & G producer it acquired in 1963. Finally, Nestlé had a relatively small share that reflected the comparatively small size of the instant sector, to which it confined its operations.

This picture evolved gradually through the 1960s toward one of somewhat higher concentration, as the share of instant (and so Nestlé's position) strengthened, while Procter and Gamble's share also rose. Procter and Gamble's acquisition of Folger had been permitted only subject to a consent decree by the Federal Trade Commission (Hilke and Nelson 1987a). The most important change in the market dates from the expiration of this consent decree in 1971. At that point, Folger set out to expand its regional operation to the national level. As Folger expanded, General Foods resisted step by step, leading to a continuing series of battles involving both price discounts and advertising and promotional expenditures (Hilke and Nelson 1984, 1985, 1986, 1987a, 1987b).

The strategies of the two rivals evolved over successive market entries. Folger's first entry, to the Cleveland market, was based on the setting of an introductory price equal to that of Hills Brothers, a second-tier producer whose prices were pitched significantly lower than General Foods's main offering, Regular Maxwell House. Following this low introductory offer, however, Folger appears to have been aiming at a price level close to that of Regular Maxwell House. General Foods's initial response to Folger's strategy—increased advertising and promotional devices (coupons)—proved ineffective, and Folger's share grew rapidly. General Foods's financial analyses, which included a simulation study of alternative strategies, led it to conclude that a strong response involving pricing below cost in the short run would afford the least costly route to maintaining its share.

The result was a new phase marked by an intensified response by General Foods. This combined a revamped advertising strategy with a counteroffensive in Folger's home markets, in which General Foods built up its advertising expenditure and began a round of aggressive price cuts. Folger, in turn, responded to General Foods's more aggressive stance; it focused its attention on competing with secondary brands, pitching its prices at a level significantly below that of Regular Maxwell House. General Foods, however, responded by meeting Folger's price, so that the secondary brands were forced to shift their prices downward in order to maintain sales, thus precipitating a spiral of successive price cuts by the two groups of sellers.

The Cleveland experience set the basic pattern for Folger's entry into Pittsburgh, Philadelphia and Syracuse. Attempts by General Foods to use a low-price (fighting) brand (Horizon) proved less effective than expected. Its attempt to switch to a less costly response following Folger's entry in Syracuse—by offering coupons redeemable by retailers as opposed to simply cutting the price to retailers —coincided with a switch by Folger to a more aggressive strategy involving the reverse move. The result was a rapid gain by Folger of a 19% share, notwithstanding prices for Regular Maxwell House below unit variable costs throughout most of 1974–1975. Thereafter, General Foods returned to a more aggressive strategy: the company concluded that it was important to maintain straight price parity with Folger in the first six months of a Folger introduction, particularly in shelf-price-sensitive markets.

The pattern by this stage had been set, and throughout Folger's expansion General Foods—with few exceptions—met Folger's highly competitive terms to retailers point by point. The main effect of Folger's expansion, which continued throughout the 1970s (finally reaching East Coast cities by the end of the decade), was a steady decline in the share of small and medium-sized roasters operating in local or regional markets. In some cases, the tougher price pressure on local firms led to their exit from the market. In one case, this led to an antitrust suit by a local brand (Breakfast Cheer, of Pittsburgh) against General Foods, following its exit from a market in which it previously had an 18% share. In 1976, the Federal Trade Commission issued a complaint regarding General Foods's promotional activities, but the case was dismissed.

The marketing war, which reached its height in 1978, was carried on through three channels. R & G advertising expenditure amounted to around 2% of the value of retail sales, or close to $100 million, in fiscal year 1978. One effect of the battle for shares in the R & G market was to shift the share of advertising expenditure away from instant coffee. In fiscal 1977, the advertising-sales ratio for instant coffee had been double that of R & G; in fiscal 1978 the ratio fell to one and a half. A second channel related to expenditure on consumer promotional activities (coupon offers, price rebates, etc.), which outweighed advertising expenditures over the period. In fiscal 1977 they stood at around $150 million, or slightly less than 3% of the value of retail sales. In fiscal 1978, however, they rose to $200 million. (This increase represented, in part, manufacturers' reactions to the continuing decline in total sales, which resulted from the worldwide rise in coffee prices in the late 1970s, following a series of shocks to coffee supplies—the Brazilian frost of 1975, civil war in Angola, an earthquake in Guatemala, and a drought in Columbia.) A third channel accounted for even greater expenditure: trade promotion (price discounts to the retailer, given to underwrite price offers to consumers) accounted for expenditures of $250 million in fiscal 1978. Thus much of firms' efforts went directly or indirectly into price cuts, which bore heavily on local and regional competition.

The effects of the marketing war on the small roasters accentuated a trend that had been evident since the 1960s; the number of roasters had already fallen from 324 in 1963 to 213 in 1972; since then, however, the number has been reduced to around half this figure. The market structure that emerged in the 1980s is one in which the Big Three dominate the R & G market; on the retail side, both General Foods and Folger have around one-third of sales. Nestlé, which concentrated on the growing instant sector through the 1960s and 1970s, has more recently responded to a leveling off in the total share of instant coffee by turning to the R & G market via a series of acquisitions. In the 1980s, Nestlé acquired three R & G companies: Hills Brothers, a regional producer with 8% of the R & G market; the MJB company, a West Coast firm; and Chase and Sandborn, a once-leading company now mainly active in the food service (catering) area. Consolidated as Hills Bros. Coffee Inc., these now account for some 12% of the retail R & G market.

12.4 A Summing Up

A central theme of this study concerns the way in which setup costs interact with endogenous advertising outlays in determining equilibrium structure. In chapter 3, it was argued that even in advertising-intensive industries, an increase in setup cost raises the equilibrium level of concentration. The extent to which this occurs, however, will depend on the impact that changes in setup cost exert on endogenous advertising outlays, and this effect will depend delicately on various industry-specific features. For this reason, a useful way to investigate the impact of setup costs in this environment lay in the pairwise comparison of similar industries. The experience of two pairs of industries examined in this chapter appears to be broadly consistent with the model. This chapter, then, has focused on the key comparative static prediction relating to the interaction between exogenous and endogenous elements of sunk cost. The next chapter explores the same issue within a dynamic context.

13

A Complex Case

13.1 Introduction and Summary

The beer industry provides an unusually complex setting in which to examine the roles played by setup costs and advertising outlays in influencing industrial structure. Over the past generation, changes in the underlying technology have—in the view of most industry observers—warranted a shift of production to larger plants. This increase in the minimum efficient scale of operation has been seen by such observers as the primary factor underlying the steady growth in concentration that has been observed in many countries over this period. (See especially Elzinga 1982; details regarding m.e.s. estimates are given in appendix 13.1, where we also note some qualifications based on recent Japanese experience, which emphasizes the importance of current trends in technology favoring relatively small and highly automated plants.)

Over the long run, as plants are retired or superseded by new lower-cost establishments, this trend toward higher setup costs might be expected to induce changes in the structure of the industry. The fact that m.e.s. levels have been rising over time affords an unusual opportunity to explore the advertising mechanism discussed in earlier chapters. In chapter 12, we looked at pairwise comparisons between industries that were broadly similar but for a difference in the level of setup costs, and this comparative static exercise allowed an examination of the interaction between setup costs, advertising outlays, and industry structure. In this chapter, the fact that the level of setup cost has been rising over time affords an opportunity to look at this same interaction in a dynamic setting.

The beer industry operates within very different institutional regimes from one country to another. Two key institutional factors have heavily influenced the very different ways in which the industry has responded to rising m.e.s. levels across different countries:

(i) the stance of the authorities vis-à-vis mergers in the industry; insofar as mergers are permitted, they offer a possible route toward accommodating changes in m.e.s.

(ii) the practice of tying retail outlets to particular brewing companies. If retail outlets are tied to particular brewing companies, the effectiveness of advertising as a way of increasing market share will be diminished.

Within the United States, mergers were strongly discouraged by the authorities throughout most of the postwar period, a stance that was not relaxed until the early 1980s. Moreover, the tying of retail outlets to brewing companies is forbidden by law.

The U.S. industry, then, satisfies the underlying assumptions of the model employed throughout in our discussion of advertising-intensive industries, and the main part of the this chapter focuses on the U.S. case.[1] In a final section, we comment on the U.K. and German markets, where the tying of outlets is important and restraints on merger and acquisition activity have been less strict. The evolution of these markets has followed a very different route to that of U.S. markets. These industries are described in full in appendix 13.1. The appendix also describes the French and Japanese markets, in which policy decisions by the authorities brought about a highly concentrated structure at an early stage, and the Italian market, which is extremely small.

The evolution of concentration in the U.S. industry has been widely studied, and the causes of rising concentration have been a matter of controversy. In what follows, the evolution of the industry is interpreted within the framework of the theory. The analytical argument, as set out in the next section, is based on the

---

1. Although these are the main institutional factors that appear to be relevant, one further factor which is much less tangible plays a role in many of these markets. This relates to the tendency for small local brands to command a premium in some submarkets. This may derive from a local reputation effect, a factor stressed in relation to many German beers. It may also derive from the fact that such beers are simply different to standard offerings, an idea that some U.S. industry observers emphasize in regard to small "boutique" brewers. Finally, it may involve a combination of both these factors, as with many local ales in the United Kingdom.

interplay between the exogenously given level of setup costs and endogenous advertising outlays. It is argued that the successive waves of escalating advertising competition that the industry has experienced, alongside the increase in industry concentration, can be traced to a single simple mechanism, described in the next section.

13.2 The U.S. Beer Market

Explaining Concentration

Two lines of explanation have been offered for the increase in concentration experienced by the U.S. beer industry[2] over the past forty years. The first of these, proposed by Greer (1970), emphasizes the role of escalating advertising outlays by major brewers. The alternative view, argued by Elzinga (1982), is that the increase in concentration is attributable to the change in m.e.s. that has occurred over time. In a later paper, Greer (1981) acknowledges that scale economies, as well as advertising, played a role in this process. These two influences are not independent. In terms of the model, the two effects emerge as part of a single integrated mechanism. The workings of this mechanism are best illustrated by recalling the basic example developed in chapter 3, the results of which are adequately summarized in figure 3.6, shown in a modified form as figure 13.1.

The figure shows how the lower bound to equilibrium concentration varies with the level of setup cost in the industry. Suppose an industry that had setup cost σ under some earlier technology has inherited a historically given level of concentration corresponding to the point marked X in figure 13.1. The point X corresponds to a no-advertising configuration (recall the discussion of this figure in chapter 3, and note that X lies to the left of the hatched line that divides no-advertising solutions from advertising solutions).

But suppose that the technology changes so that, as plants become obsolete, they are replaced with new plants corresponding to the new and higher level of m.e.s., whose construction involves a setup cost $\sigma_2 > \sigma_1$. The historically determined level of concentration, corre-

---

2. No other industry considered in this study has been so thoroughly researched as has brewing in the United States. The present section draws heavily on the work of many authors, including most notably Elzinga (1982), Greer (1970, 1981), Ornstein (1981), and the Federal Trade Commission report of 1978.

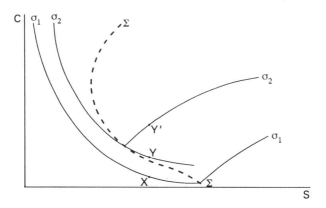

Figure 13.1
This figure, based on figure 3.6, shows how the lower bound to concentration C as a function of market size S varies with the level of setup cost σ. In the figure, $\sigma_1 < \sigma_2$. The point Y lies on a projection of the no-advertising schedule for σ_2 into the advertising zone.

sponding to point X, is no longer an equilibrium. If market size S remains unchanged, the new minimal level of concentration toward which we will move as aging plants are replaced corresponds not to point Y, the point that would be reached if advertising were ineffective, but to the higher level indicated by point Y', which is in the advertising zone. A zero-advertising configuration such as X may be destabilized either by a rise in σ as illustrated in the figure or by a fall in the unit cost (or a rise in the effectiveness) of advertising messages. The latter effect would be captured in figure 13.1 by a leftward shift in the $\Sigma\Sigma$ locus.

The Evolution of Concentration

The U.S. beer industry retained a localized, fragmented character up to the eve of Prohibition in 1919, when some 1,400 breweries were in operation. Several of today's market leaders had already built up a substantial business by that date, and firms such as Schlitz, Stroh, Pabst, and Anheuser-Busch survived Prohibition by turning to other industries.[3] The ending of Prohibition in 1933 saw a remarkably rapid influx of brewers; by 1934, over 700 were in operation. Though many of these survived only a short time, over 100 firms remained in

---

3. Confectionery, ice cream, soft drinks, and even malt syrup—which was sold as a baking ingredient, but actually used to make "home brew."

Table 13.1
The number of beer producers and breweries in the United States, 1947–1974

	Number of firms	Number of plants
1947	404	440
1954	263	301
1963	171	222
1982	67	109

Source: Census of Manufactures, various.

operation in 1940, when the top five firms accounted for only 16.3% of output, and the top ten for 24% (Greer 1981).

Over the postwar decades, the number of firms showed a fairly steady pattern of decline, while concentration increased (table 13.1 and figure 13.2. The fairly regular sigmoid shape of the curves in figure 13.1 is worth noting in view of the apparently episodic nature of the events related below.) By 1985, seven firms accounted for 97.7% of industry sales. The top two, Anheuser-Busch and Miller, alone accounted for 60%.

Before turning to the role of advertising in this process, we begin by looking at the—rather limited—role played by mergers and acquisitions in the U.S. industry. The main effect of mergers and acquisitions, up to the early 1980s, was to aid the disappearance of the small firms that had played a major role in the postwar period. The authorities' quite hostile view of mergers and acquisitions by medium or large brewers meant that such activities contributed little to the growing share of the industry leaders. The gains made by leading firms were achieved, rather—with only rare exceptions— through a process of internal growth. More recently, a relaxation in the authorities' approach to mergers among medium-size firms, from the end of the 1970s onward, led to a wave of acquisitions among second-tier brewers. This process has strengthened the position of these firms vis-à-vis the two industry leaders.

Mergers and Acquisitions

Elzinga (1982) records that the 25 leading brewers made approximately 100 acquisitions over the period 1947–1979. The acquisitions predominantly involved the takeover by middle-ranking firms of small brewers in financial difficulty. Overall, mergers and acquisitions account for very little of the observed increase in concentration

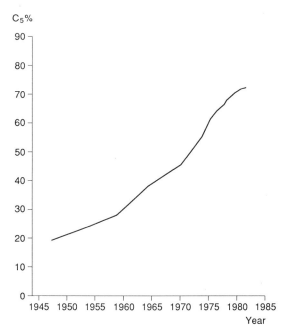

Figure 13.2
The five-firm sales concentration ratio for the U.S. beer industry. This figure is based
on table 3 of Ornstein 1981, p. 290, and table 3 of Elzinga 1982, p. 224.

that has occurred in the industry. Elzinga (1982), applying the
methodology of Weiss (1965), for example, reported a finding of no
impact on concentration due to merger over the period 1959–1972.

The industry's leading firms were dissuaded from attempting to
expand via acquisition by early intervention. In the late 1950s and
early 1960s, several of the top brewers were challenged by the antitrust division of the Federal Trade Commission.[4] The only major

4. In the first action brought by the antitrust division of the Federal Trade Commission
in 1958, Anheuser-Busch was required to resell a Miami brewer it had purchased from
American Brewing. It was argued that this purchase would eliminate American Brewing
as an independent brewer. In 1959, the antitrust division filed a complaint against the
acquisition of the Blatz Brewing Company by Pabst, an acquisition that had moved Pabst
from tenth place to fifth in the industry. The complaint finally resulted in an order to
Pabst to divest itself of Blatz. The Schlitz Brewing Company was challenged in respect
of its 1961 acquisition of the Burgermeister Brewing Corporation, and its control—
achieved through stock purchase—of General Brewing. A Supreme Court decision
confirmed the judgment of the District Court and required Schlitz to divest itself of the
assets and stock. Two minor exceptions to the blocking of acquisitions by leading firms
arose in the case of Anheuser-Busch's acquisition of the Baldwinsville, N.Y. plant from
Schlitz in 1980 and Pabst's purchase of the Blatz-Weinhard brewery in Oregon in 1979.

firm to have built up its position via acquisitions is Heilemann, which reached a share of 8%–9% through a series of purchases of older breweries.[5] Heilemann's fifteen acquisitions moved it from its position as the thirty-first largest brewer in 1960 to fourth largest in 1983.

Heilemann's experience apart, strict antitrust enforcement limited the impact of mergers until the end of the 1970s. But a changing climate of antitrust practices from 1978 onward paved the way for a new wave of mergers, which peaked in 1981–1982. The new climate was ushered in by an FTC report of 1978 that criticized the strictness of antimerger enforcement, pointing out that scale economies were more important than had generally been acknowledged in antitrust enforcement circles and arguing that mergers between regional brewers would probably increase rather than diminish competition.

All but one of the second-tier brewers were involved in the 1981–1982 wave of takeovers. Pabst purchased the Olympia company in 1982. Stroh, which ranked eighth in 1979, moved to become the third-largest brewer by acquiring the Schaeffer Brewing Company in 1980 and Schlitz in 1982. The mergers of the early 1980s, then, had the effect of strengthening the relative position of the tier of firms immediately below the two market leaders. As to the leaders, Miller's share remained level at 21%–22% over the first half of the 1980s, but Anheuser's share moved ahead from 28.2% in 1980 to 38.8% in 1985. The top seven firms, whose share totaled 78.4% in 1980, attained a share of 97.7% by 1985. The dwindling of the fringe in the early 1980s reflected, then, a phase of consolidation among second-tier brewers; it also reflected the growing share of Anheuser-Busch.

Advertising

The behavior of the industry's advertising-sales ratio over the postwar decades shows three clear phases. The ratio grew from the early postwar years to the mid-1960s, then declined to the mid-1970s; from the mid-1970s onward it has again been growing. The major shifts in the pattern of market shares over the postwar period have coincided with the two phases during which the advertising-sales ratio was rising. What both these phases have in common is that

---

5. In some cases Heilemann has shut down the brewery following acquisition and centralized production, in effect simply buying the label; by the late 1980s it had attained a total of forty-five brands. Heilemann, which was itself acquired in the mid-1980s by Alan Bond (the Australian brewer), is also alone among the top five in adopting a very low level of advertising.

• In each case the phase was sparked off by a strengthening in the market share of one or more second-tier brewers.

• One or more first-tier brewers responded to this and thereby achieved a sharp rise in (absolute and relative) market share.

• The net effect of this process was a rise in concentration, as the combined shares of the leaders and their challenger(s) rose relative to that of third-tier producers.

This squeezing out, first of small firms, and then of major regional brewers, echoes the experience of other industries. Escalating advertising competition among leading producers may lead either to the shift of such second-tier firms to a nonretail fringe (as in frozen food) or to their exit (as in coffee).

The 1953–1966 Phase

At the start of the 1950s, the three leading national brewers—Anheuser-Busch, Schlitz, and Pabst—had a combined market share of just under 20%. Below this group were a handful of major regional beer producers, among whom Carling, Hamm, Ballantine, and Falstaff enjoyed a combined share of 10%. This combined share had been rising slightly between 1951 and 1953. In the latter year, a strike halted production in Milwaukee by Schlitz and Pabst. The share of the third leading brewer, Anheuser-Busch, jumped somewhat from 1952 to 1953, as did the shares of three of the four leading regionals. In the latter year, Anheuser-Busch increased its (measured media) advertising by 85% relative to the preceding year. Schlitz, in spite of its production stoppage, followed this escalation.[6]

Over the next ten years, the advertising-sales ratio of both the major national brewers and the four leading regionals rose, as did the combined market share of each group (figures 13.3, 13.4). By 1962, however, the fortunes of the two groups began to diverge. The combined share of the four regionals actually declined slowly, while the share of the three leading nationals advanced steadily. The losers in this process were the smaller regional brewers, whose share declined steadily as that of the majors advanced (figure 13.3).

The pattern of brewers' profitability over the period is described by Greer (1970). (See also FTC 1978.) Two features are noteworthy:

---

6. So too did Miller, a company that was to play a central role in the second phase.

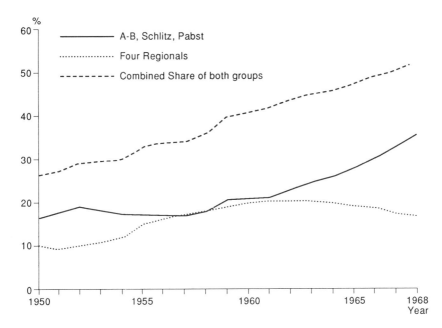

Figure 13.3
The combined market shares of the three leading U.S. brewers (Anheuser-Busch, Schlitz, Pabst) and of four leading second-tier brewers (Hamm, Carling, Ballantine, Falstaff), 1950–1968. Source: Greer 1970.

(i) The immediate postwar years saw a sharp decline in profitability for brewers of all size classes. Between 1951 and 1953, this decline showed signs of tailing off, and overall profitability in the industry fell only slightly. To what extent the profit decline of the late 1940s may be attributed to an adjustment of the industry to peacetime conditions, with more rigorous price competition favoring larger brewers, is open to debate. Throughout this period, however, a pronounced tendency was already evident for very small brewers (with annual sales of $1–5 million)[7] to have relatively low rates of return, a tendency that persisted throughout the 1960s and 1970s.

(ii) The onset of escalating advertising outlays from 1953–1954 onward was associated with a new decline in profitability among the larger brewers. As advertising levels fell, from the mid-1960s onward, the profits of the largest brewers recovered to around the levels enjoyed in the early 1950s. The case of Pabst, the third-largest

7. This group of brewers ranked about 60th to 130th among all U.S. brewers.

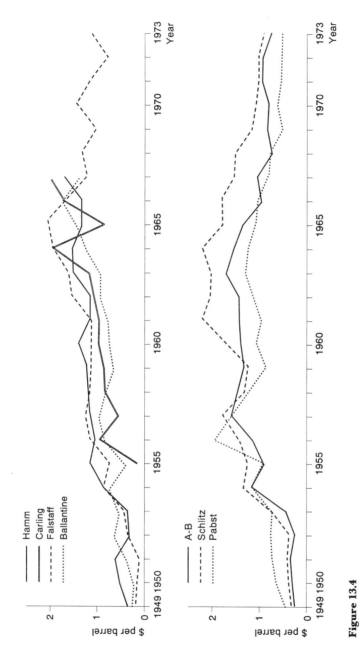

Figure 13.4
Advertising expenditure by firm for U.S. brewing, 1949–1973, in dollars per barrel. The bottom panel shows the three industry leaders (Anheuser-Busch, Schlitz, Pabst). The top panel shows four main second-tier brewers (Hamm, Carling, Ballantine, Falstaff). Source: Greer 1970, FTC, Business Trends Analysts 1987.

brewer, is particularly striking. In 1950, Pabst had a market share of 4.6%, somewhat behind Anheuser-Busch and Schlitz (both at 5.9%). Over the next few years, however, the gap between the three leaders widened until, in 1955–1956, Pabst's share had fallen to little over half of that of the two leaders.[8] In 1956, Pabst raised its advertising level per barrel ahead of the two industry leaders. During that year, its profits fell sharply. From 1959 onward, however, Pabst's advertising per barrel fell below that of the market leaders, and its profitability began to recover.

All in all, the first phase of escalating advertising outlays led to a considerable gain in the relative position of the largest brewers. The ten-firm concentration ratio, which had been 38.1% in 1953, rose to 68.4% in 1968 (Greer 1970, p. 202). Nonetheless, a substantial fringe of third-tier brewers lying outside this group still retained about one-third of the national market. In the second phase of escalation in advertising outlays, this group would virtually disappear.

The Post–1969 Phase

The second phase of advertising growth began with the acquisition of Miller by the tobacco company Philip-Morris in 1969. In 1966, Miller had been one of six second-tier firms, each with a share in the 3%–6% range, lying immediately below the three market leaders. In that year the company was acquired by a conglomerate, W. R. Grace, and over the next three years its volume share rose modestly from 4.0% to 4.5%. Following its acquisition by Philip-Morris, Miller's market share actually declined over several years, but from 1973 onward it began to increase dramatically. Miller's initial improvement in performance cannot be ascribed to the *level* of its advertising, but rather to a sudden jump in its effectiveness. The company had always maintained an advertising-sales ratio that was high relative to its rivals among the top-ten brewers. Following the company's acquisition by Philip-Morris, its advertising outlays rose further, so that by the early 1970s Miller was spending double that of the other national brands, with little impact on its share until 1973 (FTC 1978, p. 176).

---

8. The shares in 1955 were, for Anhuser-Busch, Schlitz, and Pabst respectively, 6.6, 6.8, and 4.1. In 1956, they were 6.9, 7.0, and 3.7.

The turning point came with the remarkable success of the company's Miller Lite brand in 1975. Designed to attract a young, blue-collar, heavy drinker—on the unlikely premise that a lower alcohol content allowed the customer to drink more—the product was initially greeted with considerable skepticism by rivals. So successful was the Miller Lite brand, however, that the company's share rose to 20% in some regions of the country within two years.

The response of the majors to Miller's success was to launch rival light beers and to significantly increase advertising and promotional activities. As the advertising levels rose, Anheuser-Busch strengthened its position. Throughout the 1980s Miller, having become the second-largest brewer, saw its market share settle at the 20%–22% level. Anheuser-Busch, on the other hand, kept its share of industry advertising substantially ahead of its steadily rising market share as the latter rose from 28.2% in 1980 to 38.8% in 1985 (in terms of barrels sold; see figure 13.5). This new wave of advertising was unusual both in its intensity and its effectiveness. The bull terrier that featured in Anheuser-Busch's television campaign, accompanied by the slogan

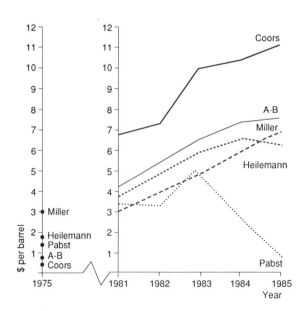

Figure 13.5

Advertising and promotional expenditure by leading U.S. brewers, 1981–1985, in dollars per barrel. The 1975 levels are shown for comparison. Source: Business Trends Analysts 1987, FTC 1978.

"It's a party animal," appears to have struck a chord even outside the United States.

The rivalry between Anheuser-Busch and Miller, now the two leading brewers, induced a number of different responses from their main rivals. Neither Schlitz nor Stroh joined in the escalation of advertising outlays. Industry analysts attributed the relatively poor performance of Schlitz over the period to its low advertising levels (Euromonitor 1987), but the cost of competing with Anheuser-Busch and Miller was such that it is by no means clear that a high advertising strategy would have been profitable. As noted earlier, Schlitz as well as the smaller Schaeffer company were acquired by Stroh in the early 1980s, leaving the new Stroh company with a market share second only to Anheuser-Busch and Miller (figure 13.6). Heilemann, as remarked earlier, had advanced its share to around 9% via a series of acquisitions. Heilemann supported this position by keeping its advertising-sales ratio close to that of the market leaders. The same strategy was followed by Genesee, one of the smallest of the top-ten brewers, whose market share stood at about 2% in the early 1980s.

Two leading firms showed a rather different pattern of response over the period. Pabst saw its share slowly decline from 11% to just over 5% between 1976 and 1985. Its initial response to the new escalation of advertising outlays was to match the advertising-sales ratios of the market leaders; from 1983–1984 onward, however, its advertising outlays were cut back sharply (figure 13.5).

Coors's experience is particularly striking. As recently as 1978, the Federal Trade Commission report on the brewing industry labeled Coors "the exception to the rule." The company, as the FTC remarked, did very little advertising, and in spite of relatively high unit (production and transport) costs, enjoyed a rate of return that compared favorably with the industry leaders, a fact that was "at odds with the popular belief that increasing sales and the establishment of premium prices require huge amounts of advertising—especially if one is to compete with the nationals" (FTC 1978, p. 112). By the early 1980s, however, Coors, whose market share had slowly declined from a high of 9% in 1976 to below 8% in 1980, dramatically reversed its advertising policy. Throughout the first half of the 1980s, Coors maintained an advertising-sales ratio substantially greater than that of the market leaders (figure 13.5). Over the same period its market share gradually recovered, to just below 9% in 1985.

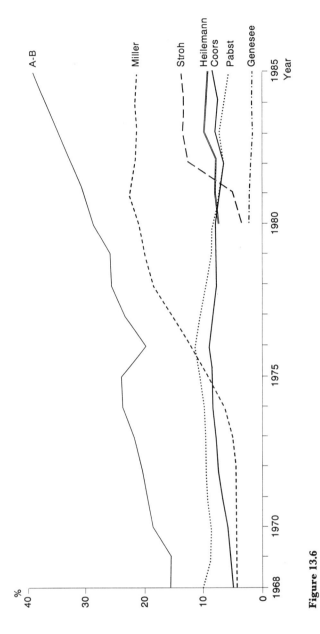

Figure 13.6
Market shares of leading U.S. brewers, 1968–1985.
Source: Greer 1981, Business Trends Analysts 1988.

As the majors strove to retain or advance their shares through enhanced advertising expenditure in the 1980s, the takeover wave among second-tier firms added to the decline of small brewers. By 1985 the top-seven U.S. brewers accounted for 97.7% of industry sales. All in all, the evolution of structure in the U.S. industry was largely shaped by a process of internal growth, with mergers and acquisitions playing a significant but secondary role. While it can indeed be argued that the initial impetus underlying the rising trend in concentration may be the changing degree of scale economies in the industry, a central role in the evolution of structure was played by the process of competitive escalation of advertising outlays that occurred over these two crucial periods.

13.3 International Comparisons

The escalation of advertising outlays that has played such a central role in the evolution of concentration in the U.S. beer industry has been much more muted in each of the other countries studied here. The explanation offered in the chapter introduction for this difference in experiences across countries hinges on two institutional differences:[9]

• the blunting of the effectiveness of advertising by virtue of the tying of retail outlets to brewing companies; and

• the stance of the competition policy authorities in respect of merger and acquisition activity.

The limited effectiveness of advertising can be captured in two ways within the model. If advertising in ineffective at all levels, then, in terms of figure 13.1, the $\Sigma\Sigma$ frontier shifts rightward, and we never enter the advertising zone, however high σ becomes. A second interpretation is that advertising works only up to some ceiling level; the analysis of this case and its equivalence to the case of advertising as an exogenous sunk cost is discussed in chapter 3, section 3.5.

The role of these factors in each of the other countries studied here is developed in appendix 13.2. The remarks that follow are limited to a brief summary of the main ideas in respect of the U.K. and

---

9. In the case of the Italian market, this difference may simply reflect the very small size of the market per se (chapter 3).

German markets, each of which affords an interesting point of comparison with U.S. experience. (As noted, the Italian market is extremely small, while the evolution of French and Japanese markets has been heavily influenced by direct policy intervention; again, details are provided in appendix 13.2.)

The United Kingdom

In the United Kingdom, a crucial early decision to limit the number of licences to sell beer led to a competitive scramble by brewers to acquire licensed premises, and as early as 1913, some 95% of all licensed premises were tied to particular brewers. The industry nonetheless was relatively fragmented throughout the first half of the century. It was not until the 1950s and 1960s that a wave of merger activity led to the dominance of seven major national brewers, which together controled over 72% of production. The Monopolies Commission report of 1969 drew attention to the way in which the tying of outlets implied that the only attractive route toward growth lay in acquisitions that would enhance the brewer's access to retail outlets (see appendix 13.2). Changes in structure since the end of the 1960s have been relatively modest, in part as a result of the increasingly hostile view taken by the competition policy authorities toward further mergers.

Advertising, on the other hand, has been relatively ineffective as a way of increasing sales, given the presence of the tie between brewers and outlets. However, over the past twenty years some success has been achieved by brewers in establishing major national brands via advertising in the newly developing lager segment, whose size has grown from less than 5% of total beer sales in the mid-1960s to over 30% in the mid-1980s. The reasons adduced by commentators to account for the rising importance of advertising in this segment are noted in the appendix; advertising levels in the United Kingdom, however, still remain very low by comparison with the United States. In 1986, the industry advertising-sales ratio was 1.0%, as opposed to 3.6% for the United States.

Germany

In Germany, as in the United Kingdom, the tying of retail outlets to particular brewers again blunts the effectiveness of advertising. Long-term contracts between the brewer and retail outlets guarantee the brewer exclusive supply rights. In addition to the existence of the tie, heavy restrictions on television advertising further increase the difficulties in establishing national brands. This difficulty goes hand in hand with an apparent tendency by German consumers to favor the image of the small local brewery. In appendix 13.2 it is argued that the relevance of this aspect of consumer tastes is evidenced by the strategies that firms have come to adopt when acquiring rival brewers. The German industry remains, overall, the most fragmented of those studied here. The structure differs between the north of the country, where a sequence of mergers during the 1970s led to a moderately concentrated structure, and the south, where small local breweries still account for the larger bulk of beer sales.

If beers are classified by price category, however, a very revealing feature emerges. The low-price category is dominated by medium- and large-scale brewers; it is here that the exploitation of scale economies becomes crucial to survival. The huge number of small local brewers, on the other hand, operates in the midprice segment, using their strong local reputation to maintain a price premium sufficient to cover the higher unit costs incurred in their small-scale operations. It appears that the effect of increasing m.e.s. levels in this instance has been confined to one price-sensitive segment of the market, while the appearance of strong advertising-generated national brands characteristic of the United States has not occurred— leaving intact the position of a wide range of local beers, each able to command a modest premium over low-priced beers within its own local market.

13.4 Summing Up

The evolution of concentration in the beer industry offers an unusual opportunity to see how changes in exogenous sunk costs over time, associated with the rising levels of m.e.s., may interact with endogenous advertising outlays in determining equilibrium structure. We have seen, in the preceding industry studies, how the pattern of adjustment has varied across countries. Only in the United States were two assumptions of our analysis satisfied: the evolution of structure was left to market forces, and the effectiveness of advertising was not blunted by the presence of ties between producers and outlets. The U.S. experience, therefore, is of particular interest.

The reasons for the rise in concentration in the U.S. industry have been a matter of controversy for some time. Some authors, notably Elzinga (1982), emphasize the primary role played by the changing pattern of scale economies. Greer (1970, 1981), on the other hand, has emphasized the role played by escalating advertising outlays among major brewers. Even if it is accepted that both of these factors played a role, it is not obvious which of the two should be seen as having initiated the steady rise in concentration that began in the 1950s. It may be argued that the advent of television advertising provided the initial impetus, though the conventional view that has emerged over the past decade stresses the primacy of scale economies.

Although considerable differences exist between alternative estimates of scale economies in brewing, industry experts generally agree that the minimum efficient scale of operation rose substantially between the early postwar years and the late 1970s. What is at issue is not whether rising m.e.s. led concentration to rise, but whether this rise in m.e.s. is in itself sufficient to explain such changes in structure as have occurred in the U.S. industry.

How, then, can we judge whether the four-firm concentration ratio of 97% attained in 1985 is attributable solely to scale economies? The theory suggests that the conventional way of deciding this issue, by way of a comparison of actual and warranted levels of concentration, is unhelpful (see chapter 1, section 1.5). One alternative route we might take is to look at how the relationship of market structure to market size differs across countries. With the exception of Japan (where the structure of the industry has been managed throughout the postwar period), the U.S. industry is the most concentrated of the six. Moreover, both the larger size of the U.S. market and its greater geographical extent might favor a relatively low level of concentration, were it not for the role played by advertising. This would suggest that scale economies per se do not tell the whole story.

A second line of argument is to look at the relationship between profitability and size across different U.S. brewers. Greer (1970) shows how the profitability of U.S. brewers varied across size classes during the period 1949–1975. Although it is clear that firms in the smallest size class had lower profitability than the largest (sixty or so) brewers over the period as a whole, the pattern across the other size classes is less clear. Certainly it does not seem to be the case that a clear size/profitability correlation existed across the top sixty brewers. It was at this time, as noted above, that a handful of leading national and regional brewers saw their share advance substantially vis-à-vis the smaller regional brewers. These two arguments, taken together, might suggest that a pure scale-economies explanation is inadequate. On the other hand, the discussion of the U.S. industry strongly suggests that the mechanism that we have found to hold in many other advertising-intensive industries (most notably frozen food, RTE cereals, soft drinks, and coffee) is closely mirrored by the process experienced by the U.S. beer industry over two key phases of its recent experience.

What, then, are the implications of the present analysis? One of the most intriguing facts to emerge in the beer industry in recent years is that changing technology now appears to make possible high levels of efficiency in small-volume plants. If future events confirm this alleged trend, how will concentration be affected? Insofar as sunk advertising outlays have created high-image national brands, and a relatively modest flow of advertising by the majors may now suffice to maintain this image (depreciation advertising), there is no reason to expect that a fall in m.e.s., however dramatic, would lead to any significant fall in the level of concentration. This point is basic to the theory and reflects the central notion of advertising as an (endogenous) sunk cost.

V
Summing Up

The hypothesis, though unproven, meets the primary criterion of a successful explanation . . . it coordinates a suite of observations which would otherwise remain unconnected.

Stephen Jay Gould

14

Drawing Some Threads Together

It is time to draw together the various lines of argument developed in earlier chapters and attempt an overall evaluation. In what follows, the main ideas of the theory are summarized briefly, and then the evidence presented in earlier chapters is summed up. Later sections deal with a number of questions regarding the implications of the theory and its relationship to various strands in the existing literature on industrial structure. .

14.1 A Brief Review of the Theory

The aim of the study is to explore whether any substantive theoretical propositions are robust to certain kinds of reasonable changes in model specification and might therefore form a basis for examining cross-industry regularities in the area of industrial structure (section 1.3). The central results of the theory pertain to the description of two basic mechanisms, each implying an associated lower bound to the equilibrium level of concentration. The first of these bounds relates to the case in which the level of sunk costs is exogenously given (chapter 2). The second becomes relevant only when sunk costs are endogenously determined (chapter 3).

If only exogenous sunk costs are present, the theory takes a very simple form. The key step in the analysis of this case lies in specifying a function linking concentration to equilibrium prices (or price-cost margins). This function summarizes what happens in the second stage of the game. The phrase "toughness of price competition," as used in the present study, refers to this functional relationship. Although this relationship is not easy to measure, it is nonetheless possible to posit a priori a number of factors that make price competition "tougher" in the present sense. These factors include product characteristics (degree of homogeneity) and institutional factors (strictness of competition policy).

The theory leads to two robust predictions in the exogenous sunk costs setting:

(i) the function specifying the lower bound to equilibrium concentration converges monotonically to zero as market size increases;

(ii) an increase in the toughness of price competition shifts this lower bound upward.

As we go from industries characterized by a high degree of product homogeneity to industries in which scope exists for differentiating rival offerings, two influences shift this lower bound. First, the relaxation in the toughness of price competition implied by the greater degree of product differentiation tends to shift this bound *downward*. Second, insofar as firms can enhance consumers' willingness-to-pay by increasing advertising outlays, a new mechanism comes into play that also constrains equilibrium structure. If it is assumed that the effectiveness of advertising, as measured by the relationship between sunk costs and consumers' willingness-to-pay, always exceeds some minimal level, then there will be some corresponding minimal level of concentration *independent of market size* that must be exceeded at equilibrium. The effects of these two influences on the lower bound to equilibrium concentration are illustrated in figure 3.9.

The theory leads to three more or less robust predictions in this endogenous sunk costs setting:

(i) concentration remains bounded away from zero as market size increases;

(ii) there is no longer any *monotonic* relationship, in general, between market size and minimal concentration levels;

(iii) the only robust comparative static result identified above is that increases in setup cost imply an increase in minimal concentration levels, even in this endogenous sunk costs regime.

14.2   A Review of the Evidence

Four types of evidence have been presented in favor of the theory.

(i)   Econometric Tests

Direct tests of the central predictions of the theory, which relate
to the difference between industries where advertising plays no important role and advertising-intensive industries, were presented in
chapter 5. The results are consistent with the theory and are not
easily reconciled with the counterhypothesis that advertising is an
exogenous barrier to entry.

(ii)   Industry Histories

While the econometric results are *consistent* with the theory, this still
leaves open the possibility that these relationships arise for reasons
quite different to those implicit in the theory. Is it possible to probe
directly whether the mechanisms postulated here are indeed at work
in shaping the evolution of structure? This leads us to much more
informal but nonetheless valuable types of evidence.

The theory explains observed patterns of structure by claiming
that they correspond to Nash equilibria in some underlying game.
This implies that configurations lying beyond the set of equilibria
(i.e., corresponding to concentration levels below the lower bounds
specified above) will be broken by the action of some deviant. Each
of the bounds rests on a different mechanism. In the exogenous
sunk cost model, nonequilibrium configurations could only be maintained in the long run if firms succeeded in holding prices above
their equilibrium levels—and any such attempt will be broken by
the action of a deviant that cuts price. The additional mechanism
that arises in the case of advertising-intensive industries is quite
different. Here, if the structure is too fragmented, it will be optimal
for a deviant to increase advertising outlays and thereby break the
configuration.

Equilibrium theories, of their nature, present a problem when it
comes to direct testing: what maintains the situation as an equilibrium is some mechanism that *would* come into play if a nonequilibrium configuration arose. The operation of such a mechanism
can be seen only when some fortunate accident means that a historically given configuration is not (or is no longer) an equilibrium. Such
scenarios are likely to arise in an industry's early days, before structure has stabilized, and at times when some exogenous shock to
technology or market demand impinges on the system. By looking at

such episodes, some insights can be gained into the relevance of the mechanisms postulated by the theory.

This line of argument has been developed at various points throughout the text. The key point of comparison is between the archetypal examples of the salt and sugar industries, as described in chapter 6, and the frozen food industry, described in chapter 8. The evolution of the salt and sugar industries appears to conform well to the exogenous sunk cost model developed in chapter 2. There seems to be clear evidence that the collapse of fragmented structures was typically precipitated by price cutting. The frozen food industry offers an illustration of the second mechanism. Here, a rapid inflow of early entrants to the U.S. and U.K. industries was followed by a phase of escalating advertising outlays, during which a set of middle-ranking firms experienced declining profitability. The culmination of this process led to the appearance of a clear dual structure in which the (advertising-sensitive) retail market came to be dominated by a handful of firms whose heavily supported brands enjoyed relatively high market shares.

This process is observed to work in a more or less similar form across a wide range of advertising-intensive industries. (Key examples in the United States include coffee, RTE cereals, biscuits, and beer. In the United Kingdom, particularly clear examples arise in RTE cereals and pet food. A striking example in France arises in the mineral water industry. However, well-documented examples are relatively rare outside the United States and United Kingdom—and this point deserves some comment (see below).) The clear contrast in the mechanisms that appear to have played a role in the evolution of concentration between these two groups of industries lends considerable support to the present interpretation of the econometric results of chapter 5.

(iii)   Comparative Static Predictions

A second type of evidence relates to the comparative static predictions of the theory. Two kinds of prediction are of interest here: Within the *exogenous sunk cost* model, it is predicted that the minimal level of concentration consistent with equilibrium should be higher, according as the toughness of price competition is greater. This prediction can be tested by looking at differences in the structure of a given industry across countries that differ in respect of the authorities' stance on competition policy. It can also be tested by looking at the effects within an industry when shifts in the toughess of price competition occur over time. These predictions were explored in chapter 6, in the context of the salt and sugar industry, whose experience appears to conform well to the predictions of the theory.

Within the *endogenous sunk cost* model, a prediction of interest is that increases in setup costs will be associated with an increase in the minimal level of concentration, but that, while such increases will initially raise the level of advertising intensity, further increases in setup cost may or may not lead to a rise in advertising intensity. Whether or not they do depends inter alia on the extent to which increases in advertising increase total *industry* sales (as opposed to the sales of an individual firm).

These predictions were tested in the context of the confectionery and coffee industries in chapter 12. In each case the industry can be separated into two subindustries, which differ widely in their levels of setup cost while being broadly similar in most other pertinent respects (chocolate versus sugar confectionery, instant versus roast and ground coffee). In both cases, the observed differences between the two industries appear to be broadly consistent with the predictions of the theory.

(iv) Other Evidence

The last kind of evidence adduced in favor of the theory relates to its apparent success in knitting together a large number of phenomena that have often been remarked upon, but that have been seen in isolation. Such phenomena include:

• The regular appearance of dual structure in advertising-intensive industries. Within the theory, such a structure is predicted to emerge once different customers differ in their responsiveness to advertising outlays (chapters 3, 8).

• Concentration is usually far above the levels considered warranted on the basis of traditional arguments (chapters 1, 6)—especially in homogeneous goods industries with large setup costs (Anderson et al. 1975). Within this theory, the minimal level of concentration consistent with equilibrium can be arbitrarily high, even when setup costs are modest, depending on the degree of toughness of price competition in the market. The evolution of a highly concentrated structure in the salt and sugar industries, for example, is immediately comprehensible within the theory.

• The existence of apparently separate influences underlying the evolution of structure in some industries has led to an eclectic view, which attributes some importance to each. Within the theory, these influences are seen to be part of a single unified mechanism. The key illustration here is the U.S. beer industry (chapter 13), and another example arises in the RTE cereals industry. In the latter case, the product proliferation mechanism can be seen as a special case arising within the present framework, and it has been argued that this mechanism merely modifies, but does not replace, the basis mechanism underlying the evolution of concentration in all advertising-intensive industries (chapter 10).

Evidence of this kind is both soft and intangible. Nonetheless, it may be extremely important insofar as it appears to confirm the view that these mechanisms play a central role in influencing the evolution of structure.

14.3   The Scope of the Theory

The scope of the theory is quite restricted in a number of different directions; in what follows we look at each of these in turn.

How Advertising Works

No attempt is made here to explain *why* advertising works. That it does is simply taken as an empirical fact. The theory is concerned only with analyzing the economic implications of this observation. It would be inappropriate therefore to take up any stance on the advertising-as-persuasion versus advertising-as-information debate (Ferguson 1988, Connor et al. 1985, p. 295). It is clear that the former view is consistent with our central assumption about advertising effectiveness (condition 2 of chapter 3), but it is less obvious whether the advertising-as-information view is. At first glance, it might seem that if advertising were a pure information-dissemination device, we should reach a saturation level at some absolute level of outlays, thus leading to a violation of condition 2. However, there are versions of the advertising-as-information argument that posit that advertising outlays are a guarantee of product quality, and that the expenditure involved must be large compared to the firm's profit flow in order for it to function as a signaling device in distinguishing high-quality from low-quality suppliers. This latter version of the advertising-as-information story might more plausibly be reconciled with the central assumption of the present analysis.

A separate issue relates to the way in which advertising outlays depreciate over time. It is central to the present treatment that advertising outlays can properly be modeled as a sunk cost, in the sense that yesterday's commitments affect the firm's environment today. In practice, a flow of advertising expenditure will be needed to maintain the firm's image over time. What is at issue here is not the rate of depreciation of advertising, which might be rapid, but rather the difference between the flow of expenditure an incumbent needs to maintain his position and that required of an entrant in establishing a similar position.

Applications to R & D

The theory can be applied in principle to any form of sunk outlays that increase consumers' willingness-to-pay for a given firm's product(s). Thus, the arguments apply also to the analysis of R & D-intensive industries. However, the extension to this area is not immediate: substantial issues arise both within the theory itself, and in relation to the testing of theory.

In advertising-intensive industries, it is a reasonable first approximation to treat a firm's stock of goodwill as a single (scalar) variable and to imagine that this goodwill, once acquired, will be maintained (subject in practice to some "flow" advertising to offset depreciation in the stock of goodwill). In R & D-intensive industries, it is necessary to imagine an industry as consisting of a sequence of discrete product markets (corresponding to successive technologies or technological frontiers). The function $F(u)$, which plays a central role in the theory, can then be interpreted as the envelope of the set of functions corresponding to successive technologies. So just as $F(u)$ is analogous to the advertising response function within the advertising literature, so also is it analogous to the envelope of the curves on an overlapping technologies diagram, in which the performance attained is plotted against cumulative R & D outlays.

The real difference, however, arises in respect of the question: to what extent do R & D outlays incurred on a given vintage carry over to the next vintage? Within the advertising context, it is reasonable to assume that the firm's image carries over to successive generations of product offerings. This is clearly untrue in general for R & D outlays. The answer varies widely from one market to another. In advertising-intensive industries, the fact that the degree of carryover is strong is crucial to the fact that industry leaders, once established, tend to retain their leadership. Where the carryover effect is weak, however, it may induce a switch from a persistence of dominance mode to one of leapfrogging, as industry leadership changes with every generation of technology.

The analysis extends in a relatively straightforward manner to the analysis of *product* innovation. There are some R & D-intensive industries, however, in which process innovation, as well as product innovation, plays a major role (the chemical sector being the most important example). An analysis of process innovation in a setting similar to that used in this study was set out in Dasgupta and Stiglitz 1980.

Finally, in some R & D-intensive industries, patent protection plays a potentially important role in influencing the pattern of technical change, and so the evolution of structure. The presence of patent laws can have the effect of modifying the payoff structure of the game in ways that make it analogous to a tournament. This observation lies at the base of a large literature on patent races (see, for example, Tirole 1989).

Welfare Analysis

No welfare analysis, and so no policy prescriptions, have been offered. There are two fundamental reasons for avoiding any such analysis:

(i) The central aim of this volume is to investigate results that are robust to certain reasonable changes in model specification. An examination of these models indicates that most if not all of the obvious welfare questions depend in a more or less delicate way on the details of the model. (Consider, for example, the outlawing of price coordination in the model of chapter 2.)

(ii) Any judgment on welfare requires that a view be taken as to how advertising affects welfare and, as noted above, this is an issue that is deliberately bypassed here.

Many economists feel that the reason the analysis of structure is worth undertaking is that strong welfare judgments and policy implications follow. This is not the view taken here. Welfare judgments are not proposed here—but neither is the usefulness of pursuing such issues questioned. The only caveat is that such results are best developed at a more market-specific level than that used here.

What *is* implicitly argued here, however, is that the resolution of the agenda of *positive* issues is properly seen as anterior to the making of any welfare judgments or the formulation of policy proposals. Such judgments and proposals deserve to be based on a theory, whether this one or some other, that is shown to be empirically successful in describing the markets in question—and not by reference to some arbitrarily selected model whose results may be fragile to reasonable respecifications of the underlying game.

Profits

The centerpiece of the traditional Bain paradigm lies in the claim that concentration and profitability are positively correlated across industries. At the empirical level, much evidence has been offered for such a correlation—and much dispute surrounds its interpretation (see Scherer 1980 for a survey of evidence and views). No such relationship is claimed in this study, nor is such a relationship deduced. The reason for this is similar to that adduced in relation to welfare judgments.

All the models used here involve free entry, yet the examples presented in chapters 2 and 3 show that intramarginal firms may earn positive profits at equilibrium. Some authors, however, would argue that the appearance of such positive profits by intramarginal firms should induce some kind of costly jockeying for position in the industry. Pushing such an argument to its logical conclusions, authors such as Dixit and Shapiro (1986) and Fudenberg and Tirole (1985) have offered symmetric games with the following features. The only pure-strategy equilibria are asymmetric, and these equilibria involve positive profits for some firms. But by modifying the game so that entry decisions are made over a (long) sequence of short decision periods, a mixed-strategy equilibrium can be obtained that has two features: (i) the probability that an excessive number of firms enter can be made arbitrarily small, while (ii) all firms obtain zero expected profits ex ante. What happens here is that competing for the prize involves outlays on the part of individual firms that are sufficient to dissipate the rents earned by successful entrants.

This example is cited merely in order to make a negative point: within the class of models on which the analysis is based, it is difficult to draw any conclusions regarding profitability that are robust to the same degree as those relationships studied in earlier chapters. Indeed, the difficulties in making the link between the kinds of model set out above and traditional discussions of profitability are very substantial. Quite apart from the theoretical issues just noted, a number of deep questions would need to be addressed as to how profitability should be measured in testing models of this kind. Such issues lie outside our scope.

14.4   The Limitations of the Theory

The theory has four kinds of limitations, two of which have been the subject of separate chapters.

Multiplicity of Equilibria

Since the theory merely implies a lower bound to equilibrium structure, it leaves open a wide range of outcomes that are consistent with equilibrium. This is an *inherent* limitation of the theory. Only by adding more structure, and thus reducing the domain of application of the theory, can more precision be obtained. This point was developed in chapter 7, which focused on the case in which the constraints implied by the theory are weakest.

The Advertising Response Function

A potentially more serious limitation relates to one of the key maintained assumptions of the theory. The notion that different industries can be classified in terms of some typical degree of reponsiveness to advertising outlays, as represented by $F(u)$ in chapter 3, is open to question. Occasional instances underline the well-known difficulties that arise in attempting to divide industries, on the basis of any observable product characteristics, into those that are responsive to advertising and those that are not. The experience of the mineral water industry, examined in chapter 11, underscores this point.

Other Mechanisms

A third kind of limitation has arisen sporadically throughout earlier chapters. This relates to instances in which the evolution of structure appears to be influenced by a mechanism that—though it includes the use of advertising outlays—also encompasses elements that lie beyond our scope. Examples of this were noted in

• the U.S. coffee industry, where the advance of the majors across successive cities involved a mixture of advertising with aggressive price competition. Predatory pricing is excluded within our present framework, in that price competition is modeled as a one-shot game (stage two of the basic game) in which, at equilibrium, all firms have prices at or above marginal cost.

• the U.S. frozen food market, where the pattern of market segmentation appears to be reinforced by the use of "tit-for-tat" entry strategies. Such cross-market strategies between majors may play an important part in some contexts, but they are excluded from the present model.

Cross-Country Differences

One of the most serious limitations of the analysis relates to country-specific influences on structure. The theory is consistent with the emergence of such differences, insofar as institutional factors specific to some country impinge on the toughness of price competition or the shape of the advertising response function. In various industries, we have noted the role played by identifiable influences of this kind (see especially chapters 6 and 13).

There is little doubt, however, that some general tendency exists for concentration to be higher in the United States, and the United Kingdom, for example, than in France, Germany, and Italy. While this difference is widely attested and is observed in the data set, this study has done little to explain it. In chapter 5 such influences were simply subsumed into country dummies. There is reason to believe that the origin of such differences lies outside the scope of this kind of model, and a proper understanding of these influences may require a model that incorporates "growth of firm" effects (see below).

A second source of systematic cross-country differences relates to the role of foreign-based multinationals. In France, Germany, and Italy, United States-based multinationals play a leading role in several of these industries. The same is true of the United Kingdom and Japan, though to a lesser degree (in the sense that some leading U.K. and Japanese firms achieved a stronger position vis-à-vis the multinational groups at an early stage). This point may be related to another difference in experience between the United States and the United Kingdom, on the one hand, and Continental European markets on the other: the apparently lesser extent to which a competitive escalation of advertising outlays has been a feature of French, German, and Italian markets. As noted in chapter 3, the presence of a strong first mover in this kind of market may lead to a preemption effect whereby a concentrated structure may be maintained while total advertising outlays remain lower than would be the case under strategic symmetry.

14.5   Relationships to Other Approaches

Some of the limitations noted above are not so much limitations of the theory per se, but rather are limitations that must attach necessarily to *any* theoretical approach that seeks to account for cross-industry differences in structure by reference to differences in the underlying pattern of technology and tastes. Not all approaches are of this kind, however. Indeed, one of the most striking features of the literature on industrial structure is that it consists of two parts, each of which has its own agenda. Between the two, there have been few points of contact.

The Time-Series Dimension

The part of the literature with which this book has been concerned focuses on the role of industry-specific features that might account for cross-sectional differences in structure. The other part of the literature focuses on time-series issues and includes two important strands: the well-known stochastic models of firm growth, and the literature on merger waves and related issues. Within the kind of model developed here, the motives for merger derive from the possibilities of relaxing price competition in the industry; and although this is doubtless one motive for merger, it is clearly not the only one. A satisfactory theory of merger and acquisition behavior might possibly begin from models of the kind developed above, but any adequate account of such behavior would certainly demand a richer theoretical structure.

The "growth of firms" literature has been heavily directed toward explaining the skew distribution of firm sizes at the aggregate level. Theories of this kind emphasize dynamic aspects of firm growth; and the classical literature on the subject (Hart and Prais 1956, Simon and Bonini 1958, and Prais 1976) is currently undergoing a renaissance in the empirical literature (Pakes and Ericson 1987, Dunne, Roberts, and Samuelson 1988). The only (modest) point of contact between this literature and the cross-sectional literature lies in some attempts to introduce the industry's m.e.s. level as a lower bound to firm size when specifying the stochastic processes underlying the size distribution.

The argument of this study suggests that the constraints on the size distribution of firms that emanate from industry-specific characteristics are much more subtle. Once endogenous sunk costs are present, it is clear that these must influence the evolution of industry structure in quite a complex manner. The meshing of the type of cross-sectional approach developed in the study with the new growth of firms literature represents one of the obvious challenges for future research.

Evolutionary Models

Since we have been much concerned with history, it is only appropriate to remark on the relationship between the theoretical framework of chapter 2 and evolutionary models of industrial structure (see, for example, Nelson and Winter 1982). The essence of any evolutionary approach lies in setting aside the notion of profit maximization in favor of some form of survivor principle. One important objection to many current game-theoretic models is that they rest on the notion that firms carry out quite subtle calculations that require an extremely detailed knowledge of the environment they face. It seems all the more attractive, therefore, to explore whether the profit-maximizing assumption might be replaced with a weaker but more compelling survivor principle.

The key difference between rival evolutionary approaches lies in the *tightness* of the survivor principle that they advocate. At one end of the spectrum, we have the approach taken in evolutionary biology (Maynard Smith 1982, Hammerstein 1989). Here, the central concept of an evolutionarily stable strategy (ESS) is closely analogous to that of the Nash equilibrium concept. While a general characterization of the relationship between the Nash equilibrium concept and that of the ESS appears to be elusive, for many games the two are identical (Van Damme 1987). A reformulation of the present results in this guise would be fairly routine. At the other end of the spectrum of evolutionary models stands the Schumpeterian approach, which has been influential within the industrial organization field. Here, a much weaker version of the survivor principle is employed, and the constraints on the data will be correspondingly weaker.

What would be required, then, to allow a reformulation of the main proposition of chapter 3 in terms of a survivor principle? An examination of the proof of the proposition makes the answer immediately clear: it requires two things. First, it requires that firms earn non-negative profits at equilibrium. This is nonproblematic, for it is precisely this result that is generated either as an approximation, or in some appropriate limit, by any appeal to a survivor principle. The second element is more controversial: this requires that, should any profit opportunity exist, it will be exploited. This notion of "no unexploited opportunities" drives a wedge between tight and weak versions of the survivor principle. The central results of this book depend crucially on an appeal to this latter notion. Even so, this permits an important relaxation in the assumptions employed in chapter 3, for it is no longer necessary to assume that each firm chooses the *optimal* product specifications, but merely that no gaps exist in the configuration that could be profitably filled.

14.6   A Summing Up

In the two preceding sections, we have seen a number of things that the present theory does not purport to do. It is time to place in perspective those things in which it does succeed. Explaining industrial structure has long been acknowledged as a somewhat intractable problem. It is clear that there are many influences at work, and a full and satisfactory theory that properly addresses all of these influences may be long in coming. Yet the fact that there *are* a few empirical regularities that have been pretty well established implies that we may reasonably hope to arrive at a theory with some (limited) explanatory power.

But while a few statistical regularities have indeed been established, the literature to date can claim only a very limited degree of success in explaining cross-sectional differences in structure by reference to industry specific factors. Meanwhile, on the theoretical front, a growing body of literature has induced a certain pessimism; for it turns out that the new generation of game-theoretic models appears to place only limited constraints on the data, first, because multiple equilibria are the norm in these models, and second, because outcomes may be delicately dependent on various market features that are difficult to measure or proxy empirically.

A central thesis of this book is that these two points are not unrelated. The main claim set out in earlier chapters is that there is a close congruence between the few statistical regularities that emerge from the data and the few robust results that emerge from the theory. This seems an encouraging result, both at the theoretical and empirical level. If this view is accepted, then some potentially weighty implications follow both for theory and for empirical work. For theory, it suggests that a potentially fruitful way forward in this area (and perhaps others) may lie in thinking explicitly in terms of a distinction between robust results and particular examples. Allied to this, on the empirical side, it suggests that the two polar forms of investigation—the traditional cross-industry regressions and the currently popular single industry studies—might in principle be merged into a single endeavor, within which the experiences of individual industries can be mapped into special cases of a general theoretical model whose robust results drive the cross-industry regularities .

Afterword

The publication of Samuelson's *Foundations of Economic Analysis* in 1947 can be seen as marking a turning point in the dominant style of research in economics. Prior to that date, the dominant style was one in which models were advanced with some diffidence, as Marshall's successors glanced nervously over their shoulders at the bewildering complexity of the world. Whether the behavior of markets could be adequately represented by simple mathematical models was widely doubted. From the 1950s onward, it is possible to trace a gradual shift of attitude, culminating in the high confidence of "positive economics" in the mid-1960s. By then the wheel had turned full circle. Much of applied economics had come to be organized around an accepted routine: write down the model, derive its comparative static properties, find some data, and run a regression to test these predictions. Equilibrium models had come into their own, and hand in hand with this development went a tendency to rely more and more heavily on purely econometric evidence.

Now it would be difficult to object to the view that hypotheses should be formulated sharply and tested rigorously. But an unfortunate side effect of these largely salutary developments lay in a widening divide between those economists who valued the power and rigor of equilibrium theory and those whose predilection lay in unraveling the messy realities of history. Against this background, it seems a little ironic that the pursuit of pure theory should have brought us full circle. The deeper we go in advancing the theory of markets beyond the safe but largely empty categories of perfect competition and monopoly, the more we discover that history matters.[1]

The ways in which history matters are many and various; first-mover advantages are only the tip of the iceberg. If robust results constrain outcomes only weakly, then there is great scope for adding structure to the model. One route lies in sticking to the basic game-theoretic models and looking to special cases. This is the route followed in the present volume. But this is not the only route, and it is already clear that it will not bring us more than part of the distance toward a full understanding of how industrial structure evolved.

The outcomes of any evolutionary process are vastly contingent, as Gould (1987) so eloquently reminds us. In seeking to explain why things went this way rather that that, we rapidly outrun those systematic and measurable influences that are the domain of the contemporary economist, and we are drawn ineluctably into the historian's realm of accident and personality.

Success in explaining industrial structure may be long in coming. But this is a problem that merits attention, for it involves an unusually nice balance between two elements. Rigorous equilibrium arguments may prove invaluable in providing a secure foundation on which to build. At the same time, the need to come to grips with historical influences is palpable. As we come to better understand the ways in which rigorous theory may be meshed with historical arguments in this field, we may also arrive at a more balanced approach to the marshaling and weighing of the many types of evidence that can serve to discriminate between rival economic models.

---

1. The dangers ahead were already clear to some critics in the 1960s. In an attempt to defend the safe havens of perfect competition and monopoly against the "empirical emptiness" of imperfect competition, Friedman (1953) argued—quite remarkably—that in looking at a market like cigarettes, we might simply treat it as perfectly competitive while analyzing some types of problem, and as a monopoly while analyzing others. (See Archibald 1961, and for a review of these issues, Sutton 1989b.)

Appendices

Appendix 1
Market Share Tables

FRANCE	MARKET SHARE 1987
1 Cie des Salins du Midi et des Salines de l'Est	about 65%
2 Solvay et Cie	about 25%
3 Saline d'Einville	very small
4 Mines de Potasse d'Alsace	very small
Number of producers marketing dry salt: about 5[1]	
Volume of production: 7,711 tons (1985)	

1. With a few artisan producers surviving.
Note: *Volume of production figures for all countries are as reported in the U.S. Bureau of Mines Mineral Yearbook and include unmarketed salt.*

Source: Company interviews.

GERMANY (F.R.)	MARKET SHARE 1981[1]
1 Deutsche Solvay-Werke GmbH	about 35%
2 Sudwestdeutsche Salzwerke AG	about 34%
3 Kali und Salz AG	about 18%
4 Norddeutscher Salinen GmbH (AKZO)	about 6%
Number of producers marketing dry salt: 8	
Volume of production: 12,300 tons (1985)	

1. Market shares changed little during the early 1980s.

Source: Bundeskartellamt.

ITALY	MARKET SHARE 1987
1 Italkali	47%
2 AIS/Monopolio	15%
3 Societe de Salines du Midi et de l'Ouest	11%
4 CIS	7%
Number of producers marketing dry salt: 3	
Volume of production: 4,688 tons (1985)	

Source: Company interviews.

Table M.1 Market shares in the salt industry

UNITED KINGDOM	MARKET SHARE[1] 1986
1 British Salt (Staveley Industries PLC)	50%
2 Imperial Chemical Industries PLC (ICI)	45%
3 New Cheshire Salt Works	about 4%
4 Ingram Thompson & Co. Ltd.	<1%
Number of producers: 5	
Volume of production: 7,856 tons (1985)	
1. Based on volume sales.	

Source: Author's estimates based on MMC 1986 and
company interviews.

UNITED STATES	CAPACITY SHARE[1] 1986
1 International (AKZO)	38%
2 Morton Salt Co.	24%
3 Cargill	14%
Number of producers marketing dry salt: about 7	
Volume of production: 39,226 tons (1985)	
1. Estimates based on 1986 ownership structure and plant capacity figures reported in 1988 by the Bureau of Mines.	

Source: Industry interviews, Bureau of Mines.

FRANCE	MARKET SHARE 1985-86
1 Générale Sucriére	25%
2 Sucre Union	24%
3 Beghin Say[1]	23%
4 Compagnie Francaise de Sucrerie	9%
5 Vermandoise Industries	
Annual consumption: 2.6 million tonnes (1985-1986)	

1. Beghin Say is France's largest producer and controls over 30%
of France's A and B quota. The greater part of its production is
exported, however (63% in 1984/85).

*Source: Source based on tonnage figures cited in MMC 1987.
All consumption figures are from USDA 1986 and relate
to centrifugal sugar (raw value).*

GERMANY (F.R.)	MARKET SHARE 1986
1 Suddeutsche Zucker	about 30%
2 Pfeifer & Langen	about 15%
3 Hannover Zucker AG	about 9%
Number of refiners: 18	
Annual consumption: 2.25 million tonnes (1985-1986)	

*Source: Author's estimates based on capacity figures published
by Verein der Zuckerindustrie.*

ITALY	MARKET SHARE 1985-86
1 Eridania	35%
2 Gruppo Sacc Veneto (Montesi)	22%
3 Gruppo SFIR	9%
4 Sadam	6%
Number of firms: 11	
Annual consumption: 1.78 million tonnes (1985-1986)	

Source: Shares based on tonnage figures cited by MMC (1987).

Table M.2 Market shares in the sugar industry

JAPAN	MARKET SHARE 1981[1]
1 Mitsui Sugar Co.[2]	14.1%
2 Taito Co. Ltd.[2]	9.5%
3 Cito Sugar Co. Ltd.	9.0%
4 Ensuiko Sugar Refining	8.9%
Number of producers: 35 (1981)	
Annual consumption: 2.8 million tonnes (1985-1986)	
1. Shares were very stable throughout the 1980s. 2. The top shareholder in both these companies is the Mitsui group.	

Source: Nikka Keizai.

UNITED KINGDOM	MARKET SHARE 1985
1 British Sugar	52.8%
2 Tate & Lyle	40.9%
Number of refiners: 2	
Annual consumption: 2.35 million tonnes (1985-1986)	
Note: Imports accounted for 6.3% of volume sales in 1985.	

Source: MMC 1987.

UNITED STATES	MARKET SHARE 1986
1 Amstar	21%
2 Great Western	10%
3 Amalgamated	8%
4 California and Hawaii	7%
Annual consumption: 7.28 million tonnes (1985-1986)	

Source: Author's share estimates based on USDA capacity
figures.

FRANCE	MARKET SHARE 1985
1 Grands Moulins de Paris	15%
2 Grands Moulins de Pantin ⎤ Grands Moulins de Corbeil ⎦	8%
3 Grands Moulins de Strasbourg	3%
4 Grands Moulins Storione	3%
Number of producers: about 1,500	
Volume of production: 4.2 million tonnes (1985)	
Note: Exports account for 34% of production.	

Source: Author's estimates based on figures reported by
Dafsa Kompass and Agra-Alimentation.

GERMANY (F.R.)	MARKET SHARE 1986
1 Kampffmeyer Mühlen GmbH	20%
2 Wehrhahn	8%
3 Georg Plange GmbH & Co. KG	5%
4 Erling	5%
Number of producers: about 600	
Volume of output: 4.2 million tonnes (1986)	
Note: Exports account for 12% of production.	

Source: Author's estimates based on interviews.

ITALY	MARKET SHARE 1985
1 Molino di Foggia	2.2%
2 Soc. Romana Macinazione S.p.A.	1.7%
3 Casillo s.r.l.	1.6%
4 Basile s.p.A.	1.2%
Number of producers: 1,144	
Volume of production: 7.0 million tonnes (1985)	
Note: Exports account for almost 15% of production.	

Source: Databank.

Table M.3 Market shares in the flour industry

JAPAN	MARKET SHARE 1985
1 Nisshin Seifun	33%
2 Nippon Seifun	22%
3 Showa Sangyo	7%
4 Nitto Flour Milling	5%
Number of producers: 161	
Value of production: 4.2 million tonnes (1985)	

Source: Yano Research Institute.

UNITED KINGDOM	MARKET SHARE 1986
1 Rank-Hovis McDougal	30-32%
2 Dalgety's	about 24%
3 Associated British Foods	about 20%
4 Heygates	2-3%
Number of producers: 48	
Volume of production: 3.7 million tonnes (1986/87)	

Source: Author's estimates based on interviews.

UNITED STATES	MARKET SHARE 1986
1 ConAgra	18%
2 ADM	13%
3 Cargill	12%
4 Pillsbury	12%
Number of mills: 208	
Volume of production: 17 million tonnes (1985)	

Source: Author's estimates based on data
        supplied by General Mills.

FRANCE	MARKET SHARE 1986
1 Pain Jacquet	about 2%
2 La Pain Turner	about 1%
3 Harry's	about 1%
4 Blé Or	about 0.5%
Number of firms: about 38,000	
Note: For measures of market size in each country, see text.	

Sources: Confédération de Boulangeries Industrielles, Agra-Alimentation.

GERMANY	MARKET SHARE 1984
1 Rugenberger Grossbackereien	2%
2 Geschi-Brot Schiesser	2%
3 B. Wandeln	1.5%
4 Wilhelm Weber	1.5%
Number of firms: about 30,000	

Source: Marketing in Europe 1985.

ITALY	MARKET SHARE 1986
1 Giannotti	Each of these producers has a share of around 1%.
2 Panem	
3 La Spiga	
4 Interplan s.r.l.	
Number of firms: about 32,000	

Source: Company interviews.

Table M.4 Market shares in the bread industry

JAPAN	MARKET SHARE 1983
1 Yamazaki Baking Kansai Yamazaki	27-28%
2 Shikishima Seipan	9-10%
3 Fuji	6-7%
4 Dai-ichi ya	4-5%

Number of firms: about 8,000

Note: Sales to institutions constitute a relatively high proportion of total sales in Japan.

Source: Fuji Keizai.

UNITED KINGDOM	MARKET SHARE 1985
1 Allied Bakeries	about 27%
2 Rank-Hovis McDougal	about 23%
3 Associated Family Bakers	about 5%
4 Warburton	about 3%

Source: Author's estimates based on company interviews.

UNITED STATES	MARKET SHARE 1986
1 Continental Baking (Ralston Purina)	10-13%
2 Campbell Taggart (Anheuser-Busch)	5-7%
3 Flowers Industries	3-5%
4 Interstate Bakeries	3-4%

Number of firms: about 1,800

Source: Author's estimates based on figures reported in Wholesale Bakery 1987 and U.S. Dept of Commerce.

FRANCE	MARKET SHARE 1985
1 Olida-Caby	about 10%
2 Morey	about 6%
3 Fluery-Michon	about 5%
4 Herta	
5 Géo	
Number of firms: about 500 industrial producers	
Volume of sales: 20.3 billion FF (1985)	
Note: Olida and Caby have, since 1985, split into two independent concerns.	

Source: Company interviews.

GERMANY (F.R)	MARKET SHARE 1982
1 Herta-Atland-Dörffler	8-10%
2 Fleiwa Flieschwaren Producktions und vertriebe GmbH	5-6%
3 Stockmeyer GMbH and Co. KG.	3-4%
4 Wilhelm Lutz KG Fleishwarenfabriken GmbH & Co.	2-3%
Number of firms: 660 (1982)	
Volume of sales: about 10 billion DM (1983)	
Note: Imports accounted for 18% of sales in 1982. The market definition includes some meats other than pork (see text).	

Source: Author's estimates based on data reported by Coop-Ag.

ITALY	MARKET SHARE 1986
1 Fiorucci	3-4%
2 Galbani	3-4%
3 Vismara	2-3%
4 Citterio	1-2%
Number of firms: about 2,500	
Value of sales: 5,046 billion lira (1983)	

Source: Databank.

Table M.5 Market shares in processed pork products

JAPAN	MARKET SHARE 1986
1 Itohan Foods Ltd.	17%
2 Nippon Meat Packers	13%
3 Marudai Foods	11%
4 Purina Meat Packers	10%
Number of firms: 250 industrial producers	
Value of sales: 603 billion yen (1986)	

Source: Yano Research Institute.

UNITED STATES	MARKET SHARE 1986
1 Oscar Mayer (Gen. Foods/Philip Morris)	over 5%
2 Geo. Hormel & Co.	about 5%
3 Morrell (United Brands)	4-5%
4 Beatrice Foods	4-5%
5 Sara Lee	4-5%
Number of firms: about 1,000 (1982)	
Value of sales: $13.354 billion (1986)	

Source: Author's estimates based on company
             interviews.

FRANCE	MARKET SHARE 1986
1 Saupiquet	15-16%
2 Compagnie Générale de Conserve (CECAB)	11-12%
3 Bonduelle	10-11%
4 SA des Propriétaires Réunies	less than 3%
Number of firms: 20-25	
Volume of retail sales: 8 billion FF (1986)	
Notes: Imports account for about 15% of sales.	

Source: Agra-Alimentation.

ITALY	MARKET SHARE 1986
1 IRI { Cimo (23-24%) / Alivar (13-14%) }	36-38%
2 Conserve Italia	24-25%
3 Columbani	13-14%
4 Star	5%
Number of firms: 80-90	
Value of retail sales: 107 billion lira (1986)	
Notes: Imports account for less than 5% of sales. See text for market definition.	

Source: Author's estimates, based on figures
supplied by Databank.

Table M.6 Market shares in the canned vegetables industry

UNITED KINGDOM	MARKET SHARE 1986
1 Hillsdown	45-50%
2 Bachelors	15-20%
3 Hartleys	7-10%
4 Pillsbury	7-8%

Number of firms: about 10
Value of retail sales: 239 million (1986)
Notes: Market shares relate to total production including production for retailers' own-labels. Imports account for 15% of sales.

Source: Author's estimates based on sector shares published by Mintel and discussions with producers.

UNITED STATES	MARKET SHARE 1986
1 Del Monte	about 20%
2 Pillsbury (Green Giant)	about 18%
3 Larsen (incl. Ocanomowoc)[1]	
4 Stokely[1]	

Value of retail sales: $2.384 million (1986)
1. Apart from the two market leaders, there are several regional canners of roughly similar importance. Market share of top-four producers lies in 45-55% range.

Source: Author's estimates based on company interviews.

FRANCE	RETAIL MARKET SHARE 1985
1 France Glace Findus (Nestlé)	17-25%
2 Cofralim, Miko (Ortiz-Miko)	14%
3 Cogesal (Unilever)	4%
4 Bonduelle	5%
Number of producers: about 70	
Value of retail sales: 29.2 billion FF (1986)	
Note: The nonretail sector accounts for 47% of total consumption in volume terms.	

Source: Author's estimates based on Agra-Alimentation, MIE.

GERMANY (F.R.)	RETAIL MARKET SHARE 1985
1 Langnese Iglo (Unilever)	35%
2 Bofrost	18-20%
3 Eisman (Co-op)	15-16%
4 Oetker Gruppe	10%
Number of producers: about 70	
Value of retail sales: 7,000 million DM (1986) [1]	
Notes: The nonretail sector accounts for 47% of total consumption by volume. 1. Incl. fruit (1.5% by volume).	

Source: Author's estimates based on company interviews.

ITALY	RETAIL MARKET SHARE 1985
1 Unilever	60%
2 Italgel	17%
3 S.I.P.A. Arena	8%
4 Frigodaunia	4%
Number of firms: about 70	
Value of retail sales: 1,400 billion lira (1986)	

Source: Databank.

Table M.7 Market shares in the frozen food industry

JAPAN	RETAIL MARKET SHARE 1985
1 Nichirei	about 16%
2 Ajinomoto	about 14%
3 Nissui	about 12%
4 Snow Brand (own-label)	about 8%
Number of firms: Over 300	
Value of retail sales: 138.4 billion yen (1986)	
Note: The nonretail sector accounts for 74% of total sales.	

Source: Company interviews.

UNITED KINGDOM	RETAIL MARKET SHARE 1985
1 Birds Eye (Unilever)	25%
2 Ross	8%
3 Findus	4%
Value of retail sales: £1,623 million (1986)	
Note: All but those above have very small retail market shares. The own-label sector accounts for 35% of retail sales. The nonretail sector accounts for about 17% of total sales.	

Source: Unilever.

UNITED STATES	RETAIL MARKET SHARE 1987
1 Campbell	15%
2 ConAgra	14%
3 Pillsbury	11%
4 Stouffer (Nestlé)	9%
5 Kraft	8%
Number of producers: 1,500-1,600	
Value of retail sales: $13,655 million (1986)[1]	
Notes: Precise figures for total nonretail sales are not available. However, it is believed that the nonretail sector is commensurate with the retail sector. 1. Incl. fruit (12% of total volume).	

Source: Euromonitor.

FRANCE	RETAIL MARKET SHARE 1988
1 Societé des Produits du Mais	43%
2 Sopad (Nestlé)	27%
3 Fralib	15%
4 BSN (Liebig)	6%
Value of retail sales: 950 million FF (1986)	

Source: Euromonitor.

GERMANY (F.R.)	RETAIL MARKET SHARE 1986
1 Maggi (Néstle)	about 38%
2 Knorr (Maizena)	about 32%
3 Novia (Unilever)	about 11%
4 Erasco (Pillsbury)	about 3%
Value of retail sales: 575 million DM (1986)	

Source: Euromonitor.

Table M.8 Market shares in the prepared soups industry

JAPAN	RETAIL MARKET SHARE 1985
1 Ajinomoto	about 55%
2 Pokka	about 6%
3 Nestlé	about 5%
4 Meiraku	about 5%
Volume of sales: 45 billion yen (1985)	

Source: Author's estimates based on figures published
by Japanscan (1985).

UNITED KINGDOM	RETAIL MARKET SHARE 1986
1 Heinz	41%
2 Bachelors	15%
3 Campbell	9%
4 CPC (Knorr)	5%
5 Crosse & Blackwell (Nestlé)	5%
Value of retail sales: £258 million (1986)	
Note: Nonretail sales account for 20% of total sales.	

Source: Euromonitor.

UNITED STATES	RETAIL MARKET SHARE 1986
1 Campbell Soup Company	63%
2 Lipton	8%
3 Progresso	2%
4 Ramada Pride	2%
Value of sales: $2,257 million (1986)	

Source: Euromonitor.

FRANCE	RETAIL MARKET SHARE 1986
1 Astra Calve (Unilever)	68%
2 Lesieur	13%
3 Vamo	-
Volume of consumption: 216,000 tonnes (1986)	
Note: Two-thirds of Vamo's output is accounted for by own-label sales.	

Source: Author's estimates based on company interviews.

GERMANY (F.R.)	RETAIL MARKET SHARE 1986
1 Union Deutsche Lebensmittelwerke	52%
2 Walter Rau Lebensmittelwerke	20%
3 Fritz Homann Lebensmittelwerke	14%
4 Margarinewerke J. Lülf	about 5%
Number of firms: about 16	
Value of consumption: 496,000 tonnes (20% nonretail)	
Notes: Most of Walter Rau's output goes to the own-label sector via the Aldi supermarket chain, whose own-label product accounts for 20% of the market. Unilever held a 50% stake in Fritz Homann and has since acquired the company (1989).	

Source: Author's estimates based on company interviews.

ITALY	RETAIL MARKET SHARE 1986
1 Van den Berghs (Unilever)	40-45%
2 STAR	23-28%
3 Kraft	13-16%
4 Tavella	about 6%
Number of firms: about 20	
Volume of consumption: 95,000 tonnes	
Note: Retail sales account for less than one-quarter of total volume	

Source: Tavella, Inchiesta Food.

Table M.9 Market shares in the margarine industry

JAPAN	RETAIL MARKET SHARE 1986
1 Snow Brand Milk Products	39%
2 Ajinomoto Co. Inc.	15%
3 Nippon Lever	12%
4 Meiji Milk Products Ltd.	10%
Number of firms: 28	
Volume of production: 238,000 tonnes (1985)	
Note: The retail market in Japan accounts for only one-third of total sales. Imports and exports are negligible.	

Source: Euromonitor.

UNITED KINGDOM	RETAIL MARKET SHARE 1986
1 Van den Berghs (Unilever)	50%
2 Achetos and Hutchinson	10%
3 Unigate	7%
4 Kraft	8%
5 Dairy Crest	4-5%
6 Coop	about 3%
Number of firms: about 8	
Volume of consumption: 422,000 tonnes (1986)	
Note: Achetos and Hutchinson's 10% share relates wholly to their production for retailer's own-label. Own-label sales account for 26% of all retail sales.	

Source: Van den Berghs.

UNITED STATES	RETAIL MARKET SHARE 1986
1 Kraft, Inc.	20%[1]
2 H.J.H. Nabisco Inc.	20%
3 Lever Bros.	9%
4 Land O'Lakes	4%
5 CPC International	2%
Number of firms: 24	
Volume of consumption: 1,232,000 tonnes	
1. Kraft's share relates to the company's position prior to its acquisition of the Chiffon brand from Anderson Clayton, which occurred in early 1987.	

Source: Euromonitor.

FRANCE	MARKET SHARE 1987
1 Pernod Ricard	over 20%
2 Schweppes	over 15%
3 Perrier	over 15%
4 BSN	over 14%
Number of firms: 40-50	
Volume of consumption: 0.9 billion liters per year	

Source: Company interviews.

GERMANY (F.R.)	MARKET SHARE 1983
1 Coca-Cola	39%
2 Pepsi	9%
3 Aldi (own-label)	6%
4 Sinalco	3%
Number of firms: about 700	
Volume of consumption: 4.0 billion liters per year	

Source: Euromonitor.

ITALY	MARKET SHARE 1986
1 Coca-Cola	61%
2 Gruppo San Pellegrino	12%
3 San Benedetto	7%
4 Crodo	4%
Volume of consumption: 1.1 billion liters per year	

Source: Marketing in Europe.

Table M.10 Market shares in the soft drink industry

JAPAN	MARKET SHARE 1986
1 Kirin Brewery	28%
2 Coca-Cola	28%
3 Asahi Brewery	28%
4 Sapporo Brewery	4%
Number of firms: about 1,500	
Volume of consumption: 2.9 billion liters per year	

Source: Yano Research Institute.

UNITED KINGDOM	MARKET SHARE 1987
1 Coca-Cola and Schweppes Beverages	about 25%
2 Britvic Corona	about 20%
3 Reckitt and Colman	about 2%
Number of firms: about 270	
Volume of consumption: 2.6 billion liters per year	
Note: Apart from the above three firms, several regional sellers have shares of around 1%.	

Source: Author's estimates based on company interviews.

UNITED STATES	MARKET SHARE 1986
1 Coca-Cola	about 40%
2 Pepsico	about 30%
3 Hicks & Hass	about 13%
4 Royal Crown	about 5.5%
5 Cadbury Schweppes	about 5%
Volume of consumption: 50 billion liters per year	

Source: U.S. Industrial Outlook 1987, chap. 39.

FRANCE	MARKET SHARE 1983
1 Kellogg	50-55%
2 Quaker	23-25%
3 Banania	13-15%
Value of market: 365 million FF (1984)	
Note: The three firms shown above account for about 90% of sales. Three further firms account for the remaining 10-11%. Most sales are supplied via imports. This industry is therefore excluded from the basic data set.	

Source: Euromonitor.

GERMANY (F.R.)	MARKET SHARE 1984
1 Kellogg Deutschland	50%
2 Schnee Koppe	15%
3 Brüggen	8%
4 Kölln	8%
Value of sales: 280 million DM (1984)	
Note: Kellogg operates a single plant in Germany, from which it supplies all Continental European markets. This industry is therefore excluded from the basic data set. See text.	

Source: Euromonitor.

ITALY	MARKET SHARE 1987
1 Kellogg	56%
2 Gram	20%
3 Quaker	19%
Value of sales: 38 billion lira (1987)	
Note: Apart from the above three firms, only three small (importing) firms were active in the mid-1980s. Most of sales are supplied via imports. This industry is therefore excluded from the basic data set.	

Source: Company interview.

Table M.11 Market shares in the RTE cereals industry

JAPAN	MARKET SHARE 1986
1 Kellogg	58%
2 Cisco	26%
3 Nisshin Foods (Nisshin Seifun)	4%
4 Nippon Shokuin Seiso	4%
Value of market: 7.2 billion yen (1986)	
Note: Kellogg imports part of their product and manufactures some locally. This industry is excluded from the basic data set.	

Source: Fuji Keizai and company interview.

UNITED KINGDOM	MARKET SHARE[1] 1986
1 Kellogg	49%
2 Weetabix	17%
3 Nabisco	8%
4 Quaker	5%
Value of sales: £423 million (1986)	
1. By volume.	

Source: Mintel.

UNITED STATES	MARKET SHARE 1986
1 Kellogg	42%
2 General Mills	24%
3 General Foods	12%
4 Quaker Oats	8%
Value of sales: $4,870 million (1986)	

Source: Euromonitor.

FRANCE	MARKET SHARE 1986
1 BSN (Evian, Badoit)	about 25%
2 Vittel	20-25%
3 Perrier/Contrexeville	20-25%
4 Volvic	7%

Volume of sales: 3,203 million liters (1986)

Note: Considerable disagreement exists as to the market share pattern in the French market. The above estimates should be treated with caution.

Source: Author's estimates based on various sources and company interviews.

GERMANY (F.R.)	MARKET SHARE 1985
1 Apollinaris	9%
2 Gerolsteiner	7%
3 H. Hövelmann	6%
4 Blaue Quellen	5%

Volume of sales: 2,800 million liters (1985)

Source: Author's estimates based on company interviews

ITALY	MARKET SHARE 1986
1 The Italfin 80 (Ciarrapico) group	21-22%
2 The Sangemini group	18-19%
3 The San Pellegrino group	14%

Volume of sales: 2,700 million liters (1986)

Note: Apart from the three major groups indicated above, there are several independent firms with shares in the 2-3% range.

Source: Databank.

Table M.12 Market shares in the mineral water industry

JAPAN	MARKET SHARE 1985
1 Suntory	43%
2 Kirin	9%
3 Nikka Whiskey	5%
4 Horinai	5%
Volume of sales: 77 million liters (1985)	

Source: Based on figures reported in Japanscan, October 1986.

UNITED KINGDOM	MARKET SHARE 1985
1 Perrier	55%
2 Evian	9%
3 Malvern	6%
4 Ashbourne	3%
Volume of sales: 75 million liters (1985)	
Note: During the mid-1980s, the U.K. market grew rapidly and the pattern of market shares changed sharply over a short period. Considerable differences of opinion exist in the industry as to share figures for this period.	

Source: Euromonitor.

FRANCE	MARKET SHARE[1] 1987
1 BSN (Vandamme Pie qui chante)	about 20%
2 General Foods France	about 16%
3 Lamy Lutti	about 10%
4 Haribo	over 5%

Imports: 19% of consumption
Volume of consumption: 144,800 tonnes (1986)
1. Shares in all tables refer to sugar confectionery, excluding chewing gum.

Source: Author's estimates based on published sources and company interviews. The volume of consumption figures in all tables are taken from the IOCCC Statistical Bulletin.

GERMANY (F.R.)	MARKET SHARE 1986
1 Haribo GmbH and Co.	14-18%
2 August Storck KG	14-18%
3 Ragolds	3-5%
4 Katjes Fassin GmbH and Co.	2-4%

Number of firms: about 107	Imports: 18% of consumption
Volume of consumption: 357,100 tonnes (1986)	

Source: Author's estimates based on various published sources and company interviews.

ITALY	MARKET SHARE 1985
1 Sperlari S.p.A.	13-14%
2 Ferrero S.p.A.	6-7%
3 Perugina	4-5%
4 Perfetti S.p.A.	4-5%

Number of firms: 145	Imports: 11.6% of sales
Volume of consumption: 117,800 tonnes (1986)	

Source: Author's estimates based on figures supplied by Databank.

Table M.13 Market shares in the sugar confectionery industry

JAPAN	MARKET SHARE 1982
1 Fujiya	about 12%
2 Mikakuto	about 11%
3 Meiji-Seika	about 10%
4 Morinaga-Seika	about 9%

Number of firms: 192   Imports: 5% of consumption
Volume of consumption: 143,200 tonnes (1986)
1. Some sources report individual shares for the top four in the mid-1980s that exceed the above by about 1%. Difficulties in market definition preclude more precise estimates.

Source: Author's estimates based on various sources
and company interviews.

UNITED KINGDOM	MARKET SHARE 1986
1 Trebor Sharp	12%
2 Rowntree Mackintosh	12%
3 Bassett Foods plc	7%
4 Wrigley Co.	7%

Number of firms: about 130   Imports: 11% of consumption
Volume of consumption: 282,600 tonnes (1986)

Source: Mintel 1986, based on figures supplied by Cocoa,
Chocolate and Confectionery Alliance (CCCA).

UNITED STATES	MARKET SHARE 1986
1 Jacobs Suchard Brach	about 10%
2 Nabisco	about 7-8%
3 Leaf Inc.	about 5%
4 Warner Lambert [1]	less than 5%

Number of firms: over 1,000   Imports: 10% of consumption
Volume of consumption: 1,011,600 tonnes (1986)
1. It is difficult to identify the fourth-largest seller, but no firm apart from the top three has a share exceeding 5%.

Source: Company interviews.

FRANCE	MARKET SHARE 1986
1 Mars	13%
2 Suchard-Tobler	9%
3 Poulain Industries	9%
4 Chocolaterie Cantalou	8-10%[1]

Number of firms: over 50	Imports: 20% of consumption

Volume of consumption: 229,100 tonnes (1986)

1. Mostly via retailers' own-labels. Cantalou's volume share is much larger; see text.

Source: Author's estimates based on MIE 1985 and company interviews. The volume of consumption figures in all tables are taken from the IOCCC statistical bulletin.

GERMANY (F.R.)	MARKET SHARE 1986
1 Jacobs Suchard AG	30-35%
2 Ferrero HG	13-17%
3 Mars GmbH	13-17%
4 Imhoff Gruppe	13-17%

Number of firms: about 125	Imports: 21% of consumption

Volume of consumption: 381,900 tonnes (1986)

Source: Author's estimates based on various published sources and company interviews.

ITALY	MARKET SHARE 1985
1 Ferrero	26-27%
2 Perugina	11-12%
3 Dolma S.p.A. (Mars)	5-6%
4 Sidalm	4-5%

Number of firms: 200	Imports: 29% of consumption

Volume of consumption: 73,600 tonnes (1986)

Source: Databank.

Table M.14 Market shares in the chocolate confectionery industry

JAPAN	MARKET SHARE 1986
1 Meiji Seika	21%
2 Ezaki Glico	13%
3 Morinaga-Seika	13%
4 Lotte	13%
Number of firms: 66 Imports: 5% of consumption	
Volume of consumption: 159,900 tonnes (1986)	

Source: Fuji Keizai.

UNITED KINGDOM	MARKET SHARE 1986
1 Cadbury Ltd.	27%
2 Rowntree Mackintosh Group	25%
3 Mars	24%
4 Terry's	4%
Number of firms: about 50 Imports: 12% of consumption	
Volume of consumption: 448,600 tonnes (1986)	

Source: Euromonitor.

UNITED STATES	CANDY BARS	MARKET SHARE 1986
1 Hershey Foods Corp.	36 %	33-38%
2 Mars Inc.	25%	33-38%
3 Nestlé Enterprises Inc.	9%	7-9%
4 Cadbury Schweppes Inc.	9%	7-9%
Number of firms: about 30 Imports: 3% of consumption		
Volume of consumption: 1,046,300 tonnes (1986)		
Note: Market shares for candy bars are relatively reliable.		

Source: Author's estimates based on various published
sources and discussion with producers.

FRANCE	MARKET SHARE 1986
1 Generale Biscuit	34%
2 Belin	18%
3 Gringoine Brossard (Pillsbury)	5-8%
4 Biscuiterie Nantaise (General Mills)	4-5%
Number of firms: over 260	
Volume of consumption: 382,400 tonnes (1986)	
Note: Several firms have shares in the range 3-6%. These include Biscuiterie Nantaise, Bahlsen, and Delacre.	

Source: Author's estimates based on Agra-Alimentation 1987 and industry interviews.

GERMANY (F.R.)	MARKET SHARE 1987
1 Bahlsen	25%
2 De Beuklaer (General Biscuit)	10%
3 Declacre	8%
4 Brandt	6%
Number of firms: 72	
Volume of consumption: 180,000 tonnes (1986) 185,000 tonnes (1987)	
Note: This table is based on a narrower industry definition than that used by the Bundesverband des Deutschen Susswaren Industrie.	

Source: Euromonitor.

ITALY	MARKET SHARE 1985[1]
1 Barilla	22%
2 Saiwa	10%
3 Pavesi	8%
4 Colussi	6%
Number of firms: 170[2]	
Volume of consumption: 300,400 tonnes (1986)	
1. These figures correspond to a narrow industry definition (see text). The four-firm sales concentration ratio for all dry bakery products is 36%. 2. All dry bakery products.	

Source: Author's estimates based on various trade publications and company interviews.

Table M.15 Market shares in the biscuit industry

JAPAN	MARKET SHARE 1986
1 Kita Nippon Shokuhin	19%
2 Yamazaki Nabisco	11%
3 Lotte	10%
4 Tohato Tokyo Seiko	9%
Number of firms: 150	
Volume of consumption: 245,900 tonnes (1986)	

Source: Yano Research Institute.

UNITED KINGDOM	MARKET SHARE 1986
1 United Biscuits	31%
2 Nabisco	13-15%
3 Rowntree	8-10%[1]
4 Burton	5-7%
Number of firms: about 30	
Volume of consumption: 559,000 tonnes (1986)	
1. Some arbitrariness arises in respect of the classification of chocolate countlines versus biscuits in this case.	

Source: Author's estimates based on various market
research reports.

UNITED STATES	MARKET SHARE 1986
1 Nabisco	40-45%
2 Keebler	15-16%
3 Sunshine	5-7%
4 Pepperidge Farm	3-5%
Number of firms: over 300	
Volume of production: 1,232,000 tons (1986)	

Source: Author's estimates based on company interviews.

FRANCE	RETAIL MARKET SHARE 1986
1 Jacques Vabre[1] 2 Grand-Mère[1]	about 40%
3 Douwe Egberts	about 15-20%
4 Café Quotidien	2-3%

1. Both Jacques Vabre and Grand-Mère are now owned by Jacobs.

Source: Agra-Alimentation.

GERMANY (F.R.)	RETAIL MARKET SHARE 1986
1 Jacobs	23%
2 Albrecht (Aldi)	18%
3 Tchibo	18%
4 Eduscho	15%

Source: Gruner and Jahr.

ITALY	RETAIL MARKET SHARE 1986
1 Lavazza	38%
2 Splendid (Procter & Gamble)	12%
3 Bourbon (Nestlé)	6%
4 Sao	4-5%

Source: Company interview.

Table M.16 Market shares in roast and ground coffee

JAPAN	TOTAL MARKET SHARE 1986
1 UCC	37%
2 KEY	23%
3 ART	7%
4 Néstle (MJB)	2%

Source: Nikka Keizai 1988.

UNITED KINGDOM	RETAIL MARKET SHARE 1986
1 General Foods (Kenco)	about 25%
2 Allied Lyons	12-18%
3 Melitta	about 10%

Source: Author's estimates based on MIE reports
and company interviews.

UNITED STATES	RETAIL MARKET SHARE 1986
1 General Foods	36%
2 Procter & Gamble (Folger)	28%
3 Néstle (Hills Bros.)	11%
4 Choc Full O'Nuts	5%

Source: Euromonitor.

FRANCE	RETAIL MARKET SHARE 1986
1 Sopad Nestlé	56%
2 Cicona	8%
3 General Foods	6%
4 Jacques Vabre	3%
Note: Instant coffee constitutes 20% of total coffee consumption by volume.	

Source: Agra-Alimentation.

GERMANY (F.R.)	RETAIL MARKET SHARE 1986
1 Nestlé	50%
2 Jacobs	18%
3 Hag (GF)	12%
Note: Instant coffee constitutes about 10% of total retail sales of coffee.	

Source: Gruner and Jahr.

ITALY	RETAIL MARKET SHARE 1986
1 Nestlé	close to 100%
Note: Instant coffee comprises 1% of retail coffee sales.	

Source: Company interview.

Table M.17 Market shares in instant coffee

JAPAN	RETAIL MARKET SHARE 1986
1 Nestlé	63%
2 Ajinomoto	24%
3 UCC	2%

Note: Instant coffee accounts for 63% of all coffee sales and about four-fifths of all retail sales.

Source: Nikka Keizai 1988 and company interviews.

UNITED KINGDOM	RETAIL MARKET SHARE 1987
1 Nestlé	45-48%
2 General Foods	21%
3 Sainsbury's own-label	7%
4 Brooke Bond Oxo (Unilever)	6-7%

Note: Instant coffee accounts for 90% of all retail coffee sales.

Source: Mintel.

UNITED STATES	RETAIL MARKET SHARE 1986
1 General Foods	43%
3 Nestlé	27%
3 Procter & Gamble	20%

Note: Instant coffee accounts for about one-third of retail sales.

Source: Euromonitor.

FRANCE	MARKET SHARE[1] 1987
1 Unisabi (Mars)	about 50%
2 Quaker France	about 20%
3 Gloria (Néstle)	about 16%

Number of firms: 30-35

Value of sales: 5,789 million FF (1987)[1]

1. All tables relate to dog and cat food only (see text).

Source: Company interviews.

GERMANY (F.R.)	MARKET SHARE 1984
1 Effem (Mars)	About 65%
2 Quaker-Latz	20%
3 Glücksklee (Carnation-Nestlé)	4%
4 Bremer Vitakraft-Werke	4%

Number of firms: about 80

Value of sales: 1.3 billion DM (1984)

Source: Euromonitor.

JAPAN	MARKET SHARE 1986
1 Nippon Petfood	17%
2 Nisshin Petfood	8%
3 Ajinomoto General Foods	7%
4 Puri Taiyo Petfood	7%

Number of firms: 22

Value of sales: about 40 billion yen (1986)

Source: Company interviews.

Table M.18 Market shares in the pet foods industry

UNITED KINGDOM	MARKET SHARE 1985
1 Pedigree Petfoods	53%
2 Spillers Ltd.	22%
3 Quaker	7.5%
4 Carnation (Nestlé)	0.5%
Number of firms: 60-80	
Value of sales: £742 million (1985)	

Source: Author's estimates based on figures published by Euromonitor and Mintel.

UNITED STATES	MARKET SHARE 1986
1 Ralston Purina	28%
2 Quaker Oats	14%
3 Carnation (Nestlé)	12%
4 Mars	10%
Number of firms: over 100	
Value of sales: $5.3 billion (1986)	

Source: Euromonitor.

FRANCE	MARKET SHARE 1986
1 BSN Gervais-Danone	40-45%
2 Nestlé (Sopad, Guigoz)	25-27%
3 Société des Produits du Mais	13-14%
4 Milupa	5-6%
Number of firms: about 9	
Value of retail sales: 2,850 million FF (1986)	

Source: Author's estimates based on data published
in Euromonitor.

GERMANY (F.R.)	MARKET SHARE 1986
1 Néstle	about 35%
2 Milupa	over 25%
3 Hipp	20-25%
Consumer expenditure: 724 million DM (1986)	
Note: Exports account for about one-seventh of production. Imports are extremely small.	

Source: Author's estimates based on data published by
Euromonitor.

ITALY	MARKET SHARE 1983
1 Plada (H.J. Heinz)	60%
2 Monda (Gerber)	15%
3 Nestlé	8%
4 Star	5%
5 Milupa	5%
Number of firms: about 10	
Value of sales: 510 billion lira (1986)	

Source: Euromonitor.

Table M.19 Market shares in the baby foods industry

UNITED KINGDOM	MARKET SHARE 1986
1 Cow and Gate (Unigate)	30%
2 Wyeth Laboratories	19%
3 Heinz	17%
4 Milupa	14%
5 Robinson's (Reckett & Colman)	8%
6 Farley (Glaxo)	5%
Number of firms: over 10	
Value of retail sales: £150 million (1986)	

Source: Euromonitor.

UNITED STATES	MARKET SHARE[1] 1988
1 Ross Laboratories	32%
2 Gerber Products	29%
3 Meade Johnson	22%
4 Beech-Nut	7%
Number of firms: about 6	
Value of sales: $2,071 million (1986)	
1. See text for market definition (which includes both infant formula and other baby foods).	

Source: Author's estimates based on data supplied by Euromonitor. See text.

FRANCE	MARKET SHARE 1985
1 BSN Gervais-Danone	about 50%
2 SOGEBRA	about 25%
3 Seb Artois	about 6%
4 Pecheur	about 2%
Number of firms: 33 Imports: 11% of consumption	
Volume of consumption: 22 million hl (1986)	

Source: Dafsa.

GERMANY (F.R.)	MARKET SHARE 1984
1 Tchiba-Reemtsma group	8%
2 Oetker group	8%
3 Hypo-Bank group	7%
4 Holsten	
Number of firms: about 1,300 Imports: <1% of consumption	
Volume of consumption: 90 million hl (1986)	

Source: Author's estimates based on various published
sources and company interviews.

ITALY	MARKET SHARE 1985
1 Perroni	24%
2 Dreher	16%
3 Wührer	8%
4 Poretti	7%
Volume of consumption: 12.4 million hl (1985)	
Note: Peroni and Wührer merged in the late 1980s. Several firms, including Poretti, have shares in the 4-7% range.	

Source: Author's estimates based on Largo Consumo 1987
and estimates published in the trade press.

Table M.20 Market shares in the beer industry

JAPAN	MARKET SHARE 1986
1 Kirin Brewing Co. Ltd.	about 60%
2 Sapporo Breweries Ltd.	about 21%
3 Asahi Breweries	about 10%
4 Suntory Ltd.	about 9%
Number of firms: 5 Imports: 0.15%	
Volume of consumption: 47 million hl (1986)	

Source: Nihon Keizai Shinbun, 28 August 1987.

UNITED KINGDOM	MARKET SHARE 1985
1 Bass PLC	23%
2 Allied Lyons PLC	13%
3 Grand Metropolitan	12%
4 Whitbread & Co. PLC	11%
5 Scottish & Newcastle Breweries PLC	10%
6 Courage Group Ltd.	9%
Number of firms: 171[1] Imports: 6-7% of consumption	
Volume of consumption: 61 million hl (1986)	
1. See text; half of these have fewer than ten employees.	

Source: MMC 1989 (figures rounded to nearest 1%).

UNITED STATES	MARKET SHARE 1986
1 Anheuser-Busch Inc.	39%
2 Miller Brewing Company (Philip Morris Group)	21%
3 Stroh	12%
4 Heilemann	9%
Number of firms: 67 (1982) Imports: 4% of consumption	
Volume of consumption: 228 million hl (1986)	

Source: Business Trends Analysts.

Appendix 3.1

Theory

This appendix is concerned with establishing a number of technical results stated in chapter 3. It deals with:

(i) The convexity conditions on the advertising response function $F(u)$ that ensure a "well-behaved" solution.

(ii) The proof that assumption 1 implies condition 1, under Cournot or Bertrand competition.

(iii) The $\Sigma\Sigma$ locus.

(i) Convexity Condition

In this section it is shown that the condition

$$\gamma > \max\left\{1, \frac{2a}{3\sigma}\right\}$$

ensures

(a) that the second order condition for a maximum of the profit function $\Pi(u|\bar{u}) - F(u)$ is satisfied,

(b) that equations (2) and (4) of the text, as illustrated in figure 3.2, determine a unique solution that corresponds to this maximum.

(a) Second-Order Condition

The profit of a deviant firm offering "perceived quality" level u, when $(N-1)$ rival firms offer $\bar{u}$, is given by

$$\Pi(u|\bar{u}) = S \left\{ 1 - \cfrac{1}{\cfrac{1}{\mathcal{N}-1} + \cfrac{u}{\bar{u}}} \right\}^2 ,$$

while the fixed cost schedule is

$$F(u) = \sigma + \frac{a}{\gamma}(u^\gamma - 1).$$

At equilibrium, we have $\Pi' = F'$ at $u = \bar{u}$, and the second-order condition $\Pi'' < F''$ can be expressed as

$$\bar{u}\frac{\Pi''}{\Pi'}\bigg|_{u=\bar{u}} < \bar{u}\frac{F''}{F'}\bigg|_{u=\bar{u}}.$$

Differentiating the above expressions with respect to u to express this in explicit form yields

$$\frac{(\mathcal{N}-1)(\mathcal{N}-3)}{\mathcal{N}} < \gamma - 1$$

or $\quad \gamma > \mathcal{N} + \dfrac{3}{\mathcal{N}} - 3.$ \hfill (5)

On the domain $1 \leqslant \mathcal{N} \leqslant 3$, this is satisfied for any $\gamma > 1$. On $\mathcal{N} \geqslant 3$, the expression on the r.h.s. is increasing, whence it suffices that this condition be solved

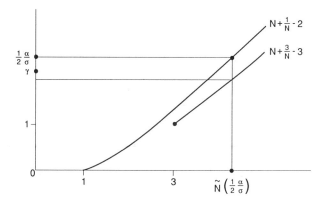

Figure 3.1.1
The expression $\mathcal{N} + (3/\mathcal{N}) - 3$, evaluated at $\tilde{\mathcal{N}}(\frac{1}{2}a/\sigma)$, is at most $\frac{1}{2}a/\sigma - \frac{1}{3}$ on the domain $\mathcal{N} \geqslant 3$. (Note that the vertical distance between the two schedules illustrated takes its minimum value of $\frac{1}{3}$ at $\mathcal{N} = 3$.)

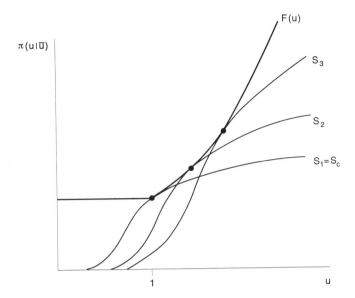

Figure 3.1.2
The functions $\pi(u|\bar{u})$ and $F(u)$. The figure shows how the equilbrium value $\bar{u}$ increases as S increases. In the figure $S_c = S_1 < S_2 < S_3$, where S_c corresponds to the "switch point" at which $\bar{u} = 1$.

for the maximal value of $\mathcal{N}$ attained over the permitted range of parameter values.

The maximal value of $\mathcal{N}$ is *either* $\tilde{\mathcal{N}}(\gamma/2)$ (attained asymptotically as $S \to \infty$) *or* it is $\tilde{\mathcal{N}}\left(\dfrac{1}{2}\dfrac{a}{\sigma}\right)$, attained at the switch point. (The notation $\tilde{\mathcal{N}}(x)$ denotes the root of $\mathcal{N} + (1/\mathcal{N}) - 2 = x$ on the domain $\mathcal{N} \geqslant 1$; see text.) But $\tilde{\mathcal{N}}(\gamma/2)$ satisfies equation (5) for all $\mathcal{N} \geqslant 3$, whereas $\tilde{\mathcal{N}}\left(\dfrac{1}{2}\dfrac{a}{\sigma}\right)$ satisfies (5) on $\mathcal{N} \geqslant 3$ if $\gamma > \dfrac{1}{2}\dfrac{a}{\sigma} - \dfrac{1}{3}$ (see figure 3.1.1). Hence the condition $\gamma > \dfrac{2}{3}\dfrac{a}{\sigma}$ is sufficient to imply that the point defined by equations (2) and (4) of the text is a local maximum of the profit function. It is easily seen that this point also corresponds to a global maximum (figure 3.1.2).

(b)   Unique Symmetric Solution

To establish that there is only one symmetric solution satisfying equations (2′) and (4) of the text, it is sufficient to show that the zero profit schedule (2′) must cut schedule (4) from below. It is intuitively clear that this requires that γ should not be too far below a/σ. By solving equation (4) of the text for F and differentiating, we obtain

$$\frac{dF}{d\mathcal{N}} = -\frac{\sigma - a/\gamma}{\left[1 - \frac{2}{\gamma}\left(\mathcal{N} + \frac{1}{\mathcal{N}} - 2\right)\right]^2}\left\{-\frac{2}{\gamma}\left(1 - \frac{1}{\mathcal{N}^2}\right)\right\}. \tag{6}$$

We require that this expression be greater in absolute value than the slope of the zero profit schedule, $F = S/\mathcal{N}^2$ at any point where the two schedules cross over the relevant range $F \geq \sigma$. This condition is required to hold for all vectors of parameters such that $\gamma \leq a/\sigma$.

Using equation (3) of the text to substitute for the denominator in (6), this condition reduces to the requirement that

$$\frac{S/\mathcal{N}}{a - \sigma\gamma}\left(1 - \frac{1}{\mathcal{N}^2}\right) > 1.$$

Using the fact that $S/\mathcal{N}^2 \geq \sigma$ and $\mathcal{N} \geq \mathcal{N}_\infty = \tilde{\mathcal{N}}(\gamma/2)$ on the relevant domain, it follows that the condition $\gamma > 2\,a/3\,\sigma$ is sufficient to ensure the result.

(ii)   Deriving Condition 1

It is proved here that assumption 1, which imposes certain properties of the standard model of horizontal and vertical product differentiation, together with assumption of *either* Bertrand *or* Cournot competition, implies condition 1 of the text.

ASSUMPTION 1:

(i) There is some bound $\bar{c}$ such that $c(u) < \bar{c}$, for all $u \geq 1$.

(ii) The utility function $U(u, d, m)$ satisfies $U_u > 0$, $U_m > 0$ and $U_d < 0$. Moreover, there exist bounds b_1, b_2, b_3 and some $\underline{m} \geq 0$ such that for all $u \geq 1$, $m \geq \underline{m}$ and $d \in [0, 1]$,

$uU_u > b_1;$

$U_m < b_2;$

$U_d < b_3.$

(iii) $\bar{Y} > \underline{m} + \bar{c}.$

(iv) For some $\underline{f} > 0, f(Y, h) \geq \underline{f}$ for all $Y \in [\underline{Y}, \bar{Y}], h \in [0, 1].$

Proof: We first define a function $P(u, Y)$ that allows us to place a lower bound on a consumer's willingness-to-pay for any product with attributes (u, h), where $u > \bar{u}, h \in [0, 1]$, given that all rival offerings lie at or below $\bar{u}$. We look first at a consumer whose most preferred value of the horizontal attribute coincides with the level h offered by the deviant firm. Note that the utility achieved by such a consumer from purchasing any of the rival products cannot exceed $U(\bar{u}, 0, Y)$. The equation

$$U(u, 0, Y - P) = U(\bar{u}, 0, Y)$$

implicitly defines the function $P(u; Y)$; and since $U_u > 0$, $U_m > 0$, we have $P(u; Y) = 0$ is strictly increasing in u. It follows that a consumer of income Y will prefer the good of quality u at price $P(u; Y)$ over the available alternative at any price $p \geqslant 0$.

Totally differentiating the above expression and using (ii) yields

$$u \frac{\partial P}{\partial u} > \frac{b_1}{b_2} \qquad \text{for any } u, Y \text{ such that } 0 \leqslant P(u; Y) \leqslant Y - \underline{m},$$

whence, noting that $P(\bar{u}; Y) = 0$, we have

$$P(u; Y) = \int_{\bar{u}}^{u} \frac{\partial P}{\partial u} du > \frac{b_1}{b_2} \int_{\bar{u}}^{u} \frac{du}{u} = \frac{b_1}{b_2} \ln \frac{u}{\bar{u}}.$$

The expression on the r.h.s. increases to $+\infty$ with u (figure 3.1.3). Hence there exists some $\tilde{u}$ such that $P(\tilde{u}; Y) \geqslant Y - \underline{m} > \bar{c}$ for $u \geqslant \tilde{u}$, where the last inequality follows from (iii).

Now choose some small (positive or negative) Δh such that $0 \leqslant h + \Delta h \leqslant 1$. From (ii), a consumer whose most preferred horizontal attribute is $h + \Delta h$ will have a willingness-to-pay for this product that is not less than

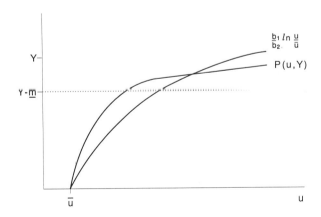

Figure 3.1.3
The function $P(u, y)$.

$$P(u; \Upsilon) - \frac{b_3}{b_2} \Delta h.$$

Hence, it follows from the above discussion that it is possible to find a vector $\{u^*, \Upsilon^*, p^*, \Delta h\}$ with $p^* > \bar{c}$ and $\Upsilon^* < \bar{\Upsilon}$ such that all consumers who have income $\Upsilon \geqslant \Upsilon^*$ and whose most preferred horizontal attribute lies in the range $(h, h + \Delta h)$ will prefer to purchase a product with attributes (u^*, h) at price p^* over any available alternative, offered at any non-negative price.

Such consumers constitute a fraction of the total population equal to

$$\mu = \int_{\Upsilon*}^{\bar{\Upsilon}} \int_{h}^{h+\Delta h} f(\Upsilon, h) \, dh dy \geqslant \underline{f} \Delta h (\bar{\Upsilon} - \Upsilon^*), \qquad \text{using (iv)}.$$

Hence by setting price equal to p^* (Bertrand competition) or output equal to $\mu \mathbf{N}$ (Cournot competition), the firm can achieve profit

$$\Pi \geqslant \mu (p^* - \bar{c}) \mathbf{N}$$

at equilibrium.

Setting

$$\alpha = \mu (p^* - \bar{c})/y > 0,$$

where y denotes the mean income of the population, we obtain assumption 1. This completes the proof.

(iii) **The $\Sigma\Sigma$ Locus**

The locus $\Sigma\Sigma$ is traced out as σ varies, for some fixed value of γ. So long as $\sigma > \underline{\sigma}$, the schedule is defined by the local condition described in the text. For σ sufficiently close to zero, the schedule must be described by reference to global deviations. An explicit formula for the schedule in this zone is difficult to obtain, but it is easy to show that the schedule cuts the horizontal axis at some finite S. To see this, consider a (candidate) equilibrium in the no-advertising zone in the limit $\sigma \to 0$, whence $\mathcal{N} \to \infty$. Take any $v > 1$ and let a deviant set $u = v$. This yields profit

$$\Pi(v|1) \to S(1 - 1/v)$$

which increases to ∞ with S, while the fixed cost

$$F(v) = \frac{a}{\gamma} (v^\gamma - 1)$$

is independent of S. Hence for some finite S a deviation to v is profitable.

Appendix 6.1

The Salt Industry

The Product

Common salt (sodium chloride) is produced either by mining natural deposits of rock salt or by evaporation of sea salt. The relative importance of the latter source varies with climate (being of particular importance in France) and the yields obtained fluctuate widely with summer temperatures. Rock salt is produced by dissolving crude rock salt in brine, followed by evaporation. The traditional open-pan method has long given way to the more efficient technique of vacuum evaporation among all but the very smallest concerns. The total volume of salt production by country is shown in table 6.1.1.

The main categories produced reflect the main use of salt: for de-icing roads, for use in the chemical industry, for sale to the food industry, and for sale to domestic users. A substantial fraction of total production is made up of salt produced by chemical companies for their own internal use; here, we will be concerned only with salt coming onto the market. The level of purity needed in the four main areas of use varies widely. Crude rock salt is suitable for de-icing roads, but a high level of purity is required for the food industry and for domestic use; and finally, a very small proportion of total volume goes to pharmaceutical uses, where an extremely high level of purity is required. Sea salt is intermediate in cost between crude rock salt and refined rock salt, and its uses span a wide spectrum of applications.

Product Homogeneity

Within any particular salt category, the products offered by rival firms differ little, except in the case of the specialist high-purity salt sold to the pharmaceutical industry. Where price differentials exist, they are usually associated with differences in the quality and appearance of packaging. Very wide retail price differentials associated largely with such differences occurred, for example, in

Table 6.1.1

Volume of production of salt, by country, 1984 (all types, including rock salt, sea salt, and *unmarketed* brine used internally by the chemical industry, etc. The latter category is relatively large.)

	Production (thousand tons)
France	7,711
Germany	12,300
Italy	4,688
Japan	1,300
United Kindgom	7,856
United States	39,226

Source: U.S. Bureau of Mines, *Mineral Yearbook 1985.*

the German market through much of the postwar period. Three price categories could be distinguished, with prices for the top category typically three times those for the bottom. While differences in packaging may reflect only differences in (unit variable) cost, they can also constitute a form of price discrimination in an imperfectly competitive market. The rather wide differentials observed in this instance led to a recommendation by the German Health Ministry that consumers should choose the cheapest salt on offer. While such packaging-based differences are common, albeit at narrower differentials, the use of (fixed) advertising outlays to promote an effective brand image is much rarer (for example, the German firm Bayer made an attempt to support its brand by long-term advertising).

In the United States, the Federal Trade Commission has on a number of occasions acted against salt producers that made advertising claims about the alleged superiority of their product. Another strategy has involved the production of salt-based seasonings, which can be differentiated and which enjoy sometimes substantial advertising support. A single product line of this kind, Morton's Seasoned Salt, enjoyed advertising support of £2.57 million in 1987, as against £1.12 million for regular household salt. (The figure for salt advertising used in computing the advertising-sales ratio reported in chapter 4 is based on the latter figure and does not include such salt-based seasonings.)

Such occasional exceptions apart, advertising levels for salt are so low as to often go unrecorded in statistics. Moreover, such outlays are effective in supporting margins only in the retail sector, which typically constitutes no more than one-tenth of the total market in the countries studied here. Throughout the remaining segments of the market, competition within any particular category of salt is focused heavily on price.

Setup Costs in the Salt Industry

The U.S. salt industry is divided between two SIC codes. Most rock salt is produced by establishments classified under SIC code 1476, details of which are provided in the *Census of Mineral Industries, 1977*. Most evaporated salt, produced from natural or artificial brine, is classified within manufacturing industry, SIC 2899 (Chemicals and Chemical Preparations, n.e.c.)[1]; but salt accounts for only a very small part of the activities of this large residual category, which encompassed a total of 1,639 establishments in 1977. Data concerning this industry are available in the *Census of Manufactures, 1977*, and the *Annual Survey of Manufacturers, 1976*. Further information on the salt industry as a whole is available in the Bureau of Mines *Annual Yearbook* for 1977 . (The volumes for these years are those most closely contemporaneous with the sources used in deriving the setup cost estimates quoted in chapter 4, Table 4.2.)

The setup cost estimate for *rock salt* cited in table 4.2 was derived as follows:

• For SIC 1476, the gross value of depreciable assets at end of year 1977 amounted to $182.7 million, while industry shipments totaled $159.8 million.

• The median plant in this industry falls in the size class of 20–40 employees. Data for this size class have been suppressed to avoid disclosing information on individual firms. Data are available for the two adjacent size classes, however, as follows. Three establishments with 10–19 employees account for annual shipments valued at $3.9 million, out of an industry total of $159.8 million. Thus the average establishment in this size category accounts for 0.8% of industry sales. Three establishments with 50–99 employees account for annual shipments of $16.8 million; thus the average establishment in this size category accounts for 3.52% of industry sales. These two figures provide a lower and upper bound to the value of m.e.s.

A similar approach for evaporated salt is not feasible, since data for this category are subsumed into a larger miscellaneous group of industries.

For the salt industry as a whole, no capital-output ratio can be computed from the published data cited above; but an estimate of m.e.s. can be derived from the breakdown of output by size of establishment cited in the Bureau of Mines *Annual Yearbook* for 1977 (p. 171). In that year, the median plant size fell in the category 100,000–1,000,000 tons per annum. Twenty-eight plants in this size category accounted for 12% of total production. Hence the average plant in this size category produced 0.43% of total output. This provides an estimate of m.e.s. for the industry as a whole.

The Markets by Country

The U.S. and U.K. markets are described in chapter 6. The Japanese market is omitted from the study. In what follows, the French, German, and Italian industries are described briefly.

---

1. In 1977, output of rock salt was 17.8 million short tons, valued at $161.0 million; output of evaporated salt was 5.6 million short tons, valued at $246.2 million. These figures exclude brine, used as such.

France

France, a substantial net exporter of salt, produces both sea salt (along the Mediterranean coast) and rock salt in the Jura mountains (Lorraine) in roughly equal proportions. The production of sea salt is centered around Aigues-Mortes (which has been a center of production since Roman times) and Salin-de-Girand, Europe's largest saltworks, both close to the estuary of the Rhône; these two saltworks together account for 90% of France 's production of sea salt. In the mid-nineteenth century, salt in this area was produced by a large number of small firms, which joined forces with a merchant from Montpellier to form the Compagnie des Salins du Midi. The company gradually acquired all of the saltworks in the Mediterranean area. Up to the early 1950s, a sizable fringe of smaller concerns continued to operate; throughout the 1960s, however, a series of mergers and acquisitions reduced the total number of producers to a handful. In particular, the Compagnie des Salins du Midi merged with Salines de l'Est et du Sud-Ouest to become Compagnie des Salins du Midi et des Salines de l'Est (C.S.M.E.), which today accounts for some two-thirds of total output. Over the same period, substantial consolidation occurred among the rock salt producers of the Lorraine area; the major result of this consolidation was the emergence of the Varangéville vacuum salt plant, owned by C.S.M.E. The only other substantial producer in France is the Belgian chemical concern Solvay. The company has major industry in the Jura region, whose output is absorbed by the company's chemical plants. Part of its output from other sites is sold on the French market, however, where it accounts for about one-quarter of sales.

Although France is a major net exporter of sea salt, it also imports a small part of its domestic needs; this largely reflects the role of transport costs, with users close to Belgian and German producers buying in from abroad. Production, imports, and exports fluctuate with climatic factors, but as a rough guide, total French production amounts to 6.7 million tons per annum; half of this is in the form of brine, used directly by the chemical industry. Some 3.5 million tons are marketed; over half a million tons are exported in a typical year, while imports amount to less than one-quarter of a million tons.

Germany (F.R.)

The German salt industry has experienced a process of gradual consolidation akin to that occurring elsewhere, but some special features of the process are worth noting. A substantial part of total industry capacity is held by public authorities, whereas the other major presence in the industry is that of international salt companies (Solvay (Belgium) and AKZO (Netherlands)), and German chemical companies (e.g., Wacker-Chemie GmbH, owned by Höechst).

A look at patterns of shareholding in the industry indicates that effective consolidation was already well established in the 1950s and 1960s. In 1952, twenty firms were in operation; by 1969, this number had fallen to eleven. Among these eleven firms, however, three identifiable groups were clearly dominant. Deutsche Solvay-Werke GmbH, a subsidiary of the Belgian salt specialist Solvay, was (and still is) the market leader. It operated two plants whose combined capacity (about one-third of total industry capacity) was more than double that of either of its nearest rivals, Salzwerk Heilbronn AG and Saline Friedrichshall. The latter concern, however, was held by the state of Baden-Wurttemberg, which also held the former jointly with the city of Heilbronn, as well as holding the smaller Südwestdeutsche Salinen. In 1971, these various interests were brought together as Südwestdeutsche Salzwerke AG, in which each of the two public authorities held a 45% share, thereby forming a group similar in size to Solvay. The fourth- and fifth-largest producers, in 1966, were Salzdetfurth AG, and Burbach-Werke AG; both of these were held by Wintershall-Konzern, and in 1970 the two companies were merged to form today's third major producer, Kali und Salz AG.

The three majors now supply almost 90% of German salt. Only three other concerns have a share exceeding 1%. They are Norddeutsche Salinen GmbH (in which AKZO is a major shareholder); Wacker-Chemie (a subsidiary of Höechst); and Bayerische Berg-, Hutten- und Salzwerke AG, which is held by the state of Bavaria, and which specializes in the supply of salt to the retail trade via its Bad Reichenhaller Salz subsidiary.

Italy

Until 1974 the production and sale of salt in Italy fell under the control of the state monopoly (Monopolio) for more than a century. The Monopolio also controlled the production of tobacco products, and retail salt was sold via a network of wholesalers—Italy's 60,000 tobacconists. The salt monopoly applied, however, only to the Italian mainland (where sea salt was produced) and excluded Sicily and Sardinia, where rock salt was mined by MSAMS (subsequently renamed Italkali). The Sicilian authorities hold a majority stake (51%) in Italkali, the remaining shares being privately held, and the company enjoys public support (in the form of favorable interest rates on borrowing, for example).

The dissolution of the state monopoly, on 1 January 1974, meant that Italkali could sell its salt nationally. The dissolution of the monopoly also prompted the formation of Compagnia Italia Sali (CIS), whose founders had formerly worked in the Monopolio and who aimed initially to play a role in distribution, buying in salt from the Monopolio for resale through new channels, in particular through grocery outlets.

In the years immediately following dissolution, strong competition developed on two fronts, as Italkali tried to expand the share of rock salt in the market while, on the other hand, CIS and Italkali both attempted to expand their shares on the distribution side. CIS continued to acquire all its salt from the Monopolio until 1978 . In that year however, the Monopolio ran out of stocks a result of climatic factors—and CIS turned to foreign sources of supply. Its two suppliers were the Dutch chemical company AKZO, for high quality vacuum salt, and the French C.S.M.E., for sea salt. In 1983/4, however, CIS reverted to purchasing its salt from the Monopolio. Over the intervening period (from 1978 to 1983), however, the Monopolio had been encountering serious difficulties in selling its salt. Not only had CIS turned to foreign sources of supply, but a number of Italian sugar producers—who at that time faced declining sales— turned to the import and distribution of salt as a way of filling their packaging capacity. Further imports were introduced by a number of new companies that entered the salt industry over the period, aiming specifically to exploit the availability of cheaper sources of supply on the international market. The Monopolio's difficulty in disposing of its supplies prompted a joint venture with Italkali in 1983/84. A new company, AIS, was formed, in which each had a 50% stake. All the Monopolio's production would go through AIS and would be sold through Italkali's distribution net.

By the mid-1980s, the Italian industry faced a twofold problem: an overall level of excess capacity, exacerbated by Italkali's expansion in the post-dissolution period, existed side by side with increasing price pressure from imports, which played an important role at the margin as small producers turned to the cheapest source of supply. Spain and Egypt have both been important sources at the margin in recent years, though the Monopolio has responded by lowering price, and total penetration has remained low (setting aside the import of high-quality salt for the chemical industry). Italkali, given its substantial resources and the availability of state support, can offer basic supplies of salt at highly competitive prices, and it is this factor, together with pressure from imports, that now sets the baseline of prices in the market. CIS, still buying in all its crude salt, has responded both by cutting employment and raising productivity in its processing plants and by attempting to focus more of its sales on high-quality, specialist segments. In 1987, CIS was acquired by France's leading producer, C.S.M.E. (their main supplier during their import phase in 1979–1984).

Appendix 6.2

The Sugar Industry

The Product

Sugar (sucrose) is produced either from cane or—in colder climates—from beet. The U.S. industry was, until the turn of the century, based on cane sugar; an indigenous beet sugar industry developed in the early part of this century. The European countries, on the other hand, produce sugar from beet, except in the case of the United Kingdom, which also refines imported cane sugar. Both products are perfect substitutes in consumption. Cane sugar production, however, involves substantially higher setup costs. Until recently, there were no good substitutes for sugar. In recent years, however, high fructose corn syrup (HFCS) has replaced sugar within the United States in many food industry uses (notably in the production of soft drinks). Sugar producers within the EC, however, enjoy effective protection vis-à-vis HFCS, which has had little impact on European markets.

Product Homogeneity

A limited range of sugar categories can be distinguished. These vary either in the degree of purification or color, on the one hand, or in the physical form (granulated, cubed, or variously shaped). The offerings of rival refiners within a category are, certain specialities apart, virtually identical. Attempts to create brand awareness have met with little success in general because of the considerable difficulty of differentiating a product in this industry from the offerings of competitors.[1] The only major wave of advertising in the United Kingdom

---

1. A rare exception arose in the United Kingdom in the 1980s. Taking advantage of the trend in consumers' thinking in favor of health foods, a small sugar firm introduced a new variety. This innovation took advantage of the fact that some consumers appear to believe purification per se "removes goodness" (contrary to the view within the industry, which holds that the only effect of whitening sugar is to remove undesirable impurities). Brown

occurred at a time when an independent sugar producer, Tate and Lyle, feared possible nationalization. This led to a round of press advertising, promoting the Mr. Cube brand name; this brand support was not, however, associated with a price premium. Within the United States, Amstar's Domino brand has for some time enjoyed a very modest degree of advertising support. On the whole, however, the level of advertising in the industry is usually so low as to pass unrecorded.

Setup Costs

Anderson, Lynch and Ogur, in analysing the U.S. industry, noted that a modern, efficient sugar beet processing plant costs about $30 million to construct. While this was a large sum in absolute terms, it was "less than the amount required in such other industries as brewing, cigarettes, petroleum and steel." They also note that, at the other extreme, entry to the shoe industry is possible for $1 million. They conclude: "Capital barriers thus appear to be moderate" (Anderson et al. 1975, p. 32). The same authors note that, in either cane or beet sugar, a firm building a single plant of m.e.s. would account for 3% to 6% of total sales of refined sugar (beet and cane) in the average marketing region.[2] On the basis of this, they argue that "there appears to be no technological reason for present high concentration levels"; indeed, they argue that there is room for twenty plants of similar size, all of them efficient, in such a region. "The level of concentration," they note, "is not explained by economies of scale in the refining process." These observations emphasize the inadequacy of a simple technical appeal to scale economies as an explanation for the levels of concentration observed (see chapter 1). The explanation developed in chapter 2 is consistent with the appearance of a highly concentrated equilibrium structure, even in the presence of moderate setup costs.

Pricing in the Sugar Industry

While some measure of intervention in the sugar industry occurs in all countries, the manner in which it impinges on price competition among sellers of refined sugar varies widely.

---

sugar is favored on these grounds, but its strong and distinctive taste is seen as a disadvantage among tea drinkers. The new and highly successful product was *partly* refined: its taste was close to that of white sugar, but its color still fell sufficiently short of white to lend it a "natural" or unrefined appearance.

2. They do note further that, because industry demand is inelastic, this may nonetheless constitute a barrier to entry sufficient to allow price to be somewhat higher than marginal cost. Even assuming a (rather high) value of 0.4 for demand elasticity, the entry of a new plant supplying 4% of industry output would necessitate a price fall of 10%.

The United States

The United States operates a system of price support directed toward sugar producers (i.e., farmers, as opposed to refiners). It bases the level of support on a calculated target price that it aims to bring about in the market. The key step in putting together the modern sugar regime lay in the Sugar Act of 1934, which set out—against a background of acute distress among sugar producers in the face of low world prices—to establish quotas both for domestic production and for imports, by country of origin. A tax on processing was introduced, out of which benefit payments were made to growers. Attempts were made, via the design of the benefit payments, to create incentives to producers to limit their acreage. By adjusting the quotas, the authorities were in a position to set a target price for refined sugar on the U.S. market. This target price, under the terms of the relevant legislation, was to be chosen to balance producer and consumer interests.

As Anderson et al. (1975) note, the target price was on some rare occasions exceeded when a shortfall in domestic production coincided with rising prices on the world market (1963 and 1973–1974), but apart from these exceptions the domestic price has been remarkably close to the target price. As these authors note, the asymmetry is easily explained, for the authorities can readily adjust quotas to raise prices on the domestic market, but they cannot reduce prices to meet the target if the world price exceeds the target price. This regime has undergone a number of modifications over time. The arrangements have been allowed to lapse briefly—in 1974–1977 and in 1980–1981—when market prices were sufficiently high to render the provisions unwarranted. For details, the reader is referred to USDA 1984.

The pertinent issue, however, is not the pricing of raw sugar but the determination of refining margins. This will depend on the level of wholesale prices of refined sugar. Wholesale prices are determined in the United States on the basis of a basing point system, according to which each refiner sets a price to a customer as a function of that customer's distance from a base point used for that region. (The base point need not be the site of any particular refinery.) Anderson et al. (1985) remark that schemes of this kind may facilitate price collusion because they make common knowledge the price each customer can expect to obtain from rival sellers. The target price system is designed on the assumption that the price of refined sugar will be determined by a process of price competition among refiners. A series of antitrust actions were brought against the refiners in the 1970s in respect of their pricing practices.

The European Community Sugar Regime

From 1968, the French, German, and Italian industries operated within the framework of the EEC sugar regime. The basic principles of the arrangement run as follows: on the formation of the regime, each country was allocated a production quota based on its output level over the preceding five years. The quota was subdivided into A and B components: sugar production up to the A + B quota could be sold within the community at a guaranteed minimum price, the balance of the A + B quota amount over community consumption being exported. The community imposed levies payable by producers, however, and the size of the levy was substantially greater for B quota sugar. These latter levies are currently set so as to impose on producers the cost to the community of selling any excess over community consumption on the world market. The original intention was that the B quotas would be adjusted over time in order to redirect production within the community toward low-cost producers—but such adjustments have been slow to appear. Any production exceeding the A + B quota (dubbed "C" sugar) must be sold by producers outside the community on the free market. The community's minimum price is typically substantially higher than the world price.

Among the community's producers, France has the lowest unit cost (of production and processing combined), and Italy the highest. The differences in unit cost reflect inter alia climatic differences: sugar beet is harvested and processed over a limited period (the "campaign") whose duration varies widely across producers, so that the number of months for which sugar beet factories are actually operating is highly variable. The levels of A + B quotas and domestic consumption are shown in table 6.2.1. France is a substantial exporter; its A + B quota is far in excess of domestic consumption. Italy is a net importer, its consumption levels being substantially greater than its A + B quotas. Germany's A + B quotas, on the other hand, moderately exceed its domestic consumption. The lower prices obtained on world markets ensure that, in most cases, production remains close to the A + B quota; in 1984–1985, for example, the community produced 12,500,000 tonnes (white sugar equivalent); of this, 9,323,000 tonnes were classified as C sugar—and of this, France accounted for almost half the total, at 638,000 tonnes, Germany for 293,000, and Italy for none.

The way in which this regime impinges on the structure of the industry within each country depends crucially on how country quotas are allocated across producers. In each of the countries considered here, the procedure adopted was

Table 6.2.1

Quotas, production, and consumption of sugar in four European Community countries (thousand tonnes)

	A & B quota	A + B sugar	C sugar	Consumption
Germany	2,602	2,600	293	2,202
France	3,802	3,619	638	1,907
Italy	1,568	1,275	—	1,614
United Kingdom	1,144	1,144	170	2,268

Source: Monopolies and Mergers Commission 1987.

to allocate quotas to firms on the same basis as had been employed by the EEC in determining country quotas, that is, in proportion to the firm's production level over the preceding five years. This had the effect, by and large, of freezing the structure attained by the industry at the time of the scheme's inception (1968). In the case of the German industry, a moderately concentrated structure had evolved by that time, but in both Italy and France, the industry of the 1960s was a quite fragmented one. The French authorities, in line with their general philosophy vis-à-vis the community, encouraged a reorganization of the industry on the eve of EEC entry. For Italy, change came later: only repeated financial difficulties among Italian sugar firms prompted a major reorganization of the industry in 1984.

Germany (F.R.)

The evolution of the German industry illustrates the appearance of some forms of intervention that have come to characterize much of Europe's sugar industry. Throughout the late nineteenth century, the growth of the various national sugar industries was fostered in many cases by government subsidies, and this process led to a severe glut on world markets. Repeated attempts were made in the latter half of the century to control this problem by way of proposed agreements to limit or abandon subsidies. In each case, the attempt failed because at least one major producer opted out (in 1864, it was Germany that stayed out; in 1877, it was the Netherlands).

Against this background, the German government decided in 1896 to limit domestic production by way of a system of taxes on output in excess of a certain quota. In the following year, the German sugar producers joined together in a single association (Verein der Deutschen Zuckerindustrie) that superseded earlier partial associations. Finally, in 1902, the first major international accord was reached at Brussels between Germany and seven other West European countries, under which all members agreed to abolish all subsidies on the production and sale of sugar. The Brussels agreement was renewed in 1907 for a further term of five years.

In the years immediately following the First World War, Germany's sugar industry was highly regulated. In 1924, however, wartime controls were lifted and a new association of producers was formed. The new association set out to limit German refiners' sales on the domestic market by setting minimum requirements on the volume of sugar to be exported. Meanwhile, attempts to establish an international accord in the spirit of the prewar Brussels agreement failed in 1927, as Britain and Java decided to opt out.

The regime of the late 1920s proved to be a comfortable one for the German industry; production levels rose and German exports doubled between 1925 and 1930. But the overexpansion of the industry that occurred in these years led to severe losses in 1930–1931. In the latter year, the government intervened, requiring producers to join an association that imposed production quotas. This restored the fortunes of the industry, and both inventory levels and the level of indebtedness fell rapidly over the next few years.

From 1934 onward, the industry came under the direct control of the government, a situation that persisted through to the early postwar years. Controls lapsed in 1950, and in 1951 a new law came into effect, under which the price of sugar would be determined by the authorities, who would regulate the level of sales by region by means of a monthly quota. Transport cost differentials, moreover, would be offset by means of subsidies. Under a later law of 1959, provision was made for the use of subsidies for factory building and closure, to facilitate mergers aimed at rationalizing production. Thus, the coming of the EEC sugar regime in 1968 involved no very dramatic discontinuity in the affairs of the industry.

Current Structure

In 1926, Konrad Schumacher brought together many small south German refineries to form Süddeutsche Zucker. Many of its factories were in areas that would form part of East Germany; following the war, it made up for the loss of these by building a number of new factories. Throughout the postwar period, it has been Germany's leading sugar producer. Its extensive net of shareholdings in the other major sugar producers give it a strong influence in the industry; in the early 1980s, its shareholdings included a 25% stake in Zuckerfabrik Franken GmbH, the fourth-largest producer. The industry's second producer throughout the entire postwar period has been Pfeifer & Langen, which has grown both through building new refineries and by way of acquisitions. It operates seven factories in the western part of the country. It is unusual, among German sugar refiners, in being widely diversified (its other interests include biscuits, confectionery, snack foods, and tea).

Germany has three major sugar beet growing areas. In the south, all factories are owned either by Süddeutsche Zucker AG or the industry's fourth producer, Zuckerfabrik Franken GmbH. In the western region, Pfeifer & Langen own six of the nine factories. In the third major beet-growing area (Lower Saxony), eight firms are active, and they operate via a common marketing organization (Verkaufsgemeinschaft) whose membership includes the number-three producer, Hannover Zucker AG, and the Nordzucker brand. There are in fact only three important brands of sugar on the German market (Nordzucker, Südzucker (owned by Süddeutsche Zucker AG), and Kölner Zucker (Pfeifer & Langen).

Indeed, the level of regional concentration accounts for the recent concerns of the competition policy authority, the Bundeskartellamt, as evidenced by its decisions to forbid Pfeifer & Langen to join a common marketing organization, and to forbid Süddeutsche Zucker AG and Zuckerfabrik Franken GmbH (which between them own all the factories in the south) to form such an organization. (The two latter firms merged in 1988 to become Südzucker AG Mannheim/Ochsenfurt.)

Italy

The Italian sugar industry faces a severe climatic disadvantage relative to its European rivals.[3] The industry has long enjoyed a degree of protection and subsidy, both before and after accession to the EEC. In the 1950s, the policy regime favored the development of the industry; many small refiners entered the market, and the area under beet cultivation was greatly extended. As a result, on Italy's entry to the EEC, it had a relatively fragmented sugar industry, in which a large number of firms operated on a small scale under adverse cost conditions. Rivalry among the small refiners took the form of competition against each other for beet supplies from domestic growers.

Price competition is heavily muted. In addition to the EEC's minimum intervention price, the Italian authorities also fix a maximum price slightly above that level. Throughout the 1970s, a combination of relatively low production within the EEC and a relatively high intervention price led to satisfactory profit levels for Italy's sugar producers. But a surge in production following a large sugar crop in 1981 led to a series of financial difficulties: two firms alone had production levels exceeding Italy's A + B quota at the beginning of the 1980s, and much of the country's production was sold on the free market.

The resulting losses for producers led to severe financial difficulties for two of the leading groups of producers, Montesi and Maraldi. Following the collapse of the Montesi group, the Italian authorities invited the industry leader, Eridania (acquired by the Feruzzi group in 1979), to participate in its restructuring. A new company, ISI, was formed in which Eridania had an indirect equity holding, and most of Montesi's factories were transferred to ISI. The Maraldi group went into bankruptcy in the early 1980s. What remains as Gruppo SFIR is at present a subsidiary of General Azucarera de Espana.

France

In 1967, France's sugar industry was the most fragmented in Europe, despite the fact that it had been undergoing a gradual process of consolidation throughout the 1960s and the number of sugar factories had fallen to 92 in 1966 from 109 in 1954/55. This process involved, inter alia, the acquisition of small refiners by the industry's two leading firms: in 1966, for example, Beghin absorbed two refineries in which it already held a majority stake, while Say acquired a majority stake in a small refiner in the Ardennes. The two industry leaders also signed an accord in the same year, arranging a regrouping of certain refineries between the two for the sake of geographical rationalization. Beghin and Say, together with the industry's third and fourth producers, Raffineries de St. Louis

---

3. The period over which sugar beet is harvested lasts a mere 50–60 days, a period far below that of many of its European competitors (the corresponding period in the United Kingdom, for example, is 100–120 days). Italy's producers face a serious and unavoidable disadvantage, therefore, which is reflected in their comparatively high level of unit cost.

and Bouchon-Pajot, had a combined turnover of 1.5 billion FF, as compared to 2.5 billion for the industry as a whole.

But this gradual process of consolidation was transformed, in 1967, by two events that effectively divided the industry into two major groups: the first of these brought together the four above-named firms, among others, into a new leading group held by a mixture of French and foreign interests. The second event related to the consolidation of a group of agricultural cooperatives and seven (later eight) private producers into a (much smaller) second grouping, Sucre-Union.

The formation of the dominant (Beghin-Say) group involved a complex series of arrangements between the companies. An international consortium, the Compagnie Européenne de l'industrie sucrière (CEIS), was formed, in which Beghin held a 33.4% stake; Italy's leading producer Eridania held a 15.6% stake; and the remaining stake was held by European Sugar France, an organization held jointly by Belgian and U.K. sugar firms (Raffinerie Tirlemontoise, Tate & Lyle).

Meanwhile, the industry's third and fourth producers Bouchon-Pajot and the Raffineries de St. Louis, together with Nouvelles Sucrières Réunis, were amalgamated to form Générale Sucrière. Both Bouchon-Pajot and Raffineries de St. Louis held a 10% stake in Say, which in turn held a 27.9% stake in Raffineries de St. Louis and a 23.77% stake in Nouvelles Sucrières Réunis.

Thus, with the acquisition of Say by CEIS in 1967, a complex network of interests was formed, which produced a new leading sugar group and led to a pattern of ownership in the French industry at least as concentrated as that prevailing among its European partners. The degree of consolidation achieved may be gauged by examining the turnover of each of France's larger refiners in 1966 (table 6.2.2).

One effect of the new regrouping, was to hasten the process of rationalization of smaller French refineries; the average level of capacity, which had been 1,180 tonnes/day in 1954/55, somewhat exceeded 3,000 tonnes/day in 1970/71 and rose to 4,550 tonnes/day over the next five years (table 6.2.3). By 1980–1981, it had reached 6,281 tonnes/day—a level exceeding that of Germany and Italy and surpassed within the EEC only by Denmark and Belgium (Dafsa 1985, p. 60).

These changes established the broad pattern of structure that has persisted over the past twenty years, though a gradual consolidation of ownership among small refiners has further accentuated the degree of concentration in the industry (Dafsa 1985, p. 58).

The United Kingdom

The U.K. sugar market differs in two obvious respects from that of its larger European Community partners: the production of beet sugar is controlled by a single firm, British Sugar, while sugar produced from (imported) cane, by Tate & Lyle, retains a sizable fraction of the market. A less obvious feature, which

Table 6.2.2
The major French groups, as of 1967 (excluding refiners with a turnover below 100 million FF)

	Turnover, 1966 (million FF)
The Beghin-Say grouping	
Beghin	642.2
Say	570.8
Générale Sucrière[a]	445.4
Sucre Union	330.0
Fransucre (Sté. de distribution Mathien et SIAS-Francois)	237.3
Lebaudy-Sommier	171.8
Union sucrière de l'Aisne[b]	N.A.
Companie sucrière[b]	130.0
Sucrerie du Soissonais et Jernynck[b]	N.A.

Source: *Agra-Alimentation*.
a. Linked via minority shareholdings to Say (see text).
b. Regrouped subsequent to 31 December 1967.
N.A. denotes "not available."

Table 6.2.3
Size distribution of refineries in the French sugar industry (in tonnes/day)

	1950–1951	1970–1971	1975–1976
below 1,000	56	—	—
1,000–3,000	44	39	20
3,000–5,000	5	22	24
5,000–7,000	—	9	12
over 7,000	—	2	12

Source: CEDUS.

plays a crucial role in the competitive process in the industry, relates to the role of imports. These constitute a mere 6% of the market and, given the Community's sugar regime, they come predominantly from other community producers.

British Sugar was established under the Sugar Industry (Reorganisation) Act of 1936, which amalgamated all existing sugar beet processors into the newly formed company, which controls all beet sugar produced in the United Kingdom. Until 1980, a minority (16.67%) share was held by the Ministry of Agriculture, Fisheries, and Foods, and a further 7.5% was held by the Treasury Solicitor. S & W Berisford plc, an international commodity trader—whose interests included the manufacture and processing of sugar—held a 9.99% stake in 1980, in which year it announced its intention of acquiring the balance of the equity (including that held by the public sector). Following a report by the Monopolies and Mergers Commission (1980–1981), Berisford completed the purchase of the equity by August 1982.[4]

Tate & Lyle plc is the holding company for the Tate and Lyle group, which controls all cane sugar refining in the United Kingdom. The company had its origin in Tate & Lyle Ltd., formed in 1921 by the amalgamation of Henry Tate & Son Ltd. and Abram Lyle & Sons Ltd. In 1976, Tate & Lyle acquired the United Kingdom's other major cane refiner. In the United States, it acquired (but later sold) a controlling interest in Refined Sugars Inc. (New York), and it purchased (and reopened) seven sugar beet factories in the Midwest from Great Western Sugar Company in 1985–1986. More recently, it has acquired Amstar.

A number of factors need to be borne in mind in understanding the determinants of shares in the U.K. market:

(i) The EC country quota for U.K. production accrues wholly to British Sugar, as the sole U.K. beet sugar producer.

(ii) The ACP (African, Caribbean, and Pacific) developing countries are guaranteed a right under the Lomé Convention to supply a quota of cane sugar to community refiners. The evidence submitted by Tate & Lyle to the Monopolies and Mergers Commission (1987) indicated that the margin available for refining ACP cane under the community's regime have been squeezed in real terms and are less than those earned by British Sugar.

(iii) The impact of high fructose corn syrup, a key threat to sugar sales in the United States, has been of negligible importance up to now in the United Kingdom, as in the rest of the European Community. (This reflects a quota set for community production of isoglucose, as well as tariff protection against imports designed to protect growers of sugar beet.)

---

4. The nonsugar interests of BSC had traditionally been confined to goods that provided outlets for its by-products (molasses, animal feed), but in the period following Berisford's acquisition of the company, it has begun to diversify rapidly. BSC is now held by Berisford via the latter's wholly owned subsidiary Bristar, whose other interests include H. R. Daniels (flavors), Haven Foods (dried fruit), Gelatin Products, and further interests in biotechnology and agribusiness.

Overall, then, the total volume of sales in the U.K. market has been more or less static for many years; but this static picture conceals a steep decline in the retail market with an offsetting increase in the (somewhat larger) industrial market, which supplies the confectionery, soft drinks, and baking industries. In the retail market, some limited brand awareness exists among consumers. As mentioned earlier, Tate & Lyle's Mr. Cube brand, introduced in the 1970s to ward off proposed nationalization, is well established. British Sugar has recently tried hard to emulate this success, by spending some £1–£2 million a year on advertising for their Silver Spoon brand.

In contrast to many other areas of the U.K. food industry, retailers' own-label products are unimportant. Sainsbury's is alone among the majors in using an own-label granulated sugar, which accounts for only one-third of their granulated sugar sales. The industrial market, on the other hand, in which the market leaders in confectionery and soft drinks are the major buyers, is extremely price competitive, with regular switching of contracts between British Sugar and Tate & Lyle. More significantly, many if not most of these larger buyers take some of their needs directly from imports. In this area, a number of major merchants are active, buying both domestic and continental supplies.

The nature of price competition in the U.K. market was characterized by the Monopolies and Mergers Commission (1987) as being one of price leadership by British Sugar, with Tate & Lyle as a follower. The commission also noted that price competition has apparently been tough in recent years, with several major industrial buyers switching suppliers (in both directions) in response to price cuts. Within the industry, indeed, the period 1984–1986 is seen as having been marked by a price war, as British Sugar adopted a more aggressive marketing stance while Tate & Lyle, operating within tighter margins, failed to hold on to its market share, which declined steadily throughout the mid-1980s. British Sugar enjoys an EC quota of 1.114 million tonnes (white sugar equivalent; A and B quotas combined), and it aims to sell its full quota on the U.K. market.

Since margins are higher in the retail sector, it might seem attractive to British Sugar to attempt to raise its share in that segment; however, its share now appears to have stabilized at 63% in retail, and it seems likely that further extentions in that share might spark off a new price war. The real source of competitive pressure in the industry, however, comes from imports: these are highly sensitive to the differential between the U.K. price and the price elsewhere in the community. Following Berisford's takeover of British Sugar, an attempt was made to raise margins, but this led to a sharp surge in imports (1982–1983). In the price war of 1984–1986, on the other hand, imports fell very steeply. It would seem that imports play a very significant part in constraining the strategies of domestic producers.

Appendix 7.1

The Flour Industry

Industry Definition and M.E.S. Estimates

In what follows, the flour-milling industry is defined to encompass all varieties of flour, whether derived from wheat or other grains (rye, etc.). The basic technology of the industry has changed little since the late nineteenth century, though newly constructed or upgraded mills have been highly automated relative to traditional mills. Figures for m.e.s. based on U.S. median plant size provide an estimate that compares closely with those obtained from engineering studies (0.68% of U.S. output as against 0.74% for SIC 2941 (Flour and Other Grain Mill Products); see Connor et al. 1985 (p. 154) and chapter 4.

The United States

The foundations of the modern milling industry lay in a series of technical innovations, centered around the introduction of steel roller mills, which dominated the American industry throughout the 1870s. During that time, Minneapolis came to prominence as the focal point of the milling industry, and the period up to the end of the following decade was one of broad prosperity for the still fragmented American industry.

The transition to the more concentrated structure that prevails a century later can be traced to three separate and well-defined waves of consolidation. The first of these phases came in the years immediately following 1889, when a group of English investors, attracted by the reputed profitability of the U.S. flour industry, acquired and merged C.A. Pillsbury & Co. (which operated the largest steel rolling mill in use at that date) with the Washburn Company. The newly formed concern was not a success; it paid no dividend at all during the nineteen years over which it operated. The industry's high profitability during the 1880s, which had attracted the investment, had in fact already begun to reverse by the end of the decade, and the industry suffered from excess capacity for the next two generations.

Be that as it may,

The size of the Pillsbury-Washburn company so disturbed its smaller competitors in Minneapolis that six of them joined in a merger of their own in 1891, thus launching Northwestern Consolidated Milling Co. The following year three others were amalgamated as Minneapolis Flour Manufacturing Co. In a sort of chain reaction, the five principal mills in New York City merged in 1892 as Hicker-Jones-Jewell Milling Co. The purpose of these cases was to obtain the supposed advantages of large scale operation, although a secondary consideration was the desire by several estates and elderly owners to retire from the business. These factors inspired the organization during the same year of Sperry Flour Co., which brought into one concern the six principal milling companies in California. (Steen 1963, p. 64)

This wave of mergers was followed by an attempt to create a milling trust, modeled along the lines of the various arrangements of this kind that were becoming common in other industries. The attempt foundered, however, largely because of its failure to incorporate two of the industry's leading firms, Pillsbury-Washburn and Washburn Crosby. The trust went into receivership in 1900.[1]

The upshot of the first phase of consolidation, as Morgan (1979) notes, was the dominance of Minneapolis milling by four families: the Washburns, Pillsburys, Crosbys, and Bells. Whereas the first wave of consolidation began as a defensive reaction to events within the flour industry itself, the second wave has been seen as reflecting inter alia a response to consolidations taking place in the bread and baking industry. The rise of industrial bakeries in the United States had been an offshoot of the development of "new process milling" in the 1870s, and by the 1920s several major bakery chains had appeared. These consolidations occurred during a decade of low industry margins following the prosperous postwar years. An FTC investigation during the 1920s sought to establish evidence of price fixing, but in fact no such evidence emerged. Wide variations in prices existed, with millers complaining of rivals' pricing practices, but there was no evidence of collusion.

The series of events that constituted the second wave of consolidations in the industry are described by Steen (1963, p. 76). The most important feature of this second wave lay in the formation of General Mills, which became the first genuinely national milling concern. As Steen describes it,

Washburn Crosby Co., Inc., acquired mills in Chicago and Kansas City in 1922, and in 1928–1929 this company, already the industry's largest, was the keystone in General Mills, Inc., which also included Red Star, Sperry, El Reno and the Kell properties in Texas and Oklahoma. It thus became the first milling company to be national in scope. Its nearest rival, Pillsbury, bought mills in Atchison and Astoria in 1922 and 1929, and built mills in Enid and Springfield. Commander Larabee Corp. was formed in 1926, becoming third largest, being a merger of Larabee Flour Mills Co. and the Sheffield-

---

1. As Steen (1963) notes, the trust was reorganized as Standard Milling Co., but while this holding company controlled more mills than did any other company in the industry, these mills "were under separate management and were not classed as a single entity."

controlled mills in Minnesota. Not far behind in size was Flour Mills of America, Inc., a 1927 consolidation of Kansas Flour Mills Corp. and Valier & Spies Milling Co. Another step of importance was the organization in 1929 of Tex-O-Kan Flour Mills Co., which brought the seven Burrus-controlled companies into one concern.

The wave of mergers that had marked the 1920s began to subside at the end of the decade. Nevertheless, several more important mergers occurred during the 1930s. In particular, three of the majors (Pillsbury, General Mills, and International) each acquired a further mill during the latter decade, while a substantial number of obsolete plants were closed down in the face of serious excess capacity.

The structure of milling thereafter remained relatively static for several decades. The 1940s and 1950s were marked by a gradual absorption and consolidation of smaller family-owned concerns. The four largest firms in the industry accounted for 29% of industry output in 1951. This figure rose to reach 32% in 1958, but thereafter fell to 24% in 1965 . During the 1970s, the share of the top-four companies grew slowly, but remained in the range 33%–38%.

The third major wave of consolidation occurred during the 1980s, when the four-firm concentration ratio rose rapidly from around 38% to around 58% between 1980 and 1985. This new wave of consolidation saw the emergence of three major conglomerates as the industry's leading firms, with Pillsbury now in fourth place. ConAgra, currently the industry's leading firm, was originally a milling company, which later expanded into feedstuffs and then into meat packing. Its main strengths developed in the unbranded sector of the food-processing industries, but more recently it has begun to expand also within the branded area. ADM, now the industry's second-largest miller, began operations in oils and grains, but it also has long-standing interest in the flour industry, having become a major miller with its acquisition of the Veneer Milling Co. of Kansas in the 1960s. The third largest miller is now Cargill, one of the country's leading meat packers, whose main interests lie in grain merchanting. It is now a major food conglomerate, with interests that include oils, poultry, and orange juice. The common denominator linking the company's major areas of interest is that transport costs play an important role in all these areas; Cargill's main area of strength appears to lie in such industries.

The United Kingdom

The evolution of structure in the U.K. flour industry is outlined in chapter 7. By the mid-1980s, some forty-eight companies, operating eighty-nine mills, belonged to the industry's trade association NABIM, which represented virtually the entire industry. The three leading companies (Rank-Hovis, Allied Mills, and Spillers) now account for over 75% of production, while ten of the remaining members are small stoneground millers. About two-thirds of output by volume goes for (industrial) bread making; the output of Rank-Hovis and Allied Mills goes to bread divisions of their respective companies (see appendix 7.2);

the same was true of Spillers until the company quit the bread industry in the late 1970s.

The industry's trade association NABIM sees the U.K. industry as highly efficient, a fact it attributes to the much greater degree of consolidation achieved in the U.K. industry, as against its counterparts in Continental Europe. The industry's technology has remained basically unchanged since the introduction of steel rollers in the nineteenth century; recent advances have been concerned with automation of production via computer control. A new, efficient green-field site mill would today involve a capital expenditure of some £15–£20 million, it is felt; though the only new mill in the United Kingdom in recent times was that built by Allied Mills at Corby with the aid of government grant, following the closure of the local British Steel plant. Only the Big Three have multi-plant operations; and the site of some mills reflects historical factors rather than the pattern that would now be optimal.

With wheat accounting for 80% of the industry's costs, differences in perfor-mance across companies depend not so much on differences in production technology, but rather on the company's ability to buy wheat well, mix types successfully, and so achieve a high extraction rate.[2]

Japan

Chapter 7 outlined the early emergence of Nippon Seifun and Nisshin Seifun as Japan's two leading millers in the prewar period. In what follows, we comment on how the market environment has evolved over the intervening half-century. In the immediate postwar period, government policy under the Food Control Act was geared toward relieving food shortages, and through a mixture of price regulation and subsidies, it encouraged entry to the industry to such a degree that the number of firms at one point exceeded 3,000 (compared to 185 in 1936). But in 1951, substantial imports of rice alleviated the need for such support, and the volume of wheat imports fell. In 1952, improving conditions on the domestic food market and in the international wheat market prompted the abolition of the government commission responsible for overseeing the flour industry, and subsidies were withdrawn. A huge shakeout of small firms occurred: the num-ber of factories fell from 2,852 in 1951 to 1,081 in 1956. Thereafter, a slow but

---

2. Prior to EEC accession, U.K. millers purchased a substantial amount of Canadian wheat, which, when mixed with domestic supplies, yielded very high-quality flour for bread making (less expensive domestic wheat, on the other hand, sufficed for biscuit flour, much of which was produced by smaller millers).

One of the effects of EEC entry, however, was to make this strategy relatively unat-tractive; U.K. millers had a strong incentive to supply their import requirements from community producers. A result of this was a gradual but important trend among U.K. breeders to develop domestic wheat strains more attuned to the needs of the bread industry, and U.K. millers have gradually learned to work to a greater degree with domestic supplies. The proportion of homegrown wheat used in the industry rose from 54% in 1979/80 to about 74% in 1986/87.

steady decline in the number of factories continued, but for the past decade numbers have been relatively stable. Between 1976 and 1985, for example, the number of factories declined only slightly, from 238 to 207.

The larger part of the wheat used by the industry is imported. The world price is substantially below the domestic price, and imports are centralized through a government agency that operates a system of duties and subsidies to local producers, and then supplies wheat to the flour firms at a uniform price. The rule determining the quota of wheat allocated to each miller was, until 1975, based on a formula involving the miller's capacity (with a 0.2 weighting factor) and his sales volume (0.8 weighting factor). This formula led to a growing misalignment between input requirements and sales, and in 1975 the rule was changed to one based on sales alone.

It might seem at first glance that the existence of administered quotas on raw material inputs might limit movements in market shares over time. At least since the reforms of 1975, this does not seem to be the case. But government policy on raw material quotas has had one clear effect: the fact that such quotas are unavailable to new entrants blocks entry to the industry. Thus the slow decline in firm numbers over the past decade can be seen as reflecting, quite simply, the asymmetry inherent in this rule. The inevitably fluctuating fortunes of small firms will lead to occasional exit; without compensating entry, concentration will tend to rise. Slow though the process is, its continuance over such a long period has led to a sizable diminution in total numbers.[3]

Mergers and acquisitions in the industry have been rare. Small firms, in the main, are not less profitable or less efficient in terms of unit costs than the majors. On the other hand, the majors do have an advantage, via their superior technical facilities, insofar as they can deliver a more consistent quality level (i.e., the variance of quality over time, for any type of flour, is argued to be less for the leading brands).

A further force determining the evolution of market structure relates to the links with bakeries. Price competition in the industry has not been severe, at least since the major contraction in numbers began to tail off in the early 1960s. Since then, nonprice competition has been the norm. The flour companies typically have long-term implicit contracts with the bakeries they supply. Small bakeries often lack expertise, a tendency accentuated by the fact that bread making represents a relatively recent Western influence. Flour companies tend to supply assistance in the form of know-how; in fact, the market leader Nisshin

---

3. The industry has also actively encouraged the exit of small millers: an association exists that pays a subsidy to small firms to close down operations. Thereafter, its wheat quota is redistributed on a pro-rata basis to the remaining firms. The scheme has not had much impact, however; the number of firms accepting the offer has been running at less than one per year, and the scheme is now effectively inoperative. On the other hand, some small firms, finding that sales are declining, have been selling some or all of their output directly to the majors, which then brand and sell it. Such sales account for around one-tenth of the total sales of the leading firms. In this way, a small firm facing a loss of sales can retain its input quota.

Seifun considers its provision of know-how on making bread and Japanese noodles its most important selling point. Nisshin sells at a premium relative to other flour producers, and it attributes its ability to do so to the services it provides its bakery customers.

All in all, the past three decades have been marked by a slow decline in the number of small millers, while the combined share of the largest four millers has remained fairly steady (fluctuating between 67% and 68% from 1970 to the present).

France

The French flour-milling industry consists predominantly of extremely small concerns—about 1,500 active firms, approximately 90% of which employ fewer than ten workers—but a handful of larger concerns, mostly founded around the turn of the century, have maintained a strong position in the industry for decades. A notable feature of the French industry is its high level of exports: some 34% of domestic production is exported. Large and medium concerns dominate the export trade; the leading firms typically sell as much overseas as they do on the domestic market (the top-three millers alone account for more than half of French exports).

Although the market shares reported in table M3 (appendix 1) suggest a rather fragmented structure, it is in fact difficult to assess the effective degree of concentration in the French market because many of the larger millers are interlinked via a complex series of financial relationships. For example, Grands Moulins de Paris holds a majority stake in Societé des Moulins Régionaux, which controls six regional mills. Grands Moulins de Pantin is the majority shareholder in Grands Moulins de Corbeil, and each of these two companies has a (directly or indirectly held) minority stake in Societé des Moulins de Beaubourg et de Coudekerque and in Malteries Franco-Belges. Grands Moulins de Corbeil in turn holds a minority share in Societé des Moulins Régionaux, in which Grands Moulins de Paris is the majority shareholder.

Other groupings also exist, which involve major millers. Grands Moulins de Strasbourg, for example, has a minority stake in Grands Moulins de Pantin. Against this complex background of financial links, any figures for concentration in the market need to be interpreted with extreme caution. This study follows the practice of the leading French trade journal, *Agra-Alimentation*, in linking Grands Moulins de Corbeil with Grands Moulins de Pantin (in which the former has a majority stake) as a single entity, but otherwise these linkages have been ignored in reporting market share figures.

The structure of the industry has been changing slowly over the past two decades, by way of a steady rate of exit of very small concerns. In the mid-1960s there were 3,500 millers; by the mid-1970s the total number of concerns amounted to some 2,300 or so, of which 1,800 were active; the number of active firms had already fallen to around 1,500 by the early 1980s (Commission de la Concurrence 1981). A number of factors played a role in this process.

The industry is subject to government control via two channels:

(a) Milling requires a permit; hence the distinction between the total number of mills and the number of active mills.

(b) Price controls on flour set an upper bound to prices over much of the past decade.

In the early 1970s, the industry faced a fairly static level of demand on the domestic market. Domestic sales fell throughout the late 1960s, but stabilized at a relatively low level from the beginning of the 1970s, leaving the industry with a serious problem of overcapacity. This problem was accentuated by a combination of rising wheat prices and price controls on flour, which squeezed margins on domestic sales. The smaller firms were hardest hit by these circumstances, partly reflecting the fact that the large and medium producers are most active in export markets.

Attempts were made by the industry—which was greatly concerned at the appearance of aggressive price competition—to solve the overcapacity problem; but these attempts finally failed in 1974, when a sufficient minority of (small) concerns voted against plans that would have led to the buying out of many small firms' milling rights, and the proposals were dropped. This failure prompted official intervention. In 1975, new regulations were introduced regarding the merger of firms, and a complex formula was developed to determine the degree to which milling rights could be transferred, while the renting of a firm's milling rights to other producers was disallowed. By the end of the decade, industry observers were reporting a more favorable climate, resulting from a combination of falling capacity, a recovery in domestic sales, the removal of price controls, and a healthy performance in export markets (*Agra-Alimentation* 1979).

Germany (F.R.)

In the mid-1980s, the Federal Republic had a total of some 1,500 flour milling concerns; all but 400 being extremely small, with an annual output of less than 500 tonnes. A very sharp difference exists between the highly fragmented structure in the southern part of the country and that in the north, where a small number of sizable concerns enjoy a substantial share of the market.[4] The number of mills per capita in Bavaria, for example, is three times as high

---

4. Concentration in some segments is moderately high. A recent Bundeskartellamt ruling on the acquisition by Germany's leading miller, Kampffmeyer, of Plange (Hamburg) defined the relevant market for retail (i.e., household) flour as north Germany. In that market, they found the two leading firms, Kampffmeyer and Plange, to have a combined market share of some 55% of all retail sales. (Retail sales of flour account for one-tenth of all flour sold.) Only two other firms (Komplet and Ströh) were found to have a substantial share of the north German market; the remaining firms were extremely small, with market shares below 1%.

as in Nord Rhein-Westphalen. Throughout the postwar period, the industry was subject to restrictions on the quantity of wheat milled by each company, as well as price controls on flour, but since 1976 free market conditions have prevailed.

The industry went through a very difficult period in the 1950s and 1960s, when total demand declined and excess capacity came to be seen as a serious problem. A program of mill closure, paid for by the industry, was introduced alongside supporting legislation that subsidized closures and forbade new entry. This program was completed in late 1975, by which time it was generally felt that capacity was reasonably in line with demand. With the freeing of prices, a period of tough competition ensued. This phase came to an abrupt end with the insolvency of Kampffmeyer, the country's largest miller, in 1984. A perhaps surprising reaction to Kampffmeyer's insolvency was a fight to capture the market share vacated by the industry leader, which took the form of a rapid surge of investment in additional capacity by medium-sized millers; in the wake of Kampffmeyer's acquisition by DG Bank and its (slow and costly) recovery of its substantial market share, the industry now finds itself once again in a state of serious overcapacity.

Differences between the industry's position in the north and in the south exist both in regard to structure and to performance. Prices are about 7% higher in the south, where margins are relatively satisfactory, and most small firms can survive reasonably comfortably. In the north, low prices and tight margins are seen as the central problem in industry circles, but views differ as to the cause. On the one hand, it is argued that price competition is much tougher in the north, but it is also the case that the main buyers—the bakeries—are far more effectively organized in the north, and their buying power squeezes margins.[5]

An alternative interpretation, widely offered but harder to sustain, attributes the current difficulties of the north German industry to structural problems, that is, to overcapacity. This seems less convincing, however, in light of reactions to the industry's attempts to reduce capacity: its recent success in closing down a mill in Lower Saxony was followed by an immediate increase in capacity by a number of existing firms, which cancelled out the gain. All in all, it seems that the difference between the problems of the north and the relative ease of the south reflects more than differences in the degree of imbalance between capacity and demand.

---

5. The distribution of flour in the German market involves some special features. There are about 25,000 small local bakeries, and these bakeries typically organize themselves into cooperative buying groups ("Bäko"), of which almost 100 are currently operating. Their activities vary sharply from one city to the next; in some areas, they compete fiercely for members, but in others they are relatively quiescent. Private wholesalers also play a major role, but the mills themselves maintain direct links with individual bakeries. Good personal relations can bypass the Bako, whether this involves a small miller whose owner deals personally with the bakery, or—as in the case of the larger millers—it is achieved by means of a large and active sales force.

How stable is the present structure? Industry observers argue that the process of exit of the very smallest mills will continue; the competition authorities will be neutral in respect of such a move, in that it is likely to lead to the growth of the smallish middle-ranking firms. On the other hand, the growth of the majors in north Germany does seem likely to be impeded by the competition authorities, in the wake of the Kampffmeyer decision. Clearly, if the present squeeze on margins in the north German industry is indeed the result of increasingly tough price competition, the incentive to merge, other things being equal, will be correspondingly great.

Italy

The Italian flour industry is highly fragmented. The leading firms are relatively small, family-owned concerns. Some interrelationships exist between mills, either because they form part of the same family group or, less formally, because different members of the same family operate (financially independent) mills. The main producer until the late 1970s was Chiari e Forti, whose market share was no more than 3%; its interests were acquired in 1976–1977 by Costato and by Lege delle Cooperative. The Costato group thereby acquired Grandi Molini, which together with its other milling interests (SEME and Costato S.p.A.) gives it around 3% or 4% of milling capacity. Its share of domestic sales is, however, much smaller. Two other groups are of similar importance: the Casillo group owns Casillo s.r.l., which has a 1.6% market share, as well as a number of smaller mills; the Ambrosio group (Italgrani) owns both the market leader, Molino di Foggia, as well as some smaller mills.

Reliable figures are not available for the market shares by group. The shares by individual firms published by Databank indicate, however, that only seven firms have a share exceeding 1%, while only four more have shares between 0.5% and 1%. Even allowing for the fact that two of the top-four mills are owned by groups that also hold a number of small mills, it is clear that the top-four producers have a market share well below 10%.

Recent events in the industry do not suggest that this fragmented structure shows much sign of changing: a small number of acquisitions of minor mills have occurred, and one major mill (Grandi Molini) has changed hands. More interesting perhaps is the acquisition of Molino Verge by Saiwa, itself part of the American multinational Nabisco, and the fact that Barilla—Italy's leading pasta and biscuit maker, and a highly dynamic company—is integrated backward into milling via its ownership of Molino Basile di Altamure and Molini Saini di Ferrara.

Some 15% of domestic production is exported; the leading exporter, Pardini F.lli, accounts for 19% of total exports and ranks first in terms of its share of domestic production (3.2%), though its share of the domestic market is much lower (0.4%). The other leading firms have a relatively modest export share (Grandi Molini 7.4%, Corticalla 3.2%, Molino di Foggia 2.8%, Casillo 2.2%).

Appendix 7.2

The Bread Industry

Market Definition

The bread market is defined here to include all types of bread, whether baked from wheat flour or not, but all related bakery products are excluded. One broad distinction is of particular relevance in what follows. In France, Germany, and Italy, where most bread is sold by small local bakers, the bulk of sales consists of loaves baked, purchased, and consumed within a single day. The short shelf life of such bread (which can be as low as ten hours, as in the case of France) diminishes, to some extent, the (quite limited) scope that might otherwise exist for reducing costs through centralizing production in one location. In these countries, industrial bakeries play a relatively small role in the market, which is dominated by the artisan sector.

In the United States, the United Kingdom, and Japan, on the other hand, the familiar supermarket loaf—variously labeled the "(sliced) pan," the "pullman loaf," and so on—is the most popular variety. Though it is typically baked and delivered for sale on the same day, its longer shelf life somewhat eases the problems of distributing fresh bread over a wide radius. In the United States, for example, a shelf life of three to five days is typical, as compared to one day or less in France, Germany, and Italy. In the United States, United Kingdom, and Japan, industrial bakeries play a much larger role, and the nature of the industry, both in terms of its production technology and its methods of distribution, is relatively similar.

These differences should not be exaggerated. Recent trends in both groups of countries suggest some convergence in these respects. In-store bakeries in the United States, and the spread of "French" bakeries in Japan, have led to a rapid growth in the share of "Continental" bread types. Meanwhile, in France, the industrial product of frozen dough for sale to local bakers has led to new possibilities for partial centralization of production in one location.

The Markets by Country

Relative Market Size

The measure of relative market size is based on the volume of household consumption of bread and rolls in 1986. This measure is widely used in the market research literature and the trade press, and it can be determined fairly precisely. It excludes the nonretail segment, which accounts for something on the order of 10%–20% of total output in these countries. Reliable figures for total production or consumption volume that admit a valid comparison across these countries are not available, however. As to value-based measures, it is possible to obtain *retail* sales figures for each country, but figures for total sales, or for the value of production, are again problematic—in part because many small bakeries may fall outside the scope of census figures for manufacturing establishments. For these reasons, it was decided to follow the practice of basing comparisons on the volume of household consumption.

In the case of the Japanese market, the figure is not available. However, figures are available for the total volume of flour used in the industry, and this can be compared with the equivalent figure for the United States, as reported in the Census of Manufactures. A cross-check on the estimate thus obtained is possible by reference to the total value of retail sales in both countries; this leads to a closely similar figure for the relative size of the two markets in 1985. The resulting estimates for relative market size are shown in table 7.2.1.

France, Germany (F.R.), and Italy

In France, Germany, and Italy, industrial bakers account for a relatively small fraction of total bread production: about 10% in Italy, 15% in France, and

Table 7.2.1
Relative market size in the bread industry

	Volume of household consumption, 1986 (thousand tonnes)[a]	Relative market size (U.S. = 1)
France	3,489	0.654
Germany	4,674	0.879
Italy	3,688	0.693
Japan	N.A.	0.263[b]
United Kingdom	2,584	0.486
United States	~5,320[a]	0.100

Source: ERC 1989.
a. Based on USDC figures of per capita consumption.
b. Author's estimate based on figures for total wheat flour inputs, as reported in the U.S. Census of Manufactures and as supplied by Yamazaki.

30% in Germany. An artisan fringe of some tens of thousands of local bakers provide the large bulk of consumption. As to the leading industrial bakers, no firm has succeeded in achieving an overall share in the bread market exceeding 2% or so.

The nature of the typical industrial bread baker varies somewhat across these three countries, both in respect of the types of bread in which these producers specialize and in terms of the outlets they supply. As to the types of bread involved, the basic sliced pan varies greatly in importance: in Germany, this type of bread accounts for one-quarter of bread consumption in the northern half of the country, where it constitutes 70% of the output of industrial bakers (in southern Germany, on the other hand, it is of very little importance). In France, such bread constitutes a mere 7% of industrial production, and its production is largely the preserve of three major industrial bakers.[1] In Italy, it is of negligible importance, industrial bakers producing a range of types similar to small local bakers.

In all three of these countries, industrial bakers sell largely to supermarkets and institutional buyers, but they also sell a substantial fraction of their output through independent retail bakers or through their own chains of outlets. This last pattern is especially prevalent in Germany; typical of this pattern is the well-known Lübig company, for example, which delivers from a single central bakery to a widespread net of its own shops throughout the Bonn-Köln area.

The scope for centralizing production has been extended recently by the advent of industrially produced frozen dough, as noted. The impact of this change has varied; it is not yet legally permissable to bake from bought-in dough in Italy, while in the French market it has been argued (in the trade press) that its rapid growth is indicative of a substantial change in the industry. Its use allows the local baker to buy in his normal range of bread products, while its production requires setup costs that are much more substantial than those of the typical industrial baker. Some of France's leading industrial bakers, including Pain Jacquet, have entered this segment in a substantial way. Its likely long-run impact on the market remains, however, a matter of conjecture.

The advent of frozen dough has been offered within the industry as an explanatory factor underlying a number of recent acquisitions of French bakeries by flour millers. Since the early 1980s, several mills have taken over bakers (including Moulin de la Brie and the agricultural cooperative SCANEB).[2] Some other tendencies toward a modest degree of consolidation in the French market have been evident over the past twenty years: Pain Jacquet owes its current position as France's leading industrial baker in part to a series of acquisitions (including L'Independente of Lille in 1971 and La Proma at Aubaque in 1974), though much of its growth has rested upon a program of rationalization and extension of its own plants. Pain Jacquet is unusual in the European bread

---

1. Sixty percent of the output of France's industrial bakers is made up of traditional types (the "baguette" and its larger equivalents); while 30% consists of "viennoiserie."

2. On the other hand, France's leading mill, Grand Moulins de Paris, has itself begun to manufacture frozen dough, competing with some of the leading industrial bakers.

industry in having some external involvement: the company was one of a trio of interests that recently acquired Germany's leading baker, Rugenberger Grossbackereien. On the other hand, Le Pain Turner, France's second baker, was acquired in 1986 by a U.S.-based multinational (Campbell Soup Co.).

Some similar developments have been at work in the German market. Wendeln, one of Germany's largest industrial bakers, acquired six smaller bakers during the mid-1980s. Cross-border sales, too, occasionally occur: one of Germany's oldest industrial bakers, Harry's, founded in the seventeenth century, enjoys a visible presence in French supermarkets, for example. Another of Germany's largest bakers, Weber GmbH, is owned by an American corporation (Borden Inc.). Again, such activities are the exception rather than the rule. All in all, the bread industries of these three countries remain among the most fragmented considered in this study.

One further factor deserves a brief comment. Price controls have long played a part in both the Italian and French bread markets. In Italy, price controls on basic bread types are the norm, but their practical impact on industrial bakers is minimal, as the majors generally contrive to sell most of their output in noncontrolled categories. For example, only 5% of Giannotti's sales in the Milan area—its main market—are of the controlled (*panne a l'olio* and Michette) varieties. In France, the price of bread was fixed until 1978; industrial bakers simply computed their prices by subtracting a retail margin of (at most) 20% from the price and, at least from the 1960s onward, they achieved satisfactory profits under the regime. The decontrol of prices in 1978 led to a decade of increasingly intense price competition; over the period 1983–1987, for example, the (nominal) price of bread actually fell, and the bakers' trade association, the Syndicat National des Industries de Boulangerie et Patisserie, reported the average net margins of industrial bakers as having fallen to zero by 1986. The effects of decontrol fell most heavily on the nonindustrial sector, where the number of bakers fell from 42,000 in 1974 to 38,000 in 1987. Responses within the industry were of two kinds. An attempt by the millers' trade associations to give a lead in suggesting a method of calculation of prices to their members was found by the Commission de la Concurrence to be tantamount to an attempt to coordinate prices, and the practice was outlawed in 1981. An alternative form of response has lain in an increasing tendency by the major industrial bakers to shift production away from the highly competitive bread area into allied products, such as frozen dough, where margins are relatively high.

Japan

Bread is seen in Japan as a modern, Western food; prewar consumption was low, and a major stimulus to the industry's growth was the government's postwar policy of encouraging flour imports and bread production.[3] It is custo-

---

3. The standard Japanese loaf is not dissimilar to a British or American supermarket loaf: styled the "pullman" loaf, it has, however, an unusual square profile and is typically

Table 7.2.2
Size distribution of bread factories in Japan, 1980

Employment size category	Factories (%)	Output (%)
less than 10	62.0	4.2
10–299	36.0	41.0
300 or more	2.1	55.0

mary to distinguish three kinds of unit: the small local bakery, baking on the premises; the medium-sized factory, which operates at a regional level, selling to various local outlets; and a handful of large national companies. The relative importance of the three kinds of firm is illustrated in table 7.2.2, which shows the size distribution of factories in 1980.

As early as the 1960s, it had become clear that a substantial number of bakers faced difficulties. The diagnosis of the Ministry of Agriculture at that time was that the future lay with a mixture of (a few) very large firms that enjoyed advantages associated inter alia with technical economies via mass-production techniques and with the small local bakery. It was felt that the middle-sized firm was the most vulnerable and that mergers and acquisitions should be encouraged in this range. The events of the early 1980s, when medium-sized firms began to experience increasing difficulties, suggest that this judgment showed some prescience. The trend that has been emerging of late has involved a pattern of acquisitions by large national firms of medium-to-small regional bakeries. At the same time, increasingly tough competition by the leading firms in the industry for certain regional markets has led to increasing difficulties for small-to-medium regional producers and has stimulated mergers and acquisitions in many cases. For instance, press reports in 1987 indicate increasingly tough competition among three leading firms (Yamazaki, Fujipan, and Ryoyu) for market shares in the Kyushu region.

These tendencies have led to a significant loss of market share by some hitherto very secure regional firms. For example, Kudo-pan once had an 80% share within its own region (the Aomori prefecture), but now it holds only 50% or so. All in all, the pattern of competition has changed; in the past, the regional firm might typically have competed on a more or less equal basis with one of the national producers, but now it is increasingly the case that a regional market is contested by several of the largest firms, with a consequent erosion in the position of the local, middle-sized firms that once dominated their respective areas.

---

eaten, in thick slices, with butter and spreads (jam, etc.). However, such loaves take only a moderate fraction of total sales, and the variety of types offered is now large reflecting, for example, the growing influence of French-style bakeries, which have spread throughout much of the country, as well as (to a lesser degree) the presence of German-style loaves in some outlets.

Why, then, have the national brands—in particular Yamazaki[4]—succeeded? The industry view is that technical scale economies are modest, insofar as unit production costs are concerned. The advantage of the major producer lies rather in his ability to deliver a consistent level of quality, in terms of both taste and shelf life, over long runs. A second advantage over the medium-sized firms lies in the extent and effectiveness of the majors' distribution net; indeed, it is marketing skills, broadly defined, that are emphasized as their key advantage.

Yamazaki's growth since the mid-1960s, when it became the first firm to distribute nationally, illustrates these trends. Like a number of other majors (Shikishina, Fuji, Kobeya), it acquired an interest in a number of medium-sized regional producers, either by acquiring a 50% share in the firm or by taking a minority interest as part of a package deal (a technological joint venture). Yamazaki's policy was based on continual investment in the latest production techniques, using relatively high-grade raw materials, and so achieving a very high quality level: it is to this latter factor that the company attributes its relatively high market share in the retail sector, in which small shops typically use a single supplier, and competition between majors for supply contracts is becoming increasingly severe.

All in all, the market appears to be in a transitional state. A handful of major companies have, via a mixture of internal growth and acquisitions, come to occupy an increasingly large share of the market. The losers in this process have been medium-sized, firms; the small local bakeries show every sign of surviving. It seems likely that this process will continue, to the detriment of medium-sized firms, for some time. The structure envisaged by the Ministry of Agriculture in the mid-1960s, in which a small number of national bakers coexist with a stable and successful population of small local bakeries, appears to be a likely focus of convergence for the industry over the next decade. The most notable feature of the industry at present is the growing tendency for the largest firms to "meet" in regional submarkets, to the detriment of the once-secure regional incumbent.

The United Kingdom

The evolution of structure in the U.K. bread market has been heavily inter-twined with the evolution of the flour industry. The close relationship between millers and bakers is a feature that extends beyond the market leaders, and it is a characteristic that distinguishes the U.K. market from the other markets

---

4. Yamazaki Baking was, until 1985, Japan's largest bread producer, with a market share slightly ahead of the second firm, Kansai Yamazaki. The two firms merged on January 1, 1986, under the name Yamazaki Baking, leaving the new firm with a preeminent position in the industry. Via its affiliate, Yamazaki Nabisco, it is also highly active in the biscuit market, producing both Japanese-style and — via its link with the American Nabisco—Western-style biscuits. Yamazaki Baking has twenty-one factories, nineteen of which produce bread and cakes.

studied here. Eighteen major plant bakers supply 75% of U.K. bread sales, and ownership links between these plant bakers and flour companies are widespread. The dominance of industrial baking is much greater in the United Kingdom than elsewhere. In part, this may be attributed to the structural shifts in the bread and flour industries described in chapter 7 and appendix 7.1. A further factor that influenced developments in the U.K. market, however, was the imposition of price controls: bakers were at times restrained from fully passing on increases in labor costs during the 1960s and 1970s. Pressures on margins over this period contributed to the exit of Spillers from the bread market, and these pressures also appear to have influenced a general shift over the period to larger bakeries in which labour productivity gains were possible. During the 1980s, this process continued. RHM, for example, reduced its number of plants from sixty-five to twenty-five) between 1980 and 1987, and it achieved a sixfold increase in total labor productivity over that period. The radius over which bread is distributed from plants is now as high as 80–100 miles.

The United States

Over the first half of the century, industrial bread baking grew very rapidly in the United States. Over that period, the drift of population from rural areas to cities combined with overall population growth to stimulate demand for commercially baked bread. Since the 1950s, on the other hand, total demand has changed little. Over its half century of rapid growth, industrial bread baking developed a highly fragmented structure, characterized by a large number of single-plant bakeries, each serving a small local area. Toward the end of this era, however, a new trend was becoming evident, which gathered momentum over the decades that followed. This trend involved both the appearance of multiplant companies selling over a wide number of more or less separate local markets and an associated rise in the average plant scale in the industry. Between 1939 and 1963, the number of plants fell by more than half, from 10,325 to 5,010. Over the same period, average plant size in terms of the value of shipments rose tenfold (FTC 1967). The number of companies operating in the industry fell from 6,000 to 4,300 over these years, a contraction that in part reflected the exit of small companies that failed over this period, and in part the absorption of acquired bakeries. Between 1952 and 1964, over 200 bakeries were acquired, mostly by a number of large companies that began to achieve a national scale over these years, by means of a process of acquisitions—including, in some cases, the acquisition of relatively sizable concerns that already operated across more than one state (FTC 1967).

By 1963, nine large multistate corporations had evolved (National Commission on Food Marketing 1966).[5] These nine companies operated 340 plants, of

---

5. They were: Continental Baking Co., Inc., American Bakeries Co., Campbell Taggart Associated Bakeries, Inc., General Baking Co., Ward Baking Co., Interstate Bakeries Corp., National Biscuit Co., Southern Bakeries Co., and C. J. Patterson Co.

which 286 were predominantly bread plants, and their combined output accounted for 40% of all commercial bread produced. The four largest (Continental Baking Co., American Bakeries Co., Campbell Taggart Associated Bakeries, Inc., and General Baking Co.) accounted for 23% of industry sales.

Over the next two decades, the four-firm concentration ratio rose slowly, to reach 31% by the mid-1980s. Two of the industry leaders to emerge by the 1960s had become the two leading bakers by the latter date. By then, both had been acquired by leading conglomerates. Campbell Taggart was owned by the leading brewer Anheuser-Busch, and Continental had been acquired in 1968 by the International Telephone & Telegraph Corporation (ITT), from whom it was purchased by Ralston-Purina in 1985.

The evolution of structure and conduct in the U.S. market over the past twenty years has attracted considerable attention. Three aspects of that development are unusual and deserve comment:

1. The early phase of development, from the late 1940s to the early 1960s, was marked inter alia by a phase of substantial advertising. The advertising-sales ratio in the industry rose over that period, reaching 1.4% in 1947 and 2.4% in 1963. The most visible advertiser over that period was Continental whose Wonder Bread brand achieved national recognition. At the other end of the spectrum, many local brands were well established. Industry observers were reporting by the mid-1960s that penetrating local markets was made difficult insofar as winning shelf space in supermarkets against local brands that had established brand recognition advertising was problematic. Continental's advertising emphasized the nutritive value of Wonder Bread, and its claims were challenged by the Federal Trade Commission, which demanded that the company cease advertising the nutritive content of its bread unless it also stated that it was no more nutritious than any other enriched bread. (The details of the complaint are set out in Fenn 1971.)

2. While national concentration levels remain low, local concentration levels are typically much higher. Connor et al. (1985) record that the FTC identified seventy-five local markets in which Continental and the leading local baker with whom it competed had an average combined share of 59.7%. This pattern has been the norm for two decades: in the mid-1960s the FTC surveyed seventeen cities and found four-firm concentration ratios ranging from 39% to 92% across the group (FTC 1967, table 15.) Against this background, charges of price fixing have been common. In its 1967 report, the FTC noted that in the preceding decade, nine price conspiracy cases had been brought against bread bakers (a total exceeded only by the dairy industry). An illustrative case is summarized by Connor et al. (1985, p. 361), involving the association of bakers in Washington, under which all members were required to set a price equal to Continental's (an exception being made for the Safeway supermarket, which was allowed to sell for one cent less).

3. In recent years, while advertising has dwindled, the continued expansion of the majors has been accompanied by charges of predatory pricing in selected cities. A full discussion of the FTC case against Continental is set out in Connor

et al. 1985 (p. 268ff). Evidence presented by the Commission in respect of Continental's behavior in the Northern Californian market suggested that the company was violating the Areeda-Turner criterion, in selling below unit variable cost. While the market leader, Campbell Taggart, more than held its own over the period in question, the third- and fourth-ranked bakers, American and Inglis, both lost heavily: American ceased selling in seven major areas of Northern California, and Inglis sold its assets to Campbell Taggart. This left Campbell Taggart and Continental as the sole wholesale bakers serving all parts of the Northern California area.

To sum up: the basic pattern driving the evolution of structure in the U.S. bread market since the 1960s has been the acquisition of local bakers with a view to buying their distribution net. This process has led to the emergence of two major national chains, and while national concentration levels remain low, local levels can be moderate to high. The advantage enjoyed by Continental is seen by observers within the industry to reside in its unparalleled strength in distribution, and this factor may have played a major part in the company's success. There are two further factors, however, that may have modified this process: the role of a wave of advertising during the critical phase of early consolidation in the 1960s, and the aggressive price competition that accompanied Continental's expansion in the 1970s.

Appendix 7.3

Processed Pork Products

Industry Definition

The meat-processing industry poses some serious problems in relation to international comparisons. The product mix consumed varies widely across countries; beef products in particular play a very different role in the United States, say, where they are of primary importance, as against Italy or Japan, where their role is relatively minor. Even within the basic run of pork products found in the countries studied here, considerable differences exist. The definition used in this study is narrow: processed pork products include bacon, ham, and sausages as primary product categories. This definition excludes all nonpork products (beef, poultry), and in so doing it excludes most canned products, with the exception of canned sausages.

The industry's primary products, then, include all ham and bacon, ranging from the full smoked ham, which is sliced in the consumer's presence and sold by weight, to the prepacked slices of bacon, ham, salami, and similar meats sold typically through supermarkets; and from cans of Spam to plastic packs of frankfurters. Gray areas exist at the boundaries of this range, but the broad conclusions of this analysis would be little affected by minor reclassifications.

The present study omits the case of the U.K. market on the grounds that somewhat over half of ham and bacon sales are satisfied by imports. In fact, the leading seller in the main (bacon) segment of the U.K. market is an association of Danish exporters.

The Markets by Country

France, Germany (F.R.), and Italy

In France, Germany, and Italy, the market is highly fragmented. The four leading firms and their combined shares are shown in table 7.3.1. In each of these markets, attempts by market leaders to establish a strong presence,

Table 7.3.1
Market concentration in processed pork products, by country

Leading firms by country	Combined share, C_4 (%)
France (Olida-Caby, Fleury-Michon, Morey, Géo)	~23
Germany (Herta-Atland-Dörffler, Fleiwa, Stockmeyer, Wilhelm Lutz)	~20
Italy (Fiorucci, Galbani, Vismara, Citterio)	~11
Japan (Ito-Ham, Nippon, Marudai, Purina)	~51
United States (Oscar Mayer, Hormel, Morrell, Beatrice)	~20

whether by way of advertising or through merger, have met with very limited success. Germany's leading firm is the product of a merger in the mid-1980s between Herta and Atland-Dörffler. The Herta brand is immediately recognised in all parts of the country. Such brand awareness is rare in the industry, however; even the name of a middle-ranking producer such as Waltner (whose market share places it in the lower half of the industry's top ten) will be recognized by only a small fraction of all consumers. Waltner, for example, markets a large fraction of its output through an intermediary (broker), Zembo, which sells under its own name. Thus Waltner products will be marketed under both the Waltner and Zembo brands. Such an approach helps the medium-size firms achieve national distribution; typically, such firms will also supply for own-label distribution—Waltner, for example, producing the Elite brand sold by the Kaufhaus chain of department stores.

Of the 600 firms in the German industry, the 20 largest account for about one-third of output. At the other end of the spectrum, an artisan fringe of some 200 firms share about 1% of sales between them, their output largely consisting of fresh sausages (würst); the industry's other two main product lines—ham and bacon, and dry sausages (salami, etc.)—are the preserve of industrial producers.

Italy's leading producers are of two kinds, and most—including Vismara, Citterio, and Negroni—grew up as large family firms. A small but important second group of leading firms have entered the industry from the dairy products sector. Indeed, Galbani and Invernizzi (which rank second and eighth respectively in processed pork products) are two of Italy's largest food firms and are leading producers in the dairy products area.[1] Against the background of an

---

1. The link between dairy products and processed pork products is one of the more unusual features of the Italian industry, and it reflects the highly fragmented nature of Italian retailing. What the two sectors have in common is the need for a well-organized distribution network that can supply a very large number of tiny retailers with fresh products. Here the dairy firms enjoy a comparative advantage, and in seeking to capitalize on their well-developed distribution net, Invernizzi and Galbani turned to processed meats as a natural area into which to diversify. Their success in the area has caused traditional processed meat producers such as Fiorucci to rethink their own distribution strategies.

artisan sector of 2,500 producers, who sell good-quality products at competitive prices and operate over a small locality with minimal distribution costs, the problem for the industry leaders is one of finding a suitable niche in which they can prosper. Two kinds of response have emerged. On the one hand, Galbani has set out to offer a broad product range at the medium-to low-quality end of the spectrum, while aiming to achieve high volumes on its lines; on the other hand, firms such as Citterio have gone for a high-price/high-quality strategy in attempting to distinguish their offerings from those of the small local producer.

This difficulty of establishing a strong presence in the market, against the background of a strong fringe of small local producers, is echoed by the French experience. France's market leader,[2] Olida-Caby, emerged from an attempt made in 1967 to create a major presence in the then highly fragmented industry. An initial agreement to merge four of the leading firms (Olida, Caby, Fleury-Michon, and Morey) fell through. Olida and Caby joined to form Olida-Caby, however, and later acquired Fleury-Michon to form France's dominant meat firm, whose 15% market share exceeded that of its nearest rivals by a factor of three. Its broad regional net of factories and its wide range of products contrasted with the narrower geographic scope and more specialized product ranges of its nearest rivals. The company's experience, however, has been mixed. The industry as a whole suffered from a squeeze on margins during the period of price controls in the 1970s; the firms that came through the period most successfully were those specializing in new products (plastic packs, etc.), and small specialist firms that specialized in a single line. Olida's financial difficulties led to its divestment of Fleury-Michon and, more recently, Olida and Caby have become independent. In 1986, Olida s newly appointed chief executive was reported in the French press as saying that the company had a sound product range, but had suffered for fifteen years from a mixture of underinvestment in plant and neglect of its Olida brand image. (*Nouvel Economiste* (April, May 1987)). On the other hand, Olida's broadly based diversification plans have achieved some striking successes (notably in certain segments of the frozen food industry, where it has taken the lead over Findus and Vivagel with its Gorey and Marie brands).

Olida's difficulties are to some degree typical of the industry's leading firms. *Agra-Alimentation*'s 1985 report on the industry indicates a long-term decline in the share of the top handful of firms, together with a strengthening of both middle-ranking and smaller firms. Crude measures of labor productivity paint

---

2. The French industry, labeled "charcuterie," covers not only processed pork products as defined here but also beef and poultry; poultry is unimportant, beef accounts for about 20%, and pork for about 80%. Thus, the industry described here corresponds only approximately to the above definition of processed pork products. Of its principal products, ham is mostly sold via retail outlets that offer it by the slice ("à la coupe," or "traditionelle"). This accounts for 87% of ham sold, in fact, whereas the modern plastic packs of ham in slices ("libre service") account for only 13% of the total. At the industry's fringe, as usual, the artisan sector—specializing in fresh sausages and pâtés—accounts for something between 15% and 20% of consumption of charcuterie.

a story consistent with this: in terms of tons of output per employee, there is little change across different size categories of firms in the upper half of the size distribution, except for a sharp fall in the case of the very top category (three firms with annual production above 20,000 tons). Labor productivity slowly declines, on the other hand, as size falls below the median level.[3]

The United States

The U.S. market differs in one important respect from the three European markets just considered. The relatively large distances that separate stock-rearing areas from the main centers of population led to the early development of a highly concentrated upstream industry. The meat-packing industry involves the slaughtering, refrigeration, and transportation of carcasses, and it is distinct from the relatively fragmented meat-processing industry. The relations between the two industries are, in one sense, quite close, in that the largest meat-processing firms are descendants of the Big Ten that dominated meat packing at the turn of the century.

The overall structure of market shares in processed pork products suggests a very fragmented structure, but this is somewhat misleading in that the market is highly segmented, and some companies have built up a very strong presence in certain sectors. The two leading firms today are Oscar Mayer and Hormel. Both have a diversified portfolio of products, but part of the reason why both survived so well throughout the difficult period of the 1960s and 1970s lies in the fact that their portfolios are neatly interlocking, so that the two rarely meet head on. Rather, each enjoys a secure leadership position in its own areas of strength. Thus Oscar Mayer focuses on bacon, (wiener and hot dog) sausages, and sliced cold meats ("luncheon meat"). Hormel, on the other hand, is strong in ham and canned products and has recently been highly successful in diversifying outside the industry, moving into processed foods generally with a strategy based on continuous product innovation.

The pattern of concentration within segments, then, can be quite different to the overall picture of five roughly similar-sized firms, each with no more than 5% or so of the market. In some segments, concentration can be relatively high.

---

3. In light of the experience of the U.S. industry, it is of interest to look at the experience of European producers in respect of vertical relations between slaughtering and meat processing. The available evidence suggests that the economies to be gained from an integrated operation are at best rather modest. Indeed, in both France and Italy, a steady trend away from an integrated operation has been evident over the past decade. Somewhat less than half of the firms in the French (charcuterie) industry now do their own slaughtering in-house, while the remainder either use public slaughterhouses or buy in carcasses. This trend is particularly evident in Italy, where the typical producer is simply too small to take on the increasingly onerous financial commitment required in establishing a modern slaughterhouse. On the other hand, a few major firms constitute exceptions to this trend: some, such as Citterio and Negroni, have integrated backward into the raising of their own livestock.

For example, in cold sliced meats, Oscar Mayer's share exceeds 25%. In hot dogs, Oscar Mayer holds a share that is believed to lie in the 10%–20% range. Hygrade (sold to Sara Lee in 1989) is the leading firm in this segment. These two firms, together with Armour and Eckrich, are believed to account for around 30% of hot dog sales. These two sectors are outliers, however: they are both highly advertised, brand-aware products. Such is not true of the other market segments, and here concentration is much lower. Oscar Mayer's share of the bacon sector (its third major focus) is believed to be somewhat over 5%.[4]

The aggregate picture is also somewhat misleading in another respect: many of the industry's medium-size producers operate on a regional basis, and it is typical that a leading regional brand can command a share of the overall market in excess of 20% of its own area (Farmer John's on the West Coast, for example, or Colonial in the Northeast).

Overall, despite these qualifications, the processed pork product market as a whole remains a very fragmented one in which a large number of small local producers can find a niche. Notwithstanding the presence of a highly concentrated upstream industry, the low setup costs involved at the processing end have allowed a low degree of overall concentration to persist for some decades, in all but a couple of exceptional segments.

Japan

The current range of products offered by the Japanese (ham and sausage) industry today corresponds quite closely to the definition set out above.[5] This was not so, however, even in the quite recent past. The present market leader, Ito-Ham, was founded in 1927, but had fewer than half a dozen employees up to the immediate postwar period, at which time the company was engaged primarily in making sausages from a mixture of meat and fish. In 1945 the company developed a form of "pressed ham" made from goat meat, mutton, and chicken—the growth of which throughout the 1950s stimulated the growth of the sector as a whole. The price of pork, which is imported, remained prohibitively high throughout the 1950s, and the main stimulus to growth through the sixties came from Ito-Ham's 1957 development of a new form of "pressed ham," which was actually based on mutton (the taste of which is disliked by Japanese consumers, but effectively masked via this newer process).

It was only from 1970 onward, however, as a result of a government initiative to stabilize pork prices and the continuing growth in disposable income, that

4. The role of private-label sales varies across market segments; in the more highly branded areas it can be significant (about 20% of the hot dogs segment, and slightly more than that in sliced cold meats).

5. Canned meat is relatively unimportant in Japan, apart from a small corned beef sector worth 19 billion yen in 1983, as compared with 570 billion yen for ham and sausages. Competition in this area has been unusually severe of late, with supermarkets pressing hard on producers to support lower prices. Some 90% of output is supplied by four firms, none of them among the market leaders in ham and sausages.

pork became the predominant input in the range of products offered by the industry (in 1986, for instance, pork accounted for 78% of inputs, while mutton had declined to 8%). Some 40% of the inputs to the industry are still imported, even though most of the fresh pork consumed in Japan is now produced domestically.

The five large firms that now dominate the industry date from the early period of industry growth in the 1950s. With few exceptions, these firms owe their present scale to internal growth. One exception is Nippon Ham, which was formed by merger and has acquired some half-dozen small firms since its formation. Ito-Ham acquired some local producers during the 1960s, though in most cases it expanded into new regions by building a factory in the area.[6]

Apart from the top-five firms—which today account for some 60% of sales—there are some twenty or so medium-size producers that sell under their own brands. These top twenty-five firms account for 80% of industry sales. The remaining firms (over 200 in all) are small and are predominantly engaged in selling on a local basis in the nonretail sector. Finally, a further 250 producers comprise a small artisan sector.

Annex: The U.S. Meat-Packing Industry

The emergence of oligopoly in the nineteenth-century U.S. meat-packing industry is the subject of a classic study by Yaeger (1981). The opening up of new cattle-rearing regions in the West, far from the main centers of population, provided an incentive for a small number of leading firms to develop large-scale operations in shipping meat in refrigerated trains. The scale economies intrinsic to this process had brought about, by the turn of the century, a situation in which ten major national firms dominated the meat-packing industry. The Big Ten typically operated in both beef and pork and were active in both slaughtering and processing; such generalists included, for example, Swift and Armour. Some others of the Ten whose interests in some cases lay primarily in pork products survive today as leading pork processors (Oscar Mayer, Morrell, Hormel, Hygrade). Meat processing, on the other hand, remained relatively fragmented. The low level of scale economies at the processing end allowed the survival of a huge number of small and medium-sized processors who purchased their inputs from major meat packers.

Antitrust proceedings in the meat-packing sector in the early part of the century ended in a consent decree, the outcome of which was a moderately concentrated structure that persisted through to the 1960s. It was at that point that the industry entered a phase of rapid restructuring that led to the current

---

6. Foreign links between the major producers and their U.S. counterparts are of some importance. Nippon Meat Packers has ties with Swift, for example, while Prima Meat Packers has a licensing arrangement with Oscar Mayer.

dominance of three major meat packers—only one of which is a descendant of the Big Ten.

The first major change came in the 1960s, when several conglomerates acquired leading meat packers: Wilson was acquired by LTV, whose main interests lay in steel and shipbuilding; Morrell was acquired by the country's leading marketer of bananas, United Brands; while the Greyhound Corporation —by origin a long-distance bus company—acquired Armour. The second major change came in the 1970s with the emergence of Iowa Beef Packers (IBP); operating from Western Nebraska and Colorado down to the Texas Panhandle, far from the traditional areas that formed the focus of the old Big Ten, IBP grew rapidly. Its growth was aided by the construction of new, low-cost plants and unhampered by the inflation-linked pay rates negotiated by its Big Ten rivals during the 1950s—rates that imposed an increasingly heavy cost burden on the majors throughout the 1970s. By the early 1980s, IBP had become the country's leading meat packer. Second to IBP was ConAgra, which incorporated both Armour and part of Swift.[7] The last of the three firms to dominate meat packing is a newcomer. Cargill, the international grain merchant, grew to its present position over the past two decades by acquiring and consolidating a series of small regional meat packers.

While the slaughtering (packing) end is now highly concentrated, the processing industry remains much less so. Among the seven major firms of national importance in pork processing, all but one (Sara Lee) are direct descendants of the old Big Ten.[8]

---

7. In 1983 Greyhound sold three Armour plants to Swift and the remaining part of Armour to ConAgra. Swift (which had been renamed Esmark in 1973) in turn spun off part of its meat-packing interest to ConAgra—although retaining some rights to market under the Swift brand—before being itself acquired by Beatrice Foods (see footnote 8).

8. Oscar Mayer, Hormel, and Morrell were all among the original Top Ten. Beatrice Foods, a major food conglomerate, acquired Esmark (formerly Swift) and Eckrich, one of the more important regional pork processors, and became one of the leading producers of processed pork products. The outsider among today's market leaders is Sara Lee, a widely diversified food firm. Its activities in the processed pork industry have involved acquiring a portfolio of strong regional producers that continue to market their products in their own regions. One of these regional brands, Hillshire Farms has recently been developed as a national brand.

Appendix 7.4

Canned Vegetables

Industry Definition

Finding a satisfactory industry definition, on the basis of which a useful international comparison of experience is possible, is rather difficult in the case of the canning industry. There are three problems. The first is that in some countries the canning industry is highly segmented, with the large majority of firms producing *either* canned vegetables *or* canned fruit (or some other single product line, such as fish). In other countries, however, a sizable fraction of the firms may produce two or more of these lines.

The second problem relates to the degree of import penetration: in Germany, domestic production accounts for less than 15% of consumption, both in canned vegetables and canned fruit. In the United Kingdom, 87% of canned fruit consumption is imported (though imports of canned vegetables are relatively low).

The third problem relates to special categories within the product mix: for example, the usual practice in the industry is to treat canned baked beans as a special category. The reasons for this are that canned baked beans (i) are produced by a separate subgroup of firms, which do not overlap much with mainstream canned vegetable products, (ii) do not compete with an equivalent frozen category, and so have been protected from the general decline in industry sales, and (iii) are much more highly branded than are canned vegetables generally—the advertising-sales ratio for canned baked beans is relatively high, whereas for other canned vegetables it is very low. The relative importance of this category varies widely across countries. In the United Kingdom, for example, sales of canned baked beans are worth over two-thirds of the sales value of all other canned vegetables combined. A second exception relates to tomatoes. In Italy, this is the single most important product, accounting for over half of canned vegetable sales. In most of the other countries, supplies are largely or wholly imported.

The approach taken here is as follows. The industry is defined as canned vegetables, excluding baked beans and tomatoes. On this definition, import penetration is high only in Germany; the German market, which is largely served by imports, is omitted from our comparison. The Japanese market differs widely in its product mix from the other countries considered here, and for that reason it too was omitted in the econometric analysis of chapter 5. A brief description of the Japanese market will be found below. All in all, no fully satisfactory approach seems possible. The present compromise is designed to minimize the problems inherent in making a cross-country comparison.

Setup Costs and Structure

We noted in chapter 4 that two widely used methods for estimating m.e.s. tend, by and large, to yield roughly similar results: the median plant size estimate, and estimates based on engineering studies. In the case of canned vegetables, however, more recent engineering estimates indicate an m.e.s. far greater than the scale of the median U.S. plant. The most plausible reason for this anomaly lies in the fact that the canning industry has for long been stagnant or declining. Associated with the decline has been a gradual consolidation of the industry, achieved alongside—and partly in response to—intensifying price competition and pressure on margins. The process of exit is slow, however, and despite continuing exit of the smallest producers, median plant size in the industry remains low relative to recent engineering estimates of m.e.s. plant size. (The median plant size estimate is used in the econometric estimates reported in chapter 5.)

The Evolution of Structure

The development of the canning industry falls into two clear phases. Its beginnings can be traced to technical innovations in the canning process in the nineteenth century. In 1809, Nicolas Appert received a prize from the French government for developing the idea of preserving food by sealing and heating it in containers. It was not until thirty years later, however, that tin cans began to be used in place of glass bottles. Although numerous patents were granted for canning over the next fifty years, problems of spoilage remained serious until the 1890s. During that decade, the realization that these problems were caused by the presence of bacteria led to the introduction of standardized heating procedures, and this development marked the start of the modern canning industry. Further technical improvements, in both canning procedures and equipment occurred throughout the first two decades of the twentieth century (Federal Trade Commission 1962). The industry developed rapidly throughout the first half of the century in all the countries considered here, and by mid-century it had reached its high point. From that stage onward, however, the industry moved into a state of stagnation or decline as the growing frozen food industry began to make rapid inroads in most countries, and this second phase of the industry's history has persisted to the present time. Some specialist categories of canned food have escaped the general pattern, but apart from these exceptions, the history of the industry since the 1950s has been one of very slow growth or of actual decline .

A second general feature of these markets is of particular relevance in what follows; this relates to the role of advertising. On the basis of the criterion adopted in chapter 3 (an advertising-sales ratio below 1%), we have classified this industry as a homogeneous goods industry. Unlike salt, sugar, bread, or flour, however, canned vegetables do enjoy a limited degree of advertising support. Moreover, during the first phase of the industry's history, canned vegetables were among the more highly advertised food products. Although a number of prominent brands were well established by mid-century in several countries, the rise of television advertising coincided with the transitional phase in which canned goods began to lose ground rapidly to frozen foods. The escalation of advertising outlays by frozen food manufacturers that occurred in the 1950s and 1960s in the United States and United Kingdom, for example, was not paralleled by any notable rise in the advertising of canned goods. Rather, these products came to be regarded in industry circles as a commodity product, sold basically on price, over the 1960s and 1970s. In spite of this, a number of successful brands still survive in the industry in certain countries (notably in the United States, France, and Italy).

The Markets by Country

The United States

The U.S. canning industry,[1] comprising both canned vegetables and the (much smaller) canned fruit category, expanded rapidly throughout the first half of the century. The FTC report of 1962 records the fact that the total number of canneries increased from 100 in 1870 to 1,800 in 1900, and to over 3,000 by 1947. After that date, numbers began to decline, falling to 2,333 in 1958. By 1985, the number had fallen to 1,209.[2] These trends in the number of firms reflected a combination of two factors. The first factor was a rise in average plant size[3] and the exit of very small plants. The second was a falling trend in total output from the 1960s onward.

---

1. This account draws on the report by the Federal Trade Commission (1962).
2. The number comprises the three four-digit SIC industries "canned vegetables" (SIC 2033), "canned specialties" (SIC 2032), and "pickles, sauces, and salad dressings" (SIC 2035), and corresponds to the pre-1954 SIC industry "canned fruit" and "vegetables" (SIC 2033) (see FTC 1962, p. 26).
3. The FTC notes that "the 2,333 canneries operating in 1958 produced 18 times the volume of the 1,800 canneries operating at the turn of the century."

Up to the early 1960s, total industry output continued to grow, with the volume of production increasing by one-third between 1947 and 1963 (FTC 1962). Thereafter, however, the industry began to decline. In 1972, fruit and vegetable canning (SIC 2033) accounted for 8.18% of value added in the food industry as a whole (SIC 2); by 1985, this figure had almost halved, to 4.27%.[4]

Over the half-century during which the industry was steadily growing, it showed many of the features of those archetypal advertising-intensive industries described in chapters 8–10. It was only as the industry began to decline that canned goods took on the character of a commodity product, but this process still left two major brands, established in the industry's early days, commanding a significant price premium.

When the U.S. canning industry first developed in the 1870s and 1880s, it was highly fragmented. Consolidation came in two waves. The first was a response to the depression of the 1890s, a period during which small canners faced increasing serious problems as price competition intensified. The outcome was the formation of the California Fruit Canners Association, a fairly loose federation of eighteen companies which together owned about half of California's canning establishments. The newly formed association chose Del Monte as its main brand, and by it 1915 was packing over fifty products under that label (the association continued, however, to use no less than seventy-two other leading brands).

The second phase of consolidation occurred in 1916, when four major companies—including the California Fruit Canneries—merged to form the California Packing Corporation. Also among the four was the J. K. Armsby Company, one of the largest wholesale grocery companies on the West Coast, whose founder had for some years been canvassing the idea of a merger of interests in the canning industry. The central theme of the new organization was clear from the start:

"One goal, one basic concept, held all these disparate elements together.... California Packing Corporation would present a solid front in the market place.... There would be only one premium Calpac label—*Del Monte*.... And it would be promoted for all it was worth.... By virtue of its size and financial resources, California Packing Corporation now had the capacity to do what none of its predecessors could do: establish a *national* market for a single brand of canned fruits and vegetables and build that market into a great consumer franchise through the new medium of mass advertising." (Braznell 1982, p. 38)

Prior to 1916, it had been customary for a typical canner to label produce under several brands and provide customers with their own "exclusive" brands in the manner of own-label producers today. Against this background, the new Del Monte strategy represented a major innovation: its advertising campaign, from 1917 onward broke new ground in the U.S. food industry. Full-color

---

4. The decline in canned specialties, SIC 2032, was slower (from 2.28% of value added in 1972 to 2.07% in 1985).

advertisements in leading magazines, together with huge mailings to the grocery trade inviting them to tie in to this national advertising campaign by featuring Del Monte brands prominently in their displays, were the key elements in the campaign. *Fortune* magazine commented in 1938 that the Calpac campaign "induced a new habit of brand buying throughout the country" (Braznell 1982, p. 49).

By mid-century, the U.S. canning industry had evolved a clear dual structure, with a small number of highly advertised brands competing alongside a large fringe of nonadvertisers. In 1959, the top-eight advertisers accounted for 82.6% of industry advertising. Of these, the five largest accounted for 61% of the industry total, and the advertising-sales ratio for this group of five firms stood at 5.7%, as against 3.2% for the industry as a whole. Another feature typical of the advertising-intensive industries related to the difference in sales concentration within the retail and nonretail sectors. The four-firm sales concentration ratio within the retail market stood at 43.2% in 1959, as against 13.4% in the nonretail market. Within certain market segments, much higher levels were reached. Of fifteen categories of canned fruit, vegetables, and juices surveyed by the FTC, the four-firm sales concentration ratio (for the combined retail and nonretail markets) exceeded 60% in seven cases.

An FTC report (1967, p. 12) noted a strong positive relationship between firm size and profitability across the entire range of size classes in the industry in 1959. This reflected two factors: as the FTC noted, the twelve largest canners, each with annual sales exceeding $25 million, enjoyed average pretax profits equal to 8.8% of their net canning sales. At the other end of the scale, firms with annual sales below $1 million had pretax profits equal to 0.7% of net canning sales.

The relatively high rate of profit earned by the top group of twelve firms can in part be attributed to the brand premia enjoyed by this group of firms; the negative relationship found across the remaining size classes, however, was indicative of the lower unit costs achieved by the larger canners. Almost 40% of the 343 smallest firms reporting to the FTC made operating losses in 1959, and 70% of all loss-making canners came from this group.

The FTC's analysis indicated that concentration in the various submarkets had increased substantially since the 1930s and the bulk of the decline in firm numbers had come from the exit (via bankruptcy or otherwise) of small firms. Merger and acquisition activity, on the other hand, was shown to involve for the most part the absorption of relatively profitable medium-size firms by major food processors—often coming from outside the canning sector.

As the industry moved into its slow decline from the 1960s onward, two trends emerged. First, the pressure on smaller firms, already emphasized by the FTC in the early 1960s, continued to induce substantial exit. Second, most major brands lost ground as the industry became more "commodity-like." Of the eight leading firms whose brands enjoyed heavy advertising support in 1959, only two (Del Monte and Green Giant) remain as strong brands today (FTC 1967, p. 54). These two alone command a significant price premium (of the order of

15%–20%), and their market shares have strengthened over time as other brands have declined. Currently, they command a combined (retail) market share of about 38%. Apart from these two brands, the rest of the market is dominated by own-label sales, which take over half the total. A sizable fringe of small producers continues to operate, but these specialize in the retailers' own label segment.

Between these two groups lie a handful of medium-sized firms operating on a regional basis. These include the cooperative S + W, a major brand on the West Coast. Libby sells in the Southeast, via a form of cooperative arrangement with growers. The Larsen Canning Co. sells under its own label. Also in this group is Stokely, which has merged with a leading private-label supplier, Oconomo-woc Canning. A very high proportion of retailers' private-label products are supplied by a number of firms in this group, and the total volume produced by the group is commensurate with the total volume of the two market leaders. Price competition in this part of the market is very strong, brand image is weak, and sellers cannot command any significant premium over own-label supplies.

At the top end of the market, however, the two leaders keep prices roughly in line and aim to maintain their respective shares. Given the substantial premium they command, the business is a steadily profitable one and formed an attractive target for expansion by leading food corporations. R. J. Reynolds acquired Del Monte (in one of a number of diversification moves by leading tobacco firms into general food products). In 1980, Pillsbury acquired Green Giant, in a move directed toward acquiring the company's frozen food business; but Pillsbury found, over time, that it can earn satisfactory returns on its canning business also.

The United Kingdom

The U.K. market has passed through a series of phases similar to those noted for the U.S. industry. In recent years, continuing price pressure on most sellers has led to a more consolidated structure, with an almost total disappearance of strong brands. Only Pillsbury's Green Giant, with a relatively modest market share, commands a substantial premium in the U.K. retail market. The report by the Commission of the European Communities (1977) on the evolution of concentration noted a number of features of the U.K. market that parallel the U.S. experience During the early stages of the industry's evolution, closeness to growing areas was relatively important, and a quite fragmented structure developed, with a large number of small local firms. Later, some canners were acquired by major food processors—but, in contrast to the United States, major brands had not emerged by the 1960s, when the industry began to lose ground to frozen foods. (Between 1966 and 1973, for example, average household spending on frozen food rose by 9.5% per annum in real terms, but spending on canned foods rose by less than 1.5%.

The failure of major brands to emerge in this area was remarked upon as surprising in the EEC report, given the access to capital enjoyed by the major food processors in the industry. By 1973, the advertising-sales ratio for canned vegetables was 0.7%. Certain special categories of canned food, including baked beans and salmon, for example, were highly advertised at this time, and leading brands were well established.

By the time the industry had entered the phase of low growth during the 1970s, canned vegetables had become a commodity product, with no strong brands present in most major segments. Throughout the 1970s, continued downward pressure on unit margins led to severe financial difficulties for many producers. It was against this background that a process of consolidation began in the early 1980s.

To understand the structure of the U.K. market, it is useful to begin by noting the main product categories. These are listed in Mintel 1985 as peas (48% of retail sales), corn (16%), carrots (14%), beans—other than baked beans—(12%) potatoes (5%), and mushrooms (3%). Apart from corn and potatoes, imports to the United Kingdom are relatively unimportant. Nonretail sales are poorly documented, but account for less than 10% of total sales.

The largest sector—peas—divides into two subsectors:

• Garden peas (16% of retail sales) are a strictly seasonal product, canned once a year during an 8–10 week period. They earn relatively high unit margins, but involve relatively high stockholding costs.

• Processed peas (32% of retail sales) are a nonseasonal, high volume low margin product and are highly price competitive.

In the early 1980s, the branded half of the peas market was divided among a handful of producers. Bachelors, a Unilever subsidiary that produced only processed peas, was clear market leader in this segment with a 23% share of retail sales. None of the others—Del Monte, Hartleys (a Chivers Hartley subsidiary), Lockwoods, Smedley, Morton (a Beecham Foods subsidiary), and Morrell—had more than 10% of retail sales in either processed or garden peas. Own-brand sales had grown to the point where they accounted for half of all retail sales by the early 1980s; most major producers sold both under their own brands and supplied retailers for their own-label lines.

Margins continued to be low throughout the early 1980s, partly as a result of price competition at the retail level and partly as an outcome of the intensity of competition for their own-label business. A number of producers faced serious financial difficulties, and it was against this background that the new and rapidly growing food conglomerate Hillsdown acquired five U.K. canners: Smedley, Lockwoods, Morrell, Morton (a small, premium producer), and Wilson (a meat canner). Hillsdown thereafter embarked on a process of rationalizing its brand structure: Smedley was to be their main brand; the Morrell brand disappeared; and the Morton brand was retained for premium products.

This series of acquisitions left Hillsdown as a clear market leader in all major categories except corn (where Pillsbury's Green Giant brand accounts for over 40% of sales) and potatoes (where Hillsdown, Hartleys, and Anglia Canners are of roughly similar importance). With an equally strong presence in the own-label half of the market, Hillsdown accounted for almost one-half of canned vegetable sales by the late 1980s. Meanwhile, Del Monte, the market leader in garden peas, decided to withdraw from the U.K. market. This left a gap at the premium end of the market, at which Hillsdown's Morton brand was targeted.

The branded half of the canned peas market thus came to be occupied by Hillsdown, Bachelors (processed peas only), and Hartley's. On the own-label side, a further handful of firms now operate: these include Anglia Canners (a part of Associated British Foods), Quantock (a Gerber subsidiary whose main activity is in orange juice, but which also packs garden peas), and the Co-op, which is a major own-label supplier whose activities extend far beyond the Co-op retail outlets. Finally, a few firms, including Stratford canners and Mid-Norfolk canners, specialize in catering sales.

The overall structure, then, is one of moderately high concentration. Price competition became less severe during the latter half of the 1980s. This was in part a result of some easing of pressure on the own-label sector by leading retails, but it also reflected the industry's experience of price cutting during the mid-1980s, when attempts by one producer to gain share led to price matching and a consequent fall in margins.

Following this phase of consolidation, the severe financial problems besetting some producers during the 1970s had become less evident by the mid-1980s, most of the remaining firms appearing relatively secure. Nonetheless, pressure on margins remained a major incentive to reduce costs. Conventional wisdom within the industry during the 1980s held that large-scale production yielded some significant advantage, but opinions differed as to the best route to increased efficiency. Bachelors chose to build a new, highly efficient plant from scratch, but they were alone in taking this avenue. For most firms, the more cautious alternative of piecemeal refurbishment and modernization of existing plant has been the norm.

France

A generation ago, the French canning industry was relatively fragmented, but a gradual process of consolidation, involving both a series of acquisitions and the exit of small producers, has led to a moderately concentrated structure in which about twenty-five producers remain active. The growing strength of own label products is also apparent: they now account for just over 40% of retail sales. Many of the smaller remaining producers focus primarily on the own-label sector, and many of the majors use own-label sales to keep up production levels when necessary.

The industry's main products are peas, beans, and mushrooms. Most producers confine themselves to canning vegetables, but half a dozen or so of the larger producers also can fruit. A few producers both can and freeze vegetables, some of these are subsidiaries of leading frozen food firms (Ortiz Miko operates via both Miko SA and Cofralim; France Glace Findus is a Nestlé subsidiary).

The cooperative sector remains a significant force, in large part because of a process of consolidation among small cooperatives. The largest cooperative group—the Compagnie Générale de Conserves, controlled by the Breton co-operative Cecab—is the leading supplier in the industry. It cans vegetables, fruit, and fish and is also active in frozen foods and prepared meals. Until 1981 it retained several brands, but since then has been following a more focused strategy, confining itself to its leading (D'Aucy) brand and attempting to build that up over time.

The only firm whose share exceeds that of Cecab is the Saupiquet group, which has wide interests: half of its 1982 turnover (1.2 billion FF) derived from canned fish, about 30% from canned vegetables (sold under the Cassegrain brand), and the rest from prepared meals. The third seller is Bonduelle, whose importance on the domestic market is somewhat less than that of Saupiquet, but whose main strength lies in export markets (mainly the United Kingdom and Germany) where it earns almost half its sales revenue. The (much smaller) fourth producer, SA Les Propriétaires Réunis, sells about half its output under its (several) own brands, and the remaining half to the own-label sector. Apart from canning vegetables, it also has interests in meat processing.

Branding in the industry remains weak, though the growing success of Bonduelle in establishing brand recognition in European markets is notable. Efforts by other producers, notably Cecab, to increase brand awareness contributed to a surge in advertising, especially on television, in the late 1970s and early 1980s. But overall levels remain modest, accounting for about 0.25% of sales revenue in 1981, and even this low figure represented a fivefold increase over the 1977 level.

Italy

The canned vegetable industry in Italy is dominated by the canned tomato segment, where Italy is Europe's leading producer and a major exporter. This segment is relatively fragmented (as tends to be the case in other countries also, notably in the United States). Here, we exclude this segment to achieve comparability across countries. The main products of the Italian canned vegetables industry, thus defined, are peas and beans.

The industry as a whole consists of two groups of firms:

• a small group of highly diversified food companies (Cirio, Alivar, and Star) whose strength lies in their strong distribution network and a highly respected brand image; and

• a large fringe of very small producers, over 400 in all. Most of these operate exclusively in canned tomatoes, and the smallest of them focus on the catering segment (which takes 20% of total output) and the export market.

Between these two groups lie two firms with roots in the cooperative movement:

• Conserve Italia, a consortium of cooperative-owned canneries; and

• Columbani, a firm with strong links to producer cooperatives, which hold shares in the company.

The leading firms operate both in tomato products and in peas and beans. However, the number of smaller firms active in the latter segment is relatively low (about eighty to ninety).

Finally, a handful of major firms operate in selective segments of the industry, employing a high image/high price strategy. The best known of these is the French firm Bonduelle, which sells via its subsidiary, Bonduelle Italia. The Del Monte corporation also operates via a domestic subsidiary, Calpak. Two domestic firms, Panigal and Daf, also operate in this segment.

One recent entrant of note is the Parmalat company, which entered the segment by launching its "tetrapack" of tomato juice in 1982. This introduction was typical of a company noted for a policy of innovative product development and package design and for the effectiveness of its advertising campaigns and national marketing strategy, and it offers a good example of an attempt to create a profitable niche against the background of a highly fragmented, price-competitive industry. In canned vegetables, Parmalat does not itself produce, but buys in products from smaller companies and markets them under its brand.

To facilitate comparison with the data for other countries, the market definition used in constructing the market share table for canned vegetables covers the canned peas and beans segment only (though the overall pattern is not greatly different for the sector as a whole, apart from the presence of a large fringe of very small tomato canners). The most notable feature of the market share pattern is the relatively high level of concentration, which becomes apparent when Cirio and Alivar are grouped: both are held by SME, which in turn is part of the public corporation IRI. (Until recently, SME also held a stake in Star, which it has relinquished; Star is now controlled by the Fossati family, via Findim.)

Overall, therefore, a large number of producers survive, but the industry is dominated by a handful of firms whose strength lies as much in the general marketing advantage they enjoy as large, diversified food firms as in the brand image attached to their products.

Japan

The Japanese canning industry has a two-tiered structure in which a large number of producers sell through a second tier of firms, the "brand owners." At the production end, there is rather less specialization than is evident in other countries: of Japan's 567 canners, about 80% can vegetables, whereas about 40% can fruit. Many factories operate only in season. The gradual growth of the frozen food industry has, as elsewhere, contributed to a slow decline in canning and to a gradual exit of producers.

The product mix is rather different from that of the other countries considered here. By far the largest canned product is sweet corn, of which 90% is grown

Table 7.4.1
Brand-owner shares in two major segments of the Japanese canning industry

Sweet corn (total sales 5.3 billion yen, 1983)		*Mushrooms* (total sales 3.1 billion yen, 1983)	
	Share, 1983 (%)		Share, 1983 (%)
Aohata Kanzume	50	Shimizu Sokuhin	24
Nichiro Gyogyo	10	Ryoshoku (Higasa)	18
Daisey Sokuhin	9	Sanyo-do	15
Cradle	9	Aohata Kansume	9

Source: Yano Research Institute.

on the northern island, Hokkaido Some 70% of canned sweet corn is sold to industrial users and 30% to retail. Other canned vegetables include mushrooms (again sold mainly to industrial buyers) and asparagus. Imports of these categories are small. Two other categories (tomato products and bamboo shoots) figure heavily in consumption and are largely or wholly imported.

Given the integrated nature of production, it is difficult to arrive at production shares in canned vegetables. A comparison of canners' turnover with the total sales of all canned goods, however, indicates that the four largest canners produce less than 20% of total output. Among the leading firms are:

• Iwate-Kanzume, an independent firm that has close relations with brand owners Sanyo and Nissui. It cans vegetables, fish, and fruit and had a 1983 turnover in the 7–8 billion yen range.

• Nihon Kanzume (owned by Meiji Milk, one of Japan's largest food firms) sells largely to Aohata Kanzume, the leading brand owner in sweet corn. It cans both vegetables and fish and had a 1983 turnover in the 7–8 billion yen range.

Thus, even the leading producers are medium-sized enterprises. Concentration by brand owner, however, is much higher. The shares of the leading brands in the two major categories are shown in table 7.4.1.

As is clear from these tables, the major brand owners tend to specialize by category: only Aohata Kanzume has a leading position in both segments. It is also clear that a concentration ratio computed in terms of brand owners instead of individual producers will be moderately high. Because of the difficulties involved in arriving at a market definition under which the Japanese industry might reasonably be compared with those of France, Italy, the United Kingdom, and the United States, the Japanese industry was omitted from the econometric analysis of chapter 5.

Appendix 8.1

Frozen Food in Japan

The Japanese frozen food market forms an interesting point of comparison with the markets described in chapter 8, and the leading multinationals, Nestlé and Unilever, play only a very small role.[1] The origins of the industry are novel: it began with the frozen fish segment, and the two pioneering firms in that area, Nichirei and Nissui, remain among the leading half-dozen firms in the industry today. The Japanese industry is also unusual in that the retail segment is relatively small: 74% of sales by volume are made in the nonretail (catering) segment. This is attributed in industry circles to a combination of several factors. One factor lies in the high rate of growth in demand by the catering sector, as female participation in the labor force increases. While the latter factor might also be expected inter alia to stimulate retail sales of convenience foods generally, much of this increase has accrued to the rival category of "chilled foods," which are very popular on the Japanese market.

Industry output was extremely low as recently as 1970, when it stood at 141,000 tonnes, compared to 26,000 tonnes in 1965. By 1986 it had reached 823,000 tonnes, corresponding to a level of per capita consumption less than half that of the United Kingdom.[2] The gradual growth of the industry has attracted a number of Japan's leading food processors. Ajinomoto, which began as a producer of monosodium glutamate, is now a widely diversified food processor. It entered the frozen food business in 1971, when consumption was still quite modest; it launched its retail brand nationally in 1975 and its catering line in 1976. Snow brand, originally a producer of milk products, is also a widely diversified food processor. Because of the dominance of Nichirei and Nissui in frozen fish, the pattern of market shares is quite different according to whether fish are included or not (see table 8.1.1). Ajinomoto's success in building up a

---

1. Nestlé entered the market over a decade ago, but its market share remains extremely small. Unilever entered more recently, selling fish cakes under the Iglo brand, and has since begun to extend its product range.

2. Japan 7.9 kilos per capita; United Kingdom, 20.9; Germany, 18.4; United States, 47.0; and France, 15.0.

Table 8.1.1
Market shares in the Japanese frozen food industry, 1986

Company	Retail market shares (%)		Catering market shares (%)	
	Total	Excl. fish		
Nichirei	16	10	Nichirei	12
Nissui	14	10	Katokichi	10
Ajinomoto	8	16	Nissui	10
Snow Brand	8	7	Yayoi	10

Source: Nikka Keizai, company interviews.

leading position in the retail segment revolves around its policy of maintaining a high rate of new product introductions. In the catering segment, Nichirei and Nissui are again among the top-four producers, followed by Katokichi and Yayoi. The overall share of the top-four sellers in catering (43%) is close to the level in retailing (46%).

The market supports a large number of independent producers; in 1986, 763 plants were in operation (though 68 of these produced 53% of total output), while the number of firms operating was around 500. The viability of this unusually large number of small firms is largely attributable to the form of relationship that has developed between the market leaders and the small producer. The main outlet for the small producer is to supply the product directly to a leading firm, which then markets it under its well-established brand. This relationship is not at all novel to this industry; it occurs in other Japanese food industries (such as canning; see chapter 7) and in the frozen food industry in some other countries (as with Birds Eye in the United States).

This relationshlp has, however, been developed to an unusual degree in the Japanese frozen food industry. The retail market is heavily driven by the constant flow of new product lines, and some of the majors invite small companies to jointly develop new products. The major producer will in such cases provide advice on quality control and processing methods, while buying in the product to be sold under its brand name.

Appendix 9.1

Prepared Soups

Market Definition

We define the prepared soups market to include both canned and dried varieties, the relative importance of which varies widely by country. We exclude the new and very small category of frozen soups, as well as a range of related products often included in standard industry definitions (bouillon cubes, sauces, etc.).

The Markets by Country

The U.S. and U.K. markets are described in chapter 9. In what follows, we describe the French, German, Italian, and Japanese markets.

France

As in much of Continental Europe, dried soups form the most important category in the French market, accounting for sales of 1.1 billion FF in 1986 as against 190 million FF for canned soups. The dried soups segment is dominated by subsidiaries of three multinational groups: Société des Produits du Mais, a subsidiary of CPC; Sopad-Nestlé; and Uniliver's subsidiary, Fralib. These three sellers accounted for 96% of total sales in this segment in 1986. A fourth seller, Potalux, sells under its own brand as well as supplying the retailers' own-label sector. In the canned sector, four-fifths of total sales volume is accounted for by one firm: Segma Liebig Maille, a subsidiary of France's leading food conglomerate, BSN.

Germany (F.R.)

As in several other European markets, dried soups form a relatively large part of total sales in the German market. In 1983, sales of canned soup were valued at 203 million DM, while sales of dried soups valued at 329 million DM (Verlagsgruppe Bauer 1984, p. 30). Some twenty-six producers are active in the soups and sauces industry. Although several indigenous producers retain a very small presence, both segments of the market are dominated by a handful of multinational companies. In the dried soups segment, the leading sellers are Maggi (Nestlé) and Deutsche Maizena (owned by CPC and selling under the Knorr brand). In the canned segment, the Unilever subsidiary Schafft Fleisch-weke has a 22%–23% market share, comprising both its sales under its Unox brand and its own-label products sold through the leading food retailer Aldi. Its leading competitors in the canned soup segment are the two leading dried soups makers Maggi (Nestlé) and Deutsche Maizena (CPC); besides these three firms, two others have canned soup shares exceeding 5%: Erasco, a Pillsbury subsidiary and Conservenfabrik Eugen Lacroix GmbH, which was acquired by Campbell in 1978 (Verlagsgruppe Bauer, 1984, pp. 8–9).

Italy

The product mix in the Italian market is substantially different from that observed in the other countries studied here, in that by far the largest category consists of frozen soups (minestrone), a category that is relatively unimportant elsewhere. This market segment is, moreover, dominated by a different group of companies (leading frozen food producers) than is the market for nonfrozen prepared soups. The latter market is extremely small. Total output in 1983 stood at 6,100 tonnes (1,400 canned and 4,700 dried), a large proportion of which was exported.[1] Imports in the same year amounted to 1,226 tonnes, with three-quarters of this total coming from West Germany. The small size of the Italian market can be gauged by comparing these figures with the volume of production in the United Kingdom, which stood at 274 million tonnes in 1983.

For this reason, the Italian market was omitted from the regressions reported in chapter 5. Within the nonfrozen prepared soups market, Knorr (CPC Italia) is the leading brand, accounting for over half of total sales. Other sellers include Campbell and two indigenous producers, Star Stabilimento Alimentare and Parmalat.

Japan

The Japanese market is relatively small, and its growth dates from the early postwar years. Campbell marketed soup in Japan from the early 1950s; at that time, the company was selling products produced in the United States via a Hong Kong trading company. While Campbell currently offers a range of products designed specifically for the Japanese market, these products are still produced in its U.S. plants and distributed in Japan by Mitsui.

---

1. Exports of soups and soup preparations amounted to 3,219 tonnes in 1983.

While Campbell retains a 25%–30% share in canned soup, the growth of the dried soup category over time has been much greater, and canned soups now account for only 10% of total sales.

The market leader in the soup market is Ajinomoto, Japan's largest food processor (see chapters 8, 12). Ajinomoto built up the market for prepared soups in Japan through a mixture of continual product innovation and heavy advertising support. The range of soups on offer is both different from, and much wider than, those found in Europe or the United States. New lines introduced in 1988, for example, included a fruit-based product and a Vichysoisse-type powdered soup made by adding milk. Ajinomoto's entry to the soup market dates from the 1960s, when they formed a link with Knorr (CPC). This move represented one of Ajinomoto's first ventures into the food and drink market; prior to that date, the company was already established as Japan's leading producer of monosodium glutamate (MSG). In 1987, CPC sold its interests in the venture to Ajinomoto. Ajinomoto's strategy in building up the market by constantly introducing new categories with heavy advertising support is typical of the company's marketing activity in other areas. Apart from Ajinomoto, no company has succeeded in gaining much more than 5%–6% of total sales. Several companies (Pokka, Nestlé, Meiraku, Campbell) have shares in the 2%–6% range. In all, some thirty-eight companies market soup, but many of these are basically packers that buy in their product.

Appendix 9.2
Margarine

Product Definition

The margarine market forms part of the wider oils and fats market, which includes a range of edible fats used for direct consumption, for cooking, or in baking, etc. Major cross-country differences exist in regard to the product mix consumed. For example, the Northern European countries have a relatively high level of margarine consumption, while consumption of oils is relatively low. In Southern Europe, the reverse is true. Differences of this kind in the composition of demand within the oils and fats markets make an overall comparison of structure rather complex. Within this study, the approach taken is to focus on one particular product market, margarine, as a representative of this group of markets.

The margarine market has gone through a series of technical innovations over the course of the century. The introduction of new products has in turn been affected by the legal framework within which the industry operates. The difficulties faced by margarine makers in the United States, up to the 1950s, were unusually stringent. However, for all of the countries studied here, some form of regulation has been in operation in the margarine industry (van Stuyvenberg 1969).

The first of two key recent developments was the introduction of soft margarine in tubs. This has in some countries almost wholly displaced the traditional hard margarine sold in packets as a butter substitute, and hard margarine has come to be used largely for cooking. The second key development related to the introduction of products involving a mix of margarine and butter. Here, legal restraints have limited developments in many countries, the United Kingdom being an exception.

The Markets by Country

The development of structure in Europe and the United States is described in chapter 9. Here, we set out the current structure of the margarine markets by country.

The United Kingdom

In 1958, some twenty-five firms were active in the U.K. margarine industry, with Unilever's subsidiary Van den Berghs and Jurgens playing a strong leading role. By 1972, however, the number of producers had fallen to fourteen.[1] The number continued to shrink over the past decade; the main pressure on smaller producers has come from cheap imports from Belgium and Holland, whose impact on the own-label market (the usual haven of the smaller margarine maker) deprived them of their natural outlet. It was against a background of severe financial difficulties, then, that a newcomer to the industry, Achetos and Hutcheson, took over several of the smaller producers to form an efficient, low-cost supplier of basic margarine products aimed at the own-label market. The company has within a few years captured some 10% of the 26% market share enjoyed by own-label products. The result of this has been a sharp decline in the number of producers.

The other major development that has changed the identity of some of the leading firms in the market during the past decade has its origin in the relatively relaxed U.K. legislation in this area. In contrast to Continental Europe, it is legal in the United Kingdom to offer a mixture of butter and margarine, though it cannot be termed "margarine" if the butter content exceeds 10%.

In 1978, Unigate, whose main interests lie in the dairy products sector, launched their St. Ivel Gold, a low-fat mixture of butter and vegetable oils. A strong marketing campaign aimed at a health image gained added impetus from two major medical reports that had appeared during the preceding ten years, both arguing in favor of a low-fat diet. The result was the strong growth of the St. Ivel brand. Over the decade, the (expensive) butter content was gradually reduced and finally phased out, thus liberating further funds to underwrite an effective marketing campaign. The result was the capture of an 8% share of the margarine market by Unigate, with a single brand.

More recently, Unigate has been joined in this market segment by Dairy Crest, a company whose origins also lie in the dairy industry (it originated as the marketing arm of the Milk Marketing Board). Their Clover product is a true mix (50% butter fat, 50% vegetable fat). Whereas Clover was a tub product, they have now launched a sister product in wrapper form called "Willow." Both are positioned as "near butters." A number of small dairy firms (such as Portadown dairies) have recently tried to enter this new market segment.

In the meantime, Kraft has been changing its strategy in the U.K. market from one of meeting Unilever head on to concentrating instead on selected high-value-added niches. Kraft now concentrates on three products

· Golden Churn, a mixed product;

· Vitalite, a polyunsaturated product, and

· Mello, a reduced-fat spread.

---

1. EEC, *The Evolution of Concentration*, p. 252.

Each product captures somewhat over 2% of the market, or around 10,000 tons/annum, which allows an efficient level of operation on all three production lines.

The Nonretail Market in the United Kingdom

Sales to catering are very much the commodity end of the market, where margins are low and price competition intense. The market is about one-third the size of the retail market; little information is available regarding market shares in this segment. Industrial sales (to bakeries) are, on the other hand, very profitable, but here the market is very service oriented, and a successful supplier will offer an extremely wide range of products to the industry, of which margarine is just one. Of the majors, Van den Berghs is an important presence in both the industrial and catering segments, as is Achetos and Hutcheson. Kraft has important interests on the catering side, while Rowallen Creameries, a subsidiary of Associated British Foods, which is extremely small on the retail side, has sizable industrial sales.

Germany (F.R.)

Unilever's main competitor in the German market comes from the own-label sector, where the Aldi supermarket chain, supplied by Walter Rau, accounts for some 20% or so of all retail sales. Fritz Homann is the only other producer selling both at retail and to the catering and industrial (baking) sector. The latter sector accounts for slightly over a quarter of total margarine sales. Smaller producers concentrate either on the retail market (typically on the own-label segment) or on the catering and industrial side.

As in the U.K. market, price pressure on German margarine makers has led to the slow but steady disappearance of small suppliers (from thirty-nine in the early 1960s to sixteen or so in the mid-1980s). This pressure has increased further as the total market size has been steady or slightly declining over the period—a trend that reflects lower prices for butter within the EEC.

The pace of new product development has been slower than in the United Kingdom; industry experts in Germany see the market as lagging the United Kingdom's by several years. Nonetheless, the shift to soft margarine in tubs has long been completed, with the wrapped bar reserved largely for cooking use. New types of packaging and new product offerings are crucial to success in the market. Walter Rau, for instance, has maintained its number-two position largely by way of a serious continuing R&D program, together with an emphasis on television advertising of its Walter Rau brand.

Indeed, the main nexus of competition in the German market lies in the "upmarket" segment, where consumers want to buy a premium product but, in choosing between alternative premium offerings, are highly responsive to a better price deal. German supermarkets, unlike those in the United Kingdom, have failed to develop any own-brands with premium status. Thus in supplying the own-label segments, producers face intense competition on price. For many years, Unilever avoided the own-label market, a factor that doubtless played a major part in allowing Walter Rau to establish itself so firmly in that niche. More recently, however, Unilever entered this segment via its acquisition of Benedikt Klein, through which it supplies margarine to Aldi.

France

In France, Unilever operates via its subsidiary Astra Calve and has long dominated the market. In 1980, a series of events led to the emergence of Lesieur, a company whose primary interests lay in vegetable oils, as Unilever's main competitor. In 1980, Unipol, a holding company with widespread interests in the food industry, decided to dispose of its margarine interests. Following the failure of negotiations with Astra Calve, it approached Lesieur, which decided to acquire the company. The Commission de la Concurrence ruled in favor of the acquisition on the grounds that:

• While Astra Calve dominated the margarine segment, Lesieur was relatively stronger in the edible oils segment of the oils and fats market;

• Astra Calve, as a Unilever subsidiary, constituted a very strong rival to Lesieur;

• Lesieur's interests rest mostly on peanut oil, Astra Calve's on sunflower oil. Given the rising trend in the relative cost of (peanut oil), Lesieur is in danger of finding itself in a weakened position in the oils and fats market. The proposed acquisition was therefore likely to strengthen the weaker of the two main firms in the overall market.

The emergence of the Astra Calve-Lesieur duopoly has left smaller firms in a relatively weak position in the retail sector. Such firms play a major role, however, in the own-label sector. Within the highly price-sensitive industrial (baking) sector, Astra Calve and Lesieur each have a 35% share, with the remaining 30% accounted for by small producers.

Italy

Margarine is a relative newcomer to the Italian market, in which consumption of oils is still very much higher. Margarine was introduced by Van den Berghs in 1954–1955. The indigenous food producer Star followed with a competing brand in 1957 and achieved a 50% market share within two years. These initial offerings were both hard margarines. Shortly afterward, however, Van den Berghs launched a soft margarine in two versions (a corn oil type, and a multiseed oil type). The U.S.-based Kraft Corporation entered the market in the early 1970s. The share of these soft margarines has grown gradually, and they now account for 10% of margarine sales. A fringe of small producers do relatively well in the industrial (baking) segment, and many such firms produce solely for the industrial market.

Japan

Margarine in Japan takes a clear second place to edible oils, the latter accounting for annual shipments of around five times (by value) the total shipments of
margarine. An unusual feature of the Japanese market is that sales are concentrated on the nonretail sector, which accounts for two-thirds of total consumption. Of the relatively small retail market (86,000 tonnes in 1985), some
85% is soft margarine in tubs, with hard margarine accounting for only 15%.
The latter is sold on price, whereas the former carries a higher margin, and
brand image plays a key role. Of the twenty-eight producers, four firms dominate the retail market. Unilever is represented by Nippon Lever, while the other
three leading sellers are among Japan's major food processors. Snow Brand Milk
Products is Japan's largest producer of dairy products; Meiji Milk Products Ltd.
has diversified widely from its core interests in milk-based products; while
Ajinomoto is Japan's largest food processor, whose other interests include frozen
food (chapter 7) and coffee (chapter 11).

The remaining margarine producers concentrate almost exclusively on the
nonretail side of the market. Of the Big Four, all but Nippon Lever sell only to
retail, while Nippon Lever divides its sales evenly between the retail and
nonretail sectors. Thus, the market is segmented rather sharply between the
highly concentrated retail sector ($C_4 = 97\%$) and the relatively fragmented
nonretail market. (If we aggregate the two segments, bearing in mind that retail
sales account for only one-third of the total, the four-firm concentration ratio
is only 36%.)

The United States

Consumption patterns in the U.S. margarine market mirror Northern Europe,
especially in the Northeastern part of the country, with soft margarine in tubs
dominating household use, whereas hard margarine in packs is used primarily
for cooking. Relatively higher consumption levels among lower-income households confirm its continued status as a cheap substitute for butter. Despite the
strong growth in the newly developing "spreads" area (where products have
50%–65% fat, as compared with 80+% for margarine proper), the U.S.
market remains less developed than that of the United Kingdom in terms of the
pace of new product innovations. Some of this difference in part reflects the
different regulatory environments, in respect of which the U.K. regime is
particularly relaxed.

The U.S. market continues to be supplied by some twenty-four firms, a
somewhat higher figure than that of its European counterparts. The most
striking feature, however, is that emphasized in chapter 9: the market is dominated at the retail end by three of America's largest food corporations, none of
which have succeeded in dominating the market. Indeed, all five of the companies now active in the retail market figure among the top-fifty food firms in
the United States. The remaining firms in the industry concentrate on the the

catering and industrial (baking) segments, where price competition is described in industry circles as fierce: producers see buyers in this segment as being little concerned about quality, relative to price. Nevertheless, with the exception of Nabisco, which confines itself to the retail sector, all of the majors are active in the nonretail market. The own-label sector is supplied by two of the majors (Land O'Lakes and Lever Brothers, via its acquisition of Shed in the early 1980's), as well as by the smaller producers.

Appendix 9.3

The Soft Drinks Industry

In this appendix, we present a description of the structure of the soft drinks industry in Germany, Italy, Japan, and the United Kingdom. The pattern of market shares in each country is shown in appendix 1, table M10.

Germany (F.R.)

The German market shows a clear difference between the cola segment, which accounts for about two-fifths of total sales by volume, and the other major segments (table 9.3.1). Within the cola segment, Coca-Cola has about three-quarters of the market; its only important rivals are Pepsico and Aldi, Germany's leading retail chain, which sells a number of own-label colas.

The other two main segments are quite fragmented, and small local firms play an important role. In all, there are around 800 firms currently operating, of which some 100 or so operate as bottlers under a franchise arrangement with Coca-Cola or Pepsico. Of the remainder, 284 are regarded (by the soft drink industry's trade association) as being primarily engaged in soft drink production; for the remaining firms, the soft drink business is a peripheral activity.

The leading domestic producers include a number of long-established, family-owned firms that offer a broad range of well-known brands. Afri-Cola Bluna GmbH of Cologne was founded in 1864, and it operates through a network of 330 franchises, both in Germany and abroad, selling a range of colas, fruit-based carbonates, tonics, and seltzers. Peter Eckes, founded in 1857, produces the leading brand of orange drink.

The other major group of producers are Germany's 190 mineral water companies. For most of these companies, the production of soft drinks is peripheral to their main activity, but they consititute a strong, widely dispersed group of local suppliers. They are particularly strong in the fruit-based sector (sparkling orange and lemon drinks), where they account for half of total sales. The only strong brand in this segment is Coca-Cola's Fanta. The small lemonade sector is particularly fragmented, with small local suppliers accounting for 80% of total sales.

Table 9.3.1
Market segmentation in Germany's carbonated soft drinks industry

Segment	Fraction of market (%)	Structure
Cola	~40	Coca-Cola ~75%; main rivals Pepsi, Aldi.
Fruit-based drinks	~30	Fanta is brand leader; 50% supplied by mineral water companies.
Lemonade	~15	80% supplied by small local firms.
Others ("low-cal" tonics and bitters)	~15	

The total share of the two main noncola sectors has been gradually declining in recent years, however, while the strongest areas of growth are in sugar-free "diet" drinks, where the major suppliers are relatively strong. Coca-Cola and Pepsico have both succeeded in increasing their share somewhat through a combination of new product introductions, a widening of their distribution net, and heavy advertising support.

France

In the French market, the asymmetry between Coca-Cola and its main rival is attenuated, in that three leading soft drink firms each offer a wide portfolio of soft drinks, and each of these commands an overall market share close to that of the spirits group Pernod Ricard, which holds the Coca-Cola franchise in France and markets Coca-Cola, Fanta, and Sprite (table 9.3.2).

The company's three main rivals are all of similar size: Schweppes, a subsidiary of the U.K.-based Cadbury Schweppes, is the market leader in the small tonics segment and is second to Orangina with its Dry de Schweppes orange drink. The leading French food processor, BSN, holds the Canada Dry franchise, with which it takes second place in the tonics segment, and it has a wide portfolio of small brands scattered across the several segments. For BSN, the soft drinks business is a natural adjunct to its interests in the mineral water market. Finally, France's leading mineral water producer, the Perrier group, holds the French franchise for the Gini soft drink from Procter and Gamble, as well as owning the Pschitt lemonade business.

The relatively fragmented lemonade segment, which was important until the early 1970s, has been in steady decline for fifteen years. Associated with that decline has been an overall rise in concentration and a gradual fall in the number of firms in the market [1] This decline is largely attributable to the growth

---

1. The total number of soft drink producers—forty to fifty—is unusually low in France, even relative to the modest size of the market. Pernod Ricard (Coca-Cola) and the other

Table 9.3.2
Market segmentation in Frances's carbonated soft drinks industry

Segment	Fraction of market (volume share, %)	Structure
Cola	33	Coca-Cola 80% +, Pepsi 15% +
Fruit-based drinks	30	Fanta and Orangina are market leaders in "low-fruit" and "high-fruit" segments respectively.
Lemonade	21	Highly fragmented; only important brand is Pschitt.
Lemon-lime drinks	6	Seven-Up 50%, Sprite 40%; own-labels account for the remainder.
Tonics, etc.	10	Schweppes 10%, BSN (Canada Dry) 15%, Perrier (Gini) 15%.

of a dozen leading soft drink brands. Advertising expenditure on the twelve top brands has been growing substantially faster than retail sales; from 1984–1988, for example, retail sales grew by about 14%, in nominal terms, while advertising on the top-twelve brands grew by over 80%. In 1987 expenditure stood at 270 million FF, and this constituted nine-tenths of total advertising on carbonated soft drinks. Thus, while advertising amounts to only 2% of total sales in the industry, it is heavily concentrated on a small number of top brands owned by the four main groups.

Italy

As in France and Germany, the soft drink market in Italy is extremely small, and the major firms in the industry include both the soft drink multinationals and a large number of domestic mineral water producers. The cola segment accounts for one-third of total sales, and of this Coca-Cola accounts for well over 90%. Orange drinks form the second major market segment, which also accounts for one-third of total sales, and here Coca-Cola's Fanta is the leading brand. A wide range of products is offered in this segment, including both higher-priced advertised brands as well as low-price alternatives. Prices per liter in this category may vary by over 50%.

The Coca-Cola Company had an overall market share of just over 60% in the mid-1980s, while Pepsico's share lay in the 1%–2% range. The only other company with a share exceeding 10% was the mineral water company San Pellegrino, which offered a wide range of soft drinks and held the franchises for

---

majors tend to own their own bottlers in France rather than franchise out the business to local operators.

Seven-Up and Royal Crown Cola. The third most important producer was San Benedetto, which also offered a wide product range and enjoyed a strong position in the orange segment, where it followed a relatively aggressive pricing policy. The company also offered a cola product (Ben-Cola), but during the late 1980s it also began bottling Pepsi.

It is possible to make a broad distinction in the Italian market between products with a "modern" image (notably cola but also some branded products in the orange drinks segment) and "traditional" products. The latter includes many products in the orange drink segment produced by domestic mineral water firms, which are heavily purchased for family consumption in large units (1.5- or 2-liter bottles). Products in the modern segment, on the other hand, are sold predominantly in cans, and these dominate sales to the 15-to-35 age group. The latter group is the focus of most soft drinks advertising. Total advertising outlays in 1985 stood at 48 billion lira. Of this, 16 billion was for cola products (Coca-Cola and Pepsi accounting for 99% and 1% of this respectively), while 12.1 billion was for orange drinks (with Fanta accounting for 38% of this).

Japan

The pattern of segmentation in the Japanese soft drink industry is somewhat different from that of the United States and Europe. It is customary to distinguish three categories of soft drinks. The first category, carbonated soft drinks, is the one we focus on here; total volume in this segment amounted to 2.9 billion liters in 1985. The second major segment is fruit-based drinks, whose output amounted to 1.8 billion liters in 1985; slightly over 10% of this volume is made of pure fruit juice, while the rest consists of non-carbonated drinks containing varying proportions of fruit juice. This last segment is omitted from our market definition for the sake of consistency—though in the Japanese case, it is arguably more appropriate to treat it as part of the same soft drinks market. Finally, "sports drinks" constitute a new and still relatively small sector that developed rapidly in the early 1980s.

Within the carbonated soft drinks area, we distinguish as usual between cola, lemonades, and (carbonated) fruit-based drinks. We also include a further category, special to Japan, consisting of "lactic" drinks. These are milk-based, carbonated drinks with a lactic acid content, modeled on the long-established Calpis soft drink, which, like Dr. Pepper in the United States, effectively defines its own category.[2] The structure of the market for carbonated soft drinks in

2. Calpis, a milk-based carbonated drink with a lactic acid content, with an annual turnover of 60 billion yen, was launched in 1919 when few soft drinks were marketed in Japan, and it became the first soft drink to be carried by the large wholesalers. The drink rapidly achieved nationwide distribution and has remained successful ever since; it is seen by consumers as a safe, traditional, healthy product. Given the highly local character of the product, the company faces effective competition only from much less successful lactic drinks offered by domestic firms.

Japan reflects two central factors: the role of the international soft drink companies and the part played by Japan's major beer producers.

The entry of Coca-Cola led to a period of very rapid growth in the cola sector, which persisted into the 1970s, but stabilized during the past decade at around 30% of the total volume of carbonated soft drink consumption. Within this sector, despite strong efforts by Pepsico, Coca-Cola retains a share of over 90% (Pepsico accounts for most of the remainder). Of some half a dozen other firms (including Canada Dry and Suntory), none accounts for as much as 1% of sales.

Since the 1960s, a substantial shakeout of the smallest firms has occurred, but some 1,500 or so firms remain active. The combined share of these small producers is less than 5%, however; some 95% of sales are made by three of Japan's four leading brewers (Kirin, Asahi, and Sapporo) together with Coca-Cola. The top brewers have a wide range of products, spanning all market segments. In the otherwise quite fragmented lemonade sector, both Kirin and Asahi have major brands.

Fanta is a strong leader in the fruit-based segment. Although the brand commands no premium in the United States where it sells at the bottom of the price spectrum in the soft drink market, it has been positioned successfully in Japan, as in Europe, as a leading premium brand. Coca-Cola also has the leading brand in the small sodas segment. The general pattern of concentration by segments mirrors that encountered in European markets (table 9.3.3). The cola sector is highly concentrated, but the other two sectors, despite the appearance of a few strong brands, each support a large fringe of very small sellers.

The role of the major brewers reflects the attractiveness of the soft drink industry as an obvious channel of diversification, given the possibility of using the same distribution net. In the Japanese market, most small sellers distribute their products via wholesalers, whereas the breweries combine the use of their own beer distribution channels with the use of wholesalers. The leading international firms, on the other hand, operate their own distribution nets.

While the cola sector has been static for the past decade, fruit-based drinks have shown a modest rate of growth; this contrasts with the picture in some of the other countries considered here, where the changing importance of the different sectors appears to favor a continuing decline for small producers. The most important growth area in the market has been in "sports drinks,"[3] whose sales volume had by 1985 reached about 10% of the level for carbonated soft drinks. The drinks were sold in powdered form, but it was not until a canned version was launched in the 1980s that the market began to develop. The leading brand, Pocari Sweat, is made by Otsuka Pharmaceuticals and commands almost one-half of total sales (47% in 1985).[4] About a dozen rival firms had entered the rapidly growing market by 1985; they included Coca-Cola, Pepsico, the

---

3. These are high-calorie drinks designed to replace the energy, minerals, and water lost during strenuous exercise.

4. It has recently begun to be manufactured under license in a number of European markets, albeit under a different name.

Table 9.3.3

Market segmentation in the Japanese soft drinks industry

Segment	Fraction of market (by volume, %)[a]	Structure
Cola	33	Coca-Cola: about 90%. Pepsico: 7%–8%.
Lemonades	29	Brand shares: Supa Light 30%, Kirin Lemon 19%, Mitsuya Cider (Asahi brewery) 19%. No other brand has over 2% of sales.
Fruit-based drinks (carbonated)	22	Fanta (Coca-Cola) 46%; only one other brand has over 10% (Mellow Yellow), but about twelve brands have share in the 2%–5% range.
Sodas, tonics, etc.	2	Fanta Club (Coca-Cola) has one-third of sales, while Suntory has one-sixth. Several firms, including Canada Dry, have shares of 10% or so.
Lactic-type drinks	4	Calpis is a clear market leader.
Other	9	

Source: *Japanscan*, vol. 4, no. 4 (June 1986), and vol. 3, no. 11 (Jan. 1986). The figures do not add to 100% due to rounding.

a. These figures relate to cabonated soft drinks only and exclude the "small bottles" category of health drinks, etc. The segment shares cited for fruit-based drinks relate to the residual category comprising fruit-based drinks and "other."

brewing companies Kirin and Suntory, and several of Japan's major food and drink conglomerates (Ajinomoto, Snow Brand). The only brands achieving a 1985 share above 5%, however, were Coca-Cola's Aquarius (25%) and Suntory's NCAA (8%).

The United Kingdom

The U.K. market for carbonated soft drinks, while far larger than that of France or Italy, is still fairly small. This is in part due to two special features of the market: the importance of tea, which accounts for over 40% of beverage consumption in the United Kingdom, and the existence of one important segment in the U.K. market that is virtually nonexistent elsewhere. Syrups or concentrates are fruit-based, noncarbonated soft drinks that are diluted before drinking. These account for about one-quarter of the value of retail sales of soft drinks in the United Kingdom (and it is estimated that they account for about one-half of soft drink consumption by volume).

This pattern has been changing, however. Aggregate consumption of carbonated soft drinks has been rising, and there has been a steady growth of the share of cola and a corresponding decline in the share of lemonade. The U.K. market was seen in the early 1980s as offering unusually good growth opportunities, and this was one of the factors that prompted a massive restructuring of the industry in the mid-1980s.

The Structure in the Early 1980s

The U.K. market remained relatively fragmented until the early 1980s. Concentration had been increasing very slowly throughout the 1970s: the total number of enterprises engaged in the soft drink industry declined from 305 in 1975 to 278 in 1980. In the latter year, 21% of output was still produced in establishments employing fewer than 100 workers, while the three largest establishments accounted for 28% of output.

The Big Three in the industry in the early 1980s were the Beecham Group; Schweppes Ltd., a subsidiary of Cadbury Schweppes; and Canada Dry Rawlings, jointly owned by leading brewers Bass (65%) and Whitbread (35%). Two other majors, both owned by brewing groups, were also of importance: Britvic, a subsidiary of Allied Lyons; and CC Soft Drinks, owned by a consortium of brewers including Grand Metropolitan.

All five of the majors had one or more brands in each market segment. The Coca-Cola franchise for the northern part of the United Kingdom was held by Beecham, while that for the rest of the United Kingdom was held by Schweppes. Throughout the early 1980s, Coca-Cola held about half the cola segment (52% in 1985), while Pepsi held about 17%. The remainder of the market was highly fragmented; though 140 different colas were on offer, minor brands accounted for little more than 10% of sales, while own-label products accounted for almost 20%.

The other segments of the U.K. market were highly fragmented. Lemonade, the most widely consumed soft drink, is produced by a large number of small, local producers. Attempts to establish some degree of brand awareness in this segment have not been successful. Canada Dry Rawlings has had television advertising campaigns for its R. White's lemonade; but only two other brands, Corona (owned by Beecham in the early 1980s) and Schweppes, have achieved the status of national brands. Many smaller companies, such as Bass, Alpine, and R. Shaw, have a very strong regional presence.

The Corona brand is the leading lemonade brand overall; its main strength lies in sales through small independent grocers and in CTNs (confectioner-tobacconist-news agents). (These two types of retail outlet together account for about 30% of soft drink sales.) Here, Corona's share of the lemonade market in 1985 was around 25% of sales. However, in grocery multiples (supermarkets, etc.), while Corona and Schweppes were the two leading brands, neither had more than 5% of sales, while the third most important brand, R. White, had a little over 1% (Mintel 1985).

In the 'fruit-based and other' category, three leading brands of canned drink had achieved a strong presence: Lilt (Coca-Cola), Cariba (Schweppes), and Tango (Beecham via Corona). These three brands accounted for 12%–14% of all sales of canned carbonates, behind Coke and Pepsi. Each of the majors had a number of offerings in the segment, but brand awareness was (and is) low, and regional specialties, with their own characteristic flavors, remain successful. Such brands include Barr's Irn Bru, claimed to be the best-selling soft drink in Scotland, J. N. Nichol's Vimto and Tizer, the latter an established drink recently remarketed by Barr's.

Restructuring

The restructuring of the mid-1980s reflected in part a response to a period of intensifying price competition in the first half of the decade. With the expansion of industry capacity associated with the introduction of modern plastic (PET) bottles, the industry had entered a phase of overall excess capacity, and this had allowed the strong own-label sector to obtain supplies at increasingly competitive rates. Meanwhile, the price of Coca-Cola, the benchmark for pricing in the industry, had been falling as importers in southern England took advantage of EEC regulations to bring in low-cost supplies of canned Coca-Cola from Europe.

The combination of pressure on margins and the apparent opportunities for expansion in the soft drink sector prompted a number of moves. In 1984, Coca-Cola acquired CC Soft Drinks, which held the franchise for Coca-Cola in the southern region, and subsequently bought out the Coca-Cola franchise from Beecham. The company's review of its U.K. operation indicated that its usual franchising system was ill suited to a market in which retailing was dominated by a handful of major supermarket chains, with whom it was essential to deal on a national basis. The company also concluded that the development of its position in the U.K. market necessitated building up a strong role in the

Table 9.3.4
Market segmentation in the U.K. soft drinks market

Segment	Fraction of market (%)	Structure
Cola	35	50% Coca-Cola, Pepsi about 17%. There are some 140 brands in all.
Lemonade	35	Fragmented, with strong regional differences in share (see text). Own-label takes about half of sales.
Tonics, sodas, etc.	8	Schweppes is a clear market leader, with its main competition coming from own-label.
Fruit-based drinks	22	Fragmented, though there are important brands, Lilt (Coca-Cola), Cariba (Schweppes), and Tango, which take 12%–14% of all canned carbonated sales. Own-label takes about half of sales.

nonretail segment (pubs, catering, etc.). With this in mind, Coca-Cola formed a joint venture with Cadbury Schweppes called Coca-Cola and Schweppes Beverages Ltd., in which the two partners had a 49% and 51% stake, respectively. Meanwhile, the major brewers merged their soft drinks interests, bringing together Britvic and Canada Dry Rawlings to form Britannia Soft Drinks. Finally, Beecham, which had held the Coca-Cola franchise for the northern region, sold its remaining soft drink interests to Britannia Soft Drinks (retaining only its health drinks, Lucozade and Ribena); Britannia, together with Beecham's soft drink business, became the Britvic Corona Co. Pepsico took a 10% stake in the new company, which now markets Pepsi.

The new structure of the U.K. soft drink market that emerged from these moves left two major groups dominating the market: Coca-Cola and Schweppes Beverages, marketing Coca-Cola and Schweppes brands; and Britvic Corona, marketing Pepsico's, Canada Dry's, and Corona's brands, among others. These two groups thereby held shares of 22% and 17% in the *total* soft drink market (including concentrates, fruit juices, and mineral water).

Appendix 10.1
The Smaller RTE Cereals Markets

The markets described here are all extremely small in comparison with those of the United States and the United Kingdom. Kellogg, the market leader in mainstream (nonmuesli) cereals in all of these countries, supplies the French and Italian markets, among others, from a single large corn flake plant in Germany.

France and Germany

The French and German markets are sufficiently similar in two respects to afford a particularly interesting comparison. In both markets, per capita consumption, though extremely low by U.S. and U.K. standards, has been growing very rapidly over the past decade; the volume of consumption approximately doubled in both countries between 1980 and 1984; in the latter year consumption was just over 200 grams per capita in France and somewhat over 400 grams per capita in Germany. In both countries, moreover, the share of muesli in total consumption was very high (40% in France, 50% in Germany). It is all the more striking therefore that the two countries diverge sharply in respect of their market structure. In both markets Kellogg is a clear leader, with about half of total sales; it offers Kellogg's Muesli in the muesli segment, as well as its range of cereals in the mainsteam segment.

In France, the second supplier is Quaker, which also has offerings in both segments, accounting for about one-quarter of total sales. The remaining quarter of the market is made up of just three more producers. Banania is an indigenous firm, which entered the industry in 1982; it offers its own Corn Flakes brand as well as a muesli product. Biscuiterie Nantaise, a leading French biscuit company, is a subsidiary of another U.S. major, General Mills, and is active only in the mainstream "presugared" segment. Finally, Sopad Nestlé, a Nestlé subsidiary, is a new entrant to the market whose declared intent is to become the "third force" behind Kellogg and Quaker.

In contrast, the German market supports a substantial fringe of small firms within the muesli segment. This difference reflects inter alia the strength of the

Table 10.1.1

Market shares in the German muesli segment and in the RTE cereals market as a whole, 1984

Muesli segment shares (%)		Overall RTE cereals shares (%)	
Schneekoppe Reform GmbH	28	Kellogg Deutschland	50
H & J Bruggen	15	Schneekoppe Reform GmbH	15
Kellogg Deutschland	12	H & J Bruggen	8
Maizena Diat GmbH	10	Peter Kolln Haferflockenweke GmbH	8
Peter Kolln Haferflockenwerke GmbH	10	Maizena Diat GmbH	7

Source: Euromonitor 1985.

environmentalist or "Green" movement in Germany: throughout the past decade, Germany has supported over 1,000 small firms operating "Reform-hauser" (health food stores).[1] A second element contributing to the more fragmented nature of the German muesli sector lies in the greater success of medium to large indigenous firms in establishing a strong market position vis-à-vis the major international producers (see table 10.1.1).

A handful of indigenous firms play a leading role in the market. Schneekoppe-Reform GmbH, a wholly owned subsidiary of the milling company Muhle Muller, concentrates on the muesli segment, in which it is the market leader. It employs 400 people and markets its muesli through grocery (supermarket) outlets rather than health food stores. Peter Kolln Haferflockenwerke is a family firm whose main interests lie outside the RTE market in the closely related but distinct "Haferflocken" (rolled oats) area. Like Schneekoppe, it confines its activities to the muesli sector. Maizena Diat GmbH also confines itself to a range of mueslis that it markets exclusively through the Reformhauser. H & J Bruggen, on the other hand, operate in both segments of the market, selling both corn flakes and muesli (Verlagsgruppe Bauer 1982, Euromonitor 1985). These firms, together with Kellogg, which ranks third in the muesli segment and is a clear leader in mainstream cereals, account for four-fifths of total sales. The remaining fifth is highly fragmented and includes a number of large and medium-sized concerns with a small presence in RTE cereals (Nestlé's subsidiary, Nestlé-Alete; Hipp; Dr. Ritter) as well as the thousand or so very small muesli makers.

Advertising expenditure in the German market has risen sharply in recent years, with Kellogg outspending all other firms combined. Kellogg's main emphasis is on television advertising, whereas all other manufacturers advertise primarily in the press (especially in women's magazines).

---

1. There were 1,100 in 1984, belonging to the Neuform-Genossenschaft. There are also up to 1,000 "Gruenladen" or "green shops," which are operations run by health food enthusiasts. The above account draws on Euromonitor 1985, "Breakfast Cereals in Germany."

Italy

The market for RTE cereals in Italy is extremely small; per capita consumption is a mere 18 grams/annum, and the total value of the market in 1987 was only 38 billion lira. The market is, however, growing very rapidly: volume sales in 1987 exceeded the 1986 figure by 28%. Kellogg has long been established in the Italian market and, up to 1980, their only effective competitor was Quaker, whose products are sold in Italy by Chiari e Forti. The only firm producing RTE cereals in Italy is Gram, a member of the GEMA group. GEMA's main interests derive from its plastics subsidiary Sirap, a firm founded in the 1960s as a producer of expanded polystyrene boards. The company later diversified into the production of plastic trays for use in food packaging. During the 1970s, like many producers of oil-based products, Gram met with serious difficulties in raw material supplies. As a result of this, the company decided to diversify into an area in which its raw materials would be locally available. Given such priorities, and the fact that the company is located in the center of Italy's corn-growing region, the decision to enter the small but growing RTE cereals market was a natural one. GEMA, through its subsidiary Gram, commenced production of corn flakes in 1980, and Gram's RTE cereal sales now account for 10% of the group's turnover.

Gram produces corn flakes using the traditional method pioneered by Kellogg,[2] which necessitates a relatively high scale of operation. In fact, 70% of Gram's production is exported to own-label producers in several countries (notably France, Germany, and Ireland). At the same time, Gram has spent heavily on advertising to build up its own brand on the domestic market. Much of Gram's advertising, which is almost exclusively in print media, has been directed toward building up the health image of corn flakes, stressing the cereals' fiber content, and toward broadening the range of usage of RTE cereal (as an ingredient in cooking, for example).

The result of heavy, consistent advertising has been a steady rate of growth in Gram's share. While Kellogg's share has remained static—supported by heavy advertising (almost all of it on television)—Chiari e Forti (Quaker) has been losing share steadily, especially in corn flakes. (Quaker's relative strength in the Italian market lies not in corn flakes but in its several muesli products.) Apart from these three producers, there are three other sellers, all very small, which import their supplies. As yet, no own-label brands have been launched, and the catering segment remains insignificant.

---

2. The traditional method involves a costly and inflexible production line, which can produce only corn flakes. The new extrusion method, pioneered by Quaker, is cheaper, largely due to its great flexibility—a huge range of cereal types can be produced on the same line, and rapid switching between types is easy. On the other hand, advocates of the traditional flake argue for its advantages in terms of color, crispness, surface texture ("bubbling"), and relatively slow pace of milk absorption.

Japan

Kellogg accounted for 58% of sales in the very small Japanese RTE cereals market in 1986. Their main rivals are three indigenous firms. Cisco is a well-established firm in the biscuit and crackers sector, whose other interests include confectionery and snack food. Cisco is the only competitor to have a share comparable with that of the market leader (24%). All remaining sellers have shares below 5%, including Nisshin Foods, a wholly owned subsidiary of one of Japan's leading flour companies, Nisshin Seifun (Nisshin Flour), and Snow Brand Milk, a leading producer of dairy products. Two of the smallest sellers, Marushinshota and Nishinoto, import their product and have share of the order of 0.5%–1%.

Appendix 10.2
In Re FTC v. Kellogg Et Al.

During the late 1960s, the Federal Trade Commission was feeling its way toward a new approach to antitrust practice. In the words of the chief of its Division of General Trade Restraints, "the issue is whether it either is or should be considered a violation of the Sherman Act and/or the Federal Trade Commission Act for, say, three or four firms to 'concentrate' 70% or 80% of an industry in their hands and then exercise the power that market share gives them to charge a price that exceeds by say 20% the price that would have prevailed had the markets remained less concentrated."[1] Fearing that the earlier emphasis on outlawing specific practices "seized the shadow and missed the substance of the problem at hand," the FTC embarked on a new approach. As part of this, in 1969 the commission issued an economic report linking profitability to concentration and advertising-sales ratios in various food-manufacturing industries. Press reports in 1971 suggested that the RTE cereals industry would be the focus of an investigation; this prompted one commentator to remark that such a case would easily be the most important antitrust action in the nation's history, one that, by its mere filing, would amount to nothing less than a challenge to the country's "industrial heartland" (cited by Wilson (1971)). To its critics, the case was an attack on "bigness" per se. The FTC's proposed remedy involved the breaking up of the majors into a number of smaller units. In this and later cases initiated in the era that followed, and notably in United States v. IBM, the question of whether market share was or was not a good indicator of market power was severely tested.

The case, however, focused on a number of specific features of the RTE industry:

• the practices of proliferating brands, differentiating similar products, and promoting trademarks through intensive advertising, resulting in high barriers to entry into the RTE cereal market;

---

1. See Harvard Business School Case Study no. 9-274-122 (1975), pp. 2–3; and Wilson 1971.

- misleading claims in advertising;
- control of shelf space;
- acquisition of competition;
- price and sales promotion practices.

These acts were alleged inter alia to have established and maintained artificially inflated prices, led to excess profits, hindered actual and potential competition, and blockaded entry.

The case ended not with a bang, but a whimper. The defense claimed certain irregularites in the (re)appointment of the administrative law judge hearing the case in 1978, when a year of hearings remained. Support for the companies came from several quarters. In the 1980 presidential election, candidate Ronald Reagan strongly criticized the action in an open letter to Kellogg's president. The AFL-CIO, alarmed about employment prospects at Kellogg's Michigan plant, added its voice. A new judge was appointed and laid down an initial decision in 1981, absolving the cereal companies in respect of virtually every contested issue.

Appendix 11.1

Mineral Water

In this appendix, we look at the structure of the mineral water market in Japan, the United Kingdom, and the United States. The markets in Japan and the United Kingdom are extremely small, though rapidly growing. The U.S. market is difficult to compare with the other markets studied here, as it consists of two quite different segments: "bottled water," sold in very large volume bottles for general household use, and "mineral water" as such. The latter submarket, which may be more appropriately compared with the other markets studied here, is extremely small; waters in this category compete with various soft drink products (seltzers, etc.).

The United Kingdom

The mineral water market in the United Kingdom is, as yet, quite tiny by the standards of Continental Europe. Total sales rose from 20 million liters in 1979 to 75 million liters in 1985 (the latter level corresponding roughly to the level of French sales in the mid-1950s). One U.K. water, Malvern, owned by Schweppes, has been available in the United Kingdom since 1850, and up to the 1970s it was the only brand generally available in Britain—one of its leading uses being as a mixer in pubs, where it was often supplied free with spirits.

The introduction of Perrier to the U.K. market in the 1970s sparked off the extremely rapid growth of the market over the past decade. Since 1978, Perrier has been winning awards for its U.K. advertisements—all involving wordplay on "Eau." Its success has been so great that its U.K. advertising agency has itself run full-page magazine advertisements, promoting its own services by reference to the success of its Perrier campaign. In 1982, Perrier's research indicated that the brand had acquired a strong social status image in the United Kingdom, and it subsequently spent an estimated £650,000 on a campaign aimed at altering the image to make the product seem more accessible. Notwithstanding such image problems, Perrier remains the clear market leader in the United Kingdom.

The boom in the U.K. market has attracted a number of new entrants (as well as further imported brands). The most important of these is Highland Spring—now the leading domestic brand—which was set up in 1979 with Arab financing, with a view to providing a low-cost source of mineral water for export to the Middle East. The company also supplies a range of products for selling under retailers own labels; its clients include Sainsburys, the leading own-label supplier. It aims quite explicitly at a relatively low-price strategy, arguing that the market will only expand as mineral water becomes more "affordable." The other leading domestic producer is Ashbourne, owned by Nestlé, which began to bottle water from a Derbyshire spring in the 1970s.

As the U.K. market has developed, the share of off-premises sales has risen steadily, and these now account for about half of total sales by value (and much more than half by volume). All in all, however, the U.K. market is at a stage where comparisons of structure with the continental European countries are not particularly helpful: imported brands (especially Perrier, Evian, and Badoit) play a major role; domestic production is developing, and the growth of Highland Spring has been a major factor in reducing the share of imported brands.

It seems likely that the present structure may change markedly as the market grows over the next decade. The key question in this respect is whether the advertising campaigns of Perrier, which have played a major part in shaping the U.K. market, will continue to ensure its dominance. Ashbourne began television advertising in 1982, as did Highland Spring in 1983, albeit on a very small scale. As with many U.K. markets, however, it may well be that the own-labels, some of which are gaining in strength, will come to dominate the market over the next decade.

Japan

In Japan, as in the United Kingdom, the market is very small and has begun to grow rapidly only over the past few years. With 1986 sales of around 80 million liters, the size of the market is close to that of the United Kingdom. The origin of this recent growth is somewhat different, however. As in the United Kingdom, mineral waters were traditionally used as a mixer for whiskey, and some whiskey producers, notably Suntory, produced mineral water for on-premises sales. The recent boom began only in 1984, however, when one of Japan's major food producers, House Food Company, launched a new mineral water[1] with an unprecedented fanfare of publicity. The advertising surrounding the new brand set off a new trend in consumption based on the use of mineral water instead of tap water in making tea and coffee (a trend that to some degree reflects consumers' dissatisfaction with tap water in some urban areas). This new market segment attracted a substantial number of new brands, and over 100 are now available. Eight long-established producers held 80% of the market in 1983, but

---

1. "Rokko-no oishi misu," or "good-tasting water from Rokko" (an area close to Osaka famous for its springs).

this share had slipped back to 75% by 1985 as the new entrants gained ground. The market leader, Suntory, still retained over 40% of the market (in volume terms), as compared with slightly over half in 1983. Apart from its own domestically produced water, it also holds the agency for Perrier in Japan. Foreign waters have had little impact on the Japanese market, where they account for about 1% of sales. The retail (off-premises) sector remains relatively unimportant, moreover, accounting for around one-tenth of sales in volume terms. As with the United Kingdom, the market is in a state of rapid change. The strong position of leading distillers and brewers in the market, and the relatively weak position of own-label products characteristic of Japan, are the main differences between the two markets.

The United States

The United States has long had a well-developed market for (still) bottled water, sold by several hundred small regional suppliers—mostly on a house-delivery basis—and used primarily as a substitute for tap water. The demand for bottled water of this kind varies greatly across regions, being greatest in hard-water areas: California and Florida are the two largest markets. The largest single supplier of such water, Hinckley and Schmidt, accounts for only about 3% of total bottled water sales by value. (The relative size of the segments is indicated in table 11.1.1.)

The market for sparkling water, used as an alternative to soft drinks, corresponds most closely to the mineral water market as defined above. The market for sparkling waters was quite insignificant until 1977, despite the availability of many domestic sparkling waters. It was the advent of Perrier in 1977 that set off a major change in this market.

Perrier had been available (though not very widely) in the United States for fifteen years when in 1976 a former Levi Strauss executive, Bruce Nevins, met Gustave Lever, chairman of Source Perrier. Nevins believed that Perrier could take advantage of Americans' growing health consciousness by promoting its product as a chic alternative to both soft and alcoholic drinks. Appointed as president of Perrier's U.S. marketing subsidiary, he launched a $2 million advertising campaign that led to a growth in Perrier's sales from $0.5 million in 1976 to about ten times that figure three years later. By 1979, advertising

Table 11.1.1
Market segmentation in mineral and bottled waters in the United States

	% of volume	% of value
Still bottled water	~77	~50
Domestic sparkling water	~8	—
Imports	~2	~7
Club soda and seltzers	~13	—

expenditure on bottled water reached a peak of $10.7 million, as other domestic and imported brands followed Perrier's lead.

Perrier, following the establishment of a strong brand image—it remains the most widely advertised brand in the United States—cut back on its spending from 1980 onward. It saw a decline in its market share through the 1980s, but reversed the trend dramatically by introducing a new range of Perrier "with a twist of lemon" (or lime, or orange) in 1985, with a consequent increase of 50% in total sales. Currently Perrier accounts for about three-quarters of the 7% of sales taken by imports.

The Perrier phenomenon proved a boon to domestic sparkling water producers. Given French requirements to bottle at source, Perrier faced a severe cost disadvantage vis-à-vis local rivals. Perrier (like other imports) sold at a price around double that of domestic sparkling waters such as Poland Spring (and five times more than the price of domestic still water).

Two major domestic producers, Beatrice Companies and McKesson, built up a major presence in the market during the late 1970s and 1980s. Beatrice Companies, with its Arrowhead, Great Bear, and Ozarka brands, held a market share of around 12% in the mid-1980s. The Arrowhead and Ozarka waters sell mostly through home-delivery channels, but Great Bear also has strong retail sales and is promoted on television with emphasis on its health aspects. In a recent acquisition, the Perrier group took over the mineral water interests of Beatrice Companies, thus making it the clear market leader in the United States. These companies apart, no mineral water maker has a share of 3% or more, and the market remains fairly fragmented.

Perrier's successes notwithstanding, advertising has remained modest, accounting for only 0.7% of sales (as compared to 1.3% for carbonated soft drinks). Perrier, despite its cutbacks in the 1980s, still accounted for over 30% of total industry advertising prior to its takeover of Beatrice, whereas Beatrice and McKesson each accounted for about 20% of the total.

In comparing the U.S. market to the other markets considered here, a choice must be made as to whether still bottled waters, used largely as a substitute for tap water, should be included. Such water forms only a small part of the market in the other countries considered, whereas in the United States, it accounts for about the same total sales value as sparkling waters and about eight times its total volume. On a narrow definition (sparkling waters only), the U.S. market is about one-sixth as large as the French, German, or Italian markets (about 120 million gallons or 530 million liters). On a broad definition, total U.S. consumption by volume is slightly higher than in these three countries.

Strictly speaking, neither the broad definition nor the narrow one is satisfactory. The data reported in the market share table correspond to the broad definition. In the regression results reported in chapter 5, we omit the U.S. mineral water market in view of these difficulties of comparison.

Appendix 12.1

The Confectionery Industries

A Note on Setup Costs

Satisfactory measures of setup cost for the confectionery sector that distinguish between the chocolate and sugar confectionery industries are not available. Given the complex pattern of segmentation within each sector, this is perhaps not surprising. It is generally agreed within the industry, however, that the setup costs for a producer of mass-market chocolate confectionery are very much greater than the outlays incurred by a typical sugar confectioner, and this impression can be confirmed by looking at the distribution of fixed assets by firms operating in both industries. Data is most easily available for the United Kingdom, where the standard trade directory *Kompass* lists (most of) the main firms operating in each sector, specifying their areas of interest sufficiently closely to permit an identification of producers either as sugar confectionery specialists (forty-nine firms), chocolate confectionery specialists (twelve firms), or producers of both categories (fifteen firms).

The median level of fixed assets for sugar confectionery specialists in 1989 was just under £1 million. The median value for the twenty-seven firms in the chocolate and combined categories was just below £3 million. The observation relevant to our concerns relates to the lower tail of these distributions, however. Of the twenty-seven firms in the chocolate and combined categories, only two had fixed assets valued below £1 million (the median value for sugar confectioners). This appears to be quite consistent with the views reported in the course of interviews: that it is possible to set up as a mainstream sugar confectioner with an outlay of "a few hundred thousand" pounds; but the outlays necessary to compete with manufacturers of mass-market chocolate confectionery products run to "a few million."

The Markets by Country

The United States

The chocolate confectionery market in the United States is largely coincident with the candy bar market, encompassing both chocolate bars and countlines and accounting for three-quarters of chocolate confectionery sales. The remaining quarter of the market consists of panned goods (chocolate-covered raisins or peanuts, sugar-coated chocolate centers, and so on), seasonal items, and assortments. The candy bar market is dominated by two producers: M & M Mars and Hershey, each accounting for over one-third of sales. Their nearest competitors, Cadbury Schweppes (U.K.) and Nestle, have shares below 10% each.[1]

The assortments market in the United States accounts for a mere 7% of the total value of production. The leading firms (Russell Stover, Whitman, Fanny Mae) tend to sell primarily through their own networks of retail outlets, and many—including Sees of San Francisco—operate on a strictly regional basis. A small but developing premium segment (with prices above $20 per pound) is dominated by Godiva Chocolatier USA, a subsidiary of the Campbell Soup Company that holds a 60% share of this segment. Its competitors in the segment include Gourmet Resources International, formed in the early 1980s by a former Godiva executive. Seasonal products, with rare exceptions, represent a fringe market in which a number of small to medium-sized firms compete on a price basis. All in all, then, the chocolate confectionery industry is dominated by the highly concentrated candy bar segment.

The sugar confectionery industry, on the other hand, is highly fragmented, with over 1,000 firms in the market and a four-firm concentration ratio below 30%. The market leader, E. J. Brach, formerly a subsidiary of the American Home Products Corporation, was acquired by the (coffee and chocolate) multinational Jacobs Suchard in 1987. Jacobs Suchard Brach is the U.S. market leader in two of the major segments, bagged candy (packaged sweets) and bulk candy (loose sweets, often sold in open supermarket displays), and the company also produces a wide range of seasonal products.

Brach's activities, then, are centered on the mainstream areas of the sugar confectionery industry, where setup costs are low and the number of active firms

---

1. Hershey, the traditional leader in the U.S. chocolate confectionery market, is now widely diversified; confectionery accounts for only 5% of its sales. Nestle, which enjoys a strong quality image in the U.S. market, has been building up its position there via a series of acquisitions of established brands. Cadbury Schweppes (U.K.) has also built up a product portfolio in the U.S. market quite different from that of the parent company, its best-known brands deriving from acquisitions (notably that of the Peter Paul Co. in the mid-1970s). A revealing aspect of Cadbury's product mix is the firm's complete opting out of the assortments market, in which it is a market leader in the United Kingdom—a reflection of the relative unimportance of this segment in the U.S. market.

is extremely high. The second-largest producer, R. J. R. Nabisco, on the other hand, focuses on the one market segment (hard roll candy) in which setup costs (associated primarily with packaging plant) are moderately high. Its Life Savers brand dominates the market for hard roll candy (mints), where it and Warner-Lambert Co. (whose main strengths lie in chewing gum, mints, and specialty confectionery) share nine of the ten leading brands. The third producer, Leaf Inc., was created by the Finnish company Huhtmaki, which formed Leaf from three U.S. confectioners acquired in 1985. It has a number of well-known brands, including Good and Plenty, Clark Bars, and Milk Duds.

For the fringe of small producers in the industry, supplying own-label products is an important activity. A handful of industry leaders—Brach included—avoid producing for own-label, but most other sugar confectioners are willing to supply to the segment in which national retail chains such as Kroger and SuperValu are major buyers. Another outlet for small fringe firms lies in seasonal products, where mass merchandisers such as K-Mart follow a policy of seeking out low-price suppliers of attractively boxed items, which are often placed side by side in store displays with well-known branded goods (from which they enjoy a certain spillover effect). Other small suppliers turn to the production of candy for sale to "rebaggers," who essentially "pack and brand" for resale, providing indirect access to broader (regional or national) markets.

The United Kingdom

The U.K. chocolate confectionery sector is dominated by three firms whose combined market share is around 80%. In all, about fifty firms are active. The three leading companies are Cadbury Schweppes PLC, Rowntree Mackintosh PLC (acquired by Nestlé in 1988), and Mars Ltd.[2] Cadbury and Rowntree operate in all three market segments (countlines, bars, and assortments). Mars is market leader in chocolate confectionery in terms of volume, though in value terms it ranks just below Cadbury and Rowntree Mackintosh. It is the only one of the Big Three that does not compete in the assortments sector, which in the United Kingdom is a relatively large sector in which margins are relatively high (most purchases being for gifts, so that lines are less price sensitive).

Although high levels of concentration in the countlines and bars segments are to be expected, a surprising feature of the U.K. market lies in the unusually high degree of concentration in the assortments sector, a segment usually associated with low setup costs, supporting a substantial fringe of smaller producers. Within the United Kingdom, however, this segment is dominated by Cadbury and Rowntree, which offer a wide range of moderately priced offerings. To find the counterpart of the assortments segment familiar in Continental Europe, one has

2. Cadbury Ltd. is the U.K. confectionery division of Cadbury Schweppes PLC, whose other main interests lie in the soft drinks sector (chapter 9).

to look to the quite small high-price end of the U.K. assortments market. Here, a small number of medium-sized firms operate, the best known of these being Thorntons, which markets widely throughout the United Kingdom via its own retail outlets.[3] While some medium and small producers operate at this top end of the market, others survive in the "children's" segment, where small local and regional firms offer low price molded chocolate items as well as sugar confectionery.

As in the case of the United States, the sugar confectionery industry in the United Kingdom is highly fragmented. Some 130 or so companies currently operate, with the top three holding around 30% of the market (as compared to 80% for chocolate confectionery). Traditionally, most of the firms in this area are specialists in sugar confectionery; however, all of the Big Three in chocolate confectionery retain a sufficient interest in sugar confectionery to rank among the top seven producers in this much more fragmented sector.

Apart from a number of smaller specialist segments, the market remains fragmented. The closest U.K. equivalent to the American hard roll candy sector is the mints sector, which—as in the United States—is relatively highly concentrated. The main producers are Rowntree and Trebor; there are many unbranded mints, but these two firms dominate on the branded end of the market with distinctive and well-advertised packeted mints. As in the United States, then, this segment constitutes an exception within sugar confectionery, in that a small number of heavily advertised brands play a leading role. At the other end of the spectrum, the boiled sugar category requires the lowest levels of capital outlay. The only majors distributing nationally in this segment are Barker and Dobson (and their Keeler business) and Trebor Sharps. Beyond these firms, the segment is the domain of the small, highly localized firm. The market is typified by long-standing relationships between distributors and local suppliers, and these relationships are notoriously hard to disrupt—indeed, it is regarded within the industry as being extremely difficult to establish a major presence in the sector.

Small firms, then, survive well in the sugar confectionery sector. The total number of firms has long been fairly stable, and no marked pattern of entry or

---

3. The difference in operation between Thornton's and the majors is well illustrated by their different approaches to the end-of-year sales peak. For the majors, the production cycle for this peak begins in January, with products being cold-stored for the better part of a year. Thornton's, by contrast, begins its production cycle for the Christmas peak in August. Shelf life, too, differs as between the mass-market assortments offered by the majors and these higher-priced offerings—a difference reflected in a different chain of supply. The majors market assortments through the same supply chain as is used for their other lines; the key distinction in the U.K. market is not so much between countlines and bars versus assortments, but between mass-market chocolate and "upmarket" alternatives. This distinction is further emphasized by a difference in approach to presentation and packaging: while the majors attain substantial scale economies in their packaging operations, Thornton's—and other small producers at the high-price end of the spectrum—will often sacrifice scale economies for a distinctive hand-produced finish.

exit is apparent.[4] The main limitation on the range of offerings by small firms lies not in production technology but rather in packaging. The smallest firms confine themselves wholly to supplying loose confectionery in jars, the traditional method of sale for small retail outlets. To produce packaged sweets requires a much heavier outlay—and so, in a segment like mints, for example, there is a sharp distinction between the branded, packeted segment where two of the majors dominate and the fringe of small producers supplying loose unbranded mints.

An interesting feature of the U.K. sugar confectionery industry relates to own-brand suppliers. In many industries this segment is very much the domain of small firms. Here, the reverse is true: the key own-brand suppliers are among the largest firms in the industry. For example, Bassett's recent acquisition of the Anglo-Bellamy business is aimed at allowing Bassett to concentrate on its branded business, while letting Anglo-Bellamy focus on the unbranded sector.[5]

The differences in structure between the sugar and chocolate confectionery industries in the United Kingdom are mirrored by a difference in advertising intensity. Chocolate confectionery is very highly advertised; in fact, the Big Three rank as second, third, and fourth in the U.K. league of advertising spenders (behind Procter and Gamble, the soap and detergent manufacturer). These three firms, with an 80% share of the chocolate confectionery market, account for 90% of the industry's advertising. The preferred advertising medium is television, which takes 90% of the total "classical" advertising expenditure. Such advertising is augmented by substantial poster advertising and heavy "below the line" promotional activities (price discounts, etc.).

Sugar confectionery is less heavily advertised (£16 million in 1986 as compared to the £19 million spent on chocolate confectionery). Mars and Rown-

---

4. A few recent events have, however, caused some commentators to feel that changes of some consequence may be starting to develop in the sugar confectionery sector. The Hillsdown conglomerate has acquired two small family concerns that are well-known regional names, Needlers (Hull) and Bluebird (near Birmingham). Barker and Dobson has acquired the confectionery business of the Scottish jam producer Keeler's. Bassett Foods PLC has purchased from Rowntree Mackintosh its Anglo Bellamy business, whose product ranges overlap substantially with Bassett's and which will operate as a separate profit center of the company (specializing in the unbranded sector, while Bassett concentrates on the branded sector). Bassett has also acquired the confectionery interests of Maynards, the brand leader in wine gums, from Ware White (which had acquired Maynards for its Zodiac toy retail chain).

5. At first glance, this feature of the industry might seem puzzling. A very natural explanation lies, however, in the high level of concentration of U.K. retailing. The major retailers need suppliers who are at least medium-sized firms; the very small confectioners lack the scale to supply at a national level. Where a major experiences a loss of share in some sector, there is a strong incentive to fill production capacity by increasing supply to the unbranded sector. Given the scale of the largest chains supplied by firms already active in own branding, and the fact that these large chains are keen to expand their own-label business, it is relatively easy to offset the effects of a fall in branded sales by building up own-label supplies.

tree strongly support their leading sugar confectionery brands (Polo Mints, Opal Fruits, and Rowntree's Fruit Pastilles, the latter two taking over £1 million per year each in the early 1980s) just as they do their chocolate confectionery lines. Some of the other leading sugar confectionery firms also advertise: Trebor spent £1 million on its Softmints launch, while Bassett has provided continuous but more modest support for its main lines. Nonetheless, these examples are the exception rather than the rule: advertising totals indicate a much lower degree of advertising support in the sugar confectionery sector.

Germany (F.R.)

About half of all sales of chocolate confectionery in Germany consists of (large-format) chocolate bars; countlines take only one-quarter of sales, and all other lines, including assortments, seasonals, etc., account for the remaining quarter (see chapter 12, table 12.2). The large chocolate bar market, consisting as it does of a wide range of products that differ little in form or quality, is highly price sensitive. The volume of output has been stagnant for some time, and the segment is marked by strong price competition and poor margins. This situation has been exacerbated by the fact that an unusually high proportion of this category (over 60%) is sold through mass retailers that exert relatively strong bargaining power vis-à-vis producers and see low prices on chocolate bars as an attractive promotional device.

The chocolate bar market is dominated by four firms; Suchard-Tobler, Ritter, Stollwerk/Sprengel, and Sarotti together account for two-thirds of sales.[6] In contrast with the relatively unified British and American industries, the count-line segment of the German industry is dominated by a quite different group of firms to those producing chocolate bars. Although many indigenous firms play

---

6. Considerable consolidation has occurred among the industry leaders in recent years (a trend attributed in the industry to the increasing pressures on margins). Jacobs Suchard AG formed as an outcome of the 1982 merger of Jacobs and the Swiss group Interfood S.A. In 1986, the Swiss parent company acquired the leading chocolate confectioner in Germany, Leonard Monheim Ag, whose subsidiaries included Lindt und Spungli GmbH and Trumpf Schokolade Fabrik. The second largest domestic producer, the Imhoff Group, restructured in 1986, includes the two major producers Stollwerk AG and Sprengel GmbH & Co., as well as a share in the Berlin-based confectioner Hildebrand. The two main component companies had hitherto been linked by joint shareholdings and operated in concert. Apart from these recent consolidations, a second form of response to competitive pressures in the industry has been to turn to other markets. With one notable exception, the major firms in the industry have preferred to turn to international markets, especially in Belgium, Switzerland, and the United States, rather than diversify within Germany. Stollwerk is a rare exception: it is involved in chemicals, industrial cleansing, and the meat industry. For the most part, however, the companies have sought to penetrate foreign chocolate markets through the acquisition of local firms (Monheim's subsidiaries include General Chocolate NV in Belgium, Van Houten and Zoon Inc. in the United States, and Comet Confectionery Ltd. in Canada; Ritter purchased Pied Piper Confectionery from Bassett Foods (U.K.) in 1980).

Table 12.1.1

Market shares by segment in the German chocolate confectionery industries in the mid-1980s

Candy bars (countlines) (%)		Chocolate bars (%)	
Mars	55–60	Suchard Tobler	25–30
Ferrero	~25	Ritter	~20
Rowntree Mackintosh	~8	Stollwerksprengel	~10
		Sarotti	~9
		Monheim Trumpf	~5

Source: Author's estimates based on various sources and interviews.

a leading role in the chocolate bar segment, the smaller but rapidly growing countlines sector is dominated by foreign producers (table 12.1.1). The countlines segment, indeed, is quite similar to its British and American counterpart, characterized by a very high level of concentration, high unit margins, and very high advertising levels (an advertising-sales ratio of 6%–10% for major producers)—in comparison with both the chocolate bar segment and the sugar confectionery industry.

The German sugar confectionery industry overlaps little with the chocolate confectionery industry, as only a handful of firms are engaged in both sectors. The leading sugar confectioner is Haribo, a private company whose turnover exceeds 400 million DM and whose market share is believed to be roughly similar to that of the other leading firm, Storck (both in the range 14%–17%). The remaining firms (including Ragolds, Katjes, and Vivel) have shares below 5%.

A striking feature of the market is the high degree of segmentation. In spite of the low overall level of concentration, particular segments can be highly concentrated, with the dominant firms being medium-sized producers that focus their production on a very narrow range of products.[7] The pattern carries over to the market leaders, which rarely compete head on, but rather specialize in different niches.[8]

Yet, in spite of the high degree of brand awareness that it achieves, Haribo's advertising budget, at 2% of sales, is modest relative to that of the leading chocolate makers. Margins, in the company's view, "don't justify higher expenditure."[9] The pattern of new product introductions in the industry reflects this.

7. Thus, for example, wine gums are sold by only a handful of producers; in throat lozenges, five small to medium-sized firms (including Ragolds) divide the market between them.
8. Storck specializes in caramels, chewing gum, and chocolate items. Haribo concentrates on wine gums, fruit gums, and licorice. Its best-known product, Gummi-Bears, has become a growth segment in the U.S. market, where they are now sold by Brach's, which import its supplies from Austria.
9. Quoted by Dafsa (1985) and attributed to a study by CFCE.

The launch of new chocolate products is accompanied by expensive advertising campaigns running into the 5–10 million DM range. Sugar confectioners such as Haribo, on the other hand, rely on the access to shelf space their brand name provides to introduce a steady stream of new products unsupported by advertising; these products are withdrawn if they fail to capture share. Haribo will introduce about twenty new products in a typical year, expecting two-thirds of them to be withdrawn in less than two years. It is simply cheaper to launch such product lines directly than to test the market: the technology lends itself to short runs of new product lines similar to the company's standard products. A fringe of small sugar confectioners survives, consisting by and large of firms operating in specialist niches. Where they have run into problems in recent years, however, takeovers by the market leaders have not been uncommon.[10]

Notwithstanding these trends, the industry remains rather fragmented. The majors have expanded over time, but their expansion derives in large part from growing overseas activities. Haribo, for example, exports 40% of its output; Storck's figure of 20% coincides with the industry average.

France

Of the markets studied here, the French market is alone in having a higher degree of concentration in sugar confectionery than in chocolate confectionery. In comparison with the other countries, France has both the highest level of concentration in sugar confectionery and the lowest in chocolate confectionery. Thus the reasons for this reversal of the usual relative concentration levels between the two industries must be sought on both sides of the market.

An unusual feature of the French chocolate confectionery industry, noted in chapter 12, is the dominance of the chocolate bar segment, which has many of the characteristics of a commodity industry. The countlines segment of the French market is, as usual, highly concentrated. Mars Alimentaire SA, a subsidiary of Mars Inc. that manufactures in France, accounts for 65% of sales, with Rowntree Mackintosh accounting for 30%. Sopad Nestlé, with about 7% of the market, is a weak third in this segment.

At the other end of the spectrum, the assortments sector is highly fragmented. Some forty-two manufacturers are present in the market, along with a fringe of artisan producers. In seasonal items, some of the major firms have established a strong presence in particular niches. For example, Rowntree Mackintosh and Ferrero account for 45% of sales of "end of year specialties," while Ferrero dominates in liqueur and cherry specialties, with 54% of sales in this area.

In the dominant chocolate bar segment, which accounts for 47% of sales in volume terms, five major chocolate firms (Suchard, Poulain, Nestlé, Lindt, and Côte d'Or) have a strong presence. Retailers own-label sales provide strong competition in the segment, however—an unusual situation with few interna-

---

10. Thus Haribo has recently acquired three firms: Munster, Klogen and Meier, and Dr. Hillers, while Storck has acquired Dickmann.

tional parallels in the chocolate confectionery industry. A single producer, Chocolaterie Cantalou, accounts for 30% of total sales volume in the chocolate bars segment, and four-fifths of this is sold under retailers' own labels.

Up to the 1960s, this sector was highly fragmented, and many artisan enterprises were active. During the 1970s, however, the sector underwent considerable consolidation. Of the major firms now active in the industry, most are foreign groups. Of the ten leading firms in the chocolate industry as a whole, only three are French: Barry (which manufactures semifinished products), Poulain Industries, and Chocolaterie Cantalou. The restructuring of the past decade, then, has led to an outcome in which a group of multinational chocolate makers compete on roughly equal terms in the main chocolate bar segment. None has succeeded in building up a strong enough brand image to make it a market leader; the growth of a strong own-label sector and the intense pressure on unit margins go hand in hand with low advertising levels in stabilizing a relatively fragmented structure.

The French sugar confectionery industry, on the other hand, is somewhat more highly concentrated than its counterpart in the other countries studied here. There are three major national brands, each of which has a strong presence in both of the main market segments (table 12.1.2). All three are major food industry groups: La Pie qui chante was acquired by BSN in 1980 (along with Vandamme and Franco-Russe, the three companies being subsequently regrouped). General Foods operates via its French subsidiary, General Foods France, selling under the Krema brand. Lami Lutti is owned by the Campbell Soup Company. The fourth-largest seller is the German Haribo Company, which retained a strong leadership position in the jellies segment up to the mid-1980s.

A number of strong regional producers were already present in the French industry in the immediate postwar years, and one brand (Krema) was well established nationally. But it was the advent of the major supermarket chains (the hypermarkets) from 1966 onward that provided the main impetus toward a substantial shift in the structure of the industry. The Krema brand was the first to become established as a leader in the new and rapidly developing

Table 12.1.2
Market shares by segment for leading companies in the French sugar confectionery industry (supermarket sales only), 1987–1988

	BSN	GF	Lami Lutti
Bagged sweets (45% of sales)	~25	~25	~9
Jellies (27% of sales)	~10	~20	~25
Other	~10		

Source: Author's estimates, based on company interviews.

supermarket segment; General Foods marketed the brand aggressively through-out the late 1960s and, by 1972, Krema had reached its peak in terms of market share, accounting for 45% of total sales in its (bagged sweets) segment. Of its main rivals, Vandamme Pie qui chante (BSN) accounted for only 5% of sales, while Lami Lutti had about half that figure. A handful of strong regional firms constitute the next tier of sellers.

Throughout the 1970s, two major trends appeared. The first involved the steady disappearance of the substantial number of small local and regional producers as supermarkets own-label sales grew in importance, rapidly gaining one-fifth of total sales. This growth in sales occurred largely at the expense of small local and regional firms as opposed to the major brands, and the leading regional producers turned to the supply of own-label products (the last major firm to begin supplying own-label was General Foods, which began as recently as 1984).

The second trend was the growth of two major rivals to General Foods. Vandamme Pie qui chante advanced its share from around 5% or so to take one-fifth of the market. Its strategy lay in launching distinctive and innovative products, each with strong advertising support. General Foods, over the same period, had a number of distinctive products, but preferred to advertise its umbrella Krema brand as opposed to promoting individual products. Its other main rival, Lami Lutti, also increased its share with a strategy of strongly advertised, distinctive products (Black Mint, Noisetor, and Magnificat), their share eventually plateauing at around one-tenth of total sales.

By the mid-1980s, the Big Three clearly dominated the market, their only serious rival being the German Haribo, with a large but declining share in the jellies segment. Rivalry between the Big Three, moreover, led to a shift in General Foods's advertising strategy as of 1985, in favor of promotions of specific products—and so to a new phase of advertising rivalry. Total advertis-ing in the confectionery segment more than doubled between 1986 and 1988, the increase in large part reflecting a substantial rise in outlays by the sugar confectionery leaders.

Italy

The Italian confectionery industries are unusual relative to the other industries studied here in two respects. First, the number of chocolate confectioners is *greater* than the number of sugar confectioners. This observation is readily accounted for in terms of the composition of demand across sectors: it merely reflects the fact that the assortments and seasonal sectors, in which setup costs are very low, are fairly large in Italy, and a substantial number of small firms operate in these segments. The second observation of interest is that both the chocolate and sugar confectionery sectors have similar—and rather high—advertising-sales ratios. This observation is less easily explained; to trace its origin we need to look in detail at some unusual features of the Italian con-fectionery market.

The Italian confectionery industry is anomalous in several respects. The level of per capita consumption is extremely low; among the countries studied here, it is equaled only by Japan. Furthermore, the Italian market is unique among our present set of countries in that sugar confectionery has been growing steadily for over a decade. Meanwhile, consumption of chocolate confectionery has grown at a relatively modest rate, and half of this rise has been supplied by imports of countlines and bars.

In looking at the sources of growth in the market, it is helpful to follow the practice of the Italian industry in segmenting the confectionery market along rather different lines to those customarily employed in other countries. This alternative approach distinguishes three segments, common to both chocolate and sugar confectionery. The first is "gift purchases"; the second consists of "traditional" (sugar) confectionery products; while the third is labeled the "modern" or the "prodotti da banco" segment. The latter term has no precise equivalent in English; it refers to products sold through certain channels of distribution, the archetypal (and dominant) example being a "bar-tabac" outlet.

These three categories mesh rather poorly with the usual segments used here. Chocolate countlines fall within the "prodotti da banco" segment, but this segment also includes an important range of sugar confectionery items—typically those sold in tube form ("caramelle in stick"). Such products are sometimes said to be impulse purchases, in contrast to such items as sugar confectionery sold loose or in bags, that are heavily purchased by housewives for routine family consumption and which fall into the traditional category. Chocolate assortments include both (more expensive) gift items as well as less expensive lines classified within the traditional category.

Industry analysts emphasize the differing nature of competition as between these three market segments. The key factor influencing success in the modern segment lies in the advertising-based image of the firm's product line. In the traditional sector, on the other hand, the single most important factor is promotional effort directed toward the retailer. The gift sector constitutes an intermediate case, with both of these factors being of commensurate importance. In looking at the pattern of market shares and advertising activity, it will be useful to refer to both the usual method of classification and to this alternative schema.

The Structure of the Market

It was noted that the predominance of the low-setup-cost categories of assortments and molded (seasonal) items offers an obvious explanation for the relatively modest overall concentration, and the relatively large number of firms, in the Italian chocolate confectionery industry. Examination of the sector, segment by segment, is broadly consistent with this interpretation.

The industry's two leading firms are both indigenous. Ferrero is 90% family-owned, while Perugina is part of the Buitoni group (which in 1985 was acquired by CIR, a holding company for the interests of the De Benedetti family). Both of these companies operate in three of the four product categories (bars, assortments, and seasonal items). The fourth-largest producer, Dolma, the Italian subsidiary of Mars Inc., is the market leader in countlines, where Rowntree Mackintosh is a relatively weak second.

In the countlines segment, where setup costs are greatest, the level of concentration is typical of the levels encountered in other countries, with the top two firms accounting for 70% of sales. The advertising-sales ratio in this segment, at around 20%, is extremely high relative to that of other segments of the Italian confectionery industry.

At the other end of the spectrum, the molded (seasonal) items are associated with a relatively fragmented structure. In its main product category (eggs), the top three firms have 41% of sales, all others being quite small; advertising amounts to less than 2% of sales revenue. Advertising outlays are also low in the chocolate bar segment, where again the advertising-sales ratio is around 2%. Finally, in the large assortments sector, the two market leaders, which each account for about one-quarter of total sales, advertise heavily, together accounting for three-quarters of total advertising in this segment.

In terms of the alternative classification scheme, only the two market leaders Ferrero and Perugina are major producers of those modern products (other than countlines) that dominate sales, having a strong presence in bar-tabac outlets. Given the marketing efforts of the two majors, it is relatively difficult for other firms to make much headway through these channels. These two firms are also among the top four sellers of sugar confectionery, the others being Perigotti, Sperlari, and Perfetti.

The firms with the highest advertising-sales ratios in the sugar confectionery industry are those specializing in the modern segment (table 12.1.3). In this small but steadily growing segment of the market, which is dominated by innovative products early in their life cycle (Facinelli 1982, Brugnoli 1985), a number of second-rank firms, notably Caremoli and Desar, have been vying with the market leaders for share. This observation suggests that the unusually high advertising-sales ratio found in the sugar confectionery industry reflects a process similar to that of the frozen food industry (chapter 8), in which a group

Table 12.1.3
Adertising-sales ratios and main sector of operation of selected leading firms in the Italian sugar confectionery industry

Firm	Advertising-sales ratios (%)	Main sector
Caremoli	15–16	modern
Desar	17	modern
Perugina	1.8	traditional
Scaramellini	2.0	traditional
Sperlari	6.5–8.5	gift

Source: Databank.

of middle-rank firms seek to establish themselves in the first tier as the market expands.

Japan

The Japanese market shows the usual pattern of differences between sugar and chocolate confectionery industries, with the latter being the more concentrated, but the difference is much less pronounced than in the United States or the United Kingdom. Within the chocolate confectionery industry, the (high-setup-cost) countlines segment is of negligible importance. The main segments are chocolate bars (15% of sales), panned products (30%), and chocolate-covered biscuits (40%). This difference in the composition of demand implies a lesser gap in setup costs between the chocolate confectionery and sugar confectionery industries, compared to the United States and the United Kingdom. This may in part explain the much narrower difference in structure between the two industries in Japan. But a second factor which may be no less important, operates to further narrow the gap between the two industries.

The Japanese sugar and chocolate confectionery markets are best seen as two segments of a single unified industry that is very much marketing driven. The same handful of major firms that came to prominence in the early postwar years in the caramels (sugar confectionery) sector today span both sugar and chocolate confectionery, in sharp contrast to the case in most other countries. In fact, it is not usual in Japan to distinguish the two as separate markets, though we shall do so in what follows in order to facilitate comparisons with other countries.

The confectionery industry developed very rapidly in the immediate postwar years. In the late 1940s and early 1950s a number of long-standing producers were in operation. They included Ezaki Glico, founded in 1922 as a small local confectioner selling caramels door to door from handcarts; the company later began to produce biscuits and subsequently introduced chocolate-coated products (biscuits, almonds, etc.). Morinaga Seika also began as a producer of caramels and moved subsequently into chocolate bars and chocolate-covered biscuits.

Caramels remain a basic confectionery product on the Japanese market. They are a highly standardized product, square in shape and packed tightly into small, plain boxes similar in size to a cigarette pack. These products formed a major focus of competition in the industry during the 1950s, following the end of sugar rationing. The focus of competition, then as now, was on sales-promotion devices. By the late 1950s, today's Big Four (Morinaga, Meiji, Ezaki Glico, Lotte) had already emerged as market leaders. In the process, many smaller sellers lost share to the point where they left the industry. The industry's product mix has broadened gradually over time. Even today, however, consumption remains very low. Consumption of chocolate confectionery (which now accounts for two-thirds of industry sales) is almost as low as Italy's and much below that of the United Kingdom, France, or Germany.

The most striking features of the confectionery market as a whole are the huge range of products on offer and the heavy emphasis on attractive packaging. In

1986 a total of 797 new items appeared on the market. Only 5% of new products last more than three years. Morinaga distinguishes three types of new product: a few are expected to last long term (ten to twenty years), and their launch is backed by extremely heavy television advertising. An intermediate category are not expected to last long: these are experimental and receive little advertising support. A third category comprises products aimed at children. Here the emphasis is on innovative and eye-catching design, both of product and packaging, and on the incorporation of "gifts"—an idea much favored by Japanese confectioners, which mirrors the marketing of breakfast cereals in the West.

Product innovation, combined with advertising and promotional expenditures, drives the market. The major manufacturers typically spend 7%–8% of their sales revenues on product development activities and about 5% on advertising. Another unusual feature of the Japanese market relates to the low degree of penetration by the major multinational groups. Foreign companies have found it very difficult to penetrate the Japanese market[11]

There are certain popular product categories in which small firms can compete very effectively. These include, besides the simple sugar confectionery products requiring minimal capital outlays, a number of traditional handmade specialties. On the other hand, a minority of small producers concentrate on the high-quality end of the market. In a manner analogous to small European confectioners, their products are usually sold via specialist outlets or in leading department stores. Leading national brands face a disadvantage in this sector— purely as an unwanted side effect of the success of their well-established national brands. In some cases, the majors have attempted to avoid this problem by setting up subsidiaries selling high-quality specialties under a separate brand name.

---

11. This difficulty reflects in part the presence of import duties. In 1983, the duty on chocolate imports was reduced from 31.9% to 20%, in part as a response to requests from Japanese manufacturers who feared that complaints from foreign companies would otherwise provoke retaliation in the West. At the same time, the levy on sugar purchases by Japanese chocolate firms was reduced from 16 to 3 yen per kilo in order to help them cope with the expected surge in imports. Prices of imported brands were cut when the duty fell and the domestic firms met these price cuts. The net effect of this, and of further cuts made in the interim, has been modest. The difficulties faced by foreign chocolate makers partly reflect the usual problems met by importers in coping with the channels of distribution. So far, foreign brands have done well in outlets specializing in imported goods, but have fared badly alongside Japanese products in general retail outlets. The variety and attractiveness of presentation of domestic products is now seen among industry observers as being a key factor in limiting the success of imported brands. Countlines, neglected by Japanese producers, remain the domain of foreign firms. Rowntree Mackintosh's Kit-Kat is the most successful countline at present; Mars sells via a wholly owned Japanese subsidiary. The limited degree of success achieved by the category, however, shows no sign of changing.

A limited number of foreign lines are imported by leading domestic firms. Morinaga, for instance, imports the well-known Pez line from Austria and packages it "Japanese style" for the domestic market.

Appendix 12.2

The Biscuit (Cookies and Crackers) Industry

Market Definition

The biscuit industry as defined here corresponds roughly to the U.S. cookies and crackers industry (SIC 2052), though the mix of products may vary considerably across countries. In Italy, and to a lesser extent in France, a range of traditional products often produced by small-scale local producers coexists with the standard range of products common to the United States, the United Kingdom, and Germany (F.R.). In Japan, two types of biscuit—flour-based and rice-based—are often included as part of the confectionery industry, broadly defined. The latter category are typically produced on a small scale and sold locally by artisan producers. We adopt a narrow definition that excludes such rice-based products; this leaves us with an industry definition roughly comparable to that employed for the other countries.

An Overview

The industrialization of biscuit making occurred during the second half of the nineteenth century. This was associated with both the development at mid-century of machinery to stamp out the appropriate shapes in dough and the advent around the turn of the century of mechanized ovens, which allowed a continuous flow of biscuits to be baked to a uniform standard.

In what follows, we trace the development of the industry in each country in turn. Within the United States, one firm (Nabisco) established an early lead by devoting intensive advertising outlays to supporting a series of distinctive products, and this lead has been maintained ever since. The level of setup costs in the industry is moderate, as is the current level of concentration in the market, but the pattern of evolution of structure is similar to that experienced throughout a wide range of advertising-intensive industries.

A more noteworthy feature of the biscuit industry is the way in which the several Western European markets have developed. In contrast to several of the industries studied in other chapters, in which the market was effectively established by the entry of a U.S.-based producer (canned soups, RTE cereal, soft drinks), each of the European countries had a well-developed biscuit industry prior to the entry of the U.S. market leader. The development of the U.K., French, and German markets presents an interesting parallel. In each case, the current market leader is an indigenous producer formed via the merging of a large number of small, independent concerns. The manner in which this has come about varies among the three countries, but in all cases, Nabisco is a weak second to the local market leader.

The Italian case is unusual. Until relatively recently, the industry was extremely fragmented. A complex series of events has over the past decade led to the emergence of a strong indigenous market leader whose success has been built inter alia on building up a distinctive image on the basis of heavy and sustained advertising outlays.

In the Japanese market, the confectionery industry as a whole, including the manufacture of biscuits, is highly integrated, as noted in chapter 12. Four firms have vied for industry leadership over the past decade, and the market-share pattern has been relatively volatile: two of these four firms are among Japan's leading confectioners (Meiji Seika and Morinaga Seika), another of the four is Nabisco's Japanese affiliate.

The Markets by Country

The United States

The advertising campaign that established the National Biscuit Company (NBC, later Nabisco) as the leading U.S. biscuit maker began in 1899. The campaign was contemporaneous with a number of major advertising initiatives in the food and drink sector, all of which were based on techniques of advertising pioneered by leading advertising agencies around the turn of the century. NBC's success lay in launching a single product with a name (Uneeda Biscuit) that lent itself to endless punning. Chicago newspapers in January 1899 featured advertisements carrying the single word "Uneeda." Subsequent runs of the advertisement extended the message ("Uneeda Biscuit"; "Do you know Uneeda Biscuit?"; and so on). The company's advertising budget ran to $7 million in the first decade. In the year following the opening of the campaign (1900), sales of Uneeda Biscuits exceeded 10 million packages a month, while the combined sales of all other packaged crackers were believed not to much exceed half a million packages a year.

The company built successfully on this early lead in the decades that followed. Two later campaigns, each based on a distinctive new product, established two brands that remain among the company's leading products. The first of these began in 1912, with the launch of Oreo cookies. The second came in the 1930s, with the introduction of Ritz crackers, which within three years became the largest-selling cracker in the world, with more than 29 million baked daily.

By the early 1980's, Nabisco retained a market share of 43%. Its nearest rival, Keebler, had a share of 13% and was in the process of expanding from being a regional seller based in the Midwest to operating on a national level . The only other biscuit maker with a share above 3% was a major regional producer, Sunshine, whose main strength was confined to the Southern part of the United States.

It is possible to distinguish two segments in the market: mainstream or "family" products account for 90% or more of total sales; a separate "adult" segment, associated with higher unit prices, accounts for between 7% and 10% of total sales. The firms operating in this latter segment are quite distinct from the mainstream producers: Pepperidge Farm accounts for over two-thirds of sales in the adult segment, their main competitors being imported brands (the French producer, Lu, imports part of its needs from France, but also manufactures in the United States, and the German Balsen company and Peek Frean from the United Kingdom are also active).

Retailers' own-label sales, together with unbranded generic products, accounted for 15% of total sales in the early 1980s. Much of this output comes from a large fringe of small, local suppliers; in all, over 300 producers are active .

The United Kingdom

At the turn of the century, two U.K. biscuit makers had already achieved a scale far larger than any of their rivals. Huntley and Palmer, founded as a partnership in 1841, employed some 6,000 people, while Peek Frean employed about half that number. A distinction had already emerged at that date between the "quality" producers, led by Huntley and Palmer and Peek Frean, and a large number of small producers selling primarily on price.

Throughout the 1890s, Peek Frean had begun to exploit the new opportunities for advertising offered by the growth of readership of newspapers and periodicals and the spread of billboards throughout the United Kingdom. Huntley and Palmer initially avoided advertising on the basis of the then-common belief that top-quality products required no such support; but the success of Peek Frean eventually provoked a defensive response, and Huntley and Palmer began to advertise, at first in its export markets and later in the United Kingdom. The campaign was focused on a single product (the breakfast biscuit) and in its first year led to a 40% increase in sales. By 1905, Huntley and Palmer's advertising almost equaled Peek Frean's, and its outlays doubled over the next six years.

The general recession that marked the first decade of the century brought serious problems to the industry, however. Up to that stage, informal attempts at price coordination had been the norm throughout much of the industry, with Huntley and Palmer being regarded as a price leader for the quality end of the market. Distress prompted the first attempts at a more formal approach, and in 1903 an association was formed in which most manufacturers apart from Huntley and Palmer and Peek Frean participated. The harmonious relations between the two market leaders degenerated throughout the decade as Peek Frean's more aggressive stance on advertising was extended to prices and discounts from 1902. It was not until 1918 that an association came into being that included the two market leaders; in that year, the National Association of Biscuit Manufacturers (N.A.B.M.) was formed. In 1921, Huntley and Palmer joined Peek Frean to form Associated Biscuit Manufacturers Ltd.

During the Depression of the 1930s, N.A.B.M. manufacturers faced intense price competition from nonmember companies. The most notable among these was Westons, which set prices at about one-half the levels of N.A.B.M. members, thus prompting substantial price cuts by the N.A.B.M. By 1939, Weston had achieved an annual sales volume of 34,500 tons—roughly equal to the combined sales of Peek Frean and Huntley and Palmer (34,960 tons).

Continued price cutting during the 1930s at the cheap end of the market prompted the formation of the British Cake and Biscuit Alliance, which operated as an independent association for firms outside N.A.B.M. By 1939, the six quality firms that had dominated the market in the first decade of the century produced only 30% of total output. In the immediate postwar period, increasing demand led to new entry to the industry. There were seventy-one producers in 1935; by 1951, there were ninety-two.

Over the same period, the share of the largest three producers fell by about one-sixth. Renewed advertising and promotional efforts in the late 1940s and 1950s began to reverse this trend, however. At the same time, the Restrictive Trade Practices Act outlawed price coordination, and N.A.B.M. consequently became merely a consultative body. The new trend in the industry, however, was toward nonprice competition. Advertising outlays rose from below £350,000 in 1951 to almost £2 million in 1960, and to £3 million by 1964.

It was over this period that retailers' own-label products, pioneered by Marks and Spencer, first appeared on the market, and much of the impetus to the rising trend in advertising outlays lay in an attempt by leading biscuit makers to retain a brand premium over own-label products. Within the industry, it was generally believed that a firm needed to maintain an advertising-sales ratio of about 5% in order to do this; many firms advertised less intensively, however, and the share of own-label products grew slowly over the period, and this appears to have been a key factor in prompting amalgamations in the industry. The consolidation process leading to the formation and growth of United Biscuits took place gradually. The company had been formed in 1948 to unite the interests of McVitie & Price Limited and Macfarlane Lang & Company Limited. By 1972, six more firms had joined United, and the group's turnover exceeded £128 million.

Though Associated Biscuits had itself expanded by way of its acquisition of W. & R. Jacobs (Liverpool) Ltd. in 1960, it was a relatively weak second to

Table 12.2.1
Recent trends in market shares in the U.K. biscuit industry

Market shares, 1978 (%)		Market shares, 1981 (%)		Market shares, 1985 (%)	
United Biscuits	34.9	United Biscuits	40	United Biscuits	31
Associated Biscuits	14.0	Huntley and Palmer Foods	19	Nabisco	15
Burtons	8.0	Burtons	12	Rowntrees	8
Other brands	16.9	Nabisco	5	Burton	8

Sources: Audits of Great Britain, as reported by the Price Commission (1979), Monopolies and Mergers Commission (1982), and Leatherhead Food RA (1986), based on figures supplied by the CCBA.
The above shares exclude the supply of retailers' own-label products.

United Biscuits by the late 1970s (table 12.2.1). By that date, retailers' own-label products had reached a share of 26.2% (Price Commission 1979).

Nabisco's impact on the U.K. market up to 1982 was fairly limited. In spite of the success enjoyed by some of its brands (notably Ritz crackers), it had made little impact on the mainstream biscuit market, and its market share stood at around 5% in 1981. Until that date Associated Biscuits (now Huntley and Palmer Foods) had retained a strong second position in the industry, with a market share around half that of United Biscuits. In 1982, Nabisco acquired Huntley and Palmer, thus establishing Nabisco as a clear second to United Biscuits (table 12.2.1).

France

The French biscuit industry remained highly fragmented up to the end of the 1960s. The leading food industry journal, *Agra-Alimentation*, reported in its survey of the French food industry in 1967 that 657 firms were active in the biscuit industry, broadly defined ("biscuiterie-biscotterie"), and only five firms had a market share exceeding 7% (l'Alsacienne, Biscuiterie Nantaise, Belin, Lefèvre-Utile, and Biscuiteries Brun).

Throughout the late 1960s and early 1970s, *Agra-Alimentation* reported the industry to be in a state of crisis. Price competition, driven in part by the large and active fringe of small suppliers, was and remains intense. At the same time, a number of U.S. multinationals had begun to attempt entry to the French market by acquiring local biscuit makers. General Mills was permitted to acquire Biscuiterie Nantaise in 1967, and Pillsbury set out to acquire Brossard in the same year.

A widely held view in French policy circles from the late 1960s onward, as noted, was that the emergence of French groups of substantial size was desirable in view of the imminent enlargement of the EEC. The consolidation of the biscuit industry that took place over the following decade can be seen as a response to a mixture of internal pressures (price competition) and external pressures (takeovers by foreign food conglomerates). The beginnings of this process had already occurred in 1966, with the merger of Biscuiterie Alsacienne, Biscuiterie Nantaise, and Biscuiteries Brun. The central thrust of the consolidation process lay in the emergence and growth of the Generale Biscuit group during the following decade.

Generale Biscuit acquired thirty-seven firms in seven European countries between 1968 and 1978. This series of acquisitions made Generale Biscuit the leading producer of biscuits in Continental Europe and the third-largest producer in the world, after Nabisco (U.S.) and United Biscuits (U.K.). Its brands include some of the most well-established names on the French market, such as Lu and Alsacienne. It has recently acquired Burry-Lu Inc. in the United States and has set up a production unit in Japan as a joint venture with one of Japan's leading confectioners, Ezaki Glico. In 1987, Generale Biscuit merged with BSN, France's leading food and drink multinational.

France's second largest biscuit producer is Belin, formerly owned by Nabisco and now part of BSN, whose market share of 18% in 1985 was somewhat over half that of Generale Biscuit. Apart from these two leading producers, the rest of the industry is quite fragmented. A handful of firms have shares of 3%–5%, including Biscuiterie Nantaise (General Mills) and Grignoire Brossard (Pillsbury). In all, some 250 small local producers continue to compete with the national brands.

Advertising levels in the French industry are moderate, the industry advertising-sales ratio in the mid-1980s being about 1.5%. Price competition is very active, especially for fairly standard products. Advertising support is concentrated on more elaborate and innovative products, where the overall growth in demand is strongest.

Italy

The Italian biscuit industry produces a wide range of product types, incorporating not only types standard in the United States, the United Kingdom, and Germany, but also a number of distinctive products ("amaretti," "grissini," etc.), some of which (notably grissini, a bread stick served in conjunction with main meals) are the traditional preserve of small local producers. The largest single category is "frollini," a type of shortbread, which accounted for a little under one-third of all biscuit sales in the early 1980s, and which also represented the fastest growing category at that time.

The industry was extremely fragmented until quite recently; the artisan fringe has almost disappeared, however, and almost all output is produced by sixty industrial firms. Among those producers, there is a high degree of specialization, with many producers confining themselves to a single product line or variety. Market leadership varies across segments, with Barilla as the market leader in rusks, Alivar in crackers, Colussi in waffles, and Lazzaroni in amaretti. A central

Table 12.2.2
Market shares in the Italian biscuit industry, 1975 and 1986

Market shares, 1975 (%)		Market shares, 1986 (%)	
Colussi	11	Barilla	22
Pavesi	10	Saiwa	10
Saiwa	8	Pavesi	8
Galbusera	5	Colussi	6

Source: Barilla.

development that influenced the transformation during the late 1970s and early 1980s of a hitherto fragmented industry into one whose structure more closely approximated that of the French or German market is the emergence of Barilla, Italy's leading pasta producer, as the leading biscuit firm.

In 1975, the biscuit industry, even on the basis of a narrow definition,[1] had a four-firm sales concentration ratio of 35%, and the pattern of market shares had been more or less stable for a decade. Over the next decade, this ratio had increased to 45%. The main change in market share patterns had been associated with the establishment of Barilla as a clear market leader (table 12.2.2).

Barilla, a family-owned concern specializing in pasta production, faced financial difficulties in the early 1970s partly as a result of the imposition of price controls on pasta. The company was acquired by Grace, an American chemical company, but was reacquired by the Barilla family a few years later. Grace, however, initiated a program of diversification at Barilla, which continued to have effects on the company throughout the rest of the decade.

One area of diversification explored by Barilla was the biscuit market. Realizing that frollini had wide appeal throughout the country and so formed a suitable candidate for a nationally established brand image, the company set out to develop an expensive, imaginative, and sustained advertising campaign throughout the latter half of the 1970s. The company's line of frollini were marketed under a new brand, Mulino Bianco (White Mill), and the advertising image was that of a relatively high-quality biscuit packaged in an unusual and attractive format. Barilla maintained heavy advertising support for the new brand, as its share grew; by the mid-1980s, when the brand was well established, Barilla still accounted for 30% of all biscuit advertising and its advertising-sales ratio for all of its bakery products stood at 5%–6%.

Barilla's success in establishing the Mulino Bianco brand led to an expansion in advertising activity by rival firms. By 1985, five of Barilla's main rivals

---

1. Just as in France, it is customary to define the biscuit industry to include such products as "biscotte" (toastbread) as part of a general category (biscuiterie-biscotterie), so in Italy it is customary to define the market as "prodotti da forno secchi" (dry bakery goods). On the basis of that broader definition, the four-firm sales concentration ratio for 1985 was 36% (Databank 1985).

were spending over 6% of their sales revenue on advertising.[2] Advertising is almost wholly confined, however, to the industry leaders. The industry advertising-sales ratio in the mid-1980s stood at around 2.5%.

A few of the industry's leading firms are held wholly or in part by foreign multinationals: Saiwa, formerly owned by Nabisco Brands, has recently been acquired by the French BSN group. The U.S.-based Campbell Soup Company has an interest in Lazzaroni. The leading French biscuit producer, Generale Biscuit, holds one of the smaller producers, Italu. Two others among the leading firms are in public ownership via the state holding company IRI (Sidalm and Alivar).

Germany (F.R.)

Although the overall structure of the German industry is closely similar to that of France, the leading German firm is a long-established family-owned concern, Bahlsen, which operates via a net of over a dozen subsidiary companies whose combined sales form over a quarter of total biscuit sales. Bahlsen's main competitor is De Beuklaer, a wholly owned subsidiary of the French market leader Generale Biscuit whose market share is somewhat smaller than Bahlsen's. Only two other firms have a market share exceeding 5%. One is a family-owned firm, Brand Zwieback Biscuits GmbH (Brandt), and the other is Delacre, a marketing subsidiary of the biscuits division of Campbell Europe, the European arm of the Campbell Soup Company (U.S.)

Japan

The Japanese biscuit market is closely integrated with the confectionery industry. Four of Japan's leading confectioners (Meiji Seika, Morinaga Seika, Lotte, and Ezaki Glico) rank among the top six sellers in the biscuit market. One of the two firms among the top six that are not general confectioners is

Table 12.2.3
Market shares in the Japanese biscuit market, 1974–1978

	Market share, 1974 (%)	Market share, 1978 (%)
Kitanihon Shokuhin	10.7	20.0
Yamazaki Nabisco	9.5	10.0
Morinaga Seika	11.9	9.3
Meiji Seika	9.7	9.3

Source: Dodwell Marketing Consultants 1980, estimates based on data of the Japan Confectionery Association.

---

2. Colussi (10.9%), Lazzaroni (9%–10%), Loacker (7%), Parmalat (17%), and Saiwa (6.5%). Source *Marketing in Europe* 1987, attributed to Databank.

Yamazaki Nabisco, established in 1970 as a joint venture between Nabisco and Japan's leading bread baker, Yamazaki. The other is a specialist domestic firm, Kitanihon Shokuhin Kogyo Co. Ltd., which began as a local firm making rice crackers and owes its position to the success of a particular biscuit brand (Lumonade; see table 12.2.3).

The company's strategy in launching the new brand was to aim at a high-quality image, with individually packaged biscuits sold in bags rather than packets. The new line was originally launched at a high price in specialist confectioners, but was then offered at low prices through supermarkets. The brand achieved a substantial market share in 1975, with annual sales of 12 billion yen; even though sales fell to half that level within two years, Lumonade biscuits remained Japan's leading biscuit line.

Appendix 12.3
The Coffee Industries

Setup Costs

In assessing the difference in setup cost between instant coffee and roast and ground (R & G) coffee, one distinction is of central relevance. At the production level, instant coffee requires very substantial capital outlays. The level of these outlays varies with the process (spray-dried versus freeze-dried) and the quality level of the product. R & G coffee, on the other hand, can be produced at the artisan level; the basic production process at this level merely involves roasting and grinding the imported coffee beans. On the other hand, the packaging of the final product can involve very substantial setup costs, if modern oxygen-free packing techniques are used to achieve a long shelf life—and this applies equally to instant and R & G coffee. Hence estimates for setup costs in R & G coffee vary widely, depending on what type of operation is envisaged. At one end of the spectrum, one can compare minimal outlays incurred in production. For the United States, Yip and Williams (1982) report a ratio of 150 : 1 for the typical instant producer relative to the typical R & G producer. Such an estimate might be appropriate in those markets where most R & G coffee is sold in traditional packs for immediate use. At the other extreme, if we compare the outlays involved in processing and packing R & G coffee in a form that ensures a long shelf life, it is possible that the total outlay for R & G coffee could be up to one-half that incurred by producers of instant coffee.

Relative Market Size

Satisfactory measures of relative market size are particularly difficult to obtain in the case of the two coffee markets. The best baseline for the size of the *total* (instant and R & G) coffee market is provided by the estimates for "total disappearance" (apparent consumption) by country, expressed in terms of the volume of green beans, produced by the International Coffee Organization.

While these figures provide a satisfactory estimate for the size of the total market, the division of total consumption between R & G and instant coffee is more problematic. The estimates used in constructing figure 12.2 in the text have been derived by applying various measures of the volume and value of instant and R & G sales, by country, compiled from various sources.[1] These figures should be regarded as approximations only.

The Coffee Multinationals

The Swiss multinational Nestlé is the market leader in instant coffee worldwide; its leading brand Nescafé dominates the retail market for instant coffee in five of the six countries studied here. Its leading international rival, the U.S.-based General Foods, outsells Nestlé only in the United States with its Maxwell House brand.

It has proved much more difficult, however, for leading multinationals to penetrate the R & G market. Both General Foods and Procter & Gamble, the leading producers in the United States, have achieved a limited degree of success by acquiring local R & G producers. In Italy, the second largest seller is Splendid (Procter and Gamble), while Hag and Onko (General Foods) play a minor role in the German R & G market. In Japan, General Foods has now succeeded in achieving a strong presence in the instant market since it entered a joint venture with Ajinomoto, one of Japan's leading food conglomerates, but it has not as yet had any impact on the R & G market.

The very different kind of market environment facing a seller in the R & G, as opposed to the instant, sector is underlined by Nestlé's approach to the R & G market. Its strategy has taken quite different forms in different groups of countries. In "tea culture" countries like Japan and the United Kingdom, instant coffee is the dominant type and enjoys a very high-quality image. Here Nestlé enjoys its greatest advantage—in that its image carries over successfully in selling R & G coffee. Thus, in its recent entry to this sector in the United Kingdom, it has marketed a range of blends under the Nescafé label—and indeed, Nestlé sells instant and R & G in the same packaging and format and under the same brand name (Gold Blend).

In some "coffee culture" countries, however, where instant coffee takes a relatively small proportion of total coffee sales, the Nescafé name would not carry the right weight to launch a premium R & G brand. Here Nestlé's strategy has been to proceed by acquisition: in Sweden, for example, it sells via Zoega's, while in the United States it acquired Hills Brothers, which now represent it in the R & G market. In France, a third strategy has emerged, in response to a market where two strong sellers dominate the R & G market (Jacobs, Douwe

---

1. Including various issues of *Coffee International*, *Coffee and Cocoa International*, *Tea and Coffee Trade Journal*. I am grateful to Mark Chopping of ERC Statistics International for advice on these problems.

Egberts). With instant coffee enjoying a relatively large share of the retail market, Nestlé's subsidiary, Sopad-Nestlé, has chosen in this case to pursue an advertising and marketing strategy directed toward building up the image of instant coffee in general.[2]

Italy and Japan

R & G Coffee

R & G coffee accounts for 95% of coffee sales in Italy. The market leader in R & G is the leading domestic coffee producer Lavazza, whose 38% retail share compares with 12% for its nearest rival, Splendid (Procter & Gamble). Lavazza's strength lies in a combination of high advertising expenditure (it accounts for 40% of Italy's coffee advertising) and a well-developed sales network. The latter was built up in the immediate postwar period and involves a force of 300 salesmen, who visit each retail outlet served by Lavazza every fifteen days. The company strategy has always rested on cultivating a high-quality image, and it is seen as the premium brand in Italy. Less well known abroad, it has a French subsidiary (with a 1% market share), and its advertisements have recently begun to be seen in the United Kingdom for the first time. Given the premium image of the Lavazza brand, the company faces severe limitations in building up its share at the low-price end of the market.

Although Lavazza's advertising-based image serves it well in the retail market, it is by way of its strength in distribution that it retains its position in the nonretail sector. Here it faces competition from some 1,000 or so small "roasters," almost all operating on a tiny scale, supplying ground coffee to local bars and similar outlets. The links between each "roaster" and the bars it supplies rest both on long-standing personal ties and on financial relationships. Bars facing cash-flow problems turn to their supplier for easy terms or straight loans; the quid pro quo involves a commitment to stay with the supplier over the long term. In this kind of situation, the multinationals in particular lack both the expertise and the inclination to become involved. Lavazza's case is interesting in that it represents an unusual example of a large and dominant concern that can compete with evident effectiveness in this kind of market.

The obvious parallel to the Italian experience is offered by Japan, which has a similarly high number of tiny bar and coffee shop clients served by R & G suppliers. The structure of the R & G market, moreover, bears a striking resemblance to the Italian case. The market leader, Ueshima Coffee (UCC brand) holds a 35% share of the retail market; like its main competitor, Key Coffee, its strength is built on its strong base in the nonretail sector. Ueshima's 1,000 salesmen deliver not only coffee, but a range of other products, to some

---

2. Its ease of preparation gives instant coffee a strong potential advantage, even in R & G-dominated markets. In France, a pronounced swing in consumption in favor of instant in recent years has been halted only by the development of coffeemakers that make R & G coffee relatively easy to prepare.

2,000 coffee shops; the company services a total of 70,000 accounts. A private company, it grew gradually via internal financing. It holds a minority stake in forty small "roasters," which it effectively controls by acting as their supplier of coffee beans. Ueshima's services to its small customers extend to lending them funds in periods of financial difficulty—in some cases taking a share in the business. As the customer's scale of operation rises, such considerations become relatively unimportant.[3]

At the other extreme of the catering market stand the major chains: Ueshima supplies McDonalds, for instance. In this area, the larger supplier enjoys a clear advantage. In recent years, for example, some of Japan's major trading companies have been involved in setting up chains of coffee shops operating under a tightly controlled franchise. Competition to supply these outlets has involved strong rivalry among some of Japan's largest R & G firms.

Instant Coffee

In Italy, where instant coffee accounts for only 5% of coffee sales, the market is supplied almost entirely by Nestlé. In spite of its virtual monopoly, Nestlé's advertising for instant coffee, which aims to promote the instant category vis-à-vis R & G, accounts for 13% of all coffee advertising in Italy. In contrast to Italy, Japan's instant coffee market is far greater than the R & G market, accounting for almost two-thirds of total coffee sales. Over 85% of instant coffee sales go to the retail sector; apart from some sales to the catering sector, there is also a small industrial market associated with the manufacture of coffee-flavored drinks. Within the retail sector, Nestlé is a clear market leader, with almost two-thirds of sales. Nestlé's main competitor is Ajinomoto, which operates a joint venture with General Foods. Two indigenous firms, the R & G maker UCC and Iguasu, manufacture instant coffee in Japan, while over thirty further firms supply imported instant coffee. Apart from Nestlé and Ajinomoto, however, no seller has a share exceeding 2%.

The instant coffee market grew rapidly from 1961–1962, prior to which imports of instant coffee were not permitted, and only the indigenous producer Morinaga operated on the Japanese market. General Foods began producing domestically in 1962, followed by Nestlé in 1965. Morinaga's share fell steadily, and Nestlé became the market leader by the late 1960s. General Foods, whose position lagged Nestlé's, subsequently entered a joint venture with Ajinomoto, in order to improve its access to, and distributional strength in, the food and drink sector generally.

Instant coffee is relatively heavily advertised in Japan; advertising amounted to some 8% of retail sales revenue in 1986. Expenditure on R & G advertising ran at about half that spent on instant coffee in the same year, amounting to

---

3. Restaurants, for example, constitute a group of medium-sized buyers. In this area, sellers emphasize a combination of production quality, price, and flexibility of service. The ability to respond with an immediate delivery whenever called upon is seen as essential.

5% of R & G sales—but given the very small amount of R & G sold on the retail market, this corresponded to almost 15% of *retail* sales of R & G coffee. Rising levels of R & G advertising in the 1980s reflected the fact that retail sales of R & G coffee were forecast to achieve double-digit growth throughout the decade (Yano Research Institute 1984).[4] R & G advertising levels rose rapidly as manufacturers vied to establish a position in the segment.

France and Germany

The major development in the European coffee market over the past decade has been the growth of two major groups, the German Jacobs and the Dutch Douwe Egberts. In instant coffee, Nestlé is dominant in most markets: in both France and Germany it accounts for slightly over half of sales. Both General Foods and Jacobs are among its leading rivals in both countries.[5] Germany, in spite of the small size of its instant segment (see table 12.4), has ten producers of instant coffee. Most of their production is exported, and Germany is an important source of supply for importers in the United Kingdom, Japan, and France.

France's R & G coffee market remained quite fragmented until the 1970s. Over 1,000 small and medium-sized suppliers operated on a local or regional basis, with a highly service-oriented approach, akin to that found among their Italian or Japanese counterparts. Moreover, no company had succeeded in gaining more than 10% of all coffee sales up to the late 1970s.

Nonetheless, as early as 1973, the main food industry trade journal *Agra-Alimentation* had pointed to Jacques Vabre, a Montpellier-based firm (formerly owned jointly by Jacobs and Douwe Egberts, Europe's two leading R & G concerns, and now owned by Jacobs), as being "the outsider who is henceforward to be reckoned with" (*Agra-Alimentation* 1973, p. 115). Active on the market for a mere four to five years, its aggressive marketing strategy had already established it as an influence on the national market.

The company's strategy was based on a successful attempt to build up a well-advertised national brand over a relatively short period. It introduced television advertising of R & G coffee to the French market; France's R & G makers had felt that their regional character—and limited budgets—made advertising on (national) television both excessively expensive and wasteful of resources. While this might indeed have been true in the short run, the financial capabilities of its parent companies allowed Jacques Vabre to take the long view, both in this regard and in others—notably in its ability to sustain extremely low margins over a prolonged period.

---

4. These high growth rates were seen within the industry as a by-product of increasing tourism in Japan, in that consumers' exposure to R & G coffee abroad improved its image domestically.

5. General Foods operating via Hag and Onko in Germany, while the Jacques Vabre and Grand-Mère brands in France are owned by Jacobs.

France's coffee market has long been subject to official controls on prices. During the 1970s and 1980s, the pressure on margins became particularly severe. Over this period, depressed margins and a loss of sales to the market leaders by medium-sized roasters caused a steady exit of these firms. While a strong middle ground of well-established regional firms had existed until the 1970s, these firms came under increasing pressure thereafter. Today, apart from the handful of majors, only ten firms operate on a regional basis. The remaining 1,000 or so firms confine themselves to very small-scale operation, servicing the needs of bars and cafes, etc., in their immediate vicinity.

A further factor that operated to favor the majors over regional suppliers during the 1970s and 1980s was the increasing importance of supermarket (hypermarket) sales, an area in which the majors enjoyed a clear advantage. On the other hand, the majors did not enjoy the same degree of strength in the nonretail sector as did their Italian and Japanese counterparts. Although Jacques Vabre operates a division servicing hotel and restaurant sales, this plays a secondary role in the company's activities.

The growth of Jacques Vabre sparked off a phase of intense competition for leadership in the R & G market. The focus of competition came to rest on a battle for acquisition of the Grand-Mère company. General Foods, hitherto a major seller of R & G coffee, withdrew from the French market following its failure to acquire Grand-Mère, which was taken over by Jacobs. Currently, Jacques Vabre, together with Grand-Mère, account for about 40% of supermarket sales of R & G coffee. Douwe Egberts, via Maison du Café, controls some 15%–20%. Thus the three major firms, which together held less than one-quarter of total coffee sales in France as recently as 1980, have now, under the aegis of Europe's two R & G majors, come to play a dominant role in the French market.

While the recent consolidation of the French market has led to the appearance of a clear market leader (Jacques Vabre), the German market supports three firms of similar importance—Jacobs, Tchibo, and Eduscho—along with Germany's leading retailer Aldi, whose own brand (Albrecht) puts it among the top four. In contrast to France, Germany has relatively few R & G producers (about fifty). All have come under pressure in recent years from the expansion of own-brand coffee and in particular from the increasing share of Aldi.

Attempts by the Big Three to expand or retain their shares have had the unlikely outcome of further stimulating the position of Aldi's own brand. Up to 1984, Jacobs held a share of 23%–24% of the R & G market. The rise in world coffee prices in that year led Jacobs to introduce a new production process that allegedly led to a 20% improvement in the yield householders could achieve from a given weight of R & G coffee. Jacobs introduced a new pack size of 400 grams, in place of the traditional 500-gram pack, and undertook an advertising campaign in support of its claims. These claims were contested by some of its rivals—who nonetheless introduced a similar process shortly afterward. As most of the leading firms competed for share on the basis of advertising, these claims came to be questioned by the industry's trade association, the Deutsche Kaffee-

Verband. Problems began to arise for the new offerings as Germany's coffee shops, which account for a high proportion of nonretail sales, reported difficulties in using the products; and, in late 1984, researchers reported a substantial switch in market share in favor of Eduscho (the only major to have retained the traditional 500-gram offering) and Aldi's own brand. By the end of 1984, Jacobs and Tchibo had reverted to a 500-gram pack, and the remaining majors followed. Jacobs's share recovered somewhat from its low of 16% in June 1984 toward 21% in the following year, but this was substantially short of its 1983 share of 23%–24%.

One side effect of this twenty-month episode—which the German press labeled the "coffee revolution"—was the accentuation in the trend, already evident in the early 1980s, of a shift in advertising expenditures away from instant coffee (where Jacobs is one of the main competitors) toward the R & G market. Between 1981 and 1983, advertising on instant coffee declined only slightly from 18.7 to 17.7 million DM, while R & G advertising rose slightly from 151 to 157 million DM. (These figures exclude full-range advertising in support of brands selling in both sectors.) The first three-quarters of 1984, however, saw an increase of 27% in advertising expenditure on R & G, while expenditure on instant coffee fell by 30% relative to the same period in 1983. As in France, advertising intensity in the unsettled R & G market rose during the 1980s to equal, and at times surpass, the levels attained in the instant sector—a pattern that was mirrored briefly in the U.K. market.

The United Kingdom

The U.K. market is largely an instant coffee market, with sales in this sector being dominated by Nestlé and General Foods. In contrast to the other countries studied here, own-label sales are quite substantial, amounting to 20% of 1986 sales. The largest own-label seller, Sainsbury's, ranked as the third-largest seller in the instant coffee market in that year, with a 7% share, just ahead of Brook Bond Oxo (Unilever).

Within the United Kingdom, the R & G market is relatively small (10% of retail sales in 1986), but it has been growing very rapidly, albeit from a very tiny base, throughout the 1980s. This growth has stimulated a series of developments in what was for long a fairly static market in which Allied Lyons had a dominant position. The most important development of the 1980s concerned a battle to acquire Kenco, one of Allied's main rivals, which was finally acquired by General Foods. This acquisition left General Foods as market leader in the retail R & G market, with a 25% share, while Allied's share fell from around 49% at the start of the decade to less than half that figure by 1986.

The attractiveness of penetration by acquisition in this market is easy to understand, given the key role of the catering segment for R & G producers. Kenco's net of contacts in this highly service-oriented business was the main attraction of the company to a potential buyer.

The United States

The retail segment of the U.S. market has been described in chapter 12. The nonretail segment, a predominantly R & G market (90%), accounts for 30% of total coffee sales. The segment is much less fragmented than is the case in Italy or Japan. Nonetheless, no seller had a share exceeding 10% up to the late 1970s, and the sector presents the same kind of difficulty to the majors as it does in other countries, albeit to a much lesser degree. All three majors maintained sales forces of around 500–600 at that time, but they called only on large and medium-sized outlets, leaving small outlets to be serviced by wholesalers. Regional roasters did not maintain sizable sales forces, but operated mainly through wholesalers or food brokers.

During the 1980s, the majors have made some limited headway in this sector. General Foods is believed to have about one-third of the market; Folger, however, in spite of gaining one-third of retail R & G sales, has had much greater difficulty in the nonretail sector, where it accounts for around 15% or so of sales. Nestlé, via its Hills Brothers subsidiary, is about half this size again in the nonretail market.

The United States represents the opposite extreme in this regard to the Japanese and Italian markets, but even in the United States, the nonretail sector is highly service oriented, and those local firms that have succeeded in developing long-term relationships with institutional clients may have considerable advantages vis-à-vis the majors.

Appendix 12.4
Pet Foods and Baby Foods

The evolution of dual structure in advertising-intensive industries has been a recurring theme (see in particular chapters 3 and 8). In discussing the experience of the confectionery and coffee industries in chapter 12, the role played by setup costs in influencing the viability of a fringe of small producers was emphasized. The fortunes of the fringe, however, depend not only on the level of setup costs, but also on whether a substantial proportion of price-sensitive buyers are present in the market. It has been assumed that nonretail buyers are more price sensitive and less responsive to advertising outlays. This is an oversimplification: even in retail markets, a substantial proportion of consumers may buy on price.

The degree of this divergence of tastes across different retail customers is likely to vary widely across markets, however. In what follows, a rare instance is highlighted, in which two industries that are closely similar in respect of technology (setup cost) and advertising intensity display one striking difference in structure. In the pet food industry, a large fringe of small producers operates alongside the majors, though doing no advertising and selling purely on price. The total number of producers exceeds 100 in the United States. In the United Kingdom and Germany, it lies in the sixty to eighty range. Even in the small Japanese and Italian markets, over twenty producers are active. Within the baby food industry, this fringe is almost wholly absent. Ten or fewer sellers operate in each of these countries, and the U.S. market is dominated by a mere three sellers, which account for virtually all sales. An obvious hypothesis here is that consumers differ sharply in their sensitivity to perceived quality across the two markets; although a substantial fraction of consumers are willing to buy on price in regard to pet food, they will not do likewise in purchasing baby food. Plausible though this explanation may seem, there does not appear to be any obvious way of testing its validity within the confines of this study. It is advanced here merely as a plausible hypothesis, consistent with the theory, which may account for a striking divergence in structure between these two industries.

In the remainder of this appendix, we describe each industry in turn.

Pet Foods

Market Definition

The origins of the pet food industry can be traced to the turn of the century, when major milling companies began introducing varieties of biscuits, and then other specialty grain-based products, for feeding to dogs. The U.K. company, Spillers Ltd., was already offering eighteen varieties of dog biscuits as early as 1914. Canned pet food was already well established in the 1930s and had become the dominant form of pet food in the United States. In the postwar affluence of the 1950s, however, the pet food market began to approach its modern form; during the late 1950s the U.S. pet food market expanded extremely rapidly and sales reached a level of $300 million by 1958.

We define the market quite narrowly to include only dog food and cat food, the two main product categories. This allows a satisfactorily precise comparison across the several countries. The nature of the industry's products has evolved over time. Once a natural channel of diversification for grain millers, the industry now serves as a natural complement to the (human) food industry, utilizing a broad range of by-products that would otherwise be wasted. Its products divide into three categories: dry (the descendant of the early grain-based products), moist (meat-based products in cans, etc.), and the most recent segment, semimoist (meat patties, which look like raw hamburger, and so on).

The market today in all the countries studied here shows a clear dual structure with a fringe of small producers operating alongside a handful of majors—among whom a small number of U.S. multinationals figure prominently in all cases. Small firms, however, can find their niche, not only in selling for own-label—a segment in which they will usually find themselves competing with the market leaders—but also by selling a low-price product locally through small specialist retailers (pet shops, feed stores, and so on). The extent to which small firms succeed in this varies across countries. They are noticeably stronger in the United States, where a large network of small local producers existed from the industry's early days, than in parts of Continental Europe, where the pet food industry was essentially created by the coming of the multinationals.

The Markets by Country

Beacuse three U.S. multinationals (Mars, Quaker, and Carnation) have an extremely strong position in all the countries studied here, we begin by looking at the U.S. market. We then turn to the U.K. market, whose development was largely shaped by the parallel development of the U.S.-based Mars group and the gradual growth, via a series of acquisitions, of its main indigenous rival, Spillers.

The United States

During its period of rapid development in the postwar years, the U.S. pet food industry was already marked by a clear difference in structure between its two main segments, dry and canned dog food. Dry (or grain-based) dog food was a relatively concentrated segment, the clear market leader being the Post division of General Foods whose Gaines brand accounted for around 30% of sales in the mid-1950s.[1]

The canned dog food segment was much more fragmented, the leading brand (Ken-L-Ration) taking only around 15% of sales in the late 1950s. The rapid growth of the market had attracted many new entrants, and by the end of the 1950s, over 2,000 brands of dog food were available. Many of these competed purely on price—especially in the canned sector. Canned products all looked very much alike, and it was felt to be much more difficult to produce a product with a distinctive appearance in this area; grain-based products could, on the other hand, be distinguished by shape and color to a much greater degree.

It was against this background that the appearance of a novel production method sparked a sequence of fundamental changes in the pet food industry. A new extruder-expander machine, invented in the early 1950s, allowed the manufacture of a grain-based product consisting of chunky, puffed-up pieces. Though the existence of the new technique was known to General Foods, the company had not marketed any product using the new method.[2] During the late 1950s, however, Ralston Purina—whose main interests lay in cereals and animal feed—used the new technique to produce a new and distinctive-looking product, Purina Dog Chow. The new product was sufficiently different to rival products to permit the creation of a strong brand image, and Ralston Purina backed the new brand with an advertising budget of the order of $5 million a year. The key marketing innovation, however, was to "take the product into grocery." Purina Dog Chow would be basically sold through supermarkets and general food stores, rather than through specialist pet shops or animal feed outlets. This new emphasis on the marketing of a pet food alongside general groceries was a sign of things to come; over the following decades, this pattern became the norm, and Ralston Purina took over as market leader in the pet food sector.

General Foods's response to these developments was twofold. In the first place, it led them to search for improvements or modifications of their own dry product, Gaines Meal, but this appeared to offer limited potential. The company also reviewed its (relatively weak) position in the canned market, but concluded that

---

1. General Foods had purchased the Gaines Dog Food Company in 1943. Its major product was Gaines Dog Meal, a dry (grain-based) product. In 1958, the Gaines business was allocated to the Post division of General Foods. By that time it was also producing a canned product, Gaines Menu, and Gaines Dog Biscuits.

2. The events in this market are strongly reminiscent of Foster's (1986) series of case studies in which the failure of an incumbent to switch to a new technology resulted in a switch of industry leadership.

it would be extremely difficult to successfully differentiate a canned dog food. This led to the notion of creating a third dog food category. Market research led it to identify an attractive opportunity in the development of a meat-based product similar in appearance to raw hamburger; its success with this type of product created the new semimoist segment of the market in which it became the industry leader.

Today, most of the majors compete across most segments, both in dog food and in the more recently developed cat food market.

A series of acquisitions during the 1980s has led to new shifts in structure. The Gaines business was sold by General Foods to Anderson Clayton, which in turn was acquired by Quaker Oats in 1986. Combined with Quaker's own interests in the area, the acquisition of the Gaines business has made the company the second-largest pet food producer after Ralston Purina. Among the remaining majors, Carnation was acquired by Nestlé (1984). The U.K. group Grand Metropolitan has bought into the U.S. industry via its acquisition of a number of smaller producers and is now among the industry's top-ten sellers.

The United Kingdom

The U.K. market is dominated by two firms, Pedigree Petfood (Mars) and Spillers (Dalgety), which together accounted for over three-quarters of sales during the past decade. Spillers, originally a flour miller, had already established a major position in the (dry) dog food industry in the prewar period. The company grew rapidly during the 1960s via a series of acquisitions. It expanded into canned foods though its acquisition of Spratts' Patent Ltd. in 1960, and four years later it tripled its share in that segment by acquiring Scottish Animal Products Ltd., a subsidiary of Robert Wilson & Sons. In 1967, Spillers acquired Tyne Brand Products Ltd., a canned food company with strong interests in own-label pet food. Subsequent acquisitions included Wright & Company (Liverpool) Ltd. (dog meal) and Stamina Foods (an own-label pet food business owned by Rank-Hovis McDougal). Finally, Spillers was itself acquired—following a bitter takeover battle—by Dalgety Plc. in 1979.

The U.S.-based Mars Corporation had just begun operations within the U.K. confectionery industry when, in 1934, it acquired Chappel Brothers Ltd., a small company selling canned offcuts of meat for sale as dog food under the brand name Chappie. Mars originally operated the business under the company name Chappie Ltd., but subsequent reorganizations led to changes in the name, first to Petfoods Ltd. and then, in 1972, to Pedigree Petfoods Ltd.

The UK market is a highly segmented one: Spillers dominates the dry dog food segment, in which its share exceeds 60%, while Pedigree's share is less than a quarter of this figure. Pedigree, on the other hand, has around 60% of the canned market, both in dog food and cat food. The remaining firms are of much smaller scale: Carnation (Nestlé) has about half the market for dry cat food, and Quaker dominates the very small semimoist sector.

The market, like the U.S. market, is very much marketing driven. Television advertising accounts for 4%–5% of sales revenue, and consumer and trade promotions are believed to account for about the same again.[3] On at least one occasion an attempt has been made to coordinate with a view to reducing these levels; in 1970, Spillers informed Pedigree Petfoods that it was limiting its marketing expenditures to 11% of sales, and Pedigree Petfoods informed Spillers that it was doing the same. This arrangement subsequently lapsed (Monopolies and Mergers Commission 1977, p. 18). The attractiveness of going for a high-advertising rather than low-price strategy is borne out by recent experience in the cat food segment, which doubled in value during the first half of the 1980s, now accounting for over 40% of total sales. This rapid growth, fueled in part by rising levels of cat ownership, was focused primarily at the premium end of the market, to the benefit of Pedigree's Whiskas brand, which alone accounts for half of cat food sales. Consumer attitude surveys, undertaken for Mintel by the British Market Research Bureau, indicated strong brand loyalty and an unwillingness to switch in response to price reductions.

This strong position of the branded sector is reflected in the difficulties faced by potential suppliers of own-label products, which account for only 10% of pet food sales. This is all the more surprising, in that the leading U.K. grocery multiples have been successful to a degree unparalleled elsewhere in achieving a high-quality image for their own-brand products.[4]

Insofar as price competition is concerned, the U.K. Monopolies and Mergers Commission described Pedigree as a price leader in the market in 1977. Indeed, Spillers informed the commission that "in order to achieve a better return on capital, it would raise its prices more if it were not restrained by the level of Pedigree Petfood's prices." Pedigree's pricing policy, on the other hand, appears to be designed to guard the level of share secured via its marketing efforts. This was particularly noticeable during 1985–1986, when Spiller launched a new premium canned dog food, Winalot Prime, and Pedigree reacted with strong price promotions on its main competing product, Pedigree Chum.

Against this background of strong price pressure and the growing strength of the premium end of the market, small suppliers have been finding it difficult to survive. Some have been absorbed by acquisitions; the market is national and grocery based, but a large number of very small producers operate on a local basis via sales through pet shops and similar outlets as in the United States. The weakness of the own-label sector reflects in part the willingness of most consumers to pay more for a premium product, and the small own-label sector is itself served by a handful of large to medium-sized firms specializing in own-label

---

3. This rough equality of advertising levels with other promotional expenditures is broadly consistent with the figures quoted by the U.K. Monopolies and Mergers Commission (1977).

4. Indeed, the conventional wisdom in some quarters is that the situation is unlikely to persist; pet food is now one of the few areas in U.K. food retailing where the balance of advantage lies with the manufacturer rather than the retailer. Leading retailers are likely to increase their efforts over the next few years to establish successful own-labels.

sales, such as Luda Petfood (which acquired Anglia Canners in 1987). The smaller sellers in the industry also include some major food companies such as Heinz whose main interests lie in other sectors.

The industry's trade association, the Petfood Manufacturers' Association, has sixty members, fifty of which produce dog and/or cat food. There are about forty more firms outside the association; a sizable fraction of these also produce dog and/or cat food, but they are relatively small producers with an annual turnover below £1 million and a combined market share of less than 5%.

France

The French pet food market has developed along the lines of the U.S. and U.K. markets only in the very recent past. Its rate of growth has been very rapid, however: at present, two-thirds of pet owners use at least some commercially prepared pet food, and such food is estimated to account for about half of all food consumed by domestic pets. Despite strong efforts by indigenous producers, the market is heavily dominated by the major multinational groups, operating via a domestic subsidiary. The first of the multinationals to enter was Mars, which acquired a local French producer in the 1960s. Via its Unisaba subsidiary, it now enjoys a share of slightly over 50%. The shares of Gloria (Carnation) and Quaker France (Quaker Oats), both of which entered in the mid-1970s, are harder to estimate, and figures reported in different studies vary widely— but all sources agree that these three suppliers together account for over 80% of sales. All three offer a range of products covering all four main types (semi-moist products are of negligible importance). Unisaba (Mars) is particularly strong in the canned segments, where its share exceeds 50% of the market. Gloria (Carnation) is active only in cat food and is strongest in the small dry cat food sector, where it accounts for about half of total sales. A fringe of some thirty or so smaller producers also operate in the market. These account for some of the supply of retailers' own-label products, which have a market share of 10–11%. The remaining part of own-label sales is supplied from imports, Spillers (U.K.) and Vewa in the Netherlands being important sources.

Germany

The German pet food market was extremely small until the mid-1960s, when the Mars subsidiary Effem GmbH began to market its canned dog food. Today the company accounts for more than 60% of dog food sales and over 80% of the (smaller) cat food sector. It has at least three leading brands in each of the three main market segments (Pal, Chappie, and Loyal in canned dog food; Frolic, Trim, and Snacks in dry dog food; and Whiskas, Kit-e-Kat, and Catkins in canned cat food).

The second largest producer, Quaker Latz, has its origins in a company founded at the turn of the century by a well-known dog breeder, named Latz, to produce dog biscuits. The company amalgamated with Ralston Purina in

1971 under the name Latz-Purina. The company was taken over in 1982 by Quaker, which formed a partnership with a major detergent producer, Henkel. The company's products are now also sold under the Henkel & Partner label.

The growth of the German market has been extremely rapid of late, and this has attracted a large number of small firms into the market. They remain, however, very small; indeed, Germany's oldest established industrial pet food manufacturer, Bremer Vitakraft-Werke GmbH, founded in 1926, today ranks fourth in the industry with less than 5% of the market[5]—behind Mars,[6] Quaker, and Nestlé[7] respectively. Although eighty firms produce pet food and allied products, and some of the smaller indigenous firms have achieved brand recognition (Matzinger, Bergephor, Schanmann, and Deuka), German consumers show a strong inclination to favor highly advertised brands. Advertising accounts for some 5% of industry sales, with brands such as Pal and Whiskas ranking among the most heavily advertised products in Germany. Many pet food manufacturers, and particularly Effem, run advisory and breeding services that build up their company's image in terms of a concern for pets' general welfare. As in the United Kingdom, own-label pet food has been remarkably unsuccessful, accounting for around 3%–4% of sales. Aldi, the leading German food chain, accounts for one-sixth of all pet food sales. The product is highly grocery oriented: only one-tenth of sales are made through specialist (pet shop) channels.

In sharp contrast to the United Kingdom, the leading manufacturers operate with considerable success across the three major categories of the market. Effem (Mars) has more than half the market in canned dog food, dry dog food, and canned cat food; and in each case, it is followed by Quaker Latz, which takes between one-fifth and one-third of sales.

Italy

Commercially produced pet foods have only recently begun to make inroads in the Italian market. With the highest level of domestic pet ownership in Europe, the Italian market nonetheless remains a relatively small one, with only one-tenth of pet owners buying commercially prepared food. A very high proportion of sales is still made up of imports. In the early 1980s, the fraction of consumption supplied by imports stood at 70%, but the opening of an Italian plant by Quaker (via its Italian subsidiary Chiari e Forti) reduced this to around 60% by the mid-1980s. On these grounds, the Italian market is omitted from the data set employed in the present study (under criterion 4, chapter 4).

---

5. It is a private company, in which Carnation (Nestlé) has an interest. Its primary areas of interest lie in dry pet foods for birds and rodents.
6. Mars operates via two subsidiaries, Effem (which produces both dog and cat food) and Unisaba, which sells tinned cat food under the Ronron label.
7. Glücksklee, a Hamburg-based company, was already owned by Carnation prior to the takeover of Carnation by Nestlé.

The market is dominated by two companies: Petfoods Italia Spa (which owns Chiari e Forti and more recently acquired one of the main domestic producers, Morando) and Quaker. Quaker is the market leader in dog food (with over 40% of sales), while Petfoods accounts for almost 60% of cat food sales. Up to now canned food has dominated both segments, but it is expected that the relatively small share of dry pet food will rise substantially over time.

Two-thirds of sales are still made through 3,000 specialist outlets. Thus the Italian market has not yet made the transition to the kind of highly advertised, grocery-based market characteristic of most other countries. Margins, to date, have been low, and firms explain the relatively modest levels of advertising by pointing out that total sales and unit margins cannot as yet justify substantial advertising. This situation is not expected to persist, however; advertising expenditure levels had reached 5,600 million lira per annum by the mid-1980s.[8] Advertising has been directed toward improving the share of the category (i.e., market size, rather than individual producers' shares). It is generally felt that the 15% per annum growth rate of the sector can be expected to persist for some time.

Several smaller firms have achieved a small but significant market share: they include the Star Group (with its Liz brand), which has slightly over 5% of total sales, as well as Raggio di Sole and Sacchi (both in dry pet foods), Fatro Spa (dried, meat-based products), and Risene Scotti. In all, there are over thirty producers currently operating.

Japan

The Japanese pet food market has developed relatively recently and is growing rapidly. With only 20% of dog-owning households using commercially prepared dog food, the market is expected to grow rapidly over the next decade. The most striking features of the Japanese market are its relatively low level of concentration and the relative strength of indigenous producers. The industry leader, Nippon Pet Food, which sells under the brand name BITA-1, is a wholly owned subsidiary of Kyodo-Shiryo, a Japanese animal feed company. Second is Nisshin Pet Food, a subsidiary of one of Japan's two leading flour millers, Nisshin Seifun. Nisshin Pet Food acts as an agent for Quaker Oats (U.S.).

The third producer, with a share almost equal to that of Nisshin Pet Food, is Ajinomoto General Foods, a joint venture between the U.S. multinational General Foods and Ajinomoto, one of Japan's leading food companies. Nestlé's Japanese arm, Nestlé KK, holds a 50% stake in Carnation Nippai. The fourth position is represented by Puri Taiyo Pet Food, a joint venture between a Japanese fish company, Taiyo, and Ralston Purina (U.S.). The prevalence of joint ventures, as in other industries, reflects to a considerable degree the

---

8. Which represents some 3%–4% of retail sales (150,000 million lira in 1984) according to industry estimates reported by *Largo Consumo*. These estimates should be treated with caution; some commentators report lower measured levels.

difficulties that foreign firms experience in penetrating the Japanese distribution system.

Three other producers have shares only slightly less than Nisshin, Ajinomoto, or Puri Taiyo. One of these is a Japanese firm, Petline, a subsidiary of Nippon-nosan-kogyo, an animal feed producer that belongs to the Mitsubishi group. The other two, Carnation Nippai and Nippon Effem, have links with the U.S. majors. Behind these come a fringe of smaller producers; in all, over twenty producers are present in the market.

The market is less than one-tenth the size of the U.S. market. Its huge growth potential, however, has begun to stimulate both the entry of new producers and an increasing use of television advertising by the leading firms. In the early 1980s, only two or three firms advertised regularly on television; by the mid-1980s, more than five firms were advertising regularly. The conventional wisdom within the industry is that only three or four firms are likely to prosper at the premium end of the market over the next decade.

Baby Food

Market Definition

There are three basic categories of baby food:

· Infant milk (baby formula), based on milk powder. Used from birth to two years, its use is concentrated in the first twelve months.

· Cereal-based products. These include both cereals served with milk and rusks, the latter product varying significantly in type across countries. These products represent the second feeding stage and are used from the time the child is a few months old.

· The third stage corresponds to the use of so-called wet meals, that is, ready formulated purees, etc., which are served without the addition of further liquids.

The Markets by Country

A small number of multinational companies have a strong presence in most countries: Heinz, Gerber (U.S.), Nestlé (Switzerland), and Milupa (Germany). In some cases, one or more strong indigenous firms retain a solid position (BSN in France, for example). The total number of firms operating in each country is no more than a dozen or so. The United Kingdom has eight producers of some importance; this market is something of an exception, however, in that it is highly segmented; within each segment the market is highly concentrated. Consumption levels vary widely; in Japan the market is particularly small, as infants progress to adult food at a relatively early stage. The Italian market has been undergoing a long period of decline in line with the fall in the birth rate. This decline has been accompanied by a gradual rise in the level of concentration as the market leader Plada (Heinz) has acquired rival producers.

One feature common to all countries is that two channels of distribution are used. The pharmacy sector is relatively strong in all countries in the supply of infant milk, whereas the other two categories aimed at older infants are sold predominantly through grocery channels.

France

The market is dominated by three groups, which operate through a number of subsidiaries. The market leader is the food conglomerate BSN-Gervais Danone, which operates through its two subsidiaries, Diepal-Jacquemaire (which has about 50% of the market in nonpharmacy pureed products) and Gallia (the second-largest seller of infant milk). Nestlé operates in the French baby food market via its main French subsidiary Sopad Nestlé (which sells about one-quarter of nonpharmacy pureed products) and Guigoz (the market leader in infant milk). Gerber products are sold in France via Societé des Produits du Mais, a subsidiary of the American multinational, CPC Inc. Two more foreign firms, Milupa (Germany) and Wyeth-Byla (U.K.) have a strong presence in the infant milk segment, while two further indigenous producers sell infant cereals (Jammet, Picot).

As in most countries, sales are divided between the pharmacy sector, which accounts for *all* sales of infant milk, and the grocery sector, which dominates in the other categories. Rivalry between these two retail channels is sufficiently strong in France to induce the major manufacturers to operate via separate subsidiary companies, each of which supplies exclusively through one or other of the retail channels. The lower margins used by the grocery sector have led to a steady decline in the pharmacists' share of all categories other than infant milk; by the early 1980s it accounted for a little over one-tenth of baby food sales, as opposed to one-quarter in the late 1970s.

Germany

In the German market, the three basic categories listed above account for 96% of sales in value terms ("wet meals" for 41% in 1984, infant milk for 33%, and cereal-based products for 22%). In addition, there is a small fourth category, "Kindertees," consisting of juices and teas or infusions prepared for young children (*Marketing in Europe* 1986). Three major producers accounted for 87% of consumption in 1984. Two are indigenous firms, Hipp AG and Milupa, the latter having a strong presence elsewhere in Europe. The third leading producer is the Nestlé subsidiary Allgäuer Alpenmilch AG, which operated in the baby food market via its subsidiary Nestlé-Alete GmbH.

In the wet meals category, Hipp KG and Nestlé divide the market almost equally. In infant milks, Milupa had a 40% share in 1984, followed by Nestlé (35%) and Hipp (12%). A handful of smaller producers also market instant milk, the most well known being Humana, with a 1984 share of 5% (*Marketing in Europe* 1986). In the cereal-based segment, Milupa accounts for half of sales, while Nestlé has a share of about one-fifth. A number of smaller producers are also active, including Aponti and Kölln Flockenwerke.

Italy

The baby food market in Italy has been in steady decline throughout the 1970s and 1980s, reflecting a major decline in the birth rate, which fell by 30% in the first half of the 1980s. This has led to increased consolidation in an already highly concentrated, and currently rather depressed, market.

The market leader, Plada, traces its origin to the Plasmon company, which was already the leading firm in the "postweaning" half of the market (biscuits, purees) prior to its acquisition by H. J. Heinz in the early 1960s. The decline in demand for baby food led to two forms of response from the early 1970s onward. The first concerned attempts to diversify out of the field, a policy in which the company achieved limited success. Its attempts to move into mass markets, where it faced direct competition from such leading Italian food firms as Star, were unsuccessful: the Plasmon image was too specifically associated with the sale of baby food to give it much of an advantage in these areas. On the other hand, its attempts to build on its positive image in more obviously related areas, such as diet and health foods (whole wheat pasta, high-fiber biscuits, etc.), have been very successful.

The second form of response to market decline has been an increasing move toward consolidation in the industry. Plasmon acquired Dieterba, now its number-two brand, in 1974. The most dramatic move in the industry in recent years came in 1983, however, when the company—now called Plada—acquired Nipiol, the dietetic division of Buitoni, thereby acquiring an overall share of 80%. Its shares within particular segments thereby reached 90% in baby juices and 95% in baby biscuits, while in purees it has 82% of the market, its only competitor being Gerber (owned in Italy by Monda S.p.A.). Plada's acquisition of Nipiol can be seen as defensive in the sense that financial problems within Nipiol's parent company favored a sale; and the most likely alternative to acquisition by Plada would have involved the sale of Nipiol to one of its competitors, such as Nestlé.

Italy's other suppliers are the multinationals Nestlé and Gerber, the German Milupa, and Mellin, a subsidiary of Star.

Japan

The market was developed by QP, which introduced Western-style baby food to Japan thirty-five years ago. The product has never enjoyed the kind of success it achieved in the West, however: whereas 80% or so of babies consume baby food in Europe, the figure for Japan is around 10%, and the consumption levels of those few babies who do eat it remains low by European standards.

Thus it is not surprising, given the small size of its market, to find a pattern in which the major domestic producers are some of the leading Japanese milk companies, which produce powdered milk for babies, while much of the nonmilk products (purees, etc.) are imported via links with leading American baby food manufacturers (Gerber and Beech-Nut). For this reason, the Japanese market was excluded from the data set employed in chapter 5 (under criterion 4 of chapter 4).

The United Kingdom

The market is highly segmented, so the relatively low overall concentration ratio for the sector is somewhat misleading. The three major segments are:

· Milk foods (44% of all sales in 1983). Here, three firms dominate the market: Wyeth Laboratories are market leaders with a 40% share in 1983, followed by Cow and Gate (30%) and Farley Health Products (Glaxo) (26%).

· Wet meals (27% of all sales in 1983). Here, Heinz dominates the market with 73% of sales, with Cow and Gate taking 25%. The only other seller of any note is the French firm Gallia, the BSN-Gervais Danone subsidiary, which launched its range of meals in jars in the United Kingdom in 1979.

· Dry meals, including cereals (22% of 1983 sales). Here, Robinson and Milupa dominate the market, each with about a 40% share. Boots and Heinz also compete in this segment.

Canned baby foods originated in the United States and were introduced on the British market by the H. J. Heinz Company in 1937. Heinz began manufacturing in the United Kingdom in 1947, and it still enjoyed a 95% market share twenty years later, by which time its main competitors were Unigate (Trufood, Cow and Gate) and Colman Foods Ltd. (with its Robinson range).

Within the United States, Heinz took second place to Gerber, whose products were introduced on the U.K. market in the 1960s. The products were first imported and later manufactured under license by Brown and Polson Ltd., which later changed its name to CPC (United Kingdom) Ltd., the U.K. subsidiary of CPC Inc. By the end of the 1960s, Gerber products had achieved a U.K. market share of 10%, with Heinz holding 84% of the market. Over the next few years, however, Gerber's share almost doubled to reach 19% by 1973. By the early 1970s, three firms (Heinz, Gerber, Unigate) held 90% of the market, with Colman Foods taking a further 5%. Over the past decade, Heinz and Cow and Gate have emerged as clear market leaders, with a combined share of 98%.

Milk-based baby food was introduced on the U.K. market at the beginning of the century by Cow and Gate Ltd. (which later acquired another baby food manufacturer, Trufood Ltd., from Unilever in 1955 and later merged with United Dairies to form Unigate in 1959). In the interwar years, Cow and Gate's main competitor was Joseph Nathan & Co., which imported dried milk powder from New Zealand for the U.K. market under the name Glaxo. The Glaxo Group Ltd. was formed in 1935 to incorporate the Glaxo department of Joseph Nathan.

The postwar baby boom stimulated demand and induced the entry of a new producer, John Wyeth & Brother Ltd. In 1960 Farley's Health products, which was long established in cereal-based baby foods, introduced milk-based products. These latter interests were acquired by Glaxo in 1968.

These three firms continue to dominate the segment; the main shift in structure over time has been the growing success of Wyeth Laboratories, which has grown to achieve the leading position in this segment, the only segment in which it operates. The company has a scientific image, and the U.K. Department of Health and Social Security has stated that its Gold Cap SMA is the closest substitute for human milk among those currently offered.

In the remaining segments of the baby food market, there has been some change in the pattern of market shares over time. Farley, now part of Glaxo, has dominated the rusks market since its inception. In the much smaller cereals segment, however, Colman Foods was slightly stronger than Farley in the early 1970s. Ten years later, however, Robinson and Milupa had come to dominate this segment, their combined share being about 80%.

Another noteworthy aspect of the U.K. market relates to own-label products. These products have had little success in this industry in most countries. Within the United Kingdom, in spite of the relative strength of own-brand products, the only notable success of own-label baby food is the range sold by Boots, the leading national chain of pharmacy outlets. Boots sells dried foods, rusks, and drinks under its own label and has achieved an overall share of 3.5% with the aid of an outstandingly strong image in the health and baby products area.

The United States

The U.S. market is unusual in that it is sharply segmented between the two main categories, infant milks and canned foods. Whereas in each of the other countries a considerable overlap exists between the market leaders in these two segments, in the case of the United States, each segment is the preserve of a different set of firms (see table 12.4.1).

The infant milk (baby formula) segment is dominated by three producers, all of which are subsidiaries of major producers of prescription and nonprescription drugs. Ross Laboratories is a subsidiary of Abbot Laboratories. Meade Johnson is owned by Bristol Myers, which in 1989 merged with Squibb, in a move that marked the growing consolidation of the U.S. drug industry. Wyeth Laboratories is owned by American Home Products, whose interests extend beyond the drug and health care sector and include a wide range of food products and household goods. The remaining part of the market is dominated by three firms,

Table 12.4.1
Market shares by segment in the U.S. baby food market, 1988

Market shares (%)			
Infant milk (baby formula) (sales: $1,465 million, 1988)		Other baby foods (sales: $935 million, 1988)	
Ross Laboratories	54	Gerber Products	67
Meade Johnson	36	Beech-Nut	17
Wyeth Laboratories	9	Heinz USA	13
Other	1	Other	3

Source: Euromonitor.

Gerber Products, Beech-Nut (a Nestlé subsidiary), and Heinz. Gerber is the world's leading producer of baby foods, from which it derived 56% of its sales revenue and 74% of its profits in 1988. (Its most important interests outside the baby food industry lie in clothing.)

The evolution of structure in the U.S. industry is relatively poorly documented, but such evidence as exists suggests some interesting parallels with the experience of many other advertising-intensive industries. In particular, Connor et al. (1985) emphasize the fact that as Gerber came to achieve clear dominance over its rivals, the advertising-sales ratio in the industry fell significantly, and by the mid-1980s, total advertising expenditure had fallen to just below 1% of sales revenue. Competition in the U.S. market now centers around the issue of which company makes the most nutritious food. Heinz and Beech-Nut have both spent millions of dollars in recent years in developing new baby foods free of salt, sugar and artificial ingredients.[9]

The most striking feature of the U.S. market, as noted earlier, is the sharp degree of segmentation between its two halves. However, by the end of the 1980s, there were clear indications that this pattern might not persist. Nestle, following its acquisition of Carnation in 1984, had begun to develop a position in the infant milk segment,[10] and in 1989, Gerber announced that it too would enter the infant milk segment.

---

9. Beech-Nut's entire line, which it calls "Stages," is aimed at first-time parents who are relatively unconfident, allowing them to introduce babies to new textures and flavors in four stages. Gerber's First Foods is also targeted at this segment on the principle that consumer loyalty in this market, once won, is not easily lost.

10. Though its progress was impeded by the intervention of the Food and Drug Administration, which in 1989 objected to certain aspects of its advertising campaign.

Appendix 13.1

Scale Economies in Brewing

It is widely accepted among industry experts that substantial economies exist in the brewing industry and that the minimum efficient scale of operation has increased steadily over the past generation. Influential in forming this view, at least among U.S. observers, was the observation that the major U.S. brewers began in the mid-1960s to construct new breweries that were more than twice as large as any then existing. Empirical estimates of m.e.s., based inter alia on engineering studies carried out in the 1970s, indicated a range of m.e.s. values that were very high compared to the prevailing size distribution. Reviews of U.S. studies will be found in FTC 1978 and Greer 1981. Elzinga, for example, in studying the U.S. industry, finds a sharp decline in cost up to a level of capacity of 1.5 million hectoliters/year, and a slower rate of decline up to 5 million hectoliters/year (Elzinga 1982, Marfels 1974). Similar results have been reported for the United Kingdom by Cockerill (1977).

It is interesting to use these figures to compare breweries found in the EEC with those in the United States. (Average output per plant for individual EEC countries is shown in table 13.1.1.)

In 1980, only 4.5% of European breweries had capacity in excess of 1 million hectoliters/year, while only 0.3% had a capacity exceeding 5 million hectoliters/year. For the United States, the corresponding figures are substantially higher: 59% had capacity exceeding 1.2 million hectoliters/year, and 27% had capacity in excess of 4.7 million hectoliters/year. A dividing line, often used to classify plant size, is a figure of 0.5 million hectoliters/year. A breakdown of plant size using this benchmark is shown in table 13.1.1.

The source of these scale economies is discussed at length in FTC 1978, which also presents detailed evidence provided by Schlitz, based on its own experience during the 1960s and 1970s. The FTC report, citing (unpublished) evidence by Scherer, identifies the main sources of the change in m.e.s. that began during the 1960s with technological improvements in the packaging process. The new generation of canning and bottling lines operated at much faster speeds than had been possible, and a greater throughput was needed to keep such a line

Table 13.1.1

Mean plant size and productivity in the beer industry by country and for the EEC as a whole

	Scale of Production		Productivity	
	Output per plant (1,000 hectoliters/year)		Output per employee	
	1970	1980	1970	1980
Germany	48	68	929	1,338
United Kingdom	312	457	608	982
France	178	339	1,186	1,988
Italy	157	286	903	2,477
EEC	83	130	810	1,207

Sources: various; see Marfels 1984.

Table 13.1.2

Large beer plants in the EEC (capacity exceeding 500,000 hectoliters/annum)

	Number of large plants		% of plants that are large		% of beer output from large plants		Average output of large plants (1,000 hectoliters/year)	
	1970	1980	1970	1980	1970	1980	1970	1980
Germany	32	48	2	4	34	51	916	972
United Kingdom	69[a]	44[a,b]	39	31	76	75	690	1,102
France	13	10	11	15	48	72	743	1,572
Italy	1	6	3	20	11	43	637	616
EEC	128	148	5	8	49	64	786	1,013

a. Total for the Big Seven.
b. Estimate.
Sources: various; see Marfels 1984.

operating at full capacity. A second important contribution to the rise in m.e.s., emphasized by Schlitz, related to the introduction of highly capital-intensive automated production processes.

The presence of multiplant operation provides indirect evidence on the importance of scale economies relative to transportation costs—which in the case of beer are quite substantial. In the United States, the average company operated 2.1 breweries; the market leader Anheuser-Busch operated ten breweries in 1980, each with a capacity exceeding 1 million hectoliters/year. In Europe, on the other hand, the average company operated 1.16 breweries in 1980.[1]

In view of the emphasis placed by Schlitz on the tendency for automation to increase m.e.s. during the 1960s, it is interesting to compare current conventional wisdom in the U.S. industry with the recent experience of Japanese brewers. During the 1980s, some Japanese brewers have found that high levels of efficiency can be attained in relatively small, highly automated, plants.

Japan's leading brewer, Kirin, with a 1984 output of 2.9 million hectoliters, operates no fewer than fourteen plants. The company operates at the forefront of beer-production technology, retiring old plants and building new ones that embody best-practice technology. Its new plants span a wide range of scales; its Sendai brewery, opened in 1983, had an annual capacity of 24 million hectoliters. Its newest brewery, on Hokkaido, has a capacity of only 0.5 million hectoliters. Kirin sees the attractiveness of such plants in terms of the higher efficiency achieved through incorporating a very high degree of automation, while, by scattering its fourteen plants across the country, Kirin enjoys relatively low distribution costs in a business where daily delivery from factory to regional wholesalers is the norm. This view as to the most efficient pattern of production contrasts remarkably with the current conventional wisdom in the U.S. industry.

---

1. Such considerations apart, economies of multiplant operation appear to be very limited. The only substantial contribution identified by Scherer et al. in their influential study was associated with the fact that a brewer selling across the entire United States enjoyed an advantage in creating a generally known brand image. This factor, as Greer (1981) remarks, is not, however, best thought of as an advantage deriving from multiplant operation per se. In our analysis, it is simply an aspect of the endogenous sunk cost mechanism.

Appendix 13.2

The Beer Industry

In this appendix, the evolution of the beer market in the United Kingdom and Germany is described in detail. A short description of the French, Japanese, and Italian markets is also included.

The United Kingdom

The pattern of market shares in U.K. brewing is rather different from that in the other countries studied here . The so-called Big Six brewers dominate the market, capturing 80% of total sales. Yet, in contrast to the other countries, none of the majors has succeeded in establishing a preeminent position. The role of advertising is very limited, while the drive toward dominance via horizontal merger has been muted by the cautious attitude of the U.K. Monopolies and Mergers Commission.

Two features of the U.K. beer market have played a key role in determining the way in which the industry has developed. The first is the "tied house" system under which the majority of "on-premise" consumption is accounted for by outlets owned by the major brewers. The importance of this factor in turn follows from the licensing laws, which limit the entry of new outlets. The second key feature of the U.K. market is that these on-premise sales make up a quite unusually high proportion of total sales (85%). These two features have molded the structure of the industry since the turn of the century.[1] In terms of our analysis, the ownership of most retail outlets by a small number of leading producers should be expected to modify the development of structure in certain ways.

1. In 1989, a report by the Monopolies and Mergers Commission challenged the tied house system; but a massive newspaper advertising campaign by the industry, focusing on the claim that the abolition of the tied house system would destroy the character of the British pub, was surprisingly successful in leading the authorities to limit the impact of these recommendations.

• There is limited scope for raising market share via price competition, as a large fraction of consumers patronize their local establishment. This tends to lead to high unit margins in on-premise sales.

• Because of the limited scope for raising market share, there is relatively little to be gained from expensive advertising campaigns. Advertising in general remains low by U.S. standards (see chapter 4, table 4.4).

• The main scope for expansion under such circumstances lies in acquiring rival brewers and so obtaining access to their retail outlets. This process began early in the history of the U.K. industry, immediately following the tightening of the licensing restrictions that limited the total number of retail outlets—a period around the turn of the century that industry historians label the "brewers' wars." The upshot of this process was the virtual domination of the retail trade by the major brewers (who owned 95% of British pubs by 1950, for example).

Once such a process has run its course, industry structure is effectively frozen, unless horizontal mergers are permitted. The attitude of the U.K. authorities on this score has been somewhat cautious. The result has been that certain mergers have been forbidden in recent years on the grounds that they were not in the public interest. In other words, the authorities have judged that the scale of operation already reached in the U.K. industry is sufficiently high that it cannot be judged a bar to productive efficiency. Indeed, by European Community standards, the U.K. industry is marked by a relatively high average scale of production; the average plant had a capacity of just below the 0.5 million hectoliters per year identified by Elzinga (1982) as the minimum efficient scale. The average EC plant was about one-quarter of this scale.

The Development of the Tied House System
Throughout the nineteenth century, the brewing industry in most countries underwent a gradual transformation as the small local brewer gave way to the large industrial concern.[2] In 1800, the London beer market was dominated by twelve brewers, many of whom had a strong tied trade with landlords to whom they extended considerable credit in return for exclusive supply rights. But from 1830 to 1869, a relaxation in the law allowed licenses to be freely purchased for a small fee, and the market value of existing licenses dwindled to the point that many were simply abandoned. But from the 1870s onward, the growth of the temperance movement led to increased pressure for a tightening in the law, while the restoration of magistrates' powers over the issuing of licenses from 1869 opened the possibility of restricting entry to the retail trade.

The turning point in the story, however, as Vaizey (1960) notes, came in 1886 when Baring's made a £6 million issue of stock in Guinness. The Dublin-based company had built up a large export business in England, so that Guinness had become a household name; its issue was subscribed many times over, and other

2. This section draws on Vaizey's (1960) excellent history of the U.K. brewing industry from 1886 to 1951.

leading brewers were quick to follow its example. By the end of 1890 there were eighty-seven publicly quoted brewing firms; brewing shares traded well above par and paid dividends of 5% or more.

At this point the scramble for tied houses began. As Vaizey (1960, p. 10) describes it,

> The reasons for the scramble, once it began, were obviously the fear of exclusion from existing or potential markets as rivals bought tied houses. The basis for the original impetus may have been the need for larger markets to absorb the bigger output achieved by modernization. Although nationally the rise was only a third of the existing proportion of tied property, the expansion of the tie by some companies was remarkable. Ansell's of Birmingham had 118 houses by 1890, and increased this by several hundreds in a few years. Burton Brewery Company bought fifty-two houses in 1889 alone. Watney's, Reid's, Barclay, Perkins, Allsopp's and the City of London were among many companies which bid against each other; the price of licensed property doubled and even trebled in the face of this competitive buying and the gradual restriction in the supply of licences.

These purchases of outlets were accompanied by acquisitions and amalgamations of independent brewers, a process that lasted until the turn of the century. Some key amalgamations of larger brewers also occurred, forming the nucleus of some of the industry's leading firms today. In 1899, for example, Watney and Co. Ltd. amalgamated with Combe and Co. Ltd. and Reid's Brewery Co. Ltd. and floated £15 million in public shares and debentures; "this was £6 million more than the combined value of the three businesses before flotation, and the watered capital was based entirely on inflated tied house prices" (Vaizey, 1961, p. 13).

The scramble for tied houses, as might be expected, led to some overshooting, as firms that had embarked too late on the process overextended themselves. For some, such as Allsopp's, it brought serious losses. By 1900, the pace had slowed greatly, and the industry passed through a decade of stability. By 1913, however, the proportion of tied houses had increased to 95%, as compared with a figure of around 70% in 1886.[3]

The war brought stricter licensing laws, diluted beer, and increased tax levies, all of which remained intact during the interwar years, and beer production never regained its 1913 levels. The effects of falling output levels on the major brewers were accentuated by the rising sales of beer through "working man's clubs," many of which bought their own breweries. These pressures led to further amalgamations as several major regional brewers extended their bases. On the other hand, beer advertising was introduced to the United Kingdom, in 1929 by Guinness, the one major brewer to stand outside the tied house system, a departure that in turn prompted a wave of generic ("beer is good for you") advertising by the Brewers' Society. Throughout the postwar years, the growth of advertising was closely associated with the rising popularity of bottled

---

3. There was little price competition in the period; "the price of beer was a conventional one; at 2d a pint the possibility of variation was not great, and there were never any variations in the costs of materials or duty sufficient to lead to a rise in price of beer" (Vaizey 1960, p. 17).

beer, which required careful brewing and in which the larger firms enjoyed a technical advantage over the small local brewer. Vaizey records the fact that, in 1952, the large national brewers had about 80% of all press advertising for beer. By that date, the number of brewers, which had fallen from over 16,000 in 1881 to less than 3,000 in 1920,[4] had declined further to around 540 (Vaizey 1960). Of these, 150 or so were small noncommercial plants. The remaining 390 or so breweries were owned by 310 independent firms, many of which operated one or more subsidiaries. About one-third of beer production was accounted for by fifty-two large establishments (those employing over 300 persons). Up to 1952, however, the level of concentration remained moderate. The pattern of shares to which the industry had converged, in the scramble for retail outlets, changed only slowly via a sequence of mergers and acquisitions. Over the intervening generation, the industry's development has been driven by the interplay of scale economies, advertising, and—crucially—a renewed scramble for outlets via mergers and acquisitions.

Consolidation by Merger
A Monopolies Commission investigation in 1969 remarked on the role of the tied house system in creating incentives to expand by merger and acquisition. They found

> that competition among brewers principally takes the form of competition to acquire captive portions of the retail market and to improve the amenities of their captive outlets; that as a result the retail trade is generally more uncompetitive than it would be in any event in conditions of restrictive licensing; and that, in particular, in the on-licensed retail trade price competition is practically absent and licensees tend to conform to a type which is content to avoid active competition. (MC 1969, p. 113)

They further noted the dual effects of tying; on the one hand it allowed inefficient firms to remain solvent, while on the other hand, it provided incentives to more efficient firms to take these over simply to capture their outlets.[5]

---

4. As measured by the number of "brewing for ale" licenses issued. See Monopolies Commission 1969.
5. As the report remarks,

> In one sense it might be said that ownership of tied houses on the part of brewers with inefficient or high-cost brewing capacity has provided an incentive to concentration of production; the exapanding brewers have bought up complete businesses for the sake of the additional captive outlets and closed down the inefficient plant as a result. But it would not have been necessary for them to buy inefficient or high-cost breweries at all, or breweries not required after the take-over, if these had not had tied houses attached to them. Moreover, the ownership of tied houses has, in itself, afforded the less efficient brewers some protection. The brewers themselves have told us that the tied house system has allowed a number of small brewers who could not otherwise have survived to co-exist with the large brewers. We think that this is true and it suggests that concentration of brewing capacity, and the elimination of the less efficient brewers, have not proceeded as far or as fast as they would have done if a large part of the industry had not already been vertically integrated.

By the time of the 1969 report, the industry had arrived at its modern pattern through a series of mergers in the 1950s and 1960s, and the Big Seven dominated the industry with over 72% of U.K. production (today the Big Six account for about 80%). Ind Coope had merged with Taylor Walker and Ansells to form Allied Breweries, now part of Allied Lyons PLC. On the eve of the 1967 report, Bass Mitchells and Butler Ltd. merged with Charrington Ltd. to form the new ' industry leader, Bass Charrington Ltd. (now Bass PLC).

Over the past twenty years, a series of further consolidations has brought the industry to the point where U.K. restraints on horizontal mergers constitute a serious bar to any major advances in concentration. Watney Mann and Truman, Hanbury and Buxton were acquired by Grand Metropolitan, one of a number of non-beer firms to enter the industry over the period. Whitbread continued a long-standing process of building up an "umbrella" over a series of smaller breweries, in which it holds a (minority or majority) stake.[6]

The industry is now dominated by the Big Six, which together accounted for 78% of industry sales in 1985. No one of the six, however, has succeeded in achieving a preeminent position (see market share table M20 in appendix 1).

The Rise of Lager and the Role of Advertising
The forms of beer that have traditionally dominated the U.K. market are not typical of those popular in the other countries studied here. The leading type, "bitter," is a beer brewed using a top-fermenting strain of yeast. Bitter and its variants ("ales"), together with "stouts" (made from roasted barley) dominated the U.K. market until quite recently. Bottom-fermented "lager-type" beers, which dominate beer sales in the other five countries, accounted for only 3% of the U.K. market twenty years ago. Their gradual growth over the intervening period, however, brought them level with bitter by the early 1980s (31% of 1982 sales, as against 33% for bitter).

Advertising played a very modest role within the U.K. industry up to the early 1970s, and this can in large part be attributed to the fact that 82% of U.K. beer sales are consumed on-premises, and 79% of such sales were made through premises that were tied to particular brewers (Monopolies and Mergers Commission 1989).[7] The only brewer that advertised heavily was Guinness, a company that was unusual in that it had no tied outlets. From the

---

6. Given the difficulties in expanding within the beer market, the majors have in recent years begun to diversify more heavily outside the industry, particularly in the wines and spirits area. In 1986, Grand Metropolitan acquired Heublen, the wines and spirits division of RJR Nabisco, as well as acquiring a premium brewer, Ruddles Brewery, which has now launched a £1.3 million advertising campaign for its "country premium bitter." Allied Lyons acquired a 51% stake in Hiram Walker, whose better-known brands include Ballantine, Tia Maria, and Courvoisier. Guinness, which retains a 2% share in the beer market, became, with its acquisition of Distillers, the second largest company involved in the U.K. beer industry.

7. Figures based on MMC 1989, table 2.17, p. 32. The proportion of tied premises had fallen to 57% in 1985, but these premises accounted for four-fifths of total on-premises sales at that date.

early 1970s onward, however, as the lager segment of the market grew, the U.K. brewers—which produced most of the U.K.'s lager under license from foreign firms—began to promote their products as national brands. It has been argued on a number of grounds that the scope for increasing share through advertising in this market segment is greater than in the traditional ales segment. The reasons adduced include the fact that

(a) Most tied houses do stock some beers other than those produced by the brewery to which they are tied, and "guest beers" include a disproportionate share of lagers.[8]

(b) In the relatively small off-premises segment, where the tie is relatively unimportant, lager represents a much higher proportion of sales than it does in the on-premises segment. (Off-license sales accounted for 25% of all lager sold in 1985, but for only 15% of sales of ales.)

(c) The age distribution of lager drinkers is heavily biased toward younger consumers. Some commentators see this as being relevant; it can be argued that younger consumers are more responsive to national brand advertising, but there seems to be little hard evidence for this.[9]

(d) The Monopolies and Mergers Commission (1989) suggested a further factor:

Different approaches have generally been adopted for ale and lager. Ale is a mature product with a traditional background. Attempts to market national brands of ale in the 1970s ... were generally unsuccessful. Since that time the national branding of ales has been greatly reduced and brands are now offered that stress their local origins even if, as in the case of some large brewers, they are produced at breweries many miles away from their original home.... Lager, however, has grown to prominence by means of a strategy of national branding enhanced by major advertising campaigns, with consumers generally demanding products that have a national credibility and often an international origin, although there have been successful local and regional lagers not stressing international origins. Indeed some lager has been promoted on the base of being a "world brand." Stout has been marketed in a manner similar to lager. (MMC 1989, p. 19)

Be that as it may, the lager segment of the U.K. market has attracted much more advertising than the traditional segment. Guinness was the most heavily advertised U.K. beer, as it had been for decades, but the remaining nine of the ten most heavily advertised brands were all lagers (see table 13.2.1). As the lager

---

8. The Monopolies and Mergers Commission Report of 1989 reported that three-quarters of the tied outlets they surveyed stocked at least one beer not supplied by the brewer to which they were tied; but these "guest beers" were more often lagers. The commission asked the landlords of tied houses whether they would like to sell more guest beers; two-thirds of those questioned indicated they would like to do so. Fifty-seven percent of those cited the fact that the brewer would not permit such sales as the reason for not offering more guest beers.

9. In 1987, consumers under thirty-five accounted for 51% of all beer consumption, but for 69% of draught lager sales.

Table 13.2.1
Advertising outlays on lager in the United Kingdom

	Share of total beer sales (%)	Share of total beer advertising (%)
1967	4	14
1987	45	67

Source: Author's estimates based on MEAL.

segment has grown, the advertising levels in the industry—though still very modest by U.S. standards—have grown too.

Lager prices are higher than those of other beers, to an extent that is not explicable by differences in production cost. In the off-premises trade, however, where the tie is much less important and competition is consequently more effective, this price differential is lower—though a subcategory of premium lagers is the highest-price beer category in the off-license trade (Monopolies and Mergers Commission 1989, paragraph 2.219).[10]

The German Beer Market

The German market is the most striking outlier among the several cases examined. Of the 1,200 or so breweries operating in Germany, over 800 are found in Bavaria alone. The south German market is highly fragmented, the typical brewery being a small family-owned concern, selling beer on its own premises or in its immediate vicinity and brewing less than 20,000 liters a year. The north German market, on the other hand, is much closer in structure to the other markets examined here. A wave of mergers in the late 1960s and early 1970s played an important role in fostering the emergence of three major groups, which together account for somewhat over 30% of Germany's total beer sales— and a much higher proportion of sales within the north German market. The second peculiarity of the German market relates to the relatively high number of beer types; the market is a highly segmented one, and—within north Germany at least—a relatively low level of aggregate concentration may conceal substantially higher levels of concentration within certain market segments.

Market Segmentation
"Pils"-type beers are the most popular throughout Germany, but especially within Nord Rhein-Westphalia, where one-third of Germany's beer is consumed. Within Nord Rhein-Westphalia, other major types include "Alt" (similar to British ale) and Kölsch, a product peculiar to the Cologne area, in which

---

10. The sales concentration ratio is lower for standard lagers in the off-premises trade than it is for beers generally, but is very high in the case of premium lagers. Chilvers (1989) cites brand shares for both categories in the off-premises segment. The four leading brands account for 33% of all sales of standard lager, while the four leading premium brands account for 59.5% of sales of all premium brands.

it constitutes a major submarket. The regional nature of these latter types is evident; Kölsch and Alt account for a mere 3.6% and 2% of total German consumption, respectively, but for 13% and 8% in Nord Rhein-Westphalia. In the south, there are a large number of regional specialities, including "Hell" (similar to lager) and "Weissbier," a pale, wheat-based beer.

Of ten major categories that together account for 95% of total sales in 1984, Pils accounted for 52%, Export for 18%, Hell for 7%, and Alt for 6%; each of the others account for less than 5% of the sales (*Marketing in Europe* 1986). Within major beer types, the market can be further segmented by price and quality. Within the Pils market—apart from a small specialty segment—there are three major categories:

· "Premium" brands account for 40% of Pils sales. There are high-quality beers, which generally enjoy advertising support.

· "Konsumbier" types are midprice beers, typically the regular brands of medium to small regional breweries. They are not heavily advertised, and sales tend to be confined to the locality of the brewery.

· "Billig" or "cheap" beers, so called because of their regular use as special offers or loss-leaders by supermarket chains, are of two kinds. Some medium-sized brewers specialize in offering such beers; they sell purely on price and receive no advertising or promotional support. This type of beer is also sold by some of the larger breweries, which fill their production capacity by marketing high-quality Pils beers at prices close to short marginal cost, though not under their own brand name.

As for the smaller brewer, none can compete in the price-sensitive "billig" segment. Here, all producers have capacity exceeding 200,000 hectoliters/year (Schwalbach and Müller 1984). The small brewer depends on a local reputation for quality that, without advertising support, allows him to sell in the midprice range, at which he can cover costs.

Market Size and the Scale of Breweries
Beer output rose steadily in Germany from 1950 to 1976, as per capita consumption increased from 35.6 liters/year to its peak of 150.9 liters in the latter year. Over the succeeding decade, however, this trend was reversed. While per capita consumption of beer remains high in Germany, the decline in demand since the mid-1970s has led to a situation of overcapacity (of the order of 15% or more, according to industry sources).

Overcapacity has fuelled increasingly tough price competition in the off-premises sector. Between 1980 and 1985, beer prices rose by less than 15%, while the retail price index rose by 21%. The widening disparity between off- and on-premises prices has caused a slow rise in the share of off-premises beer. In the period 1980–1985, on-premises sales accounted for slightly less than 10% of total sales, and the on-premises share of bottled beer sales fell from 12% in 1981 to 11% in 1985.

The size distribution of breweries has changed gradually over the same period. In 1962, only sixteen breweries had a capacity exceeding 500,000 hectoliters/year; in 1984, there were forty-seven breweries of that size. Meanwhile, the gradual exit of small breweries reduced the total number of (commercial) breweries from 2,155 in 1962 to little over 1,000 by the mid-1980s. The forty-seven large breweries, operating with a capacity of half a million hectoliters/year, accounted for 54% of German beer production in 1984; at the other end of the scale, the 798 small breweries with a capacity below 30,000 hectoliters/year produced only 7% of total output (Verlagsgrüppe Bauer 1987).

Concentration levels have risen substantially since the 1960s (see table 13.2.2.) Research by Schwalbach and Müller (1984) has shown that virtually all of the increase derives from mergers, the most important jump in concentration being associated with a series of mergers during the period 1965–1971.

In that period, the present-day leadership structure emerged. The single most important event concerned a series of acquisitions by a Munich-based bank, the Bayerische Hypotheken und Wechselbank AG (the "Hypo-Bank"). The Hypo-Bank already ranked as the industry's fifth most important concern; its holdings in the brewing industry amounted to a total of just below 2% of total output. Its key move lay in bringing together the industry's second and third firms, Dortmunder Union and Schultheiss, thus making the Hypo-Bank the new market leader (table 13.2.3).

Table 13.2.2
Four- and eight-firm concentration ratios for the German beer industry

	C_4 (%)	C_8 (%)
1958	11.8	19.6
1965	12.9	20.9
1971	33.6	41.5
1974	37.8	45.2
1979	34.3	43.6

Source: Schwalbach and Müller 1984.

Table 13.2.3
Market shares of the four leading German beer concerns, 1963–1979

Market shares (%)

1963		1971		1979	
Oetker	4.4	Hypo-Bank	12.5	Hypo-Bank	15.4
Dortmunder Union	4.0	Reemtsma	10.7	Reemtsma	7.6
Schultheiss	2.4	Oetker	7.7	Oetker	7.3
Dortmunder Actien	2.2	Holsten	2.7	Holsten	3.9

Source: Schwalbach and Müller 1984.

The second major force to emerge in the 1965–1971 period was the cigarette and coffee concern Reemtsma, which became the industry's second-largest firm. Reemtsma controls three of Germany's thirty largest breweries: Bavaria-St. Pauli Brauerei AG, Hannen Brauerei GmbH, and Brau AG. Oetker, a large diversified food and drink producer, hitherto the largest firm in the industry, fell to the third position. Oetker owns two of the three largest German breweries: Binding Brauerei AG and Dortmunder Actien Brauerei. (The largest of the German breweries, Beck und Co., is an independent.) No other concern controls more than 5% of output.

The sudden rise in merger activity in the late 1960s and early 1970s was followed by a decade of relative stability. The three majors, far from gaining further ground, actually weakened—Oetker and Reemtsma only marginally, the Hypo-Bank quite substantially. (See market share table M20 in appendix 1.)

Marketing, Advertising, and National Brands
Many of the early mergers failed to generate the hoped-for results. With the wisdom of hindsight, it is possible to identify one factor that appears to be of relevance. The key (Hypo-Bank led) merger between Dortmunder Union and Schultheiss aimed primarily at cost reductions achievable through rationalization on the production side. On the marketing side, the idea was to build up one brand at the expense of the other. As it happened, the combined sales steadily declined relative to the sum of the individual market shares of the companies acquired. In the case of those, like Oetker, that have been more successful in their acquisition strategy, the emphasis has been on continuing to market and support all brands acquired, while still rationalizing through closing down the breweries purchased and shifting production to other Oetker sites.

The experience of the 1970s appears to have convinced most German brewers that success in expansion-by-acquisition is most easily achieved through a policy of the latter kind. Recent successful acquisitions have been based on a strategy of building upon the good will associated with the long-standing image of the acquired brand. Indeed, within the German market, premium status is to a large degree associated with production at a well-known and long-established brewery.[11]

The other side of this coin relates to the noticeable failure by any of the German brewers to successfully establish a national brand enjoying strong

---

11. Dortmunder Union, for example, more recently acquired Iserlohner, a specialty beer from the Saarland region. The company intended, initially, to shift production away from the Iserlohner brewer. In the event, however, it continued production on the old site, as part of its strategy of building up the brand's premium image. The same pattern can be seen in the recent acquisition by Wicküler, one of Germany's top-ten brewers, of Sion—a small, private brewery, well established as a premium producer of the local Cologne speciality, Kölsch. Wicküler's acquisition has left the production side unaffected, and the former owner remains involved, dealing with the sales side of the business. As a result, Wicküler has become the only major brewer with a presence in the premium end of the Kölsch market.

market penetration across the country—a fact that stands in sharp contrast to U.S. experience. The majors have learned rather to advance through acquiring a portfolio of small, premium brands, carefully retaining the identity of each.[12]

Now it is true in all countries, to a greater or lesser degree, that leading brewers find it worthwhile to offer various identifiable brands, each targeted at a distinct group of consumers. What makes the German market different is the degree to which premium status is identified with long-existing breweries, generally of small or medium size. The image most closely correlated with this in the United States, for example, is arguably that of the new, small, "boutique" breweries, whose recent success has not even begun to impinge significantly on the majors. In the United Kingdom a more precise equivalent is the return to "real ale"—a movement to which the majors belatedly responded, by acquiring and building up small, long-established local breweries.

The difference in perception regarding what constitutes premium status has clear implications for the economics of beer advertising. The scale economies achievable in promoting the Budweiser name in the United States cannot be duplicated if expenditure must be split among many brands, each promoted in isolation. And yet, this latter pattern appears to be increasingly the norm in the German industry. Wicküler, for example, recently revamped its product line, introducing new, different names for several of its beer types and simultaneously raising price.[13]

Nonetheless, a small number of beers enjoy a high level of brand awareness, at least in the premium Pils market, a sector that accounts for one-fifth of German beer sales, carries high margins, and receives a disproportionate share of advertising support. In this segment, the only brands with a segment share exceeding 10% in 1984 were König Pilsner (25%), Bitburger (19%), Warsteiner (18%), and Krombacher (13%). Some—though not all—of these enjoy a high level of brand recognition among consumers. A survey reported by Springer-Verlag for 1984 gave the percentage of adults familiar with various premium Pils brand names; Beck's Bier scored 69% and Bitburger Pils, 55%. Beck's Bier, the most highly visible on export markets, scored highest, at 69%, despite its relatively small domestic share. A number of other beers, whose share of sales in this segment were no more than 5%, still commanded wide recognition: Furstenburg Pilsner and Jever Pils, for example, were both familiar to about 40% of consumers.

A second factor that has limited the rise of advertising expenditures lies in the extent of tied sales. For the smallest brewers, their premises may provide an

---

12. Schwalbach and Müller (1984) emphasize several causes of poor postmerger performance. Apart from considerations of rationalization in production and brand management, they also identify managerial weaknesses and a failure to coordinate the two firms effectively following the merger.

13. In this respect, advertising in the German beer industry appears to share some characteristics of the RTE cereals market. As noted in chapter 8, such brand-focused advertising admits the possibility of a more fragmented structure in the absence of first-mover advantages or large-scale economies in production.

outlet for a significant share of their modest production levels. Even for medium-sized brewers, one of their most valuable assets may be in their supply links: these often take the form of very long-term contracts (twelve years in many cases). The maximum contract length is twenty years, and contracts may either wholly or partially exclude sales of rival brewers' products. Some debate exists as to the degree of such tying, with brewers citing a figure of 50%, and the outlets themselves citing 70%–80% (Schwalbach and Müller 1984). A major motive for acquisition, in the German market, lies in capturing these "Gastronomie" outlets (premises serving both beer and food). Acquiring a brewery becomes more worthwhile the wider its net—and so the main targets for acquisition are not the smallest breweries but those of medium scale.

A further factor inhibiting the effectiveness of advertising relates to restrictions on television advertising that limit the times at which beer may be advertised. This has resulted in a relatively high concentration of advertising expenditures on print media. In 1985, television took only 16% of expenditures, radio took 14%, and the remaining 70% was divided between magazines, newspapers, and the trade press. (Some observers forecast that the development of private television stations will ease advertising restrictions and may lead to a significant shift in this ratio.)

The Decline in Profitability

The increasing intensity of price competition, linked with the industry's over-capacity, has resulted in steadily falling profits. Schwalbach (1985) calculates that the post-tax rate of return on assets has fallen from 6.6% in 1961 to 3.9% in 1981, as compared with a much smaller decline for all manufacturing industry over the same period (from 4.9% to 3.9%). The larger firms, scale economies notwithstanding, did not fare better than average: the figures for the sixty-nine major brewers identified by Schwalbach show a slightly greater fall than that suffered by brewers generally (from 6.8% to 3.7%). Some of the largest brewers did, however, fare relatively well. Schwalbach's analysis suggests that the relatively successful large brewers were, on the whole, those who (inter alia) advertised more heavily and diversified more successfully into the (relatively attractive) soft drinks area. Indeed, as Schwalbach and Müller (1984) note, while the market share of the Big Three has fallen slightly in recent years, the next-largest tier of brewers have strengthened their overall share as price and advertising competition have intensified. It is the third group of brewers—those in the 80,000–200,000 hectoliters/year range— that have suffered in this process. Indeed, but for long-term contracts with outlets, which have been a major stabilizing influence, a substantial exit of brewers would be likely to occur.

Foreign Competition

While Germany exports about 5% of its beer production, imports have, up to now, remained well under 1% of consumption. The limited degree of import penetration is often attributed to the German "Rheinheitsgebot," a sixteenth-century purity law that limits acceptable ingredients to malted barley, hops, yeast, and water. A recent EEC directive has found the law unacceptable, however, and much speculation exists within the industry as to whether or not this will lead to a surge in imports.

The purity law notwithstanding, a few well-known foreign beers have long been available in Germany, but have had little impact (they include Tuborg as well as a Czech-made Budweiser). The failure of foreign firms to gain a foothold in the past is widely attributed within the industry to their failure to secure "Gastronomie" outlets and to shortcomings in their marketing strategies—a fact emphasized by the minority of observers within the industry who feel that the ending of the Rheinheitsgebot may usher in a new phase in the development of the industry's structure.

France and Japan

The structure of the beer industry in both France and Japan has been primarily shaped by public policy, which favored a highly consolidated structure. In the case of Japan, a very concentrated structure has been maintained throughout the postwar period via a licensing system that limits entry. In France, policy initiatives have led to the dominance of the industry by two major brewing groups. In both countries, price competition is extremely muted (whether via overt price controls or tacit understandings), and advertising competition plays an important role. In Japan, advertising forms one strand in a complex and changing mix of marketing devices through which firms compete actively for market share. In France, on the other hand, the main focus of advertising effort lies in limiting the growing importance of high-image foreign beers. In neither case, however, did advertising play any part in the process that led to the currently high level of concentration in these industries.

The French Market
The French beer industry, the second smallest of those considered (table 13.2.4), is also one of the most highly concentrated. The number of brewers fell from almost 1,000 in 1937 to 86 by 1974. The number of firms has fallen over the

Table 13.2.4
Beer output by country, 1982

	1982 output (million hectoliters/year)
France	22
Germany	95
Italy	10
Japan	47
United Kingdom	60
United States	228

Table 13.2.5
Size distribution of beer producers in France and Germany

1981	France	Germany
Total number of firms	43	1,292
Number with production ≥ 500,000 hectoliters/year	7	46
Number with production ≤ 60,000 hectoliters/year	8	1,050

Source: Dafsa 1984.

past two decades from 122 in 1966 to 58 in 1974, and to 30 by the mid-1980s. This process has been accompanied by a steady shift in the size distribution of firms (table 13.2.5). Between 1966 and 1974, for example, the average output per brewery had risen from 130,000 hectoliters to 250,000—a figure far in excess of that found in most European countries (the corresponding figure for Germany was 52,000, while that for Belgium, 75,000).

But the most striking feature of this process of consolidation lies in the emergence of two major groups of breweries that now jointly account for three-quarters of French beer production. Among the factors underlying the relatively rapid rate of consolidation in the French industry over the past twenty years appear to have been:

• The imposition of price controls, which hold price increases below the rate of increase of raw materials at some periods, notably during the 1970s (*Agra-Alimentation* 1974).

• French producers suffered within the European market from their lack of an image as a beer producer comparable to that of Germany, Belgium, and the Netherlands. The export potential for French beer was consequently limited, and even though domestic consumption rose slowly in real terms, export penetration rose faster. Between 1964 and 1974, imports almost quadrupled (0.56 million hectoliters in 1964; 1.96 in 1974).

• The larger part of French beer sales (55%) is sold for home consumption, and of this some 30% is sold through supermarkets. Both of these features favor the well-established brands of the larger firms over the small local brewer.

All these factors led to increasing pressure on small and medium brewers, many of which were facing serious financial difficulties by the mid-1970s (*Agra-Alimentation* 1974).

But the single most striking difference between the French experience and that of the United States, the United Kingdom, and Germany lay in the view of the French authorities as to the efficiency case for mergers. This view was not specific to the beer industry but formed part of a general approach favoring consolidation across a range of industries, the better to meet competition within the EEC. This view was particularly persuasive in the case of the beer industry, however, given the relatively low level of total beer sales in France and the initially fragmented state of the industry.

The two major effects of this policy in favor of consolidation were

• the fostering of the development of BSN as France's leading food conglomerate as well as the country's leading brewing group;

• the permissive approach toward the formation, in 1984, of the new Sogebra group as a counterweight to BSN, whose share by then amounted to some 50% of French beer sales.

The origins of BSN's leading role in the French industry date back to 1972. BSN (Boussois-Souchon-Neuvesal), originally a plate glass maker whose interests had expanded into packaging and—via the Kronenbourg brewery—into the food and drink industry, took over the Sté Européenne de Brasseries in that year. The latter company operated twenty-three breweries and accounted for almost one-third of French beer sales (6 million hectoliters/year out of 19 million; corresponding to annual sales of 400 million FF out of an industry total of 1,300 million). Together with BSN's existing interests, this acquisition gave the group a 45% share in the domestic market and some 60% of French exports.

In the same year, BSN, encouraged by the French authorities, merged with the leading food group Gervais-Danone to form what the trade press described as the new "French Nestlé." Besides its position in the beer market, the group would also have a 30% share in the mineral water market, 70% of the baby food market, 35% of yogurts and desserts, 37% of fresh cheese, and 25% of prepared meals. Its beer output made it one of Europe's largest brewing groups, and it was hoped that the group would compete on equal terms with the European market leaders. From 1979 onward, BSN, through Kronenbourg, began to build up a sizable presence in other European markets. By 1982, it controlled Belgium's third-largest brewer and both Italy's and Spain's second-largest.

In the early 1970s, BSN's main competitors on the French market were Union de Brasseries, Société Alsacienne de Brasseries, Brasserie Pelforth, Brasserie Motte Cordonnier, and Grande Brasserie Moderne. Together with BSN, these five breweries accounted for 80% of beer sales, but each of these firms was extremely small in comparison with the industry leader.

In 1984 the French authorities approved a merger that led to the creation of a second pole within the French beer industry. This comprised the five breweries owned by the Société Générale de Brasseries, two owned by Pelforth, and Heineken's interest; in all, this amounted to a 25% share of the French market, as compared with BSN's 50% share. The breweries that remain outside these two groups are quite small; they include Brasseries du Pêcheur SA (whose output was 0.6 million hectoliters in 1984), Grande Brasserie Moderne SA (about 0.4 million), and Grande Brasserie Alsacienne d'Adelshoffen (0.3 million).

The advertising-sales ratio for the French industry is shown in table 13.2.7. The levels are comparable with those achieved in the United States throughout much of the period studied here, but advertising is not directed at gaining share from domestic rivals. Rather, it primarily represents a response to the increasing

Table 13.2.7
The advertising-sales ratio for the French beer industry

	1979	1980	1981	1982
Advertising-sales ratio	3.1	3.4	3.7	3.7

difficulties French brewers have experienced in recent years in retaining share against imported beers. The steady rise of imports, noted above, has led French firms to the view that efforts to improve the image of their offerings relative to German, Belgian, and Dutch beers is vital to the future of the domestic industry.

The Japanese Beer Industry
Japan is the fifth-largest beer producer in the world after the United States, West Germany, the Soviet Union, and the United Kingdom. As the industry began to develop in the 1870s, the number of brewers ran to about twenty, but this number gradually declined thereafter. Only two firms operated during the war; and in 1946, the larger of these, Dainihon-Beer, was broken up by the authorities into two independent companies, Asahi-Beer and Nippon-Beer. Only three new brewers were granted entry licenses in the succeeding years; the Sapporo brewery was established in 1949, and in 1957 Takara-Syruzo opened (the latter was acquired by Kirin in 1967). Finally, in 1963, Japan's oldest and largest distiller, Suntory, entered the beer market. Today, the big four (Kirin, Sapporo, Asahi, and Suntory) account for 99% of sales; only one further producer—the small local Orion brewery in Okinawa—is now in operation.

The striking absence of entry in a large and growing market is a direct outcome of government policy.[14] Foreign firms, moreover, have found market penetration very difficult; and those foreign beers currently available in Japan are marketed by the domestic brewers.[15] Alongside these restrictions on entry to the market is a strongly muted degree of price competition. Prices are not controlled, but they reflect an implicit understanding between the firms and the

---

14. The rationale sometimes cited for the government's apparent reluctance to allow (or encourage) entry is that beer tax is a major source of revenue and that this policy helps to maintain a large and stable flow of tax. It is not clear, however, that this is a convincing explanation.

15. Gaining adequate access to the channels of distribution seems to have been a major reason for the currently dominant practice of selling through one of the Big Four. By government regulation, beer is distributed only through wholesalers; some of these sell only for one brewer; others operate on a national basis, selling all four of the major brands. Gaining access to a sufficiently wide net of wholesalers appears to pose serious difficulties; Heineken, for example, was formerly distributed through Kokubu, but could only reach those retail outlets served by that wholesaler. Since 1984, however, Heineken has switched strategy and is now produced under license by Kirin. Suntory brews Budweiser under license from Anheuser-Busch. Other major beers are also distributed via domestic brewers: Sapporo imports Miller from the United States and Guinness from Ireland.

authorities. It is not surprising therefore that the industry is marked by intense nonprice competition for market share.

The shares of the three major producers in the first postwar decade were roughly equal; indeed, this reflected in part the outcome of a policy of rationing raw materials across producers. Since the mid-1950s, however, the main changes have been:

• There was slow but steady growth in the market share of Kirin, the current market leader. By the mid-1960s, Kirin accounted for half of all beer sales, and by the mid-1980s it accounted for almost two-thirds of total sales.

• Suntory entered the market in 1963, and drew level with Asahi in the mid-1980s.

• Over the same period, both Sapporo and Asahi have experienced a slow decline in share.

Over the past twenty years, the battle for market share has centered around a series of waves of innovations in both products and packaging. Throughout the early 1960s, the emphasis was on extending the range of offerings as firms sought out unoccupied niches.

In the early 1980s, Suntory, the smallest of the Big Four, sparked off a new round of competition by introducing a new range of uniquely packaged products (in animal shapes, etc.). The success of the new wave of packs was such as to induce the only setback to Kirin's market share in a decade. Kirin and the other brewers responded with similarly innovative offerings. Within a few years, however, the new packages fell out of fashion and were virtually nonexistent by 1986.

In the 1980s firms turned from packaging innovations to product innovations. Kirin, which had produced only regular (pasteurized) lager-type beer, introduced a wide range of new beer types (unpasteurized, "light", etc.). Its rivals responded in kind, but Kirin nonetheless recouped the loss in market share that it had experienced in the "packaging" episode of the 1970s.

Italy

The Italian industry is extremely small; total beer consumption in the mid-1980s was less than half that of France (table 13.2.4). Some thirteen companies were active in 1984, operating twenty-seven breweries. These domestic brands competed against more than 300 imported brands. The total share of imports stood at 16% in 1985; most of these imports came from other EC countries, West Germany and France being the main suppliers. The market has been growing slowly but steadily over the past decade; between 1974 and 1984, production rose by 25%, and this trend was maintained into the late 1980s.

The leading domestic producer, Peroni, retained a share slightly above 20% throughout the first half of the 1980s, and three other domestic firms (Dreher, Wuhrer, and Henninger) each had shares in the 8%–12% range. The most important foreign brewer in the market was Heineken, whose share in the early 1980s lay in the 3%–4% range. Most industry observers argued, in the mid-1980s, that the fragmented structure of the industry was unlikely to persist for much longer in the face of competition from leading EC brewers, which operated on a substantially larger scale than their Italian counterparts. By the late 1980s, indeed, the structure of the market had begun to alter substantially as a wave of consolidation began (see the market share table M20 in appendix 1). The industry currently appears to be in a transitional phase.

References

Market research reports, official publications, and company histories are listed separately on pages 542–550.

Adam, James S. (1977), *A Fell Fine Baker: The Story of United Biscuits*, London: Hutchinson Benham Ltd., for the company.

Anderson, Keith B., Michael P. Lynch, and Jonathan D. Ogur (1975), *The Sugar Industry*, Washington, D.C.: U.S. Federal Trade Commission.

Andres, Carl (1984), "Campbell Soup Company: R&D Profile," *Food Processing*, May.

Archibald, G. C. (1961), "Chamberlin versus Chicago," *Review of Economic Studies*, vol. 29, pp. 2–28.

Bain, Joe S. (1956), *Barriers to New Competition*, Cambridge, MA: Harvard University Press.

Bain, Joe S. (1966), *International Differences in Industrial Structure: Eight Nations in the 1950's*, CT: Greenwood Press.

Ballinger, Roy A. (1975), *A History of Sugar Marketing through 1974*, Agricultural Economic Report no. 382, Washington, D.C.: U.S. Department of Agriculture.

Baumol, William J., John C. Panzar, and Robert D. Willig (1982), *Contestable Markets and the Theory of Industry Structure*, San Diego: Harcourt Brace Jovanovich.

Baumol, William J., and Robert D. Willig (1981), "Fixed Costs, Sunk Costs, Entry Barriers and Sustainability of Monopoly," *Quarterly Journal of Economics*, vol. 46, pp. 405–431.

Bernadin, M. P. (1975), *Le Sucre (Documentation Pratique de CEDUS)*, Paris: CEDUS.

Bonanno, Giacomo (1985), *Topics in Oligopoly: Local Equilibria, Chocie of Quality, Entry Deterrence*, unpublished Ph.D. diss., University of London.

Bonanno, Giacomo (1987), "Product Differentiation and Entry Deterrence Revisited," *Review of Economic Studies*, vol. 54, pp. 37–46.

Börgers, Tilman (1985), "Existence of Sequential Entry Equilibrium in Product Differentiation Models," unpublished ms.

Börgers, Tilman (1987), *Extensions and Refinements of the Nash Equilibrium Concept*, unpublished Ph.D. diss., London University.

Braznell, William (1982), *California's Finest: The History of the Del Monte Corporation and the Del Monte Brand*: published by the Del Monte Corporation.

Bresnahan, Timothy F., and Peter C. Reiss (1990), "Entry in Monopoly Markets," *Review of Economic Studies*, forthcoming.

Broadbent, Simon (ed.) (1981), *Advertising Works: Papers from the IPA Advertising Effectiveness Awards*, London: Holt, Rheinhart and Winston.

Brugnoli, Aldo (1984), "La produzione e la distributione di surgelati," *Largo Consumo*, no. 4/1984.

Cahn, William (1969), *Out of the Cracker Barrel*, New York: Simon and Schuster.

Calvert, Albert Frederick (1913a), *A history of the Salt union; a record of 25 years of disunion and depreciation, compiled from official reports, with an introduction by Albert F. Calvert*, London: Effingham Wilson.

Calvert, Albert F. (1913b), *Salt in Cheshire*, London: Effingham Wilson.

Caves, Richard E. (1989), "International Differences in Industrial Organisation," in Richard Schmalensee and Robert Willig (eds.), *Handbook of Industrial Organisation*, Amsterdam: North Holland.

Chilvers, Lloyd (1989), *Drink in the UK: An Analysis of Alcoholic Drinks Markets and Distribution*, London: Economist Intelligence Unit.

Christensen, C. Roland (1977), "Note on the Soft Drink Industry in the United States," Harvard Business School Case Study no. 377–213.

Cockerill, A. (1977), "Economics of Scale, Industrial Structure and Efficiency," in A. P. Jacquemin and W. de Jong (eds.), *Welfare Aspects of Industrial Markets*, Leiden: H. E. Stenfert Kroese B. V.

Compagnie des Salines du Midi et des Salines de l'Est (1985), *Le Sel*, Presses Universitaires de France.

Connor, John M., Richard T. Rogers, Bruce W. Marion, and Willard F. Mueller (1985), *The Food Manufacturing Industries: Structure, Strategies, Performance and Policies*, Lexington, MA: Lexington Books.

Corley, T. A. B. (1972), *Huntley & Palmers of Reading 1822–1972: Quaker Enterprise in Biscuits*, London: Hutchinson.

Culbertson, John D., and Rosanna Mentzer Morrison (1983), "Economies of Scale Data for the Food Manufacturing Industries," Unpublished ms.

Dasgupta, P., and J. E. Stiglitz (1980), "Industrial Structure and the Nature of Innovative Activity," *Economic Journal*, vol. 90, pp. 266–293.

Dasgupta, P., and J. E. Stiglitz (1988), "Potential Competition, Actual Competition and Economic Welfare," *European Economic Review*, vol. 32, pp. 569–577.

D'Aspremont, C., J. Jaskold Gabszewicz, and J. F. Thisse (1979), "On Hotelling's 'Stability in Competition,'" *Econometrica*, vol. 47, pp. 1145–1170.

Davies, Stephen (1980), "Minimum Efficient Size and Seller Concentration: An Empirical Problem," *Journal of Industrial Economics*, vol. 28, pp. 287–302.

Dixit, A. K., and C. Shapiro (1986), "Entry Dynamics with Mixed Strategies," in L. G. Thomas (ed.), *Strategic Planning*, Lexington, MA: Lexington Books.

Dixit, A. K., and J. E. Stiglitz (1977), "Monopolistic Competition and Optimum Product Diversity," *American Economic Review*, vol. 67, pp. 297–308.

Dunne, T., M. J. Roberts, and L. Samuelson (1988), "Patterns of Firm Entry and Exit in U.S. Manufacturing," Working Paper, Pennsylvania State University.

Eichner, Alfred S. (1969), *The Emergence of Oligopoly*, Baltimore: John Hopkins University Press.

Elzinga, Kenneth G. (1982), "The Beer Industry" in W. Adams (ed.), *The Structure of American Industry* (6th ed.), New York: Macmillan.

Enrico, Roger (1986), *The Other Guy Blinked: How Pepsi Won the Cola Wars*, London: Bantam Books.

Evely, R., and I. M. D. Little (1960), *Concentration in British Industry*, Cambridge: Cambridge University Press.

Fenn, Dan H., Jr. (1971), *Continental Baking and the FTC*, Harvard Business School Case Study no. 9-371-528.

Ferguson, Paul R. (1988), *Industrial Economics: Issues and Perpectives*, London: Macmillan.

Fisher, R. A., and L. H. C. Tippett (1928), "Limiting forms of the frequency distributions of the largest or smallest member of a sample," *Proceedings of the Cambridge Philosophical Society*, vol. 24, pp. 180–190.

Fost, Carolyn Ann (1970), "The Salt Industry: A Case Study in the Evaluation of Public Policy," unpublished Ph.D. diss., Southern Illinois University.

Foster, Richard N. (1986), *Innovation: The Attacker's Advantage*, New York: Summit Books.

Friedman, James W. (1986), *Game Theory with Applications to Economics*, Oxford: Oxford University Press.

Friedman, Martin, and Bryan Savage (1987), "Geo. A. Hormel & Co.: New Products Company of the Year," *Processed Food* (New Products Annual).

Friedman, Milton (1912), *Essays in Positive Economics*, Chicago: University of Chicago Press.

Fudenberg, D., and J. Tirole (1985), "Preemption and Rent Equalisation in the Adoption of New Technology," *Review of Economic Studies*, vol. 52, pp. 383–401.

Gabszewicz, J. Jaskold, and J.-F. Thisse (1980), "Entry (and Exit) in a Differentiated Industry," *Journal of Economic Theory*, vol. 22, pp. 327–338.

Gabszewicz, J. Jaskold, Shaked, A., Sutton, J., and Thisse, J. F. (1981), "Price Competition among Differentiated Products: A Detailed Study of a Nash Equilibrium," ICERD Working Paper no. 37, London School of Economics.

George, Kenneth, and T. S. Ward (1975), *The Structure of Industry in the EEC*, Cambridge: Cambridge University Press.

Gould, Stephen Jay (1987), *An Urchin in the Storm*, New York: Norton.

Greer, Douglas F. (1970), "Product Differentiation and Concentration in the Brewing Industry," *Journal of Industrial Economics*, vol. 18, pp. 201–219.

Greer, Douglas F. (1973), "Some Case History Evidence on the Advertising-Concentration Relationship," *The Antitrust Bulletin*, vol. 38, pp. 307–332.

Greer, Douglas F. (1981), "The Causes of Concentration in US Brewing," *Quarterly Review of Economics and Business*, vol. 21, pp. 87–106.

Gumbel, E. J. (1958), *Statistics of Extremes*, New York: Columbia University Press.

Hammerstein, Peter (1989), "Biological Games," *European Economic Review*, vol. 33, pp. 635–644.

Hannah, Leslie, and John A. Kay (1977), *Concentration in Modern Industry: theory and measurement and the U.K. experience*, London: Macmillan.

Harris, Christopher (1985), "Existence and Characterization of Perfect Equilibrium in Games of Perfect Information," *Econometrica*, vol. 53, pp. 613–616.

Harris, Donald (1987), "DPP takes off with new technology," *Retail and Distribution Management*, March–April, pp. 9–12.

Hart, P. E., and R. Clark (1980), *Concentration in British Industry, 1935–75*, Cambridge: Cambridge University Press.

Hart, P. E., M. A. Utton, and G. Walshe (1973), *Mergers and Concentration in British Industry*, Cambridge: Cambridge University Press.

Hayenga, Marvin, V. James Rhodes, Jon A. Brandt, and Ronald E. Deiter (1985), *The U.S. Pork Sector: Changing Structure and Organisation*, Ames, IA: Iowa State University Press.

Headen, Robert S., and James W. McKie (1966), *The Structure, Conduct and Performance of the Breakfast Cereal Industry: 1954–64*, Cambridge, MA: Arthur D. Little Inc.

Hendricks, Kenneth, and Robert H. Porter (1988), "An Empirical Study of an Auction with Asymmetric Information," *American Economic Review*, vol. 14, pp. 301–314.

Hilke, John C., and Philip B. Nelson (1984), "Noisy Adertising and the Predation Rule in Antitrust Analysis," *American Economic Review (Papers and Proceedings)*, vol. 74, no. 2, pp. 367–371.

Hilke, John C., and Philip B. Nelson (1985), "A Note on the Economics of Network Television Adertising," FTC Working Paper no. 132.

Hilke, John C., and Philip B. Nelson (1986), "Retail Featuring as an Entry of Mobility Barrier in Manufacturing," FTC Working Paper no. 144.

Hilke, John C., and Philip B. Nelson (1987a), "Caveat Innovator: Strategic and Structural Characteristics of New Product Innovation," *Journal of Economic Behaviour and Organization*, vol. 8, pp. 213–229.

Hilke, John C., and Philip B. Nelson (1987b), "FTC v General Foods: The Newest Learning in Attempted Monopolisation Law," forthcoming in John Kwoka and Larry White (eds.), *The Antitrust Revolution*: Scott Foresman.

Hilliam, M. (1986), *Bakery and Cereal Products in the UK*, Leatherhead: Leatherhead Food R. A.

Hoffman, W. G. (1969) "100 years of the Margarine Industry," in J. H. van Stuyvenberg (ed.), *Margarine: An Economic, Social and Scientific History, 1869–1969*, Liverpool: Liverpool University Press.

Horowitz, Ira, and Ann R. Horowitz (1965), "Firms in a Declining Industry: The Brewing Case," *Journal of Industrial Economics*, vol. 13, pp. 129–153.

Hotelling, H. (1929), "Stability in Competition," *Economic Journal*, vol. 39, pp. 41–57.

Jenks, J. W. (1888), "The Michigan Salt Association," *Political Science Quarterly*, vol. 3, pp. 78–98.

Kaldor, N. (1950), "The Economic Aspects of Advertising," *Review of Studies*, vol. 38, p. 13.

Katz, Barbara G. (1978), "Territorial Exclusivity in the Soft Drink Industry," *Journal of Industrial Economics*, vol. 27, pp. 85–96.

Kelton, Christine M. L., and W. David Kelton (1982), "Advertising and Intra-industry Brand Shift in the US Brewing Industry," *Journal of Industrial Economics*, vol. XXX, pp. 293–303.

Kessides, Ioannis N. (1988), "Toward a Testable Model of Entry: A Study of the U.S. Manufacturing Industries," unpublished (University of Maryland).

Kostick, Dennis S. (1985), "Salt," *Mineral Yearbook 1985*, Washington, D.C.: U.S. Bureau of Mines.

Kreps, D., and R. Wilson (1982), "Reputation and Imperfect Information," *Journal of Economic Theory*, vol. 27, pp. 253–279.

Kreps, D. M., and J. A. Scheinkman (1983), "Quantity Precommitment and Bertrand Competition yield Cournot Outcomes," *Bell Journal of Economics*, vol. 14, pp. 326–337.

Lambin, Jean Jacques (1976), *Advertising, Competition and Market Conduct in Oligopoly over Time: An Econometric Investigation in Western European Countries*, Amsterdam: North Holland.

Lane, W. (1980), "Product Differentiation in a Market with Endogenous Sequential Entry," *Bell Journal of Economics*, vol. 11, pp. 237–260.

Marfels, Christian (1974), "A New Look at the Structure of Oligopoly," *Zeitschrift für die gesamte staat wissenschaft*, vol. 130, pp. 249–270.

Marfels, Christian (1984), *Concentration, Competition and Competitiveness in the Beverage Industry of the European Community*, Luxembourg: Commission of the European Communities.

Maunder, P. (1970), *The Bread Industry in the United Kingdom*, Nottingham: University of Nottingham (Dept. of Agricultural Economics).

Maynard Smith, J. (1982), *Evolution and the Theory of Games*, Cambridge: Cambridge University Press.

Messenger, Robert (1987a), "Meat Processors Fight Back!" *Processed Food*, April.

Messenger, Robert (1987b), "The Mysteries of M&M/Mars," *Prepared Foods*, May.

Messenger, Robert (1987c), "Consolidation Re-shapes industry," *Prepared Foods*, July.

Messenger, Robert (1987d), "Nestlé's Sweet Dreams: A Nightmare for Competitors," *Prepared Foods*, August.

Milgrom, P., and J. Roberts (1982), "Predation, Reputation and Entry," *Journal of Economic Theory*, vol. 27, pp. 280–312.

Morgan, Dan (1979), *Merchants of Grain*, London: Weidenfeld and Nicholson.

Mueller, Willard F., and Larry G. Hamm (1974), "Trends in Industrial Market Structure, 1947 to 1970," *Review of Economics and Statistics*, vol. 66, pp. 511–520.

Müller, J., and J. Schwalbach (1980), "Structural Change in West Germany's Brewing Industry: Some Efficiency Considerations," *Journal of Industrial Economics*, vol. 28, pp. 353–368.

Nelson, Phillip (1978), "Advertising as Information Once More," in David G. Tuerck (ed.), *Issues in Advertising*, Washington, D.C.: American Enterprise Institute.

Nelson, S., and D. Winter (1982), *An Evolutionary Theory of Economic Change*, Cambridge, MA: Harvard University Press.

Neven, D. (1985), "Two Stage (Perfect) Equilibrium in Hotelling's Model," *Journal of Industrial Economics*, vol. 33, pp. 317–326.

Norman, Donald A. (1975), *Structural Change and Performance in the US Brewery Industry*, unpublished Ph.D. diss., UCLA.

Oliver, Thomas (1986), *The Real Coke, The Real Story*, Random House.

Ornstein, Stanley I. (1977), *Industrial Concentration and Advertising Intensity*, Washington, D.C.: American Enterprise Institute.

Ornstein, Stanley I. (1981), "Antitrust policy and market force as determinants of Industry structure: case histories in beer and distilled spirits," *The Antitrust Bulletin*, Summer, pp. 281–313.

Ornstein, S. I., and S. Lustgarten (1978), "Advertising Intensity and Industrial Concentration—an empirical enquiry 1947–1967," in D. G. Tuerck (ed.), *Issues in Advertising*, Washington, D.C.: American Enterprise Institute.

Pakes, Ariel, and Neil Ericson (1987), "Empirical Implications of Alternative Models of Firm Dynamics," Working Paper, University of Wisconsin.

Palesy, Stephen R., and Walter J. Salmon (1978), "Planning at Pepsi," Harvard Business School Case Study no. 9-579-108.

Panzar, John C., and Robert D. Willig (1981), "Economies of Scope," *American Economic Review*, vol. 71, pp. 262–272.

Parravicini, Patrizia (1984), "La caratteristiche merceologiche degli alimenti surgelati," *Largo Consumo*, no. 4.

Parravicini, Patrizia (1986), "I piatti pronti surgelati e i precucinate: un'analisi merceologiche," *Largo Consumo*, no. 2.

Phlips, L. (1971), *Effects of Industrial Concentration: A Cross-Section Analysis for the Common Market*, Amsterdam: North Holland.

Prais, S. J. (1976), *The Evolution of Giant Firms in Britain*, Cambridge: Cambridge University Press.

Pryor, Frederick L. (1972), "An International Comparison of Concentration Ratios," *Review of Economics and Statistics*, vol. 54, pp. 130–140.

Rogers, Richart T. (1984), "Concentration Change in Food and Tobacco Product Classes, 1958–1977," Working Paper no. 74, Madison, WI: University of Wisconsin.

Sacchi, Pier Mario Curtz (1984), "Il mercato degli oli di semi e della margarina," *Inchiesta Food*, no. 7–8.

Samuelson, Paul (1947), *Foundations of Economic Analysis*, Cambridge, MA: Harvard University Press.

Scherer, Frederick M. (1980), *Industrial Market Structure and Economic Performance* (2nd ed.), Chicago: Rand McNally.

Scherer, Frederick M. (1982), "The Breakfast Cereal Industry," in W. Adams (ed.), *The Structure of American Industry* (6th ed.), New York: Macmillan.

Scherer, F. M. et al. (1975), *The Economics of Multi-plant Operation in an International Study*, Cambridge, MA: Harvard University Press.

Schmalensee, Richard (1978), "Entry Deterrence in the Ready-to-Eat Breakfast Cereal Industry," *Bell Journal of Economics*, vol. 9, pp. 305–327.

Schmalensee, Richard (1989), "Inter-Industry Differences of Structure and Performance," in Richard Schmalensee and Robert Willig (eds.), *Handbook of Industrial Organisation*, Amsterdam: North Holland.

Schwalbach, J. (1985), "Rentabilitätsentwicklung Deutscher Brauereiaktiengesellschaften," in G. Bombach, B. Gaheln, and A. E. Ott (eds.), *Industreökonomik: Theorie und Empire*, Tübingen: J. C. B. Mohr (Paul Subeck).

Schwalbach, J., and J. Müller (1984), "Brauereiindustrie," in Peter Oberender (ed.), *Markstruktur und Wettbewerb in der Bundesrepublik Deutschland*, Munich: Verlag Vahlen.

Selten, R. (1975), "A Re-examination of the Perfectness Concept for Equilibrium Points in Extensive Games," *International Journal of Game Theory*, vol. 4, pp. 25–55.

Selten, R. (1978), "The Chain Store Paradox," *Theory and Decision*, vol. 9, pp. 127–159.

Shaked, Avner, and John Sutton (1982), "Relaxing Price Competition through Product Differentiation," *Review of Economic Studies*, vol. 49, pp. 3–13.

Shaked, Avner, and John Sutton (1983), "Natural Oligopolies," *Econometrica*, vol. 51, pp. 1469–1484.

Shaked, Avner, and John Sutton (1987), "Product Differentiation and Industrial Structure," *Journal of Industrial Economics*, vol. 36, pp. 131–146.

Shaked, Avner, and John Sutton (1990), "Multiproduct Firms and Market Structure," *Rand Journal of Economics*, vol. 21, pp. 45–62.

Shepherd, W. Geoffrey (1961), "A Comparison of Industrial Concentration in the United States and Britain," *Review of Economics and Statistics*, vol. 43, pp. 70–75.

Shubik, M., and R. Levitan (1980), *Market Structure and Behavior*, Cambridge, MA: Harvard University Press.

Simon, Herbert, and Charles P. Bonini (1958), "The Size Distribution of Business Firms," *American Economic Review*, vol. 48, pp. 607–617.

Slade, Margaret (1987), "Interfirm Rivalry in a Repeated Game: An Empirical Test of Tacit Collusion," *Journal of Industrial Economics*, vol. 35, pp. 499–516.

Smith, Richard L. (1985), "Maximum Likelihood estimation in a class of non-regular cases," *Biometrika*, vol. 72, pp. 67–92.

Smith, Richard L. (1989), "Extreme Value Analysis of Environmental Time Series: An Application to Trend Detection in Ground-Level Ozone," *Statistical Science*, vol. 4, pp. 367–393.

Smith, Richard L. (1990), "Nonregular Regression," *Biometrika* (forthcoming).

Steen, Herman (1963), *Flour Milling in America*, Minneapolis: T. S. Denison & Co. Inc.

Stern, Louis W. (1966), *Studies of Organization and Competition in Grocery Manufacturing*, Technical Study no. 6, National Commission on Food Marketing, Washington, D.C.

Suchors, Cheryl, and C. Roland Christensen (1977), "Seven-Up Company (A)," Harvard Business School Case Study no. 378-097.

Sutton, John (1986), "Vertical Product Differentiation: Some Basic Themes," *American Economic Review (Papers and Proceedings)*, vol. 76, pp. 393–398.

Sutton, John (1989a), "Endogenous Sunk Costs and Industrial Structure," in G. Bonanno and D. Brandolini (eds.), *Market Structure in the New Industrial Economics*, Oxford: Oxford University Press.

Sutton, John (1989b), "Is Imperfect Competition Empirically Empty?" in George R. Feiwel (ed.), *The Economics of Imperfect Competition and Employment: Joan Robinson and Beyond*, London: Macmillan.

Tirole, Jean (1989), *Theory of Industrial Organization*, Cambridge, MA: MIT Press.

Tousley, R. D. (1969), "Marketing," in J. H. van Stuyvenberg (ed.), *Margarine: An Economic, Social and Scientific History, 1869–1969*, Liverpool: Liverpool University Press.

Trembaly, Victor J., and Carol Horton Tremblay (1988), "The Determinants of Horizontal Acquisitions: Evidence from the US Brewing Industry," *Journal of Industrial Economics*, vol. 37, pp. 21–46.

U.S. Department of Agriculture (1984), *Sugar: Background for 1985 Farm Legislation*, Economic Research Service, Agriculture Information Bulletin no. 47B.

U.S. Department of Agriculture (1986), *Sugar, Molasses and Honey*, FS1-86, May.

Vaizey, John (1960), *The Brewing Industry, 1886–1951: An Economic Study*, London: Pitman.

Van Damme, Eric (1987), "Stability and Perfection of Nash Equilibrium," Berlin, New York: Springer-Verlag.

van Stuyvenberg, J. H. (ed.) (1969), *Margarine: An Economic, Social and Scientific History, 1869–1969*, Liverpool: Liverpool University Press.

Vickers, John (1986), "The Evolution of Market Structure When There is a Sequence of Innovations," *Journal of Industrial Economics*, vol. 35, pp. 1–12.

Walsh, G. (1974), *Recent Trends in Monopoly in Great Britain*, Cambridge: Cambridge University Press.

Watt, Richard S. (1962), "A Method of Analyzing Demand for Mineral Commodities: A Case Study of Salt," U.S. Bureau of Mines Information Circular 8057, Washington, D.C.: U.S. Government Printing Office.

Weiss, Leonard (1965), "An Evaluation of Mergers in Six Industries," *Review of Economics and Statistics*, vol. 42, pp. 172–179.

Weiss, Leonard W. (1972), "The Geographic Size of Markets in Manufacturing," *The Review of Economics and Statistics*, vol. 54, pp. 245–257.

Wilson, Charles (1954), *The History of Unilever* (2 vols.), London: Cassell & Co. Ltd.

Wilson, Charles (1968), *The History of Unilever*, vol. iii, London: Cassell & Co. Ltd.

Wilson, Rufus E. (1971), "The FTC's Deconcentration Case Against the Breakfast Cereal Industry: A New Ballgame in Antitrust?" *Antitrust Law and Economics Review*, Summer, pp. 70–71.

Yaeger, Mary (1981), *Competition and Regulation: The Development of Oligopoly in the Meat Packing Industry*, Greenwich, CT.: JAX Press.

Yip, George S., and Jeffrey R. Williams (1982), *US Retail Coffee Market (A)*, Harvard Business School Case Study no. 582-087.

Market Research Reports and Related Sources

General

Own Brands, Keynote, 1986.

Sugar

Agra-Alimentation, Annual Reviews of the French Food and Drink Sector, 1965, 1967.

"L'Industrie Européen du Sucre," *Dafsa Kompass*, 1979.

Nikkan Keizai Tsushinya (Yosabu Hen), *Sakerui-Syokuhin-Sangyo no Seisan Hanbai Share* (Production and Sales Share of the Food and Drink Industry), Tokyo, 1983.

Statistiches Tabellenbuch (Teil 4), Verein der Zuckerindustrie, Bonn, 1987.

Zucchero, Dati e Analisi, Databank, 1986.

Zuckerindustrie—Entwicklung in Einzeldarstellungen, Verein der Zuckerindustrie, Bonn, 1977.

Flour

Japanscan, vol. 4, no. 6 August 1986, p. 21.

"L'industrie alimentaire francaise," *Agra-Alimentation*, 1974, 1975, 1977.

"La Meunerie," Dafsa Kompass, 1982.

Molitoria, Databank, 1986.

Nippon-Seifun-Kabushikigaisya, *Present Position of the Flour Industry*, Tokyo: Nippon Seifun, 1987.

"Panorame de l'industrie alimentaire francaise, en 1979," *Agra-Alimentation*, 1979.

Report on the Food Industry, Tokyo: Kaidanren-Yoseimondai-Kondankai, 1986.

Bread

Annual Report 1987, Wholesale Bakery.

"A White Paper Report: The Changing Face of Breadstuffs," *Milling and Baking News*, 1983.

"Baking Executives Report 1987," *Milling and Baking News*.

"Bread and Pastries in Germany," *Marketing in Europe*, no. 269, April, 1985, pp. 52–57.

The Market for Flour-Based Products in Europe, ERC Statistics International Limited, 1989.

Market Shares in Japan, Yano Research Institute, 1986.

Processed Meat

Der Fleisch und Fleischwaren-Markt in der Bundesrepublik Deutschland, Coop Ag, 1985.

Salumi, Databank, 1986.

"Olida-Caby cherche la bonne recette," *Nouvel Economiste*, 22 May 1987.

"Olida-Caby objectif equilibre," *Nouvel Economiste*, 24 April 1987.

Canned Vegetables

Canned Food, Keynote, 1984.

"Canned Foods in Italy," *Marketing in Europe*, 1986.

"Canned Vegetables," *Market Intelligence* (Mintel), November 1985.

"Les Industries de Conserves," *Dafsa Kompass*, December 1983.

Market Shares in Japan, Yano Research Institute, 1985.

Frozen Food

"A Marketing Retrospective," *Frozen Food Age* (35th Anniversary Issue), vol. 36, no. 1, August 1987.

Alimenti Surgelati, Databank, 1986.

"Company Report: Nichirei," *Japanscan*, vol. 4, no. 4, June 1986.

Der Märkt dür Tiefkühlkost, Verlagsgruppe, Bauer, 1977.

"Frozen Food in Germany," *Marketing in Europe*, 1985.

"Frozen Food," *Market Intelligence* (Mintel), August 1985.

Frozen Foods, 4th ed., Keynote, 1984; 7th ed., 1987.

Frozen Foods: A Review of the Market in 1986, Walton-on-Thames: Birds Eye Walls Limited.

"Frozen Foods in France," *Marketing in Europe*, no. 272, July 1985.

"Frozen Foods in Itay," *Marketing in Europe*, no. 290, January 1987.

Growth Opportunities in Convenience Food, E.R.C., 1987.

Japan's Food & Kindred Products Market and Industry, Yano Research Institute, 1984.

Les Surgelés: Production et Distribution, Dafsa, 1978.

"Market Report: Frozen Foods," *Japanscan*, vol. 4, no. 4, June 1986, and vol. 5, no. 1, March 1987.

MÄRKTE: Tiefkühlkost, Axel Springer Verlag, 1978.

Prepared Soups

"*Campbell vs. Lipton*," *Advertising Age*, August 3, 1987.

"Canned Soup in Germany," *Marketing in Europe*, no. 260, July 1981.

Der Märkt für Suppen, Sossen, Würzen und Gewürze, Verlagsgruppe Bauer, July 1984.

EEC, *Market Research Great Britain*, London: Euromonitor Publications, chapters 5 and 6.

Japanscan, vol. 2, nos. 11, 12, January/February 1985.

Market Shares in Japan, Yano Research Institute, 1985.

"Soups in Italy," *Marketing in Europe*, 1984.

"Soups in Italy," *Market Research Europe*, 1984.

"Soups," *Market Research Great Britain*, 1982, 1985.

Margarine

"Cooking Fat and Oils," *Market Intelligence*, (Mintel), April 1980.

Der Märkt für Speisefette, Verlagsgruppe Bauer, 1984.

Japanscan, vol. 4, no. 8, October 1986; vol. 3, no. 5, July 1985; vol. 4, no. 6, August 1986.

"Les Industries alimentaires fâce à l'élargissement du marché commun," *Agra-Alimentation*, 1972.

"L'Industrie alimentaire francaise," *Agra-Alimentation*, 1974.

"Oils and Fats in West Germany," *Marketing in Europe*, 1986.

"Yellow Fats," *Market Research Great Britain*, 1986.

Soft Drinks

"Carbonates," *Euromonitor*, 1985.

"Carbonates," Mintel, 1985.

"Coca Cola set to drive the market forward," *Retail Confectioner and Tobacconist*, April 1988.

"Coke Adds Life," *Markets*, June 4, 1987.

"Concentrated Drinks," *Euromonitor*, 1984.

"Drinks Mixers," *Euromonitor*, 1985.

The Future of the Soft Drink Industry 1985–90, Boston Consulting Group, 1987.

Soft Drinks, Keynote, 1983.

US Industrial Outlook 1987, U.S. Dept. of Commerce, chapter 39 (Food and Kindred Products).

RTE Cereal

"Breakfast Cereals in Germany," *Marketing in Europe*, 1985.

Breakfast Cereals, Keynote, 1983.

"Breakfast Cereals," *Market Research Great Britain*, 1985.

"Breakfast Cereals," *Mintel*, 1987.

"Cereals in France," *Marketing in Europe*, 1985.

"Champion of Competition vs. the Breakfast of Champions: The Case of Ready-to-Eat Cereals," Harvard Business School Case Study no. 9-373-249 (1972).

Der Märkt für Fertige Früstückskost, Verlagsgruppe Bauer, 1982.

"The Global Marketplace," *Prepared Foods*, May 1987.

"The Kellogg Company Inc.," Harvard Business School Case Study no. 9-274-122 (revised 1975).

Confectionery

The American Candy Market, Business Trends Analysts, 1986.

Brugnoli, Aldo, "I prodotti a base di cacao," *Largo Consumo*, no. 6, 1985.

"Chocolate Confectionery in France," *Marketing in Europe*, 1986.

"Chocolate Confectionery in Italy," *Marketing in Europe*, 1982.

"Chocolate," *Mintel*, 1985.

Confectionery, Keynote, 1984.

Der Märkt für Schokolade und Süsswaren, Verlagsgruppe Bauer, 1983.

Facinelli, Bruno, "I prodotti non da forno a base di zucchero e di cacao," *Largo Consumo*, no. 9, 1982.

Japanscan, vol. 4, no. 5, July 1986, pp. 17–19; vol. 2, no. 7, September 1984, p. 1; vol. 4, no. 3, May 1986, pp. 13–16; vol. 4, no. 5, July 1986, pp. 11–15; vol. 4, no. 12, February 1987, pp. 16–18.

Ladd, Edward H. *Cadbury Schweppes Ltd.*, Harvard Business School Case Study no. 9-274-105 (1973).

"Le Marché Francais des Produits Alimentaires," *Agra-Alimentation*, 1987.

L'Industrie de la Chocolaterie et de la Confiserie en Europe, (Collection "Analyse de Secteurs"), Dafsa, 1985.

Prodotti a base di Cacao, Databank, 1986.

Prodotti a base di Zucchero, Databank, 1986.

Schokolade und Süsswaren: Marketing Anzeiger, Axel Springer Verlag AG, 1987.

Statistical Bulletin of the International Office of Cocoa, Chocolate and Sugar Confectionery (IOCCC), Hermann Pöhlmann (ed.), Brussels, 1988.

"Sugar Confectionery," *Mintel*, 1986.

"Sugar Confectionery," Special Report no. 3, Retail Business, 1986.

The US Confectionery Market, Euromonitor, 1987.

Coffee

Brugnoli, Aldo, "La Produzione e la distribuzione di caffe," *Largo Consumo*, no. 2, 1985.

"Instant Coffee," *Market Research Great Britain* (Euromonitor), May 1984.

Japan's Food & Kindred Products Market and Industry, Yano Research Institute, 1984.

"L'Industrie alimentaire francaise," *Agra-Alimentation*, 1973, p. 115.

"L'Industrie alimentaire francaise," *Agra-Alimentation*, 1977, p. 129.

Märkte: Information für die Werbeplannung, Axel Springer Verlag AG-Marketing Anziegen, 1985.

"Roast and Ground Coffee," *Market Research Great Britain*, February 1986.

Biscuits

"Biscuits," *Market Research Great Britain*, Nov.–Dec. 1983.

"Biscuits in France," *Marketing in Europe*, January 1981.

Biscuits in the United States, Euromonitor, 1987.

Centre Francais du Commerce Extérieure, *Le Marché Américain de la Biscuiterie*, Paris: Direction des Produits Agro-Alimentaire, 1983.

Flour Confectionery, Keynote, 1986.

"Fusion B.S.N. et Generale Biscuit," *Le Soir*, 20 February 1987.

"La Structure de l'industrie francaise de la biscuiterie," *Agra-Alimentation*, November 1967.

Le Marché Francais des Produits Alimentaires (3rd ed.), Paris: Agra-Alimentation, 1987.

"L'industrie alimentaire francaise," *Agra-Alimentation*, 1965/6, 1967, 1978.

Market Shares in Japan, Yano Research Institute, 1985.

Market Survey on Biscuits in Japan, Tokyo: Dodwell Marketing Consultants, 1979.

Prodotti da forno secchi, Databank, 1985.

Your Market in Japan: Biscuits, JETRO.

Pet Food

"Cat Food," *Market Research Great Britain*, Euromonitor, 1984.

"Cat and Other Pet Food," *Market Intelligence* (Mintel), 1986.

"Dog Food," *Market Intelligence* (Mintel), 1986.

"Dog Food," *Market Research Great Britain*, Euromonitor, 1985.

"General Foods: Opportunities in the Dog Food Market," Harvard Business School Case Study no. 9-578-162.

"General Foods'—Post Division (A): 'Going to the Dogs,'" Harvard Business School Case Study no. 9-510-008.

"General Foods—Post Division (B): 'Going to the Dogs,'" Harvard Business School Case Study no. 9-510-009.

"Market Leaders in Dog and Cat Food," *Japanscan*.

"Petfood in France," *Market Research Europe*, 1978, 1981, 1985.

Petfoods, Keynote, 1987.

"Petfoods," *Market Research Great Britain*, Euromonitor, 1986.

"Petfoods in Germany," *Marketing in Europe*, Special Report no. 1, April 1986.

Baby Food

"Baby Foods in West Germany," *Marketing in Europe*, 1986.

Beer

The American Beer Market, Business Trends Analysts, 1987.

"Anheuser-Busch Cos.," *Advertising Age* (Special Issue), 1986.

Beer in the U.S., Euromonitor, 1987.

"Beer in West Germany," *Marketing in Europe*, no. 284, July 1986.

The Beer Market in France, Keynote, 1982.

Breweries, Keynote, 1983, 1987.

Der märkt für Bier, Verlagsgruppe Bauer, 1987.

Japanscan, vol. 5, no. 2, April 1987; vol. 5, no. 3, 6 August 1983; vol. 5, no. 4, 2 April 1986; vol. 5, no. 2, 8 October 1984; vol. 5, no. 1, 6 August 1983; vol. 5, no. 1, 7 June 1983.

"La Brasserie en Europe," *Dafsa Kompass*, 1984.

"Les Industries Alimentaires fâce à l'élargissement du Marché Commun 1972," *Agra-Alimentation*, 1972.

"L'Industrie Alimentaire Francaise," *Agra-Alimentation*, 1974.

"Marketing Fact Sheet," Anheuser-Busch, Inc.

Official Reports

France

Commission de la Concurrence (1981), *Ententes dans la Meunerie et la Boulangerie*.

"Rachat Par Lesieur de la Division Alimentaire d'Unipol," *Journal Officiel de la République Francaise*, 17 April 1984, pp. 28–30.

Germany (F.R.)

Monopolkommission (1984/5), *Gesamtwirtschaftliche Chancen und Risiken wachsender Unternehmensgrössen*.

Monopolkommission (1986/7), *Die Wettbewerbsordnung erweitern*.

Monopolkommission (1985), *Die Konzentration im Lebensmittelhandel*, Sondergutachten 14.

United Kingdom

Commission of the European Communities, *A Study of the Evolution of Concentration in the Food Distribution Industry for the U.K.*, vol. 1, chap. 5, October 1977.

Monopolies Commission (1969), *Beer: A Report on the Supply of Beer* (HC216).

Monopolies Commission (1973), *Breakfast Cereals: A Report on the Supply of Ready Cooked Breakfast Cereal Foods* (HC.2).

Monopolies and Mergers Commission (1976), *Frozen Foodstuffs* (HC.674).

Monopolies and Mergers Commission (1977), *Flour and Bread*.

Monopolies and Mergers Commission (1980–81), *S & W Berisford Ltd. and British Sugar Corporation Ltd. A Report on the proposed merger* (HC 241).

Monopolies and Mergers Commission (1983), *Nabisco Brands Inc. and Huntley & Palmers Foods PLC. A Report on the Proposed Merger*, Cmnd. 8680.

Monopolies Commission (1986), *White Salt*, Cmnd. 9778.

Monopolies and Mergers Commission (1987), *Tate and Lyle plc and Ferruzi Finaziaria SpA and S & W Berisford plc. A report on the existing and proposed mergers*, Cmnd. 89.

Monopolies and Mergers Commission (1989), *The Supply of Beer: A report on the supply of beer for retail sale in the United Kingdom*, Cmnd. 651.

National Board for Prices and Incomes (1964–65), *Prices of Bread and Incomes (1964–65)*, *Prices of Bread and Flour*, Cmnd. 2760.

National Board for Prices and Incomes (1969–70), *Bread Prices and Pay in the Baking Industry: First Report*, Cmnd. 4329.

National Board for Prices and Incomes (1970), *Margarine and Compound Cooking Fats*, Cmnd. 4368.

National Board for Prices and Incomes (1970–71), *Bread Prices and Pay in the Baking Industry: Second Report*, Cmnd. 4428.

Price Commission (1977), *Coffee: Prices, Costs and Margin*, Report No. 29.

Price Commission (1979), *United Biscuits (UK) Ltd—Biscuits, Crisps, Nuts and Savoury Snacks*.

United States

Federal Trade Commission (1962), *Economic Inquiry into Food Marketing*, Part II, The Frozen Fruit, Juice and Vegetable Industry, Washington, D.C.: U.S. Government Printing Office.

Federal Trade Commission (1967), *Economic Report on the Baking Industry*.

Federal Trade Commission (1978), *The Brewing Industry*, Staff Report of the Bureau of Economics, December.

Federal Trade Commission, *In re Kellogg et al.*, docket no. 8883.

National Commission on Food Marketing, *Organisation and Competition in the Milling and Baking Industries*, Technical Study No. 5, June 1966.

Company Histories

Braznell, William (1982), *California's Finest: The History of the Del Monte Corporation and the Del Monte Brand* (published by the company).

Kirin Biru Kabushiki–Gaisha Gojyu-nen-shi (a fifty-year history of the Kirin Brewery Co. Ltd.), Tokyo: Kirin Brewery Co. Ltd., 1957.

Le Salin d'Aigues-Mortes, Compagnie des Salins du Midi et des Salines de l'Est (company brochure).

90 Nenshi (a ninty-year history), Tokyo: Nippon Flour Mills Co. Ltd., 1987.

Nisshin-Seifun Kabushikigaisha 70 Nenshi (A seventy-year history of the Nisshin Flour Milling Company), Tokyo: Nisshin Flour Milling Co., 1970.

Interviews

France

Agra-Alimentation	Michel de St. Albin
Cie des Salins du Midi et des Salines de l'Est	Philippe Tardieu
Comité Français du Café	M. Ruault
Confederation Français de la Conserve	M. Mulot
Générale Sucrière	Guillemette Chapuis
GEO	Charles Gazan
GLORIA	François Jobelot
Sopad Nestlé	Claude Desmont
Suchard Tobler	Marc Oliver Bernard
Syndicat national de la biscuiterie française (UNIBREM)	Gilles Cantreau
Syndicat National des Industries de la Boulangerie et Patisserie	

Germany

ADH-Mühlenverband, Bonn	Rechtsanwalt Ehrhart Schäfer
Apollinaris-Brunnen Actien-Gesellschaft	Arnold Wolters
Bundeskartellamt	Helmut Bethke
Dr. August Oetker Zentralverwaltung	Dieter Baader
Fleischwarenfabrik Waltner	Manfred Schenkewitz
Georg Plange GmbH & Co.	Jurgen Plange
GFK Handelsforschung Gmbtt & Co. K G	Walter Berthold
Hansa Tiefuhlmenu Gmbtt & Co.	Friedhelm Kurlfinke
	Otto Rasch
IFO Institut fur Wirtschaftsforschung	Michael Breitenaker
Klosterbrauerei Andechs	Georg Orthuber
Lehrstuhl für Marktforschung Bonn	R. Wolfram
Lubig GmbH	Hans Lubig
Monopolkommission	Rainer Feuerstack
	Horst Greiffenberg
	Bernd Noll
Schultheiss-Brauerei A G	Peter Mihm
Verband der deutschen Brot-und Backwarenindustrie e V	Helmut Martell
Verein der Deutchen Salzindustrie e V	Karl-Heinz Irlenborn
Walter Rau Lebensmittelwerke	Karl W. Abt
Wicküler Gruppe	Wolfgang Feidner

Italy

Barilla	A.I. Ganapini
Buitoni Spa	Dott. Citernese
GRAM, GEMA Spa	Benetto Riva
Heinz Italy	Emilio Terzaghi
Invernizzi	Dott. Boschin
	B. Lorenzetti
Lavazza	Alberto Lojacono
	Tullio Toledo
Pepsico	A. Ritteri
S.A.G.I.T. SpA	Dott. Rigetti
Simmenthal Spa	Dott. Notte
STAR Spa	Vittorio del Mastro

Japan

Ajinomoto General Foods Inc.	Yohnosuke Tsujimoto
Calpis Food Industry Co.	Kazuo Ino
	Tetsuo Yoshiya
Campbell Japan Inc.	Kenneth G. Boston
Dentsu	Ryosuke Shibata
Ezaki Glico Co. Ltd.	Toshio Morita
	Katsuyuki Nogi
Japan Canners' Association	Susumu Mishima
	Toshiaki Miura
Japan Soft Drink Bottlers' Association	Tadeo Mizuuchi
	Tadahisa Miyake
Kirin Brewery Co. Ltd.	Shigeo Sakurai
Meiji Seika Kaisha Ltd.	Akira Horie
	Makoto Kobayashi
	Tetsuo Nakamura
	Yoshinobu Yoshimura
Mitsui Sugar Co. Ltd.	Masafumi Kurosu
Morinaga & Co. Ltd.	Kazuhiko Kuriiwa
	Hiroshi Tsukamoto
National Federation of Agricultural Cooperative Associations	Atsushi Iwasaki
	Koji Yoshida
National Research Institute of Agricultural Economics	
Nippon Flour Mills Co. Ltd.	Yoshiyuki Onodera
	Takehiro Hosokawa
	Kiichi Inazuki
	Yoshio Iwasaki
Nippon Suisan Kaisha Ltd.	Yoshio Kurita
	Mitsuhiro Ozawa

Nisshin Four Milling Co. Ltd.

Isao Iijima
Hidetaka Niikura
Ted Shiragami

QP Corporation

Hidenari Jikuhara
Takashi Nishitai
Hidefumi Tachibana

Snow Brand Milk Products Co. Ltd.

Sanae Enju
Naoyuki Motomura
Yashuhiro Noda
Tadashi Oura
Sadaaki Yokote
Yukio Yokozawa

Suntory Ltd.

Kiyotoshi Andoh
Hiroyuki Fujita

Ueshima Coffee
Yamazaki Baking Co. Ltd.

Shoji Kinoshita
Kimiyasu Otani

Switzerland

Nestec Ltd. (Nestlé)

Serge Milhaud

United Kingdom

Birds Eye Wall's Ltd.

Ron Green
Eric Walsh

British Sugar
Campbell Grocery Products Ltd.

R. B. Begy
Jim Harrington
Peter H. Scott

Coca-Cola Schweppes Ltd.
General Foods
Geo Bassett & Co. Ltd.

Colin Gamble
R. J. S. Bell
Rose Hunt
David J. Lake

Hillsdown Ltd.
The Nestlé Co. Ltd.
Rank-Hovis McDougall
Van den Berghs & Jurgens Ltd. /

Steve Saunders
E. Humphries
M. Handley
J. Stowell

United States

Anheuser-Busch Inc.
Frozen Food Age
General Mills Inc.

Michael J. La Monica
A. H. Rosenfeld
James J. Feeney
Robert W. Rowe

Jacobs Suchard Brach Inc.

Bert J. Nelson
N. Mitchell

Land O'Lakes Inc.
Nestlé Foods Inc.
Oscar Mayer Foods Corporation
Pepperidge Farm Inc.

The Pillsbury Co.
Ralston Purina Co.

Salt Institute
Schweppes USA
Thomas J. Lipton Inc.
U.S. Department of Agriculture
U.S. Department of Commerce

Duane Bethune
Jeff Caso
Patrick J. Luby
Patrick Callaghan
William R. Encherman
Dan Locke
Terry Block
Betsy Cohen
Bruce Bertram
Randy C. Papadelis
G. B. Boycks
Robert D. Barry
Donald A. Hodges
William V. Janis

Index